VISUAL QUICKSTART GUIDE

VISUAL BASIC .NET

FOR WINDOWS

Harold Davis

Visual QuickStart Guide

Visual Basic .NET for Windows

Harold Davis

Peachpit Press
1249 Eighth Street
Berkeley, CA 94710
510/524-2178
800/283-9444
510/524-2221 (fax)

Find us on the World Wide Web at: http://www.peachpit.com
To report errors, please send a note to errata@peachpit.com
Published by Peachpit Press, a division of Pearson Education

Editor: Jill Marts Lodwig
Production Coordinators: Judy Zimola and Connie Jeung-Mills
Copyeditor: Judy Ziajka
Compositor: Maureen Forys, Happenstance Type-O-Rama
Indexer: Karin Arrigoni
Cover Design: The Visual Group
Cover Production: Nathalie Valette

ISBN 0-321-18088-7

9 8 7 6 5 4 3 2 1

Printed and bound in the United States of America

Dedication

For Phyllis, the love of my life

Acknowledgments

I'd like to thank everyone at Peachpit Press who helped make this book happen, particularly my editors Jill Marts Lodwig and Judy Ziajka. Jill and Judy put a tremendous amount of intelligence, effort, and energy into this project.

For me, writing books is a family affair. In that connection, thanks are due to both Martin Davis and Phyllis Davis, who read much of this book in draft form and made many helpful suggestions.

CONTENTS AT A GLANCE

TABLE OF CONTENTS

INTRODUCTION

I wrote this book to help meet the needs of a number of different kinds of people:

- Perhaps you are a VB6 programmer in the process of making (or considering making) the leap to VB .NET.
- Maybe you've been coding in .NET for a while and need a quick visual reference that shows you how to perform important tasks.
- Maybe you want to understand all the fuss about .NET.
- Perhaps you understand procedural programming, but want to get up to speed with the next paradigm: object-oriented programming.
- Then again, maybe you've never programmed at all or have written just a few macros and have decided that now is the time to learn programming.

There is something for each of these kinds of readers in my book. While I do assume that you are familiar with the basics of using the Microsoft Windows operating system, I don't assume any prior knowledge of programming.

I can also guarantee that more advanced readers will not be bored! Programming in VB .NET is fun and stimulating.

If you are already working in VB .NET, you don't need me to tell you how exciting it is, as you've seen this for yourself. If you're new to .NET, I envy the fine adventure you are about to embark upon!

If you are a VB6 programmer (and, possibly, a reader of the best-selling previous edition of this book), you'll find that VB .NET begins where VB6 ends, and you have a brave new world to conquer and explore!

The approach of this book is to provide a step-by-step, visual guide to performing Visual Basic .NET tasks. The many graphics in this book work well for a learning a development environment like Visual Studio .NET for Visual Basic—which is visual to the max.

Each chapter shows you how to accomplish specific tasks, many of which come up frequently in the real world. In this book, I'm not big on theoretical disquisition: you learn the hows and whys of .NET, objects, and programming in the course of doing actual projects.

While it is theoretically possible to create a Visual Basic .NET program using a text editor and command-line compilation, in the real world Visual Studio .NET is the development environment used to create VB .NET programs. In other words, you need to know your way around Visual Studio to create Visual Basic programs.

For that reason, the first chapter in this book, "Introducing Visual Studio .NET," explains how to work with Visual Studio .NET.

The next few chapters in this book explain some of the exciting new aspects of the VB .NET language. I show you right off the bat how to create Web services and how to work with interfaces, objects, and classes in a fully object-oriented way. (So if you read only the first four chapters of this book, you will know how to use Visual Studio, how to create a Web service, and how to program in a full object-oriented fashion!)

The great advantage of proceeding by tackling these important topics early is that we can then use the vocabulary of Web services and—most important—of object-oriented programming in the rest of the book as you learn how to create Windows applications, work with exceptions, animate sprites, explore the objects in the .NET Framework, use XML, and much, much more!

VB .NET is so exciting, and so much fun, that I can only ask, "Why wait?" With this book you can get started now. As Hillel put it, "If not now, when?"

Visual Basic .NET

Visual Basic is the programming language used by more programmers than any other in the history of the world (over 5 million and counting). It combines extraordinary ease of use with great power and flexibility. Visual Basic is used in many ways by people at many different levels: from programmers just taking their first baby programming steps to veritable Jedi knights of the art of programming.

The Visual Basic language is a descendant of the original BASIC (Beginner's All-Purpose Symbolic Instruction Code). BASIC was invented in the early 1960s by two Dartmouth professors, John G. Kemeny and Thomas Kurtz. It was intended to be as easy to understand and as close to everyday language as possible.

In this respect, Visual Basic has kept the BASIC tradition intact. It is one of the easiest computer languages to work with and understand.

With the immensely popular Visual Basic 6, Microsoft's sixth version of its Visual Basic development environment combining visual design tools and the VB language, many observers thought that VB had come as far as it could. Not so, it turns out!

Visual Basic .NET is not your father's Visual Basic, and it is not "VB7." I can't emphasize enough that Visual Basic .NET is not just an improved version of VB6.

VB .NET is a powerful, graceful, fully object-oriented modern language, every bit the equal of C# or Java. VB .NET somehow manages to preserve the simplicity of syntax that has always been the hallmark of the BASIC family of languages.

Visual Basic .NET preserves keywords and syntax that are, for many of us, familiar. For those who are not familiar with any version of BASIC, its semantics are still close enough to everyday language to be easy to learn quickly.

But it is a big mistake to go about learning Visual Basic .NET as though it is Visual Basic business as usual. As I'll show you in this book, programming effectively in VB .NET (as compared to VB6) requires a whole new way of thinking.

What is .NET?

There's a great deal of confusion surrounding the term *.NET,* since it is primarily a marketing term—and its meaning as a marketing term changes as the wind blows from different directions in Redmond, Washington.

While *.NET* has been used to label a variety of Microsoft products, significantly including the Microsoft enterprise server line, for programmers *.NET* primarily means:

- .NET programming languages, such as Visual Basic .NET (and C#.NET)
- Visual Studio .NET, the development environment used to create programs in the .NET programming languages
- The .NET Framework, which is a huge class and runtime library that provides objects used to enable many different kinds of programs

Of these .NET aspects, the .NET Framework deserves a little more comment. To say that the .NET Framework is a runtime library means that the files containing the .NET Framework runtime must be present on any system for a compiled .NET program to run.

The best way of thinking of the .NET Framework class library is as a giant code layer that provides tools for creating applications that run on Windows and the Web. This kind of giant code layer is sometimes called an *abstraction* layer, and it is much like the Java virtual machine environment required to run Java programs.

So when you write a program in VB .NET, you are no longer really writing a Windows or Web program. You are writing a program for the abstraction layer (the .NET Framework). The .NET Framework will know how to run your code on versions of the Windows operating system (or as a Web application on the Web).

More about Visual Studio .NET

Microsoft's Visual Studio .NET is an umbrella development environment used to create applications in languages including Visual Basic .NET, C# .NET, and C++.

Tying .NET, Visual Basic, and Visual Studio together, Visual Basic .NET programs are written in the VB language, use the .NET Framework, and are created using Visual Studio .NET. (As I've mentioned, you can create VB .NET programs without Visual Studio, but this is a relatively unfriendly process and not covered in this book.)

Visual Studio .NET provides a sophisticated Code Editor that is used to create, edit, and debug Visual Basic .NET code.

Visual Studio also supplies objects and tools that visually and easily—almost magically—assemble into Windows, Web, and Web services user interfaces (and much more).

As already noted, the first chapter in this book shows you how to accomplish the tasks you need to create Visual Basic .NET programs using Visual Studio. So the first chapter is all you really need to read to start playing!

By the way, the programs shown in this book were written and tested in Visual Studio .NET 2002. I also tested them in a release candidate version of Visual Studio .NET 2003.

Design Time Versus Runtime Environments

It's important to understand that you will be using Visual Studio .NET in two different modes as you work through the tasks presented in this book. These modes are called *design time* and *runtime*. In design time mode, you create a VB .NET program, so this is a mode that only programmers see. In runtime mode, a VB .NET program is running for the benefit of end users.

In the Visual Studio .NET design time environment, you create and modify objects and enter code. The runtime environment compiles the code and runs it in an environment that is pretty much like the runtime environment that end users will see, but is still somewhat under the control of Visual Studio. This mode has advantages when debugging a program, as I explain in Chapter 9, "Exceptions and Debugging." However, you can always compile, or *build*, a project and then run the compiled program—so that the Visual Studio .NET runtime environment is not involved at all. (As explained earlier, VB .NET programs do still require the .NET Framework to be installed on the system running the program.)

Line Continuation

Unlike programming languages that have a specific end-of-line character (such as a semicolon), a code statement in Visual Basic .NET ends only at the end of the line the statement is in. This means that VB .NET statements can get quite long. Presenting code, particularly VB .NET code, is problematic in the context of a book whose text is displayed within two-columns (such as this one). There's no perfect solution to this display problem. I've chosen to break code within the text of this book using the VB .NET line-continuation marker, which is a space followed by an underscore (_), to show that a line is continued. (The other option would have been to use an artificial character that is not part of the VB .NET language, such as an arrow, to show that a line is continued.)

Using the VB .NET line-continuation marker,

```
this is all one line
```

is the same thing as

```
this is all one _
  line
```

You should understand that code presented within tasks and text in this book will break onto lines differently than the same code when you first enter it in the Visual Studio Code Editor due to line breaks and line-continuation characters in the text of the book.

However, the code appearing in the text columns of the book is functionally exactly equivalent to code entered in the Code Editor in unbroken lines without using the line-continuation marker.

In addition, code in program listings in the book is two columns wide and appears (for the most part) as it would within the Code Editor.

Operating Systems

Visual Basic .NET is part of Visual Studio .NET, and, as such, can be installed on the Windows NT (Version 4.0 or later), Windows 2000, or Windows XP operating systems.

You should know, however, that while Visual Studio .NET (and VB .NET) can be installed on the "Home" version of Windows XP, the full features of the development environment will not be available unless you are running Windows XP Professional. Specifically, applications that require a Web server (this means ASP.NET Web Services applications and ASP.NET Web applications) can only be created using VB .NET (and Visual Studio .NET) running on Windows XP Professional (and not the Windows XP Home version of that operating system).

Visual Studio .NET 2002 and 2003

The projects (and code) that comprise the tasks in this book were written using Visual Studio . NET 2002. These projects were also tested using the release candidate version of Visual Studio .NET 2003.

Contacting the Author and Downloading Source Code

I have made every effort to be as accurate as possible. However, it is inevitable in life that some errors may have crept in. I'd greatly appreciate any corrections. Please drop me a line at vbnetvqs@bearhome.com with any suggestions or comments.

I encourage you to follow the examples in the book by re-creating the objects in the projects and using your keyboard to enter the source code as you follow the tasks explained in this book. You will learn the most if you do this.

However, for some people, typing is unbearably tedious. For those of you, I have placed the source code for the projects in the book, organized in zipped archives by chapter, on the companion Web site for you to download. The URL for the companion Web site is http://www.peachpit.com/vqs/vbnet/.

What are you waiting for? Let's get started right away!

1 Introducing Visual Studio .NET

While it's possible to create a Visual Basic .NET program in any text editor such as Notepad and then compile the program at the command line, this isn't a very convenient or easy way to work. A much better approach is to use the world-class integrated development environment (IDE) provided by Microsoft: Visual Studio .NET. Visual Studio is the development tool designed for use with .NET languages such as Visual Basic .NET and is used throughout this book to create Visual Basic .NET programs.

This chapter introduces you to Visual Studio and its most important features. First it explains how to get started with Visual Studio and configure its most important settings. Then it shows you how to work with modules, projects, and solutions—the building blocks for the programs you can create using VB .NET.

The Start Page

When you first run Visual Studio, it displays the Start page (**Figure 1.1**). The Start page provides a great deal of functionality, but you can access this same functionality via the Visual Studio development environment, so ultimately it's up to you to decide whether you want to see the Start page each time you open Visual Studio.

✔ Tip

- If the Start page doesn't appear when you open Visual Studio, click the Visual Studio Help menu and choose Show Start Page.

As I describe the Start page in this section, I'll also mention alternate ways of accomplishing the same thing using the Visual Studio development environment. (For example, choosing File > New Project is the same as clicking the New Project button on the Start page.) In addition, if you decide you aren't really fond of the Start page, you can explore the other options presented in the "At Startup Alternatives" section later in this chapter.

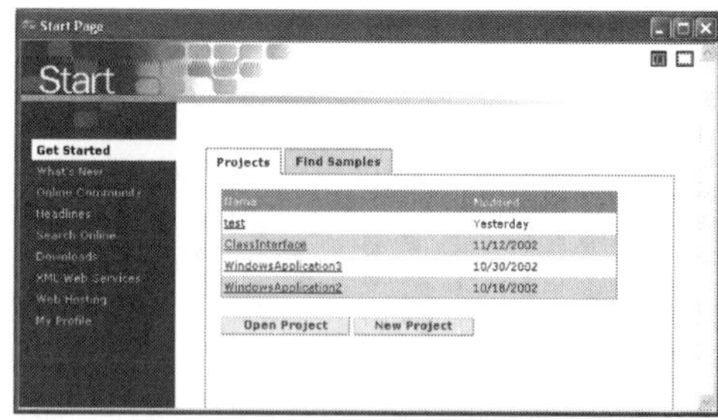

Figure 1.1 You can use the Visual Studio Start page to open projects, gather information, set your profile, and much more.

Figure 1.2 The hyperlinks along the left side of the Start page give you access to its functionality.

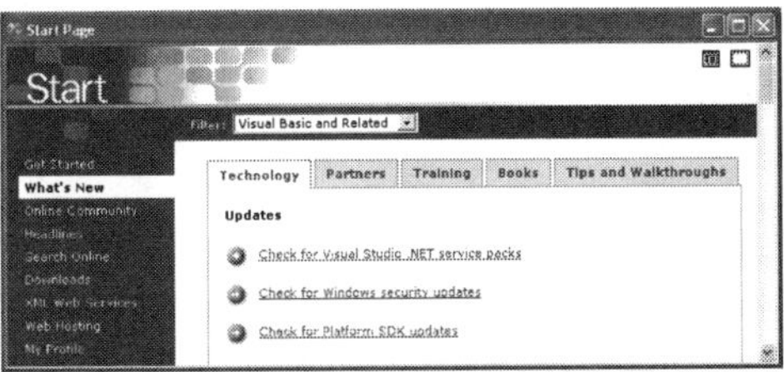

Figure 1.3 The Updates section of the Technology tab provides a link that allows you to check for Visual Studio service packs (bug fixes).

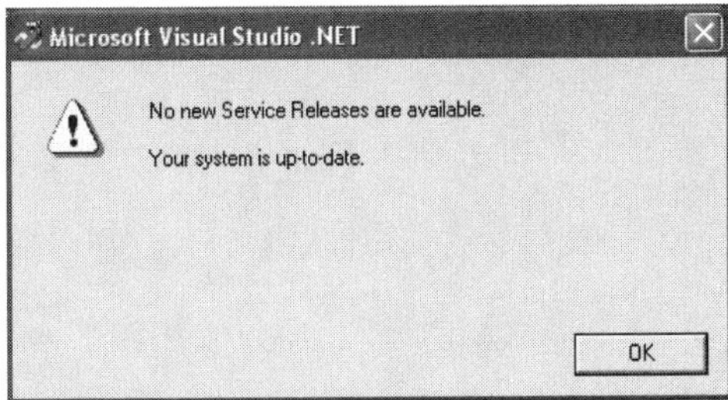

Figure 1.4 If your copy of Visual Studio is up-to-date, you'll see a message box saying so.

Checking for updates

Before you begin using Visual Studio and VB .NET, you should make sure you have the most recent bug fixes, called a *service pack*, for your version of the software.

To check for Visual Studio updates:

1. On the Start page, move the cursor to highlight the What's New link (**Figure 1.2**).
2. Click What's New.

   The Technology tab opens, with the Updates links shown at the top of the tab (**Figure 1.3**).
3. Click the Check for Visual Studio .NET Service Packs link (shown at the top of Figure 1.3).

   If your software is up-to-date, a message will appear saying so (**Figure 1.4**); if service packs are available, the download screens for the updates will be displayed.

✔ Tip

- For the Visual Studio update procedure to work, you must be connected to the Internet.

Setting your profile

Your Visual Studio profile determines the keyboard layout, the default layout of Visual Studio windows, and—perhaps most important—the Help documents you'll see. (For more information about working with Visual Studio's Help system, see Appendix A, "Getting Help.")

To set your profile:

1. On the Start page, click the My Profile link.
   The My profile page opens (**Figure 1.5**).
2. Select a Profile, such as Visual Basic Developer.

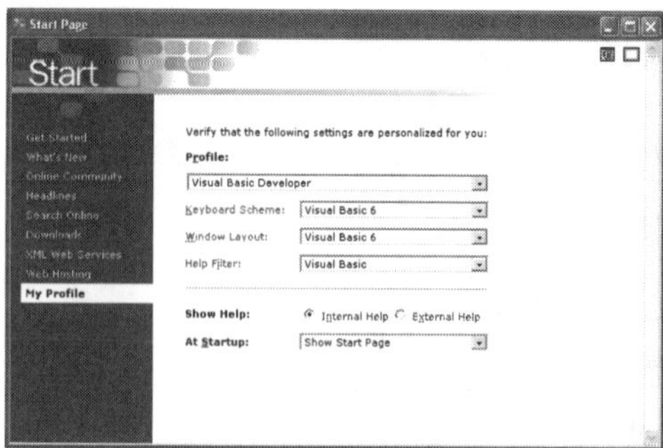

Figure 1.5 Use the My Profile page to customize Visual Studio.

✔ Tips

- I recommend that you modify the Visual Basic Developer profile by changing Keyboard Scheme to Default Settings, Window Layout to Visual Studio Default, and Help Filter to Visual Basic and Related. There is no good reason to keep settings inherited from Visual Basic 6 because the two languages and development environments are so different. In addition, you'll find this more expansive Help Filter setting likely to better help you find all the information you need as you work.
- If you make these changes as shown in **Figure 1.6**, then your Profile will be listed as Custom.

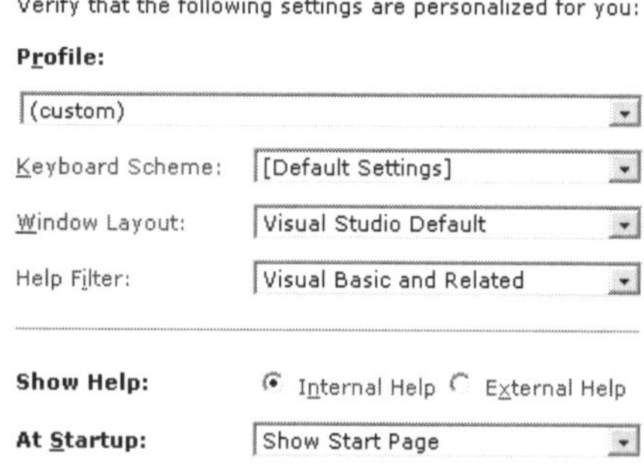

Figure 1.6 Suggested profile settings for a Visual Basic programmer.

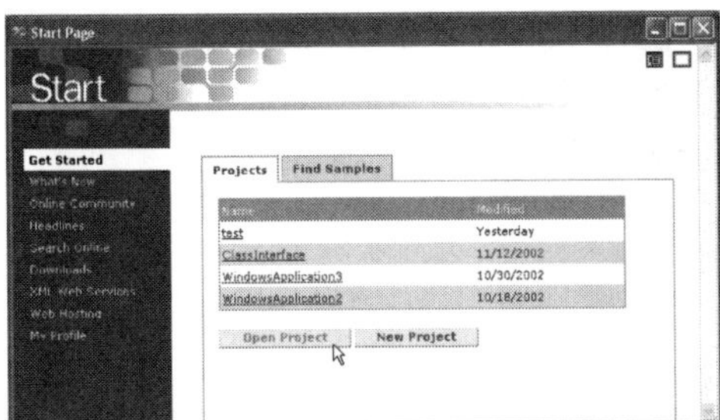

Figure 1.7 Use the Open Project button on the Projects tab to open an existing project.

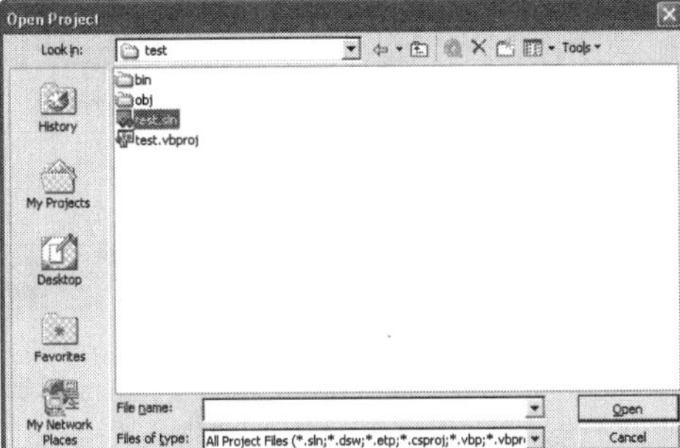

Figure 1.8 Use the Open Project dialog to select a solution or project.

Opening an existing project

Often when you start Visual Studio, all you really want to do is open an existing project that you need to work on.

To open an existing project (or solution):

1. Click the Get Started link on the left side of the Start page to display the Projects tab if it is not already displayed (**Figure 1.7**).
2. Click the Open Project button.
3. Use the Open Project dialog (**Figure 1.8**) to select a Solution (.sln) file or a Visual Basic Project (.vbproj) file.
4. Click Open.

   The project (or solution) opens in Visual Studio.

✔ Tips

- The relationship between projects and solutions is explained in "Solutions, Projects, and Modules" later in this chapter.
- You can also open an existing project—if it is on the most recently used (MRU) list—by clicking its link on the Start page. (The MRU links appear in the box above the Open Project button of the Projects tab, as shown in Figure 1.7.)
- You can also access the Open Project dialog from the Visual Studio menu bar by choosing Open > Project.

Importing VB6 projects

You can easily import VB6 projects into Visual Studio .NET. Although code converts from VB6 to VB .NET without huge problems, you'll find that you need to hand-tweak the conversion, and that the converted code doesn't really use the .NET Framework to the fullest.

To import a VB6 project into VB .NET:

1. In the Open Project dialog, select a VB6 project (.vbp) file.
2. Click Open.

   The Visual Basic Upgrade wizard opens (**Figure 1.9**).
3. Fill in the information requested by the wizard (mainly the location for the converted project).
4. Click Next on the final pane of the wizard.

   The wizard now converts the VB6 code to VB .NET code, storing the converted project in the location you designate. It then creates a task list of things you need to review (**Figure 1.10**), places comments regarding potential issues in the code, and adds a conversion report to the converted project (**Figure 1.11**).

✔ Tip

- The Visual Basic Upgrade wizard does a very creditable job of converting VB6 code to VB .NET code. However, the automated conversion is only the starting point for a VB .NET project. Usually, you'll be better off starting a new VB .NET project rather than relying on the wizard, because you'll have cleaner code that takes better advantage of .NET features.

Figure 1.9 The Visual Basic Upgrade wizard converts VB6 code to VB .NET.

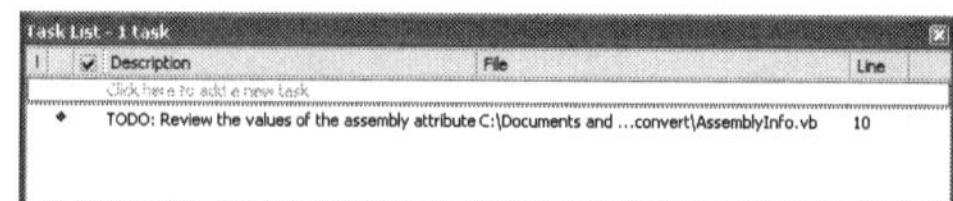

Figure 1.10 After the wizard completes the code conversion, it provides a task list of further steps.

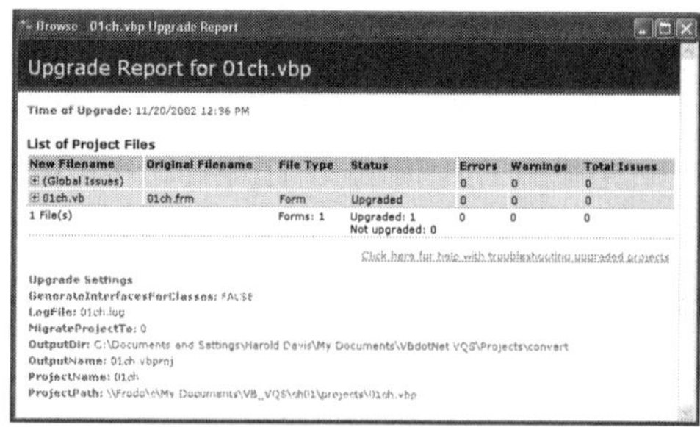

Figure 1.11 The wizard also creates an upgrade report, which details the steps taken in the conversion process.

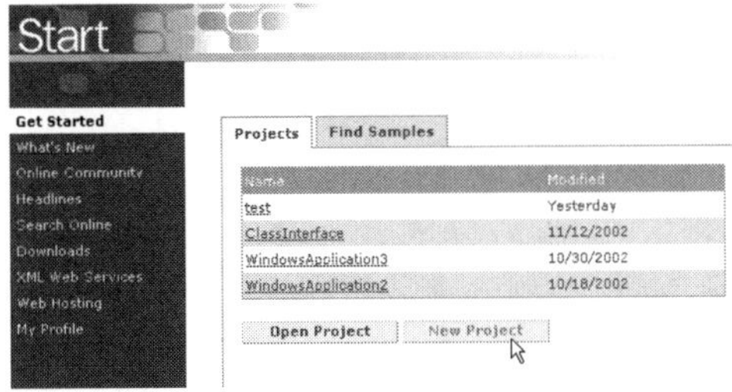

Figure 1.12 Use the New Project button on the Projects tab to open the New Project dialog.

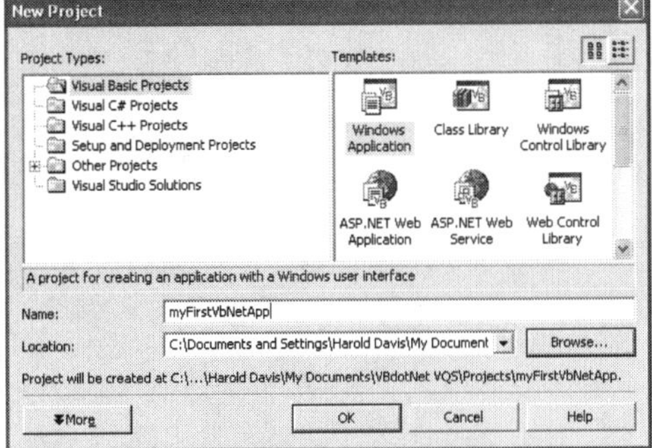

Figure 1.13 Use the New Project dialog to specify a project type, template, name, and location.

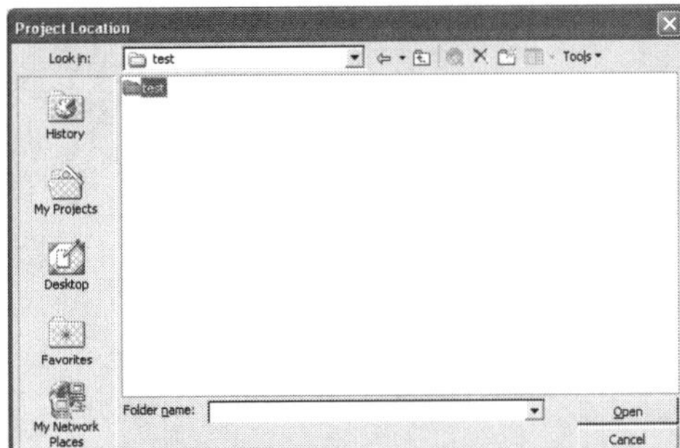

Figure 1.14 You can use the Project Location dialog to select a location for project source code files.

Starting a new project

If you don't want to open an existing project, the chances are good that you've fired up Visual Studio to get to work on a new project.

To open a new project:

1. Click the Get Started link on the left side of the Start page to display the Projects tab if it is not already displayed.
2. On the Projects tab, click the New Project button (**Figure 1.12**).

   The New Project dialog opens (**Figure 1.13**).
3. In the Project Types pane, select Visual Basic Projects.
4. In the Templates pane, select a project template: for example, Windows Application, which is used to create a project with a Windows user interface.

   (The various project templates are described later in this chapter.)
5. In the Name text box, provide a name for the project.
6. Provide a starting location for the project source files by doing *one* of the following:
   - Accept the Visual Studio suggestion.
   - Select a location from the Location drop-down list box.
   - Type a location in the Location list box.
   - Click Browse to open the Project Location dialog (**Figure 1.14**); then specify a location.
7. After you specify the project type, template, name, and location provided, click OK.

   The project will be created, ready for use in the Visual Studio environment.

✔ Tip

- Anther way to open the New Project dialog is to choose File from the Visual Studio menu bar and then select New > Project.

Configuring Visual Studio .NET

Configuring Visual Studio means customizing it to meet your particular needs. You specify the most important configuration settings for Visual Studio in the Options dialog.

There are also some configuration items that you may want to set on a per-solution or per-project basis; these are discussed in "Solutions, Projects, and Modules" later in this chapter.

In this section, you'll learn about a few of the key configuration items that can be set using the Options dialog.

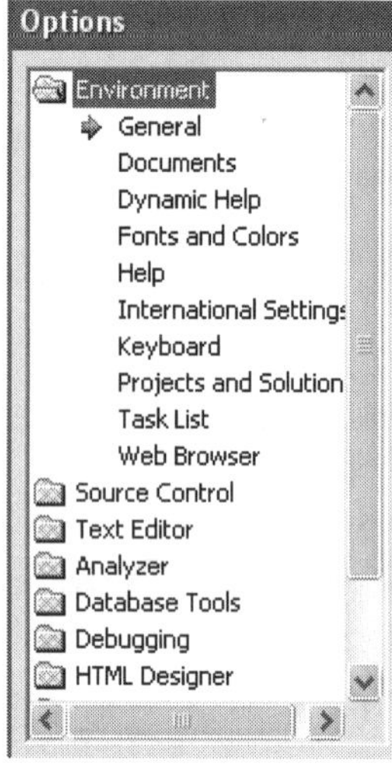

Figure 1.15 You can set many configuration items in the Options dialog, navigating through the various items using the visual folder metaphor shown here.

To open the Options dialog:

- From the Visual Studio menu bar, choose Tools and then select Options.

  The Options dialog opens. As you can see in **Figure 1.15**, you can set many options using the Options dialog.

You won't usually need to change the default settings for the configuration items shown in the Options dialog. But if you are curious about a particular setting, you can easily find out more about it by clicking the Help button on the tab where the configuration item is located.

Tabbed versus MDI environment

Windows in Visual Studio can be displayed in either of two modes: a tabbed or a multiple document interface (MDI) environment.

You'll probably have to play with the two modes to get a feel for them, but generally, the tabbed environment organizes windows as tabbed groups, making it easy to navigate multiple document windows by clicking the tab for the window (**Figure 1.16**). In contrast, in the MDI environment, some of the

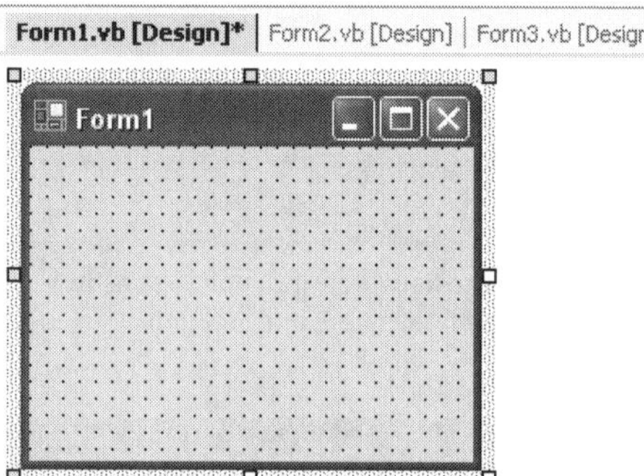

Figure 1.16 In the tabbed environment, you use the tabs at the top of the Form designer to navigate between forms.

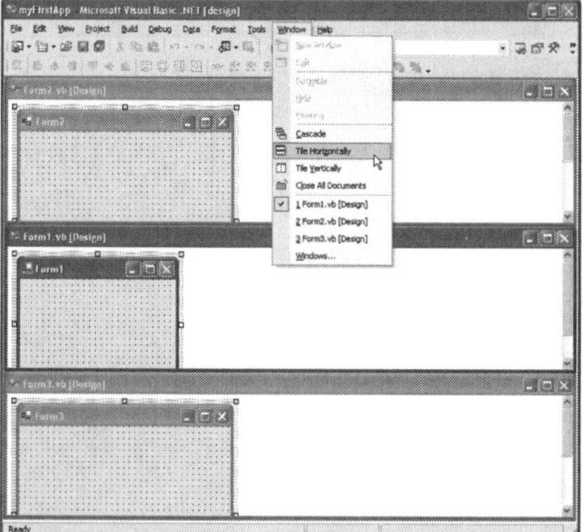

Figure 1.17 In the MDI environment, tabs do not appear at the top of the document window, and you can arrange windows using the Cascade and Tile commands on the Window menu.

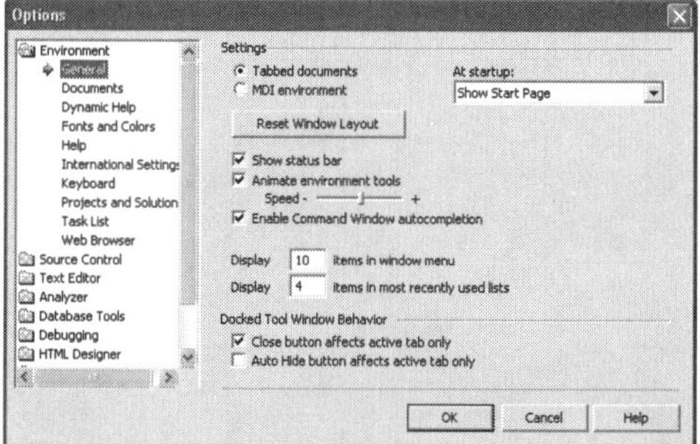

Figure 1.18 Use the Environment General page of the Options dialog to set the style of the Visual Studio environment (and much more).

space that is otherwise occupied by the tabs is reclaimed. (Somewhat confusingly, some of the windows that are part of the Visual Studio IDE in an MDI environment can still have tabs.) You can navigate between windows by pressing Ctrl+Tab on the keyboard or by using one of the organizational options on the Visual Studio Window menu, such as Tile (**Figure 1.17**). (These Window menu items do not appear when the environment is set to Tabbed.)

To switch between MDI and tabbed environments:

1. From the Tools menu, select Options.

   The Options dialog opens.

2. Expand the Environments tab and select General.

   The Environment General page of the Options dialog appears (**Figure 1.18**).

3. In the Settings area at the top of the dialog, do *one* of the following:

   ▲ To switch to a tabbed environment, select the Tabbed Documents radio button.

   or

   ▲ To switch to an MDI environment, select the MDI Environment radio button.

4. Click OK.

✔ Tips

■ To make an environment change take effect, you must close and reopen Visual Studio.

■ You can restore the environment to its default layout by clicking the Reset Window Layout button, located just below the Settings options in the Options dialog.

At-startup alternatives

In the Options dialog, you can also specify whether you want the Start page to appear when Visual Studio opens (the default), or you can specify an alternative that you prefer. At the upper right of the Environment General page in the Options dialog, you'll find the At Startup drop-down list (**Figure 1.19**). You can choose among the following alternatives to the Start page:

- The last solution that was loaded in Visual Studio
- The Open Project dialog (explained earlier in this chapter)
- The New Project dialog (explained earlier in this chapter)
- An empty environment, ready for whatever you want to do with it

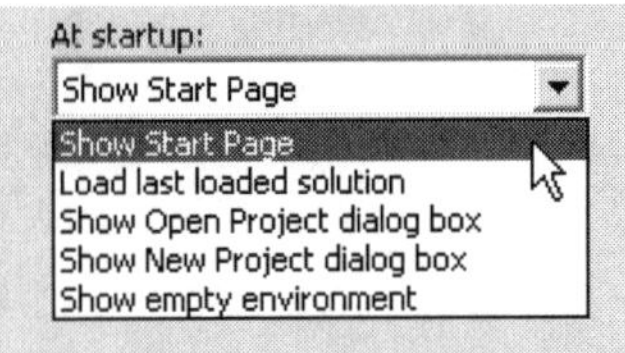

Figure 1.19 Use the At Startup drop-down list to select an alternative to showing the Start page when you open Visual Studio.

Saving source files

Another important setting in the Options dialog determines the way source files are saved. These are your choices:

- **Save Changes to Open Documents.** Choose this option to automatically save all changes you've made to source files when you close a module, project, or solution.
- **Prompt to Save Changes to Open Documents.** When you select this option, you are prompted to save changes to source files when you close them. This is the setting I recommend; it gives you the flexibility to discard changes when you want to, but minimizes the risk of accidentally losing your work.

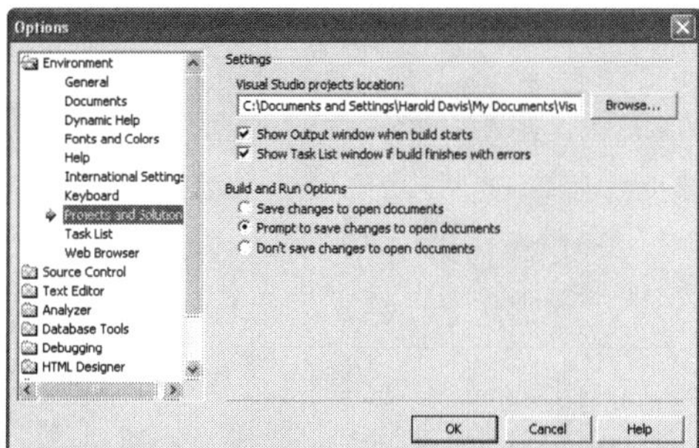

Figure 1.20 You can use the Projects and Solutions page of the Options dialog to set Visual Studio to prompt you to save changes to open documents.

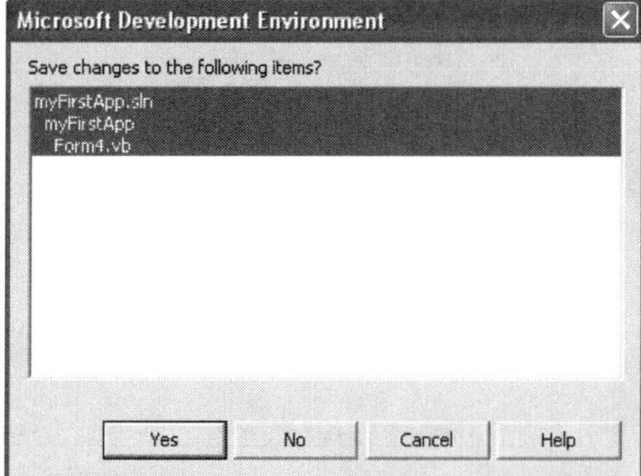

Figure 1.21 If you select Prompt to Save Changes to Open Documents, you will be prompted to save any source files containing unsaved changes when you close Visual Studio.

- **Don't Save Changes to Open Documents.** This is the default setting when you first install Visual Studio. When you select this option, Visual Studio doesn't save changes to source files when they are closed, so you should probably switch to one of the other options. Otherwise, you could inadvertently lose some of your work.

To prompt to save changes:

1. With the Options dialog open, expand the Environment folder in the left pane and then select Projects and Solutions.

   The Projects and Solutions page of the Options dialog opens (**Figure 1.20**).

2. Under Build and Run Options, select Prompt to Save Changes to Open Documents.

3. Click OK.

   The next time you make a change to a source file and then attempt to close Visual Studio, you'll be prompted to save the change if you haven't already done so (**Figure 1.21**).

✔ Tip

- The option named Don't Save Changes to Open Documents is risky because you can easily accidentally lose unsaved work.

Solutions, Projects, and Modules

A *project* is a group of source files, or *modules*, that, when compiled and run, form a single application, such as an executable program, a library, a Web service, or an ASP.NET Web application.

A *solution* is a container for a project or related projects and is used to organize projects. If you create a project—for example, using the New Project dialog—it is always placed in a solution (which is given by default the same name as the project).

When a solution contains multiple projects, they are generally related. Here are some fairly typical scenarios in which it would make sense to organize several projects into one solution:

- One project within a solution compiles to an executable application, and another project in the same solution compiles to a library that the executable uses.
- One project within a solution compiles to an executable application, and another project in the same solution compiles to the setup program for the application.
- One or more projects within a solution are the source files for custom controls used by another project within the solution.

However, most of the time—particularly at first—you will be working with solutions that contain one project, with the solution and the project having the same name.

Error Messages: Creating a Web Application

If you get an error message when you try to create an ASP.NET Web Application project or an ASP.NET Web Service project, check to make sure that Internet Information Services (IIS) is installed on your system; it is an optional component when you install Windows XP Professional. Also check to ensure that you have developer access to IIS on a remote host.

If the error message still appears, make sure that you installed Web Development Server Components as part of Visual Studio (this is another installation option) and that the user name you logged in with is registered with the VS Developers Group (which authorizes access for Web development).

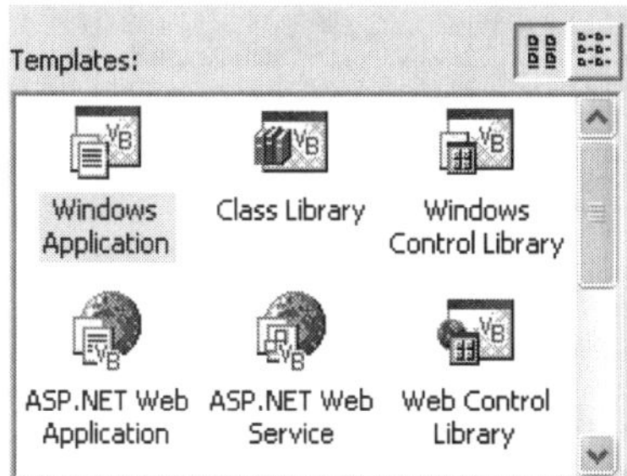

Figure 1.22 Use the Templates pane of the New Project dialog to select a project type.

Types of projects

You select a type of project by choosing a template from the Templates pane of the New Project dialog (**Figure 1.22**). (If you forget how to access the New Project dialog, see "To open a new project" earlier in this chapter.)

These are the most important project types:

- **Windows Application.** Used to create a Windows form executable application, usually with an .exe file extension. This is the standard kind of application you generally find running on the Microsoft Windows operating system.
- **Class Library.** Used to create a library file, usually with a .dll file extension.
- **Windows Control Library.** Used to create a custom Windows control (or controls).
- **ASP.NET Web Application.** Used to create ASP.NET Web applications hosted by Internet Information Services (IIS).
- **ASP.NET Web Service.** Used to create a Web service and a test project for the Web service.
- **Web Control Library.** Used to create custom Web controls to be used with ASP.NET Web applications.
- **Console Application.** Used to create executable applications that run from the command-line console.

Using Solution Explorer

Solution Explorer is the Visual Studio tool for navigating among projects in a solution, and—more often—between modules within projects.

To open Solution Explorer:

- From the View menu, choose Solution Explorer.

  Solution Explorer opens, showing the currently loaded solution and project or projects (**Figure 1.23**).

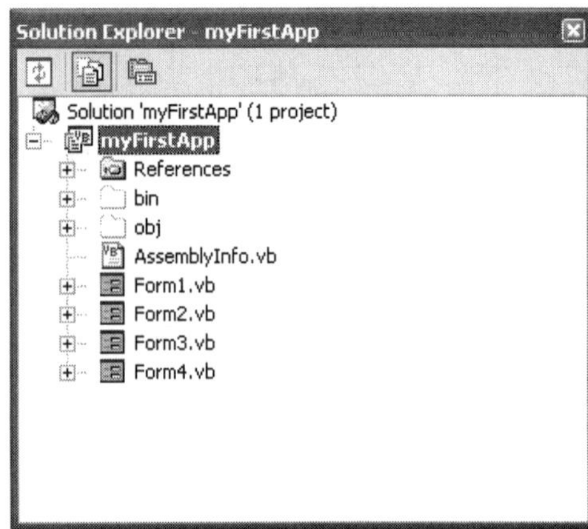

Figure 1.23 Use Solution Explorer to navigate through project modules and projects in a solution.

✔ Tips

- To see all of the modules in a project, expand the items in Solution Explorer by clicking the icons to the left of the items.
- The Show All Files button, located on the toolbar that runs across the top of Solution Explorer, toggles Solution Explorer between two modes: one in which only the modules for a project are displayed, and the Show All Files mode, in which the source files that underlie the module files are also displayed.

If you want to use a solution to manage multiple projects, you need to be able to add new (or existing) projects to a solution.

To add a new project to an existing solution:

1. With Solution Explorer open, select the solution to which you want to add a project (at the top of the Solution Explorer window).
2. Right-click to open the context menu for the solution.
3. Choose Add from the context menu.
4. From the submenu that opens, choose New Project (**Figure 1.24**).

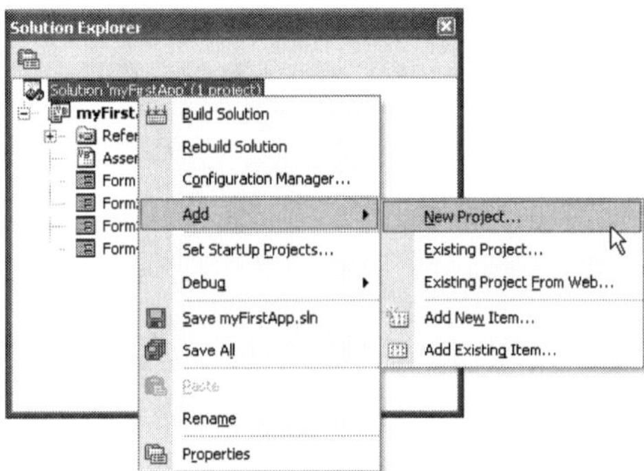

Figure 1.24 You can add a new project to an existing solution using the context menu for the solution in Solution Explorer.

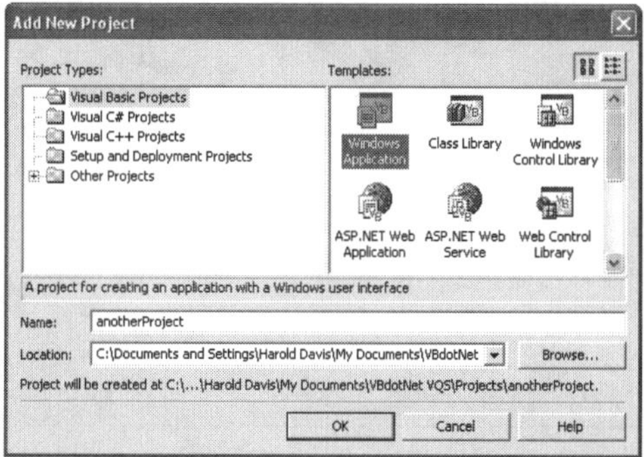

Figure 1.25 Use the Add New Project dialog to add a new project to a solution. (Note that this is a slightly different dialog than the New Project dialog, shown in Figure 1.26.)

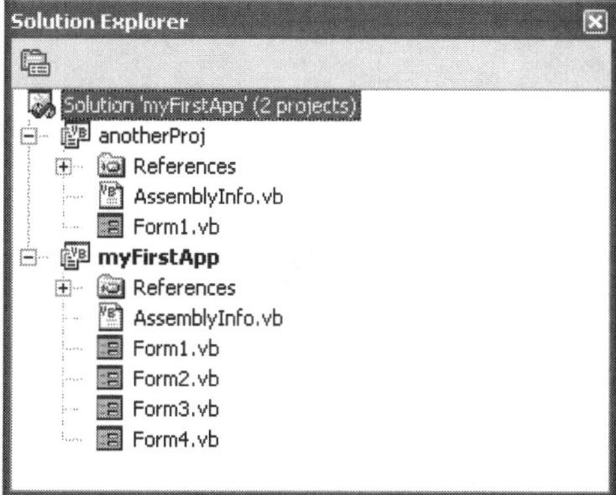

Figure 1.26 You can also add a new project using the New Project dialog if the Add to Solution option is selected. (Note that this dialog differs slightly from the Add New Project dialog shown in Figure 1.25.)

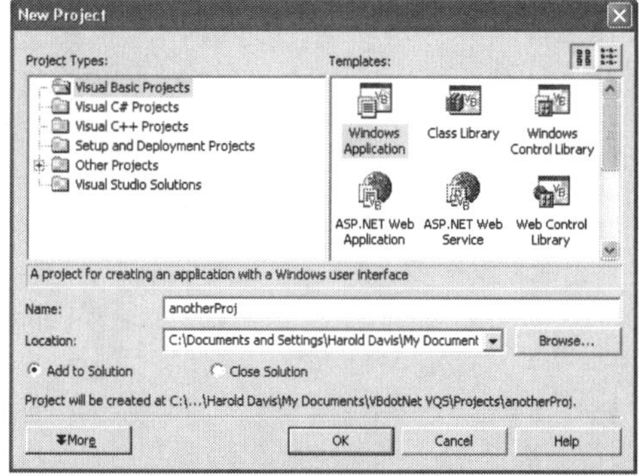

Figure 1.27 If a solution contains multiple projects, Solution Explorer shows all projects.

The Add New Project dialog opens (**Figure 1.25**).

5. Give the new project a name and click OK.

   The new project is added to the existing solution, which now contains multiple projects (**Figure 1.26**).

✔ Tip

- Another way to add a new project in Visual Studio is to choose File > New Project. The New Project dialog appears. In this dialog, provide a name for the new project and make sure that Add to Solution is selected (**Figure 1.27**). When you click OK, the project will be added to the solution.

To add an existing project to a solution:

1. With Solution Explorer open, select the solution to which you want to add an existing project.
2. Right-click to open the context menu for the solution and choose Add from the context menu.
3. From the submenu that opens, choose Existing Project.

✔ Tip

- Another way to add an existing project in Visual Studio is to choose File > Open Project. Be sure that when the Open Project dialog appears, Add to Solution (rather than Close Solution) is selected.

Property pages for a solution

Some configuration properties are set on a per-solution basis. This is done using the Property Pages dialog for the solution. The most important settings this dialog controls are the order in which projects run (assuming that a solution contains multiple projects) and the designation of the Startup project.

If a solution contains multiple projects, you may need to specify whether multiple projects or only one project will run. If more than one will run, you may also need to specify which project runs first. You do this by specifying the Startup project.

To set the Startup project:

1. With Solution Explorer open, select a solution (at the top of the Solution Explorer window).

   If you forget how to open Solution Explorer, see "To open Solution Explorer" earlier in this chapter.

2. Open the Property Pages dialog for the solution (**Figure 1.28**), either by clicking the Properties icon on the Solution Explorer toolbar or by choosing Properties from the solution's right-click context menu.

3. To set a single Startup project, select the Single Startup Project radio button and then select the Startup project from the drop-down list shown in Figure 1.28.

   or

   To run more than one project at startup, select the Multiple Startup Projects radio button (**Figure 1.29**). Then use the Move Up and Move Down buttons to set the execution order of the projects.

✔ Tip

- You can also set the Startup project by first selecting the project in Solution Explorer and then, from the Visual Studio Project menu, choosing Set as Startup Project.

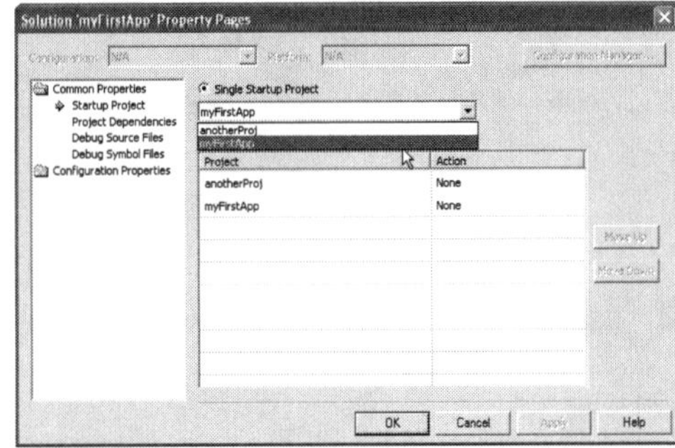

Figure 1.28 Use the Property Pages dialog for a solution to specify a Startup project.

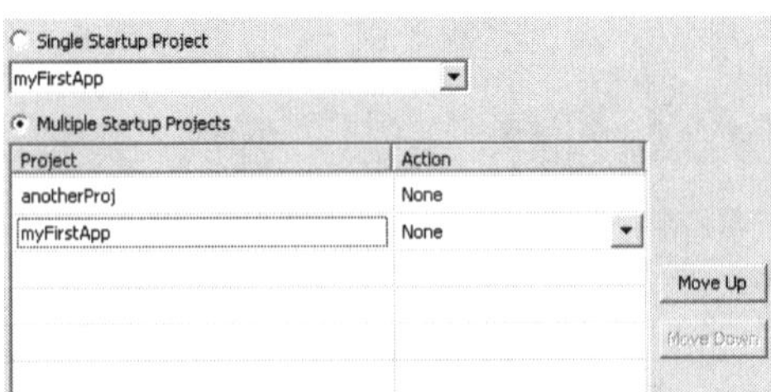

Figure 1.29 If Multiple Startup Projects is selected, you can use the Move Up and Move Down buttons to set the execution order.

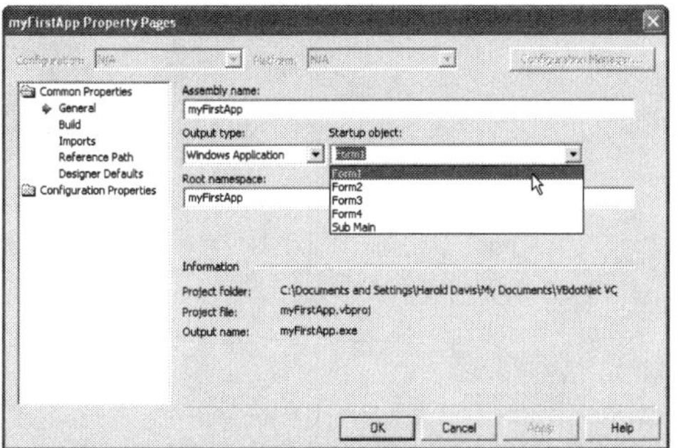

Figure 1.30 Use the General page of the Property Pages dialog to specify a Startup object for the project.

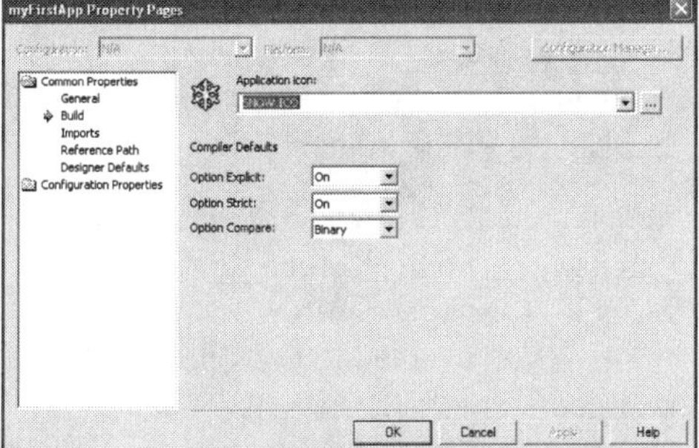

Figure 1.31 Use the Build page of the Property Pages dialog for a project to designate an application icon and set important compiler options.

Setting property pages for a project

Many configuration options are set on a per-project basis using the Property Pages dialog for the project.

One of these options is the project Startup object. In the case of a Windows application, this is either a class derived from the Form class or a Sub Main procedure, as explained in Chapter 5, "Windows Forms."

To set the Startup object for a project:

1. Select the project in Solution Explorer.
2. Right-click to open the context menu for the project and then select Properties.

   The Property Pages dialog for the project opens (**Figure 1.30**).
3. On the General page, select the Startup object using the drop-down list shown in Figure 1.30.
4. Click OK.

You also set a number of important options on the Build page of the Property Pages dialog for a project (**Figure 1.31**). You use this page to designate the icon associated with an application.

✔ Tip

- You can use the icons that shipped with VB .NET if you want. They are located in the Common7\Graphics\icons folder installed with the rest of Visual Studio (usually, the path is \Program Files\Microsoft Visual Studio .NET\Common7\Graphics\icons).

You can also use the Build page to set important compiler options for the project:

- **Option Explicit**, which can be set to On or Off. If set to On, this option requires explicit variable declaration and will throw a syntax error at compilation if you attempt to use an undeclared variable. By default, Option Explicit is set to On, and I recommend that you keep it this way.
- **Option Strict**, which can be set to On or Off. When set to On, Option Strict requires explicit type conversion for any type of conversion that might conceivably cause loss of data. Setting this option to On requires a bit more effort on the part of the programmer, but this is the right approach and reduces the possibility of errors in the long run. By default, Option Explicit is set to Off, but I recommend that you change it to On.
- **Option Compare**, which can be set to Binary or Text. When Binary is specified, string comparisons are case sensitive; when Text is specified, they are case insensitive. There is seldom a good reason to change Option Compare from the default, which is Binary.

To set Option Explicit and Option Strict compiler options:

1. On the Build page of a project's Property Pages dialog, use the drop-down lists to set Option Explicit and/or Option Strict to On or Off.
2. Click OK when your selections are complete.

Setting Option Explicit and Option Strict in Code

Using the Property Pages dialog for a project, you can set Option Strict and Option Explicit on a per-project basis.

You should also know that these options can be set in code on a per-source-file basis. To turn both options on in this manner, you would add the following statements in the Code Editor before any other code in a module:

```
Option Explicit On
Option Strict On
```

(Note: If you don't know how to open the Code Editor, see "To open the Code Editor" later in this chapter. If you're not familiar with the term *module*, a module is a source code file that is part of a project. Modules are explained more fully in the next section.)

Generally, you should run with these options turned on (unless you like living dangerously or sloppily), so you may as well just turn them on at the project level, unless you want to add the code statements to every module in your project. If you do this, you do gain the advantage of explicitly informing anyone reading your code that these options are enabled.

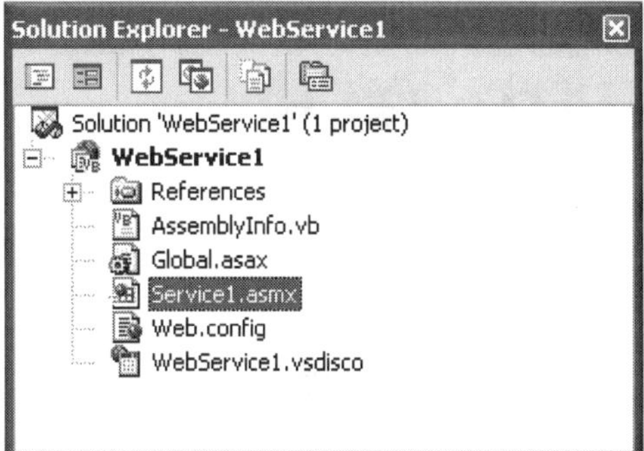

Figure 1.32 The default ASP.NET Web Service project in Solution Explorer includes a Web Service module, a Web.config file, and other files.

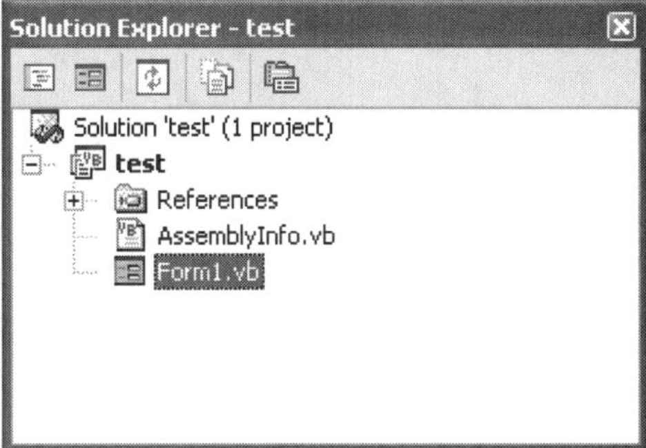

Figure 1.33 The default Windows Application project in Solution Explorer includes a Form module and other files.

Types of modules

Projects are made up of modules that contain source code. The type of modules that make up a project—and which are available to be added to a project—depends on the type of project. For example, an ASP.NET Web Service project is made up of modules that are very different from those of a Windows Application project, as you can see by comparing **Figure 1.32** and **Figure 1.33**.

Some module types, such as a Class module, can be opened only in the Code Editor (see the "Using the Code Editor" section later in this chapter). Other module types, such as Windows Form or Web Form, can be opened in the Code Editor to edit the source code. In addition, they can be visually designed using the appropriate Form designer.

continues on next page

The types of modules you can add to a project include the following:

- **Windows Form.** Used as the basis for a window in a Windows application (**Figure 1.34**).
- **Web Form.** Used as the basis for an ASP.NET Web application (**Figure 1.35**).
- **Web Service.** A module used for creating an ASP.NET Web service.
- **Class.** A code module containing an empty class declaration.
- **Module.** An empty code module.
- **User Control.** The basis for a Windows custom control, created using a visual designer.
- **Web User Control.** The basis for an ASP.NET server control, created using a visual designer.
- **DataSet.** Used to hold tables of data (see Chapter 15, "XML, Data, and ADO.NET," for more information).
- **XML.** An XML data file (see Chapter 15 for more information).
- **XMLSchema.** An XML schema file (see Chapter 15 for more information).

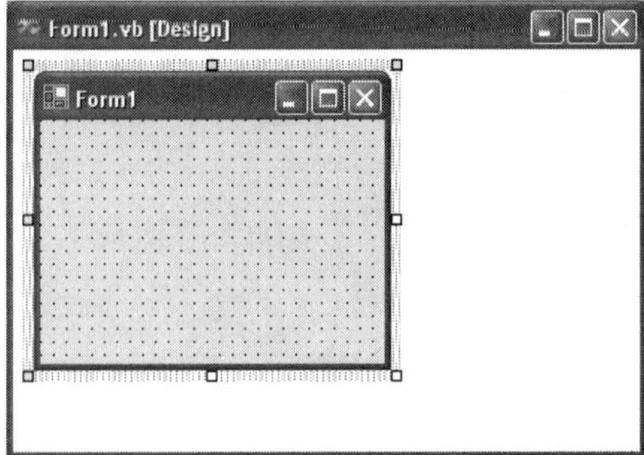

Figure 1.34 Use a Windows Form module to create a window in a Windows desktop application.

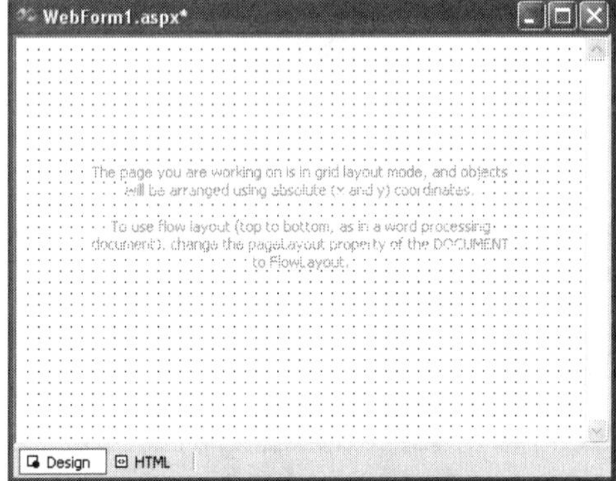

Figure 1.35 Use a Web Form module as the basis for an ASP.NET Web application.

✔ Tips

- You can use a project to create an ASP.NET Web application or a Windows form application, but not both at the same time. Thus, as you'd expect, a single project cannot have both a Web Form and a Windows Form module.
- In the same way, User Control modules can be used as part of Windows applications (but not ASP.NET applications), and Web User Control modules can be part of an ASP.NET application (but not a Windows application).

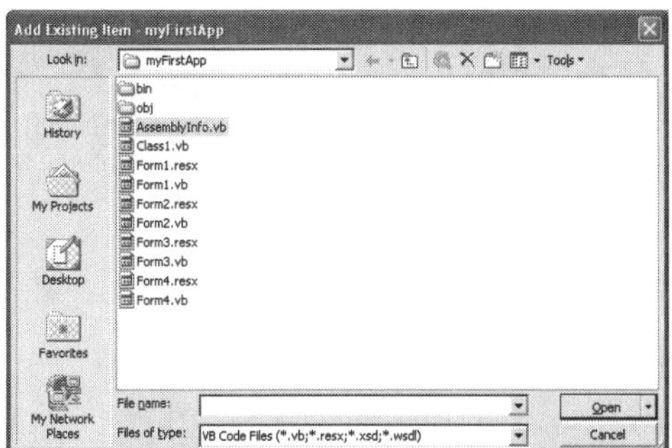

Figure 1.36 Use the Add Existing Item dialog to add an existing module to a project.

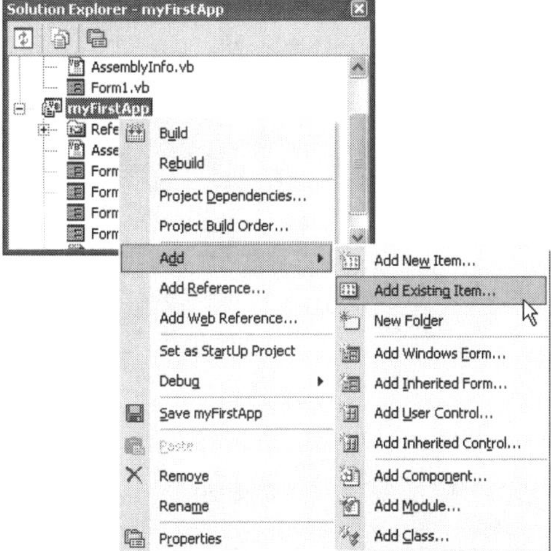

Figure 1.37 You can use the context menus in Solution Explorer to open the Add Existing Item dialog.

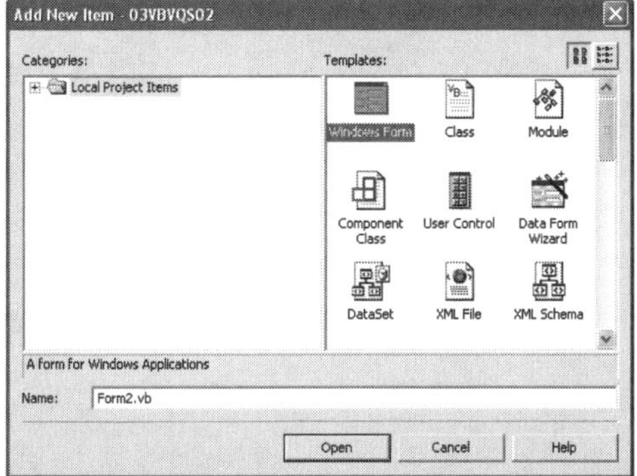

Figure 1.38 Use the Add New Item dialog to add a new module to a project.

It's easy to add an existing module or a new module to a project.

To add an existing module to a project:

1. Open the Add Existing Item dialog by doing *one* of the following (**Figure 1.36**):
   - ▲ From the Visual Studio Project menu, select Add Existing Item.
   - ▲ Right-click within a project in Solution Explorer and choose Add > Add Existing Item (**Figure 1.37**).
2. Select the module you want to add.
3. Click Open.

   The module is added to your project.

To add a new module to a project:

1. Open the Add New Item dialog by doing *one* of the following: (**Figure 1.38**)
   - ▲ From the Visual Studio Project menu, select Add New Item.
   - ▲ Right-click within a project in Solution Explorer and choose Add > Add New Item.
2. From the Templates pane of the Add New Item dialog, select the type of module to add: for example, Windows Form.
3. Give the module a file name (or accept the default name).
4. Click Open.

   The new module is added to your project.

✔ Tip

- You'll notice various items on the Project menu (and the Solution Explorer context menu) that add specific kinds of new modules. Choosing one of these items, such as Add Windows Form or Add Class, opens the Add New Item dialog with the module type preselected in the Templates pane. This approach amounts to a slight shortcut, but the results are the same as if you'd opened the generic Add New Item dialog and then selected a template.

Visual Studio Tools

This section briefly introduces four of the most important Visual Studio tools: the Code Editor, Form designers, Toolbox, and Properties window.

✔ Tip

- Other Visual Studio tools are covered later in this book. You'll find a discussion of the Class View window in Chapter 3, "Working with Classes"; the Object Browser in Chapter 14, "The Object Browser"; and Server Explorer in Chapter 15, "XML, Data, and ADO.NET."

Using the Code Editor

The Code Editor is, of course, the heart of Visual Studio. It's what you'll use to enter the Visual Basic .NET code that is the primary subject matter of this book.

You'll gather information on many of the nifty features of the Code Editor as we go along, but for now we'll focus on just one important feature: statement auto-completion.

To see how this feature works, let's examine a trivial example. You may remember that earlier in this chapter, I told you how to add Option Explicit On and Option Strict On statements at the beginning of any code file.

If you start by adding the keyword Option at the top of a code file and then enter a space, the Code Editor auto-completion feature will supply a drop-down list of the keywords that can legally continue the statement (**Figure 1.39**). If you select a keyword from the drop-down list, such as Explicit, then auto-completion will show you the keywords that can follow it (On or Off).

This is a very handy feature because with it, you don't have to remember much about a code statement to get the syntax right; you just need to remember how the statement begins.

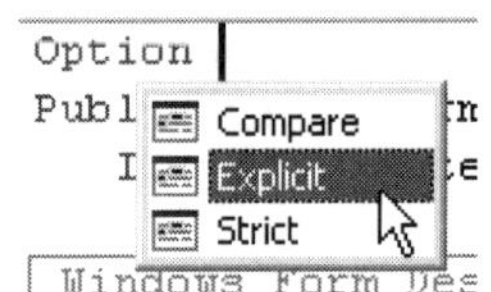

Figure 1.39 The Code Editor's auto-completion feature supplies the possible keywords that can correctly continue a statement.

To open the Code Editor:

1. Select a module that contains code in Solution Explorer.
2. Do *one* of the following:
   - ▲ In Visual Studio, choose View > Code.
   - ▲ In Solution Explorer, double-click a module that contains only code, such as a Class file.
   - ▲ For a module that contains code but can be modified using a designer, such as a Windows Form or Web Form module, select the module in Solution Explorer and, from the right-click context menu, choose View Code.

Using the Form designers

As already noted, some kinds of modules—notably Windows Form, Web Form, and Web Service modules—can be edited visually using a special designer.

✔ Tip

- Ultimately, the designer merely serves as a convenience, because it is easier to set some things visually than to set them in code. But you can always achieve the same results as you can in a designer by modifying the code related to the module in the Code Editor. For further discussion, see Chapter 4.

To open a form in its designer:

- Do *one* of the following:
  - ▲ Double-click a Windows Form, Web Form, or Web Service module in Solution Explorer.
  - ▲ Select a module in Solution Explorer that provides a designer and then, in Visual Studio, choose View > Designer.
  - ▲ In Solution Explorer, select a module that provides a designer and then, from the right-click context menu, choose View Designer.

To resize a form:

1. Open a form in its designer.
2. Move the mouse over one of the *handles* (shown as small boxes in **Figure 1.40**) on the bottom or right of the form until the mouse pointer changes to a double-headed arrow.
3. Drag the form by its handles to the new size you desire.

✔ Tip

- To change both the vertical and horizontal size of the form simultaneously, drag the handle in the lower-right corner.

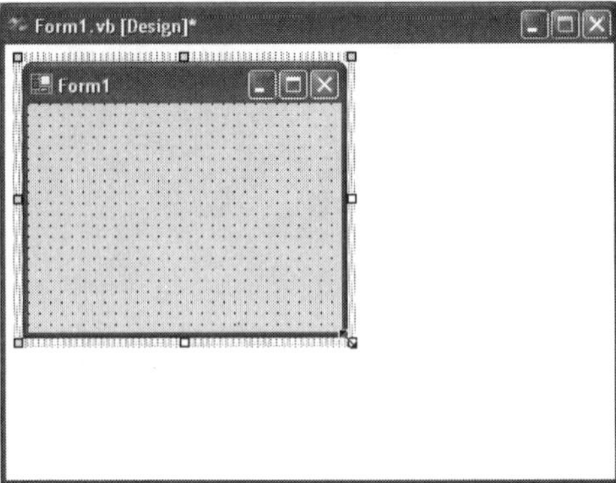

Figure 1.40 To resize a form, drag the handles shown in the form's designer.

Using the Toolbox

You can use the Toolbox to visually add controls and components to a Windows form, Web form, or Web service in its designer.

✔ Tip

- Controls and components are reusable blocks of code that can be hosted by a container such as a form. Controls have a visual user interface, whereas components do not.

The controls and components in the Toolbox can be customized, as you'll see in Chapter 10, "Controls That Accept User Input."

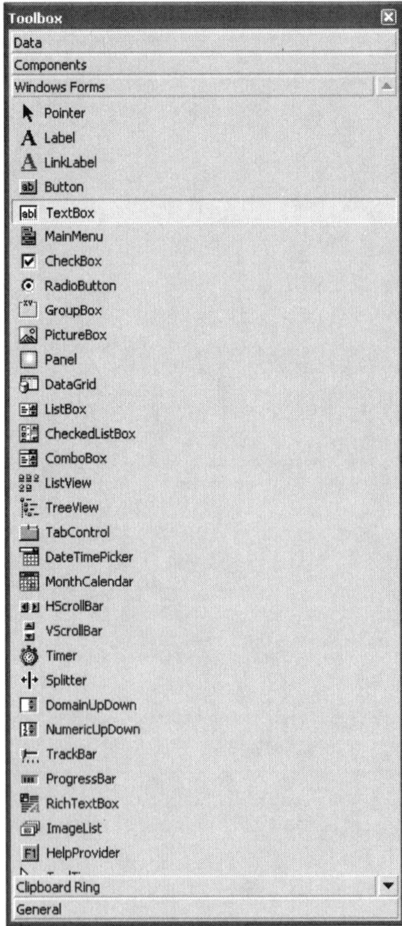

Figure 1.41 Out-of-the-box Toolbox for use with a Windows form.

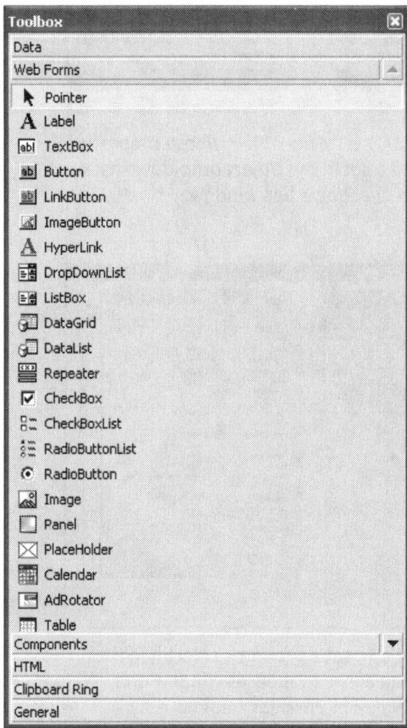

Figure 1.42 Out-of-the-box Toolbox for use with a Web form.

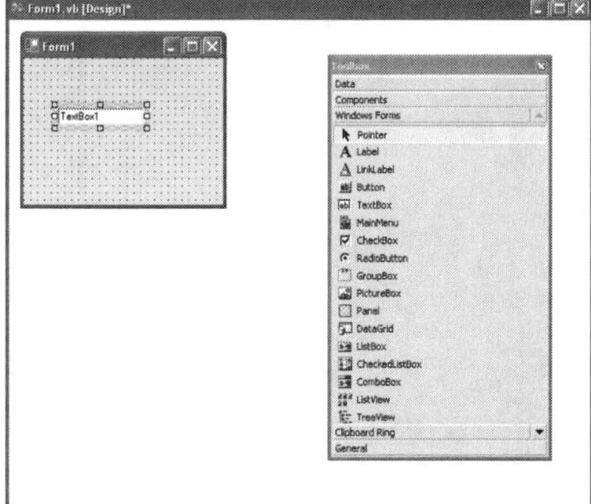

Figure 1.43 Double-click, or drag and drop, a control or component on the Toolbox to place an instance of it on the form in its designer.

The out-of-the-box controls and components available in the Toolbox depend on the type of project and module—that is, the items for a Windows form (**Figure 1.41**) are different from the items for a Web form (**Figure 1.42**).

To open the Toolbox:

- With a module open in its designer, in Visual Studio choose View > Toolbox.

To add a control to a Windows form:

1. Open a Windows form in its designer.
2. Open the Toolbox.
3. Double-click a control or component in the Toolbox.

   An instance of the control or component is placed on the form (**Figure 1.43**).

✔ Tip

- Alternatively, you can drag and drop a control or component from the Toolbox to place an instance on the form.

Using the Properties window

The Properties window provides a convenient way to set *properties.* A property is a setting that describes something about an object such as a form or control.

✔ Tip

- The Properties window is an important tool that helps make Visual Studio a rapid application development (RAD) environment. However, every property set in the Properties window can also be set strictly using code.

To open the Properties window:

- In Visual Studio, choose View > Properties Window.

To set a form property:

1. Open a form in its designer.
2. Open the Properties window.
3. Make sure that the form is selected in the Object drop-down list at the top of the Properties window (**Figure 1.44**).
4. In the left column of the Properties window, select the property you want to set (the Text property, which sets the form caption, is shown in **Figure 1.45**).
5. In the right column of the Properties window, enter the new property value.
6. Click some other property in the Properties window, or click outside the Properties window, to apply the new property to the form.

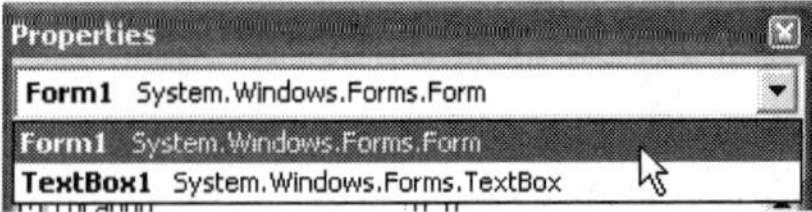

Figure 1.44 Select the object whose properties you want to set in the Object drop-down list at the top of the Properties window.

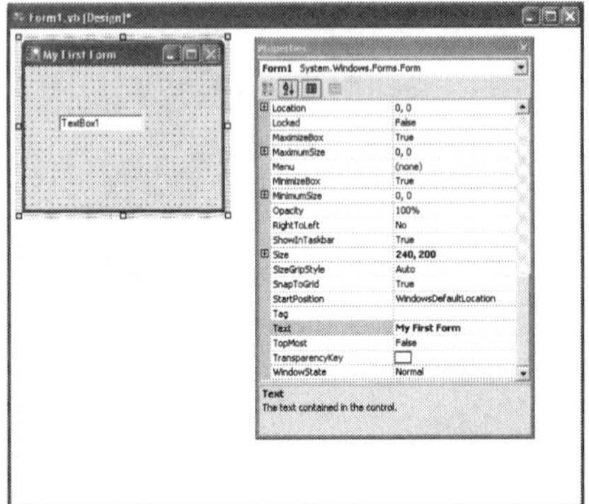

Figure 1.45 To set a property, select it in the left column of the Properties window and enter its value in the right column.

Properties in the Properties window can be viewed as a single alphabetical list or categorized into functional groups.

To switch between alphabetical and categorical property lists:

- To view properties by category, click the Categorized (left-most) button on the Properties window toolbar.

  or

- To view all properties alphabetically, click the Alphabetic (second from left) button on the Properties window toolbar.

Setting the property of a control that has been seated on a form works the same way as setting the property of the form itself.

To set a control property:

1. Open a form in its designer.
2. Add an instance of a control, such as a TextBox control, to the form.
3. Open the Properties window.

Figure 1.46 The Text property of the TextBox control is set to Hello!.

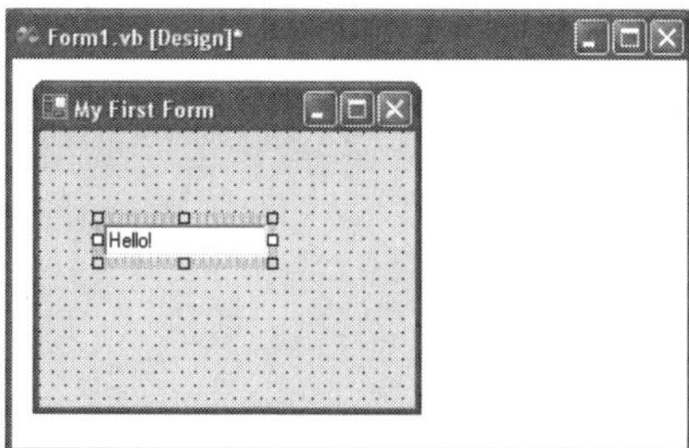

Figure 1.47 When you check the form in its designer, you'll see that the new property value has been applied to the TextBox control.

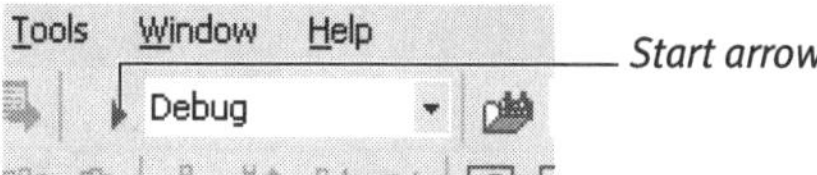

Figure 1.48 You can use the Start arrow to run a project.

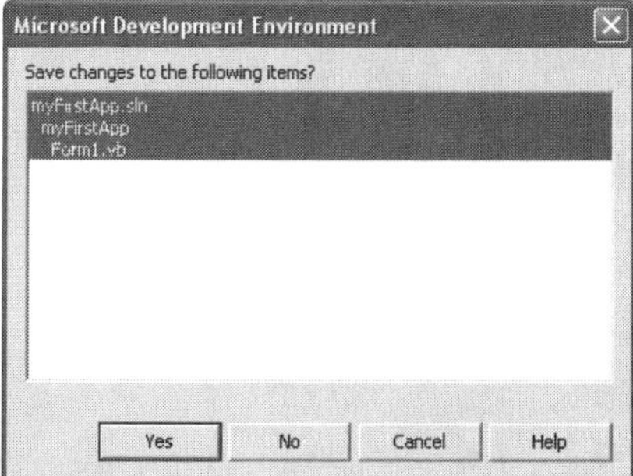

Figure 1.49 If you've set the Build options to Prompt to Save Changes, as suggested earlier in this chapter, you will be prompted to save any changes to open files when you run a project.

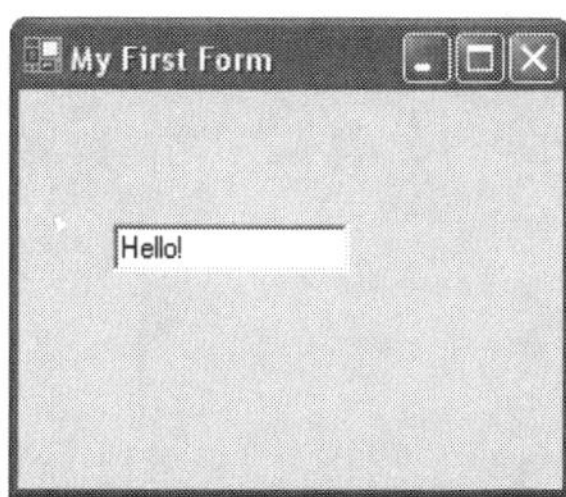

Figure 1.50 The form and control property values set using the Properties window are displayed when the project is compiled and run.

4. Make sure that the control (the TextBox control) is selected in the Object drop-down list at the top of the Properties window.

5. In the left column of the Properties window, select the property you want to set. (The Text property, which sets the initial text displayed in the TextBox control, is shown in **Figure 1.46**.)

6. In the right column of the Properties window, enter the new property value (in Figure 1.46 it is Hello!).

7. Click with the mouse on some other property in the Properties window, or click outside the Properties window, to apply the new property to the control. You can look at the control seated on the form in its designer (**Figure 1.47**) to verify that the property has been changed.

If you run the project, you will see the new form caption and the new control property as they really look at run time, and not just in the Visual Studio design-time environment.

To run a project:

1. Do *one* of the following:
   - ▲ From the Visual Studio Debug menu, choose Start.
   - ▲ Press the F5 key.
   - ▲ On the Visual Studio toolbar, click the Start arrow to the left of the Configuration drop-down list (**Figure 1.48**).

2. Click Yes when prompted to save changes (**Figure 1.49**).

   The project will compile and run, showing the changes you made to properties using the Properties window (**Figure 1.50**).

Summary

In this chapter, you learned how to:

- Use the Visual Studio Start page
- Open an existing project
- Import a VB6 project in VB .NET
- Start a new project
- Configure Visual Studio options
- Describe the different kinds of projects
- Describe solutions and how they relate to projects
- Work with Solution Explorer
- Set Option Explicit and Option Strict
- Describe the different kinds of modules
- Add a module to a project
- Work with the Code Editor
- Work with Form designers
- Add a control to a form
- Set control and form properties
- Compile and run a project

2

Creating a Web Service

Now that you know how to navigate around the Visual Studio .NET development environment, it's time to create your first Visual Basic .NET program.

Because the ability to easily and quickly create Web services is one of the most exciting features of Microsoft's .NET initiative, this chapter shows you how to create and test an ASP.NET Web service as your first program.

Understanding Web Services

What is a Web service? In its simplest form, a Web service offers a method (or methods) that can be invoked over the Web using open standards for communication, including Hypertext Transfer Protocol (HTTP) and eXtensible Markup Language (XML). (If you're new to the term *method,* you should know that it refers to a function or procedure that is associated with an object. In other words, when a method is invoked, it executes an action of some sort.)

Web services are exciting because they offer a way to create programs that are completely cross-platform. These programs can be accessed over the Web independent of the tools used to create them and the operating system they run on.

Another defining characteristic of a Web service is that it must supply discovery information about itself. This means that you should be able to query a Web service and have it tell you the names of the methods it provides, the arguments accepted by each method, and the return values for the methods. In other words, you don't have to know very much about a Web service, other than that it exists, to be able to use it in your programs.

The purpose of Web services is to provide components that can communicate with each other regardless of the language in which they are written and the operating system on which they run. These components make their methods available for use, or *consumption*, by other programs. To consume a Web service, a program makes a request running over HTTP to use the methods via HTTP GET, HTTP POST, or—most commonly—Simple Object Access Protocol (SOAP).

Since Web services use SOAP requests, it is important that you understand the gist of SOAP, although .NET insulates you from having to code the SOAP details as you create Web services.

I mentioned earlier that Web services provide a universal discovery mechanism. To implement this mechanism, .NET automatically creates a Web Services Description Language (WSDL) document, which other applications (or humans) can read to understand how to use the Web service. Again, .NET saves you from having to create your own WSDL documents to create a Web service, but you should know that these documents exist and what their purpose is.

Web services also make use of Universal Description, Discovery, and Integration, or UDDI. UDDI is a kind of Yellow Pages for Web services, and you need to use UDDI if you want to find a Web service—or if you want to ensure that your Web service can be found.

The remainder of this section introduces you to the fundamentals of these three key components of a Web service—SOAP, WSDL, and UDDI—and provides the background information that you will need to build sophisticated Web services using .NET.

SOAP

Essentially, the SOAP standard, which is overseen by the World Wide Web Consortium (W3C), is based on XML. The standard consists of three parts:

- An *envelope* that defines rules for describing a message and processing it
- A set of *encoding rules* for instances of application-defined data types
- A *convention* for representing remote procedure calls and responses

If you think that hand-coding a Web service that follows the SOAP standard sounds fairly complex and tedious, you are absolutely right. Fortunately, when you create an ASP.NET Web service project in Visual Studio, all of the coding is taken care of for you. However, if you are interested in learning more of the details of the SOAP specification, you can read it at http://www.w3.org/TR/SOAP/.

WSDL

WSDL is used to create documents that describe the methods supported by a Web service, the arguments that the methods accept, and what the Web service returns. In other words, the WSDL document tells a program (or programmer) what's needed to consume a Web service.

Because WSDL documents are usually read by computers—not people—they must be in a form that can be manipulated in software. That's why the format of a WSDL document is an *XML schema*—XML that itself specifies the format of an XML document.

When you create an ASP.NET Web service project in Visual Studio, you don't have to worry about coding a WSDL document. Visual Studio automatically takes care of this for you when you run the ASP.NET Web service project. However, if you are curious to know more about the WSDL specification, you can find more information at http://www.w3.org/TR/WSDL.

If you find yourself in the position of having to write a VB .NET program that *consumes* rather than *creates* an ASP.NET Web service, the Visual Studio development environment creates a *proxy* based on the Web service's WSDL document. The proxy class contains code that enables you to use the Web service's methods in your Visual Basic code. For details, see Chapter 6, "Consuming the Web Service."

UDDI

If a tree falls in a forest and no one sees it fall, has it really fallen? The same kind of conundrum could apply to Web services, except that we have UDDI (Universal Description, Discovery, and Integration) to let us know the services are there.

For instance, if you have a Web service that others may want use, you can use UDDI to list your service so that people can find it. Similarly, you can use UDDI to find Web services that may fit your needs.

Unlike SOAP and WSDL, which you must understand conceptually but which the .NET user interface insulates you from, you may find yourself interacting at an early stage with UDDI.

To find a Web service:

1. On Visual Studio's Start page, click the XML Web Services link.

   The Start page opens with the Find a Service tab displayed (**Figure 2.1**).
2. Make sure that the UDDI Production Environment radio button is selected.
3. From the Category drop-down list, select a category such as Financial.
4. In the Search For text box, enter a search term (or leave the box empty to see all of the Web services in the selected category).
5. Click Go.

   A list of available Web services and their descriptions will be displayed.

✔ Tips

- See Chapter 1 for more information about the Visual Studio Start page.
- For greater control over the search, click the Advanced button.
- To list a service with UDDI, select the Register a Service tab and click the Register Your XML Web Service Today link.

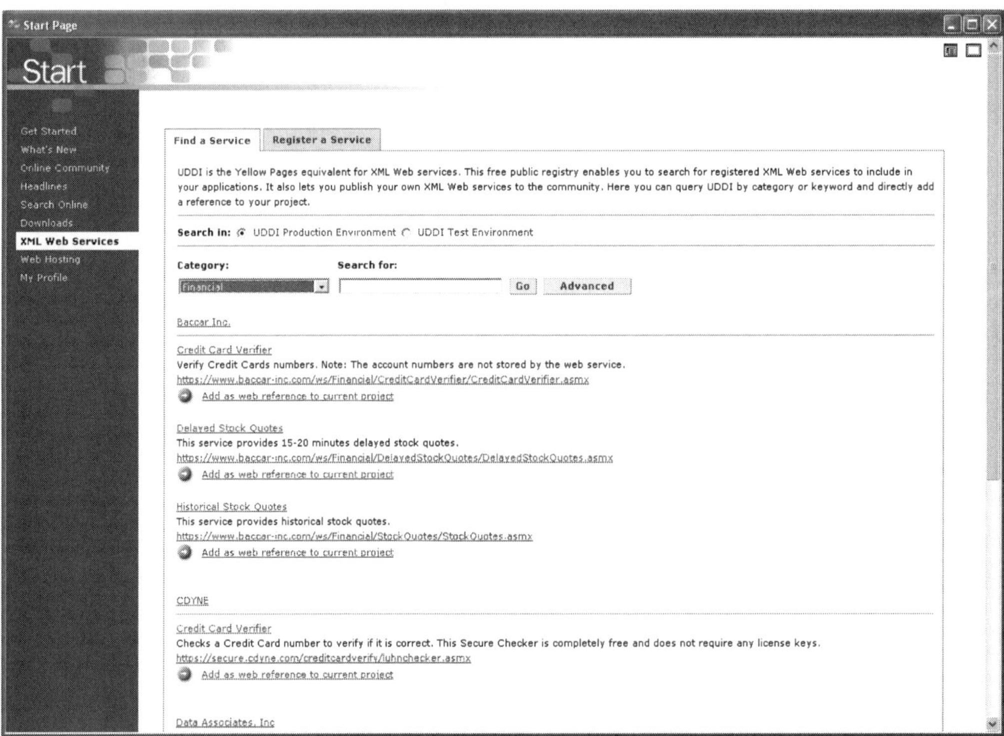

Figure 2.1 Use the XML Web Services page to find an existing Web service and to register your service so that others can find it.

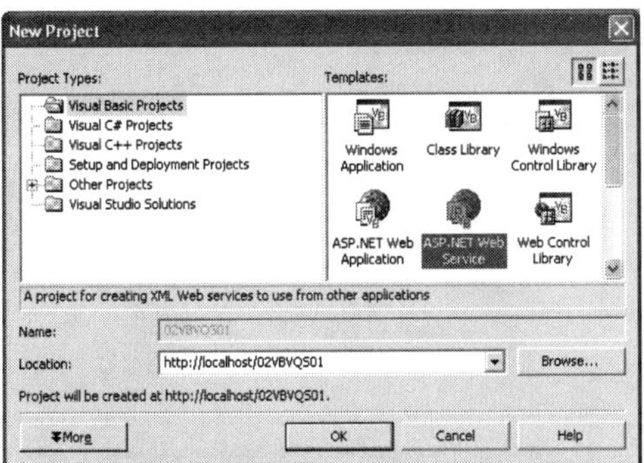

Figure 2.2 Choose ASP.NET Web Services in the Templates pane of the New Project dialog to open a new Web service project.

Creating a Web Service

Web services are extraordinarily easy to create using Visual Basic .NET, so let's get started right away.

In Chapter 1 you learned that programs are based on VB .NET projects. So the kind of program you create depends entirely on the kind of project you choose, whether it's a Windows Application project, ASP.NET Web Application project, ASP.NET Web Service project, and so on.

The first step in creating a Web service is to open a new ASP.NET Web Service project.

To open a new ASP.NET Web Service project:

1. Open the New Project dialog (**Figure 2.2**) by selecting File > New Project or by clicking the New Project button on the Start page.
2. In the Project Types pane, select Visual Basic Projects.
3. In the Templates pane, select ASP.NET Web Service as the project type.
4. Give the project a name by typing a name after the URL http://localhost/ in the Location text box.
5. Click OK.

   The new ASP.NET Web Service project will be created.

continues on next page

✔ Tips

- The URL, or Uniform Resource Locator, provided in Step 4 assumes you are running and testing your Web service on a local instance of Internet Information Services (IIS). If you are using a remote host, enter the appropriate URL in the Location text box.
- If you get error messages when trying to create the project, see the sidebar "Error Messages: Creating a Web Application" in Chapter 1 for some troubleshooting tips.
- Although the Name text box is disabled (dimmed), the text you type in the Location text box following http://localhost/ becomes the project name and will be automatically entered into the Name text box.
- By default, http://localhost/ points to the Inetpub\wwwroot folder. So, for example, a Web service project named 02VBVQS01 would be placed in the Inetpub\wwwroot\02VBVQS01 folder. However, you can place your projects in other locations and create virtual URLs to point to them by using the Internet Information Services administrative applet, accessed through the Administrative Tools group on your computer's Control Panel.

Now open Solution Explorer (**Figure 2.3**) and look at the files in the project you created. Note that the project includes a Web Service module, named by default Service1.asmx. (If you forget how to open Solution Explorer, see "To open Solution Explorer" in Chapter 1.)

When you create a new project, the Web Service module most likely will be open in its designer (this happens by default). If your project isn't open, double-click it in Solution Explorer and it will appear.

You can use the Web Service designer to visually add components to the Web Service class module (**Figure 2.4**). However, while it generally makes sense to design Windows forms

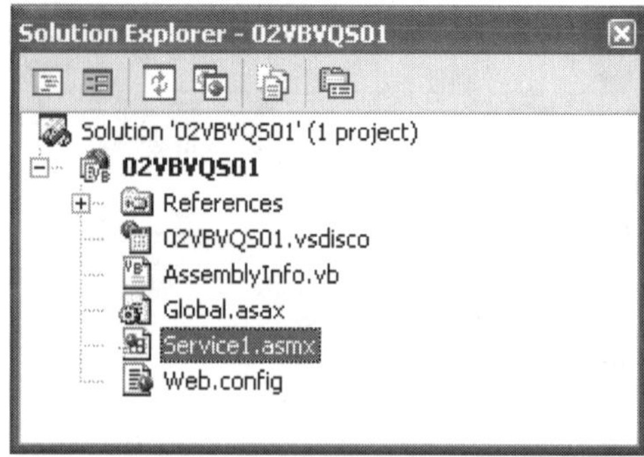

Figure 2.3 If you look in Solution Explorer, you'll see a Web Service (.asmx) module.

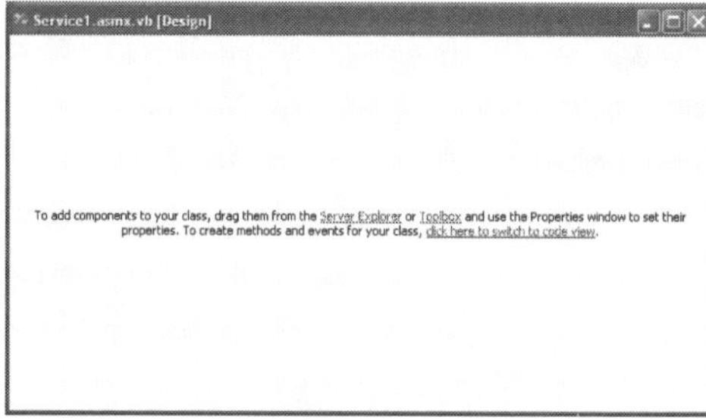

Figure 2.4 You can use the Web Service designer to visually add components to the Web Service class.

visually (and most Web forms have a significant visual component), most of the time you won't be visually designing a Web Service module. This is because a Web service consists of methods (or functions), which are simply code, so there is not much to be gained by using visual design tools. (For information about using designers to speed development of Windows and Web applications, see Chapter 5, "Windows Forms," and Chapter 16, "ASP.NET Web Applications.")

Once you've opened your new ASP.NET Web Service project, you need to switch to the Code Editor so that you can examine the Web Service module in more detail.

To open the Code Editor:

- In Solution Explorer, select the Web Service module and then choose View > Code.

  or

- In the Web Service designer, click the Switch to Code View link.

When you look at the Web Service module in the Code Editor (**Figure 2.5**), you'll see that the program starts with an Imports statement:

```
Imports System.Web.Services
```

This statement tells the compiler that the code can use classes and class members from the System.Web.Services namespace.

Next, you'll see the following three lines of code (actually, all are part of a single code statement):

```
<WebService(Namespace:= _
   "http://tempuri.org/")> _
   Public Class Service1 Inherits
   System.Web.Services.WebService
```

The first part of this, the <WebService> tag, tells Visual Basic that this code is a Web service.

continues on next page

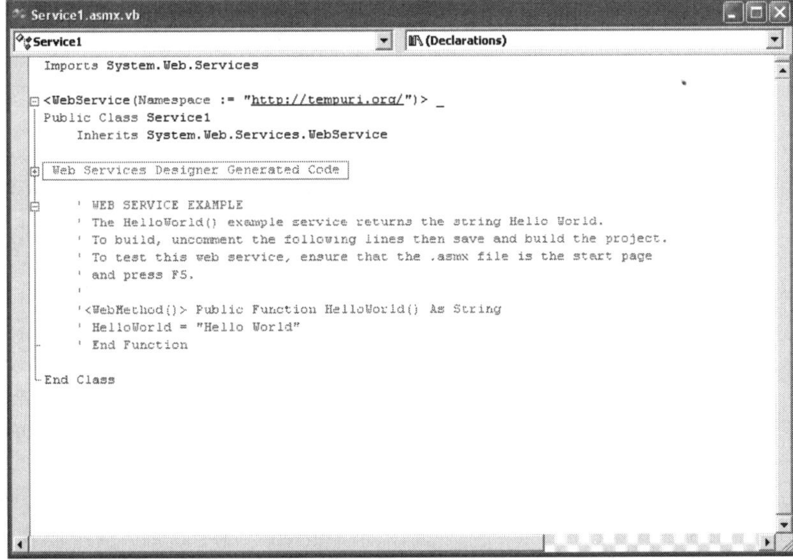

Figure 2.5 If you look in the Code Editor, you'll see that it includes a commented-out Hello World Web method.

The conclusion of the statement names the class (Service1) and specifies that it inherits (or derives) from the class System.Web. Services.WebServices. (For more about class inheritance, see Chapter 3, "Working with Classes.")

✔ Tip

- On the next line, the Code Editor displays a gray + (plus) sign followed by the label "Web Services Designer Generated Code." If you click this, the designer-generated code will be expanded and displayed. This is the code that facilitates visual deployment of components in the Web Services designer.

Continuing downward in the Code Editor, you'll see a Web service example: a Web method named HelloWorld that returns the text string `"Hello World"`. You can see this commented out—with each line preceded by a single apostrophe (')—in Figure 2.5. So if you simply took out the comment markers, you'd have a skeleton Web method packaged in a Web service.

Finally, the code concludes with the statement

```
End Class
```

Now that you've seen what comes in a Web Service module out of the box, it's time to make it your own. You'll start by changing the default URI.

Uniform Resource Identifiers

By default, a new Web service created in Visual Studio is given the Namespace attribute http://tempuri.org/. This is a URI—Uniform Resource Identifier—which should be a text string pointing to a location under your control (although it need not be a path you can navigate to, unlike a URL).

If you don't change the default URI, every time you run the Web Service test page, you'll get a suggestion that you change it.

To change the default URI to a custom value:

- Change the URI in the WebService tag to a custom value:

```
<WebService(Namespace:= _
   "http://peachpit.com/webservices")> _
   Public Class Service1 Inherits
   System.Web.Services.WebService
```

Next, let's add a Web method to the service.

To add a Web method to the service:

1. Add a <WebMethod> attribute tag.

   This tag will mark the function that is the Web method.

2. Create a function.

   This function is the Web method.

   Listing 2.1 shows the entire Web service, including a new Web method that returns a string.

✔ Tip

- The statement

  ```
  HelloVQS = _
     "Visual Basic .NET is cool!"
  ```

  assigns the string `Visual Basic .NET is cool!` to the function, which becomes the return value for the Web method.

Listing 2.1 A Web service and Web method that returns a string.

```
Imports System.Web.Services

<WebService(Namespace:="http://peachpit.com/webservices")> Public Class Service1
   Inherits System.Web.Services.WebService
   <WebMethod()> Public Function HelloVQS() As String
      HelloVQS = "Visual Basic .NET is cool!"
   End Function
End Class
```

Testing the Web Service

You can easily test Web services and their related methods by running the Web service in Visual Studio, which generates test pages on the fly.

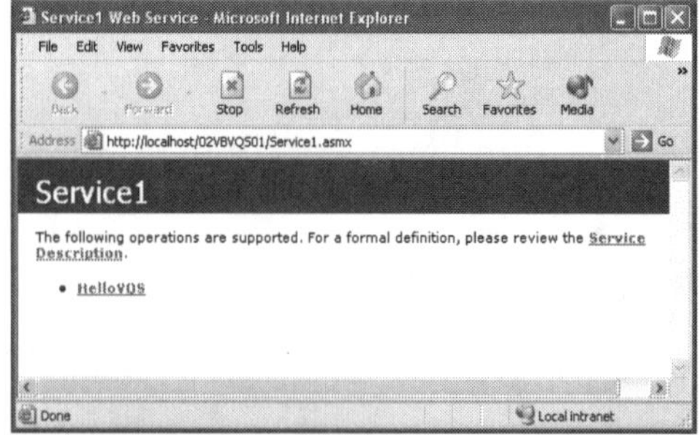

Figure 2.6 The test page generated by Visual Studio for the Web service includes links to the methods provided by the service.

To test the Web service and method:

1. Run the project in Visual Studio by choosing Debug > Start (or clicking the Start arrow).

   The Service test page opens (**Figure 2.6**).
2. Click the link for the Web method that appears in the Web service test page. A test page for the specific Web method will open (**Figure 2.7**).
3. Click the Invoke button.

   The program returns a page that is formatted in XML and that includes the Web method return value and data type (string) (**Figure 2.8**).

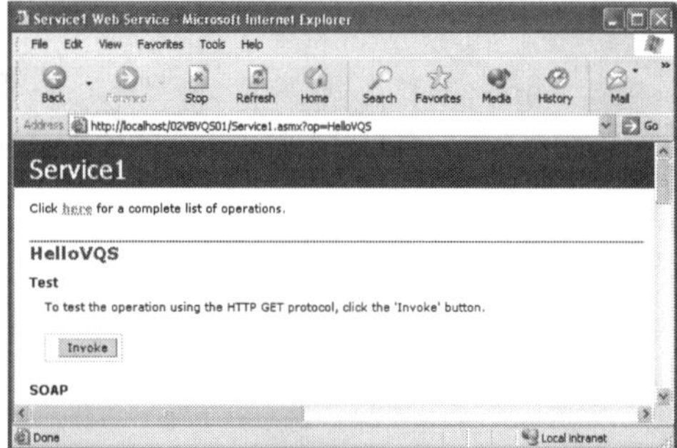

Figure 2.7 To test the Web method, click the Invoke button.

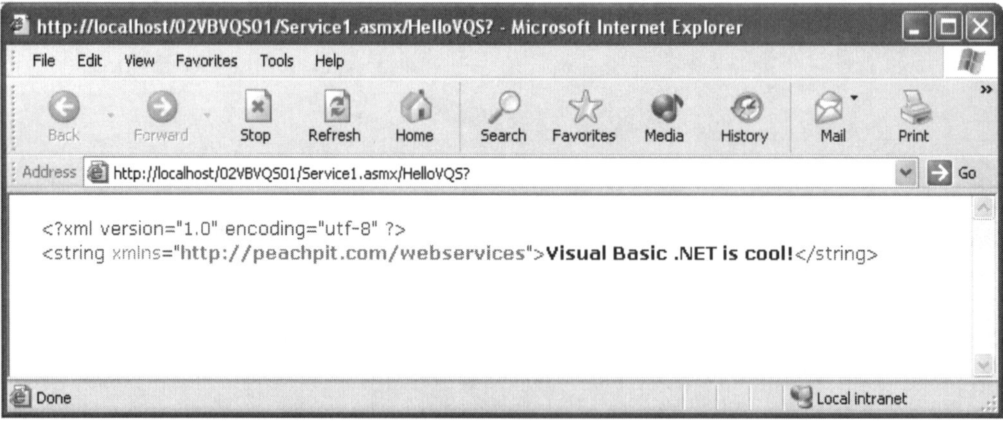

Figure 2.8 The return value for the Web method is displayed in XML.

Adding Web Methods

A Web service can have many Web methods. But to be useful, a Web method needs to do more than simply return a string. You need to be able to create Web methods that can receive varying inputs. Let's start by adding a Web method to the service that calculates the sum of two long integer inputs.

To add a Web method that calculates the sum of two integers:

1. Add a `<WebMethod>` attribute tag.

   This tag will mark the function that is the Web method.

2. Create the function AddTwoNums that accepts two long integers as arguments and returns a long integer.

3. Perform the arithmetic and assign the results to the function as shown in **Listing 2.2**.

✔ Tip

- There are no checks in this code to verify that the user has actually entered integers. If the user enters a text string instead of a number on the test page, the program will generate an exception. For an example of how to validate user input to ensure it's numeric, see Chapter 6, "Consuming the Web Service." To understand how exceptions work, see Chapter 9, "Exceptions and Debugging."

Listing 2.2 A Web method that adds two long integers.

```
<WebMethod()> Public Function AddTwoNums(ByVal numOne As Long, ByVal numTwo As Long) As Long
   AddTwoNums = numOne + numTwo
End Function
```

Testing the Web Method

As mentioned before, you can easily test a new Web method: by running the ASP.NET Web service that contains the method.

To test the Web method that adds two numbers:

1. Run the project in Visual Studio by choosing Debug > Start (or by clicking the Start arrow).

   The Service test page, showing both Web methods, opens (**Figure 2.9**).

2. On the test page, click the link for the AddTwoNums Web method.

   A test page for AddTwoNums, with places to enter the arguments accepted by the Web method, opens (**Figure 2.10**).

3. Enter values for numOne and numTwo and then click the Invoke button.

   The program returns a page that is formatted in XML and includes the Web method return value (the sum of the two numbers entered) and the data type (long integer) (**Figure 2.11**).

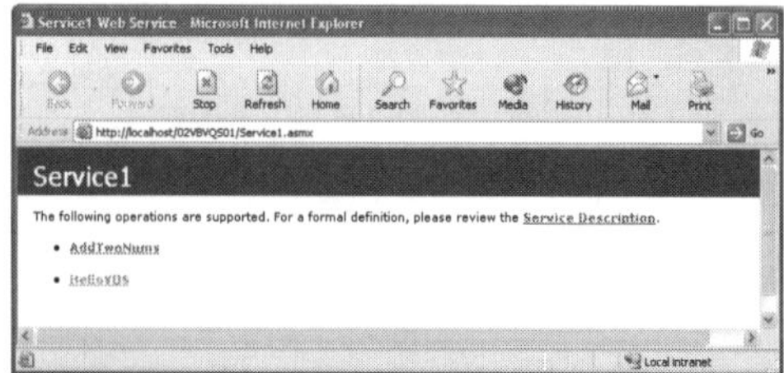

Figure 2.9 The new Web method appears as a link on the Web Services test page.

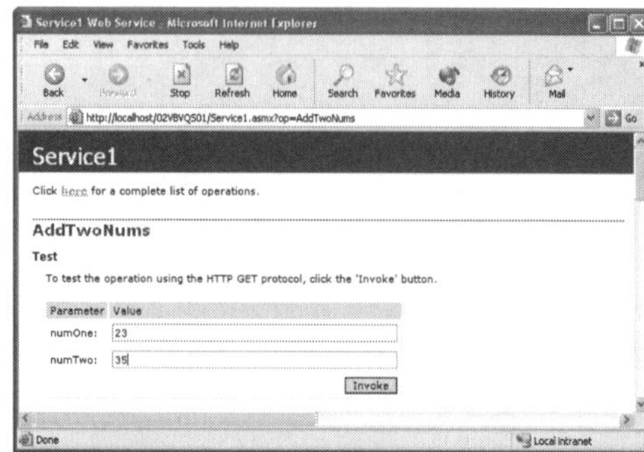

Figure 2.10 The test page provides input boxes for the arguments accepted by the Web method.

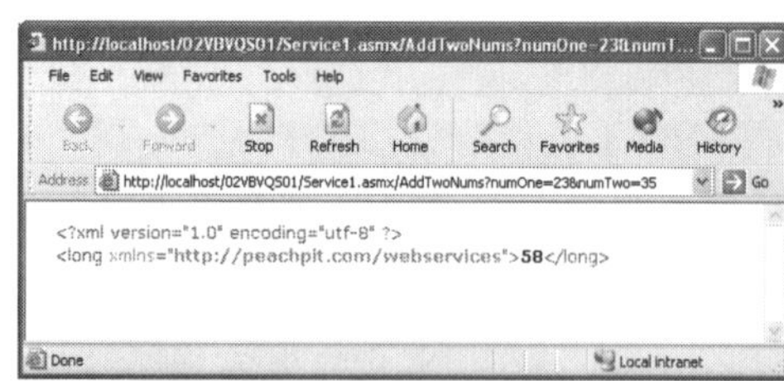

Figure 2.11 The result of running the Web method with the input provided appears in XML format.

Summary

In this chapter, you learned how to:

- Describe Web services and the standards related to Web services, such as SOAP, WSDL, and UDDI
- Create a Web service project
- View the Web Service module in the Code Editor
- Add a Web method to a Web service
- Test a Web service and method using the Visual Studio test pages
- Add and test a Web method that accepts user input

3 Working with Classes

Perhaps the biggest difference between Visual Basic .NET and Visual Basic 6 is the fact that VB. NET is a fully object-oriented (OO) programming language, whereas VB6 is not.

To say that a programming language is fully OO means that it provides a consistent and rich way to program with objects and classes. The many benefits of programming in an OOP fashion include being able to frequently reuse code, model complex systems more easily, and create maintainable code.

However, to get the most out of an OO programming environment, you must have a basic understanding of OO concepts and the mechanics, or craft, of working with objects and classes. This chapter introduces you to objects and classes and the way they work in Visual Basic .NET. By laying down the foundation and mechanics of the craft of class-based programming early, I hope you'll be able to take advantage of the concepts and techniques presented in this chapter and apply them throughout the rest of the book.

Understanding Objects and Classes

We'll begin by briefly touching on some object-oriented concepts and terminology and exploring their relevance. If you're already experienced with object-oriented programming, you may wish to skim or even skip this section. If you're new to the topic, be aware that this chapter isn't extensive enough to enable you to design a complex OO system. If that's what you're after, I recommend picking up some of the many good books devoted solely to subjects such as object-oriented programming practice, Unified Modeling Language (UML), and the theory and practice of using object-oriented design patterns. The classic book on this topic is *Design Patterns: Elements of Reusable Object-Oriented Software* by Erich Gamma, Richard Helm, Ralph Johnson, and John Vlissades (Addison-Wesley, 1995). A somewhat more readable introduction to UML, design patterns, and OO design is Alan Shalloway and James R. Trott's *Design Patterns Explained: A New Perspective on Object-Oriented Design* (Addison-Wesley, 2002).

Why OOP?

Programming in an object-oriented style encourages and facilitates the following:

- Code reuse, which saves time and debugging headaches
- Code systems that are modeled on their real-life counterpart systems (a good thing!)
- Disciplined, component-based, modular code
- Code, and code systems, that are easily maintained
- Code mechanisms that can be used to solve complex problems in a conceptually simple fashion

Because the .NET Framework is, in essence, a gigantic object-oriented class library, you won't be able to figure out how to best use it and unlock the wonderful resources it contains if you don't have a solid understanding of OOP.

Furthermore, the out-of-the-box .NET code for forms, Web services, and so on is all class-based. This code will simply not be intelligible to you if you don't understand how objects and classes work.

✔ **Tip**

- One use of the dot operator (.) in .NET is to indicate class hierarchy and the relationship of classes to namespaces (which are used to internally organize .NET classes). For example, the expression System.Windows.Forms.Form is used to name the Form class within the Windows.System.Forms namespace (the class used as the basis for windows and dialogs in Windows applications). You'll find information about .NET namespaces and class hierarchy in Chapter 14, "The Object Browser."

Key principles

Achieving the OOP benefits outlined in the previous section involves implementing a few of the following key concepts, principles, and abilities:

- **Objects.** Intuitively, in every day life, you deal with a great many objects (for example, this book). From an OOP viewpoint, an object is a structure that stores data and the related procedures for working with that data. For example, an OO program might have a printer object that manages the data and procedures necessary for interacting with printers.
- **Abstraction.** In OO terms, abstraction means filtering out the extraneous properties and attributes of objects, so that users of the object can focus on the properties that matter.

- **Aggregation.** Aggregation means the ability to create an object that is a composite of other objects. Aggregation, sometimes also called *containment*, is a very powerful way to model real-life processes and to simplify coding.
- **Encapsulation.** Encapsulation is the process of hiding (or encapsulating) the data used by an object and granting access to it through specific interactions with the object. This grouping of related attributes and methods is used to create a cohesive entity. There are lots of real-life analogues to encapsulation. Think, for example, about requests for information from the president of the United States. If all requests for information from the president must be directed to the Press Office, then the Press Office is practicing encapsulation.

✔ Tip

- Controlling access via encapsulation is a good way to create maintainable code that has fewer bugs.

- **Inheritance.** Inheritance is the practice of organizing objects into a hierarchy in which objects are categorized according to their common characteristics and purpose. This practice makes programming easier and more intuitive because you can easily find objects based on their classification in the hierarchy. You can also create new *child* objects that inherit the prebuilt characteristics of their *parent.*
- **Polymorphism.** From an OO viewpoint, polymorphism means the ability of two different objects to respond to the same request in their own unique ways. For example, a print text message might cause a printer object to print the text. The same message, when received by a screen object, might cause the text to be displayed on the screen. When a message, or instruction, to an object causes different (polymorphic) results depending on its context—the number and type of arguments it passes—this action is called *overloading* (explained in more detail later in this chapter).

Objects and classes

You must understand the distinction between objects and classes.

You can think of a class as a generalized blueprint, or template. In contrast, an object is a specific *instance* of the class. That's why the term *instance* is used to mean an object—in other words, a specific instance of a class. When you create a new object, you are *instantiating* the object, based on a class.

The process of creating an OO programming system involves first conceptualizing and creating the classes (and class hierarchy) that will be used as the template, or blueprint, for objects and relationships needed to solve the problem.

A subsequent part of the process involves creating mechanisms for instantiating objects based on these classes and getting the objects to interoperate appropriately with each other, users, and program data.

To understand the relationship between objects and classes, you can think of it this way: The class is like a cookie cutter, and the object is like the cookie. So there is only one class—the cookie cutter—whereas you can make as many objects from that class—the cookies made by the cookie cutter—as you like.

✔ Tip

- In .NET, classes are named with an uppercase first letter, whereas object names start with a lowercase first letter.

Adding a Class to the Web Service

To get started understanding the mechanics of classes and objects in Visual Basic .NET, let's add a class module (containing, in fact, a class named Vqs) to the Web service project we developed in Chapter 2, "Creating a Web Service."

Within the Vqs class, we'll add a property named Text, intended to encapsulate a text string. We'll also add a method to the class, ReverseText, that reverses the text string stored in the Text property. So if the value of the Text property is the string `"Tom Marvolo Riddle"`, following the action of the ReverseText method, it would become the string `"elddiR olovarM moT"`. (Class members, including properties and methods, are discussed more fully later in this chapter.)

To use these class members, you must first set the Text property to the value that is to be reversed. The Text property is then operated on by the ReverseText method, and the changed string value is retrieved from the Text property.

The ReverseText method itself uses some of the built-in members of the .NET String class: the Length property and the Substring method. Within ReverseText, the expression Me.Text is used to refer to the property that is to be manipulated.

✔ Tip

- The Me keyword is used to refer to the current instance of an object. You don't really need to use the keyword in this example, since the reference to the Text property is unambiguous, but it does help to make the code clearer.

Where Do Classes Go?

In a Visual Basic .NET project, classes don't have to be placed in class modules. They can be added anywhere—in any kind of module—where they are syntactically legal. You can even nest one class within another, which is sometimes an effective way to manage complex classes.

As you might assume from the fully OO nature of VB .NET, each kind of module contains, in fact, a class itself. For example, when you create a new Web Service module, the out-of-the box code created is a class that inherits from the System.Web.Services.WebServices class. And when you create a Windows form module, the class created inherits from the System.Windows.Forms.Form class.

So why would you place a class (or classes) in one or more class modules? Primarily, you use this as an optional technique for helping programmers organize source code, making it easier to find things later.

A `for` loop iterates the number of times there are characters in Me.Text (from `0` to `Me.Text.Length - 1`). Each character at the front of the string is peeled off using the Substring method and added to the end of a new string (stored in the local variable stringNew) using the string concatenation operator (&). When the iteration is complete, the reversed string, stored in StringNew, is assigned back to the Text property.

Listing 3.1 shows the complete code for the Vqs class, including its members the Text property and the ReverseText method.

Listing 3.1 Vqs class containing a property and a method.

```
Public Class Vqs
   Private m_text As String = ""

   Public Property Text() As String
      Get
         Text = m_text
      End Get
      Set(ByVal Value As String)
         m_text = Value
      End Set
   End Property

   Public Sub ReverseText()
      Dim newString As String = ""
      Dim i As Integer
      For i = 0 To Me.Text.Length - 1
         newString = Me.Text.Substring(i, 1) & newString
      Next
      Me.Text = newString
   End Sub
End Class
```

To add a class module to the Web service project:

1. With the Web service project open in Visual Studio, open the Add New Item dialog by doing *one* of the following:
   - ▲ From the Project menu, select Add Class or Add New Item.
   - ▲ From the project's right-click context menu in Solution Explorer, select Add Class or Add New Item.
2. In the Add New Item dialog that appears (**Figure 3.1**), make sure Class is selected in the Templates pane.
3. Provide a name for the code module, such as Vqp.vb, in the Name text box.
4. Click Open. The Code module will open in the Code Editor (**Figure 3.2**) with an initial class declaration created using the module name without the file suffix.

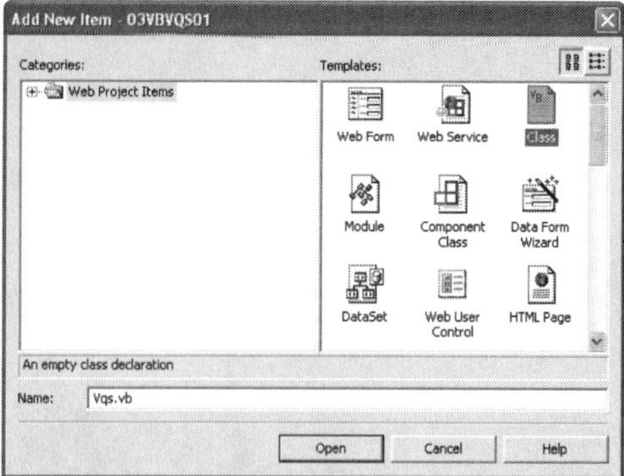

Figure 3.1 Use the Add New Item dialog to add a class module to the project.

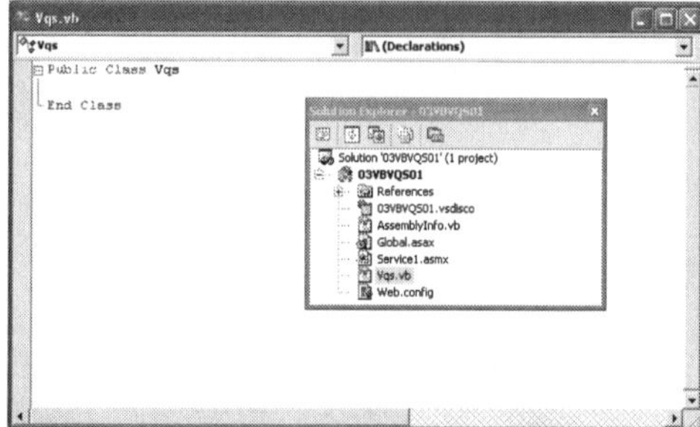

Figure 3.2 The class module and the default class created by the IDE are shown in the Code Editor and Solution Explorer.

✔ Tips

- You can change the class name provided by Visual Studio to any legal identifier you like. You can also add more than one class to a single class module.
- Project module files that contain Visual Basic code are usually named with a .vb file suffix.
- You can put class declarations in any kind of code module, as explained in the sidebar "Where Do Classes Go?" Class modules are purely optional, existing to help you organize the source code contained in your project.

The next step is to add the Text property to the class.

As a general matter, a property is a class member that serves to encapsulate a variable that stores object information. The variable is declared so that it is private to the object, and special property procedures, using the keywords Get and Set, are used to store and access the private variable from outside the object. The property procedures can be used to initialize or validate values, or for many other purposes. In other words, the property procedures function like gatekeepers. If you want to "talk" to the underlying variable that stores the property value, you have to go through the property procedures.

If you type the keyword `Property` to create a property in the Code Editor, Visual Studio will create the framework of the Get and Set property procedures for you. All you have to do is enter the "guts" of the property procedures so that they actually interact with a private variable.

For example, to add a property named MyProperty of type long integer (`Long`) to a class, you would start by typing the first line of the property definition:

```
Property MyProperty() As Long
```

As soon as you press the Enter key to accept this line, Visual Studio will add the framework for the property procedures, so that the outline for your new property looks like this:

```
Property MyProperty() As Long
   Get

   End Get
   Set(ByVal Value As Long)

   End Set
End Property
```

To add the Text property to the class:

1. Create a private variable typed as a String that is initialized to the empty string:
```
Private m_text As String = ""
```
2. Type the first line in the declaration for the property typed as a String:
```
Public Property Text() As String
```
The development environment will supply the framework for the property procedures:
```
Public Property Text() As String
   Get


   End Get
   Set(ByVal Value As String)


   End Set
End Property
```
3. Add code to the Get property procedure that assigns the value of the private variable to the property (this is also a place to add any special initialization or validation code):
```
Get
   Text = m_text
End Get
```
4. Add code to the Set property procedure that assigns the value of the property to the private variable (this is also a place to add any special initialization or validation code):
```
Set(ByVal Value As String)
   m_text = Value
End Set
```
5. Run the project (from the Debug menu, choose Start) to verify that there are no syntax errors.

✔ Tips

- It is traditional to name the private variable that is encapsulated by a property using a lowercase *m*, followed by an underscore (_), followed by the name of the property with its first letter lowercased: for example, m_text.
- Properties are generally named with an uppercase first letter: for example, `Text`.
- The empty string can also be referred to using the `Empty` constant of the String class, so the private variable declaration for this property could be rewritten (possibly with greater clarity) as:
```
Private m_text As String = _
   String.Empty
```
- Listing 3.1, presented earlier, shows the complete code for the Text property.

Adding a method to a class is a matter of creating a function, or if the method doesn't return a value, a procedure using the Sub keyword.

✔ Tips

- The `Sub` keyword, which may be a little unintuitive, is a holdover from the old days of Visual Basic programming. It is short for *subroutine*.
- If you are coming to VB .NET from a language such as Java, C++, or C#, you should recognize a function declared as type `void`—meaning it returns nothing—as based on the same concept as a Sub procedure.

In our case, the ReverseText method merely operates on the Text property—it does not return a value—so it can be declared as a Sub.

To add a ReverseText method to the class:

1. Enter the declaration for the procedure:

   ```
   Public Sub ReverseText()
   ```

   Visual Studio will supply the End statement for the procedure, so it now looks like this:

   ```
   Public Sub ReverseText()


   End Sub
   ```

2. Enter the code for the method that uses the Text property value to build a new, reversed string and then assigns it back to the Text property:

   ```
   Public Sub ReverseText()
      Dim newString As String = ""
      Dim i As Integer
      For i = 0 To Me.Text.Length - 1
         newString = _
            Me.Text.Substring (i, _
            1) & newString
      Next
      Text = newString
   End Sub
   ```

3. Run the project (from the Debug menu, select Start) to verify there are no syntax errors.

✔ Tips

- Listing 3.1, presented earlier, shows the complete code for the Vqs class, including the ReverseText method.
- You'll find an explanation of how the ReverseText method works earlier in this section.

The next step in this exercise is to use the new class and its members from the Web service. (Actually, this is pretty easy compared to creating the class!)

To invoke the class and members from the Web service:

1. Open the Web service in the Code Editor.
2. Create a new Web method using the <WebMethod> attribute as explained in Chapter 2. The Web method will be a function named ReverseString that accepts a string—the text to be reversed—and returns a string, the reversed text:

   ```
   <WebMethod()> Public Function _
      ReverseString (ByVal inString As _
      String) As String
   ```

3. Declare a variable named vqs and use the New keyword to instantiate it as a new object based on the Vqs class:

   ```
   Dim vqs As New Vqs()
   ```

   You'll know you are on the right track if auto-completion supplies the name of the class as you start to type it (**Figure 3.3**). This means that in the eyes of the development environment, the Vqs class exists, and instantiation based on it is syntactically correct.
4. You can now set the vqs object's Text property value using as the input the Web method:

   ```
   vqs.Text = inString
   ```

   Note that the members of the instantiated class will appear in the auto-completion drop-down list (**Figure 3.4**), so you can choose them from the list as you write your code without having to know the names or types.

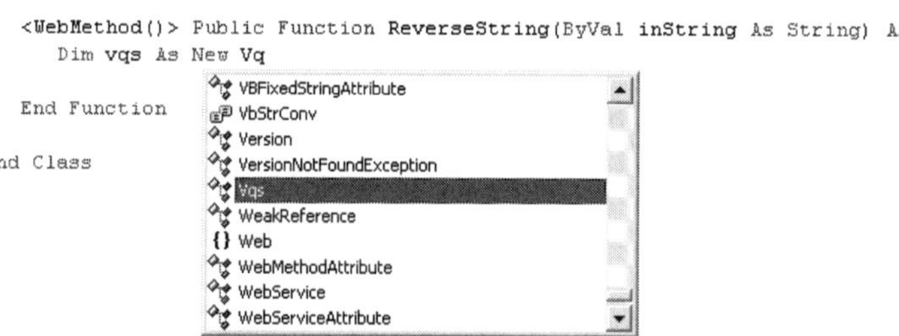

Figure 3.3 When you attempt to instantiate an object based on the Vqs class, the Vqs class should appear in the auto-completion drop-down list in the Code Editor.

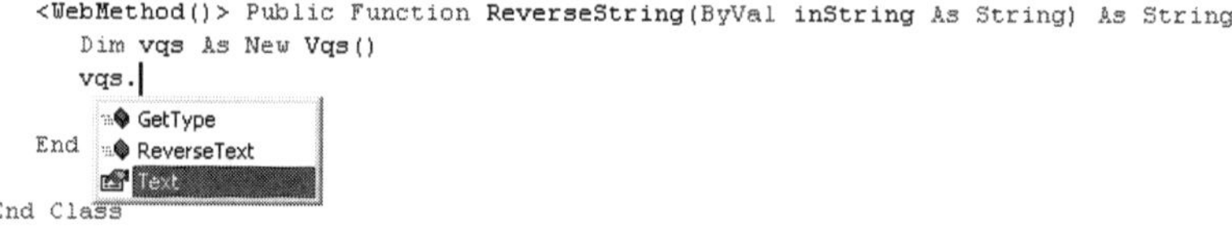

Figure 3.4 With the class instantiated, class members should appear in the auto-completion drop-down list.

5. Next, invoke the method:

   `vqs.ReverseText()`

6. Finally, assign the value of the object's Text property—presumably, it has been reversed—back to the Web method as its return value:

   `ReverseString = vqs.Text`

✔ Tips

- **Listing 3.2** shows the complete code for the Web method that uses the class.
- The statement `Dim vqs As New Vqs()` does two things: (1) it declares the variable vqs as of type Vqs, and (2) it instantiates a new instance of the Vqs class and stores a reference to it in the variable vqs. Alternatively, you'll see it written as two statements (the first a variable declaration, and the second the object instantiation):

  ```
  Dim vqs As Vqs
  vqs = New Vqs()
  ```

- In Visual Basic, identifiers are case insensitive, so vqs and Vqs are one and the same, and the statement

  `Dim vqs As New Vqs()`

  effectively names the object with the same identifier as the class. If there is any chance of confusion, it's better to name objects differently than the classes they are based on. So, for example, you might give the name *the_Vqs* to an object based on the Vqs class.

Listing 3.2 Instantiating the class and using its members from a Web service.

```
Imports System.Web.Services

<WebService(Namespace:="http://peachpit.com/webservices")> Public Class Service1
   Inherits System.Web.Services.WebService

...
   <WebMethod()> Public Function ReverseString (ByVal inString As String) As String
      Dim vqs As New Vqs()
      vqs.Text = inString
      vqs.ReverseText()
      ReverseString = vqs.Text
   End Function

End Class
```

To test the invoked method:

1. Run the Web service project to display the Visual Studio–generated Web Service test page (**Figure 3.5**), as explained in Chapter 2.
2. Click the ReverseString link to test the Web method.
3. On the ReverseString test page (**Figure 3.6**), enter an input string to reverse.
4. Click Invoke. The results will be returned in XML format (**Figure 3.7**).

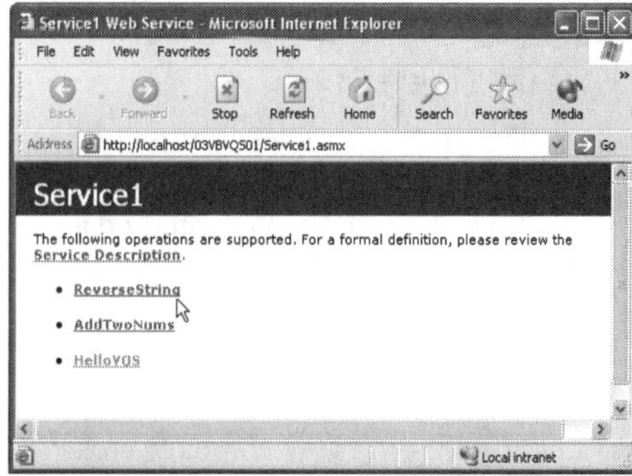

Figure 3.5 The new Web method should appear on the Visual Studio test page for the Web service.

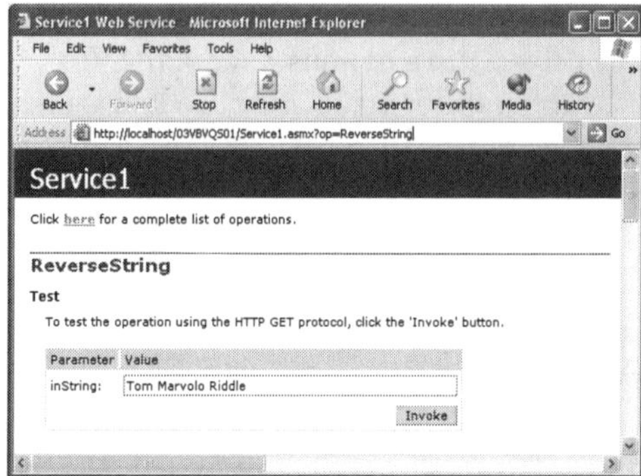

Figure 3.6 You can test the class method by entering a string to reverse.

Figure 3.7 If the class property and method are working properly, then the Web method should return the string reversed.

Adding a Class to a Windows Application

Now we're going to switch and build Windows applications rather than Web services, using the same class, Vqs, and class module, Vqs.vb, that we developed in the Web service context. There are several reasons for making this switch.

First, although Web services are way cool and the ability to create them is one of the key new features of VB .NET, the truth is that most programmers spend much of their time creating desktop applications—meaning Windows Application projects. So it's important to be comfortable with objects and classes in the context of Windows programming.

Second, some of the mechanics of using the development environment are simpler when you're creating Windows programs. There are some things you don't have to worry about, so you can concentrate more easily on programming and working with VB .NET, which is what this book is primarily about. For example, if you don't have access to the Internet Information Services Web server—and have it properly configured and successfully interacting with Visual Studio—you can't create ASP.NET or ASP.NET Web Service projects using Visual Basic .NET (or any other .NET language).

So with these considerations in mind, we'll be working with classes using Windows Application as the example project for the rest of this chapter. In addition, most of the examples presented from this point forward in the book will be in the context of Windows desktop applications, with the exception of those in Chapter 6, "Consuming the Web Service," and Chapter 16, "ASP.NET Web Applications."

However, bear in mind that most of the techniques of OO and class-based programming can be applied to any type of .NET project, not only Windows applications.

By using the same class, Vqs, and class module, Vqs.vb, in the Windows application example as in the Web service example, I'm demonstrating an equally important but more subtle point: the wisdom of programming in a class-conscious fashion. When you understand that you can use one single class in multiple types of projects, with no recoding of the class, it becomes crystal clear that organizing your code in classes fosters code reuse—and saves you work.

To get the ball rolling, I'll show you how to open a new Windows Application project. Then I'll show you a variety of ways to add the Vqs class we created in the last section to this project. Finally, I'll show you how to add a rudimentary user interface to the Form class that is an out-of-the box part of a Windows Application project and use it to invoke the members of the Vqs class. You probably won't be too surprised to learn that the invocation code is essentially the same for the Windows form as it was for the Web service.

To open a new Windows Application project:

1. From the Visual Studio File menu, choose New Project.

   The New Project dialog opens (**Figure 3.8**).
2. In the New Project dialog, make sure Visual Basic Projects is selected from the choices in the Project Types pane.
3. In the Templates pane, choose Windows Application.
4. In the Name text box, provide a name for the project.
5. In the Location text box, provide a path for the project source files (or use the Browse button to select the location).
6. Click OK.

   The new Windows Application project will be created in Visual Studio.
7. Open Solution Explorer (View > Solution Explorer) to verify that a Windows Application project containing a form module has been created (**Figure 3.9**).

✔ Tip

- You'll find a great deal of information about creating and working with projects in Chapter 1, "Introducing Visual Studio .NET."

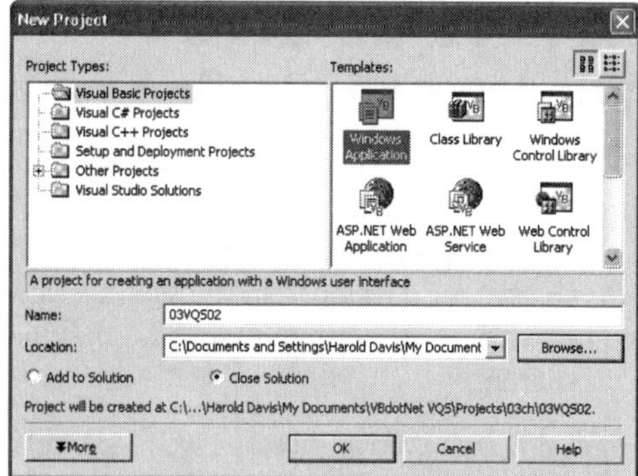

Figure 3.8 To open a new project, in the New Project dialog select Windows Application from the Templates pane, give the project a name, provide a location, and click OK.

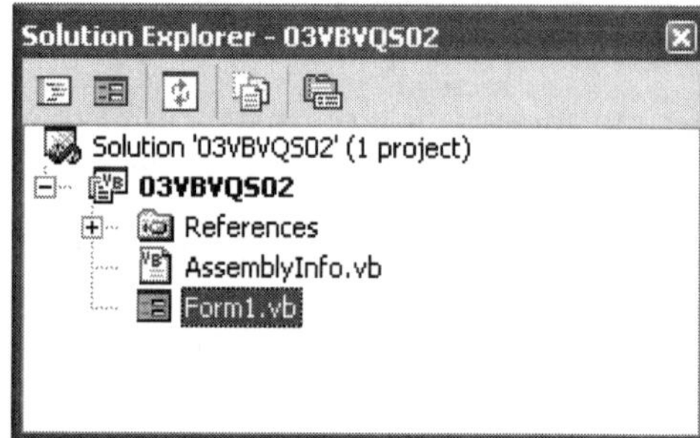

Figure 3.9 You can see the new project, including the Form module, in Solution Explorer.

As mentioned earlier, we are going to use the unaltered Vqs class and class module with this new Windows project. You can do this in several ways:

- You can follow the same steps as described for the Web service project and manually enter the class code, with object invocation working the same way as in the Web service project.
- You can add a reference to the Web service project and then instantiate the class in the Windows project. The wrinkle here, which you'll see how to deal with in a moment, is that you'll need to refer to the external project's namespace in order to access its classes.
- You can add the file containing the class—in other words, the class module—to the project and then use it like any other class in a project.

The differences among these techniques will become clear if you work through each in the context of your new Windows Application project and the Vqs class.

To add a new class:

- Follow the steps outlined for the project in the section "Adding a Class to the Web Service," using the New Item dialog to add a class module named Vqs to the Windows Application project and typing the code for the class and its members.

✔ Tip

- Copying and pasting works! If you are as averse to retyping code as I am, you can always open two instances of Visual Studio: one for the Web service project and the other for the Windows Application project. Then you can add the new (empty) class module named Vqs to the Windows Application project and simply copy and paste the contents of the Vqs class module from the Web service project to the new module.

You can use a class that is incorporated in another compiled .NET project without any additional work. To do this, you must add a reference in the current project that points to the external project.

To add a reference to a different project:

1. From the Visual Studio Project menu, choose Add Reference.

   The Add Reference dialog opens (**Figure 3.10**).

2. In the Add Reference dialog, select the Projects tab.

3. Click the Browse button.

   The Select Component dialog opens (**Figure 3.11**).

4. Select a component file, such as a .dll or .exe file, for the project you want to reference.

5. Click Open.

   The file you chose will be added to the Selected Components pane on the Projects tab of the Add Reference dialog (**Figure 3.12**).

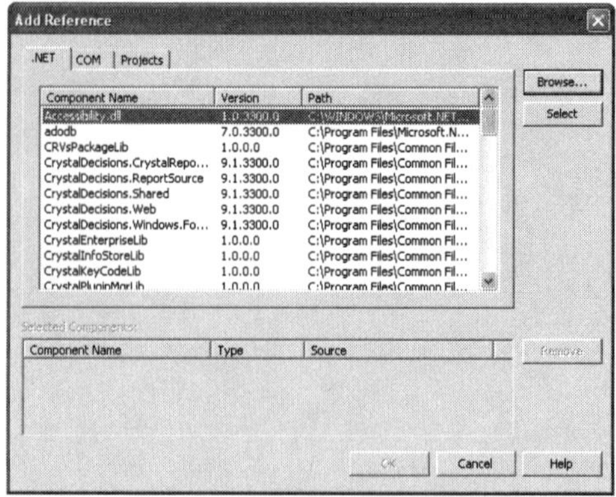

Figure 3.10 Use the Add Reference dialog to add references to external components.

Figure 3.11 Select the compiled file containing the class you want to reference.

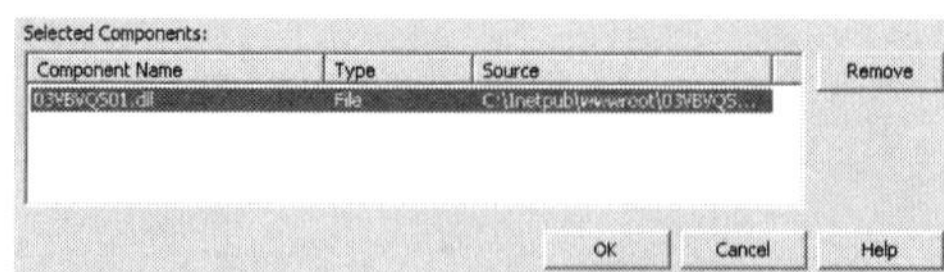

Figure 3.12 The selected program will appear in the Selected Components pane of the Add Reference dialog.

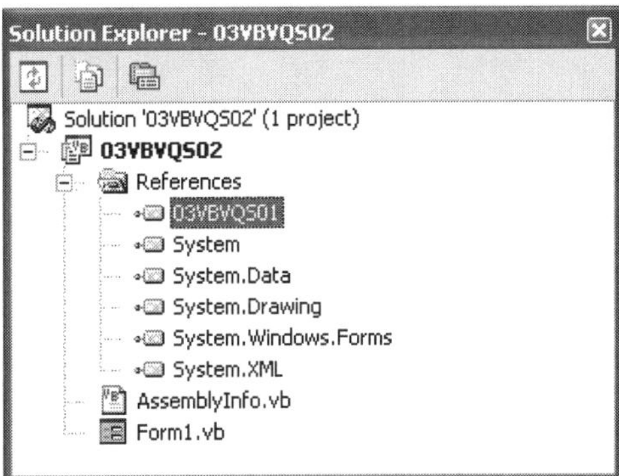

Figure 3.13 If you expand the References folder in Solution Explorer, you can see the added reference.

6. Click OK.
7. To verify that the reference has been added to the current project, open Solution Explorer.
8. Expand the References folder in Solution Explorer by clicking the plus icon (+) next to the highest-level References folder.

   You should see the external project present as a reference (**Figure 3.13**).

✔ Tips

- Compiled project files are normally found in the bin folder, located below the folder created for the project source code files.
- Don't confuse the use of an object that is based on a class included in the Web service project with the use of a Web service. Chapter 6 explains the use of Web services.
- You can use the Object Browser to inspect the class hierarchy, classes, and class members supplied by the referenced components. For information on working with the Object Browser, see Chapter 14.

To instantiate the class in the external project once it has been referenced, you need to use a slightly different syntax than that for instantiating a class that is present in a project. Specifically, the instantiation needs to include the namespace that the class is part of. As you'll see in Chapter 14, you can easily add (and name) your own namespace hierarchies to contain classes. However, if you haven't provided a namespace, the default is the project name preceded by an underscore: for example, _03VBVQS01. So the object declaration statement and instantiation becomes:

```
Dim vqs As New _03VBVQS01.Vqs()
```

In some respects, it's easier to simply add the existing module file containing the Vqs class to the new project (as you probably recall, the file is named Vqs.vb). To do this, you can leave the file where it is, although, of course, you must be able to locate it in your file system. (Remember that ASP.NET and ASP.NET Web project source files are saved in a location below that pointed to by the Internet Information Services default virtual directory. This directory is called the Default Web Site in the IIS Administrative tool, normally \inetpub\wwwroot.)

Alternatively, you can use Windows Explorer to copy the class module file to the folder that contains the new project's source code files. The advantages of this process are that all of the source code for your project is in one place, and you can change the new project's class code without affecting the old project.

Of course, these advantages become disadvantages if you make changes to the code and then want to use the changed class code in the old project. If issues involving source code management and versioning become troublesome to you, you should probably investigate the use of Visual SourceSafe, which integrates well with the Visual Studio environment. This will help take care of most of these issues for you and is particularly important in a team development context.

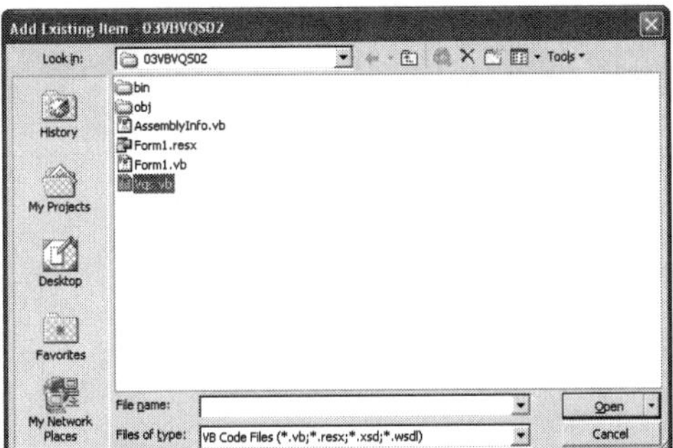

Figure 3.14 Use the Add Existing Item dialog to add a file—such as class module file—to a project.

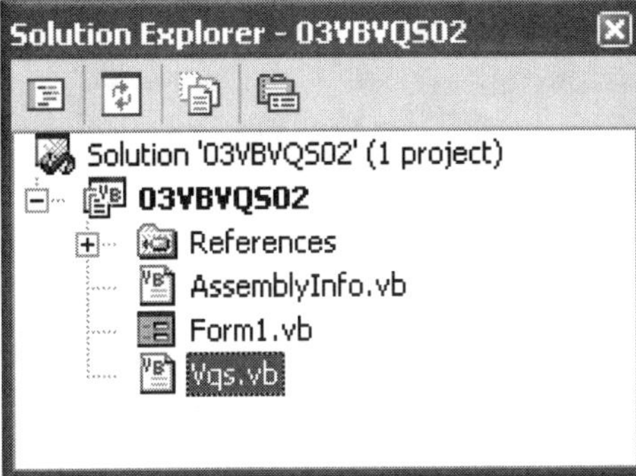

Figure 3.15 The class module is now shown in Solution Explorer.

To add an existing class module:

1. From the Visual Studio Project menu, choose Add Existing Item.

   The Add Existing Item dialog opens (**Figure 3.14**).
2. Select the class module file.
3. Click OK.
4. Open Solution Explorer to verify that the class module has been added to the project (**Figure 3.15**).

To make use of the Vqs class in the Windows application, we'll need to construct a "rough and ready" user interface based on the Form class so that the user can enter a text string, click a button, and see the string reversed.

With this interface, the user enters the text to be reversed in a TextBox control. Next, the user clicks a Button control to invoke the class members. The results of the reversal are displayed using a Label control.

✔ Tip

- You'll find more information about constructing forms-based user interfaces, and working with classes derived from the Form class, in many parts of this book, beginning with Chapter 5, "Introducing Windows Forms."

To add a user interface to the Windows form:

1. To open the form in its designer, from the Visual Studio View menu, choose Designer (or use one of the alternatives described in Chapter 1).

   The blank form in the designer is like an empty canvas (**Figure 3.16**), ready to be embellished using the Toolbox and Properties window.

2. From the View menu, choose Toolbox to open the Toolbox (**Figure 3.17**).

3. On the Windows Forms tab of the Toolbox, double-click the Label, Button, and Text controls to add one instance of each control to the form (**Figure 3.18**).

4. Drag and drop the controls on the form to size and place them visually in a way that makes sense.

5. If you'd like, shut the Toolbox.

6. From the View menu, choose Properties Window to open the Properties window (**Figure 3.19**).

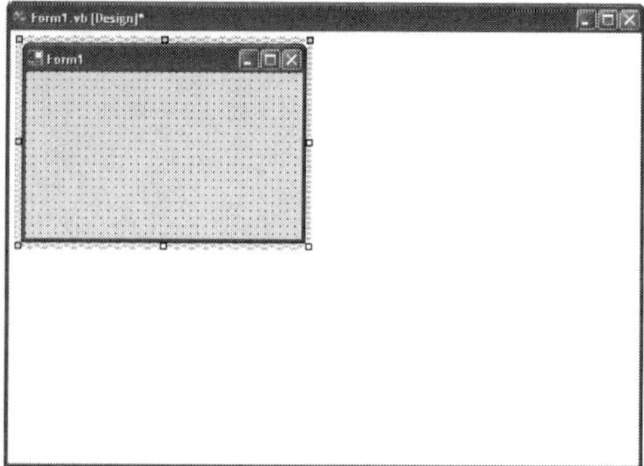

Figure 3.16 A form in its designer is like a blank canvas.

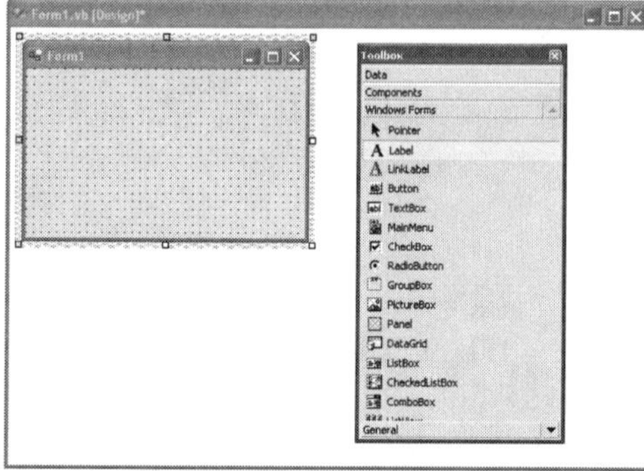

Figure 3.17 Use the Toolbox to add instances of controls—such as Labels, Buttons, and TextBoxes—to the form.

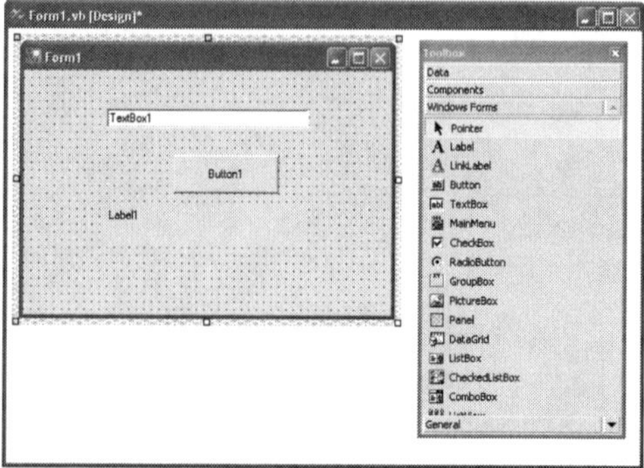

Figure 3.18 Once a control instance has been added to the form from the Toolbox, it can be visually positioned and sized.

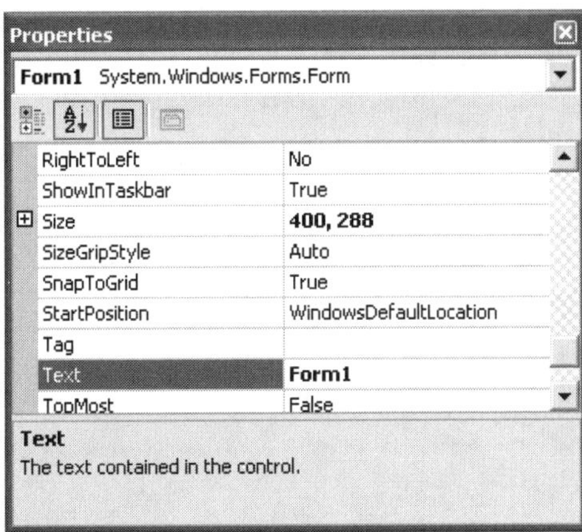

Figure 3.19 Use the Properties window to set the properties of the form and control object instances.

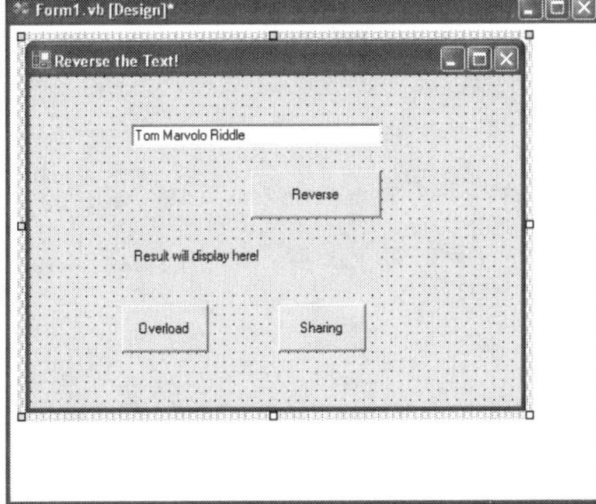

Figure 3.20 You can use the Text property to set initial values and provide descriptive information for the user.

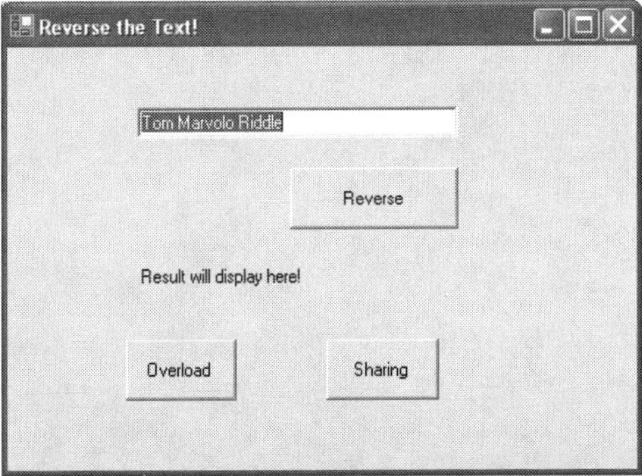

Figure 3.21 To see what the window will "really" look like, compile and run the form.

7. Use the Object drop-down list in the Properties window to select the objects and change their Text properties to the values shown in **Figure 3.20**.

8. From the Debug menu, choose Start to compile and run the project and see how the user interface actually appears (**Figure 3.21**).

✔ Tips

- The default, or initial, value of the TextBox control's Text property is set using the Properties window—but it can, of course, be changed at runtime by the user.
- In a real project, you'd probably want to take more care with the appearance of the user interface and include labels with text that explain the purpose of user interface elements.
- In the interest of simplicity, I accepted the default names of the instances of controls placed on the form: for example, `Label1`, `TextBox1`, and `Button1`. These names can be easily changed using the Properties window, and it's better practice to name control instances that are used in code—as all of these will be—in a way that reflects their purpose. (It may be hard to know what `Button1` does, particularly when you have many buttons on a form, but btnReverse is pretty clear.) I'll provide some examples of appropriately named control instances in Chapter 5.

The final piece of this demonstration instantiates an object based on the Vqs class and uses it from the Windows form. As already explained, the code for doing this will be almost exactly like the code for doing it from a Web service.

To invoke the class members from a Windows form:

1. With the form open in its designer, double-click the Button control.

   This creates an event framework to handle the Button's Click event and opens the framework in the Code Editor (**Figure 3.22**).

2. Within the Click event handler—that is, after the auto-generated procedure definition

   ```
   Private Sub Button1_Click(ByVal _
      sender As System.Object, ByVal _
      e As System.EventArgs) Handles _
      Button1.Click
   ```

   add code to declare and instantiate an object based on the Vqs class. If the class is part of the Windows Application project, you approach this exactly the same way as in the Web service project:

   ```
   Dim vqs As New Vqs()
   ```

   On the other hand, if the class is being accessed through an external component reference, then you need to use the external project's namespace in the instantiation—for example:

   ```
   Dim vqs As New _03VBVQS01.Vqs()
   ```

3. Assign the value of the TextBox Text property to the class instance Text property:

   ```
   vqs.Text = TextBox1.Text
   ```

4. Invoke the ReverseText method:

   ```
   vqs.ReverseText()
   ```

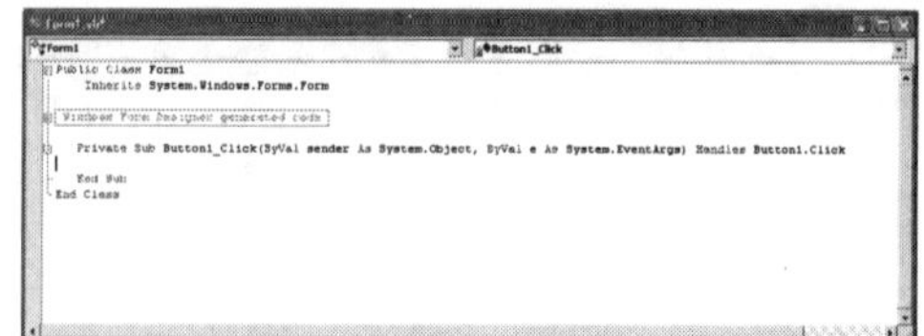

Figure 3.22 Visual Studio automatically creates the framework for an event handler procedure.

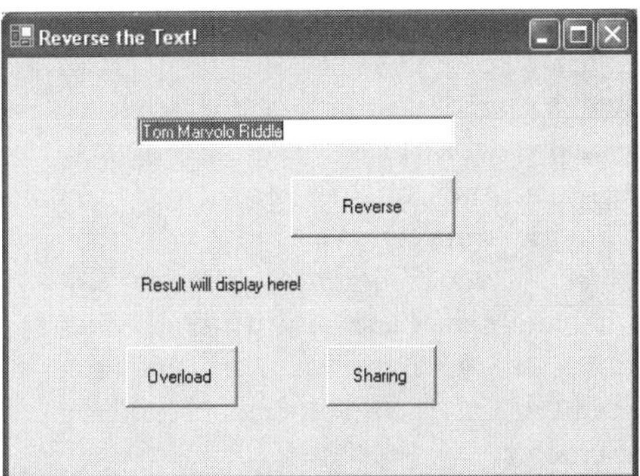

Figure 3.23 The form opens with the default value for the text string.

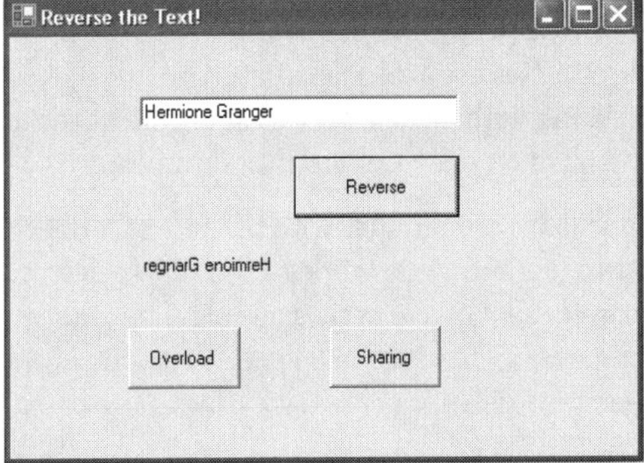

Figure 3.24 If you enter a text string and click Reverse, you can verify that the class instance operates correctly.

5. Assign the updated class instance Text property value to the Label's Text property:

   `Label1.Text = vqs.Text`

6. To compile and run the project, from the Debug menu choose Start.
7. When the form window opens (**Figure 3.23**), enter a text string in the text box.
8. Click Reverse and view the results to make sure that the class method works (**Figure 3.24**).

✔ Tips

- **Listing 3.3** shows the complete code for the Button click event (with the referenced component instantiation commented out). Note that all lines beginning with an apostrophe are comments, not code, in VB .NET.
- Events are discussed in the overview of the next section, "Class Members," and in Chapter 5. In Chapter 9, "Exceptions and Debugging," you'll find detailed information about writing code that handles events.

Listing 3.3 Instantiating the class and using its members from a Windows form. (The instantiation of the class as part of an externally referenced component is shown commented out.)

```
Private Sub Button1_Click(ByVal sender As System.Object, ByVal e As System.EventArgs) _
   Handles Button1.Click
   'Do it for a referenced component
   'Dim vqs As New _03VBVQS01.Vqs()

   'Do it for the class and class module file part of the project
   Dim vqs As New Vqs()

   'the rest is the same, no matter how you get the class instance
   vqs.Text = TextBox1.Text
   vqs.ReverseText()
   Label1.Text = vqs.Text
End Sub
```

Class Members

Classes are made up of members, so programming a class means programming the members of that class. In other words, if you don't understand class members, you don't understand classes—so this is a very important topic.

The members of a class are the properties, methods, fields, and events that you use to take advantage of a class's functionality. (Together, the members of a class are also said to "define the class.")

Besides public members, a class can, of course, contain variables and functions for the internal use of class instances. The whole point of public members is to encapsulate the internal workings of the class so that when you are programming with the class, you don't need to know about them. But even though you use only public members associated with a class, you shouldn't forget that the class has internals.

If you actually create or modify class code, you will most likely have to work with internals such as variables. These are marked as *local* in scope using the Private keyword. An example is the m_text variable we used to store property values in the Vqs class example in the previous section. The statement that declares m_text, `Private m_text As String = ""`, says that m_text is local in scope to the class. This means that code within the class (the local scope) can use the variables, but no other code can. For more on scope and on the uses of the Public and Private keywords, see the "Scope" section later in this chapter.

This section also shows you how to work with shared members, which do not require instantiation to be accessed. In the OO world, shared members are analogous to global variables in a procedural program. In other words, by sharing a member, you potentially make it available to all of the objects in your program. This section also introduces the Class View window, which is a quick and easy interface to help you understand classes, their relationships, and their members.

Properties

You've already seen the general form that properties take, but it's worth reviewing because properties are so important. Properties are an encapsulated means of dealing with values, and, as such, are at the heart of object-oriented programming.

If you are not familiar with properties, understanding how they work is probably easiest in the context of a generic example. The following example is general enough that you can easily modify it to create your own properties.

Suppose that you want to implement a property named Prop that stores and retrieves a Long value. To do this, you set up a private local variable named m_prop by declaring the variable using the Private keyword to actually store the value.

Within the Prop property procedure, a Get accessor retrieves the value stored in m_prop, and a Set accessor saves a new value to m_prop. (Accessors are a special kind of procedure that work with properties. They are designed to retrieve—and save—property values.) Code that serves gate-keeping, validation, or other purposes can also be placed in either the Get or Set accessor.

Here's what this looks like in code:

```
Public Class Demo
    Private m_prop As Long
    Public Property Prop() As Long
        Get
          ' Validation or other code here
            Prop = m_prop
        End Get
        Set(ByVal Value As Long)
          ' Validation or other code here
            m_prop = Value
        End Set
    End Property
End Class
```

One important point you should know is that you can easily create read-only or write-only properties by omitting the appropriate accessor.

To create a read-only property:

1. Add the ReadOnly keyword to the property procedure declaration.
2. Omit the Set accessor from the property procedure.

   Here's an example of a read-only property:

   ```
   Private m_prop As Long
   Public ReadOnly Property Prop() _
       As Long
       Get
           Prop = m_prop
       End Get
       ' No Set accessor because
       ' read-only
   End Property
   ```

✔ Tip

- In reality, if you create a property without the ReadOnly keyword and include a Set accessor that contains no code, the property operates in a read-only fashion—no changes to the property value are saved. The only problem is that no notification is sent to the calling code whose attempted changes to the property value were simply ignored.

To create a write-only property:

1. Add the WriteOnly keyword to the property procedure declaration.
2. Omit the Get accessor from the property procedure.

   Here's an example of a write-only property:

   ```
   Private m_prop As Long
   Public WriteOnly Property Prop() _
       As Long
       ' No Get accessor because
       ' write-only
       Set(ByVal Value As Long)
           m_prop = Value
       End Set
   End Property
   ```

✔ Tip

- If you create a property that omits the WriteOnly keyword and includes an empty Get accessor, you will always get back the uninitialized value of the property (`0` in the case of a numeric property, and the empty string if the property is of type String).

Methods

Methods are active. They do something, most often to the object that they are part of, but the action can also be applied to other objects. Without methods, objects based on classes wouldn't be able to do anything—so you need to know how to work with methods if you are to get anything done.

Under the covers, a method is a public function, or procedure (using the Sub keyword) if it does not return a value.

For example, here's the framework for a method that accepts a string as an argument and has no return value:

```
Public Sub Meth1(ByVal arg As String)

End Sub
```

If the method will return a value, then it must be created using the Function keyword. For example, here's the framework for a method that accepts a long integer argument and returns a string value:

```
Public Function Meth2(ByVal arg As _
   Long) As String

End Function
```

✔ Tips

- The declaration of a method, including its name, argument types, and return type, is called its *signature*.
- You can omit the Public keyword, since by default procedures and functions are public in scope. However, it's better practice to include it explicitly.

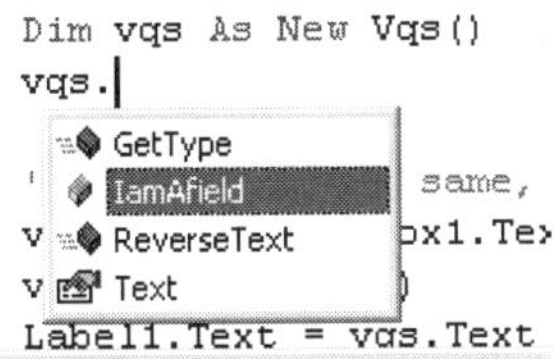

Figure 3.25 Auto-completion in the Code Editor lists the public members of a class instance.

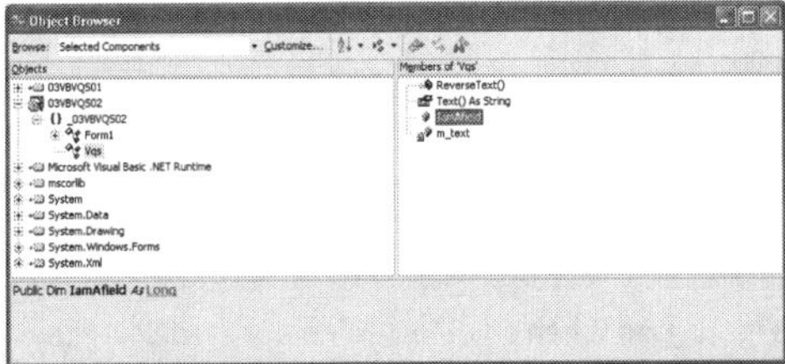

Figure 3.26 The Object Browser shows the members of classes you create.

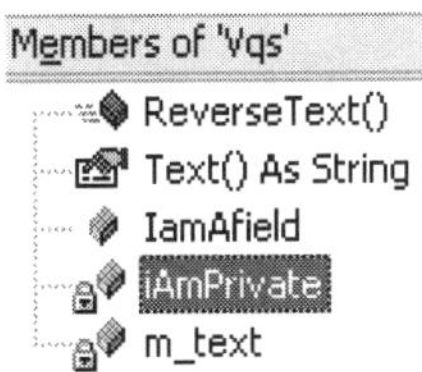

Figure 3.27 Private or local variables are marked with little padlocks in the Object Browser.

Fields

Fields are variables belonging to class instances that can be directly manipulated by outside code.

In terms of implementation, a field is simply a class variable declared with a public scope so that it is accessible to instances of the class—for example:

```
Public IamAfield As Long
```

You'll know that you're on the right track with a field declaration when you instantiate the class in the Code Editor and auto-completion shows the field in the list of class members (**Figure 3.25**).

The Object Browser, primarily discussed in Chapter 13, "The Common Dialog Controls," is a great tool for inspecting the members of your classes (**Figure 3.26**). (To open the Object Browser, from the Visual Studio View menu choose Other Windows; then select Object Browser.)

✔ Tip

- If you omit the access modifier and simply declare a variable in a class with a statement such as `Dim iAmPrivate As String`, the variable declared is private by default. You can see this visually in the Members pane of the Object Browser because the variable is marked with a little padlock (**Figure 3.27**).

You should use fields sparingly, because overuse violates the OO principles of encapsulation and code hiding. It is often better practice to use properties instead of fields.

Events

An *event* is a placeholder for code that is executed when the event is triggered (which is also called *firing* the event). Events are fired by a user action, program code, or the system. When the event is fired, a message goes out to all objects that have "subscribed" to the event. The message tells the objects to process any code that may have been placed in the related event-handling framework.

Earlier in this chapter, you saw how to add code that responded to the built-in Click event that comes with a Button control.

It's pretty easy to add your own custom events to a class and to arrange to handle them in another class when they are fired.

As an example, I'll show you how to add an OnPalindrome event to the Vqs class—fired, naturally, when the user enters text that is a palindrome (a string that reads the same both backwards and forwards) and invokes the ReverseText method.

To add a custom event to a class:

1. Declare the event in the class with any arguments you'd like (in this case, none):

   ```
   Public Event OnPalindrome()
   ```

2. At the appropriate point in the class—in this case, when the reversed string matches the original one—fire the event using the RaiseEvent keyword:

   ```
   If (Me.Text = newString) Then
      RaiseEvent OnPalindrome()
   End If
   ```

   You'll know you're on the right track if, after you type the RaiseEvent keyword in the Code Editor, it supplies a drop-down list of events, including OnPalindrome (**Figure 3.28**).

```
    If (Me.Text = newString) Then
       RaiseEvent
    End If         OnPalindrome
    Me.Text = newString
End Sub
```

Figure 3.28 The available events appear in the autocompletion drop-down list when you enter the RaiseEvent keyword.

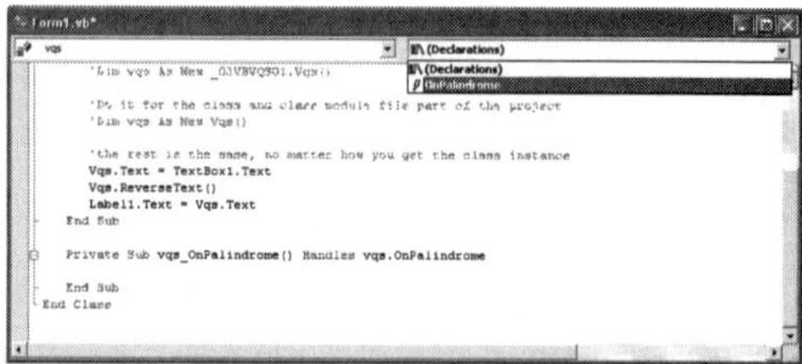

Figure 3.29 When an object is instantiated using the WithEvents keyword, you can use the Objects and Procedures drop-down lists to auto-generate the framework for an event-handling procedure.

✔ Tips

- Events appear in the Code Editor procedure list marked with a lightening bolt icon, as you can see in Figure 3.28 and **Figure 3.29**.
- If the event was declared with arguments, then you must raise, or invoke, it with a matching number and parameter type.
- It is important to understand that you're entirely responsible for causing the event to be fired appropriately.

  A common approach to firing an event is to keep checking over time to see if a condition has been fulfilled. Then, if it has, you can actually fire the event using a RaiseEvent statement. You can use the Timer component, explained in Chapter 11, "The Timer Component," to facilitate this kind of arrangement.
- **Listing 3.4** shows the complete code for the Vqs class with the added OnPalindrome event.

Listing 3.4 Vqs class with the OnPalindrome event added.

```
Public Class Vqs
   Private m_text As String = ""

   Public Property Text() As String
      Get
         Text = m_text
      End Get
      Set(ByVal Value As String)
         m_text = Value
      End Set
   End Property

   Public Sub ReverseText()
      Dim newString As String = ""
      Dim i As Integer
      For i = 0 To Me.Text.Length - 1
         newString = Me.Text.Substring(i, 1) & newString
      Next
      If (Me.Text = newString) Then
         RaiseEvent OnPalindrome()
      End If
      Me.Text = newString
   End Sub

   Public Event OnPalindrome()
End Class
```

Next, you'll see how to handle the OnPalindrome event when it is fired from the instance form class that is used to enter text that is to be reversed. Remember, however, that an event can be handled from many kinds of objects, not just forms.

To handle the event in the form:

1. Revise the declaration for the class instance to add the WithEvents keyword:

   ```
   Private WithEvents vqs As New Vqs()
   ```

2. When an object, such as vqs, is declared at the class level using the WithEvents keyword, it appears in the Objects drop-down list at the upper left of the Code Editor (Figure 3.29). Select vqs in the Object list.
3. When vqs is selected in the Object list, events associated with the object appear in the Procedures drop-down list at the upper right of the Code Editor (Figure 3.29). Select the OnPalindrome event from the Procedures list to have the Code Editor automatically create the framework for the event handler:

   ```
   Private Sub vqs_OnPalindrome() _
      Handles vqs.OnPalindrome

   End Sub
   ```

4. Within the event handler framework, add code that responds to the event, by using the Text property of the form to change the caption of the form when the event is fired (the form is referred to using the Me keyword):

   ```
   Private Sub vqs_OnPalindrome() _
      Handles vqs.OnPalindrome
      Me.Text = _
   "You've entered a palindrome, _silly!"
   End Sub
   ```

5. Start the project.
6. Enter a palindrome in the text box and click Reverse.

   The OnPalindrome event will be fired and the form caption changed (**Figure 3.30**).

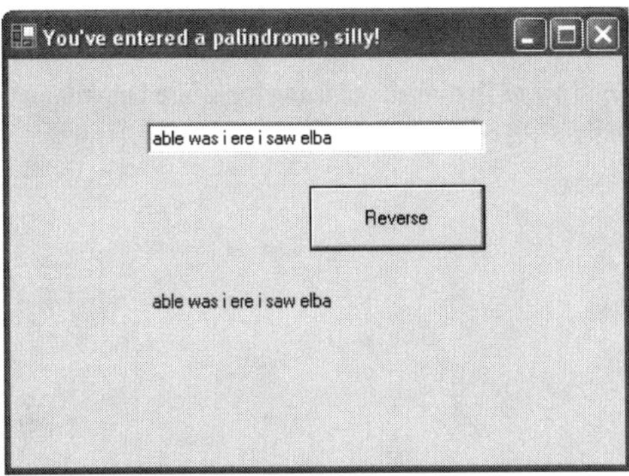

Figure 3.30 When a palindrome is entered and the Reverse button clicked, the event is fired and the window's caption is changed.

✔ Tips

- When entering palindromes, be aware that string comparison differentiates between lowercase and uppercase letters. So, for example, "Madam I mAdam" will not register as a palindrome because "Madam I mAdam" does not equal "madam I madam." (You could easily enough change this in the code by doing comparisons, using only uppercase or lowercase letters.)
- An object declaration using the WithEvents keyword must take place at the class level. It cannot be placed within a method.
- **Listing 3.5** shows the code for the Form1 class with the OnPalindrome event handler (note that the listing does not include code generated using Windows Form Designer).

Listing 3.5 The Form1 class is shown with the OnPalindrome event handler (excluding Windows Form Designer–generated code).

```
Public Class Form1
    Inherits System.Windows.Forms.Form

   Private WithEvents vqs As New Vqs()

   Private Sub Button1_Click(ByVal sender As System.Object, ByVal e As System.EventArgs) _
      Handles Button1.Click
      Vqs.Text = TextBox1.Text
      Vqs.ReverseText()
      Label1.Text = Vqs.Text
   End Sub

   Private Sub vqs_OnPalindrome() Handles vqs.OnPalindrome
      Me.Text = "You've entered a palindrome, silly!"
   End Sub
End Class
```

Shared members

Shared members are methods, properties, and fields that are marked with the Shared keyword. They're different from class members in that they exist independent of object instantiation. All instances of a class share these methods, properties, and fields.

For example, the logarithmic, trigonometric, and other methods provided by the System. Math class are all static. This means that you do not have to instantiate a Math object to use these methods—you can just go ahead and use the class member directly in your code, which is certainly convenient. Let's look at how to do that.

✔ Tip

- In some programming languages, the term *static* is used instead of *shared*; since instantiation isn't involved when the member is shared, the member is thought of as being static.

To use the shared members of the Math object:

- Invoke the constants and methods of the System.Math class without creating an instance of the class.

  For example, within a form class, if you want to display the first 10 numerical places after the decimal point of the constant Pi, you would type this statement in the form caption:

  ```
  Me.Text = _
   Math.Round(Math.PI, 10).ToString()
  ```

  Figure 3.31 shows the results.

✔ Tip

- Members of the System namespace can be referred to without the namespace qualifier. So, for example, Math, as used in this code fragment, means the System.Math class.

Figure 3.31 The results of using the shared members of the Math class appear in the form caption.

Shared members are also very useful for communicating values between object instances. You can use them in much the same way as you may have used global variables in the past. But be careful not to abuse this approach! Too much reliance on shared members for sharing values can lead to objects that are effectively unencapsulated.

The next exercise, in which you'll create a custom object, should enhance your understanding of sharing. We'll create a simple class, WhatIf, which has an instance member field (named NotShared), a shared field (named IamShared), and nothing else. Here's what it looks like:

```
Public Class WhatIf
   Public NotShared As String = ""
   Public Shared IAmShared As _
      String = ""
End Class
```

✔ Tip

- As I've said before, you have a great deal of flexibility as to where you place class code. I put this in the Vqs.vb class module.

The procedure that we'll use to test this code has been placed in a button click event handler in the form class. Here's what the declaration looks like:

```
Private Sub Button2_Click(ByVal sender _
   As System.Object,ByVal e As _
   System.EventArgs) _
   Handles Button2.Click
```

Let's get started.

To show the difference between the shared and unshared members:

1. Create two instances of the WhatIf class: thing1 and thing2:
   ```
   Dim thing1 As New WhatIf()
   Dim thing2 As New WhatIf()
   ```
2. Assign values to both the shared and unshared members of thing1:
   ```
   thing1.NotShared = _
      "thing1 not shared"
   thing1.IAmShared = "thing1 shared"
   ```
3. Assign values to both members in thing2:
   ```
   thing2.NotShared = _
      "thing2 not shared"
   thing2.IAmShared = "thing2 shared"
   ```
   The point this code demonstrates is that the unshared member of thing1 is not overwritten by assigning a value to the (same-named) unshared member of thing2. In contrast, assigning a value to the shared member of thing2 overwrites the value that was assigned to the shared member of thing1.
4. Demonstrate the preceding point by displaying the values of the shared and unshared thing1 members in a Label control (**Figure 3.32**):
   ```
   Label1.Text = thing1.NotShared & _
      " - " & thing1.IAmShared
   ```

Here's the complete code for the demonstration:

```
Private Sub Button2_Click(ByVal sender _
   As System.Object,ByVal e As _
   System.EventArgs) _
   Handles Button2.Click
   Dim thing1 As New WhatIf()
   Dim thing2 As New WhatIf()
   thing1.NotShared = "thing1 not shared"
   thing1.IAmShared = "thing1 shared"
   thing2.NotShared = "thing2 not shared"
   thing2.IAmShared = "thing2 shared"
   Label1.Text = thing1.NotShared & _
      " - " & thing1.IAmShared
End Sub
```

✔ Tip

- The string concatenation operator (&) is used to display both values in a single statement.

Figure 3.32 The value of the shared member has been overwritten by another instance of the class.

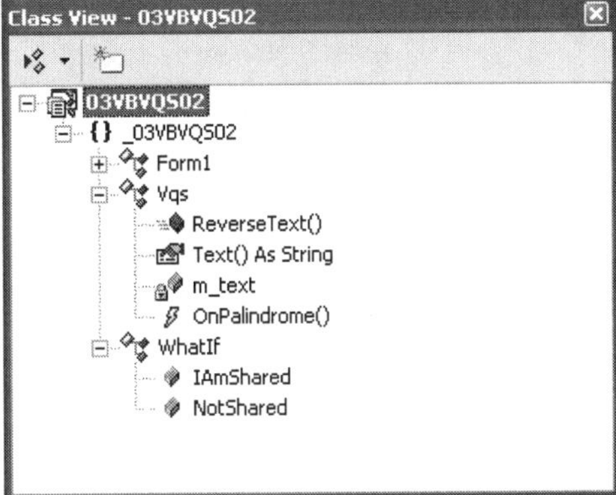

Figure 3.33 The Class View window is a useful tool for inspecting classes and members.

Class View window

The Class View window is a useful Visual Studio tool for inspecting classes and their members.

To inspect classes and members:

1. From the View menu, choose Class View.

   The Class View window opens (**Figure 3.33**).

2. Click the plus arrows to the left of each class in the hierarchy to expand the tree so that you can view classes and members as appropriate and necessary.

✔ Tips

- If you choose Go to Definition from the right-click context menu in the Class View window, the Code Editor takes you to the place where the class or member is defined in code.
- If you choose Browse Definition from the right-click context menu in the Class View window, you will be taken to the class or member as shown in the Object Browser (see Chapter 14 for more information about the Object Browser).
- C# .NET programmers may notice that the class member wizards, which help to build framework code for the various types of class members and are accessible in C# .NET from the Class View context menus, do not exist in Visual Basic .NET.

Scope

The *scope* of a class or class member is a means of referring to the objects that can access the class or member. For example, a privately scoped variable within a class cannot be accessed outside of instances of that class.

You've already seen a number of examples in this chapter of class members whose scope is defined using access modifiers (the keywords Public, Private, and so on) You've probably also noticed that a class itself has a defined scope.

Table 3.1 shows the full set of five access keywords for class and member scope, and their meanings. In addition, some common-sense restrictions apply. For example, the scope of a member can't be broader than the scope of its container—such as the class that it's in—regardless of the access identifier. Also, types declared with a Private scope must be contained within another type (otherwise, the access modifier would be meaningless).

Although all of this may sound a bit complicated, the good news is that the syntax checker in the Code Editor will stop you from making any egregious errors in this area before you've gone too far.

Table 3.1

Scope Access Keywords

KEYWORD	MEANING
Public	Public allows access without restrictions.
Private	Private access is the most restricted; access is restricted to within its class.
Protected	Members specified using the Protected keyword can be accessed only from within the class or from a derived class. Protected can apply only to members of a class—which can, of course, themselves be *nested* classes. In other words, a protected member must be contained and cannot be a highest-level class.
Friend	Friend access means that access is restricted to the program that contains the class or member.
Protected Friend	Protected Friend members can be accessed from the class or a class derived from it and/or the project that contains the member. In other words, a Protected Friend member has both Protected and Friend access. (An uncontained class cannot be modified with Protected Friend.)

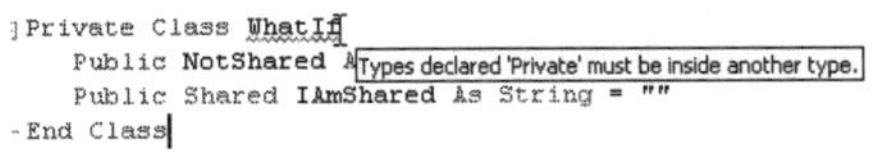

```
Private Class WhatIf
    Public NotShared A[Types declared 'Private' must be inside another type.]
    Public Shared IAmShared As String = ""
End Class
```

Figure 3.34 When you try to use the Private access modifier with an uncontained class, the compiler notes the error and supplies an informative message.

✔ Tips

- If you've used a syntactically inappropriate access keyword, the modified identifier will be underlined with a blue squiggle in the Code Editor, and an informative error message will appear when your mouse hovers over the offending identifier (**Figure 3.34**).
- Although it's better practice to explicitly provide a scope access modifier, you can declare classes and members without one. In this case, the default access scope for a class or class member is Public, except for variables declared with Dim, which are private in scope by default.
- As the defaults suggest, most of the time you'll do just fine using only the Public and Private access modifiers, unless you're exploring the subtleties of OO programming. I've included the other three access modifiers for completeness and because you'll see them used in common code. For example, you can see these access modifiers in the code supplied with the out-of-the box Form class, discussed in Chapter 5.

Method Overloading

You may remember that earlier in this chapter we briefly discussed polymorphism. Well, one way to achieve polymorphism is through method overloading, in which a class provides several versions of a method that all have the same name but different signatures. From an implementation standpoint, this means that with method overloading the number and types of arguments differ. In addition, the return type of the method's overloaded versions can vary.

The overloaded method can be called in any of its versions, and the class instance that is invoked determines the version called according to the arguments sent with the method call.

If this discussion seems overly theoretical to you, try creating an overload method using the process defined in the following task.

To create an overloaded method:

◆ Within a class, create a number of same-named methods that have different signatures. Here's an example:

```
Public Class OverMe
   Public Sub HowManyArgs()
      ' Does nothing
   End Sub
   Public Function HowManyArgs _
      (ByVal inStr As String) As _
      String
      HowManyArgs = _
         "One argument passed to me!"
   End Function
   Public Function HowManyArgs _
      (ByVal inStr As String, _
      ByVal inStr2 As String) _
      As String
      HowManyArgs = _
        "Two arguments passed to me!"
   End Function
End Class
```

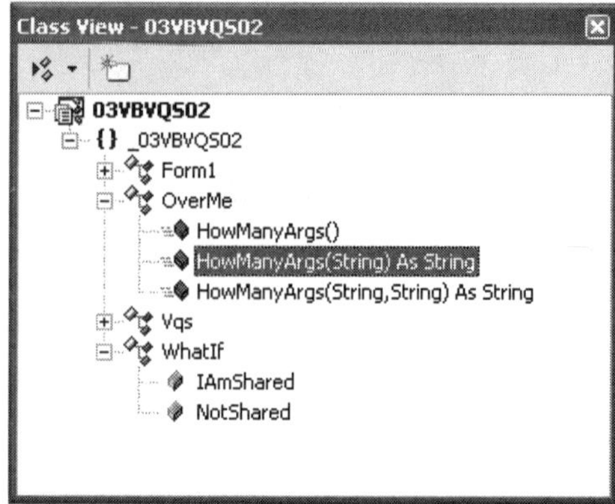

Figure 3.35 The overloaded methods can be seen in the Class View window.

✔ Tips

- The arguments of the overloaded methods don't have to all be the same type.
- You can view the overloaded methods in the Class View window (**Figure 3.35**).

```
Private Sub Button3_Click(ByVal sender As System.Object, _
    ByVal e As System.EventArgs) Handles Button3.Click
    Dim overme As New OverMe()
    overme.HowManyArgs("Only one arg"
                ▲2 of 3▼ HowManyArgs (inStr As String) As String
End Sub
```

Figure 3.36 A drop-down list of the possible method overloads appears in the Code Editor.

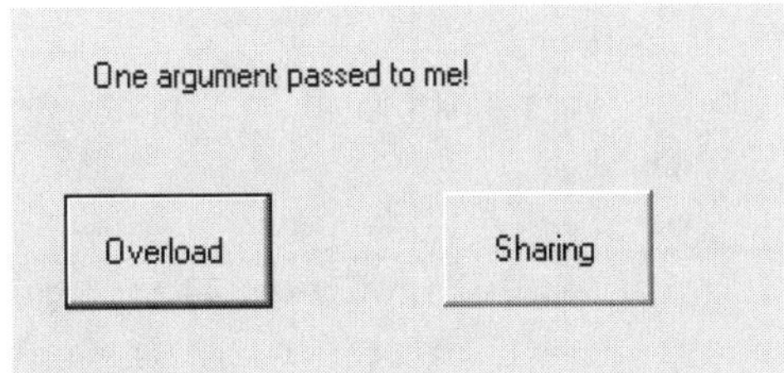

Figure 3.37 The version of the method called depends on the number (and type) of arguments passed to it.

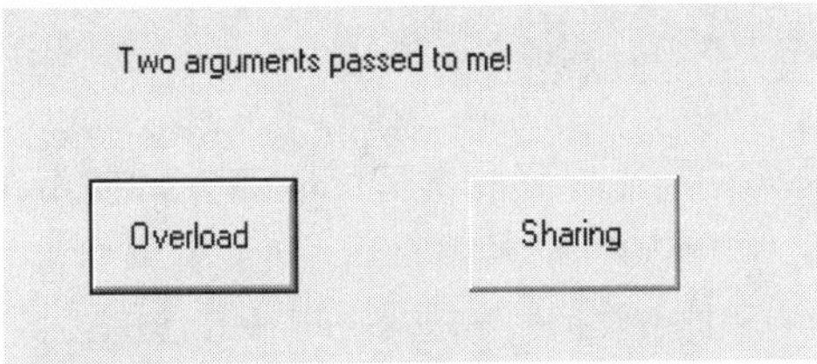

Figure 3.38 Passing two arguments to the overloaded method calls a different version of the method (with a different return value).

To test the overloaded methods:

1. Add a Button control to the form class.
2. Double-click the Button control to create a click event handler in the Code Editor.
3. Within the click event handler, instantiate an object based on the class containing the overloaded methods:

   ```
   Dim overme As New OverMe()
   ```

4. Invoke the overloaded method.

   As you start typing arguments, the Code Editor displays a drop-down list that provides signature information about the overloads (**Figure 3.36**).

5. Invoke the method with one argument and then with two arguments, so that you understand the difference.

   If you invoke the method with one argument and display the results in the Label's Text property—

   ```
   Label1.Text = _
      overme.HowManyArgs("Only one arg")
   ```

   it returns the value for the appropriate overload (**Figure 3.37**), whereas, if you invoke the method with two arguments—

   ```
   Label1.Text = _
      overme.HowManyArgs("arg1", "arg2")
   ```

   it returns appropriate (but different) results (**Figure 3.38**) based on a call to another version of the overloaded method.

Here's the code for the click event that invokes the overloaded method:

```
Private Sub Button3_Click(ByVal sender _
   As System.Object, ByVal e As _
   System.EventArgs) Handles _
   Button3.Click
   Dim overme As New OverMe()
   ' Label1.Text = _
   ' overme.HowManyArgs("Only one arg")
   Label1.Text = _
      overme.HowManyArgs("arg1", "arg2")
End Sub
```

Class Constructors

A class constructor is a method called when an object is instantiated. In Visual Basic .NET, you add an explicit constructor to a class by creating a method named New (generally referred to as the constructor).

When the class is instantiated, the New method is invoked. A typical use for the constructor is to initialize class variables.

So far, none of the classes we've created in this chapter have New methods. However, if you examine the auto-generated code for either the Form class or the Web Service class provided by the Visual Basic .NET environment, you will find New methods.

Since New methods can be overloaded, one way to use them is to allow the programmer to decide when instantiating the class whether to pass a value to the constructor. If a value (or values) is passed, then it can be used to initialize the newly minted object.

For example, let's provide two New constructors for the Vqs class. One of these overloaded methods does nothing—in other words, it does not change the status quo. The other supplies an initial value for the Text property (as you'll recall, this is the property on which the ReverseText method operates).

To add overloaded New methods to the class:

- Add the New methods to the class just as you would add any other overloaded methods—for example:

```
Public Class Vqs
   Sub New()
      'Does nothing
   End Sub

   Sub New(ByVal inString As String)
      m_text = inString
   End Sub
...
End Class
```

✔ Tip

- The New method is a procedure declared with Sub (rather than Function) and cannot return a value.

As you'll recall, we originally instantiated an object based on the Vqs class, saved the value of the Form TextBox.Text property in the object's Text property, and invoked the ReverseText method as follows:

```
Dim vqs As New Vqs()
Vqs.Text = TextBox1.Text
Vqs.ReverseText()
```

```
Dim vqs As New Vqs(TextBox1.Text)
Vqs.ReverseText[▲2 of 2▼ New (inString As String)]
Label1.Text = Vqs.Text
```

Figure 3.39 The overloads for the New method—the class constructor—appear in the Code Editor.

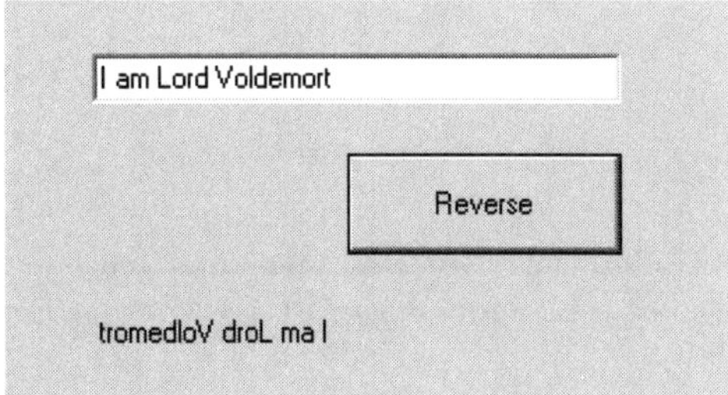

Figure 3.40 The ReverseString method works with the initial text value supplied in the constructor.

This will still work perfectly well, as we made a point of including a New overload that does nothing. However, we can eliminate one step if we take advantage of the overloaded New method that accepts a text value as an argument and initializes the Text property.

To invoke the overloaded class constructor:

◆ Instantiate the object, and at the same time pass it the value of the TextBox.Text property, as follows:

```
Dim vqs As New Vqs(TextBox1.Text)
```

Note that, as with any other call to an overloaded method, the overloads appear in the Code Editor drop-down list (**Figure 3.39**).

✔ Tip

■ Here are the two lines of code using the overloaded class constructor, instead of the original three (this more compact approach works, as you can see in **Figure 3.40**):

```
Dim vqs As New Vqs(TextBox1.Text)
Vqs.ReverseText()
```

Inheritance

Inheritance is the *sine qua non* of OO, and in some ways, the whole point of working with classes in the first place. You'll find many examples of programming using class inheritance throughout this book, so this section will focus on a few of the mechanics.

In VB .NET, classes can inherit from *one* other class at most. The class that inherits is said to *derive* from its *base* class.

To derive one class from another, you have to add an Inherits clause on a new line immediately following the class definition.

For example, when you open a new Windows Application project, the out-of-the box Form1 class that is generated by Visual Studio uses the following declaration to inherit from the general .Net Framework Windows Form class (System.Windows.Forms.Form):

```
Public Class Form1
    Inherits System.Windows.Forms.Form
```

In one brief fell swoop of code, the new Form1 class now has access to all members of the Form class (except those that are protected with Private access scope).

The general idea is to use inheritance to grab most of the functionality that you need without having to do any work, and then add some new functionality on top of the base class functionality. Subsequent derived classes can behave similarly, piggybacking on your new class and adding their own new bits.

One of the great things about inheritance is that it generally does not violate encapsulation—you don't have to know *how* the members of a base class were implemented to be able to use them in a derived class.

✔ Tip

- The concept of an abstract base class is explained in Chapter 4, "Class Interfaces."

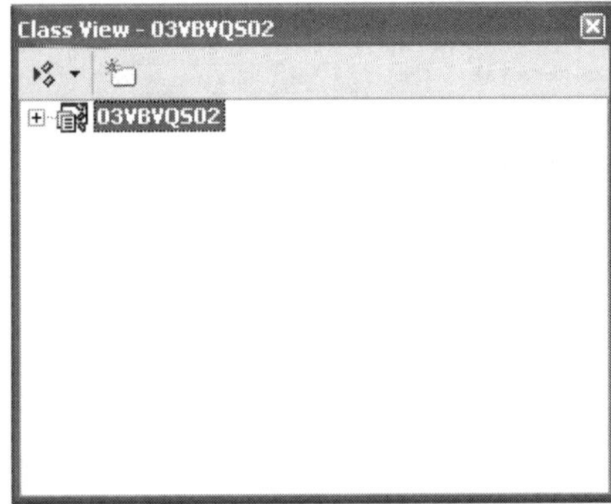

Figure 3.41 Expand the project in Class View to see its classes.

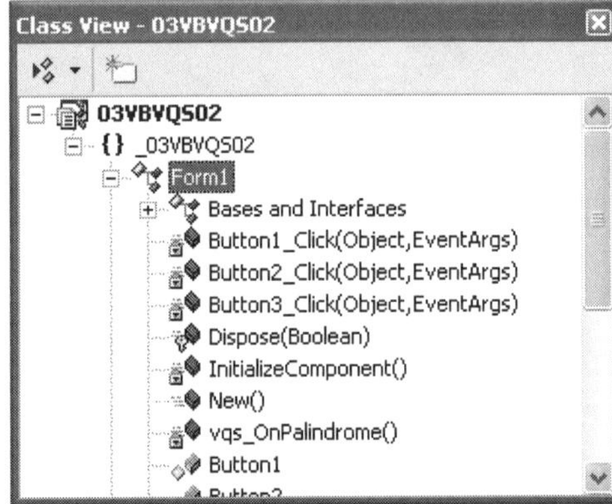

Figure 3.42 The Form1 node shows its own members and a node for derived members.

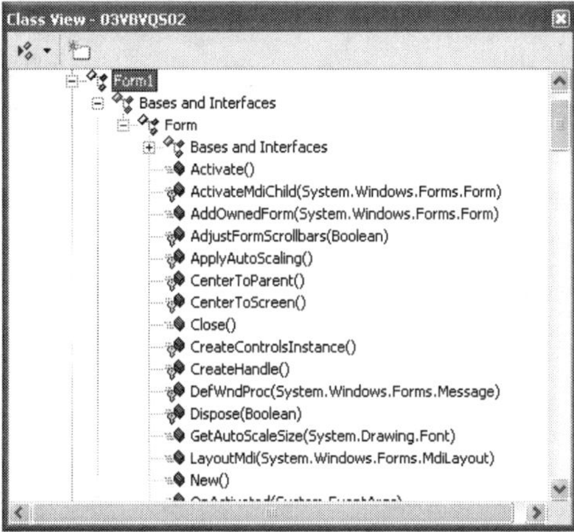

Figure 3.43 Expand the Bases and Interfaces node to see the inherited members of the class.

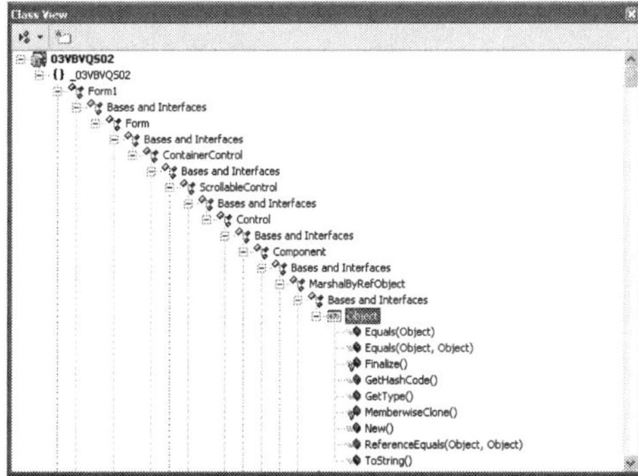

Figure 3.44 If you look far enough down the inheritance tree, you'll find that all .NET classes have Object as an ancestor.

To inspect the inheritance of a class derived from the Form class:

1. With a Windows Application project open in Visual Studio, open Class View (**Figure 3.41**).
2. Expand the project and namespace nodes until you see the class derived from Form (Form1 in **Figure 3.42**).
3. Expand the node next to Form1 to view the members of Form1 along with a node labeled Bases and Interfaces (Figure 3.42).
4. Expand the Bases and Interfaces node to see the members of Form, the base class for Form1 (**Figure 3.43**).

✔ Tips

- .NET Framework classes do not spring fully grown out of the head of Zeus. Each base class probably has its own Bases and Interfaces node in Class View, going a long way back. In fact, if you go far enough back, you'll find that System.Object—the Adam and Eve—is an ancestor of all classes that are part of the .NET Framework. This is shown for the Form class in **Figure 3.44**. If you think about it, this reinforces the sense that .NET itself was built in an OO way using class inheritance.
- The meaning of *Interfaces* in the name "Bases and Interfaces" is explained in Chapter 4.
- The Object Browser, explained in detail in Chapter 14, is another great tool for inspecting .NET class inheritance.

Here's another simple example; the following declaration creates a new class with all the functionality of the original Vqs class:

```
Public Class Vqs2
   Inherits Vqs


End Class
```

You can now see the new class in Class View along with its inherited members (**Figure 3.45**). It would be perfectly reasonable to add some new functionality to this derived class. You could also verify that it performs in the same way as its base by instantiating an object based on the derived class (Vqs2) rather than the base (Vqs)—for example:

```
Private WithEvents vqs As New Vqs2()
...
vqs.Text = TextBox1.Text
Vqs.ReverseText()
...
```

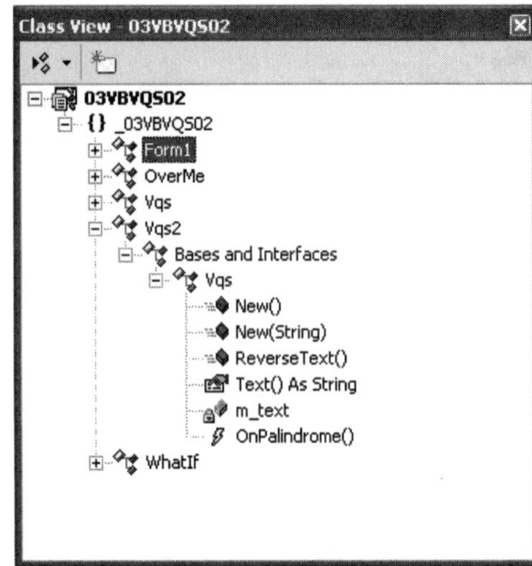

Figure 3.45 It's easy to see the base class and members for the derived Vqs2 class.

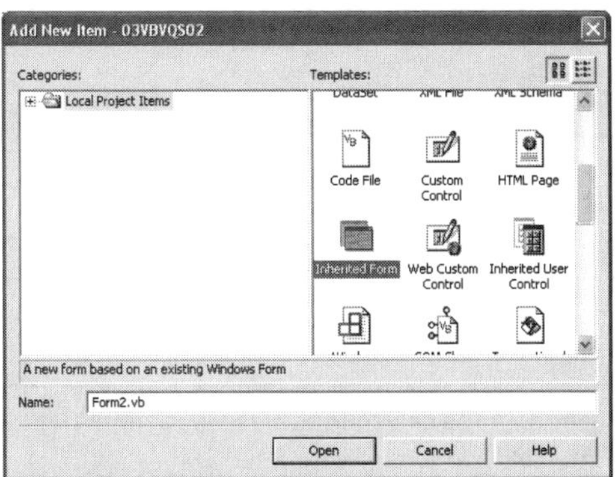

Figure 3.46 To visually inherit a Form, select Inherited Form in the Add New Item dialog.

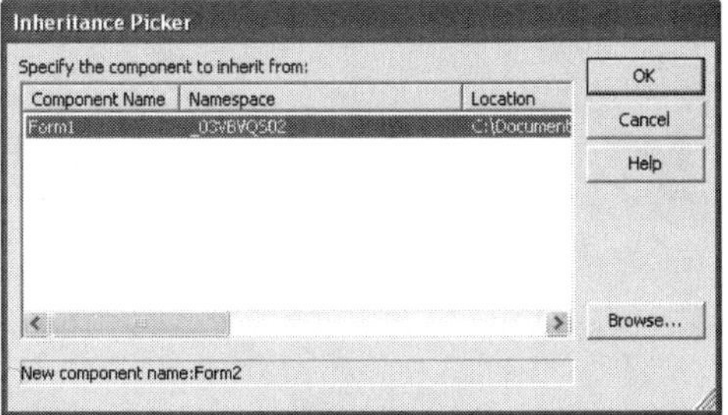

Figure 3.47 Choose the base Form class in the Inheritance Picker.

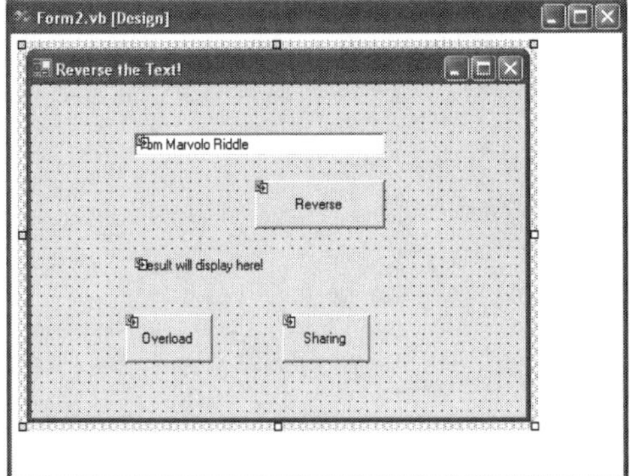

Figure 3.48 The derived form class will be opened in the project.

Visual Inheritance

Visual inheritance is a Visual Studio .NET user interface mechanism that allows you to inherit one class from another without having to—uggh!—add an Inherits clause programmatically in the Code Editor.

✔ Tip

- Visual inheritance is limited to certain types of classes, such as Forms, that have a visual component.

As the preceding paragraph suggests, I do not feel that visual inheritance is a very big deal. However, since you are likely to hear the phrase mentioned as one of the big benefits of VB .NET, you should know what it is.

To visually inherit a Form class:

1. Open the Add New Item dialog (**Figure 3.46**) by selecting Add Inherited Form from the Project menu.
2. In the Templates pane of the Add New Item dialog, make sure Inherited Form is selected.
3. Give the new, derived form class module a name, such as Form2.vb.
4. Click Open.

   The Inheritance Picker dialog opens (**Figure 3.47**).
5. Choose a component to derive from in the Inheritance Picker. (If you want to select a form from another project, click Browse.)
6. With the base component selected, click OK.

   The derived form opens in its designer (**Figure 3.48**).

continues on next page

✔ Tips

- Of course, you can view the new form module in Solution Explorer (**Figure 3.49**).
- If you open the new form in the Code Editor (Figure 3.49), you'll see that the only code in it is an Inherits clause:

```
Public Class Form2
    Inherits _03VBVQS02.Form1
Windows Form Designer generated code
End Class
```

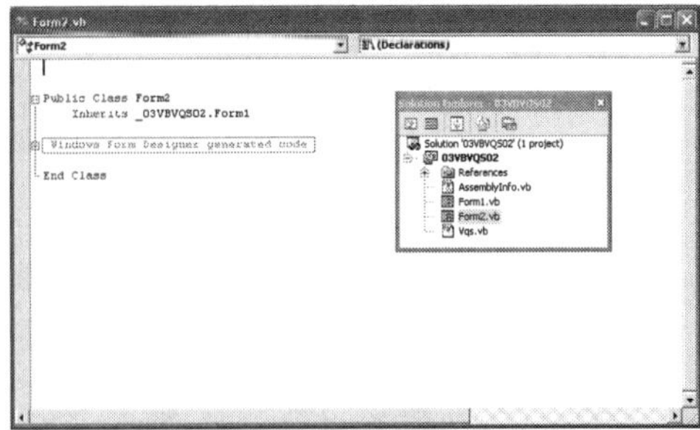

Figure 3.49 The only code added to the derived class is an Inherits clause.

Summary

In this chapter, you learned how to:

- Explain the principles of OOP
- Add a class to a Web service project
- Describe class members
- Describe fields
- Describe properties
- Describe methods
- Create a custom event in a class
- Handle the class event
- Describe shared class members
- Use the Class View window
- Describe class and member scope
- Describe method overloading
- Describe class constructors
- Describe class inheritance
- Describe visual inheritance

CLASS INTERFACES

Now that you're on solid ground in all things class-related—that is, you know how to instantiate objects based on classes and how a class can derive, or inherit, from its base—it's time to delve a little deeper.

In this chapter, we'll examine *abstract base classes* and *class interfaces*. First, we'll look at abstract base classes, which are classes that cannot be used to instantiate objects, but can be used to derive classes. Then we'll examine class interfaces and how to implement them. As you'll see in this chapter, class interfaces are a kind of contract that implementing classes must comply with and are very important for creating large, consistent applications. Finally, you'll learn why you might want to create your own custom interface—and how to do it.

This is fun material and not really very difficult, so let's get started!

Abstract Base Classes

Abstract classes are great for creating families of classes. These classes share a common ancestor in the taxonomy of the application—the abstract base class—but differing details of implementation can be left to the classes derived from the abstract class. The result is a pattern of classes that are homogeneous in the places they need to be, but differ elsewhere—which is an extremely important feature for large and complex applications.

While abstract base classes themselves can't instantiate objects, they can be used to derive nonabstract, or *concrete*, classes. These concrete classes, in turn, can be used to instantiate families of objects.

In .NET, one reason that abstract classes cannot be used directly as the basis for objects is that they're often not fully implemented. The intention is to provide an outline and allow derived concrete classes to override the (often sketchily implemented) abstract members.

On the other hand, abstract class members that *are* fully implemented offer another benefit: a single code base to debug and manage.

You probably remember from Chapter 3, "Working with Classes," that a class can be thought of as a cookie cutter, or pattern, for instantiating objects (the cookies). Now you can think of an abstract base class as a template for the cookie cutter—or the pattern for creating patterns. As you'll see, this approach makes conceptual management of classes easier, because there is a pattern for the classes.

As you will see in the next task, marking a class as abstract is a simple process.

To mark a class as abstract:

- Use the MustInherit keyword as a modifier in the class definition.

✔ Tip

- In some languages, including C#, C++, and Java, the Abstract keyword is used, rather than MustInherit.

As the task shows, marking a class as abstract is easy. But to get a good feel for what abstract classes do, it is helpful to compare an abstract class with a concrete class (otherwise, the differences won't seem that compelling). Let's start with the concrete class Dinosaur. (Creating this class should be easy, since you already learned how to create concrete classes in Chapter 3.) Dinosaur contains one field, named *Size*, and one property, called *Name*. Later, we'll transform Dinosaur into an abstract class, so you can compare it in its concrete and abstract manifestations, and create specific concrete dinosaur classes that inherit from the abstract Dinosaur class.

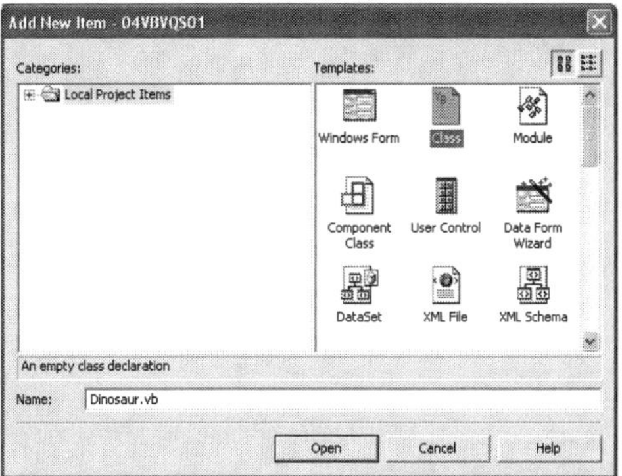

Figure 4.1 Use the Add New Item dialog to add a class module to the project.

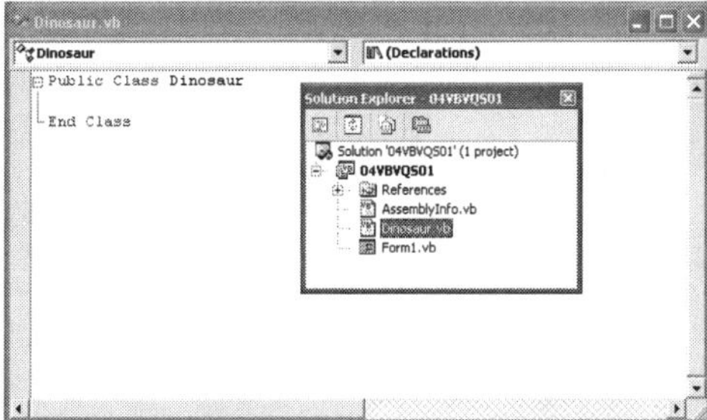

Figure 4.2 The class module, along with the default class created by the IDE, is shown in the Code Editor alongside Solution Explorer.

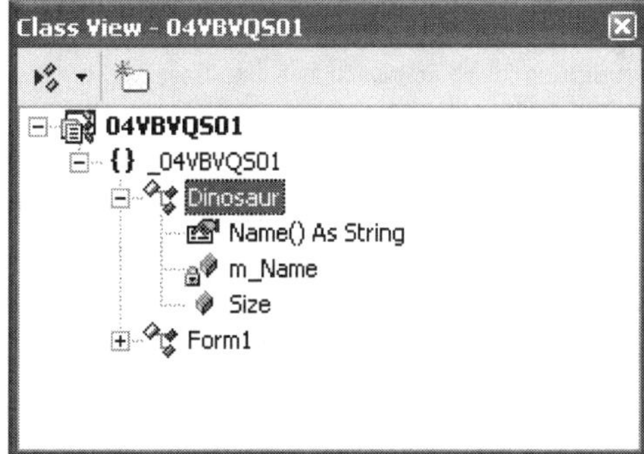

Figure 4.3 The Dinosaur class and its members are shown in Class View.

To add a concrete class to a Windows Application:

1. Open a new Windows Application project in Visual Studio. (If you need a refresher, see Chapter 1, "Introducing Visual Studio .NET.")
2. Add a class module named *Dinosaur* to the project using the Add New Item dialog as shown in **Figure 4.1**. For a discussion of how to add the class module and code, see "Adding a Class to a Windows Application" in Chapter 3.

   The new class will appear in Solution Explorer (**Figure 4.2**).
3. Open the class module in the Code Editor.

   It will consist of a class definition, as shown in Figure 4.2.
4. Using the Code Editor, add the Size field and the Name property to the Dinosaur class as explained in Chapter 3.

   The complete class code should now look like this:

```
Public Class Dinosaur
   Private m_Name As String
   Public Size As Integer
   Public Property Name() As String
      Get
         Name = m_Name
      End Get
      Set(ByVal Value As String)
         m_Name = Value
      End Set
   End Property
End Class
```

5. Open Class View to see the Dinosaur class and its members (**Figure 4.3**).
6. Save the project by selecting File > Save All.
7. Start the project by selecting Debug > Start to make sure there are no syntax errors.

To create a user interface to test the class:

1. Open the Windows form associated with the project in its designer.
2. Open the Toolbox (View > Toolbox).
3. Use the Toolbox to add three labels, two textboxes, and one button to the form (**Figure 4.4**). You'll find detailed instructions for adding these controls to the form in "To add a user interface to the Windows form" in Chapter 3.
4. Choose View > Properties Window to open the Properties window (**Figure 4.5**).
5. Using the Properties window, set the Text properties of the controls as shown in **Figure 4.6**.
6. Use the Properties window to change the Name property of the first text box from TextBox1 to txtName (**Figure 4.7**), the second text box from TextBox2 to txtSize, and the label that will display results to lblResults.
7. Run the project (by selecting Debug > Start) to make sure you are happy with the way the form looks at runtime (**Figure 4.8**).

Next, we'll instantiate based on the concrete class. The point of doing this is to compare and contrast the concrete class with an abstract class (since, of course, you cannot instantiate based on an abstract class).

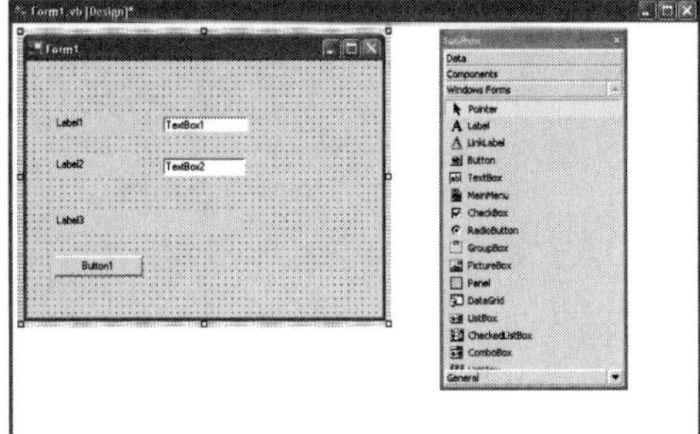

Figure 4.4 Use the Toolbox to add labels, text boxes, and a button to the form.

Figure 4.5 Use the Properties window to set the properties for objects such as an instance of the button class.

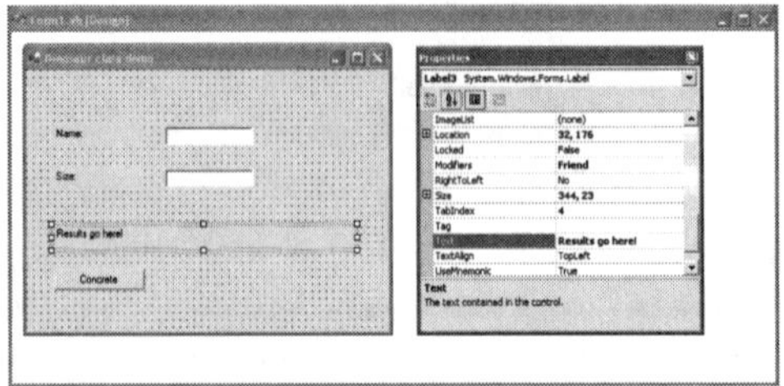

Figure 4.6 Use the Properties window to set the Text properties of the objects contained by the form to the values shown.

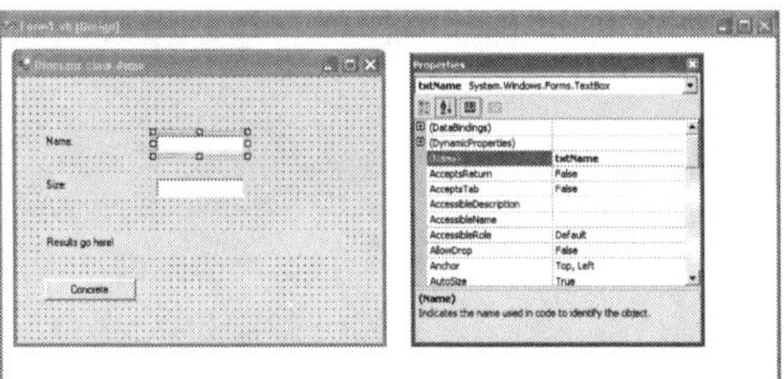

Figure 4.7 Set the Name property of the first text box (TextBox1) to `txtName`.

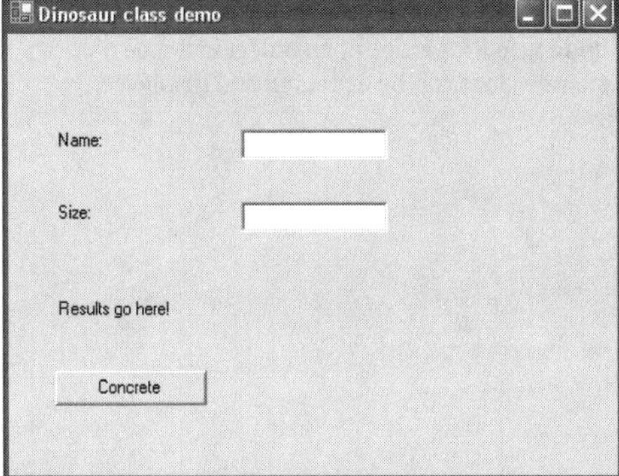

Figure 4.8 Start a project to see the way a form looks at runtime.

```
Private Sub Button1_Click(ByVal sender _
    As System.Object, ByVal e As _
    System.EventArgs) Handles Button1.Click
    Dim dino As New Dinosaur()
    dino.|
End S  GetType
nd Clas Name
        Size
```

Figure 4.9 The class members will appear in the auto-completion drop-down list in the Code Editor.

To instantiate based on the concrete class:

1. To create a click event procedure for the Concrete button you created in the previous stepped list, double-click the button and open the procedure in the Code Editor.

   Here's the framework code for the event that will be auto-generated:

   ```
   Private Sub Button1_Click _
      (ByVal sender _
      As System.Object, ByVal e As _
      System.EventArgs) Handles_
      Button1.Click


   End Sub
   ```

2. Declare a new variable and instantiate it as an object of the Dinosaur class:

   ```
   Dim dino As New Dinosaur()
   ```

3. Assign the values of the appropriate text boxes to the object's Name and Text properties.

   As you start the assignment code, you should see the members of the Dinosaur class in the drop-down list in the Code Editor (**Figure 4.9**). Here's the assignment code:

   ```
   dino.Name = Me.txtName.Text
   dino.Size = _
      Convert.ToInt16(Me.txtSize.Text)
   ```

4. Display the value of the Name property of the instantiated object:

   ```
   Me.lblResults.Text = _
      "Object created: " & _
      dino.Name
   ```

continues on next page

5. Run the project with the completed event procedure (shown here) to verify that the object can be instantiated.

```
Private Sub Button1_Click _
   (ByVal sender _
   As System.Object, ByVal e As _
   System.EventArgs) Handles _
   Button1.Click
   Dim dino As New Dinosaur()
   dino.Name = Me.txtName.Text
   dino.Size = _
     Convert.ToInt16(Me.txtSize.Text)
   Me.lblResults.Text = _
      "Object created: " & _
      dino.Name
End Sub
```

6. With the form running, enter a name and number (for the size) and click the Concrete button. The Name property of the instance will be displayed (**Figure 4.10**).

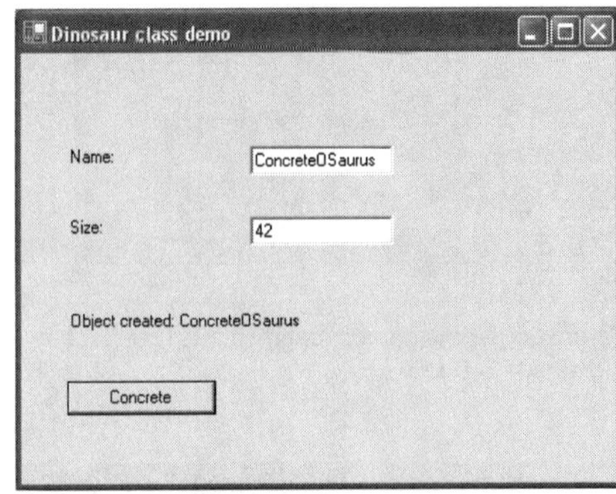

Figure 4.10 Properties of an object instance of a concrete class can be accessed and displayed.

✔ Tips

- Since the Text property of the txtSize text box is a string, you must explicitly convert it to an integer type before you can save it in the Dinosaur instance field (if you're running your project with Option Explicit On, which I recommend). You use the System.Convert.ToInt16 method to do this.
- This code does not check whether the user has entered a text string in the txtSize `text box` that can be converted to an integer—that is, the code doesn't check whether the input is an integral number. (For information about techniques for verifying user input, see Chapter 10, "Controls That Accept User Input.") If the text string is anything other than an integral number, a runtime syntax error, called an exception, will be generated. (Exceptions are explained in Chapter 9, "Exceptions and Debugging.")

So in the past few exercises we've created a regular class, Dinosaur, that can be instantiated. Now let's create an AbstractDinosaur class that is identical to the Dinosaur class except that includes a MustInherit modifier—which makes the AbstractDinosaur class truly abstract.

To make a class abstract:

◆ Add the MustInherit keyword to the class declaration—for example:

```
Public MustInherit Class
AbstractDinosaur
```

The entire AbstractDinosaur class code now looks like this:

```
Public MustInherit Class
AbstractDinosaur
   Private m_Name As String
   Public Size As Integer
   Public Property Name() As String
      Get
         Name = m_Name
      End Get
      Set(ByVal Value As String)
         m_Name = Value
      End Set
   End Property
End Class
```

As previously noted, you cannot instantiate an object based on the abstract class. You might give it a try by using the Windows Form class developed in the section "To instantiate based on a concrete class" earlier in this chapter (of course, you need to modify the code to instantiate based on the abstract class with the statement `Dim dino As New AbstractDinosaur()`). Making this attempt causes a syntax error in the Visual Studio Task List, shown in **Figure 4.11**.

✔ Tips

- The Task List is explained in Chapter 9.
- Although you can fully implement abstract classes, they are usually implemented only partially or not at all. Partial implementation serves to encapsulate common functionality for inherited classes. (To understand what I mean by encapsulate, see the definition toward the beginning of Chapter 3.)

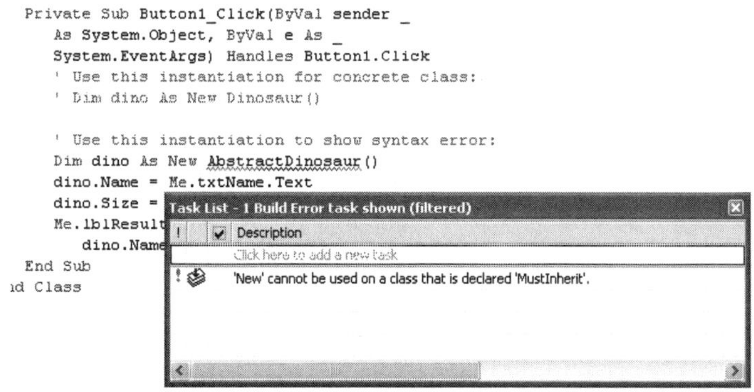

```
Private Sub Button1_Click(ByVal sender _
   As System.Object, ByVal e As _
   System.EventArgs) Handles Button1.Click
   ' Use this instantiation for concrete class:
   ' Dim dino As New Dinosaur()

   ' Use this instantiation to show syntax error:
   Dim dino As New AbstractDinosaur()
   dino.Name = Me.txtName.Text
   dino.Size =
   Me.lblResult
      dino.Name
End Sub
id Class
```

Task List - 1 Build Error task shown (filtered)

!	✔	Description
		Click here to add a new task
!		'New' cannot be used on a class that is declared 'MustInherit'.

Figure 4.11 If you try to instantiate an object from an abstract class, you'll get a syntax error.

Let's make the AbstractDinosaur class work as it is intended by rolling out some concrete classes based on it.

To derive concrete classes from an abstract class:

- Derive the concrete classes from the abstract class using the Inherits keyword. (For more information on deriving classes, see "Inheritance" in Chapter 3.)

  For example, here are some classes derived from AbstractDinosaur:

```
Public Class Allosaurus
   Inherits AbstractDinosaur
End Class

Public Class Diplodocus
   Inherits AbstractDinosaur
End Class

Public Class TRex
   Inherits AbstractDinosaur
End Class
```

✔ Tip

- Each of these concrete dinosaur classes inherits the members of the AbstractDinosaur class (Name and Size) out of the box, which is pretty neat.

You'll likely want to differentiate these concrete classes from one another using members that are specific to each class. For example, since the real dinosaur Diplodocus was not a meat eater, the Diplodocus class might have a `FavoriteVeggie` field. And since the number of claws on their short front hands was a key differentiator between the dinosaur Allosaurus and the dinosaur Tyrannosaurus Rex (Allosaurus had three and T-Rex had two, in case you wanted to know), the classes representing these dinosaurs might each have a `NumClaws` field.

Here are the concrete classes derived from AbstractDinosaur with some class-specific members added:

```
Public Class Allosaurus
   Inherits AbstractDinosaur
   Public NumClaws As Integer
End Class

Public Class Diplodocus
   Inherits AbstractDinosaur
   Public FavoriteVeggie As String
End Class

Public Class TRex
   Inherits AbstractDinosaur
   Public NumClaws As Integer
End Class
```

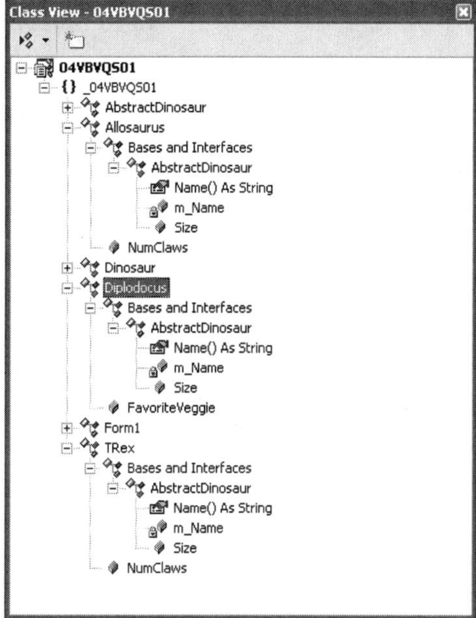

Figure 4.12 The concrete classes, their members, and the members derived from their base class (AbstractDinosaur) are shown in Class View.

Figure 4.12 shows the concrete classes derived from AbstractDinosaur in Class View.

As you can see, abstract base classes are used essentially to create taxonomies, or hierarchies of classes that share common characteristics and, as mentioned earlier, to encapsulate the common functionality.

For example, instead of deriving specific dinosaur classes directly from AbstractDinosaur, two new abstract classes—CarnivoreDino and VeggieDino—might each be derived from AbstractDinosaur. In turn, specific dinosaur classes might be derived from one of these classes, depending on whether the specific dinosaur was a carnivore. All this makes conceptual management of classes easier, because there is a pattern for the derived classes.

In addition, you don't have to recode the inherited members of the derived class—which saves work and results in fewer bugs. Finally, by marking a class with the MustInherit keyword, you ensure that it cannot be instantiated—presumably because it doesn't contain enough specifics (in other words, it is too abstract) to be appropriate as an object.

Now we can instantiate objects based on the classes derived from the abstract class.

To instantiate an object based on one of the derived classes:

1. Using the instructions provided in "To create a user interface to test the class" earlier in this chapter, add a button to the Windows form.
2. Use the Properties window to change the button's Text property to Abstract.
3. Add the framework code in the Code Editor for the button's click event by double-clicking the Abstract button. (This procedure was explained more fully in "To instantiate based on the concrete class" earlier in this chapter.)
4. Within the click event, add code that instantiates an object based on the derived class, assigns values to its property and fields, and creates a display of object member values, as shown in **Figure 4.13** (the display demonstrates that the object really was created).

   The code is as follows:

```
Private Sub Button2_Click _
   (ByVal sender _
   As System.Object, ByVal e _
   As System.EventArgs) _
   Handles Button2.Click
   Dim trexy As New TRex()
   trexy.Name = Me.txtName.Text
   trexy.Size = _
     Convert.ToInt16(Me.txtSize.Text)
   trexy.NumClaws = 3
   Me.lblResults.Text = _
      "Object created: " & _
      trexy.Name & " with " & _
      trexy.NumClaws.ToString() & _
      " claws on her front legs."
End Sub
```

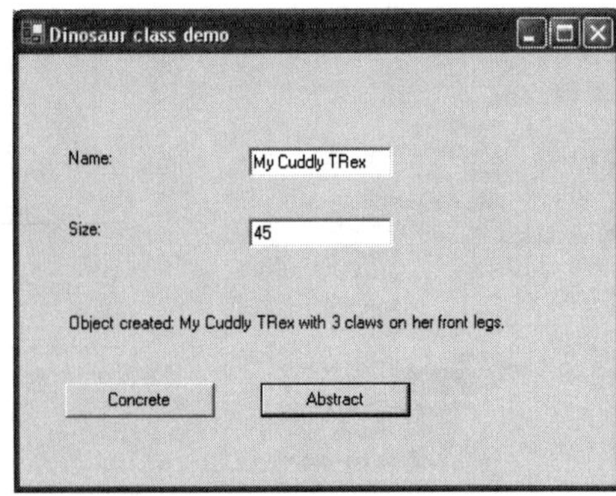

Figure 4.13 Objects based on the class that inherits from the abstract base class can be instantiated.

Table 4.1

Some Important .NET Framework Class Interfaces

INTERFACE	PURPOSE
ICloneable	Supports *cloning*, which creates a new instance of a class with the same values as an existing instance of the class.
ICollection	Defines size, enumerators, and synchronization methods for all *collections*, or groups of objects.
IComparable	Specifies that the class must provide a CompareTo method, allowing comparison between a current instance of the class and another object of the same type.
IEnumerable	Allows iteration using an enumerator over a collection.
IFormattable	Provides functionality to format an object as a string.
IHttpHandler	Defines the contract that ASP.NET implements to synchronously process HTTP Web requests using custom HTTP handlers.
IHttpModule	Provides ASP.NET module initialization and disposal events to the implementing class.

Understanding Class Interfaces

Now let's move on to class interfaces, which you should by no means confuse with user interfaces. User interfaces are visual and relate to the way a user interacts with a program. Class interfaces relate to the ways objects based on a class interact with a program. They aren't visual at all.

When a class implements an interface, the class must contain specified members—in other words, the class must comply with a kind of contract. Class interfaces are widely used as part of the .NET Framework, primarily to enforce consistency across many classes that do similar things.

The use of class interfaces has proved vital in programs that implement large and complex systems, in team development situations, and in situations in which one team of developers is creating class libraries that will be used by other developers.

A good example of this last situation is the .NET Framework. One team—that is, programmers working for Microsoft—developed the class libraries that make up the .NET Framework. Another team—that is, you and me—use VB .NET to create applications. The Microsoft .NET team used class interfaces to ensure that many aspects of application creation are done the right (and presumably the best) way. **Table 4.1**, which briefly describes some of the most important .NET Framework class interfaces, lists some of the .NET Framework class interfaces used in this way.

However, the virtues of class interfaces go beyond implementation of those written by others. If you are in a situation in which you need to enforce implementation clarity and consistency—for example, because you are involved in a team development project, or because others will use your classes—then you should consider employing custom class interfaces, as explained later in this chapter.

Unlike abstract base classes, which create a pattern that is used to supply functionality and taxonomic relationships to derived classes, a class interface does not supply functionality. It merely provides a specification to a class, in effect saying to a class, "You must comply." Compliance means that the class includes members that match the specification provided in the interface by name and signature.

In addition, a class interface does not imply a taxonomic or hierarchical relationship with other classes (other than that the implementation of a certain class interface by multiple classes implies a commonality of some of the members and functionality of the classes).

Abstract classes should be used primarily to provide common functionality among objects that are closely related, whereas interfaces are best suited for ensuring that unrelated classes provide some common functionality.

A difference in Visual Basic .NET between class interfaces and abstract base classes—indeed, between class interfaces and any base class, not just abstract ones—is that in VB .NET a class can derive from only one base class, but it can implement many interfaces.

Don't worry! The concepts related to class interfaces are not very difficult to comprehend, and if some of this seems murky, it will undoubtedly become clearer as we look at some examples.

✔ Tip

- It is conventional (although not required) to name a class interface with a capital *I*, followed by a capitalized first letter.

```
Public MustInherit Class AbstractDinosaur
    Implements IComparable
    Private m_Name As '_04VBVQS01.AbstractDinosaur' must implement 'Overridable Overloads Function CompareTo(obj As Object) As Integer' for interface 'System.IComparable'.
    Public Size As Integer
    Public Property Name() As String
        Get
            Name = m_Name
        End Get
        Set(ByVal Value As String)
            m_Name = Value
        End Set
    End Property
End Class
```

Figure 4.14 If your class specifies the implementation of an interface without the actual implementation of the interface, you will get a syntax error.

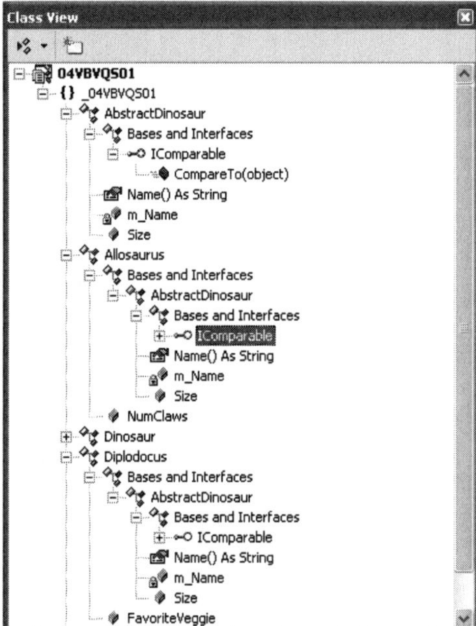

Figure 4.15 You can use Class View to determine the interfaces that a class must implement.

To specify that a class implement an interface:

- Immediately following the class declaration, add the Implements keyword followed by the interface name.

  For example, returning to the Abstract Dinosaur class, the following class declaration and implementation clause will specify the implementation of the .NET Framework class interface named *IComparable* (explained in Table 4.1):

```
Public MustInherit Class _
    AbstractDinosaur
    Implements IComparable
```

✔ Tips

- The implementation clause merely specifies that the interface must be implemented; it doesn't actually implement it. If your class code contains an implementation clause without the required implementation, you will get a syntax error (**Figure 4.14**). The purpose of this syntax error is to enforce programmer compliance with the strictures of the interface.
- When the interface implementation specification is added to the abstract base class, implementation is necessarily also required in the derived classes, as you can see in Class View in **Figure 4.15**.
- To specify more than one interface for implementation by a class, simply add it to the Implements clause in a comma-delimited list.

How do you know what you have to do to implement a specified interface in a class? Read on!

To implement an interface in a class:

1. Determine the members specified by the interface by *one* of the following means:
   - Read the error message you get when your class specifies an interface that it doesn't implement, as shown in Figure 4.14.
   - Expand the Interface node in Class View (for example, you can see the node for IComparable in Figure 4.15) to examine its members.
   - Use the Object Browser to inspect the details of the interface's members (the Object Browser is explained in detail in Chapter 14, "The Object Browser.")
   - Use Help, as explained in detail in Appendix A, "Getting Help."

   For example, to implement IComparable, your class should have a CompareTo method for comparing objects based on the class, or derived classes, with one another.

2. Add the framework code for the required members to the class by providing member definitions.

3. Add an implements clause to each member, specifying the interface member that it implements.

   Here's the framework code for the Abstract Dinosaur class implementation of the IComparable CompareTo method, including the method's Implements clause:

   ```
   Public Function CompareTo(ByVal obj _
      As Object)As Integer Implements _
      IComparable.CompareTo

   End Function
   ```

4. Add the code to the member, such as the CompareTo method, that actually does the work to implement the method.

Listing 4.1 The AbstractDinosaur class implementing the IComparable interface.

```
Public MustInherit Class AbstractDinosaur
   Implements IComparable
   Public Function CompareTo(ByVal obj As _
      Object) As Integer Implements _
      IComparable.CompareTo
      Dim dino As AbstractDinosaur
      dino = CType(obj, AbstractDinosaur)
      Return Me.Size.CompareTo(dino.Size)
   End Function
   Private m_Name As String
   Public Size As Integer
   Public Property Name() As String
      Get
         Name = m_Name
      End Get
      Set(ByVal Value As String)
         m_Name = Value
      End Set
   End Property
End Class
```

For example, the CompareTo method is supposed to provide a way to determine an ordered ranking of objects of the same type. In the case of the dinosaur classes, this might be done by comparing the Size field of each instance ultimately derived from AbstractDinosaur. This uses the fact that Size is of type Integer, which already comes with a CompareTo method that can be used. Here's the implementation code for the AbstractDinosaur class CompareTo method:

```
Public Function CompareTo(ByVal _
   obj As Object) As _
   Integer Implements _
   IComparable.CompareTo
   Dim dino As AbstractDinosaur
   dino = CType(obj, _
      AbstractDinosaur)
   Return _
      Me.Size.CompareTo(dino.Size)
End Function
```

✔ Tips

- Creating a member framework without any implementation code is sufficient to satisfy the legalistic "letter of the law" for implementing an interface, although, of course, it doesn't provide any functionality.
- The System.Ctype method used in this code converts an object of one type to another (specified) type, a process sometimes also called *casting*. In this case, an Object type, saved in the variable obj is converted to the AbstractDinosaur type and saved in the variable dino. This gives us access to the Size field of the comparison dinosaur class object.
- **Listing 4.1** shows the complete code for the AbstractDinosaur class, with the IComparable interface implementation.

Next, we should test the class implementation interface to see if it delivers on its promise—that is, provides a way to order (or compare) two objects that are instances of the class with the implementation.

To test this, why not instantiate an Allosaurus and a TRex and let the greater (larger) beast eat the smaller one for dinner?

To test the interface implementation:

1. Using the instructions provided in "To create a user interface to test the class" earlier in this chapter, add a button to the Windows form.
2. Use the Properties window to change the button's Text property to Imp Test.
3. As explained in "To instantiate based on the concrete class" earlier in this chapter, double-click the Imp Test button to add the framework code in the Code Editor for the button's click event.
4. Within the click event, add code that instantiates objects based on the TRex and Allosaurus classes:

   ```
   Dim trexy As New TRex()
   Dim ally As New Allosaurus()
   ```

5 Provide values for the Name and Size properties of these monsters:

   ```
   trexy.Name = "trexy"
   trexy.Size = 48
   ally.Name = "ally"
   ally.Size = 45
   ```

6. Use the CompareTo method of one of the objects to determine which is "greater" and display the results.

Here's the complete code for the click event procedure, including the use of the CompareTo method:

```
Private Sub Button3_Click _
   (ByVal sender _
   As System.Object, ByVal e _
   As System.EventArgs) Handles _
   Button3.Click
   Dim trexy As New TRex()
   Dim ally As New Allosaurus()
   trexy.Name = "trexy"
   trexy.Size = 48
   ally.Name = "ally"
   ally.Size = 45
   If trexy.CompareTo(ally) > 0 Then
      ' trexy is bigger
      Me.lblResults.Text = _
         "trexy the T-Rex" _
         & " ate ally the Allosaurus" _
         & " for dinner."
   ElseIf trexy.CompareTo(ally) = 0 _
     Then
      ' same size
      Me.lblResults.Text = _
         "No dinner tonight!"
   Else
      ' ally is bigger
      Me.lblResults.Text = _
         "ally the" & _
         " Allosaurus ate" _
         & " trexy the T-Rex" & _
         " for dinner."
   End If
End Sub
```

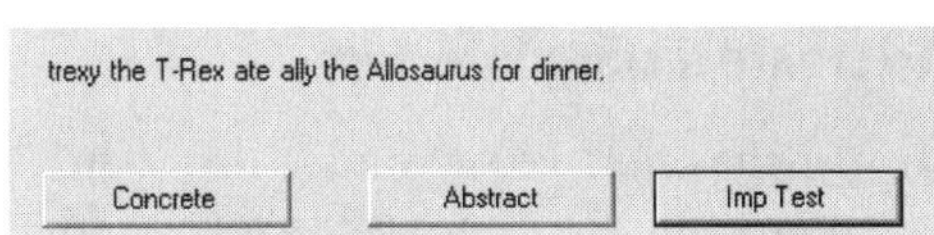

Figure 4.16 Since trex.Size is greater than ally.Size, it is Allosaurus for dinner!

7. Run the project and click the Imp Test button to verify that the CompareTo method works and displays the right results (**Figure 4.16**).

✔ Tips

- The CompareTo method returns a signed integer that indicates the ordering of the compared objects. A positive value means that the instance invoking the method is greater than the object being compared, a value of zero means the two objects are equal, and a negative value means that the invoking instance is less than the object being compared.
- You might want to play with changing the size values for the instances to make sure that the code works as it is supposed to.

Creating a Custom Class Interface

The .NET library of classes contains a great many useful and wonderful class interfaces. Even so, it's a very good thing that you can easily create your own custom class interfaces.

As already noted, one reason for creating a custom class interface and requiring that it be implemented as part of a project's coding standards is to help ensure consistency of code in a multiprogrammer team development project. You also might want to create class interfaces if you expect your classes to be used by other programmers and you want to make sure that they use them correctly.

Interfaces can declare fields, properties, methods, and events. These members are declared without actual implementation code. Instead, the interface members become a contract that any implementing classes must live up to. Every class that implements a custom interface must include the members identified by the interface—even though the implementation details are not specified by the interface.

To create a class interface:

1. Use the Interface keyword to define an interface in the same way as you would define a class—for example:

   ```
   Public Interface ICarnivore


   End Interface
   ```

2. Within the interface, declare each member that belongs to the interface by placing the signature—the member type, name, arguments, and return type—of each member in the interface, as in this example:

   ```
   Public Interface ICarnivore
      Function CanIEatU(ByVal dino _
         As AbstractDinosaur) As
   Boolean
   End Interface
   ```

As the CanIEatU method is defined here, it accepts as an argument only the objects that are based on classes derived from AbstractDinosaur. This approach differs from the more general construction in which a method accepts an Object type (as in the CompareTo method belonging to IComparable). This limits the applicability of the ICarnivore interface (for example, as defined, it could not be used with objects of a Tiger class, assuming that the class is not derived from AbstractDinosaur).

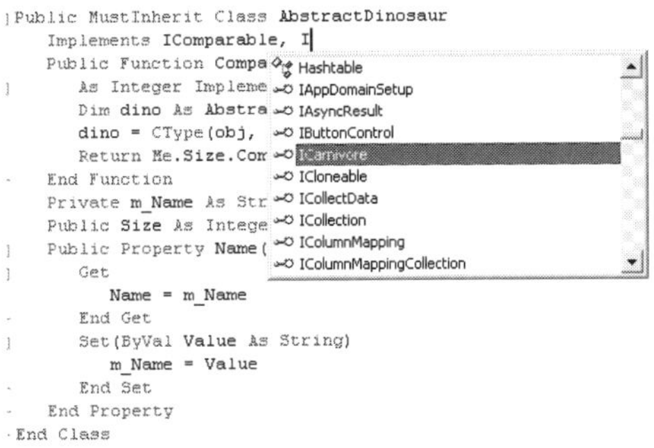

```
Public MustInherit Class AbstractDinosaur
    Implements IComparable, I
    Public Function Compa
        As Integer Impleme
        Dim dino As Abstra
        dino = CType(obj,
        Return Me.Size.Com
    End Function
    Private m_Name As Str
    Public Size As Intege
    Public Property Name(
        Get
            Name = m_Name
        End Get
        Set(ByVal Value As String)
            m_Name = Value
        End Set
    End Property
End Class
```

```
Hashtable
IAppDomainSetup
IAsyncResult
IButtonControl
ICarnivore
ICloneable
ICollectData
ICollection
IColumnMapping
IColumnMappingCollection
```

Figure 4.17 The newly created ICarnivore interface appears in the auto-completion list in the Code Editor along with .NET Framework interfaces.

Perhaps the ICarnivore interface can be justified alongside the IComparable interface on the grounds that a dinosaur might want to know whether it could successfully defeat another dinosaur before actually attempting to do so.

To specify the interface in the class definition:

- Add the interface to the Implements clause of the class definition—for example:

```
Public MustInherit Class _
    AbstractDinosaur
    Implements IComparable, _
      ICarnivore
```

The custom interface you just created (ICarnivore) should show up in the auto-completion list in the Code Editor just like the interfaces that are part of the .NET Framework (**Figure 4.17**).

Implementation of the custom ICarnivore interface works just like implementation of the IComparable interface. The members specified by the interface must be placed in the class. In this example, this means adding a CanIEatU method to the AbstractDinosaur class. The implementation, once again, relies on bigger is better: If I am bigger in my Size property than you are, I can eat you.

To implement the interface:

1. Add the members to the class specified by the interface, each with an Implements clause.
2. Add implementation code to the members—for example:

```
Public Function CanIEatU(ByVal dino _
   As AbstractDinosaur)As Boolean _
   Implements ICarnivore.CanIEatU
   If Me.Size > dino.Size Then
      CanIEatU = True
   Else
      CanIEatU = False
   End If
End Function
```

This implementation of the AbstractDinosaur class is in some respects simpler than that of the AbstractDinosaur CompareTo method. Because CanIEatU accepts an argument of type AbstractDinosaur rather than of type Object, there's no need to perform type conversion to use the members, such as the Size property, of the passed object.

Listing 4.2 shows the complete code for the AbstractDinosaur class, including the implementations for both IComparable and ICarnivore.

Listing 4.2 The Abstract Dinosaur class, including IComparable and ICarnivore implementations.

```
Public MustInherit Class AbstractDinosaur
   Implements IComparable, ICarnivore
      Public Function CanIEatU(ByVal dino As AbstractDinosaur) As Boolean Implements _
         ICarnivore.CanIEatU
         If Me.Size > dino.Size Then
            CanIEatU = True
         Else
            CanIEatU = False
         End If
   End Function
   Public Function CompareTo(ByVal obj As Object) As Integer Implements IComparable.CompareTo
      Dim dino As AbstractDinosaur
      dino = CType(obj, AbstractDinosaur)
      Return Me.Size.CompareTo(dino.Size)
   End Function
   Private m_Name As String
   Public Size As Integer
   Public Property Name() As String
      Get
         Name = m_Name
      End Get
      Set(ByVal Value As String)
         m_Name = Value
      End Set
   End Property
End Class
```

We can test the ICarnivore implementation in pretty much the same way as we tested IComparable. To make the experience a little more user interactive, we'll instantiate one TRex object with a Size value of 48, let the user pick a size for an Allosaurus object, and see whether the TRex is having dinner.

To test the interface implementation:

1. Using the instructions provided in "To create a user interface to test the class" earlier in this chapter, add a button to the Windows form.

2. Use the Properties window to change the button's Text property to ICarnivore.

3. As explained in "To instantiate based on the concrete class" earlier in this chapter, double-click the ICarnivore button to add the framework code in the Code Editor for the button's click event.

4. Within the click event, add code that instantiates objects based on the TRex and Allosaurus classes:

```
Dim trexy As New TRex()
Dim ally As New Allosaurus()
```

5. Provide values for the Name and Size properties of the TRex:

```
trexy.Name = "trexy"
trexy.Size = 48
```

6. Assign the values of the user inputs to the properties of the Allosaurus object as explained in "To instantiate based on the concrete class" earlier in this chapter:

```
ally.Name = Me.txtName.Text
ally.Size = _
   Convert.ToInt16(Me.txtSize.Text)
```

continues on next page

7. Invoke the trexy.CanIEatU method, with the Allosaurus object as the argument, and display a message depending on the result:

```
If trexy.CanIEatU(ally) Then
   Me.lblResults.Text = _
      "Yum...yum...yum. Tasty."
Else
   Me.lblResults.Text = _
      "I'm so hungry!" & _
      " No Allosaurus for dinner" & _
      " tonight."
End If
```

8. Run the project.

9. Enter a name and a size value for the Allosaurus.

10. Verify that the implemented CanIEatU method, part of the ICarnivore interface, returns appropriate results (**Figure 4.18**).

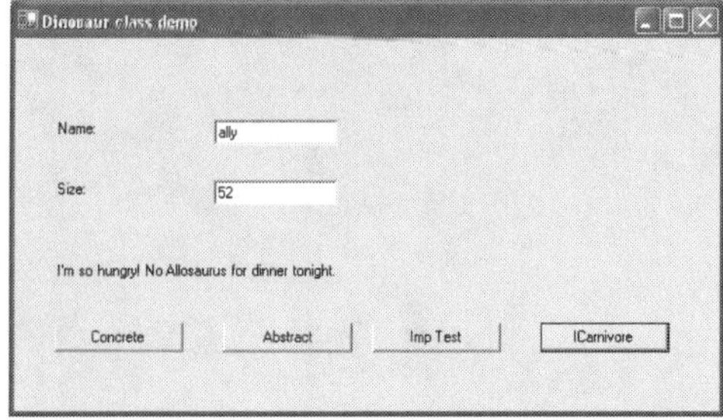

Figure 4.18 The CanIEatU method, specified by the ICarnivore interface, provides a way to determine whether one object based on a class derived from AbstractDinosaur can eat another object based on a class derived from AbstractDinosaur.

Here's the code for the entire click event procedure:

```
Private Sub Button4_Click(ByVal sender _
   As System.Object, ByVal e _
   As System.EventArgs) Handles _
   Button4.Click
   Dim trexy As New TRex()
   Dim ally As New Allosaurus()
   trexy.Name = "trexy"
   trexy.Size = 48
   ally.Name = Me.txtName.Text
   ally.Size = _
      Convert.ToInt16(Me.txtSize.Text)
   If trexy.CanIEatU(ally) Then
      Me.lblResults.Text = _
         "Yum...yum...yum. Tasty."
   Else
      Me.lblResults.Text = _
         "I'm so hungry!" & _
         " No Allosaurus for dinner" & _
         " tonight."
   End If
End Sub
```

Summary

In this chapter, you learned how to:

- Define abstract base classes
- Derive concrete classes from an abstract base class
- Use the MustInherit keyword
- Describe .NET Framework class interfaces
- Implement .NET class interfaces, such as IComparable
- Test the implementation of a class interface
- Define a custom class interface
- Implement the custom class interface
- Test the custom class interface

5

WINDOWS FORMS

Windows forms are the basis of the user interface in Windows applications. With VB .NET, Windows forms are fully object oriented—a first in the history of Visual Basic. Now that you have a solid understanding of OO programming, let's take a closer look, from an OO perspective, at the features of a Windows form.

In this chapter, you'll learn how to manipulate a Windows form in its designer and at runtime, how to work with form properties, and how to program using Form class instances.

Even if this is your first foray into Visual Basic, you'll likely find Windows forms easy and fun to design and create. If you're an experienced VB6 programmer, you'll also find that VB .NET offers some powerful new ways to design forms. For example, the Opacity property, which lets you set the visual transparency of a form, enabling all sorts of fancy visual effects, is completely new. You'll also find that the way in which you program effectively with forms has changed drastically.

The Form Class

When you create a new form, by either opening a new Windows Application project or selecting Windows Form from the Add New Item dialog, you are adding to your project a class that derives from the System.Windows.Forms.Form class, often referred to as Form class for short. (For more information on starting a new Windows Application project or adding Windows forms to a project, see Chapter 1, "Introducing Visual Studio .NET.")

Unless you change the default name suggested by Visual Studio, the new Form class (and module) you create will be named Form1. (If your project already contains a Form1, the new class will be named Form2, and so on.)

To say that a new Form class derives from the Form class means that the new class inherits all the members of the existing class, as explained in Chapter 3, "Working with Classes." However, before we begin exploring what you can do with a derived Form class, let's examine the derivation of System.Windows.Forms.Form and the code that a new form class inherits from it.

The origin of forms

If you expand the Form class in Class View (**Figure 5.1**), you can see the parent-child relationship between the Component class and the Form class. The Component class is the parent of the Control class, which is the parent of the ScrollableControl class, which is the parent of the ContainerControl class, which, in turn, begets the Form class. (If you're wondering about the origin of the Component class, it inherits from the Object class via the MarshalByRefObject class, which enables object sharing between applications.)

The relationship of the Control class to ScrollableControl is pretty obvious: the latter is a version of the control that scrolls as needed by providing scrollbars. In the same way, ContainerControl is a control with scrollbars (since ScrollableControl is the ContainerControl's parent) that also can contain other controls. But what about the relationship between the Component and Control classes? These classes are very important to a great many VB .NET projects, but they're easily confused with each other. Here are capsule explanations of both, as well as their relationship to the Form class:

- **Component:** A component is generally understood to be a reusable object that can interact with other objects. So a Component class provides the basic functionality required for object reuse and interactivity.

  In addition, a .NET component must implement the IComponent interface, or derive from a class that implements it. (Class interfaces are explained more fully in Chapter 4, "Class Interfaces.")

  One thing that the members of IComponent do is specify methods that enable the visual design of objects based

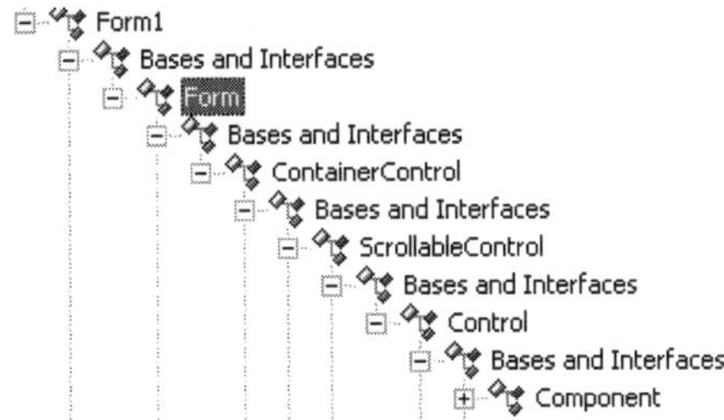

Figure 5.1 This portion of the Class View window shows the inheritance derivation of the Form class.

Figure 5.2 The Form class adds members mostly related to window manipulation, as shown in this snippet of Class View.

on a class that implements IComponent. For example, objects based on a class that implement IComponent can be added to the Visual Studio Toolbox and dragged and dropped on a design surface, such as a Form designer.

- **Control:** A control is a component that provides user-interface capabilities—so every control is a component, but not every component is a control. (For example, the very useful Timer component, explained in Chapter 11, "The Timer Component," is a component but not a control—and it has no interface visible to the end user.)
- **Form:** So far, you have learned that the Form class is used to create objects that are components, or reusable objects. However, because they inherit from the Control class these objects also have an end-user interface. And because they inherit from the ScrollableControl class and the ContainerControl class, they are also scrollable and can contain other controls.

If you look at the members of the Form class that are added to its inherited derivation, you'll see that most of these members have to do with the manipulation of the form, or window, on the screen (**Figure 5.2**). This chapter shows you how to create the windows that constitute the user interface for your Windows Application project, using the members that are grafted onto the Form class's somewhat generic inheritance.

Locating the form code

It's not that difficult to find the hidden Form code, sometimes also called the Form's *code behind*—after all, this isn't a search for Carmen Sandiego! If you open a newly created Form class in the Code Editor, you'll see a class definition and no other code:

```
Public Class Form1
    Inherits System.Windows.Forms.Form

End Class
```

However, within the class definition, you'll also see a gray Windows Form Designer Generated Code box—this is where you'll find most of the Form class code (**Figure 5.3**).

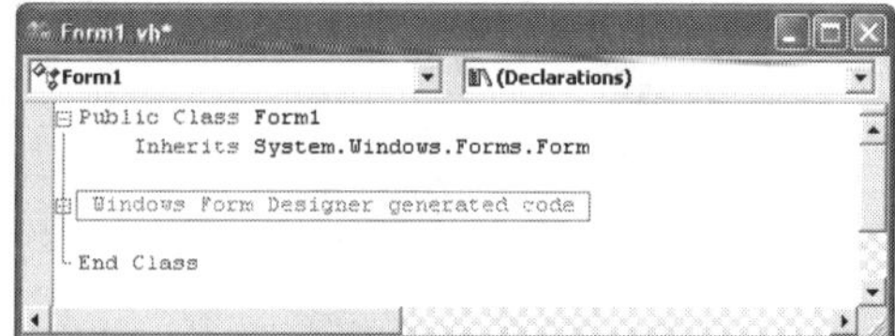

Figure 5.3 Most of the Form class code is hidden in the Windows Form Designer Generated Code region.

To view the hidden form code:

- Click the + (plus) icon to the left of the Windows Form Designer Generated Code box.

  The Code Editor expands to show the full source code for the project (**Figure 5.4**).

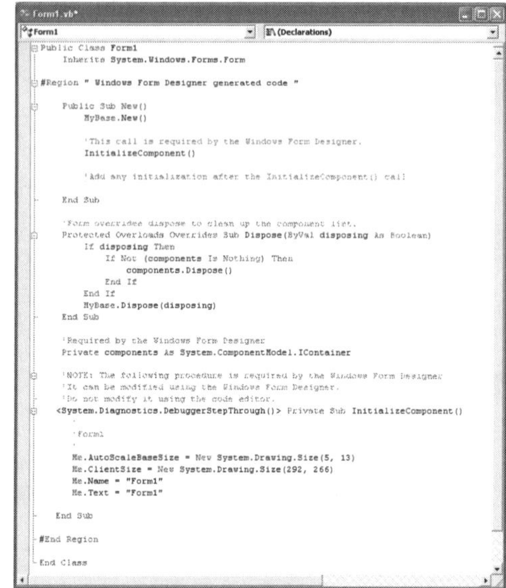

Figure 5.4 The complete Form class code displayed in the Code Editor.

Listing 5.1 shows the full source code for the Form class.

✔ Tips

- If you want to create hidden code regions in your own code, you can do it using the same syntax used by the Windows Form designer. Start the hidden region with `#Region "Text you want to appear instead of the code"` and conclude it with `#End Region`.
- Just because you can get at the Form class code, that doesn't mean you should edit it manually. If you do, you risk losing your changes the next time you change or save the form, or even losing the capability to open the form in its designer. But looking at this code is educational.

Listing 5.1 Full listing—including hidden code—for a newly minted Form class.

```
Public Class Form1
    Inherits System.Windows.Forms.Form

#Region " Windows Form Designer generated code "

    Public Sub New()
        MyBase.New()

        'This call is required by the Windows Form Designer.
        InitializeComponent()

        'Add any initialization after the InitializeComponent() call

    End Sub

    'Form overrides dispose to clean up the component list.
    Protected Overloads Overrides Sub Dispose(ByVal disposing As Boolean)
        If disposing Then
            If Not (components Is Nothing) Then
                components.Dispose()
            End If
        End If
        MyBase.Dispose(disposing)
    End Sub

    'Required by the Windows Form Designer
    Private components As System.ComponentModel.IContainer

    'NOTE: The following procedure is required by the Windows Form Designer
    'It can be modified using the Windows Form Designer.
    'Do not modify it using the code editor.
   <System.Diagnostics.DebuggerStepThrough()> Private Sub InitializeComponent()
      '
      'Form1
      '
      Me.AutoScaleBaseSize = New System.Drawing.Size(5, 13)
      Me.ClientSize = New System.Drawing.Size(292, 266)
      Me.Name = "Form1"
      Me.Text = "Form1"

   End Sub

#End Region

End Class
```

Analyzing the hidden form code

Let's examine the Form class code to see what it actually does.

The first part is a class constructor (Sub New), which calls the constructor of the Form's base class, or System.Windows.Forms.Form, and then calls the InitializeComponent class method. (Class constructors are explained in Chapter 3.) We'll look a little more closely at InitializeComponent in a moment, but for now just be aware that this method is used to convert visually added form properties, and the properties of the controls placed on the form, into code.

✔ Tip

- If you need to add initialization code to the Form class, place it in the Sub New constructor just after the call to the InitializeComponent method.

Next, the hidden form code provides an overloaded Dispose method. The Dispose method is invoked when an object is destroyed, or *disposed*. (Overloaded methods are explained in Chapter 3.) In the case of a form, the form is disposed when the form is unloaded. The overloaded Dispose method checks the list of components added to the form. If any of them have not themselves been disposed, then their Dispose methods are called.

Finally, the base class Dispose method is called:

```
MyBase.Dispose(disposing).
```

Now let's return to the InitializeComponent method and examine it a bit more closely. This method is used to save, or *persist*, information about form and form objects that were created visually in the IDE.

One way to clearly see what the InitializeComponent method is doing is to compare the code before and after you make a visual change to the form.

To compare form code before and after making a visual change:

1. Look at the contents of the InitalizeComponent method in Listing 5.1.
2. Resize the form in its designer by dragging the edges of the form.
3. Use the Properties window to change the form's name to frmDemo and its Text property to Demo (we'll take a detailed look at form design and at the Properties window a little later in this chapter).
4. Look in the Code Editor, expanding the hidden code region if necessary.

   You'll see that the values for the relevant properties have been changed in code to something like the following (depending on how you resized the form):

   ```
   Me.ClientSize = New _
      System.Drawing.Size(840, 518)
   Me.Name = "frmDemo"
   Me.Text = "Demo"
   ```

Changing the Name property means changing the class name, so if you made the change suggested in this example, the class declaration will now read:

```
Public Class frmDemo
   Inherits System.Windows.Forms.Form
```

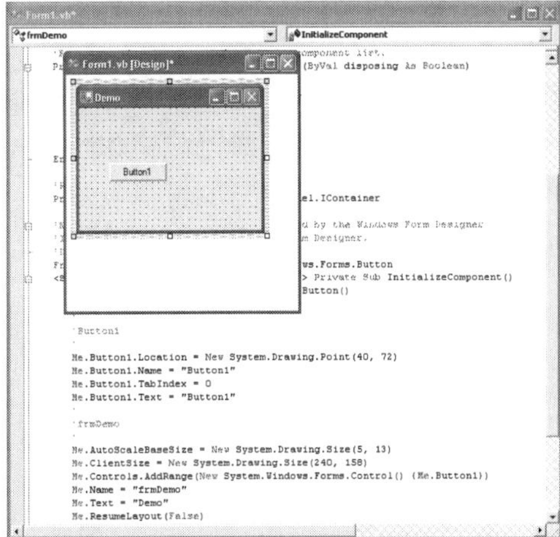

Figure 5.5 When you visually add a button to a form, the button's properties persist in the Initialize-Component method of the Form class.

The InitializeComponent method is also used to save the information involved in visually adding a control (such as a Button control) to a form. This information might include the size, location, name, and text values for the control.

To view the code when a control is visually added to a form:

1. Add a button to the form.
2. Accept the default name, Button1, for the new button class (**Figure 5.5**).
3. Open the form in the Code Editor.

   You'll find that code representing your visually added settings for the new button has been added to the InitializeComponent method:

```
...
Me.Button1 = New _
   System.Windows.Forms.Button()
...
'
'Button1
'
Me.Button1.Location = New _
   System.Drawing.Point(40, 72)
Me.Button1.Name = "Button1"
Me.Button1.TabIndex = 0
Me.Button1.Text = "Button1"
...
Me.Controls.AddRange(New _
   System.Windows.Forms.Control() _
   {Me.Button1})
```

Two points are worth noting about the mechanism used to persist values in the Form code behind. First, although this code can be educational and helpful to look at it to see what the Form is actually doing, you shouldn't modify it by hand. If you do, your changes will probably be overwritten. Second, if you are a VB6 programmer, you may remember that VB6 has a similar mechanism to persist form properties. However, unlike in VB .NET, in VB6 the persisted values are stored in project files and can't be accessed by programmers using the development environment.

In one respect, the Form class in VB .NET is still a bit anomalous. In VB6, forms are completely unique objects and different from anything else. In contrast, forms in VB .NET are simply classes, except that when you set a form as the Startup object in a project's Property pages (**Figure 5.6**), an instance of the Form class is loaded when the program runs. However, the instance of the Form class isn't named, which explains the extensive references to the instance using the Me keyword. Even if you don't know an instance name, you can always access it using Me.

Sometimes, of course, the Me keyword simply will not do when you need to access a form instance programmatically. For example, you might need to programmatically change object properties on one form from another form. This is an important and confusing topic, and one that you must get right in a fully OO environment, because most applications do consist of more than one form. You'll learn some techniques for managing form classes and instances later in this chapter in "Working with Form Instances."

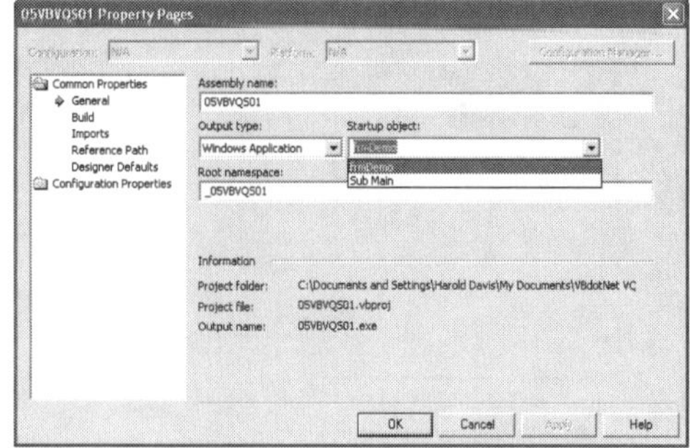

Figure 5.6 If a form is selected as the Startup object, then an instance of the form class is loaded when the project is run.

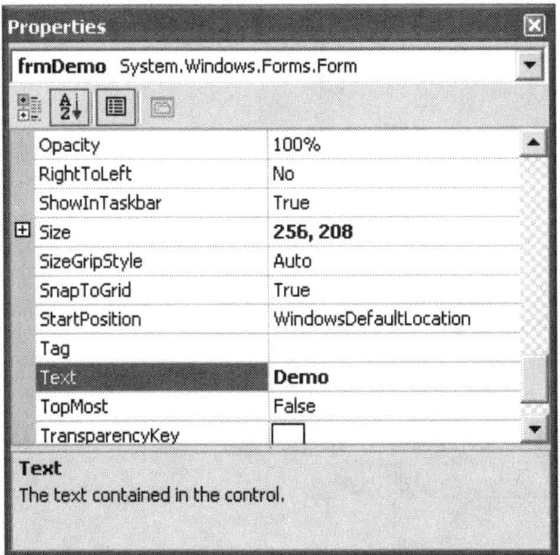

Figure 5.7 Use the Properties window to set form (and other object) properties.

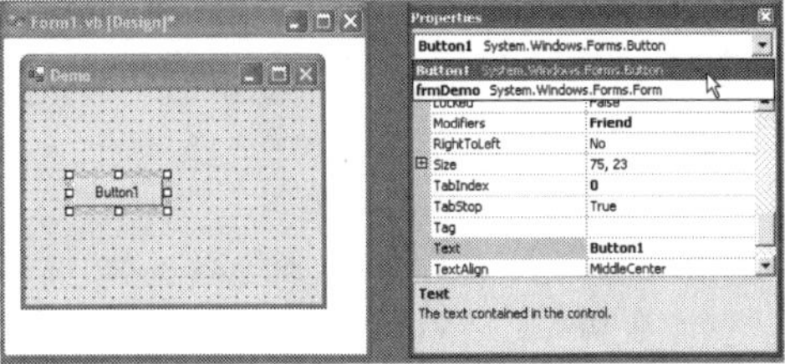

Figure 5.8 When you select an object in the Properties window, it is also selected in the Form designer.

Form Properties

As the hidden Form class code illustrates, you can set form properties in code. This approach is sometimes desirable. For example, you can set a form property in code when you want a property to change dynamically in response to a user action while an application is running. You can also use code to set form properties when you want to make the list of the properties set apparent to another programmer at a glance.

More often, however, you'll find it easier to use the Visual Basic .NET Rapid Application Development (RAD) environment to set form properties visually using the Properties window. This is particularly true when you want to set a form's initial characteristics.

In this section, you'll see how to set the most important form properties using both the Properties window and code.

To open the Properties window for a form:

- With the form open in its designer, select View > Properties Window.

  The Properties window appears (**Figure 5.7**).

If a form includes controls or components, you can use the Properties window to select these objects in addition to the form. Once you have selected the object, you can set its properties.

To select an object in the Properties window:

- From the Objects drop-down list at the top of the Properties window, choose an object such as a Button control (**Figure 5.8**).

✔ Tip

- When you select an object in the Properties window, it is also automatically selected in the Form designer.

The Text property

The Text property of a form sets the caption of the form. An object's Text property usually controls the text that the object displays.

To set the Text property in the Properties window:

1. With the form open in its designer, select the form from the Objects drop-down list in the Properties window.
2. Choose Text from the list of properties that appears on the left.
3. Enter text for the new Text property in the right column: for example, *Snappy caption!*
4. Tab away from the Text property to apply the changes.

   You'll now see the new caption on the form in its designer (**Figure 5.9**). If you run the project, the new value of the Text property will appear as the form's caption (**Figure 5.10**).

To set the Text property in code:

1. Open the Code Editor.
2. Use the Me keyword to refer to the instance of the Form class within a button click event:

```
Private Sub Button1_Click _
    (ByVal sender As System.Object, _
    ByVal e As System.EventArgs) _
    Handles Button1.Click
    Me.Text = "I am new text!"
End Sub
```

3. Run the project, and on the form click the button.

   The form's caption changes to the new value (**Figure 5.11**).

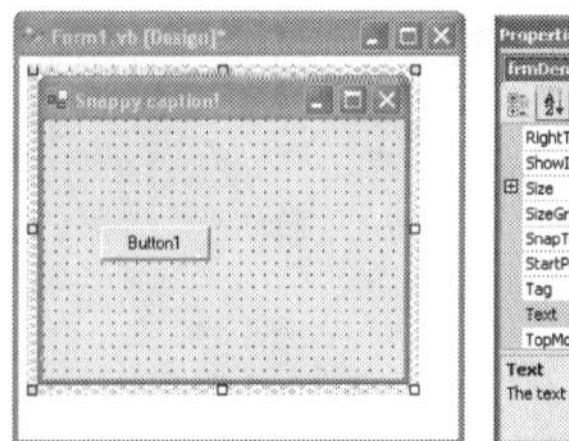

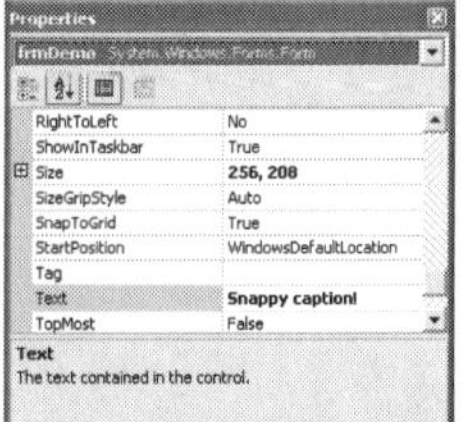

Figure 5.9 When you set the form's Text property in the Properties window, it is also set in the Form designer.

Figure 5.10 The form Text property appears as the form caption when the form is run.

Figure 5.11 You can change the form caption in code in response to a user action.

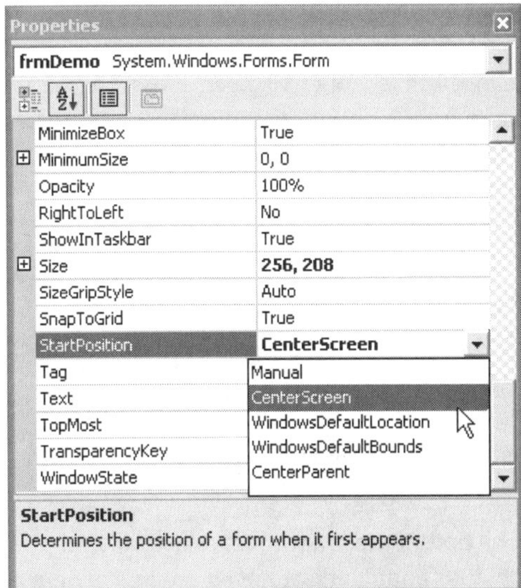

Figure 5.12 The StartPosition property controls the initial position of a window.

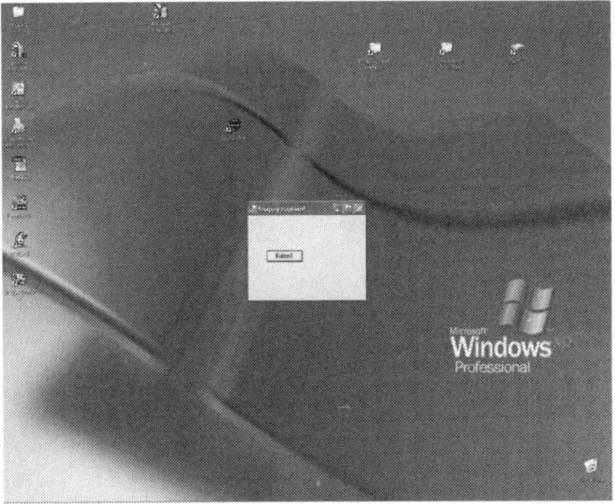

Figure 5.13 If StartPosition is set to CenterScreen, then a window appears in the center of the screen when a form loads.

The StartPosition property

The StartPosition property determines the position of a form when it first runs. (Normally, after a form is running, the user can move it.)

To start a form in the middle of the screen using the Properties window:

1. With the form open, select StartPosition in the Properties window.
2. In the right column, select CenterScreen (**Figure 5.12**).
3. Run the project.

   The window based on the form appears in the center of the screen (**Figure 5.13**).

You can easily, of course, accomplish the same thing in code.

To start a form in the middle of the screen using code:

1. Open the Code Editor.
2. The code centering the form needs to be processed before the form is actually loaded, so locate the Form class constructor, which, as explained in Chapter 3, is the New procedure, declared as `Public Sub New ()`.

   You'll find a comment added by the VB .NET IDE following the call to the InitializeComponent method indicating the proper placement of initialization code.
3. Assign a FormStartPosition constant to the StartPosition property.

To view the property assignment, see **Listing 5.2**.

The Size property

A form's Size property sets in pixels (the standard unit of measurement for computer monitors) the height and width of the form window. You can set a form's size in three ways:

- By dragging the bottom and/or the right side of the form window in its designer to the desired size.
- By setting the Width and Height dimensions using the Properties window.
- By setting the Width and Height values in code.

The first of these approaches is intuitively obvious enough not to need much explanation, although you should understand that you are setting the form window's size, not its location, which is why you cannot move the top or left borders of the form. Changes made visually in this way to a form's dimensions are reflected in the Width and Height values expressed in pixels in the Properties window.

Listing 5.2 Starting a form in the center of the screen.

```
Me.StartPosition = System.Windows.Forms.FormStartPosition.CenterScreen
```

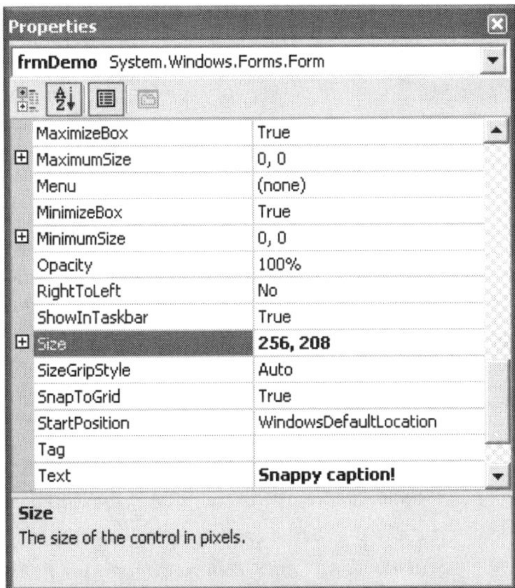

Figure 5.14 Select Size in the Properties window to change the dimensions of a form.

⊟ Size	123, 34
Width	123
Height	34

Figure 5.15 Expanding the Size node allows you to set the Width and Height properties individually.

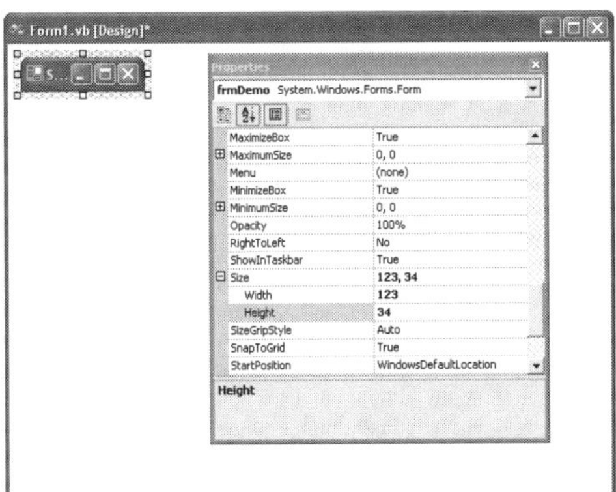

Figure 5.16 Changing the dimensions of a form in the Properties window changes the form's size in the designer as well (the form shown here is 123 pixels wide and 34 pixels high, which is as small as a standard form window goes).

The next two tasks show you how to set the form size via the other two methods: using the Properties window and using code.

To set the Size property in the Properties window:

1. With a form open in its designer, open the Properties window.
2. In the left column, select Size (**Figure 5.14**).
3. Set the Width and Height property values by entering a comma-delimited pair of values in the right column of the Properties window as shown in Figure 5.14.

   or

   Click the plus icon to the left of the word Size in the Properties window to expand the entry (**Figure 5.15**). Now enter Width and Height property values on their own individual lines.
4. Check the form in its designer to verify that the changes to the form size have been applied correctly.

   Figure 5.16 shows a form set to its minimum size using the Properties window.

As you may have already begun to suspect, Size can be applied not only to forms, but to many objects. Size belongs to the System.Drawing namespace, and it is technically a *structure*.

A structure, declared with the Structure keyword and called a *struct* in many languages, is a lightweight alternative to a class that supports members such as properties, methods, and fields. However, a structure does not support inheritance. In addition, structures in .NET are value types, whereas classes are reference types (see sidebar on the next page).

The Size structure itself represents a rectangle and always has Width and Height properties. You can used it to set new dimensions for a form window at runtime in response to a user action (such as a button click).

To change a form's size in code:

1. Create the event handler that will be used to change the form size when the user clicks the button:

```
Private Sub Button1_Click _
    (ByVal sender As System.Object, _
    ByVal e As System.EventArgs) _
    Handles Button1.Click

End Sub
```

2. Within the event handler, declare a variable (I have named it *theSize*) of type Size:

```
Dim theSize As System.Drawing.Size
```

3. Assign values to the Width and Height properties of the theSize variable:

```
theSize.Width = 500
theSize.Height = 300
```

4. Assign theSize variable to the form's Size property:

```
Me.Size = theSize
```

   Here's the complete code for the click event:

```
Private Sub Button1_Click _
    (ByVal sender As System.Object, _
    ByVal e As System.EventArgs) _
    Handles Button1.Click
    Dim theSize As System.Drawing.Size
    theSize.Width = 500
    theSize.Height = 300
    Me.Size = theSize
End Sub
```

5. Run the program, click the button, and verify that the form size changes.

Value Types and Reference Types

Value types, such as structures, hold their values, or data, within their own memory allocation. These values are stored in memory allocated to the particular value type within a program's *stack*, or data structure, and can be accessed from within the program as long as they are in scope.

In contrast, reference types, such as classes, are implemented using global memory called the *runtime heap*. The important thing to understand is that reference types contain instances: for example, an instance of a class. These instances are pointers to objects stored in memory on the heap and do not themselves contain the actual values of the instances.

✔ Tip

- Because `Me.Size.Width` and `Me.Size.Height` are values, you can't directly assign new values to them. So a statement such as `Me.Size.Width = 500` will produce the syntax error, "Expression is a value and therefore cannot be the target of an assignment."

Figure 5.17 The X and Y coordinates of the Location property control the locations of the form window.

The Location property

As you might expect, you set the Location property in pretty much the same way as you set the form's Size property. TheLocation property is a System.Drawing.Point structure, with Point defining a point in two-dimensional space using X and Y coordinates.

To set the Location property in the Properties window:

1. In the Properties window, set the StartPosition property to Manual.
2. Select the Location property.
3. Set the X and Y coordinates, if necessary expanding the Location node (**Figure 5.17**).

   The form will now load in the position set.

To set a form position at any time other than when it first loads, you will need to change the Location coordinate values in code. This process is similar to that for changing the size in code (except that you use a structure of type Point instead of type Size).

Here's how to change the form location in response to a user's action in a click event procedure.

To change a form's location in code:

1. Create the event handler that will be used to change the form location when the user clicks the button:

```
Private Sub Button1_Click _
   (ByVal sender As System.Object, _
   ByVal e As System.EventArgs) _
   Handles Button1.Click

End Sub
```

2. Within the event handler, declare a variable (I have named it *theLoc*) of type Point:

```
Dim theLoc As System.Drawing.Point
```

3. Assign values to the X and Y properties of theLoc:

```
theLoc.X = 450
theLoc.Y = 125
```

4. Assign the theLoc variable to the form's Location property:

```
Me.Location = theLoc
```

   Here's the complete code for the click event:

```
Private Sub Button1_Click _
   (ByVal sender As System.Object, _
   ByVal e As System.EventArgs) _
   Handles Button1.Click
   Dim theLoc As System.Drawing.Point
   theLoc.X = 450
   theLoc.Y = 125
   Me.Location = theLoc
End Sub
```

5. Run the program, click the button, and verify that the form size changes.

✔ Tip

- Because `Me.Location.X` and `Me.Location.Y` are values, you can't directly assign new values to them. So a statement such as `Me.Location.X = 500` will produce the syntax error, "Expression is a value and therefore cannot be the target of an assignment."

The FormBorderStyle property

A form's FormBorderStyle property determines the basic appearance and behavior of the window that the form creates when it is run. In other words, this property setting determines whether a form will be viewed as a general-purpose window, a dialog, or a toolbox-style window.

One key issue is whether a window is *sizable*. If a window is sizable, when the window is running, the user can change its size (usually by dragging the window border).

It is unusual to change the FormBorderStyle property at runtime in code, because users don't usually expect their windows to change styles midstream. However, it can be done, and I've provided an example later in this section (see "To dynamically change window styles").

The possible settings for a form's FormBorderStyle property include the following:

- **None.** Sets no border or border-related elements. This is the setting to use when you want to create a splash screen that appears as your application is loading.
- **FixedSingle.** Sets a normal window, but resizable only with the Minimize and Maximize buttons, if they are present.
- **Fixed3D.** Sets a fixed—that is, not resizable—window with a three-dimensional look.
- **FixedDialog.** Used to create dialogs. If the FormBorderStyle property is set to FixedDouble, the dialog cannot be resized.
- **Sizable.** Sets a normal, resizable window. This is the default—and most common—setting.
- **FixedToolWindow.** Displays a nonsizable window with a Close button and reduced-size title bar text. Unlike with the preceding settings, FixedToolWindow forms do not appear as icons on the Windows taskbar.
- **SizableToolWindow.** Similar to FixedToolWindow but sizable.

To create a dialog-style window in the Properties window:

1. Make sure that the form you want to use as a dialog is open in its designer.
2. Open the Properties window.
3. In the left column, select FormBorderStyle.
4. From the pull-down menu in the right column, choose FixedDialog (**Figure 5.18**).
5. Run the form to view it as a dialog (**Figure 5.19**).

✔ Tip

- To make this window look as much like a classical dialog as possible, I set its ControlBox, MinimizeBox, and MaximizeBox properties to `False` using the Properties window.

To dynamically change window styles:

1. Add a button to the form.
2. Create a click event procedure that will be used to change the form style when the user clicks:

```
Private Sub btnFixed3D_Click(ByVal _
   sender As System.Object, ByVal _
   e As System.EventArgs) Handles _
   btnFixed3D.Click

End Sub
```

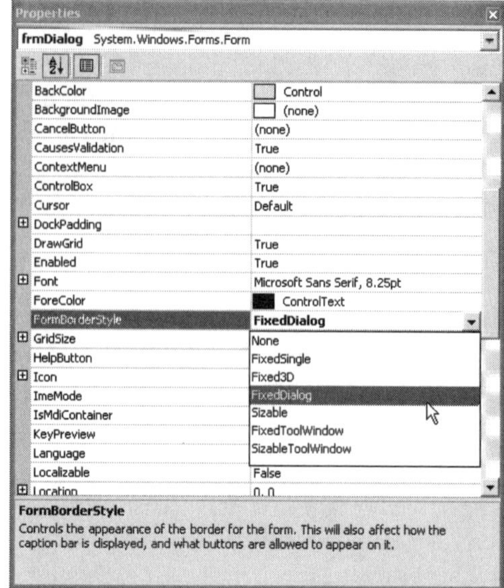

Figure 5.18 To create a dialog, set the FormBorderStyle property to FixedDialog.

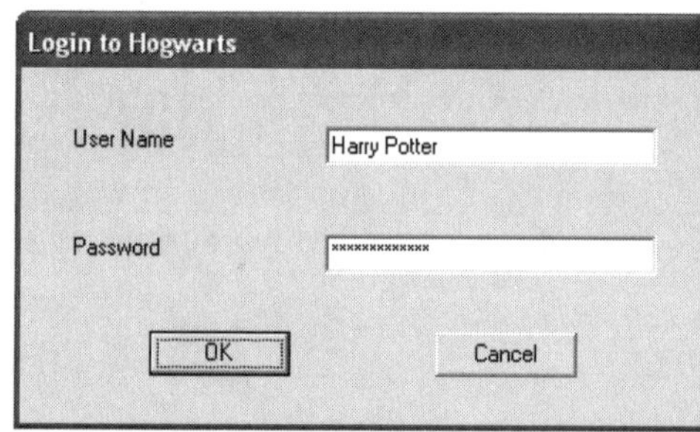

Figure 5.19 You cannot resize dialogs by dragging the form border.

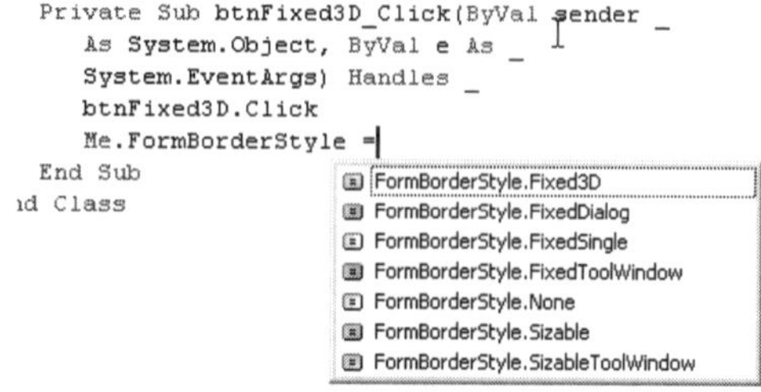

Figure 5.20 The Code Editor displays the possible values of the FormBorderStyle enumeration.

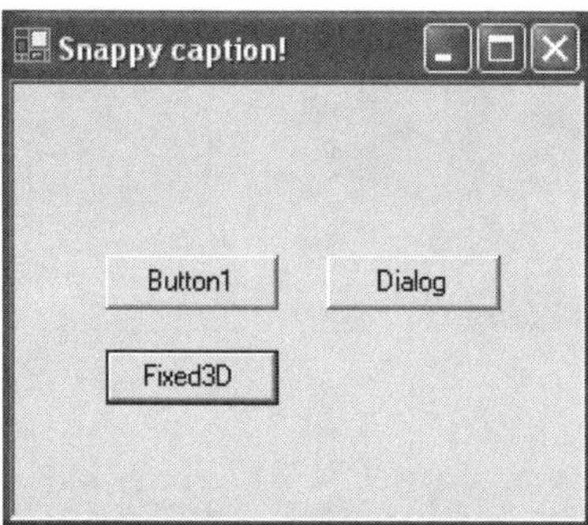

Figure 5.21 The Fixed3D FormBorderStyle displays sculpted borders that the user cannot resize.

Enumerations

Enumerations are lists of named constants, called *enumeration constants*, of the same type. The list of constants within an enumeration is also called the *enumeration list*.

You can create your own enumerations using the Enum keyword, and there are also plenty of enumerations built into the .NET Framework. For example, as you've just seen, the FormBorderStyle enumeration provides the constants that determine the style of a form-based window.

Using enumerations is a better practice than using numerical constants or constants that are named in ad-hoc fashion for the following reasons:

- It's impossible to supply a value that is not an enumeration list member without generating an immediate syntax error.
- The Code Editor will automatically supply a drop-down list of possible enumeration constants.
- Enumerations are generally named to provide clarity about their purpose.

3. Start typing the statement that will assign a value to the FormBorderStyle property.

   As soon as you type the assignment operator (=), the Code Editor displays a drop-down list of the possible enumeration values (see the Enumerations sidebar) for the property (**Figure 5.20**). This makes coding really easy, because you don't have to remember the names of the enumeration constants.

4. Choose an enumeration constant for the value: for example, `FormBorderStyle.Fixed3D`.

   The click event procedure now looks like this:

```
Private Sub _
   btnFixed3D_Click(ByVal
   sender As System.Object, ByVal _
   e As System.EventArgs) Handles
   btnFixed3D.Click
   Me.FormBorderStyle = _
      FormBorderStyle.Fixed3D
End Sub
```

5. Run the project.
6. Click the button and verify that the form style has changed (**Figure 5.21**).

✔ Tip

- Do your users a favor and don't make them dizzy with too many window style changes.

The ForeColor and BackColor properties

Form colors are set, either in code or in the Properties window, by assigning a color property value to the System.Drawing.Color structure.

The ForeColor property sets graphics and, most important, text. The BackColor property sets the background color.

It is important to note that when you set the ForeColor or BackColor property for a form, you are also setting the default values for any control seated on the form. In other words, unless a color value has been set individually for a control, the control will use the values supplied by the form. This helps you design the look and feel of a form and all of its controls in one fell swoop.

Since the ForeColor and BackColor properties work in the same way, I'll show you how to set one in the Properties window and the other in code. But be aware that each property can be set in either way.

To set the ForeColor property in the Properties window:

1. Open a form in its designer.
2. In the Properties window, choose ForeColor in the left column.
3. In the right column click the down arrow to open a tabbed color palette (**Figure 5.22**).

   The tabs are Custom, Web, and System.
4. Choose a color visually from one of the palettes.

   The name of the corresponding color property value will be assigned to the form ForeColor property (for example, *White*).

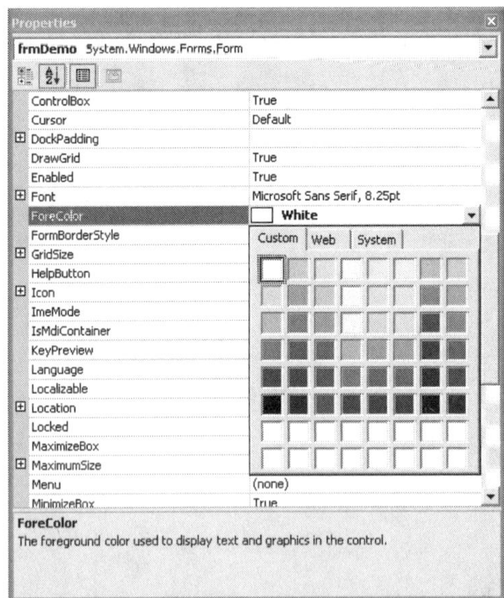

Figure 5.22 You can select a color property value visually from a palette in the Properties window.

✔ Tip

- If you know the name of the color property value, you can type it in the right Properties window column, rather than selecting the color visually from a palette.

```
Private Sub btnColor_Click(ByVal sender _
   As System.Object, ByVal e As _
   System.EventArgs) Handles _
   btnColor.Click
   Me.BackColor = System.Drawing.Color.
End Sub
d Class
```

Figure 5.23 The Code Editor provides a list of all system-defined color property values.

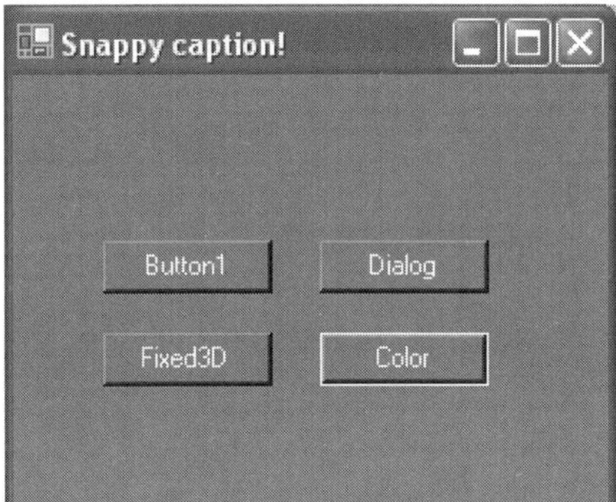

Figure 5.24 Although it's difficult to see in black and white, the form background is red and the text is white.

To set the BackColor property in code:

1. Add a button to the form.
2. Create a click event procedure that will change the form background color when the user clicks:

```
Private Sub btnColor_Click _
   (ByVal sender As System.Object, _
   ByVal e As System.EventArgs) _
   Handles btnColor.Click


End Sub
```

3 Start typing the statement that will assign a color property value to the form's BackColor property. This statement begins

```
Me.BackColor = _
   System.Drawing.Color.
```

When you type the dot operator (.) following the reference to the Color structure, the Code Editor supplies a list of system-defined color property values (**Figure 5.23**).

4. Choose a color from the drop-down list: for example, Red.

The click event procedure now looks like this:

```
Private Sub btnColor_Click _
   (ByVal sender As System.Object, _
   ByVal e As System.EventArgs) _
   Handles btnColor.Click
   Me.BackColor = _
      System.Drawing.Color.Red
End Sub
```

5. Run the project.
6. Click the button and verify that the form background color has changed (**Figure 5.24**).

The Opacity property

Opacity sets the transparency of a form. A form that has an Opacity property of 0 percent is completely transparent (or invisible). On the other hand, a form with an Opacity property of 100 percent is opaque (this is the default setting for forms out-of-the-box).

The ability to set form opacity is new with Visual Basic .NET.

To set the Opacity property using the Properties window:

1. With a form open in its designer, open the Properties window.
2. Select Opacity in the left column (**Figure 5.25**).
3. In the right column enter a number between `0` and `100` (don't worry about the percent sign; the Code Editor will add this for you as needed).
4. Run the form to observe the effect of the Opacity setting (**Figure 5.26**).

You can also create a neat effect by setting opacity at runtime, possibly in response to a user action. Here's how to do so.

To set form opacity at runtime:

1. Add a text box (for the user to enter an Opacity value) and a button (to set the new Opacity value) to a form. It's sometimes helpful from a design perspective to group related controls using a GroupBox control (**Figure 5.27**).
2. In the Properties window, name the text box *txtOpacity* and the button *btnOpacity*.
3. Set the initial value in txtOpacity to `0` and change the Text property of btnOpacity to `Set`.

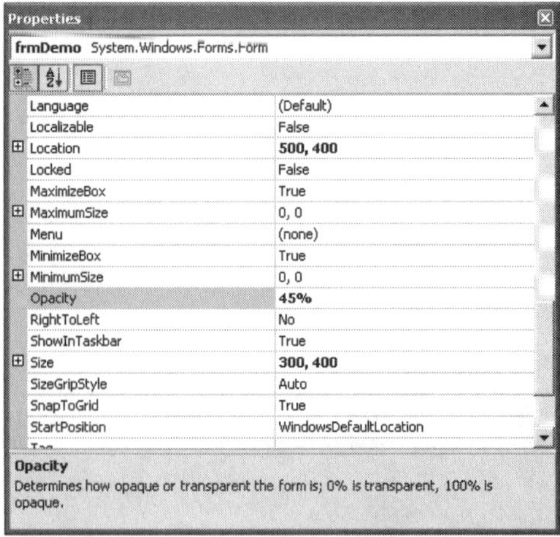

Figure 5.25 You can set the form Opacity property, which controls form transparency, in the Properties window.

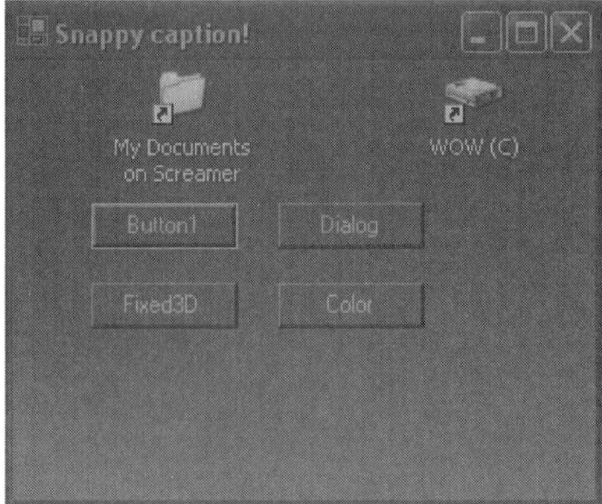

Figure 5.26 With Opacity set to 45 percent, the form is partially transparent (note the desktop icons you can see through it).

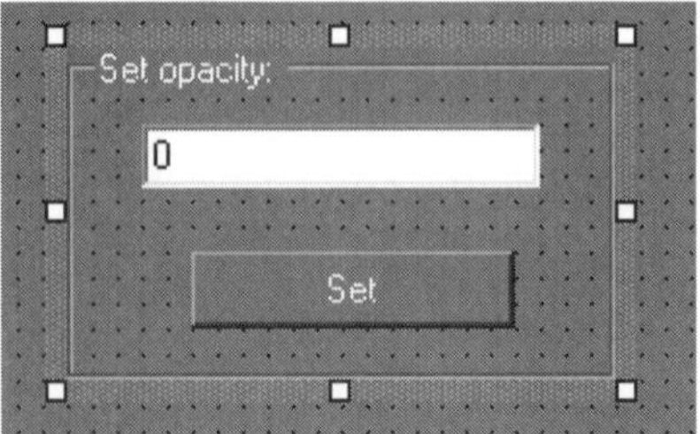

Figure 5.27 Controls, such as those used here to set form opacity at runtime, can be grouped into cohesive units.

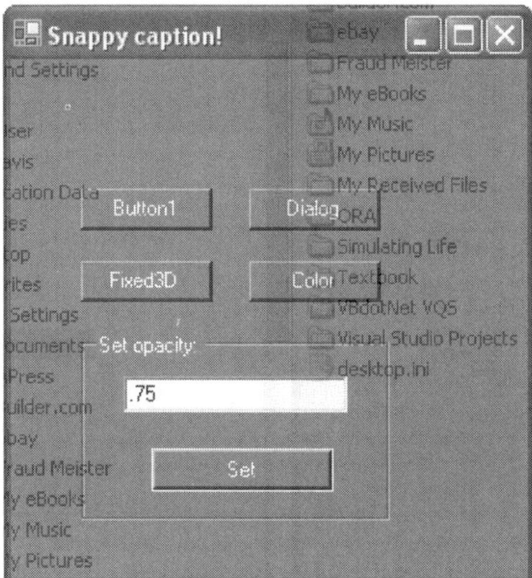

Figure 5.28 With opacity set to 75 percent (0.75), the form is barely transparent, so you can just see File Explorer through it.

4. In the Form designer, double-click btnOpacity to open a click event procedure for it in the Code Editor.

   The code framework that is created looks like this:

   ```
   Private Sub btnOpacity_Click(ByVal _
      sender As System.Object, ByVal _
      e As System.EventArgs) Handles _
      btnOpacity.Click


   End Sub
   ```

5. Use the ToDouble method of the Convert class to convert the value entered by the user in txtOpacity from a string type to a double type and assign the converted value to the form's Opacity property:

   ```
   Me.Opacity = _

   Convert.ToDouble(txtOpacity.Text)
   ```

   Here's the complete click event code:

   ```
   Private Sub btnOpacity_Click(ByVal _
      sender As System.Object, ByVal _
      e As System.EventArgs) Handles _
      btnOpacity.Click
      Me.Opacity = _
         Convert.ToDouble _
            (txtOpacity.Text)
   End Sub
   ```

6. Run the project.

7. Enter a value between `0` and `1` in the text box. For example, a value of 0.75 produces a slightly transparent form.

8. Click Set to view the effect of the change to the Opacity property (**Figure 5.28**).

One caveat: Don't actually let users directly enter an Opacity value, as we did this example! There's no way you can be sure that the user will enter a string that can be converted to a value between 0 and 1, and anything else may cause erratic results. For example, trying to set the Opacity property value to a number greater than 1 seems to cause the Visual Studio environment to hang. At the very least, you should use exception handling to catch problems if the user enters an inappropriate value (see Chapter 9, "Exceptions and Debugging"). An even better solution is to ensure at least some validation of the user's input. But perhaps the best solution is to use a visual metaphor for the user's input, such as that supplied by the TrackBar control, to make sure that all inputs are appropriate. (Input validation and the TrackBar control are both explained in Chapter 10, "Controls That Accept User Input.")

✔ Tips

- Transparent forms are supported only in Windows 2000 and later, so forms run on earlier operating systems (such as Windows Me) will be fully opaque no matter what their Opacity setting.
- The Opacity property in the Properties window is expressed as a percentage (from 0 to 100 percent); however, in code it is expressed as a number of type Double between 0 and 1.

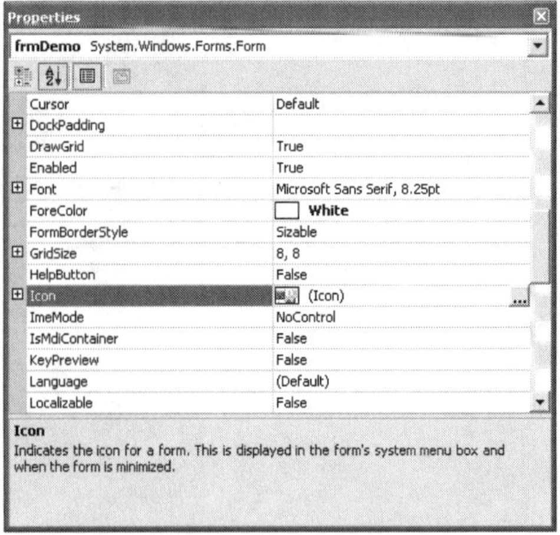

Figure 5.29 You can set the icon associated with a form by changing the form's Icon property.

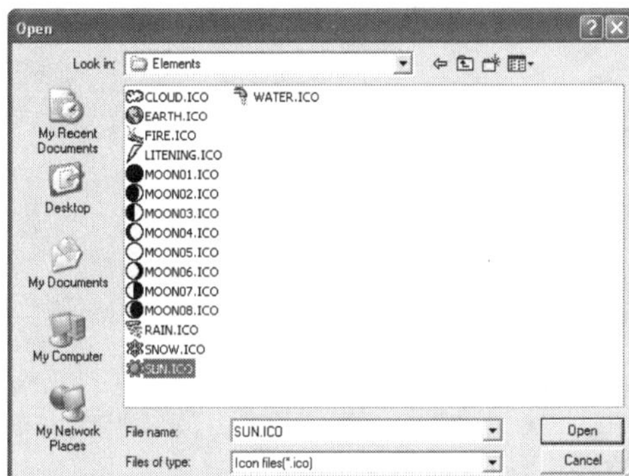

Figure 5.30 Select the icon (*.ICO) file using the Open dialog.

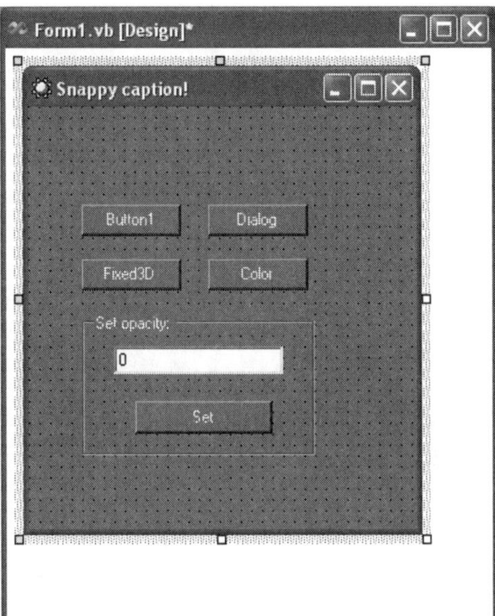

Figure 5.31 The new icon will appear on the form's caption bar in the Form designer.

Figure 5.32 You'll see the icon on the form's caption bar when the form is running.

The Icon property

Icons represent an application (or a form within an application) when it is minimized. An icon associated with a form also appears on the form caption bar and, when the form is running, on the Windows taskbar.

It's easy to use the Properties window to associate an icon with a form.

To assign an icon to a form:

1. With a form open in its designer, open the Properties window.
2. Select Icon in the left column (**Figure 5.29**).
3. In the right column, click the button marked with three dots ....

   The Open dialog appears (**Figure 5.30**).
4. Select an icon (*.ICO) file. (See the tip that follows to find the standard location of the icon files that ship with Visual Studio .NET.)
5. Click Open.

   The new icon will be displayed in the Properties window and on the form caption bar (**Figure 5.31**).
6. Run the project.

   The icon will appear on the running form's caption bar (**Figure 5.32**) and on the Windows taskbar (**Figure 5.33**) if Sizable has been selected for the value of the FormBorderStyle property (described earlier in this chapter).

continues on next page

Figure 5.33 The icon also appears on the Windows taskbar when the program is running.

✔ Tips

- By default, unless you installed Visual Studio .NET in a different location, you'll find the icons that ship with the product organized in folders in the following location: \Program Files\Microsoft Visual Studio .NET\Common7\Graphics\icons.
- You can assign a background image to a form using the BackgroundImage property in the Properties window. You can choose from a broad range of graphics files, and the process is similar to that for assigning an icon to a form.

As you might suspect, you can change the value of a form's Icon property in code and assign an icon to a form. There are a number of ways to do this, all of which require instantiation of an icon. The simplest way to create an icon is to use the first overloaded New constructor of the Icon class, which accepts as its only argument a string that is the name of a file containing the icon.

The following example assumes that the icon file (snow.ico) has been copied to the directory that contains the project's executable file (which in a Visual Studio development project is the bin directory automatically created for the project). This means that you do not need to provide path information along with the icon file name. If your icon file is in some location other than the project bin directory, you need to supply the path information in the New constructor.

To assign an icon to a form in code:

1. Declare a variable, theIcon, and instantiate it as an instance of the Icon class, passing the New constructor the name of the file that actually contains the icon:

   ```
   Dim theIcon As New Icon("snow.ico")
   ```

2. Assign the variable that references the icon the form's Icon property:

   ```
   Me.Icon = theIcon
   ```

Changing the Shape of Forms

There is no reason that your form windows need to be square! A Form class is like any other .NET class, so you can use the Drawing and Graphics classes of the .NET Framework to do some pretty weird, funky, and wonderful things to the shape of a form.

Here's how to create a click event procedure that changes the shape of a form from a rectangle to an ellipse.

To alter a form shape:

1. Add a button to a form.
2. Using the Properties window, name the button *btnShape*.
3. Double-click the button to create a click event procedure in the Code Editor:
   ```
   Private Sub btnShape_Click _
      (ByVal sender As System.Object, _
      ByVal e As System.EventArgs) _
      Handles btnShape.Click

   End Sub
   ```
4. In the Code Editor, above the Form class declaration, add an Imports statement that imports the System.Drawing.Drawing2D namespace into the project:
   ```
   Imports System.Drawing.Drawing2D
   ```
5. Within the click event, create a new instance named *theGP*, based on the GraphicsPath class:
   ```
   Dim theGP As New GraphicsPath()
   ```
6. Use the AddEllipse method of the theGP instance, with an instance of the Rectangle class as an argument, to define an elliptical region:
   ```
   theGP.AddEllipse(New Rectangle _
      (0, 0, 400, 400))
   ```

continues on next page

7. Assign the region defined by theGP to the form's Region property:

```
Me.Region = New Region(theGP)
```

Here's the complete code for changing the form's shape:

```
Imports System.Drawing.Drawing2D
...
Private Sub btnShape_Click _
   (ByVal sender As System.Object, _
   ByVal e As System.EventArgs) _
   Handles btnShape.Click
   Dim theGP As New GraphicsPath()
   theGP.AddEllipse(New Rectangle _
      (0, 0, 400, 400))
   Me.Region = New Region(theGP)
End Sub
```

8. Run the project.

9. Click Shape to reshape the form.

   The form will now be roughly circular (**Figure 5.34**).

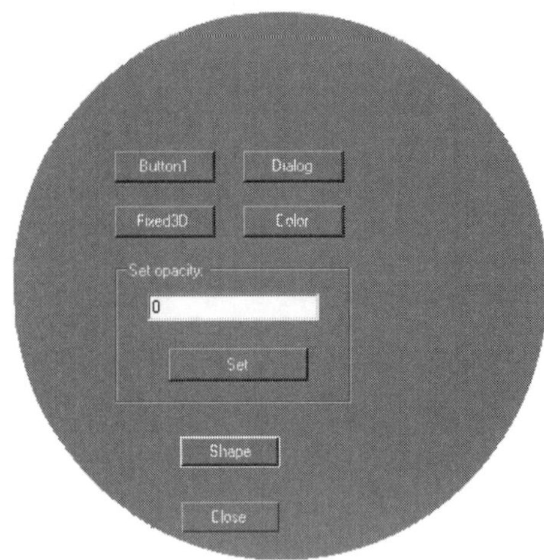

Figure 5.34 Why should all windows be square?

✔ Tips

- The Imports keyword is used to reference the classes in a namespace without fully qualifying them. So you could leave the Imports statement out of this example, but then you'd have to fully qualify each class reference. This gets pretty clunky; for example, you'd have to use `System.Drawing.Drawing2D.GraphicsPath()`
- instead of simply `GraphicsPath()`. You'll find more information about namespaces and the Imports keyword in Chapter 14, "The Object Browser."
- If you change the coordinates supplied to the Rectangle class, you will change the region occupied by the form. So go to it—play with this and have fun!
- In addition to the AddEllipse method, you can use a number of other GraphicsPath methods to create interesting effects.

When you run the preceding example, you may notice that the caption bar containing user mechanisms for initiating the closure of the form have been removed (Figure 5.34). The ellipse simply doesn't include these items in its region. So if you are going to change the shape of a form, it's a very good idea to supply a mechanism to let users close a form even if its top portion is missing.

To close a form in code:

1. Add a button to a form.
2. Using the Properties window, name the button *btnClose*.
3. Double-click the button to create a click event procedure in the Code Editor:

```
Private Sub btnClose_Click _
    (ByVal sender As System.Object, _
    ByVal e As System.EventArgs) _
    Handles btnClose.Click


End Sub
```

4. Call the Close method of the form instance by adding `Me.Close()`.

   Here's the complete code for the click event:

```
Private Sub btnClose_Click _
    (ByVal sender As System.Object, _
    ByVal e As System.EventArgs) _
    Handles btnClose.Click
    Me.Close()
End Sub
```

5. Run the project and verify that the form closes when you click the Close button.

Working with Form Instances

In the previous section, you saw how to close a form in code. However, this example, like all the examples so far in this chapter, refers to the current instance of a form using the Me keyword rather than using a specific variable for the form instance.

Often, the Me keyword simply won't get you where you want to go—for example, when you need to refer to specific instances of form classes that are not the current instance. Passing information between form instances is also something that requires effective methods for referring to the various instances in code.

This section shows you how to:

- Navigate among different form instances in multiform applications
- Invoke form instance members from other instances (which are often based on different form classes)
- Share information among multiple instances of form classes

Earlier in this chapter, you saw how to create a window that has the look and feel of a dialog by setting the underlying form's FormBorderStyle property to FixedDialog (see Figure 5.19). Let's suppose you want to open a dialog, based on this second form class and named frmDialog, from the main form in an application.

To add a new form to a project:

1. In the Add New Item dialog, make sure that Windows form is selected (**Figure 5.35**).
2. Supply a name for the new Form class, such as frmDialog.
3. Click Open.

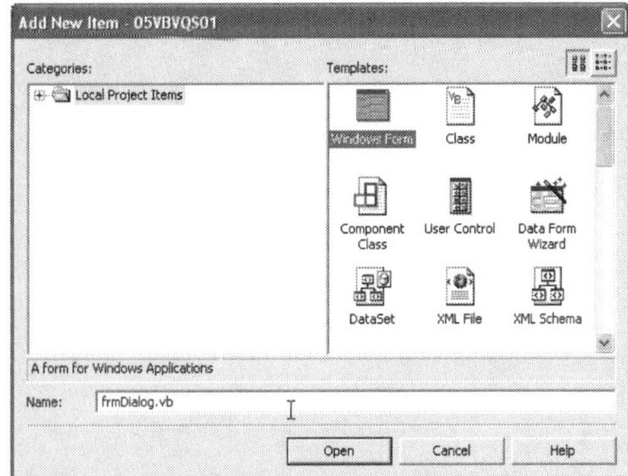

Figure 5.35 Use the Add New Item dialog to add a new form to a project.

The next series of examples assumes that frmDialog has been designed to match Figure 5.19 in appearance, and it includes two text boxes (one is named *txtUserName* and the other *txtPassword*). The project has been set to start from a primary form instance named *frmDemo*. The first task is to open an instance of the dialog form class (frmdialog) from the instance of the primary form class (frmDemo).

To open the dialog form from another form:

1. Add a button to the primary form, frmDemo.
2. Using the Properties window, name the button *btnDialog*.
3. Double-click the button to create a click event procedure in the Code Editor:
   ```
   Private Sub btnDialog_Click _
      (ByVal sender As System.Object, _
      ByVal e As System.EventArgs) _
      Handles btnDialog.Click

   End Sub
   ```
4. Declare and instantiate a variable representing the new form class instance:
   ```
   Dim frmDialog As New frmDialog()
   ```
5. Use the Show or ShowDialog method to display the new instance (see the Tips that follow for an explanation of the difference between these two methods). For example, enter
   ```
   frmDialog.ShowDialog()
   ```

continues on next page

Here's the complete code of the click event procedure:

```
Private Sub btnDialog_Click(ByVal _
    sender As System.Object, ByVal _
    e As System.EventArgs) Handles _
    btnDialog.Click
    Dim frmDialog As New frmDialog()
    frmDialog.ShowDialog()
End Sub
```

6. Run the project.
7. Click Dialog.

   The second form opens (**Figure 5.36**).

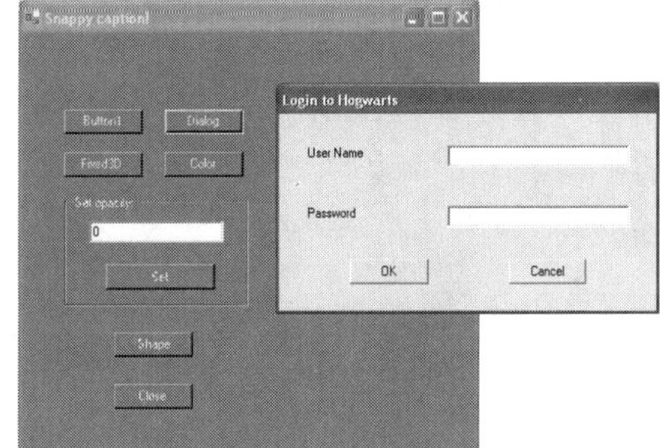

Figure 5.36 When the user clicks the Dialog button, an instance of the dialog form opens.

✔ Tips

- If you open a form instance using the ShowDialog method, the form is opened modally, meaning that the user is restricted within the application to the modal form until the form is closed. In contrast, when a form instance is opened using the Show method—for example, `frmDialog.Show()`—the form is not modal, meaning that the user can click other forms in the application along with the nonmodal form.
- If you're going to have only a single instance of a form class within a particular scope, it's often handy to name the variable that holds the instance using the same identifier as the class. This avoids having extra identifiers floating around and has the benefit of simplicity as long as you are clear that the variable is not the same thing as the class, even though they share the same name. For example, the statement `Dim frmDialog As New frmDialog()` instantiates an instance of the frmDialog class and stores it in the variable frmDialog (both class and instance variables have the same name).

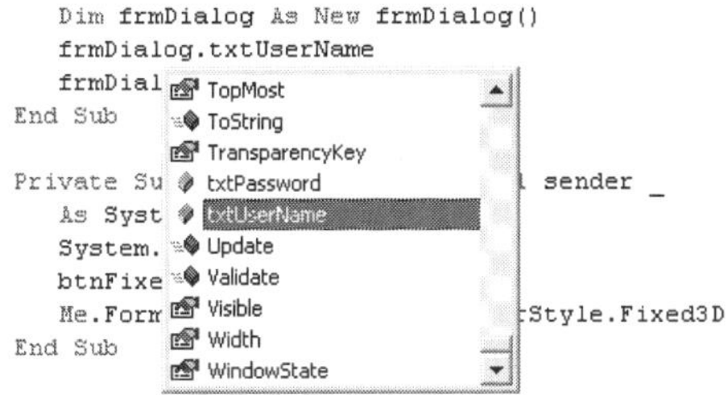

Figure 5.37 The Code Editor supplies a list of available members of a form instance.

Figure 5.38 When the dialog opens, it has been populated with the values from the form that instantiated it.

Now let's kick things up a notch by prefilling some information in the dialog form. You can reference public controls, properties, and fields belonging to the class instance in the code that invokes the instance. Specifically, you'll prefill the Text property values of the two text box controls that are members of the frmDialog class. These text boxes are named *txtUserName* and *txtPassword.*

To prefill information in the dialog:

1. After declaring and instantiating a dialog form instance, save the values of the dialog form members. You'll know you are on the right track when the members you need to set appear in the auto-completion drop-down list in the Code Editor (**Figure 5.37**).

   For example, here's the code to save string literals as the values of the dialog form's TextBox.Text properties:

   ```
   frmDialog.txtUserName.Text = _
      "Albus Dumbledore"
   frmDialog.txtPassword.Text = "Secret"
   ```

   Here's the revised code for the click event that invokes the dialog form.

   ```
   Private Sub btnDialog_Click(ByVal _
      sender As System.Object, ByVal _
      e As System.EventArgs) Handles _
      btnDialog.Click
      Dim frmDialog As New frmDialog()
      frmDialog.txtUserName.Text = _
         "Albus Dumbledore"
      frmDialog.txtPassword.Text = _
         "Secret"
      frmDialog.ShowDialog()
   End Sub
   ```

2. Run the project.

3. Click the Dialog button.

   The dialog form opens with the information prefilled (**Figure 5.38**).

continues on next page

✔ Tips

- Depending on how your code works, you may need to scope the variable storing the reference to the form instance so that it is available outside the click event procedure—that is, at the form level.
- Notice in Figure 5.38 that asterisks (*) appear in txtPassword rather than the characters of the Text property value. This is implemented by setting the PasswordChar property of the txtPassword text box to the character to be used as a mask. You can set this property in the Properties window (**Figure 5.39**).

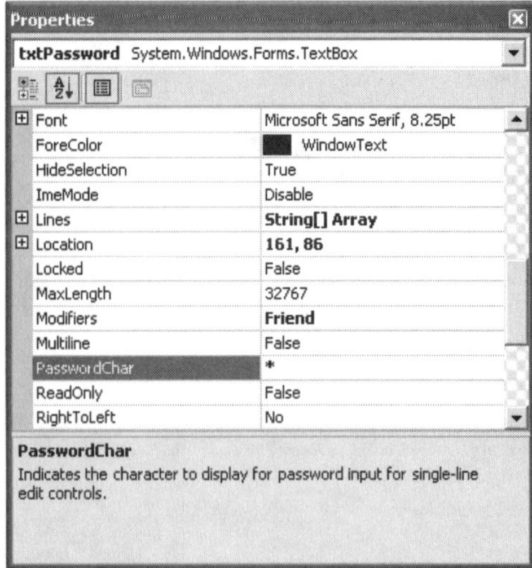

Figure 5.39 When you set the PasswordChar property, a masking character (such as *) appears in the text box rather than the characters of the Text property value.

Communication, as they say, is a two-way street. As you can see from the preceding example, it is pretty easy to get information into a form instance. But it's a little harder to see how to move information in the opposite direction and get it out of an invoked dialog form, because the primary form has no instance variable that is available to the dialog form.

In the next section, "Sending Information Back," you'll learn a couple of strategies for getting around this limitation, which involve, in one way or another, accessing a variable that points to the instance of the original form class.

In the meantime, here's how to retrieve information from a dialog. For the technique presented here to work, the dialog must be opened using the ShowDialog method (not the Show method), and the dialog form must be opened modally. In addition, an overloaded version of the ShowDialog method must be used that accepts, as an argument, the parent form instance. In this context, a *parent* means a form instance that invokes and controls another form.

For this example, we'll retrieve the user name entered as the value of the txtUserName.Text property so that when the user clicks OK in the dialog, the name that the user entered will appear on the caption bar of the primary form.

In the real world, you might want a user name and password to be retrieved by other parts of an application for a variety of reasons, such as user authentication.

To retrieve information from a dialog:

1. With the dialog form in its designer, double-click the OK button to create an event handler procedure:

```
Private Sub btnOK_Click(ByVal _
    sender As System.Object, ByVal _
    e As System.EventArgs) Handles _
    btnOK.Click


End Sub
```

2. In the Code Editor, within the event handler, assign the constant value DialogResult.OK to the DialogResult property of the dialog form class instance, so that this value will be assigned when the user clicks OK:

```
Me.DialogResult = DialogResult.OK
```

3. Use the Close method to close the current instance of the dialog form.

   Here's the complete event handler procedure:

```
Private Sub btnOK_Click(ByVal _
    sender As System.Object, ByVal _
    e As System.EventArgs) Handles _
    btnOK.Click
    Me.DialogResult = DialogResult.OK
    Me.Close()
End Sub
```

4. Back in the btnDialog click event in the frmDemo instance, add code that opens the dialog modally with the ShowDialog method, passing it the current form instance as an argument.

   This code is wrapped in an If statement that checks to make sure that the return value from the ShowDialog method is the constant value DialogResult.OK, which was assigned as the return value of the modal dialog form in Step 2 of this task:

```
If (frmDialog.ShowDialog(Me) = _
    DialogResult.OK) Then


End If
```

5. Add code to the If statement that assigns the value of the txtUserName.Text property to the current form instance's Text property:

```
If (frmDialog.ShowDialog(Me) = _
    DialogResult.OK) Then
        Me.Text = "User is " & _
            frmDialog.txtUserName.Text
End If
```

   Here's the complete code for the click event:

```
Private Sub btnDialog_Click(ByVal
    sender As System.Object, ByVal _
    e As System.EventArgs) Handles _
    btnDialog.Click
    Dim frmDialog As New frmDialog()
    If (frmDialog.ShowDialog(Me) = _
        DialogResult.OK) Then
            Me.Text = "User is " & _
                frmDialog.txtUserName.Text
    End If
End Sub
```

continues on next page

6. Run the project.
7. Click the Dialog button.
8. In the Login to Hogwarts dialog, enter a user name (**Figure 5.40**).
9. Click OK. The user name entered in the dialog will appear on the caption bar of the primary form (**Figure 5.41**).

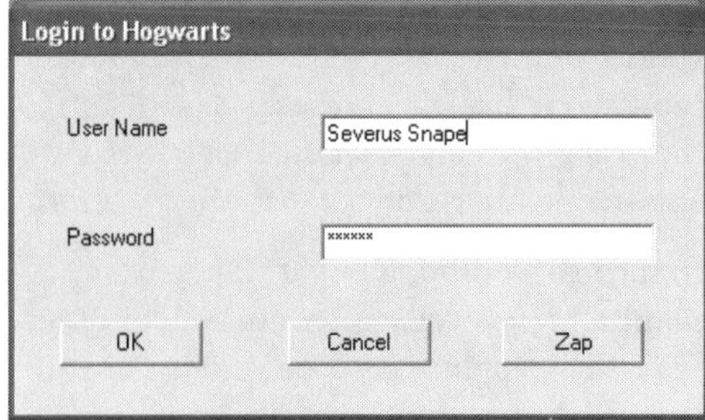

Figure 5.40 Text entered in the Login dialog can be used by the dialog's parent form when the user clicks OK.

Figure 5.41 You can use values entered in a dialog to populate the form that called the dialog.

✔ Tip

- You'll find everything you always wanted to know about If statements in Chapter 7, "Message Boxes and If Statements."

There's no great difficulty involved in closing a form instance using the Close method—provided you have access to a variable that references the instance. Putting the statement that closes the form in the same click event that instantiates it makes no sense, because you'll never see the form (it will close faster than the blink of an eye).

For example, if you run code along these lines in a click event procedure:

```
Dim dlg As New frmDialog()

dlg.Show()

dlg.Close()
```

you'll never see the instance of frmDialog because it will appear to close before you see it open! (Depending on the speed of your system, you might see a quick onscreen blink.)

Figure 5.42 One button is used to open a form instance, and the other to close it.

As you'll see, the issue comes down to giving the form instance variable the right scope by declaring it at the form class level, not within a procedure.

To close the remote form:

1. Add two buttons, named *btnOpDlg* and *btnClDlg*, to the primary form.
2. Give the first button the Text property value `Open Dlg` and the second button the value `Close Dlg` (**Figure 5.42**).
3. Double-click each button to add a click event handler framework in the Code Editor.
4. In the Code Editor, declare `dlg` as a variable of type frmDialog at the Form class level, meaning the declaration needs to be within the class, but not within any method or procedure:
   ```
   Dim dlg As frmDialog
   ```
5. Within the Open button's click event, create a reference to a new frmDialog instance in the variable dlg:
   ```
   dlg = New frmDialog()
   ```
6. Show the form instance:
   ```
   dlg.Show()
   ```
7. Within the Close button's click event, use the Close method to close the form instance:
   ```
   dlg.Close()
   ```

continues on next page

Here's the variable declaration and the Open and Close click events:

```
Dim dlg As frmDialog
Private Sub btnOpDlg_Click _
   (ByVal sender As System.Object, _
   ByVal e As System.EventArgs) _
   Handles btnOpDlg.Click
   dlg = New frmDialog()
   dlg.Show()
End Sub

Private Sub btnClDlg_Click _
   (ByVal sender As System.Object, _
   ByVal e As System.EventArgs) _
   Handles btnClDlg.Click
   dlg.Close()
End Sub
```

8. Run the project.
9. Click the Open Dlg button.
   The frmDialog instance opens.
10. Press Alt+Tab to return to the primary form.
11. Click the Close Dlg button to verify that the frmDialog instance closes.

✔ Tips

- For this example to work, the frmDialog instance must be invoked so that it isn't modal by using Show (not ShowDialog). If the form instance were modal, the user would never get back to the original form to click the Close button.
- Declaring the variable dlg, which references the dialog form instance, at the Form class level makes it available to all procedures within the class.

Sending information back

Communication may be a two-way street, as I've already noted, but so far the dialog form has been a passive partner. You've seen how to code the primary form instance to open a dialog form instance, populate it with information, retrieve information from it, and close it. But I haven't shown you how the instance of the dialog form can become an equal participant, by being able to send information back to the original form instance.

There are occasions when it's important to send information back: for example, when information keyed in by users or obtained in some other way needs to be loaded into several different forms, or when a value on one form changes when a value on another form changes.

There are a number of viable ways to send information back to an original form, but they all rely on the ability of the dialog form to access a variable that references the initial form instance.

To explore some examples of the ways to accomplish this task, let's add to our frmDialog class a button named *btnZap* that contains the text *Zap*, which is short for *Zap it back*. As a final preliminary, we will create a click event procedure in the frmDialog class for btnZap. It will be used to zap back the contents of the txtUserName.Text property to the original form.

To send information back to the first form instance using a shared variable:

1. In the primary form, begin by using the code we developed to open and shut a dialog form instance in "To close the remote form" earlier in this chapter.

2. At the form class level, declare a shared variable named *theForm* of type Form:

```
Public Shared theForm As Form
```

3. Before showing the instance of the dialog form, save a reference to the current form instance in the shared variable theForm using the Me keyword:

```
theForm = Me
```

Here's the code in the primary form:

```
Dim dlg As frmDialog
Public Shared theForm As Form
Private Sub btnOpDlg_Click _
   (ByVal sender As System.Object, _
   ByVal e As System.EventArgs) _
   Handles btnOpDlg.Click
   theForm = Me
   dlg = New frmDialog()
   dlg.Show()
End Sub

Private Sub btnClDlg_Click _
   (ByVal sender As System.Object, _
   ByVal e As System.EventArgs) _
   Handles btnClDlg.Click
   dlg.Close()
End Sub
```

continues on next page

4. In the click event for the frmDialog class's Zap button, add code that uses the shared variable member theForm in the frmDemo class to set the Text property of the original form instance:

```
frmDemo.theForm.Text = _
   "Hello, " & Me.txtUserName.Text
```

   Here's the complete code for the Zap button's click event:

```
Private Sub btnZap_Click(ByVal _
   sender As System.Object, ByVal _
   e As System.EventArgs) Handles _
   btnZap.Click
   frmDemo.theForm.Text = _
      "Hello, " & _
      Me.txtUserName.Text
End Sub
```

5. Run the project.
6. Click the Open Dlg button.
7. Enter some text in the User Name text box.
8. Click the Zap button.

   The text from the User Name text box is now displayed in the caption of the primary form instance (**Figure 5.43**).

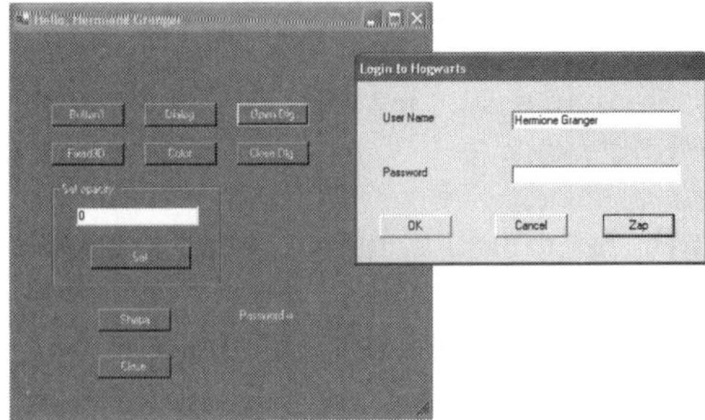

Figure 5.43 You can use a shared variable to zap information back to another form class instance.

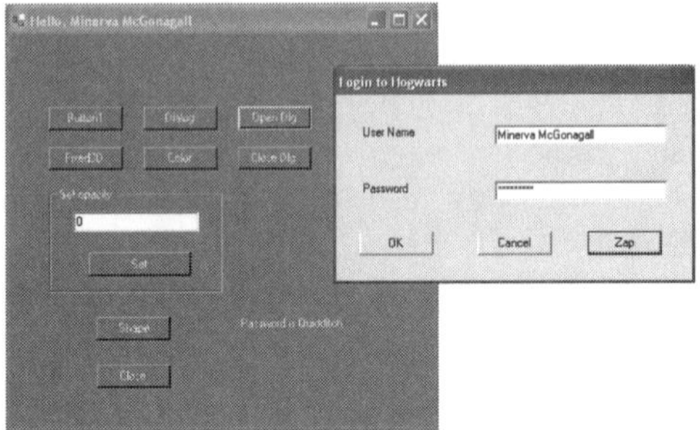

Figure 5.44 The text of the label on the primary form is set using a public field variable.

✔ Tips

- For more on shared variables and OO, see Chapter 3.
- You can place the Shared variable declaration in any Public class in your project. In particular, it doesn't have to be within the Form class.

You can easily send information from the form dialog back to the original instance of the form, but the process is also problematic because, at least to some degree, it violates OO principles of encapsulation. Use of a shared public variable does not constitute gated access. In fact, wide use of a shared public variable is the OO analog to the (naughty) habit of making extensive (and possibly expensive) use of global variables in procedural coding.

One way to avoid the architecturally inappropriate use of shared variables is to create a public field in the dialog form's class to hold a reference back to the primary form.

To demonstrate how to send information back to an original instance using a field, I've added a Label control named *lblZap* to the primary form to display the information that will be zapped back. The setup for this task is very similar to that for the task we just completed.

To send information back to the original form instance using a field:

1. In the frmDialog class, add a Public field of type frmDemo at the class level:
```
Public frm As frmDemo
```
2. In the Open button's click event on the primary form, frmDemo, after an instance of the frmDialog class has been created and a reference saved in the variable dlg, assign the current form instance using the Me keyword to the frm field:
```
dlg.frm = Me
```
Here's the relevant code from the primary form:
```
Dim dlg As frmDialog
Private Sub btnOpDlg_Click _
   (ByVal sender As System.Object, _
   ByVal e As System.EventArgs) _
   Handles btnOpDlg.Click
   dlg = New frmDialog()
   dlg.frm = Me
   dlg.Show()
End Sub

Private Sub btnClDlg_Click _
   (ByVal sender As System.Object, _
   ByVal e As System.EventArgs) _
   Handles btnClDlg.Click
   dlg.Close()
End Sub
```
3. Back in the frmDialog instance, add code to the click event for the Zap button that assigns a value from the current form to the Text property of the lblZap Label control found on the form instance that is referenced by the frm field:
```
frm.lblZap.Text = "Password is " & _
   txtPassword.Text
```
Here's the relevant code from the frmDialog class:
```
Public frm As frmDemo
Private Sub btnZap_Click(ByVal _
   sender As System.Object, ByVal _
   e As System.EventArgs) Handles _
   btnZap.Click
   frm.lblZap.Text = "Password is " _
      & txtPassword.Text
End Sub
```
4. Run the project.
5. Click the Open Dlg button.
6. Enter some text in the Password text box.
7. Click the Zap button.
The text from the Password text box is now displayed in the label on the primary form instance (**Figure 5.44**).

✔ Tip

- In this example, the frm field was declared as type frmDemo rather than plain-vanilla type Form. However, the derived class, frmDemo, inherits many members from the Form class, such as Text. So if these members are all that you need to make your application work, you could just declare the field type as Form. But remember that Form has no lblZap control, so if you need to work with this or other elements that have been added to the frmDemo class, you must declare the field to match the derived class.

Using a class field to pass a reference to the original form instance is a nifty approach. But you can add a finishing OO touch by creating a property—which is, after all, intended to encapsulate information—rather than a field.

To send information back to the original form instance using a property variable:

- In the Code Editor, in the frmDialog class, declare a property:

```
Private m_frm As frmDemo
Property frm() As frmDemo
   Get
      frm = m_frm
   End Get
   Set(ByVal Value As frmDemo)
      m_frm = Value
   End Set
End Property
```

  This property replaces the public field declaration in the class, so it is no longer needed:

```
' This is the field declaration
' We won't be using it now
'
' Public frm As frmDemo
```

✔ Tip

- See Chapter 3 for an explanation of the mechanics of properties.

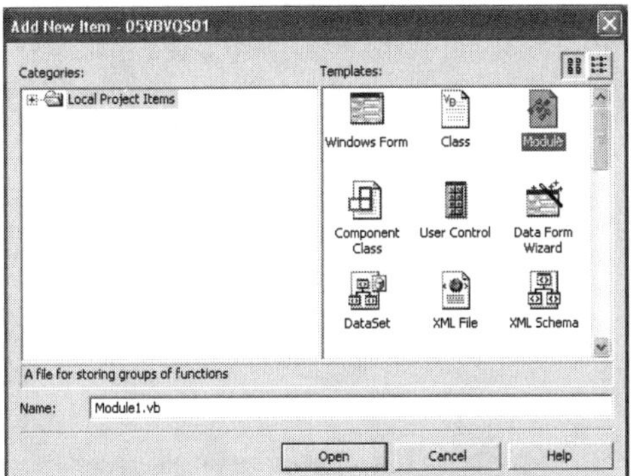

Figure 5.45 Use the Add New Item dialog to add a code module to a project.

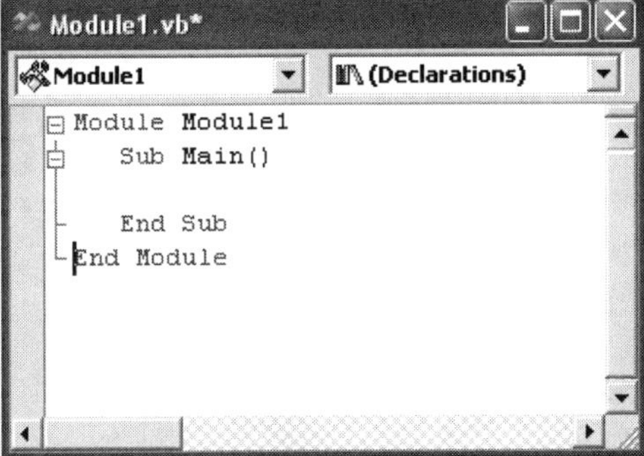

Figure 5.46 A Sub Main procedure is added to the module in the Code Editor.

Launching an Application from Sub Main

So far in this chapter, we've assumed that our application starts from a single, primary form instance that, in turn, invokes other forms (such as an instance of the frmDialog class).

There's no reason that applications necessarily have to be organized in this way. It's often better from an architectural perspective to start an application from a code procedure that serves as a traffic cop, calling different form instances as required and passing information between the forms.

In Visual Basic .NET, as in VB6, the procedure used to launch an application that doesn't start from a form is called Sub Main.

To add a Sub Main procedure to a project:

1. Use the Add New Item dialog to add a code module to your project (**Figure 5.45**).
2. In the Code Editor, add a procedure named Main to the module (**Figure 5.46**).

```
Module Module1
    Sub Main()


    End Sub
End Module
```

To start the application from the Sub Main procedure:

1. Open Solution Explorer.
2. In Solution Explorer, select the project file (**Figure 5.47**).
3. Right-click and select Properties from the context menu.

   The Property Pages dialog for the project opens (**Figure 5.48**).
4. Select Sub Main from the Startup Object drop-down list.
5. Click OK.

✔ Tip

- In the Startup Object drop-down list, you can choose among modules that contain a Sub Main procedure. However, if you select the generic Sub Main item on the list and you have more than one Sub Main procedure in your project, you'll get a syntax error.

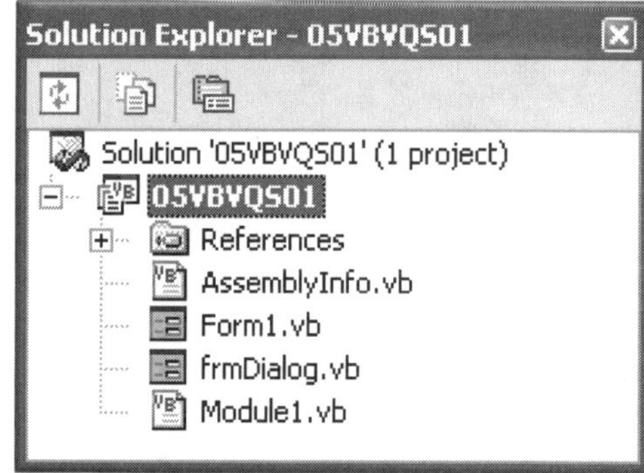

Figure 5.47 Open Solution Explorer to access the Property Pages dialog for a project.

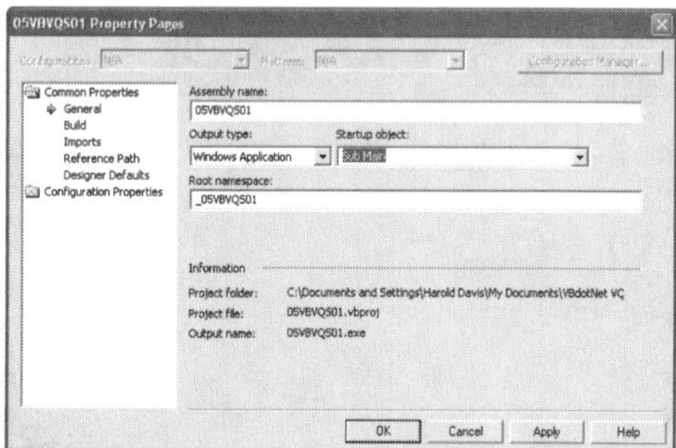

Figure 5.48 To start an application from the Sub Main procedure, in the Startup object drop-down list select Sub Main.

Starting an application from Sub Main is all very well and good, but so far our Main procedure is an empty one—it doesn't really do anything. If you run the project this way, it will start and shut down before you know it.

One response to this is that some applications do not need a user interface. They start, perform a calculation, and terminate. However, most of the time you will want to display something to the user. Furthermore, your application probably needs to interact with the user. This means that you need to know how to display forms from a Main procedure.

You might think to display forms with code along these lines:

```
Sub Main()
    Dim dlg As New frmDialog()
    Dim frm As New frmDemo()
    dlg.Show()
    frm.Show()
End Sub
```

But if you run this, you may see a flicker or two as the forms load on the screen and then unload. You won't get anything more permanent.

The best solution to the problem of the form that disappears before it is seen is to use the ShowDialog method to open the forms from the Sub Main procedure modally.

A typical arrangement is to put calls to procedures that execute initialization code required to load form variables in the Sub Main procedure before the form is displayed. You can also use Sub Main to display a splash screen while the rest of a program is loading.

As you'll see in a moment, not only can you use Sub Main to initialize values and display forms; you can use it to pass information between form class instances.

To display multiple form instances from the Sub Main procedure, passing information between them:

1. Instantiate more than one Form class—for example:
```
Dim dlg As New frmDialog()
Dim frm As New frmDemo()
```
2. Use an If statement to display the first form and check its return value:
```
If (dlg.ShowDialog = _
   DialogResult.OK) Then

End If
```
3. If the return value is `DialogResult.OK`, use the values of the dialog to initialize the other form and display it:
```
frm.Text = "Hello " & _
   dlg.txtUserName.Text
frm.ShowDialog()
```
   Here's the complete Sub Main:
```
Sub Main()
   Dim dlg As New frmDialog()
   Dim frm As New frmDemo()
   If (dlg.ShowDialog = _
      DialogResult.OK) Then
      frm.Text = "Hello " & _
         dlg.txtUserName.Text
      frm.ShowDialog()
   End If
End Sub
```
4. Run the project.
   The Login to Hogwarts dialog opens (**Figure 5.49**).
5. Enter a user name and click OK.
   The Login dialog closes and the primary form opens, displaying the user name (**Figure 5.50**).

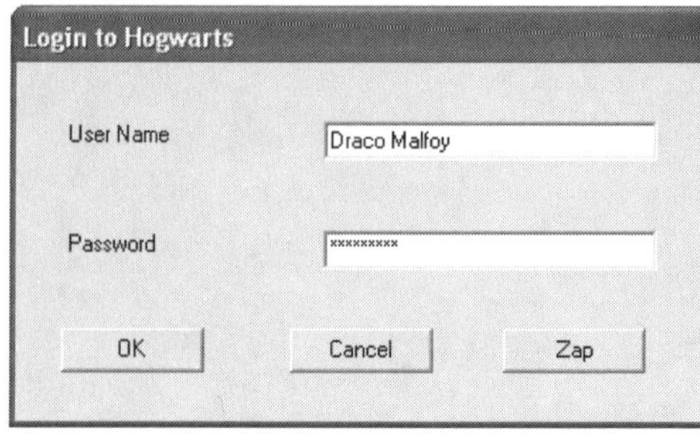

Figure 5.49 The Login to Hogwarts dialog comes up by itself.

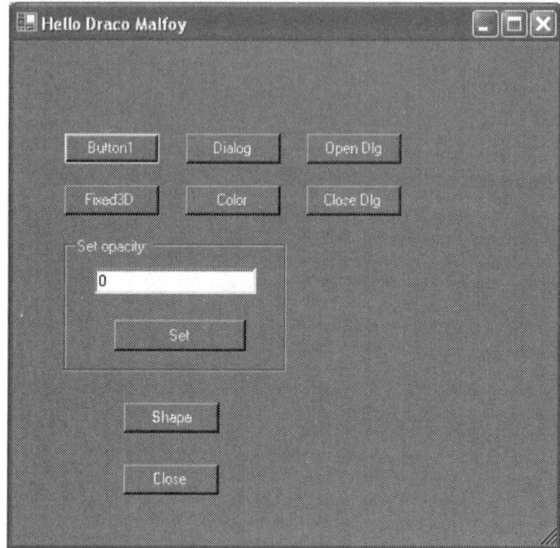

Figure 5.50 When the user clicks OK, he or she is greeted by name on the primary form (in the real world, after some authentication process).

✔ Tip

- The code shown in this task assumes that the frmDialog class has code in the OK button's click event that sets its return value to `DialogResult.OK`, as shown earlier in this chapter in "To retrieve information from a dialog."

If you want to open a nonmodal form from Sub Main, you can do so using the Application.Run method. For example, enter:

```
Dim frm As New Form1()

Application.Run(frm)
```

or (equivalently, if you don't need access to a variable referencing the form):

```
Application.Run(New Form1())
```

Summary

In this chapter, you learned how to:

- Explain the ins and outs of the Form class
- Use the Properties window to set form properties
- Set form properties in code
- Change the shape of a form
- Describe form instances and how to work with them
- Send information to and from dialogs
- Use variables that store references to form instances
- Start a project from Sub Main

6 Consuming the Web Service

So far, you've learned how to create an ASP.NET Web service, extend the service by adding classes and form-based interfaces, and test the service to verify that its methods are working. But what good is a Web service if it merely returns a string of XML? In order to be useful, a Web service needs either to respond to user input or to be invoked in program code (or both).

This chapter shows you how to use, or *consume*, in a Windows form application, the Web service you created and extended in Chapters 2 and 3. But before we can use the Web service, we first need to create a user interface to provide input for the service and add a Web reference to refer to the service. This chapter shows you how to accomplish these steps and add a little polish by validating the user input along the way.

Creating a User Interface

As you may recall, the Web service we created in Chapters 2 and 3 includes a method (ReverseString) that reverses a string. It also includes a method, AddTwoNums, that adds two long integer numbers. We'll build a user interface for using these two methods.

You can view these methods in the auto-generated page that serves as an ad hoc table of contents for the testing capability that is "baked" into a Visual Studio ASP.NET Web services project (**Figure 6.1**). (We'll ignore the third Web method shown, HelloVQS, which merely returns a constant text string.)

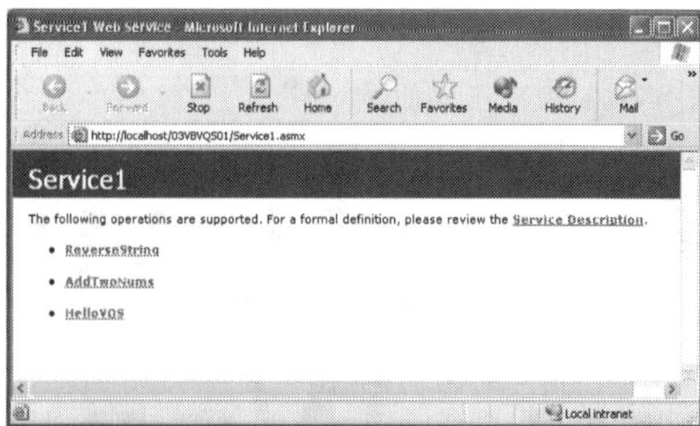

Figure 6.1 The test pages automatically generated by Visual Studio can be used to check that a Web service is working.

The first step is to start a new Windows Application project.

To open a new Windows Application project:

1. Open the New Project dialog (**Figure 6.2**) either by choosing New > Project from the File menu or clicking New Project on the Start page.
2. In the Project Types pane, make sure Visual Basic Projects is selected.
3. In the Templates pane, select Windows Application.
4. Provide a name and location for the project.
5. Click OK.

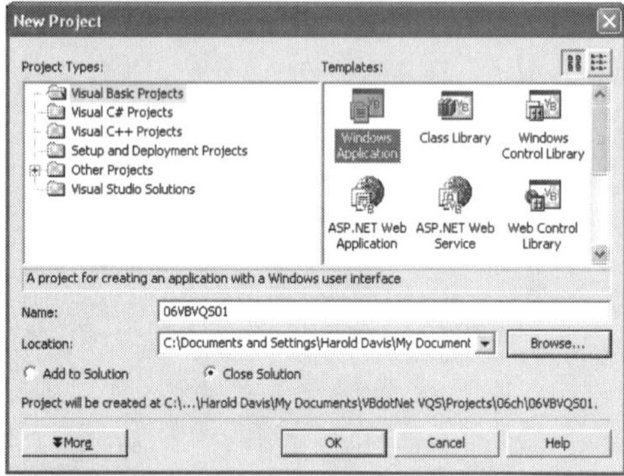

Figure 6.2 Use the New Project dialog to open a new Windows Application project.

✔ Tip

- See Chapter 1, "Introducing Visual Studio .NET," for detailed instructions related to opening new projects and project management.

Table 6.1

User Interface Controls

Name	Text	Purpose
btnAdd	Add	User clicks the button to add the two numbers
btnRev	Reverse	User clicks the button to reverse the string
lblAdd		Displays the results of the addition
lblRev		Displays the reversed text string
txtNumOne		Text box for the first user input
txtNumTwo		Text box for the second user input
txtStr		Text box for the string to be reversed

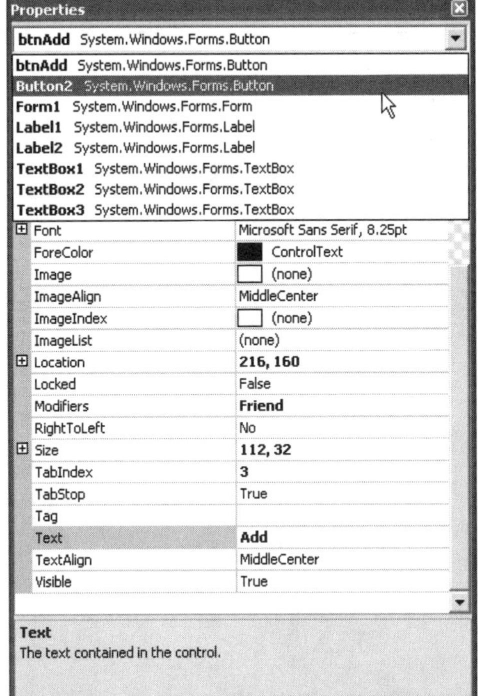

Figure 6.3 Select each item in the Objects list of the Properties window to set its Name and Text properties.

The next step is to create the user interface using the Windows form provided by the project. This will require you to add two buttons, two label controls, and three text boxes to the form. **Table 6.1** lists the Name property value, the Text property value, and the purpose of each control.

To add the controls to the form:

1. Open the form in its designer.
2. Open the Toolbox by choosing View > Toolbox.
3. Add two button, two label, and three text box controls to the form by dragging and dropping them from the Toolbox to the form or by double-clicking each control in the Toolbox.
4. Open the Properties window by choosing View > Properties Window.
5. Select each control in the Objects list (**Figure 6.3**) and set its Text and Name properties as indicated in Table 6.1.

continues on next page

When these values have been set, your form will look similar to the form shown in its designer in **Figure 6.4**.

6. Run the project to view the user interface at runtime to see the way it will actually appear to users (**Figure 6.5**).

✔ Tip

- In the form shown in its designer in Figure 6.4 and at runtime in Figure 6.5, I've added a few label controls to illustrate the purpose of each text box for the user. I've also added group boxes to visually organize the interface. Because these controls are not used programmatically, I've accepted the default names for them (Label1, Label2, GroupBox1, and so on), they do not appear in Table 6.1, and they will not be discussed further.

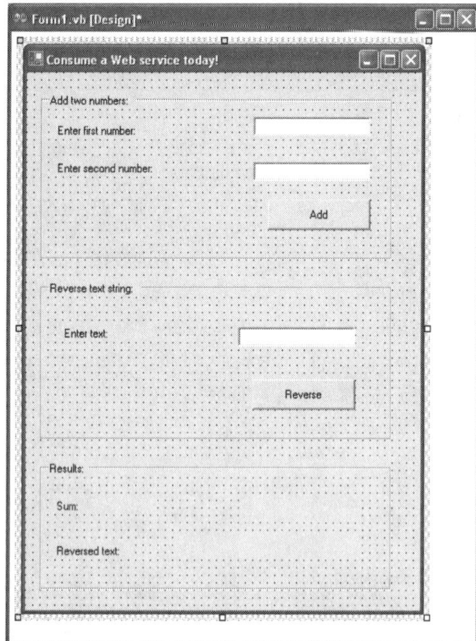

Figure 6.4 The Windows form in its designer with the completed user interface should like more or less as shown.

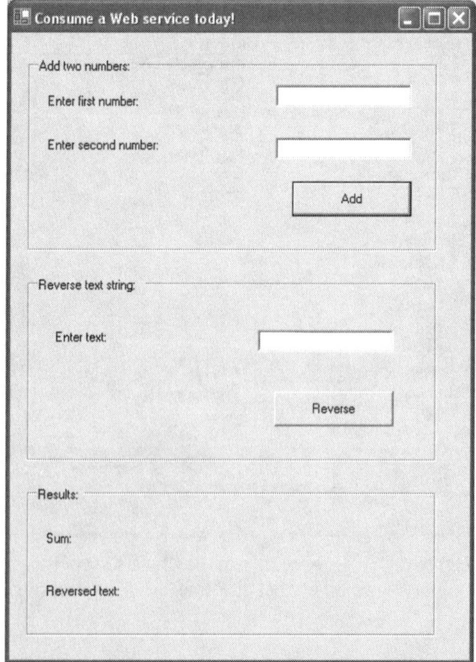

Figure 6.5 It's a good idea to run the form so that you see what it will look like to users.

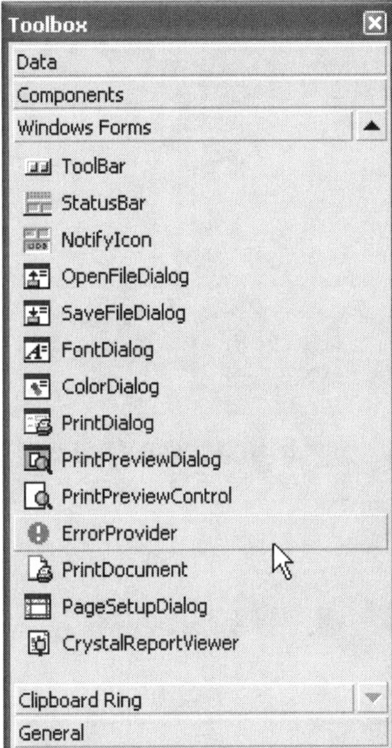

Figure 6.6 The ErrorProvider component, found on the Window tab of the Toolbox, helps validate user input.

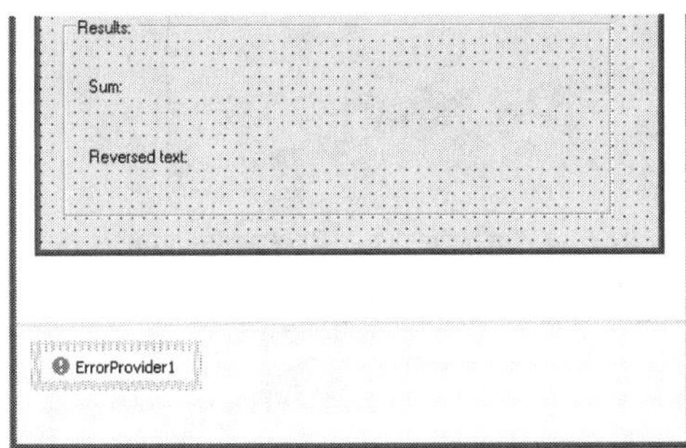

Figure 6.7 When you add an ErrorProvider component to a form, it appears in a tray at the bottom of the form's designer, not on the form itself.

Validating User Input

Let's improve the guts of this user interface a bit by adding a mechanism to check that the user actually adds numerical values in the txtNumOne and textNumTwo TextBox controls.

One way to do this is to add an ErrorProvider component to the form and then add an appropriate handler for the Validating event of each control.

To add an error provider to the form:

1. With the form open in its designer, open the Toolbox.
2. On the Windows Forms tab of the Toolbox, scroll down to the ErrorProvider component (**Figure 6.6**).
3. Double-click ErrorProvider to add it to the form. It will appear in the tray at the bottom of the form's designer (**Figure 6.7**).

✔ Tips

- Nonvisual components that have been added to a form appear in the tray at the bottom of the designer rather than on the form itself.
- You'll find information about working with Toolbox tabs in Chapter 8, "Working with MDI Forms."

The next step is to add the code that tells ErrorProvider to take some kind of action. You can do this by adding a Validating event handler that invokes ErrorProvider when a user enters a nonnumeric value. The advantage of this approach is that you can write one event handler that works for both text boxes. The disadvantage is that if Option Strict is turned on for the project (as I recommend), you're running with strict typing turned on, which means that this method takes a little bit of work. (For more information about Option Strict, see "Setting property pages for a project" in Chapter 1.)

To add a Validating event:

1. In the Code Editor, select txtNumOne from the Objects list.
2. Select the Validating event from the Procedures list (**Figure 6.8**).

   The event procedure is created:

```
Private Sub
txtNumOne_Validating(ByVal _
   sender As Object, ByVal e As _
   System.ComponentModel. _
   CancelEventArgs) _
   Handles txtNumOne.Validating

End Sub
```

To add the second control's Validating event to the handler:

1. At the end of the Validating event procedure for txtOneNum, in its Handles clause, add a comma, followed by the name of the second control, followed by the dot operator.

   The Code Editor's auto-completion facility supplies a list of possible events (**Figure 6.9**).

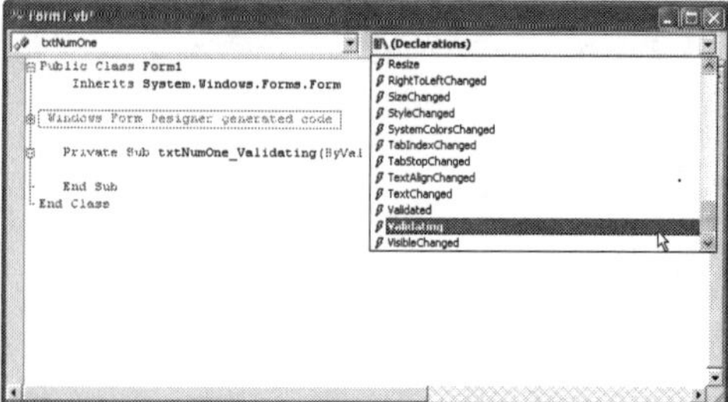

Figure 6.8 To add an event procedure in the Code Editor, select the object from the Objects list and the event from the Procedures list.

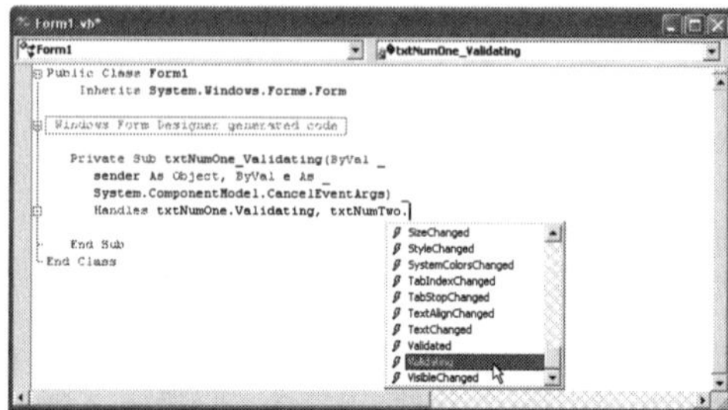

Figure 6.9 When you add another control's event to the first event's handler, auto-completion supplies a list of possible events.

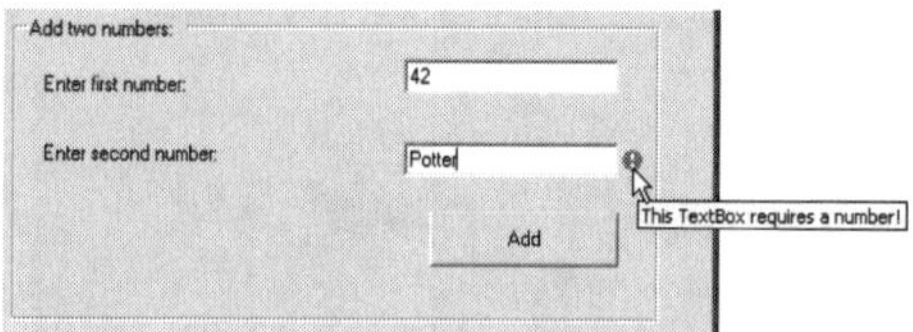

Figure 6.10 When the user enters a nonnumeric value and attempts to move focus away from the control, an error provider supplies an error message.

2. Select Validating from the list.

   The event framework now reads as follows:

```
Private Sub _
   txtNumOne_Validating(ByVal _
   sender As Object, ByVal e As _
   System.ComponentModel. _
   CancelEventArgs) _
   Handles txtNumOne.Validating, _
   txtNumTwo.Validating

End Sub
```

To wire the event:

1. Within the event handler procedure, declare a variable of type Control named *myControl*:

```
Dim myControl As Control
```

2. Use the CType method to convert the sender parameter of the event handler to the Control type and save a reference to it in myControl:

```
Dim myControl As Control
myControl = CType(sender, Control)
```

3. Use the IsNumeric method to check the value entered:

```
If Not IsNumeric(myControl.Text)
Then
```

4. If the value is not numeric, invoke the ErrorProvider component with an appropriate message:

```
ErrorProvider1.SetError(myControl, _
  "This TextBox requires a number!")
```

5. If the value is not numeric, take appropriate action, such as setting the focus on the control so that the user can't perform any other action until a number is entered:

```
myControl.Focus()
```

6. Make sure to clear ErrorProvider if a number is entered:

```
If Not IsNumeric(myControl.Text)
Then
   ...
Else
   ErrorProvider1.SetError _
      (myControl, "")
End If
```

   Here's the complete code for the event handler:

```
Private Sub
txtNumOne_Validating(ByVal _
   sender As Object, ByVal e As _
   System.ComponentModel. _
   CancelEventArgs) _
   Handles txtNumOne.Validating, _
   txtNumTwo.Validating
   Dim myControl As Control
   myControl = CType(sender, Control)
   If Not IsNumeric _
      (myControl.Text) Then
      ErrorProvider1.SetError _
      (myControl, _
   "This TextBox requires a number!")
     myControl.Focus()
   Else
     ErrorProvider1.SetError _
        (myControl, "")
   End If
End Sub
```

7. Run the project and verify that whenever a user attempts to enter anything other than a number and then to leave the control, the ErrorProvider message appears in both text boxes (**Figure 6.10**).

Adding a Web Service Reference

Now that the user interface is complete, it's time to add a reference to the Web service we created in Chapter 2. Adding a reference to the Web service allows us to invoke it from within the program just like one would invoke the method of a local class.

To add a Web service reference:

1. Determine the URL and file name of the ASP.NET Web service you created in Chapter 2.

   If you have developed the Web service locally, the URL will probably be an address relative to localhost, such as http://localhost/03VBVQS01/. You can find the URL and file name (which has an .asmx suffix) by running the ASP.NET Web service and looking at the address bar in the browser—for example, http://localhost/03VBVQS01/Service1.asmx (**Figure 6.11**).

2. Choose Add Web Reference from the Project menu.

   The Add Web Reference dialog opens (**Figure 6.12**).

3. Type, or copy and paste, the URL and file name for the Web service in the Address box.

4. Press Enter.

   The Visual Studio test pages for the Web service and other information about it will appear in the Add Web Reference dialog (**Figure 6.13**). (You can use the links in the left pane to test the Web methods provided by the Web service.)

Figure 6.11 You can find the URL and file name for an ASP.NET Web service by running the Web service in Visual Studio and reading the information in your browser's address bar.

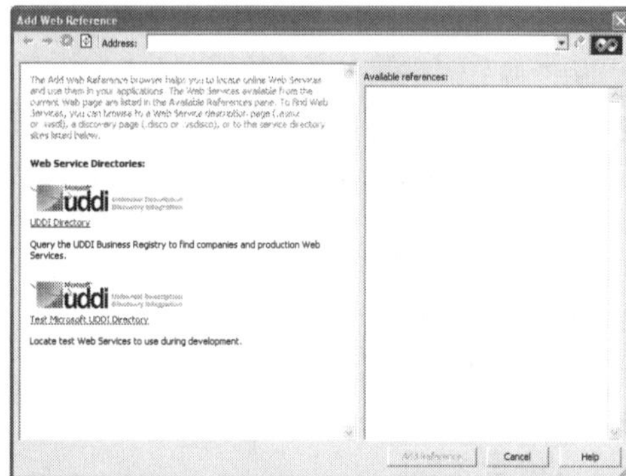

Figure 6.12 You can use the Add Web Reference dialog to add references to ASP.NET Web services.

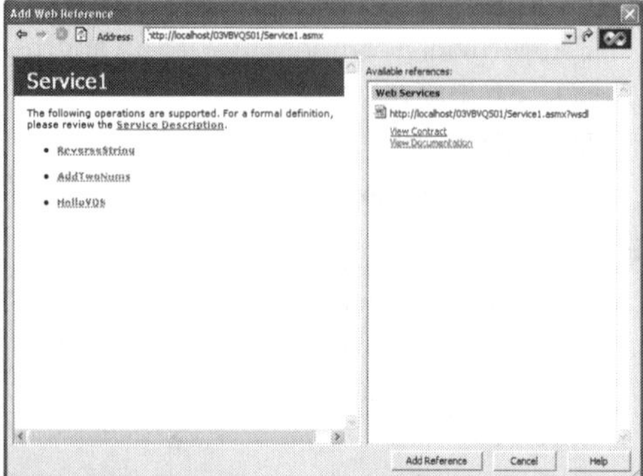

Figure 6.13 When a URL is supplied, the Web service's test pages and WDSL file are accessible from the Add Web Reference dialog.

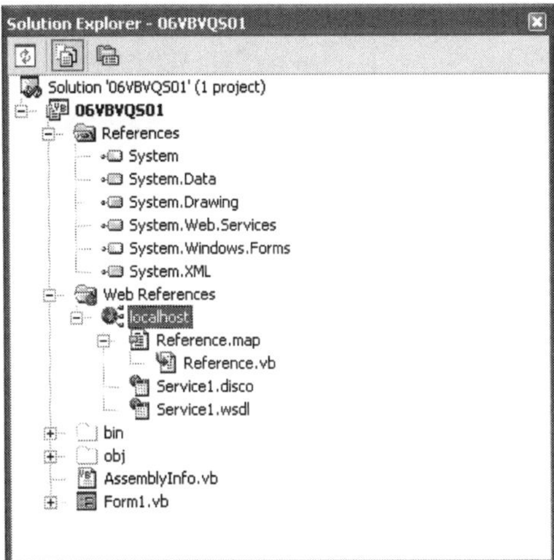

Figure 6.14 Once a Web reference has been added to your project, you'll find oodles of new things in Solution Explorer.

Figure 6.15 It's a good idea to rename the Web service reference to something distinctive.

5. Click Add Reference.
6. Open Solution Explorer and note that a number of references (System.Web.Services) and an entire hierarchical folder (Web References) have been added to the project (**Figure 6.14**).
7. Select the Web reference you just added.
8. The name of a Web reference by default is the hostname of its URL. Change it to something more descriptive or user friendly (as you can see in **Figure 6.15**, I changed the name to *myService*).

✔ Tip

- To see all of the files shown in Figure 6.14, you may need to click the Show All Files button in Solution Explorer.

Consuming the Service

The last thing we need to do is add code mechanisms for consuming the Web methods that are the members of the Web service.

To consume the service:

1. In the Code Editor, double-click the Add and Reverse buttons to create the click event procedures.
2. Declare and instantiate a variable, thisServ, that will hold a reference to the Web service:

```
Dim thisServ As New _
   myService.Service1()
```

   The Web service is accessed via the Web reference that you added to the project in the previous procedure. You'll see the reference in the auto-completion list (**Figure 6.16**). Note that this variable declaration and instantiation take place at the class level, so that both click event procedures can take advantage of the reference.
3. In the click event procedure for the Add button, invoke the AddTwoNums Web method, which appears on the auto-completion drop-down list (**Figure 6.17**).
4. Provide the Text properties of the text boxes, converted to long integer values, as arguments to AddToNums.
5. Convert to a string the results of the Web method callback and then assign this string to the Text property of the lblAdd control.

Figure 6.16 When you instantiate the Web service reference in the Code Editor, the reference will appear in the auto-completion list.

```
    Dim thisServ As New myService.Service1()
    lblAdd.Text = thisServ.

  End Sub
nd Class
```

Abort
AddTwoNums
AllowAutoRedirect
BeginAddTwoNums
BeginHelloVQS
BeginReverseString
ClientCertificates
ConnectionGroupName
Container
CookieContainer

Figure 6.17 Web methods that are members of the Web service can be selected from the auto-completion list.

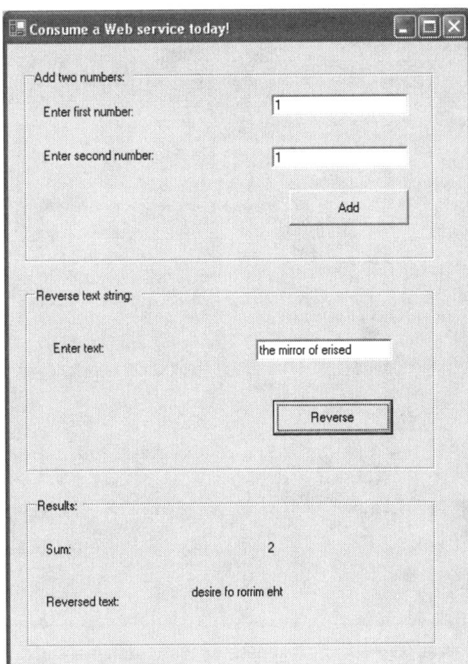

Figure 6.18 When the application is run, calls to the Web service perform as expected.

Here's the complete code for the click event:

```
Private Sub btnAdd_Click(ByVal _
   sender As System.Object, ByVal e _
   As System.EventArgs) Handles _
   btnAdd.Click
   lblAdd.Text = _
(thisServ.AddTwoNums _
(Convert.ToInt64(txtNumOne.Text), _
Convert.ToInt64(txtNumTwo.Text) _
)).ToString
End Sub
```

6. In the click event for the Reverse button, use the ReverseString method to reverse the input string.
7. Assign the results back to the Text property of the lblRev control.

   Here's the complete click event code:

```
Private Sub btnRev_Click(ByVal _
   sender As System.Object, ByVal _
   e As System.EventArgs) Handles _
   btnRev.Click
   lblRev.Text = _
      thisServ.ReverseString _
      (txtStr.Text)
End Sub
```

8. Run the project.
9. Enter some numerical values and click Add, add some text, and click Reverse to make sure that the application invokes the Web service correctly (**Figure 6.18**).

CONSUMING THE SERVICE

You may be scratching your head, wondering "Where did these Web methods come from?" This is a valid question, the answer to which can be found in the code module file Reference.vb, which was added to the project when the Web reference was added. (You can see this file in Solution Explorer in Figure 6.14.)

If you open Reference.vb in the Code Editor, you'll see all of the Web methods used in this chapter as well as the methods that are members of this service (**Figure 6.19**). This code module, sometimes referred to as a *proxy* class because it intermediates between the application and a Web service, is auto-generated as part of the process of adding the Web reference to the project.

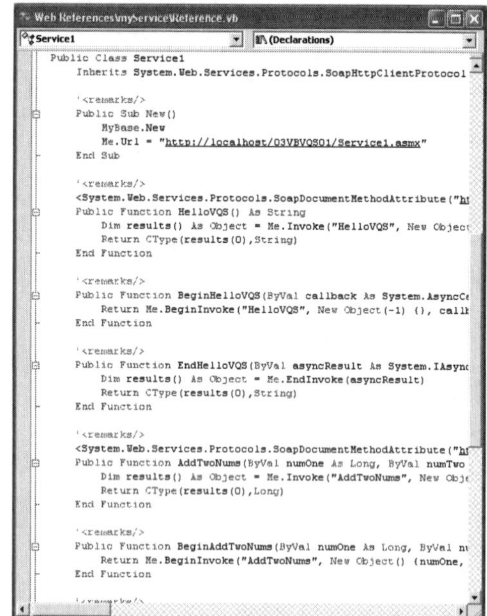

Figure 6.19 The auto-generated Web reference code module contains all of the Web methods that are members of the Web service.

If you look carefully at the proxy class, you'll see that it provides not only the methods that are members of the Web service class, but two additional methods for each Web service method. One of these additional methods is prefixed with *Begin*, and the other with *End*. So, for example, in addition to the AddTwo Nums method, BeginAddTwoNums and EndAddTwoNums methods are present.

These Begin- and End- methods are used for asynchronous calls to Web service methods—that is, invocations of Web service methods that allow other processing to occur until the Web service method returns a value. (In contrast, the calls to the Web methods shown in this chapter have been synchronous.)

You'll find more information about coding asynchronous Web service method calls in the VB .NET documentation online. The best overview information on this topic can be found by searching online Help for the article "Communicating with XML Web Services Asynchronously [Visual Basic]." (For more information about using Visual Studio's Help system to find documentation, see Appendix A in the back of this book.)

Summary

In this chapter, you learned how to:

- Create a user interface to consume Web service methods
- Validate input to make sure it is numeric
- Add a Web service reference
- Consume Web service methods

Message Boxes and If Statements

7

This chapter shows you how to create instant dialogs called *message boxes*. Message boxes can be used to display a message to or provide choices for the user. (There are also some arcane uses for message boxes, as you'll see later in this chapter, such as to create an entry in the System logs for use for auditing or diagnostic purposes.)

Message boxes are useful in and of themselves: it is the rare Windows application that does not use them as part of its user interface. In addition, message boxes can be handy as ad-hoc debugging tools, deployed during the development process but not making it into the final application.

You can create a surprising variety of message boxes using the .NET Framework. As you'll see, the syntax used to create them is easy to use and flexible.

In this chapter you'll also learn how to use some VB .NET programming statements, notably the If statement, in combination with some new Windows form controls: radio buttons and check boxes. You can't get very far in programming without using conditional statements, and the If statement is the most important one. I tie these seemingly disparate strands together by showing you how to build an application that displays most of the available message box variants and evaluates the user's response (in other words, determines which button in the message box the user clicked).

The MessageBox Class

The MessageBox class, which itself is a member of System.Windows.Forms, is used to create message boxes. Specifically, the class's Show method is used to display all message box variants.

The Show method is shared, meaning you don't need to (and cannot) instantiate an object based on the MessageBox class to use the MessageBox.Show method. (See Chapter 3, "Working with Classes," for more information about shared members.) The various overloaded versions of the Show method account for the possible variants of message boxes that you can display, such as a message box that displays text, a caption, and a button (but no icon). In essence, each overloaded version represents a message box variant.

At minimum, the Show method needs to be supplied a text string for display (although the string can be empty, resulting in a message box with no display text). For example, here's how to create a message box that displays text:

```
MessageBox.Show _
   ("This displays a message!")
```

However, you can also use an overloaded version of the MessageBox.Show method to return a value, usually the user's choice of buttons displayed by the message box. (In the overloaded versions of the Show method that return a value, Show is, of course, internally coded as a function, which returns a value, rather than as a procedure, which does not.)

The MsgBox Statement

If you are a VB6 programmer, you are probably quite familiar with the VB6 analog to the MessageBox.Show method: the MsgBox statement. This statement has been retained in Visual Basic .NET for reasons of backward compatibility, and you can still use it just as you would in prior versions of VB. However, there is no good reason to do so, and MsgBox is considerably less elegant syntactically than MessageBox.Show. Probably the better approach, therefore, is to review the material in this chapter and switch to the .NET syntax, which uses the Show method of the MessageBox class.

Here is an example that shows the use of a message box that is intended to return a value:

```
Dim answer As DialogResult
answer = MessageBox.Show _
   ("I return a value!")
```

Later in this chapter, you'll see how to add the buttons to the message box that are used to send a response value to the DialogResult variable, and how to evaluate the response.

Putting a message box together

In addition to a possible return value, the MessageBox.Show method has six possible parts, also called *arguments*. The first four arguments—Text, Caption, Buttons, and Icon—are the most commonly used. The text that is supplied as the Text argument appears within the message box, the Caption `argument` appears in the caption bar, the Buttons argument determines which buttons will be displayed, and the Icon argument determines the icon. As noted earlier, only the first of these, the Text argument, is actually required, and it is quite common to display a message box with text and no other distinctive characteristics.

The general syntax for the Show method is

```
DialogResult = MessageBox.Show (Text, _
    Caption, Buttons, Icon, _
    DefaultButton, Options)
```

To use the MessageBox.Show method to display a message box without returning a value, just use it in a statement without an equal sign:

```
MessageBox.Show (Text, Caption, _
   Buttons, Icon, DefaultButton, _
   Options)
```

Here's the meaning of the arguments, which must be entered in the following order and separated by commas:

- Text contains the text that will be displayed in the message box. The contents of a variable in the Text position must evaluate to a string, meaning that the variable must be alphanumeric. One approach to supplying the text value is to use string literals. To create a string literal, enclose an alphanumeric sequence in quotation marks, like this: `"This is a text string!"`
- Caption, which is optional, contains the text that will go in the caption bar of the message box. Like the Text argument, the Caption argument must be of type string.
- Buttons, which is optional, tells VB .NET which buttons will be displayed. This argument is an enumeration constant of type MessageBoxButtons.
- Icon, which is optional, tells VB .NET which icon will be displayed. This argument is an enumeration constant of type MessageBoxIcon.
- DefaultButton, which is optional, tells VB .NET which button is activated by default (when the user presses the Enter key). This argument is an enumeration constant of type MessageBoxDefaultButton.
- Options, which is optional, allows you to select some special options for the message box. For instance, you can make the text right-aligned, specifying a right-to-left reading order, or add an item, called a *service notification*, to the System log. This argument is an enumeration constant of type MessageBoxOptions.

In each case, the Code Editor's auto-completion features will show you the list of possible values (that is, the enumeration constants) for each of these settings, so you don't need to memorize them. In addition, so that you can easily see them all in one place, **Table 7.1** lists the possible MessageBoxButtons values. and **Table 7.2** lists the available MessageBoxIcon values.

You will also need to know the possible return values for the MessageBox.Show method (provided you've used an overloaded version of it that returns a value). In other words, what are the possible values of type DialogResult? **Table 7.3** lists these enumeration constants.

Table 7.1

MessageBoxButtons Values

Enumeration constants	Meaning
MessageBoxButtons.AbortRetryIgnore	Displays Abort, Retry, and Ignore buttons.
MessageBoxButtons.OK	Displays an OK button only.
MessageBoxButtons.OKCancel	Displays OK and Cancel buttons.
MessageBoxButtons.RetryCancel	Displays Retry and Cancel buttons.
MessageBoxButtons.YesNo	Displays Yes and No buttons.
MessageBoxButtons.YesNoCancel	Displays Yes, No, and Cancel buttons.

Table 7.2

MessageBoxIcon Values

Enumeration constants	Meaning
MessageBoxIcon.Asterisk	Displays an information icon.
MessageBoxIcon.Error	Displays an error icon.
MessageBoxIcon.Exclamation	Displays an exclamation icon.
MessageBoxIcon.Hand	Displays an error icon.
MessageBoxIcon.Information	Displays an information icon.
MessageBoxIcon.None	Does not display an icon.
MessageBoxIcon.Question	Displays a question icon.
MessageBoxIcon.Stop	Displays an error icon.
MessageBoxIcon.Warning	Displays an exclamation icon.

Table 7.3

DialogResult Values

Enumeration Constants	Meaning
DialogResult.Abort	Abort button was clicked.
DialogResult.Cancel	Cancel button was clicked.
DialogResult.Ignore	Ignore button was clicked.
DialogResult.No	No button was clicked.
DialogResult.None	None of the buttons were clicked.
DialogResult.OK	OK button was clicked.
DialogResult.Retry	Retry button was clicked.
DialogResult.Yes	Yes button was clicked.

Visual Basic Comments

Comments, which the compiler ignores, are an important means of documenting your code, or adding notes to your programs. Any time something is likely to be unclear to a reader of your code, or to you after some time has elapsed, you should add a comment.

Since some of the examples in this chapter include comments, this is a good place to explain the rules that apply to comments.

In VB .NET, the usual way to add a comment to code is to enter a single quotation mark (') to denote the beginning of the comment. `REM`, followed by a space also works, although this is an older syntax going back to the roots of Basic, and it is better practice to use a single quotation mark. (If you are interested, `REM` is short for Remark.)

If a line starts with a single quotation mark (or `REM`), then the entire line is a comment (and the compiler does not process it).

To enhance readability, it's good practice to place at least one space after the comment marker and before the comment itself, though this isn't required.

Here are some examples of comments:

```
' Comments are good!
REM Comments are fine!
i = 42 ' This comment is mine!
```

A very nice feature of the VB .NET Code Editor allows you to comment and uncomment selected blocks of code. You can access this facility by selecting multiple code statements in the Code Editor and then choosing Edit > Advanced and selecting Comment Selection or Uncomment Selection.

Message box examples

To give you a better understanding of the practicalities of using the Show method, we'll create some message boxes that use the MessageBox.Show method.

By the time you've completed the tasks in this section, you will have learned about most of the significant aspects of creating message boxes. I've combined these examples into one application where clicking a different button launches each message box.

We'll start with one of the simplest message boxes: one that merely displays text and a caption. For this first message box, we'll also look at the details of setting up the button that invokes it.

To add a button to the form:

1. Open a new Windows Application project.
2. With a Windows form open in its designer, select Toolbox from the View menu to open the Toolbox (**Figure 7.1**).
3. Drag and drop a Button control from the Toolbox onto the form (or double-click the control in the Toolbox to add it to the form).

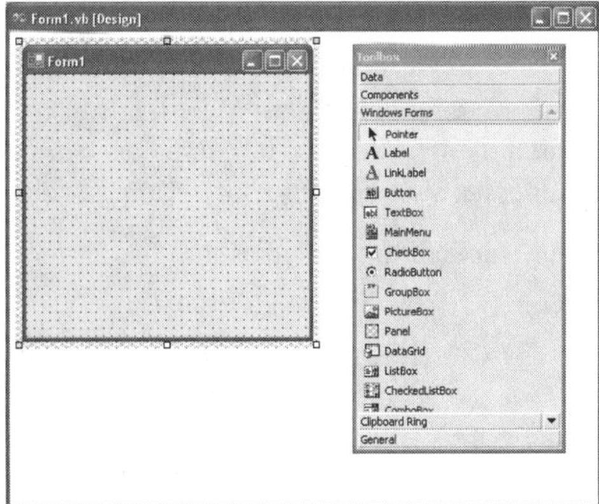

Figure 7.1 You can use the Toolbox to add a button to the form.

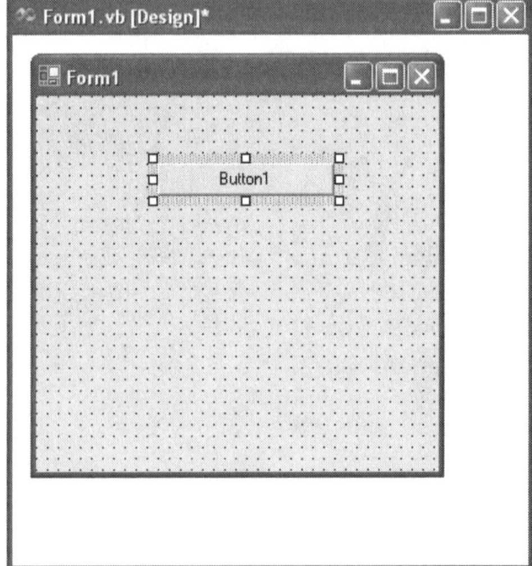

Figure 7.2 You'll see the Button control positioned on the form.

Figure 7.3 It's a good idea to use the Properties window to change the name of each control to something that makes clear what the control is.

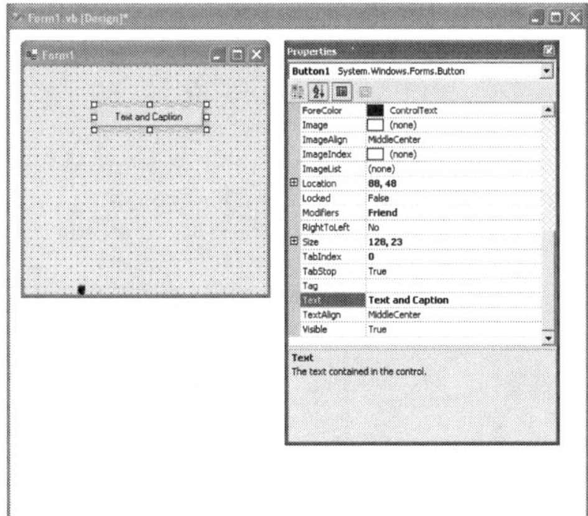

Figure 7.4 Use the Properties window to set the Text property of the button.

To set the button's Name and Text properties:

1. Select the button on the form (**Figure 7.2**).
2. Choose Properties Window from the View window to open the Properties window.
3. With the button still selected, choose Name in the left column of the Properties window (**Figure 7.3**).
4. In the right column of the Properties window, set the Name property to `btnTextandCaption`.
5. In the left column of the Properties window, select Text.
6. In the right column of the Properties window, set the Text property to `Text and Caption` (**Figure 7.4**).

Look at the top button in **Figure 7.5**; this is the way the button will look when the application is run. Figure 7.5 also shows the way the application that is used to demonstrate message boxes in this section will appear when it is complete (one button is used to display each message box variation).

To add a click event handler to the button:

- Double-click the button to open the Code Editor and create a click event procedure (**Figure 7.6**).

  or

1. Open the Code Editor.
2. Select the button from the Objects list (**Figure 7.7**).
3. Choose Click from the Procedures list (**Figure 7.8**).

   The click event procedure framework is created in the Code Editor (**Figure 7.9**).

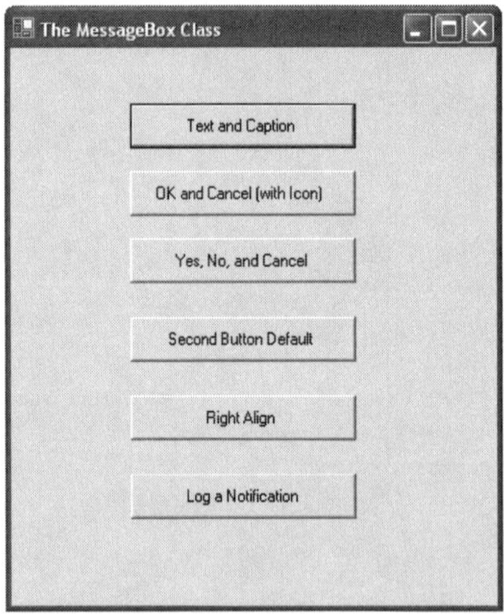

Figure 7.5 When the interface for the application explained in this section (used to demonstrate message box syntax) is complete with all six buttons, it will look like this.

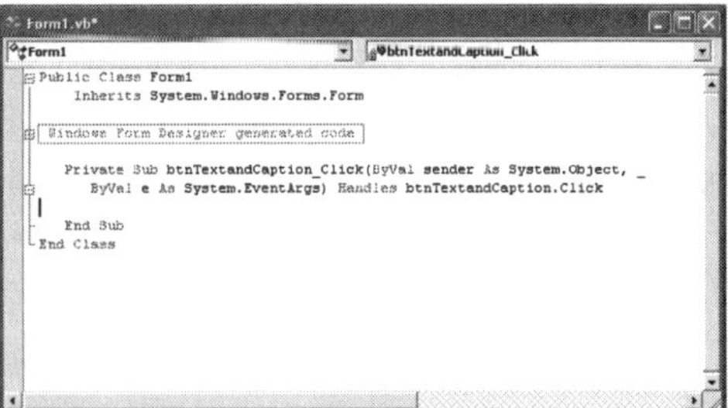

Figure 7.6 When you double-click the button, a click event handler is created in the Code Editor.

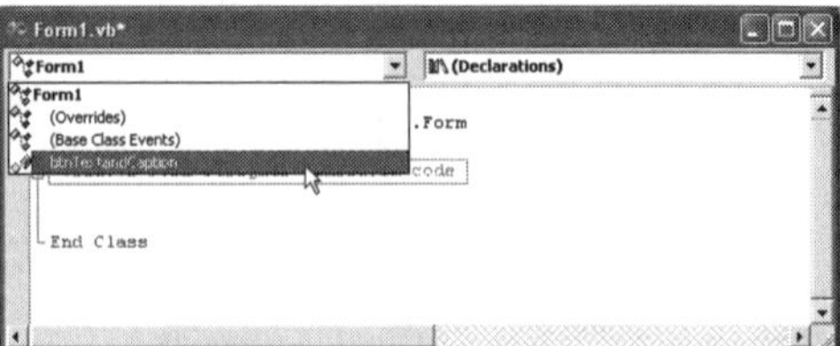

Figure 7.7 To create a click event procedure within the Code Editor, first select the object that will be firing the event from the Objects list.

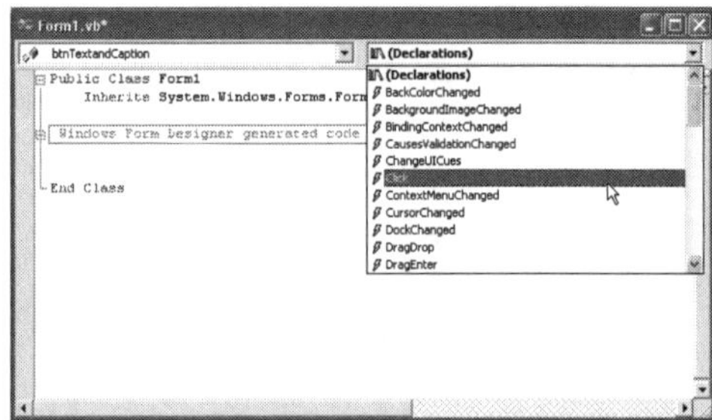

Figure 7.8 With the object selected, choose the desired event procedure from the Procedures list.

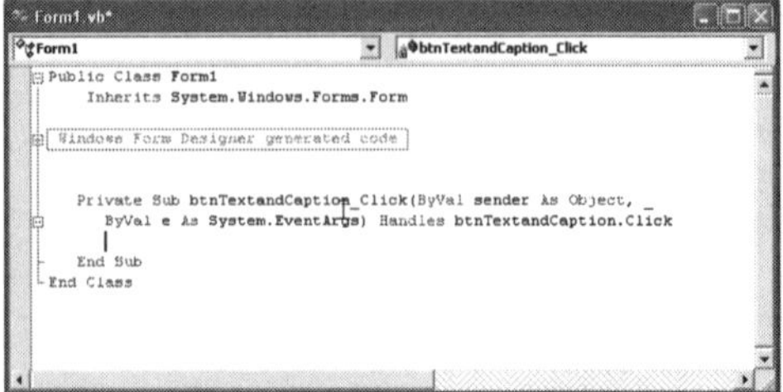

Figure 7.9 A click event procedure can be generated using the drop-down lists in the Code Editor.

```
Private Sub btnTextandCaption_Click(ByVal sender As Object, _
    ByVal e As System.EventArgs) Handles btnTextandCaption.Click
    MessageBox.Show |
1 of 12  Show (text As String, caption As String, buttons As System.Windows.Forms.MessageBoxButtons, icon As
         options As System.Windows.Forms.MessageBoxOptions) As System.Windows.Forms.DialogResult
text: The text to display in the message box.
```

Figure 7.10 As you start to type the Show method in the Code Editor, the syntax of the possible method overloads is displayed.

```
    MessageBox.Show("This is the text!",
1 of 12  Show (text As String, caption As String, buttons As System.V
         options As System.Windows.Forms.MessageBoxOptions)
caption: The text to display in the title bar of the message box.
```

Figure 7.11 As you proceed through the Show method, the type of each argument is described in the Code Editor.

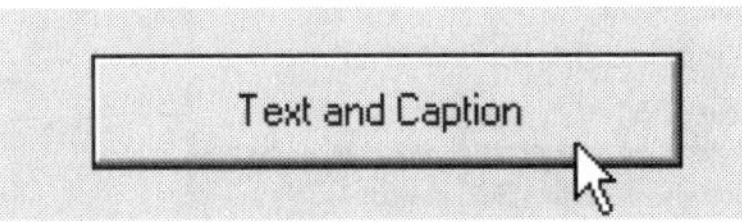

Figure 7.12 To view the message box, click the Text and Caption button.

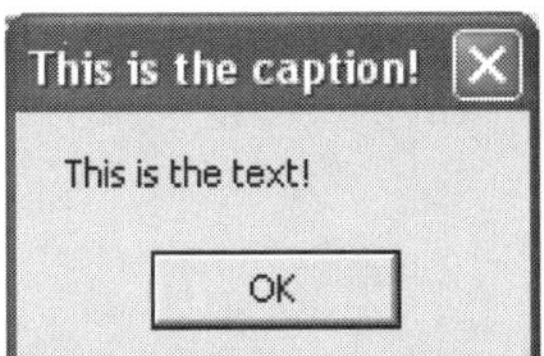

Figure 7.13 If only the text and caption are specified, the message box also displays an OK button.

To display text and a caption in a message box:

1. In the Code Editor, within the event handler framework, create a MessageBox.Show statement. As you start entering the statement, the Code Editor will show you the overloads for the method and the type required for each argument (**Figure 7.10** and **Figure 7.11**).

2. Enter a Text and Caption text string argument for the Show method.

   The click event handler now looks like this:

   ```
   Private Sub btnTextandCaption_Click _
      (ByVal sender As Object, ByVal _
      e As System.EventArgs) Handles _
      btnTextandCaption.Click
      MessageBox.Show _
         ("This is the text!", _
         "This is the caption!")
   End Sub
   ```

3. Run the project.

4. Click Text and Caption (**Figure 7.12**).

   The message box displaying the Text and Caption opens (**Figure 7.13**).

✔ Tip

- If you end the Show method before specifying a MessageBoxButtons value, the message box will have an OK button (as you can see in Figure 7.13).

You can add a little bit in the way of social graces to your message box by including a Cancel button (dubbed by some wags as a "Not OK" button). Displaying an icon in the message box also adds that certain decorative savoir faire.

To display OK and Cancel buttons and an icon:

1. Add a button named *btnOKIconCancel* to the form.
2. Create a click event handler for the button.
3. Within the click event handler, start a MessageBox.Show method with a text string for the Text value (`Press OK to continue, Cancel to escape!`), and another text string for the Caption value (`Do you want to continue?`).
4. After entering the Caption string, enter a comma (`,`).

   The Code Editor supplies a drop-down list of MessageBoxButtons values (**Figure 7.14**).
5. Select MessageBoxButtons.OKCancel from the drop-down list.
6. Enter a comma (`,`).

   The Code Editor supplies a drop-down list of MessageBoxIcon values (**Figure 7.15**).

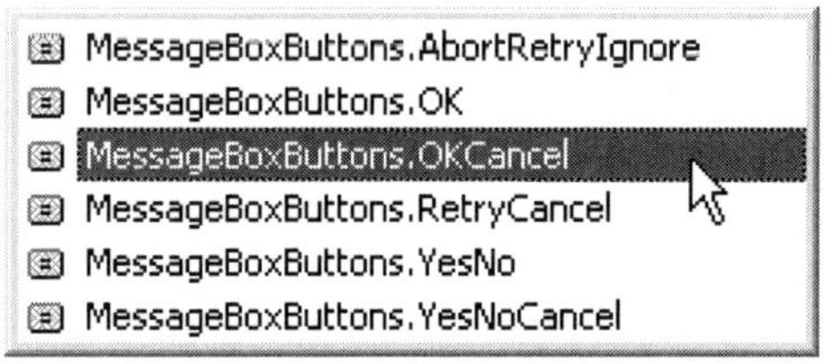

MessageBoxButtons.AbortRetryIgnore
MessageBoxButtons.OK
MessageBoxButtons.OKCancel
MessageBoxButtons.RetryCancel
MessageBoxButtons.YesNo
MessageBoxButtons.YesNoCancel

Figure 7.14 Auto-completion in the Code Editor displays the possible enumeration values for the buttons parameter.

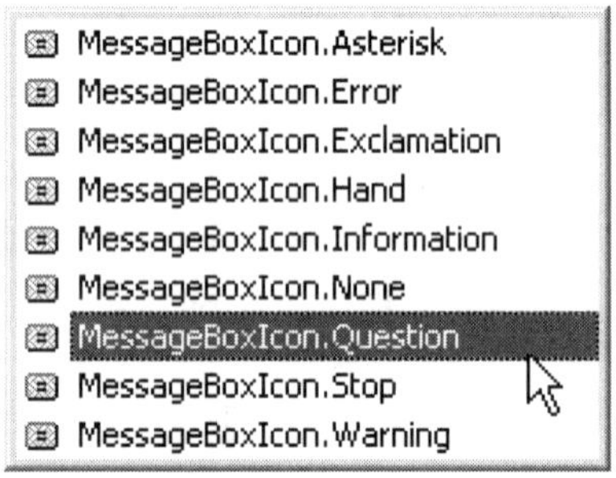

MessageBoxIcon.Asterisk
MessageBoxIcon.Error
MessageBoxIcon.Exclamation
MessageBoxIcon.Hand
MessageBoxIcon.Information
MessageBoxIcon.None
MessageBoxIcon.Question
MessageBoxIcon.Stop
MessageBoxIcon.Warning

Figure 7.15 The available icons are displayed in a drop-down list.

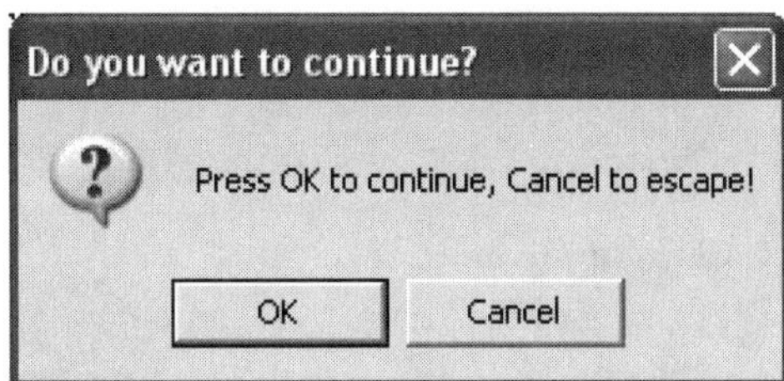

Figure 7.16 The message box displays OK and Cancel buttons, as well as the icon specified.

7. Select MessageBoxIcon.Question from the drop-down list.

   Here's the click event procedure as it now stands:

   ```
   Private Sub _
      btnOKIconCancel_Click(ByVal _
      sender As Object, ByVal e As _
      System.EventArgs) Handles _
      btnOKIconCancel.Click
      MessageBox.Show _
         ("Press OK to continue," & _
          "Cancel to escape!", _
         "Do you want to continue?", _
         MessageBoxButtons.OKCancel, _
         MessageBoxIcon.Question)
   End Sub
   ```

8. Run the project.
9. Click the OK and Cancel buttons.

   The message box displaying the text, caption, OK and Cancel buttons, and icon selected opens (**Figure 7.16**).

If you do include both OK and Cancel buttons, most likely you'll want to know which button the user clicked. To determine this, you need to slightly modify the code we just used.

To display the button that was clicked:

1. Within the click event procedure shown in the previous task, add a declaration for a variable of type DialogResult that will be used to retrieve the button clicked:

```
Dim answer As DialogResult
```

2. Revise the Show method statement so that it returns a value:

```
answer = MessageBox.Show _
   ("Press OK to continue," & _
   "Cancel to escape!", _
   "Do you want to continue?", _
   MessageBoxButtons.OKCancel, _
   MessageBoxIcon.Question)
```

3. Add a statement that shows a second message box with the user's button choice, using the ToString method to display the value of the DialogResult variable:

```
MessageBox.Show("You clicked " _
   & answer.ToString())
```

Here's how the click event procedure as modified now stands:

```
Private Sub _
   btnOKIconCancel_Click(ByVal _
   sender As Object, ByVal e As _
   System.EventArgs) Handles _
   btnOKIconCancel.Click
   Dim answer As DialogResult
   answer = MessageBox.Show _
      ("Press OK to continue," & _
      "Cancel to escape!", _
      "Do you want to continue?", _
      MessageBoxButtons.OKCancel, _
      MessageBoxIcon.Question)
   MessageBox.Show("You clicked " _
      & answer.ToString())
End Sub
```

4. Run the project.
5. Click the OK and Cancel buttons.

   The message box shown in Figure 7.16 opens.
6. Click OK.

   The message box closes, and a new message box showing that you clicked OK opens (**Figure 7.17**).

Now let's move on to a message box that displays Yes, No, and Cancel buttons. For this example, we'll start by returning a value from the Show method, because what is the point of having three buttons if you can't do something based upon which button was clicked?

To display Yes, No, and Cancel buttons:

1. Add a button named *btnYesNoCancel* to the form.
2. Create a click event handler for the button.
3. Within the click event handler, add a declaration for a variable of type DialogResult that will be used to retrieve the button clicked:

```
Dim answer As DialogResult
```

4. Start an answer = MessageBox.Show method call with a text string for the Text value (`Press Yes for the Snitch, No for a Bludger, and Cancel for the Quaffle!`), and another text string for the Caption value (`Which Quidditch ball is it?`).
5. After entering the Caption string, enter a comma (`,`).

   The Code Editor will supply a drop-down list of MessageBoxButtons values (**Figure 7.18**).

Figure 7.17 You can display the button clicked by the user.

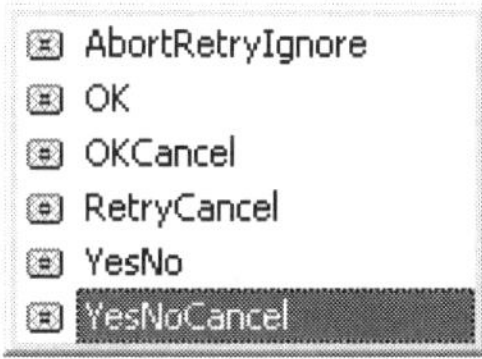

Figure 7.18 The Code Editor displays the button enumeration constant values.

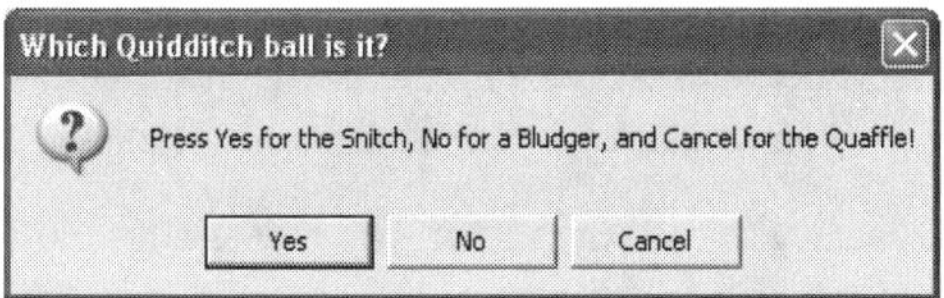

Figure 7.19 The message box displays Yes, No, and Cancel buttons as well as the specified icon.

6. Select MessageBoxButtons.YesNoCancel from the drop-down list.
7. Enter a comma (,).
   The Code Editor will supply a drop-down list of MessageBoxIcon values.
8. Select MessageBoxIcon.Question from the drop-down list.
   The code as it now stands looks like this:

```
Private Sub btnYesNoCancel_Click _
   (ByVal sender As Object, _
   ByVal e As System.EventArgs) _
   Handles btnYesNoCancel.Click
   Dim answer As DialogResult
   answer = MessageBox.Show _
     ("Press Yes for the Snitch," & _
     " No for a Bludger," & _
     " and Cancel for the Quaffle!", _
     "Which Quidditch ball is it?", _
     MessageBoxButtons.YesNoCancel, _
     MessageBoxIcon.Question)
End Sub
```

9. Run the project.
10. Click the Yes, No, and Cancel buttons.
    The message box opens (**Figure 7.19**).

With this code, when the user clicks a button, the value, expressed as a DialogResult enumeration constant, is stored in the variable answer. Earlier in the chapter, you saw how to display a text string representing the button that the user clicked. Now we'll go a step further and do something if the user clicks a particular button: We'll display another message box if the user clicks Yes. The point here is not that this is an important action, but rather that evaluating the choice is a step beyond merely displaying a string representation of the choice.

To do something with the user's choice:

1. Starting with the code explained in "To display Yes, No, and Cancel buttons" earlier in this chapter, after the Show method statement, add an If statement that evaluates the contents of the answer variable using the ToString method:
   ```
   If (answer.ToString() = "Yes") Then

   End If
   ```
2. Within the If statement, add code that displays another message box:
   ```
   If (answer.ToString() = "Yes") Then
      MessageBox.Show _
      ("Lucky you got the Golden Snitch!")
   End If
   ```
   Here's the click event code as it now stands:
   ```
   Private Sub btnYesNoCancel_Click _
      (ByVal sender As Object, _
      ByVal e As System.EventArgs) _
      Handles btnYesNoCancel.Click
      Dim answer As DialogResult
      answer = MessageBox.Show _
        ("Press Yes for the Snitch," & _
        " No for a Bludger," & _
        " and Cancel for the Quaffle!", _
        "Which Quidditch ball is it?", _
        MessageBoxButtons.YesNoCancel, _
        MessageBoxIcon.Question)
     If (answer.ToString() = "Yes") Then
         MessageBox.Show _
   ("Lucky you got the Golden Snitch!")
     End If
   End Sub
   ```
3. Run the project.
4. Click the Yes, No, and Cancel buttons.
   The message box shown in Figure 7.19 opens.
5. Click Yes.
   The message box closes, and the new message box indicating that the Yes button was clicked opens (**Figure 7.20**).

Normally, the first button in a message box (reading left to right) is the default button, meaning that it is preselected when the message box opens, and that it is the button deemed selected when the user presses the Enter key rather than clicking a button.

It is easy to set any button you like as the default button (that is, of the one, two, or three buttons available in any given message box).

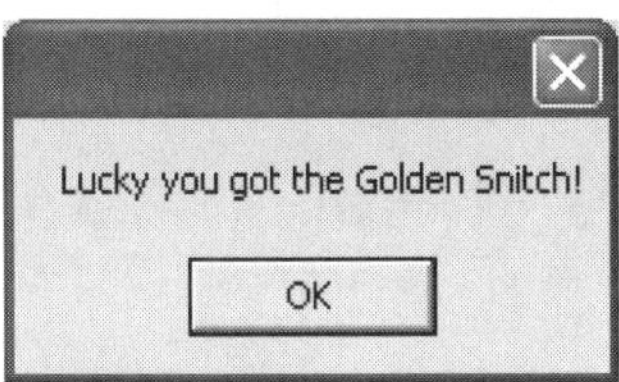

Figure 7.20 You can use the DialogResult variable to take appropriate action based on the user's choice.

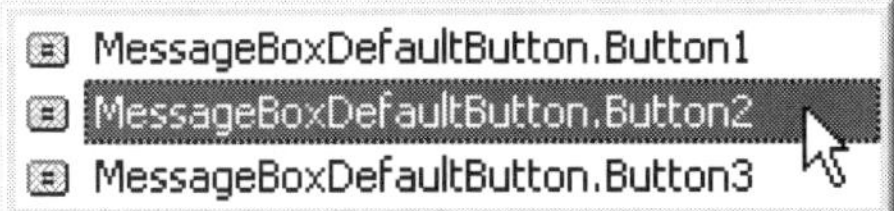

Figure 7.21 The Code Editor displays the default button enumeration values.

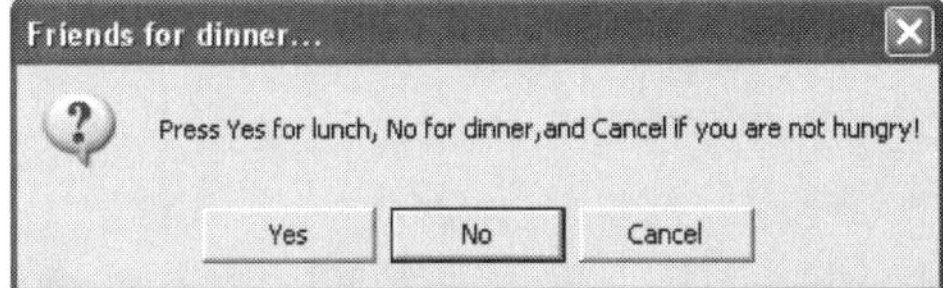

Figure 7.22 When the message box opens, the second button (No) is selected.

To set the second button as the default:

1. Within a Button click event, use the MessageBox.Show method to display Text, Caption, MessageBoxButtons, and MessageBoxIcon values.
2. After inserting the MessageBoxIcon value, select the second button by choosing the enumeration constant MessageBoxDefaultButton.Button2 from the drop-down list (**Figure 7.21**).

   The code now looks like this:

```
Private Sub btnSecond_Click(ByVal _
   sender As Object, ByVal e As _
   System.EventArgs) Handles _
   btnSecond.Click
   Dim answer As DialogResult
   MessageBox.Show("Press Yes " & _
     "for lunch, No for dinner," & _
     "and Cancel if you are not " & _
     " hungry!", _
     "Friends for dinner...", _
     MessageBoxButtons.YesNoCancel, _
     MessageBoxIcon.Question, _
     MessageBoxDefaultButton.Button2)
End Sub
```

3. Run the project.
4. Click the button to display the message box.
5. Verify that the second button is the default (you can see that it is initially selected in **Figure 7.22**).

I'm not entirely sure why you would want to right-align the text in a message box. It may be no more than a good way to get a bit of extra attention for your message boxes. But it is easy enough to do. I'll use the process of right-aligning a message box to show you how to do something else that is probably more useful: create a string that contains line breaks.

To create a string that contains line breaks:

1. Declare a string variable:

   ```
   Dim msg As String
   ```

2. Use the concatenation operator (&) and the VB .NET control character constant CrLf, ControlChars.CrLf, which places a carriage-return character followed by a line-feed character in a string, to build a string that contains line breaks:

   ```
   msg = "Right" & _
      ControlChars.CrLf & _
      "Does" & ControlChars.CrLf & _
      "Not" & ControlChars.CrLf & _
      "Make" & ControlChars.CrLf & _
      "Might!"
   ```

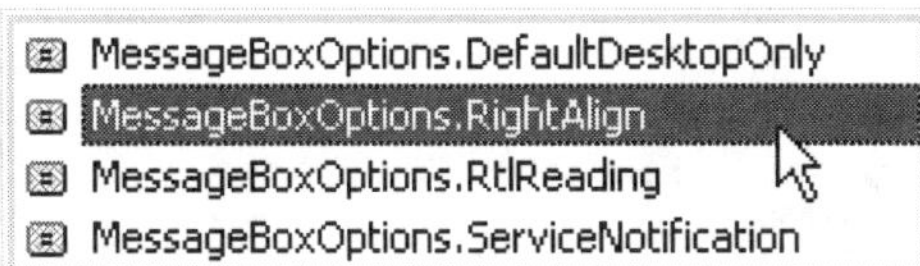

Figure 7.23 The Code Editor displays the message box options enumeration constants.

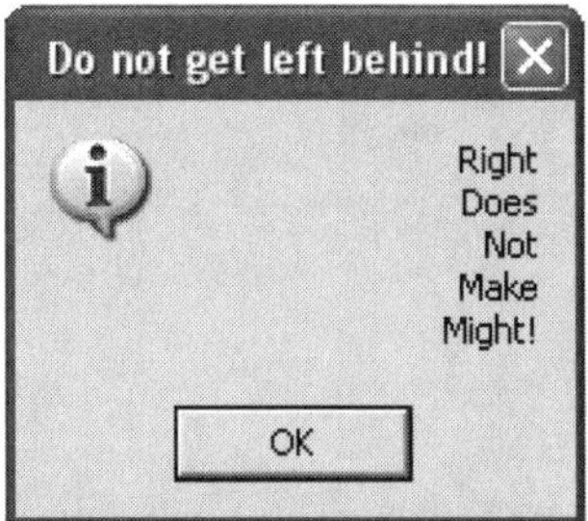

Figure 7.24 Text in the message box is aligned along its right side.

To right-align the text in a message box:

1. Within a Button click event, use the MessageBox.Show method to display Text, Caption, MessageBoxButtons, MessageBoxIcon, and MessageBox-DefaultButton values. For Text, use the string containing line breaks explained in "To create a string that contains line breaks" earlier in this chapter.
2. After inserting the MessageBoxDefault-Button value, select the right-alignment option by choosing the enumeration constant MessageBoxOptions.RightAlign from the drop-down list (**Figure 7.23**).

   The code now looks like this:

```
Private Sub btnRightAlign_Click _
    (ByVal sender As System.Object, _
    ByVal e As System.EventArgs) _
    Handles btnRightAlign.Click
    Dim msg As String
    msg = "Right" & ControlChars.CrLf & _
    "Does" & ControlChars.CrLf & _
    "Not" & ControlChars.CrLf & _
    "Make" & ControlChars.CrLf & _
    "Might!"
MessageBox.Show(msg, _
    "Do not get left behind!", _
    MessageBoxButtons.OK, _
    MessageBoxIcon.Information, _
    MessageBoxDefaultButton.Button1, _
    MessageBoxOptions.RightAlign)
End Sub
```

3. Run the project.
4. Click the button to view the message box.

   The text is aligned along the right and contains line breaks in the positions determined by the CrLf constant (**Figure 7.24**).

Service notifications are important for a number of reasons. They are used to create log entries that cannot easily be modified by users. These logs can be used for security purposes (they create an audit trail) or for diagnostic purposes.

There are more elegant and flexible ways to create a service notification in VB .NET than by using a MessageBox.Show statement, but using a message box statement to write an item to the System log is extremely easy and perfectly effective.

To log a service notification:

1. Create a MessageBox.Show statement.
2. For the options argument (the last argument in the statement) select the ServiceNotification constant (see **Figure 7.25**).

   The code invoking the Show method might look like this:

   ```
   Private Sub btnLog_Click(ByVal _
   sender As System.Object, _
   ByVal e As System.EventArgs) _
   Handles btnLog.Click
   MessageBox.Show _
   ("Report condition red!", _
   "Go to Level 3!", _
   MessageBoxButtons.OK, _
   MessageBoxIcon.Information, _
   MessageBoxDefaultButton.
   Button1, _
   MessageBoxOptions.ServiceNotification)
   End Sub
   ```
3. Run the project.
4. Click the button to show the message box.

   A normal-looking message box is displayed (**Figure 7.26**).

Figure 7.25 If the ServiceNotification option is selected, a System log notification is written when the message box is displayed.

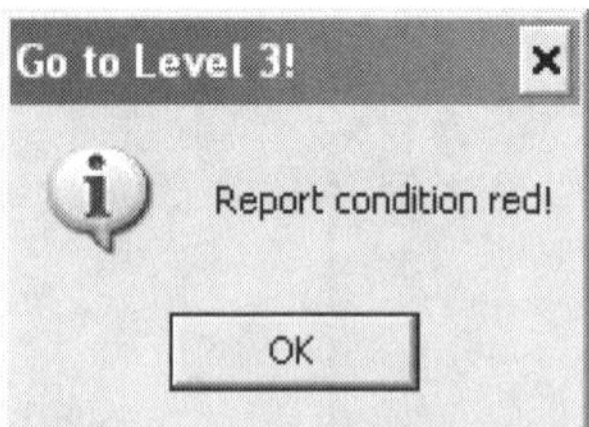

Figure 7.26 The message box is displayed normally.

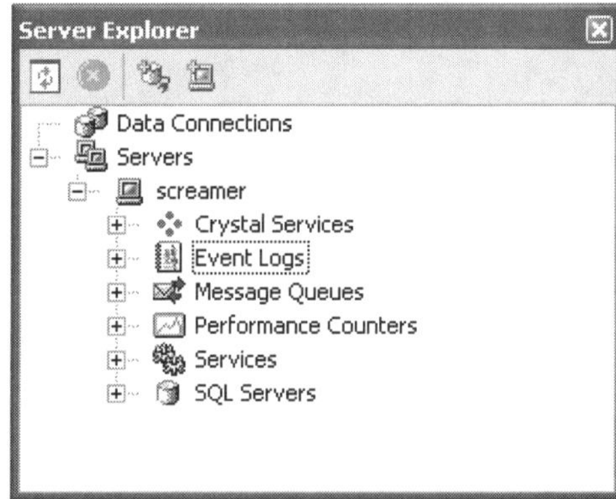

Figure 7.27 Server Explorer includes an Event Logs category.

THE MESSAGEBOX CLASS

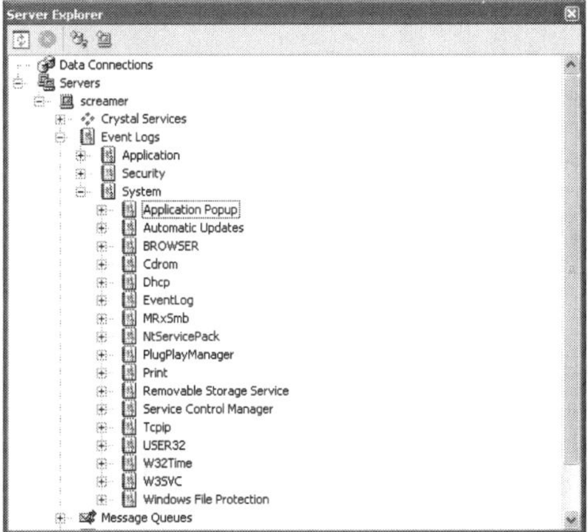

Figure 7.28 You'll find the service notification within the Application Popup folder (which is a System notification).

Figure 7.29 Each time the message box opens, it writes an entry to the log.

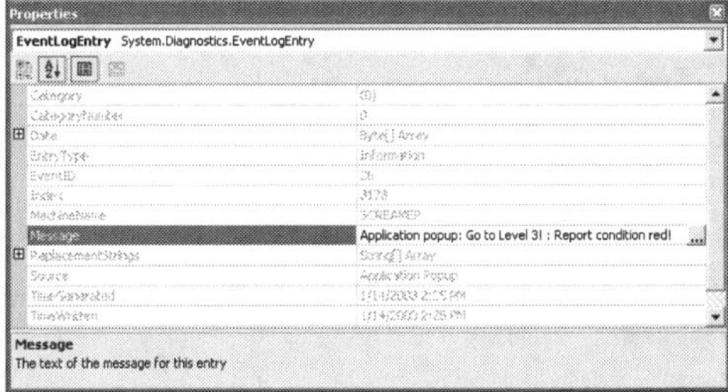

Figure 7.30 You can use the Properties dialog for the service notification to view the text and caption of the message box.

There is no indication from just looking at the message box shown in Figure 7.26 that it has actually created a service notification (which means writing a log entry), so we had better verify that it has.

To read the entry created by a notification in the System log:

1. Choose Server Explorer from the View menu.

   Server Explorer opens (**Figure 7.27**).

2. Expand the nodes of the active server until you see an Event Logs node like that shown in Figure 7.27.

3. Expand the Event Logs node until you see a System node (**Figure 7.28**).

4. Expand the System node shown in Figure 7.28 to view the Application Popup node.

5. Expand the Application Popup node to see the items that have been written to this portion of the System log (**Figure 7.29**).

6. Locate the entry written by the message box statement.

   You can probably determine this by looking at the time in which the entries were written. (In addition, the first characters of the item text, corresponding to the Text argument of the Show message, appear in this list of entries.)

7. Right-click the entry and select Properties from its context menu.

   The Properties page for the log entry shows the full Text and Caption arguments of the message box (**Figure 7.30**).

You can also view entries written to the System logs using Event Viewer, which is one of the administrative tools that ships with Windows XP. (To do this, you will, of course, need appropriate permissions and server access.)

To use Event Viewer to verify the service notification:

1. From the Windows Control Panel, double-click Administrative Tools to open the Administrative Tools applet (**Figure 7.31**).
2. Double-click Event Viewer.
   The Event Viewer opens (**Figure 7.32**).
3. In Event Viewer, expand the System folder.
4. In the System pane, locate the service notification.
5. Right-click the service notification entry and select Properties from its context menu to view log entry details (**Figure 7.33**).

As the tasks and examples in this section have shown, you can do a great deal with the lowly message box. **Listing 7.1** shows the complete code for the click event procedures developed in this section.

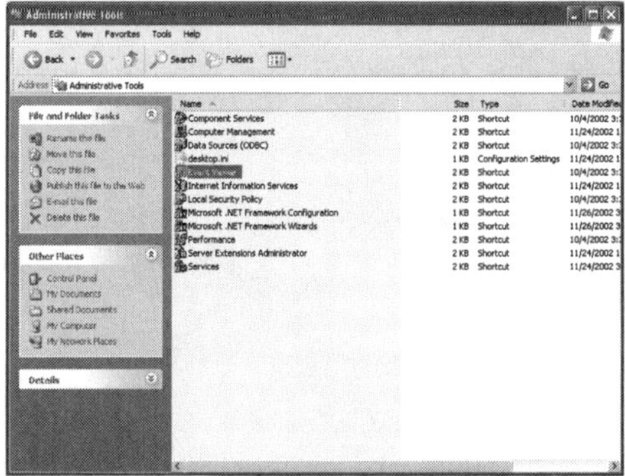

Figure 7.31 The Administrative Tools applet lets you open Event Viewer.

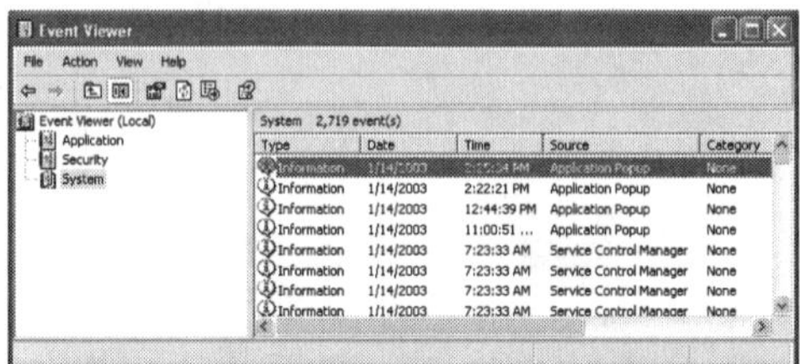

Figure 7.32 Within Event Viewer, each System notification appears on a single line.

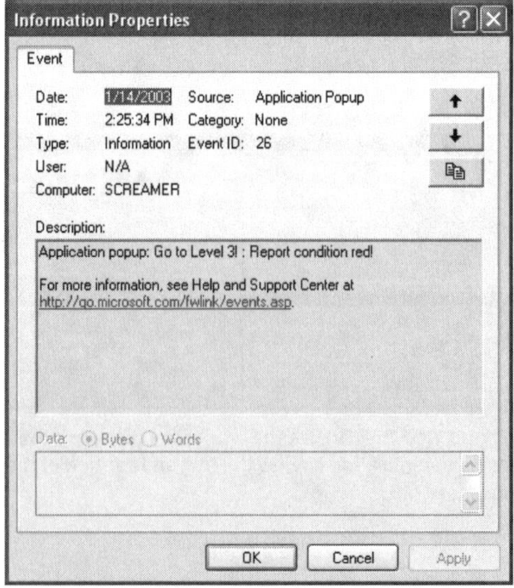

Figure 7.33 Once again, the Properties dialog for the System notification displays the message box text and caption.

Listing 7.1 Demonstration of various ways to use the MessageBox.Show method.

```
Public Class Form1
    Inherits System.Windows.Forms.Form
...
Private Sub btnTextandCaption_Click(ByVal sender As Object, ByVal e As System.EventArgs) _
   Handles btnTextandCaption.Click
   MessageBox.Show("This is the text!", "This is the caption!")
End Sub

Private Sub btnOKIconCancel_Click(ByVal sender As Object, ByVal e As System.EventArgs) _
   Handles btnOKIconCancel.Click
   Dim answer As DialogResult
   answer = MessageBox.Show("Press OK to continue, Cancel to escape!", _
      "Do you want to continue?", MessageBoxButtons.OKCancel, MessageBoxIcon.Question)
   MessageBox.Show("You clicked " & answer.ToString())
End Sub

Private Sub btnYesNoCancel_Click(ByVal sender As Object, ByVal e As System.EventArgs) _
   Handles btnYesNoCancel.Click
   Dim answer As DialogResult
   answer = MessageBox.Show("Press Yes for the Snitch, No for a Bludger," & _
      " and Cancel for the Quaffle!", "Which Quidditch ball is it?", _
      MessageBoxButtons.YesNoCancel, MessageBoxIcon.Question)
   If (answer.ToString() = "Yes") Then
      MessageBox.Show("Lucky you got the Golden Snitch!")
   End If
End Sub

Private Sub btnSecond_Click(ByVal sender As Object, ByVal e As System.EventArgs) _
   Handles btnSecond.Click
   Dim answer As DialogResult
   answer = MessageBox.Show("Press Yes for lunch, No for dinner," & _
      "and Cancel if you are not hungry!", "Friends for dinner...", _
      MessageBoxButtons.YesNoCancel, MessageBoxIcon.Question, MessageBoxDefaultButton.Button2)
   MessageBox.Show("You clicked " & answer.ToString())
End Sub

Private Sub btnRightAlign_Click(ByVal sender As System.Object, ByVal e As System.EventArgs) _
   Handles btnRightAlign.Click
   Dim answer As DialogResult
   Dim msg As String
   msg = "Right" & ControlChars.CrLf & "Does" & ControlChars.CrLf & _
      "Not" & ControlChars.CrLf & "Make" & ControlChars.CrLf & "Might!"
      answer = MessageBox.Show(msg, "Do not get left behind!", MessageBoxButtons.OK, _
      MessageBoxIcon.Information, _
      MessageBoxDefaultButton.Button1, MessageBoxOptions.RightAlign)
   MessageBox.Show("You clicked " & answer.ToString())
End Sub

Private Sub btnLog_Click(ByVal sender As System.Object, ByVal e As System.EventArgs) _
   Handles btnLog.Click
   MessageBox.Show("Report condition red!", "Go to Level 3!", MessageBoxButtons.OK, _
      MessageBoxIcon.Information, _
      MessageBoxDefaultButton.Button1, MessageBoxOptions.ServiceNotification)
End Sub
End Class
```

Building a User Interface

With examples of many of the most important kinds of message boxes now under your belt, let's put together an application that lets the user specify the message box options that he or she wants displayed. This will give you an opportunity to review message box concepts and techniques as well as to see how to put together an application.

The application will display the message box text and caption information that the user enters. It will also allow the user to choose the buttons and icon that will be part of the message box. The user can also specify that the message box log a service notification. Finally, the application will evaluate the user response to the message box—which message box button did the user click?

Adding group boxes

The form that serves as the user interface for this project will be divided into four group boxes.

GroupBox controls, along with some other controls, such as Panels, serve to visually organize other controls—the text boxes, radio buttons, and so on that make up the actual user interface. A GroupBox control also lets you add a value, as specified by the control's Text property, that explains what the controls within the group box do.

In addition to providing visual organization, a group box serves as a *container* for the controls that are placed in it. In some important ways, the controls that are placed in a container control function as a single, cohesive group. For example, if you place a bunch of radio buttons in a container such as a group box, automatically only one of them can be selected at any one time (as indicated by the property value `Checked = True`). Pretty cool!

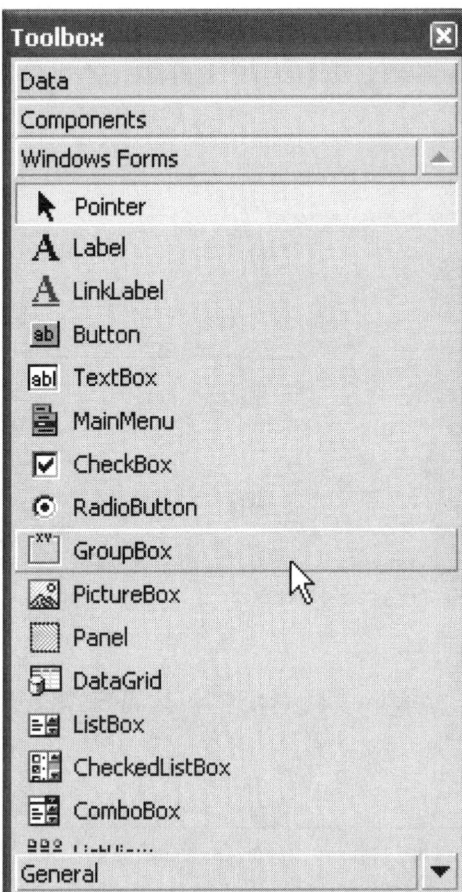

Figure 7.34 You use a GroupBox control to group other controls.

✔ Tips

- GroupBox and Panel controls are more or less functionally interchangeable, except that group boxes allow you to add a line of text at the top, and panels have more visual options.
- GroupBox inherits from the Container class, as does Form itself. You might therefore suspect that a form is also a container, and it is. However, if an application contains multiple groups of controls, you need to divide them into their own containers—otherwise, all of the controls will function as one giant group.

The application we'll build uses four group boxes:

- At the top of the form, for the user to enter the Text and Caption arguments
- In the left center, to accept the user's choice of buttons
- In the right center, to accept the user's choice of icon (this area also includes the CheckBox control used to determine whether this container will include a service notification)
- Along the bottom, to hold the button used to launch the message box display

To add GroupBox controls to a form:

1. Open a new Windows Application project.
2. Open the Windows form in its designer.
3. Choose Toolbox from the View menu to open the Toolbox (**Figure 7.34**).
4. Double-click the GroupBox control shown in Figure 7.34, or drag and drop it, to add an instance of the control to the form.

continues on next page

5. From the View menu, choose Properties Window to open the Properties window.
6. Set the Text property for the GroupBox control.
7. In the left column of the Properties window, select the Dock property.
8. In the right column of the Properties window, click the arrow to open the Dock position selector (**Figure 7.35**).
9. For the first group box, click the top panel in the Dock position selector, as shown in Figure 7.35.

   The group box will now be aligned with the top of the form, as shown in **Figure 7.36**.
10. Repeat the process for each of the other three group boxes, selecting a Dock property of Left, Right, or Bottom as appropriate.

Before setting up the radio button groups, let's add the TextBox controls to the top group box so that users can enter text and caption information for the message box.

To add text boxes to the group box:

1. Drag a TextBox control from the Toolbox onto the group box.
2. Use the Properties window to name the text box instance *txtText*.
3. Use the Properties window to set the text box's Text property to the empty string (**Figure 7.37**).
4. Repeat the process for the Caption text box, naming it *txtCaption*.

✔ Tip

- Be sure to drag the TextBox control onto the group box container, rather than onto the form itself.

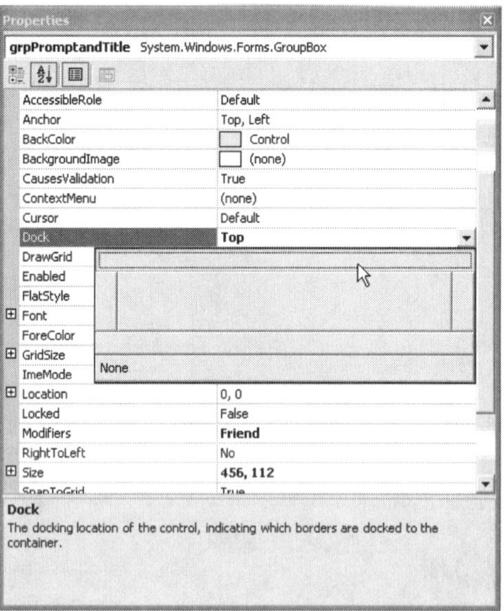

Figure 7.35 If the Dock property of the group box is set to Top, then the group box docks at the top of the control.

Figure 7.36 No matter how you resize the form, the group box remains aligned with its top.

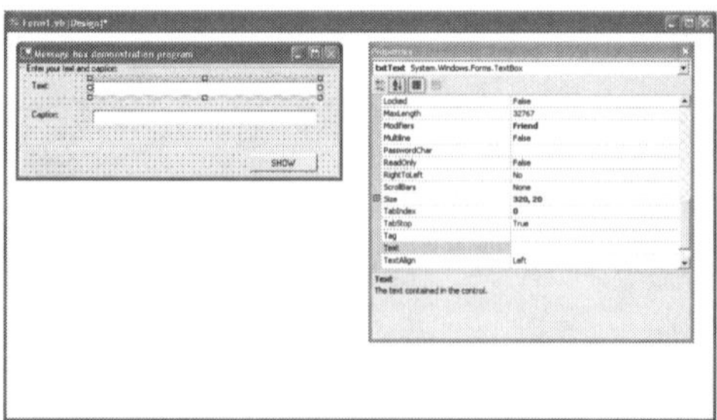

Figure 7.37 Set the text boxes so that their Text properties are empty.

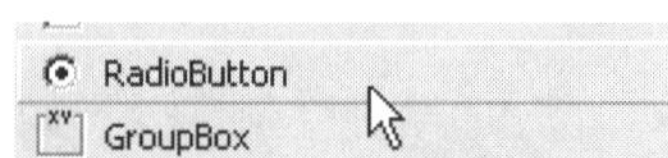

Figure 7.38 You use RadioButton controls when you want the user to make one, and only one, choice.

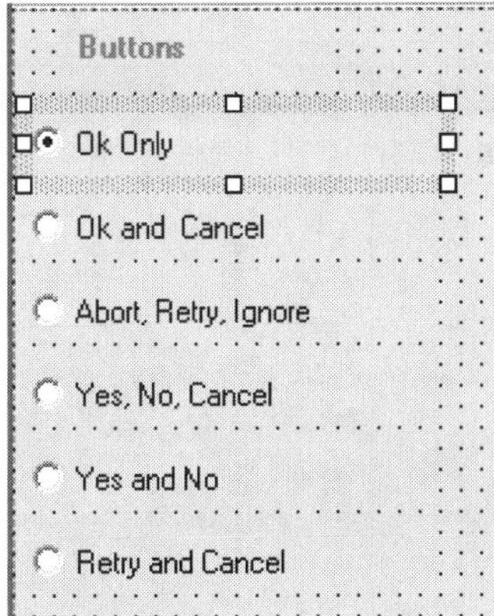

Figure 7.39 Make sure to set the Checked property to True for the first radio button in each group so that this button is initially selected.

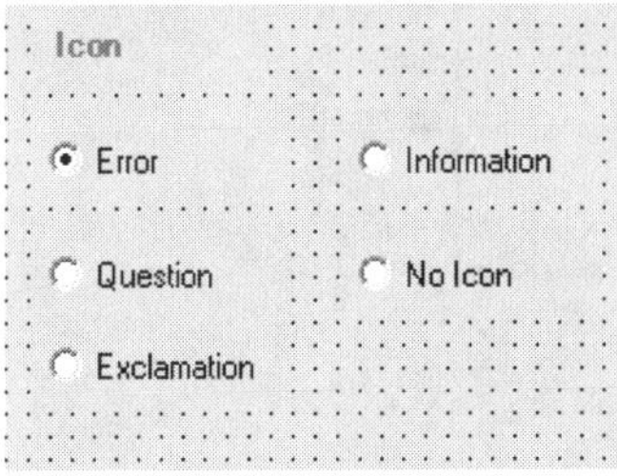

Figure 7.40 The icon choices appear as another group of RadioButton controls.

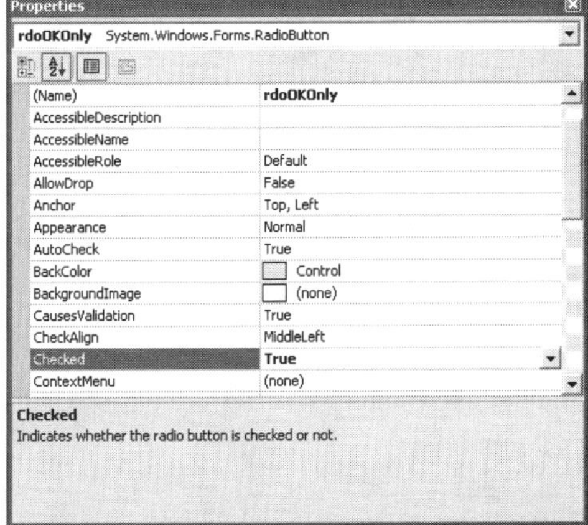

Figure 7.41 Use the Properties window to set the first radio button in the Icon group so that its Checked property is True.

Working with radio buttons

RadioButton controls, sometimes also called option buttons, are used to allow the user to select one, and only one, choice. There are other ways to make sure that the user can choose only one item from a list; for example, you can use a ListBox control, as explained in Chapter 10, "Controls That Accept User Input." The important point here is that the RadioButton control intrinsically has a very different purpose (it compels the user to make a single choice) than the CheckBox control, which allows the user to choose, or not choose, any number of individual options, including none at all.

To add radio buttons to a group box:

1. In the ToolBox, select the RadioButton control (**Figure 7.38**).
2. Drag the control to the group box, making sure drop it on the desired group box (as opposed to another group box or the form itself).
3. Use the Properties window to set the Text property, which will appear on the screen, and the name of the radio button instance.
4. Repeat the process for each radio button in each group.

   Figure 7.39 shows the RadioButton controls in the Buttons group box, and **Figure 7.40** shows the RadioButton controls in the Icon group box.
5. Use the Properties window to set the Checked property of the first radio button in each group to `True` (**Figure 7.41**).

   This step sets the first radio button as the one initially selected.

✔ Tip

- You could choose a radio button other than the first as the initial selection if you desire, but initially selecting the first one usually makes visual sense.

For the message box application developed in this chapter, **Table 7.4** shows the Name and Text values for the first group of RadioButton controls (for choosing the buttons), and **Table 7.5** shows the Name and Text values for the second group of RadioButton controls (for choosing the icon).

Table 7.4

Name and Text Values for the Buttons Radio Buttons

NAME	TEXT
rdoOKOnly	Ok Only
rdoOKCancel	Ok and Cancel
rdoAbRetry	Abort, Retry, Ignore
rdoYesNoCancel	Yes, No, Cancel
rdoYesNo	Yes and No
rdoRetryCancel	Retry and Cancel

Table 7.5

Name and Text Values for the Icon Radio Buttons

NAME	TEXT
rdoError	Error
rdoQuestion	Question
rdoExclamation	Exclamation
rdoInformation	Information
rdoNoIcon	No Icon

Adding a check box

We also want to add a CheckBox control instance to the application, so that if the user prefers, the message box can log a service notification entry. This check box could really go anywhere, but to keep things visually simple, we'll add it at the bottom of the Icon group box.

To add a CheckBox control:

1. Select the CheckBox control in the Toolbox (**Figure 7.42**).
2. Drag the control to the desired location.
3. Use the Properties window to change the control's name to `chkService`.
4. Use the Properties window to change the control's Text property so that it will display appropriate text on the screen, as shown in **Figure 7.43**.

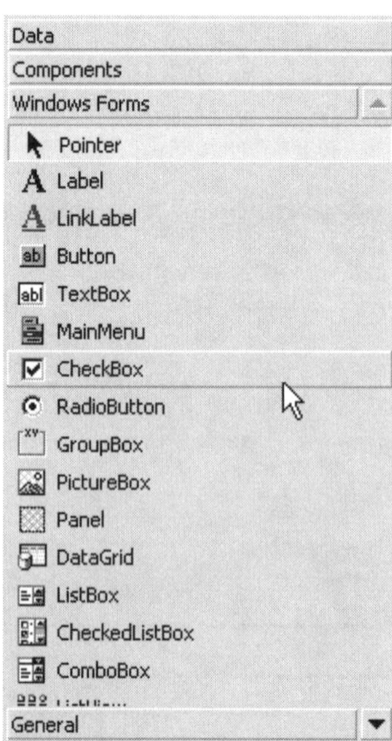

Figure 7.42 From the Toolbox, add a CheckBox control to the form.

Reviewing the form and setting the tab order

This is a good time to review the user interface we've created. As you can see in **Figure 7.44**, it looks pretty functional.

A last, important step in creating a good user interface, and one that is often overlooked, is to set the tab order: the order in which controls are accessed using the Tab key.

Figure 7.43 Use a CheckBox control to allow users to select or deselect an option.

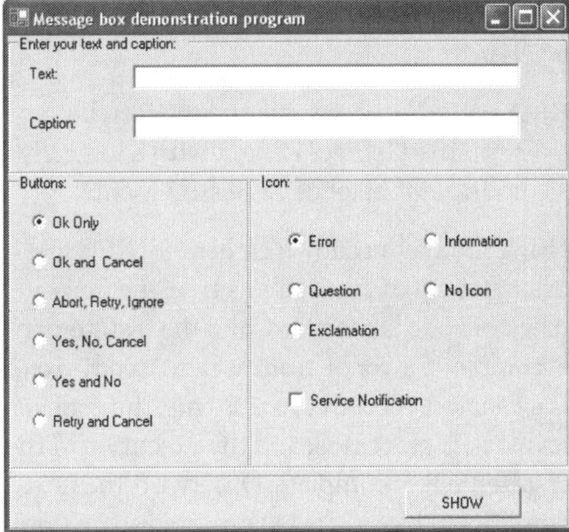

Figure 7.44 The message box demonstration program user interface is almost complete.

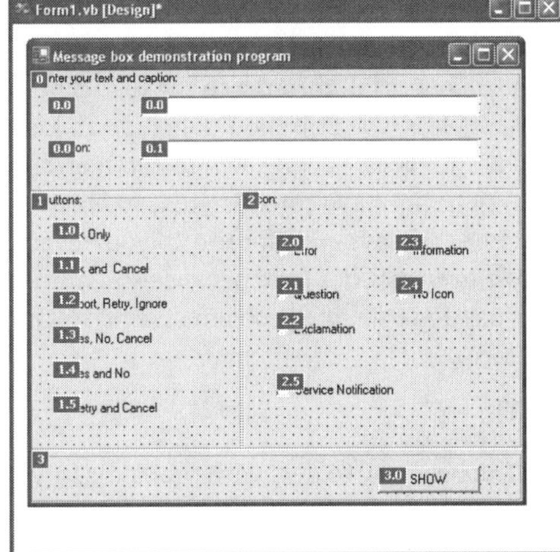

Figure 7.45 Setting the tab order allows users to tab to controls on a form in an intuitive way.

To set the tab order:

1. With a form open in its designer, choose Tab Order from the View menu.

   Numbers indicating the tab order appear over the controls on the form (**Figure 7.45**).

2. Click each control to set its position on the tab order.

✔ Tips

- Each time you click a tab stop indicator, it increments as it cycles through the possible tab stop values for the control whose tab stop it represents.
- Controls within a group, such as radio buttons contained in a group box, can only have their tab order set relative to the group container. That's why these controls appear in Figure 7.45 with their tab order indicated by a number following a decimal point (the number before the decimal point represents the tab order of the group container). From the user's viewpoint, the Tab control is used to navigate to the first control in the group; the arrow keys are then used to navigate within the group, and the Tab key to move to the next group.
- To remove a control from the tab order, use the Properties window to set its TabStop property to `False`.
- You can also set the tab order by changing the TabIndex property for each control (either in code or in the Properties window). If you do this, be sure to remember that TabIndex values are relative to the container for a given control.

Using If Statements

The message box application is now ready to be "wired"—meaning that the user interface is complete and in place. All that is missing is the code that ties the various pieces of the user interface together and lets the application do its thing (which in this example, in case you've lost track, is to display variations of the MessageBox.Show method).

To help achieve this wiring, we will use If statements. You probably know what If statements are, but just in case you don't, If statements are one type of conditional statement used in programs to allow a program to make decisions based on conditions. In other words, the program will do one thing if something is true, and do another thing if it is not.

To write good If statements, you need to understand the scaffolding and syntax of the If statement in a particular language and also what it means for something to be true. (For example, the condition `0=42` will always evaluate to false.)

The form of the VB .NET If statement that we will use to wire our message box form is as follows:

```
If condition1 Then
   first block of code
ElseIf condition2 Then
   second block of code
...
Else
   final block of code
End If
```

Before actually writing the code that will be triggered for any If statement, you should build the complete structure of the statement with the conditions and space for the blocks of code that the conditions will trigger. If statements can get complicated, particularly when they're nested one within another. If you try to write everything all at once, you can easily bollix the syntax of the statement and cause something you didn't intend when the program launches.

✔ Tip

- A complex If statement can often be simplified by replacing it with a logically equivalent Select...Case statement.

Using the syntax shown earlier, VB .NET first evaluates `condition1`. If it is true, the first block of code is executed, and the If statement is complete. If `condition1` is false, `condition2` is evaluated. If `condition2` is true, the code in its block is processed, and the execution of the If statement is complete. Otherwise, the next conditional block is evaluated, and so on until, if no conditionals have evaluated to true, the final block of code following the Else statement is executed.

In many cases, you'll think that certainly one of the conditions will be true and that execution will never fall through to the Else clause. Nevertheless, you still should include an Else clause and block of code, just to catch errors you might not have considered. Good programmers always code for those "you never know" eventualities (and because sometimes you just don't see the problem staring you in the face).

✔ Tip

- The best way to deal with problems in VB .NET code involves the use of exceptions. Exception handling code in VB .NET is explained in Chapter 9, "Exceptions and Debugging."

Wiring the Form

Now that we've designed the user interface and briefly discussed If statements, it is time to wire the form.

The entire programmatic logic for the application takes place in the click event handler for the Show button. Let's run through it piece by piece.

To create a click event procedure:

1. Double-click the Show button to create a click event procedure in the Code Editor.

   Here's the framework code for the click event:

   ```
   Private Sub btnShow_Click _
      (ByVal sender As Object, ByVal _
      e As System.EventArgs) Handles _
      btnShow.Click

   End Sub
   ```

2. Within the event procedure, declare variables to hold the user's choice of buttons and icon and the return value of the message box:

   ```
   Dim buttonchoice As _
      MessageBoxButtons
   Dim iconchoice As MessageBoxIcon
   Dim answer As DialogResult
   ```

To determine the user's button selection:

1. Create a comment at the head of the code block that says that it will be used to determine button choice.
2. Create an If statement that checks each radio button's Checked property to see which is set to `True`.
3. Within each choice in the If statement, create an assignment statement that stores the appropriate MessageBoxButtons constant in the buttonchoice variable if the choice is true.

Here's the code that is used to determine the user's button selection:

```
' Determine Button Choice
If rdoOKOnly.Checked = True Then
   buttonchoice = MessageBoxButtons.OK
ElseIf rdoOKCancel.Checked = True Then
   buttonchoice = _
      MessageBoxButtons.OKCancel
ElseIf rdoAbRetry.Checked = True Then
   buttonchoice = _
      MessageBoxButtons.AbortRetryIgnore
ElseIf rdoYesNoCancel.Checked = True Then
   buttonchoice = _
      MessageBoxButtons.YesNoCancel
ElseIf rdoYesNo.Checked = True Then
   buttonchoice = MessageBoxButtons.YesNo
ElseIf rdoRetryCancel.Checked = True Then
   buttonchoice = _
      MessageBoxButtons.RetryCancel
Else
   MessageBox.Show ("Unexpected error!")
End If
```

To determine the icon selection:

1. Create a comment at the head of the code block that says that it will be used to determine icon choice.
2. Create an If statement that checks each radio button's Checked property to see which is set to True.
3. Within each choice in the If statement, create an assignment statement that stores the appropriate MessageBoxIcon constant in the iconchoice variable if the choice is true.

Here's the code that is used to determine the user's icon selection:

```
' Determine Icon Choice
If rdoError.Checked = True Then
   iconchoice = MessageBoxIcon.Error
ElseIf rdoQuestion.Checked = True Then
   iconchoice = MessageBoxIcon.Question
ElseIf rdoExclamation.Checked = True Then
   iconchoice = _
      MessageBoxIcon.Exclamation
ElseIf rdoInformation.Checked = True Then
   iconchoice = _
      MessageBoxIcon.Information
ElseIf rdoNoIcon.Checked = True Then
   iconchoice = MessageBoxIcon.None
Else
   MessageBox.Show("Unexpected error!")
End If
```

To see if a service notification was requested:

- Create an If statement that checks the value of chkService's Checked property:

```
If chkService.Checked = True Then


Else


End If
```

To display the message box:

1. Add a comment explaining what the code block does.
2. Create one message box if a service notification was requested (with added arguments), and another if it was not.
3. Use the standard MessageBox.Show syntax, explained earlier in this chapter, together with the buttonchoice and iconchoice variables to construct the message boxes.

Here's the code that is used to show a message box based on the user's text and caption entries and choice of buttons and icon, and with (or without) a service notification:

```
' Display the Message Box (and service
     ' notification if selected)
If chkService.Checked = True Then
   answer = MessageBox.Show _
      (txtText.Text, txtCaption.Text, _
      buttonchoice, iconchoice, _
      MessageBoxDefaultButton.Button1, _
      MessageBoxOptions.ServiceNotification)
Else
   answer = MessageBox.Show _
      (txtText.Text, txtCaption.Text, _
       buttonchoice, iconchoice)
End If
```

All that remains is to find out which button in the displayed message box was clicked and to display the information.

To determine and display the button that was clicked:

1. Add a comment explaining what the code block does.
2. Declare a variable, evaluate, to store a text string based on the button selected.
3. Use If statements to check the value stored in the answer variable.
4. Display an appropriate message box in response to the If statement conditions, using the evaluate variable to generate the text of the new message box.

Here's the code block that evaluates the response to the message box and displays the results:

```
' Evaluate the answer
Dim evaluate As String
If answer = DialogResult.OK Then
   evaluate = "You clicked OK!"
ElseIf answer = DialogResult.Cancel Then
   evaluate = "You clicked Cancel!"
ElseIf answer = DialogResult.Abort Then
   evaluate = "You clicked Abort!"
ElseIf answer = DialogResult.Retry Then
   evaluate = "You clicked Retry!"
ElseIf answer = DialogResult.Ignore Then
   evaluate = "You clicked Ignore!"
ElseIf answer = DialogResult.Yes Then
   evaluate = "You clicked Yes!"
ElseIf answer = DialogResult.No Then
   evaluate = "You clicked No!"
Else
   evaluate = "Nothing was clicked!"
End If

' Show the user choice
MessageBox.Show(evaluate, _
   "Message Box Evaluation", _
   MessageBoxButtons.OK, _
   MessageBoxIcon.Information)
```

That's the entire application, which you can see in **Listing 7.2**. on the next page.

continues on next page

Listing 7.2 The complete message box demonstration program.

```
Public Class Form1
    Inherits System.Windows.Forms.Form
...
Private Sub btnShow_Click(ByVal sender As Object, ByVal e As System.EventArgs) _
   Handles btnShow.Click
   Dim buttonchoice As MessageBoxButtons
   Dim iconchoice As MessageBoxIcon
   Dim answer As DialogResult

   ' Determine Button Choice
   If rdoOKOnly.Checked = True Then
      buttonchoice = MessageBoxButtons.OK
   ElseIf rdoOKCancel.Checked = True Then
      buttonchoice = MessageBoxButtons.OKCancel
   ElseIf rdoAbRetry.Checked = True Then
      buttonchoice = MessageBoxButtons.AbortRetryIgnore
   ElseIf rdoYesNoCancel.Checked = True Then
      buttonchoice = MessageBoxButtons.YesNoCancel
   ElseIf rdoYesNo.Checked = True Then
      buttonchoice = MessageBoxButtons.YesNo
   ElseIf rdoRetryCancel.Checked = True Then
      buttonchoice = MessageBoxButtons.RetryCancel
   Else
      MessageBox.Show("Unexpected error in button selection!")
   End If

   ' Determine Icon Choice
   If rdoError.Checked = True Then
      iconchoice = MessageBoxIcon.Error
   ElseIf rdoQuestion.Checked = True Then
      iconchoice = MessageBoxIcon.Question
   ElseIf rdoExclamation.Checked = True Then
      iconchoice = MessageBoxIcon.Exclamation
   ElseIf rdoInformation.Checked = True Then
      iconchoice = MessageBoxIcon.Information
   ElseIf rdoNoIcon.Checked = True Then
      iconchoice = MessageBoxIcon.None
   Else
      MessageBox.Show("Unexpected error in icon selection!")
   End If
```

continues on next page

Listing 7.2 *(continued)*

```
' Display the Message Box (and service notification
   ' if selected)
   If chkService.Checked = True Then
      answer = MessageBox.Show(txtText.Text, txtCaption.Text, buttonchoice, iconchoice, _
         MessageBoxDefaultButton.Button1, _
         MessageBoxOptions.ServiceNotification)
   Else
      answer = MessageBox.Show(txtText.Text, txtCaption.Text, buttonchoice, iconchoice)
   End If

   ' Evaluate the answer
   Dim evaluate As String
   If answer = DialogResult.OK Then
      evaluate = "You clicked OK!"
   ElseIf answer = DialogResult.Cancel Then
      evaluate = "You clicked Cancel!"
   ElseIf answer = DialogResult.Abort Then
      evaluate = "You clicked Abort!"
   ElseIf answer = DialogResult.Retry Then
      evaluate = "You clicked Retry!"
   ElseIf answer = DialogResult.Ignore Then
      evaluate = "You clicked Ignore!"
   ElseIf answer = DialogResult.Yes Then
      evaluate = "You clicked Yes!"
   ElseIf answer = DialogResult.No Then
      evaluate = "You clicked No!"
   Else
      evaluate = "Nothing was clicked!"
   End If

   ' Show the user choice
   MessageBox.Show(evaluate, "Message Box Evaluation", MessageBoxButtons.OK, _
      MessageBoxIcon.Information)
End Sub
End Class
```

It's a good idea to test any program with as many different inputs as possible, so let's run the program and play with it a bit!

To test the program:

1. Run the program.
2. Enter some text and a caption.
3. Make a Buttons selection.
4. Make an Icon selection.
5. At this point, do not check Service Notification.
6. Click Show.

   The message box you specified should open (**Figure 7.46**).
7. Verify that the message box is the one you chose.
8. Click a button.

   The message box should close and a new message box should open.
9. Make sure that the message box correctly states the button you clicked.
10. Enter new text, caption, buttons, and icon, and this time check Service Notification (**Figure 7.47**).

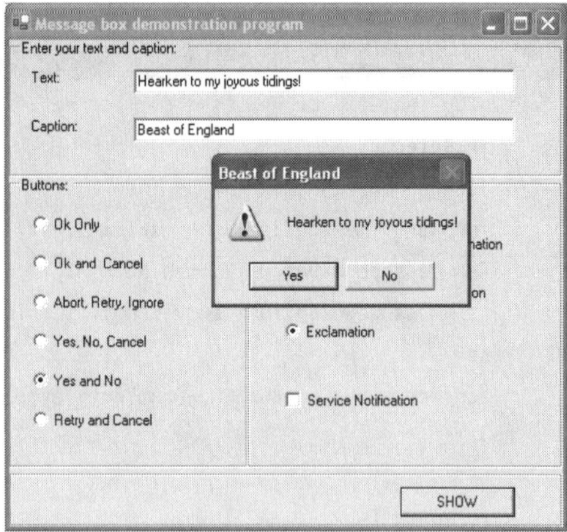

Figure 7.46 If possible, you should test every possible combination of choices in a program.

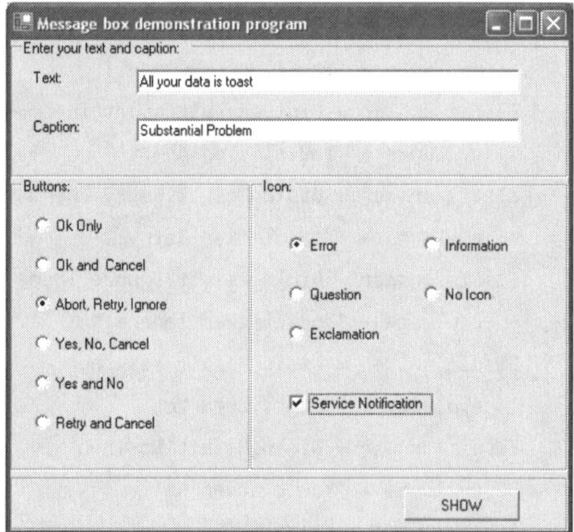

Figure 7.47 If Service Notification is checked, a service notification event will be logged when the message box is displayed.

Figure 7.48 It is easy to create alarming messages with little real content, but this is not a good general practice.

Figures 7.49 The application evaluates which button the user clicked.

11. Click Show.

    The message box you specified should open (**Figure 7.48**).

12. Click a button.

    The message box should close, and a new message box should open (**Figure 7.49**).

13. Make sure that the button you clicked is correctly identified.

14. From the View menu, choose Server Explorer.

15. Using Server Explorer, verify that a service notification was written to the System log (**Figure 7.50**).

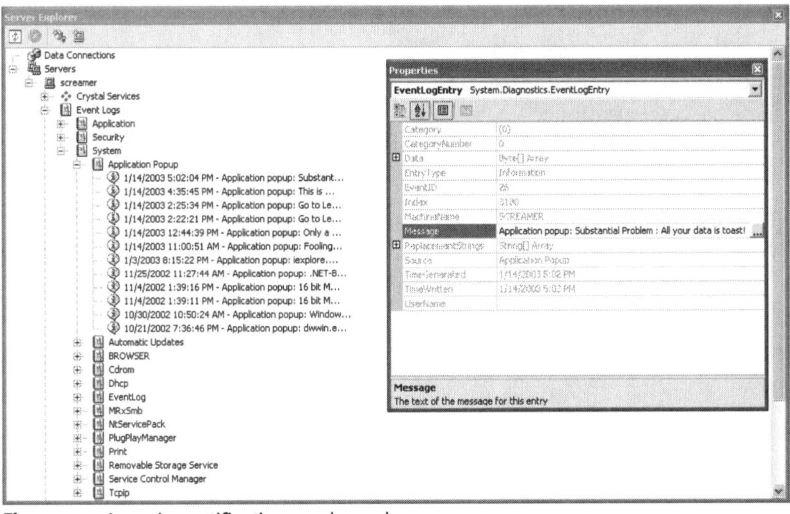

Figure 7.50 A service notification was logged.

Summary

In this chapter, you learned how to:

- Work with the MessageBox class
- Create a message box
- Display buttons and an icon in a message box
- Right-align the text in a message box
- Determine the button clicked in a message box
- Log a service notification using a message box
- Read service notifications in the System log
- Work with GroupBox controls
- Work with RadioButton controls
- Work with CheckBox controls
- Set the Tab order
- Work with If statements
- "Wire" a user interface that uses group boxes, radio buttons, and check boxes to display message box variations

8

Working with MDI Forms

So far, the Windows Applications projects you have worked with have used single standalone forms, meaning they have relied on a *single document interface* (SDI). This chapter introduces the other kind of Windows Application project interface: the *multiple document interface* (MDI).

An MDI application has one MDI—or parent—form. It can have many MDI child forms, and the child forms can be of more than one type. But all of the children must fit in the *client* space of the parent MDI form, meaning the form area exclusive of the title bar, toolbars, status bars, panels, and form border.

Creating an MDI application is a good choice for your primary user interface design when users will be working on multiple forms or documents that share the same visual characteristics.

There are many popular MDI applications. For example, depending on how you configure it Visual Studio is largely an MDI application. If you selected MDI Environment on the General Environment tab of the Visual Studio Options dialog, then you can have many open and visible child windows, such as one for the Code Editor, Form designers, and more.

continues on next page

Microsoft Excel is an MDI application (workbooks containing spreadsheets are the child forms). And Microsoft Word is partially an MDI application: Word documents are the children, but in some cases Word behaves like an SDI application rather than an MDI application because each document is opened in a separate program window rather than having multiple documents open in a single window.

In addition to MDI applications, this chapter introduces you to arrays in VB .NET. Most applications of any complexity include arrays, which are used to store objects of the same type and access them by index. You'll see how you can use an array consisting of the child forms in an MDI application, along with the form reference-passing techniques explained in Chapter 5, "Introducing Windows Forms," to easily manage all of the children in an MDI application.

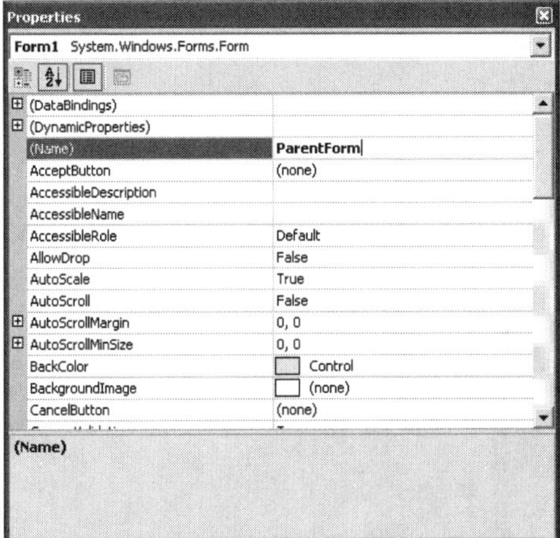

Figure 8.1 Use the Properties window to set the name of the application's form to `ParentForm`.

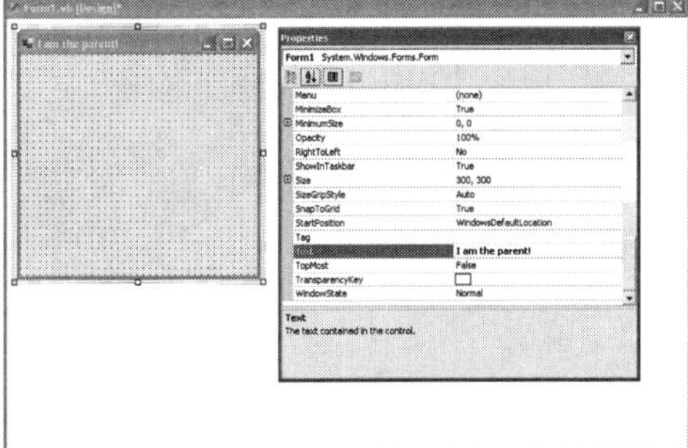

Figure 8.2 Set the text of the form to `I am the parent!`

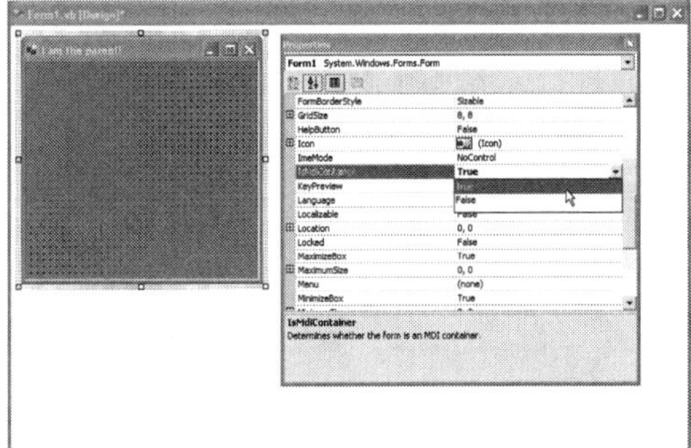

Figure 8.3 When you set the form's IsMdiContainer property to True, the background (client area) of the form changes color.

Working with the MDI Parent

The MDI parent form serves as the container for an MDI application. Normally, you would have only one MDI parent form, although (as already noted) you can have many child forms, and these child form instances do not all have to be based up the same form class.

To create a parent form:

1. Open a new Windows Application project.
2. Open the application's form in its designer.
3. Use the Properties window to set the form's Name property to `ParentForm` (**Figure 8.1**).
4. In the Properties window, set the form's Text property to `I am the parent!` (**Figure 8.2**).

   The new Text value appears in the caption bar of the form in its designer.
5. Using the Properties window, set the form's IsMdiContainer property to True (**Figure 8.3**).

   Note that after you change this setting from False to True in the Properties window, the background appearance of the form changes to reflect its new role as a container.

A very important part of any MDI application is the MDI Window menu, which allows the user to navigate among child forms and to arrange child forms within the client space of the parent form. You'll learn how to add a Window menu to an MDI application in Chapter 12, "Menus."

Usually, you'll run a status bar along the bottom of an MDI application to help users keep track of things. (For example, the main windows in both Visual Studio and Word each have a status bar at the bottom.) You can easily add a status bar to your own MDI applications by using a StatusBar control.

To add a status bar:

1. With the MDI parent form open in its designer, find the StatusBar control in the Toolbox (**Figure 8.4**).

   You may have to scroll down toward the bottom of the long list of Windows Forms controls to find the StatusBar control.

2. Double-click the StatusBar control in the Toolbox, or drag and drop it, to add it to the form.

3. In the Properties window, set the initial Text property for the status bar (**Figure 8.5**).

Often, status bars display the current time and date. In Chapter 11, "The Timer Component," you'll learn how to add this feature to a status bar and keep it updated so that the time is always current.

In an MDI application, you may want a user interface that is part of the parent form, rather than part of the children. You can achieve this by using container controls, such as toolbars or panels. If you use a Panel control, then you place other controls, such as Button and TextBox controls, on the panel. The client area of the parent form then excludes the panel (and other containers).

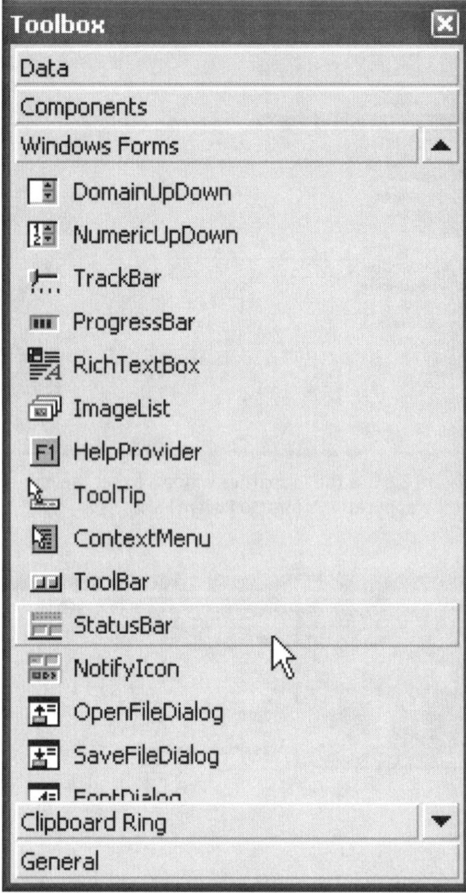

Figure 8.4 To add a StatusBar control, choose it from the Toolbox.

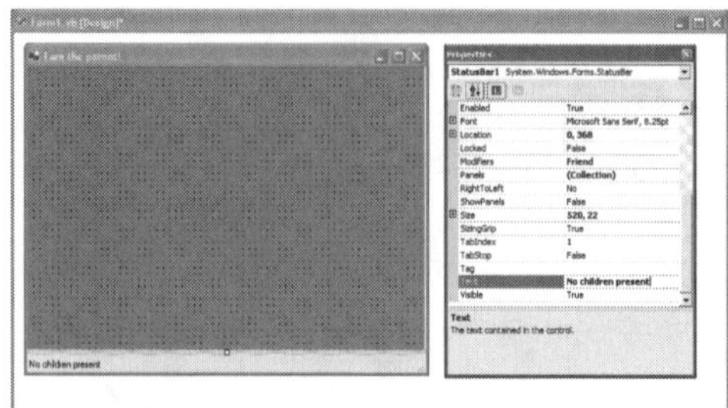

Figure 8.5 You can set the Text property for the StatusBar using the Properties window.

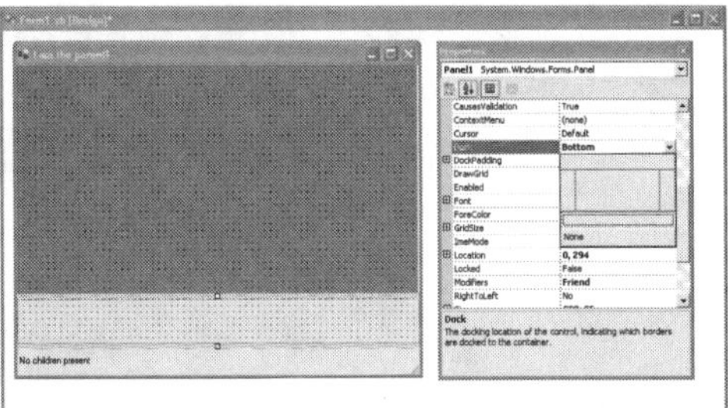

Figure 8.6 Set the Dock property of the Panel control to Bottom to align it along the bottom of the form (just above the status bar).

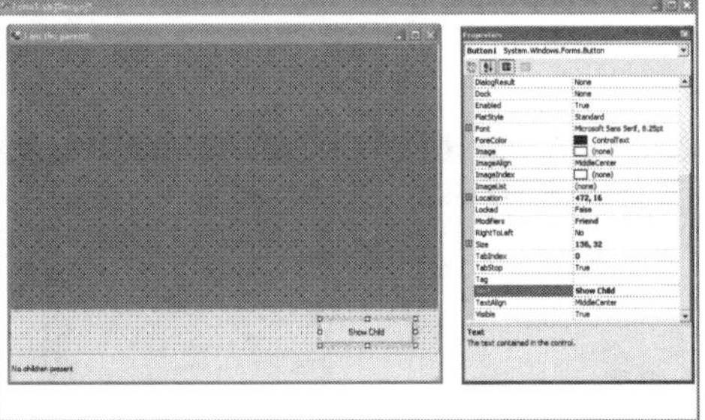

Figure 8.7 You can add controls such as buttons to the panel.

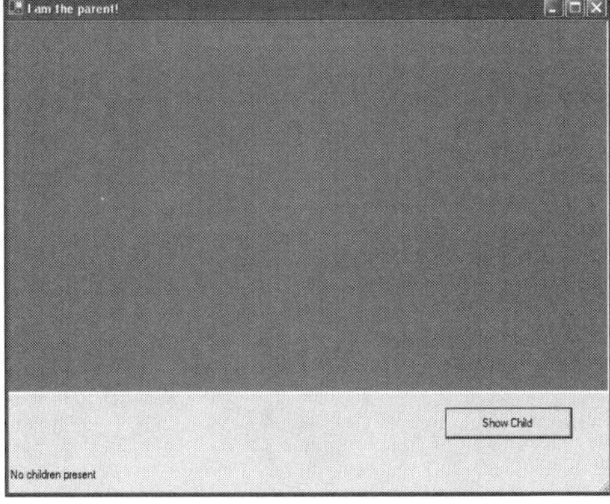

Figure 8.8 The stage is now set for you to add child forms.

In our sample MDI application, we're going to add a panel right above the status bar. To start, this panel will host a Button control for creating new instances of MDI children.

To add a panel containing a button to display child forms:

1. With the MDI parent form open in its designer and the Toolbox open, drag and drop a Panel control onto the form (or double-click the Panel control).
2. With the panel selected, use the Properties window to set the Dock property of the panel to Bottom (**Figure 8.6**).
3. Drag a Button control from the Toolbox onto the panel.

   Be sure to drag the button onto the panel and not the client area of the MDI form.
4. Make sure the Button is selected; then use the Properties window to set the Name property of the button to `btnShowChild`.
5. Set the Text property of the Button to `Show Child` (**Figure 8.7**).
6. Run the project to see the completed MDI parent form (**Figure 8.8**).

Working with MDI Children

Generally, any Windows form class can serve as the basis for an MDI child. To turn a run-of-the-mill instance of a form class into an MDI child, you need to assign an MDI parent to the MdiParent property of the child. By the way, if you add a RichTextBox control to an MDI child form, you'll almost have a standard text editor application without having to do much at all. (See Chapter 13, "The Common Dialog Controls," for information on working with a RichTextBox control.)

To see how this works in practice, we'll add a new form to the project that contains the MDI parent form and then use the click event of the Show Child button to use the new form as the basis for child instances.

To add MDI children:

1. Use the Add New Item dialog to add a new Windows form to the project (**Figure 8.9**).
2. With the new form open in its designer, use the Properties window to change the value of its Name property to `ChildForm` and the value of its Text property to `Child form` (**Figure 8.10**).
3. Back on the parent form, double-click the Show Child button to create a click event handler for the button in the Code Editor:

```
Private Sub btnShowChild_Click _
   (ByVal sender As System.Object, _
   ByVal e As System.EventArgs) _
   Handles btnShowChild.Click


End Sub
```

4. Still in the Code Editor, within the click event, declare and instantiate a new child form:

```
Dim theKid As New ChildForm()
```

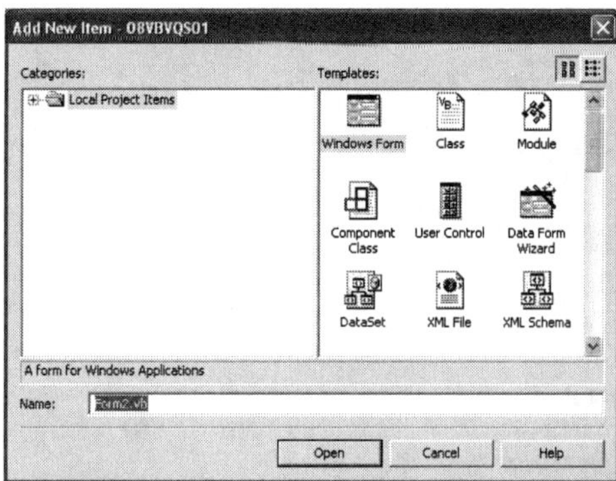

Figure 8.9 The form that will serve as the basis for the child forms is added to the project using the Add New Item dialog.

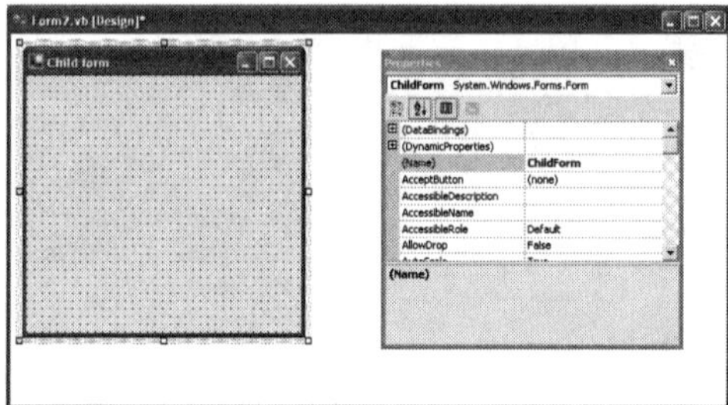

Figure 8.10 Change the Name and Text properties of the form that will be used as the basis for the application's children to reflect its role in life.

5. Following the child form declaration, assign the MDI parent form to the new child's MdiParent property:

```
theKid.MdiParent = Me
```

6. Within the click event, show the MDI child:

```
theKid.Show()
```

Here's the complete click event code that creates an instance of the new form, sets its MdiParent property so that it is a child of the container form, and opens the new child:

```
Private Sub btnShowChild_Click _
    (ByVal sender As System.Object, _
    ByVal e As System.EventArgs) _
    Handles btnShowChild.Click
    Dim theKid As New ChildForm()
    theKid.MdiParent = Me
    theKid.Show()
End Sub
```

So far, so good! But let's make this application a bit more useful by providing a mechanism for tracking the child form instances. Often in a real-world application, you need a mechanism for separately tracking the information in a number of different MDI children—for example, when each MDI child contains a spreadsheet.

As a stand-in for this complexity, we'll have each child form display a number that identifies which child it is. Adding a message that includes the form's sequential number as part of its Text property will accomplish this. The number will appear in the child's caption bar. In a "real" application, you could use the child form number to track all kinds of information related to the child form (for example, the details of a spreadsheet).

In addition, we'll display the total number of open child forms on the parent's status bar.

To track the number of children:

1. In the Code Editor, add a property, NumForms, to the MDI parent form to track the total number of forms (for instructions on how to create a property, see Chapter 3, "Working with Classes"):

```
Private m_numForms As Integer = 0
Public Property NumForms() As
Integer
    Get
        NumForms = m_numForms
    End Get
    Set(ByVal Value As Integer)
        m_numForms = Value
    End Set
End Property
```

2. Still in the Code Editor, add a method, WriteStatus, to the MDI parent form that uses the NumForms property to display the total number of forms on the status bar (for instructions on how to create a method, see Chapter 3):

```
Public Sub WriteStatus()
    StatusBar1.Text = _
      "Number of child forms is: " & _
      CStr(Me.NumForms)
End Sub
```

3. In the Code Editor, proceed to the Show Child button's click event and increment the NumForms property each time a child form is created:

```
Me.NumForms += 1
```

4. After the NumForms increment, display the new form's number by assigning a value to the new form's Text property:

```
theKid.Text = "Child Number " & _
    CStr(Me.NumForms)
```

continues on next page

5. Still in the click event handler, call the WriteStatus method to display the total number of open forms on the status bar:

```
WriteStatus()
```

6. Run the project.
7. Click Show Child.

   A single child form is displayed (**Figure 8.11**).
8. Click Show Child repeatedly.

   Each time you click the button, a new child instance is displayed (**Figure 8.12**), and the status bar shows the total number of forms opened.

✔ Tip

- The WriteStatus method uses the .NET conversion method CStr to convert the integer number of forms to a string representation that can be displayed.

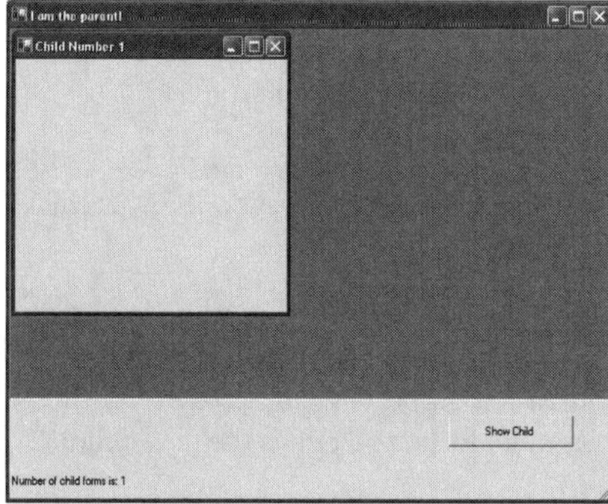

Figure 8.11 When you instantiate a child form and set its MdiParent property to the parent form, the new form appears as a child within the client area of the parent.

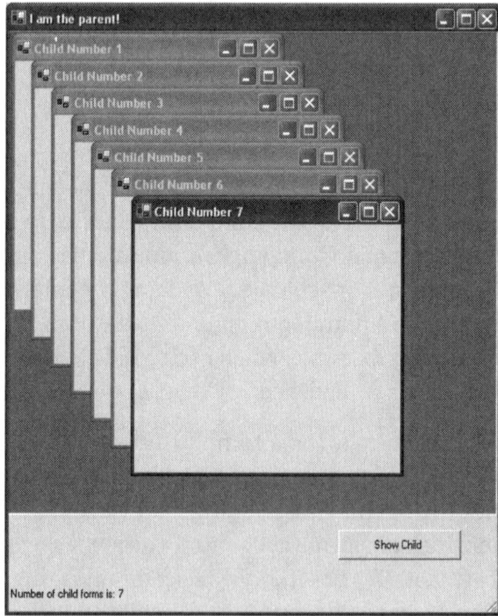

Figure 8.12 You can display many instances of child forms.

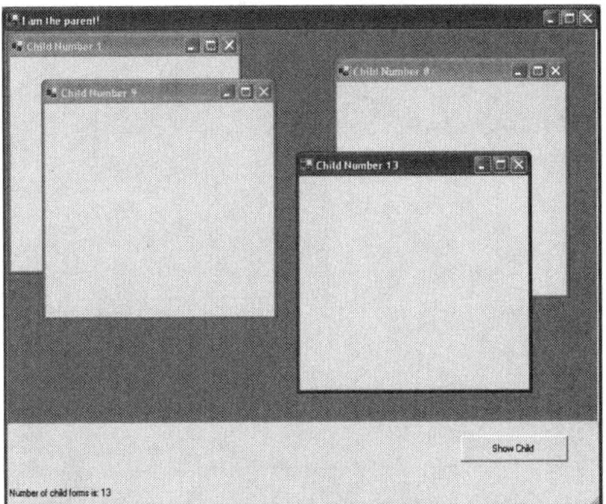

Figure 8.13 Problems arise in the child form count when you delete children (the count at the lower left says that there are 13 children, but only 4 are actually displayed).

Here's the revised Show Child click event code, incorporating the changes that display the sequential child number in the child's caption bar (the code also tracks the number of open children):

```
Private Sub btnShowChild_Click _
   (ByVal sender As System.Object, _
   ByVal e As System.EventArgs) _
   Handles btnShowChild.Click
   Dim theKid As New ChildForm()
   theKid.MdiParent = Me
   Me.NumForms += 1
   theKid.Text = "Child Number " & _
      CStr(Me.NumForms)
   theKid.Show()
   WriteStatus()
End Sub
```

However, there is a problem with this code: when you add a new child instance, the global child form counter, NumForms, goes up. The number assigned to each form is based on the global form counter, which only goes up, and never down, even when forms are closed. Thus, if you delete forms, you can easily get into situations like that shown in **Figure 8.13**, in which the status bar indicates that 13 forms are open, but in fact only 4 forms are open.

To fix this problem, we'll add a mechanism to the child form that updates NumForms (by subtracting 1) when a form is closed. We'll place this code in the child form class Closing event, which is fired when a form is closed.

For this approach to work, each child needs to be able to reference the instance of the MDI parent class that invoked it (because that's where the global NumForms property lives). For a refresher on how to pass form instance information around an application, see "Working with Form Instances" in Chapter 5.

To decrement the child form count when a child form closes:

1. In the child form class, add a public field declared as type ParentForm to hold the parent's form instance information:
   ```
   Public theDad As ParentForm
   ```
2. In the parent form's Show Child click event, add a line of code that uses the Me keyword to pass the current form instance information to each child as it is instantiated:
   ```
   theKid.theDad = Me
   ```
3. Back in the child form class, create a form Closing event procedure framework in the Code Editor by selecting Base Class Events from the Objects list and selecting Closing from the Procedures list.
   ```
   Private Sub ChildForm_Closing(ByVal _
      sender As Object, ByVal e As _
      System.ComponentModel. _
      CancelEventArgs) _
      Handles MyBase.Closing

   End Sub
   ```
4. Within the Closing procedure, add code that references the MDI parent instance to decrement the form counter and update the status bar display:
   ```
   theDad.NumForms = theDad.NumForms - 1
   theDad.WriteStatus()
   ```

Here's the complete code for the child form Closing event:

```
Private Sub ChildForm_Closing(ByVal _
   sender As Object, ByVal e As _
   System.ComponentModel.CancelEventArgs) _
   Handles MyBase.Closing
   theDad.NumForms = theDad.NumForms - 1
   theDad.WriteStatus()
End Sub
```

Listing 8.1 shows this code incorporated into the Show Child click event (and associated code) in the MDI parent form and into the Closing event of the child form class.

This code is a big improvement over the prior versions; the NumForms property will now accurately reflect the number of open children in the MDI parent.

Listing 8.1 Opening and tracking child forms (without using the MdiChildren array).

```
' in ParentForm
Private Sub btnShowChild_Click(ByVal sender As System.Object, ByVal e As System.EventArgs) _
   Handles btnShowChild.Click
   Dim theKid As New ChildForm()
   Me.NumForms += 1
   theKid.MdiParent = Me
   theKid.Text = "Child Number " & CStr(Me.NumForms)
   theKid.Show()
   WriteStatus()
   theKid.theDad = Me
End Sub

Private m_numForms As Integer = 0

Public Property NumForms() As Integer
   Get
      NumForms = m_numForms
   End Get
   Set(ByVal Value As Integer)
      m_numForms = Value
   End Set
End Property

Public Sub WriteStatus()
   StatusBar1.Text = "Number of child forms is: " & CStr(Me.NumForms)
End Sub

' in ChildForm
Public theDad As ParentForm

Private Sub ChildForm_Closing(ByVal sender As Object, ByVal e As System.ComponentModel.CancelEventArgs) _
   Handles MyBase.Closing
   theDad.NumForms = theDad.NumForms - 1
   theDad.WriteStatus()
End Sub
```

However, some problems still remain in paradise! For example, try opening five child forms, deleting the second child, and then adding another new form. As you can see in **Figure 8.14**, although the global form count is right, two child forms now are marked as number 5 in their caption bars.

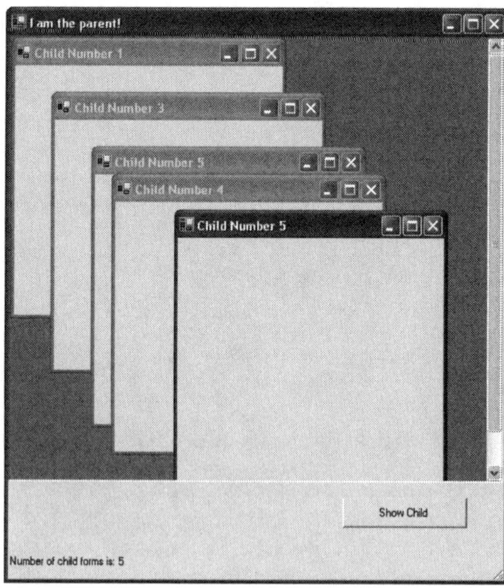

Figure 8.14 You can use code placed in the Closing event of the child form to correct the problem with the total child form count.

When you are writing a real-world MDI application, you need to be a virtuoso at tracking child forms. Specifically, if someone closes a child (for example, a spreadsheet), the information in that spreadsheet will probably be saved (to a disk file or to a database) or thrown away. In either case, you don't want to waste project resources by continuing to track the contents of deleted children within your application. (For information on saving files, see Chapter 13. For some examples of how to work with a database, see Chapter 15, "XML, Data, and ADO.NET.")

The way to solve the problem of duplicate tracking numbers is to use the MdiChildren array associated by VB .NET with every MDI parent. But before we discuss how to use the MdiChildren array, we'll explore the general topic of working with arrays in VB .NET.

Table 8.1

Important Array Methods

METHOD	DESCRIPTION
`Clear`	Sets a range of elements in an array to 0, false, or a null reference, depending on the type of the array elements.
`Copy`	Copies a range of elements from one array to another.
`GetLength`	Gets the number of elements in a specified dimension of the array.
`GetLowerBound`	Gets the lower bound of the specified dimension in the array. Note that if the array has been created using normal syntax—for example, not using `CreateInstance`—the lower bound of each dimension will be 0.
`GetUpperBound`	Gets the upper bound of the specified dimension in the array.
`GetValue`	Gets the value of the specified element in the array.
`IndexOf`	Returns the index of the first occurrence of a value in a one-dimensional array (or in a portion of the array).
`Reverse`	Reverses the order of the elements in a one-dimensional array (or in a portion of the array).
`SetValue`	Sets the specified element in the current array to the specified value.
`Sort`	Sorts the elements in a one-dimensional array.

Table 8.2

Important Array Properties

PROPERTY	RETURN VALUE
`IsFixedSize`	A Boolean value indicating whether the array has a fixed size.
`IsReadOnly`	A Boolean value indicating whether the array is read-only.
`Length`	The total number of elements in all of the dimensions of an array.
`Rank`	The number of dimensions in an array.

Working with Arrays

Arrays, arrays, arrays—arrays are an extremely important topic. Sooner or later, almost every program in the world uses one. Fortunately, VB .NET makes working with arrays easy.

As noted at the beginning of this chapter, an array stores objects of the same type that can be accessed using an index. In .NET, you create arrays using the System. Array class. This means that you can use the members—properties and methods—of the Array class when you work with arrays. Many of these members are shown in **Table 8.1** and **Table 8.2**.

The methods and properties shown in Tables 8.1 and 8.2 will allow you to work with arrays. But first, you have to know how to declare and initialize an array.

To declare a single-dimensional array:

- Declare the array as you would an ordinary variable, using the Dim...As statement, and add one pair of parentheses after the variable name. Here are two examples, one that declares an array of integers, and another that declares an array of form instances:

```
Dim myIntArray() As Integer
Dim theForms() As Form
```

You can also specify the size of the array dimension when you declare it. For example, the statement `Dim myIntArray(5) As Integer` creates an array with five integer elements (and an index running from 0 to 4).

A *multidimensional*, or *n-dimensional*, array uses multiple indices to identify values. You can easily picture a two-dimensional array as a table consisting of columns and rows. A three-dimensional array might be used to store stock price and volume information over time.

To declare a multidimensional array:

- In the array declaration, add commas inside the parentheses to separate the dimensions. For example, here's the declaration for a three-dimensional array of strings:

  ```
  Dim theStrings (,,) As String
  ```

As with single-dimensional arrays, you can initialize multidimensional arrays in their declaration statements. For example, the statement `Dim myIntArray(3,2) As String` creates a 3 x 2 array of strings. A two-dimensional array, such as the one in this example, is exactly like a spreadsheet table. The 3 x 2 array declared in the statement could be filled with the following strings:

DOG	CAT	BIRD
SNAKE	IGUANA	GEKKO

In Visual Basic .NET, you can resize array dimensions by using the ReDim statement. If the statement includes the Preserve keyword, existing element values are saved (if the Preserve keyword is left off, all element values are lost).

To resize an array (preserving the elements):

- Use the ReDim statement combined with the Preserve keyword to declare the new size of the array. For example, if you start with a five-element, single-dimension array declared as `Dim myIntArray(5) As Integer`, you can resize it so that it has seven elements (with the first five elements populated from the original array) as follows:

  ```
  ReDim Preserve myIntArray(7)
  ```

✔ Tip

- When you use ReDim, you are actually creating a new array with the same name as the old one. If you used the Preserve keyword, the elements from the old array are used to initialize the corresponding elements in the new array.

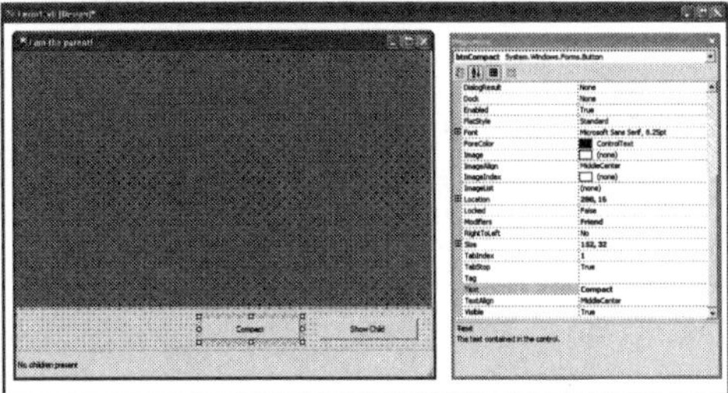

Figure 8.15 You can add other controls, such as the Compact button, to the panel along the bottom of the parent form.

Now that you understand the basics of working with arrays in VB .NET, let's return to our sample MDI application and write a procedure that allows us to track MDI child forms by *compacting* the open forms contained by the MDI parent. Compacting means making sure that the children are numbered consecutively because nonconsecutive children have been discarded.

To set up this procedure, in the sample MDI application you created earlier you'll add a Compact button to the panel that runs along the bottom of the MDI parent. The click event of the Compact button will be used to launch a method, CompactKids. The CompactKids method will perform the compaction on the MDI children using the array that is the value of the parent form's MdiChildren property.

To compact the children:

1. With the MDI parent form open in its designer, select the panel at the bottom.
2. Use the Toolbox to add a button to the panel (**Figure 8.15**). Be sure to place the button on the panel and not on the client portion of the MDI parent form.
3. Use the Properties window, as shown in Figure 8.15, to change the name of the button to `btnCompact` and its Text value to `Compact`.
4. Double-click the Compact button to create a click event procedure framework in the Code Editor:

```
Private Sub btnCompact_Click(ByVal _
   sender As System.Object, ByVal e _
   As System.EventArgs) Handles _
   btnCompact.Click

End Sub
```

continues on next page

5. In the Code Editor, within the click event procedure, add a line of code that invokes the CompactKids method:

```
Private Sub btnCompact_Click(ByVal _
   sender As System.Object, ByVal e _
   As System.EventArgs) Handles _
   btnCompact.Click
   Me.CompactKids()
End Sub
```

6. Create the declaration for the CompactKids method:

```
Public Sub CompactKids()


End Sub
```

7. Within the CompactKids method, declare an array of forms (named *frmArray*) with the same number of elements as the array returned by the MDI form's MdiChildren property:

```
Dim frmArray(Me.MdiChildren().GetUpperBound(0)) As Form
```

8. Assign the array returned by the MdiChildren property to frmArray:

```
frmArray = Me.MdiChildren()
```

9. Use a For statement to loop through frmArray, which has now been populated with references to all of the children.

   This will correctly number each form. As before, the child form numbers are displayed using each child's Text property.

```
Dim i As Integer
For i = 0 To _
   Me.MdiChildren().Length - 1
   frmArray(i).Text = _
      "Child Number " & CStr(i + 1)
Next i
```

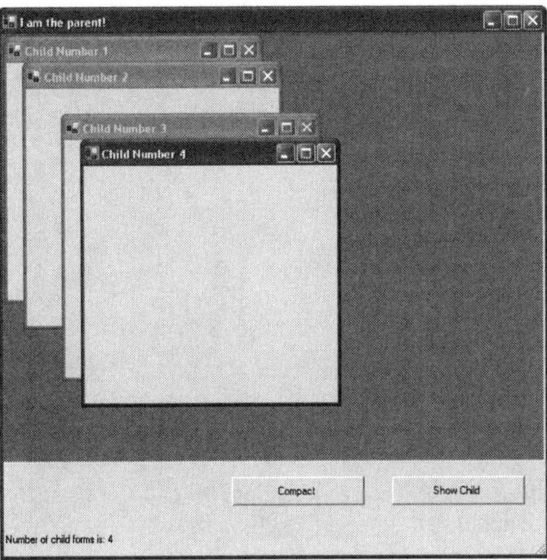

Figure 8.16 The compaction process ensures that child forms are numbered consecutively.

10. Update the NumForms property, which is used to keep global track of the total number of children, using the Length property of the MdiChildren array:

```
Me.NumForms = Me.MdiChildren().Length
```

11. Write the updated total of children to the status bar:

```
Me.WriteStatus()
```

12. Run the project to test it.

13. Create a lot of child forms and then close some of them.

14. Delete some of the lower-numbered forms.

15. Click the Compact button.

    After the CompactKids method runs, the child forms will always be sequenced correctly (**Figure 8.16**).

✔ Tips

- Despite its potentially confusing name, you should understand that the variable frmArray refers to an array (and not a form).
- If you are wondering why I created a new array for the child forms rather than operating directly on the array referenced by the MdiChildren property, it is because the MdiChildren array is read-only.

Listing 8.2 shows the complete code for the CompactKids method, as well as the event handler that invokes it.

In one sense, clicking the Compact button works fine: it always properly sequences the child forms. However, a problem remains. You must invoke the CompactKids method from the parent form (as you just saw, one way to do this is in a click event). But when you close a child form, sequencing anomalies may arise. For example, if you open three child forms, close the middle form, and then open another form, you will get two forms numbered 3 and none numbered 2 (**Figure 8.17**). True, clicking the Compact button properly resequences the forms, but this may not be good enough, depending on the needs of your application.

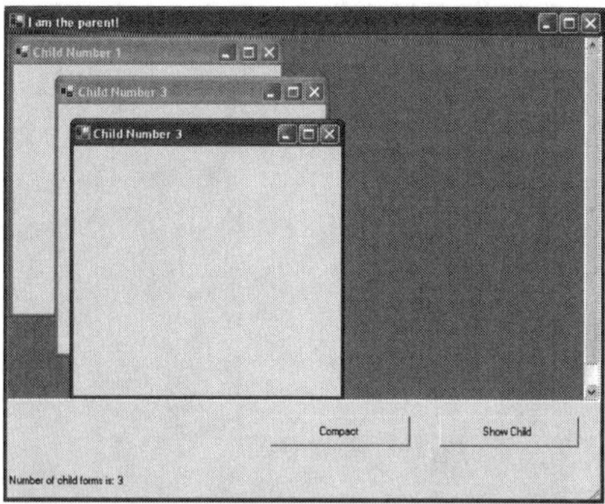

Figure 8.17 Without compaction, the child forms are not numbered consecutively—a problem that can be fixed.

You might consider solving the problem by putting a call to the CompactKids method in the Closing event of the child form class—for example:

```
theDad.CompactKids()
```


Listing 8.2 Using the MdiChildren array to compact the child forms.

```
Private Sub btnCompact_Click(ByVal sender As System.Object, ByVal e As System.EventArgs) _
   Handles btnCompact.Click
   Me.CompactKids()
End Sub

Public Sub CompactKids()
   Dim frmArray(Me.MdiChildren().GetUpperBound(0)) As Form
   frmArray = Me.MdiChildren()
   Dim i As Integer
   For i = 0 To Me.MdiChildren().Length - 1
      frmArray(i).Text = "Child Number " & CStr(i + 1)
   Next i
   Me.NumForms = Me.MdiChildren().Length
   Me.WriteStatus()
End Sub
```

However, this does not work as desired because, as far as .NET is concerned, the child form is still alive—and part of the array returned by the MdiChildren property—in its Closing event. In fact, there is no child form event in which you can place code for execution and be sure that the instance of the child does not still exist. The technical reason for this is that in .NET (as in Java), when an object is closed, the memory used by the object is marked for reclamation, but exactly when this will actually happen cannot be known. (This is called *indeterminate garbage collection.*)

So what to do? One viable approach is to renumber all of the child forms that are higher in the sequence than the form that is closing. (Forms with lower sequential numbers should be properly ordered already.) Here's how to implement this.

To renumber the forms when closing a child form:

1. In the Code Editor, within the Closing event procedure of the child form class, add a line of code to the end of the procedure that invokes a method to resequence the forms higher in number than the closing child:
   ```
   Me.Renumber()
   ```
2. Create the declaration for the Renumber method:
   ```
   Public Sub Renumber()

   End Sub
   ```
3. Within the Renumber method, declare an array of forms (named frmArray) with the same number of elements as the array returned by the MDI form's MdiChildren property:
   ```
   Dim frmArray(theDad.MdiChildren(). _
      GetUpperBound(0)) As Form
   ```
   Note that this code uses theDad, the variable containing a reference to the MDI parent form.
4. Assign the array returned by the MdiChildren property to frmArray:
   ```
   frmArray = theDad.MdiChildren()
   ```
5. Use a For loop to determine the number of the current child form (that is, the form that is closing) and store the number in the variable j:
   ```
   Dim i As Integer
   Dim j As Integer = 0
   For i = 0 To _
      theDad.MdiChildren().Length - 1
      If (frmArray(i) Is Me) Then
         j = i
         Exit For
      End If
   Next i
   ```
   This code uses the Is operator, which checks to see if two objects are the same. In this case, the Is operator is used to determine when the form referenced in the array is the one being closed (as indicated by the Me keyword).
6. Use another For statement to start at one greater than the number of the child form that is being closed (this number was saved in the j variable). This other For statement renumbers all child forms that have a higher number than the current (closing) child.
   ```
   For i = j + 1 To _
      theDad.MdiChildren().Length - 1
      frmArray(i).Text = _
         "Child Number " & CStr(i)
   Next i
   ```
7. Run the project to test it.
8. Add lots of children, delete some of them, and add more child forms to verify that the form numbering remains correct.

continues on next page

Listing 8.3 shows the complete code for the Renumber method, as well as the Closing event that invokes it.

Listing 8.3 Resequencing forms in the child class Closing event.

```
Private Sub ChildForm_Closing(ByVal sender As Object, ByVal e As _
   System.ComponentModel.CancelEventArgs) Handles MyBase.Closing
   theDad.NumForms = theDad.NumForms - 1
   Me.Renumber()
End Sub

Private Sub Renumber()
   Dim frmArray(theDad.MdiChildren().GetUpperBound(0)) As Form
   frmArray = theDad.MdiChildren()
   Dim i As Integer
   Dim j As Integer = 0
   For i = 0 To theDad.MdiChildren().Length - 1
      If (frmArray(i) Is Me) Then
         j = i
         Exit For
      End If
   Next i
   For i = j + 1 To theDad.MdiChildren().Length - 1
      frmArray(i).Text = "Child Number " & CStr(i)
   Next i
End Sub
```

Table 8.3

.NET Collection Classes

Class	Purpose
ArrayList	Used to create an array-like structure whose size is dynamically altered as items are added and removed.
CollectionBase	Provides the abstract base class for a collection—meaning that the class cannot be instantiated, only inherited, as explained in Chapter 4, "Class Interfaces."
DictionaryBase	Provides the abstract base class for a dictionary-style collection of key/value pairs.
Queue	Used to create a first-in, first-out collection of objects.
SortedList	Used to create a collection of key/value pairs that are sorted by the keys and are accessible by key and by index—so it combines the features of an array with those of a dictionary.
Stack	Used to create a last-in, first-out collection of objects.

Using Collection Classes

Just so you don't get the impression that an array is the only structure that you can use to organize groups of objects, you should be aware that .NET provides quite a few other structures for this purpose that are derived from the general *collection* class. Many of these "based on a collection" structures are very useful.

A collection is a data structure that holds objects and gives you ways to access, add, and remove objects in the collection. From this definition, you can see that an array is a particular kind of collection that adds the access-by-index functionality to general collection functionality.

A data structure that is not an array (but is derived from the collection class) is often better suited to solving a specific organizational problem than an array. For example, a *stack* provides a mechanism for storing objects and retrieving them in a last-in, first-out (LIFO) fashion without having to worry about how many objects there are or having to index them.

This last section of this chapter provides an overview of the collection classes available to you in .NET.

You'll find most of the .NET collection classes in the System.Collections namespace. **Table 8.3** lists some of the most useful collection classes.

When a class in .NET is a collection class, the class likely implements some collection-related interfaces. The point of class interfaces, which were explained in Chapter 4, is to provide a standard and familiar way to work with objects based on classes that implement the interface.

Table 8.4 shows some of the interfaces that are commonly implemented by collection classes. To fairly easily understand how to work with a given collection class, you can use online help to determine which interfaces the class implements and then look up the interface documentation. An alternative information discovery technique is to use the Object Browser, explained in Chapter 14, to view the actual "contract," or members specified, for each interface that the particular collection class implements.

Summary

In this chapter, you learned how to:

- Create MDI parent forms
- Work with the StatusBar control
- Create MDI children
- Work with arrays
- Use the array returned by a parent form's MdiChildren property
- Describe the nature of the .NET collection classes and the interfaces that they implement

Table 8.4

.NET Selected Interfaces Related to Collection Classes

Interface	Description
`ICollection`	Defines the size, enumerators, and synchronization methods for all collections.
`IComparer`	Exposes a method that compares two objects.
`IDictionary`	Represents a collection of key/value pairs.
`IDictionaryEnumerator`	Enumerates the elements of a dictionary.
`IEnumerable`	Exposes the enumerator, which supports a simple iteration over a collection.
`IEnumerator`	Supports a simple iteration over a collection.
`IList`	Represents a collection of objects that can be individually accessed by index.

9 EXCEPTIONS AND DEBUGGING

An *exception* is caused when a program encounters an extraordinary condition. Usually, but not always, the extraordinary condition is caused by an error of some kind. For example, an exception is caused, or *thrown*, when a program attempts to divide by zero or access a resource (such as a network drive) that is not available, or when an attempt to connect to a database fails because the database server is down.

To keep the code reasonably simple, the code examples presented in all the other chapters of this book except this one don't include structured exception handling. In real life, however, all .NET production code should always include exceptions and structured exception handling for a number of reasons.

The first part of this chapter explains the concepts involved in adding exception handling to programs and how to work with the relevant syntax. The second part explores debugging in the .NET environment: What are the categories of bugs that can crop up in a program? What are the most practical tools in the Visual Studio .NET environment that help avoid these problems? And how should you approach testing a program to ensure (as much as possible) it's bug free?

Structured Exception Handling

Industrial-strength programs need to be able to anticipate run-time errors, because somewhere down the line these errors *will* occur. For example, a network resource might not be available because the network is down. Or maybe a file can't be written to disk because the disk drive is full. Even with the best code in the world, these kinds of errors can happen. In the release version of a program, these and other errors must be handled. In VB .NET, these errors are handled using exceptions.

Code written using structured handling is less likely to be buggy. And, if it does contain bugs, these will be handled cleanly without displaying obscure error messages to the user. Also, using structured exception handling gives you the chance to execute clean-up code even if a program has ended with an error condition.

By definition, an exception is exceptional because it is an unexpected condition, or error, in a program. It is in the nature of life that some of these unexpected conditions cannot be anticipated. To deal with, or handle, all exceptions regardless of whether the exception can be reasonably anticipated, a rigorous framework is required, which is often referred to as *structured exception handling*.

In structured exception handling, exceptions are handled in an organized way, accomplished by using the Try...Catch...Finally statement and the methods and properties of objects based on the Exception class. Exception objects are used to store information about errors and abnormal events that occur in an application.)The next section explores the Try statement; later in the chapter you'll see how to work with the members of the Exception class.)

What does "handling" an exception actually mean? Here are the minimum requirements you should aim for when designing a solid framework for exception handling:

- Your program should not crash no matter what.
- If recovery from the situation is possible and the program can reliably continue execution, it should.
- If program execution cannot continue, a message that is comprehensible to the user should explain that the program is terminating and, if appropriate, explain why.
- Data should not be lost because of an unplanned failure.
- The program should shut down gently, meaning that the shutdown should be planned, should not involve mad disk spinning, and should not cause windows to open and close on the desktop for five minutes.
- It is an absolute priority that information necessary for identifying, debugging, and resolving the problem be saved, either to a disk file or the system event log, or to both. As discussed in Chapter 7, "Message Boxes and If Statements," it's very easy to use a MessageBox.Show statement to simultaneously send the user a message and write to the system log.

Using Try Statements

In Visual Basic .NET, you implement structured exception handling using Try...Catch... Finally statements. For exception handling to be fully functional, all program code must be included in one of the clauses (also called blocks) of a Try...Catch...Finally statement. Here's the meaning of each block:

- **Try:** Code in the Try block is the main body of the program being monitored for exceptions.
- **Catch:** Code placed in Catch blocks is executed in response to specific exceptions.
- **Finally:** Code in the Finally block is executed last of all, whether or not an exception has been caught.

The general form of the Try...Catch...Finally statement is as follows (elements enclosed in square brackets are optional):

```
Try
   Program statements
   ...
[Catch1 [exception [As type]]
   [When expression]
   ...
[CatchN [exception [As type]]
   [When expression]
   ...
[Finally
   Final program statements]
End Try
```

To implement exception handling so that it really catches all exceptions (in particular, unexpected exceptions as well as those that you might reasonably expect), be sure to include a general exception catcher as the last Catch clause. This generic Catch clause handles all exceptions that haven't been handled by specific Catch clause exception handlers.

This kind of generic Catch clause follows a fairly standard format. For example, here's a Try...Catch...Finally statement that uses both a Catch clause designed to handle divide-by-zero exceptions and a general Catch clause:

```
Try
   Program statements
   ...
Catch excep As DivideByZeroException
   ' Handle divide by zero
Catch other specific errors
   ...
Catch excep As Exception
   ' Generic exception handler
Finally
   ' Cleanup code goes here
End Try
```

This form of the Try...Catch...Finally statement is probably the approach most often used.

By the way, you might wonder what would happen if you put the generic exception handler block at the beginning (rather than the end) of the Catch blocks. The answer is that it would catch all exceptions, including the ones addressed by specific Catch clauses, so the exception-specific Catch clauses would never execute.

You'll probably find Try...Catch...Finally blocks easier to understand in the context of some examples, so let's look at how you might use them to handle exceptions.

We'll start by creating a simple user interface that can be used to cause and catch exceptions. The user interface will consist of a text box, a button, and a status bar.

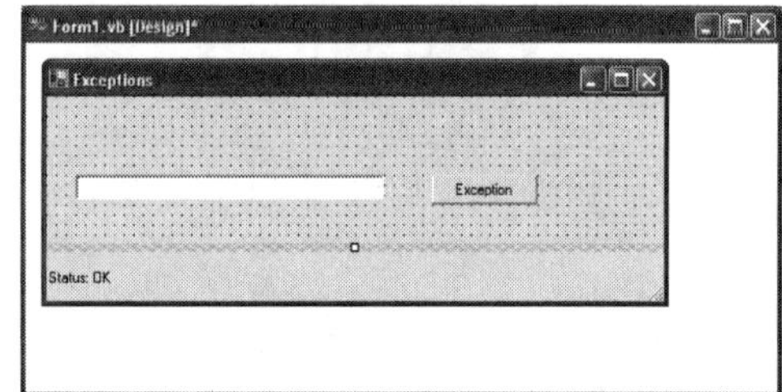

Figure 9.1 A simple user interface is used to generate exceptions.

To create a user interface for generating and catching exceptions:

1. Open a new Windows Application project.
2. Open the application's form in its designer.
3. Use the Toolbox to add a TextBox control, Button control, and StatusBar control to the form.
4. Open the Properties window.
5. Use the Properties window to change the name of the TextBox control to `txtInput` and the value of its Text property to the empty string.
6. Use the Properties window to change the name of the Button control to `btnExc` and the value of its Text property to `Exception`.
7. Use the Properties window to change the value of the Text property of the StatusBar control to `Status: OK` (accept the default name for the control instance, StatusBar1).

   The interface is complete and should look like the form shown in its designer in **Figure 9.1**.

Next, let's set up the user interface to generate an unhandled exception. By observing an unhandled exception in action, we'll be better able to see how (and why) exceptions should be handled.

The first exception we'll cause is a type-casting error known as an invalid type cast exception. This error occurs when you try to convert one type to another type but conversion is not possible. Specifically, we'll try to convert a text string to an integral number. No exception occurs if the text string is numeric—for example, 1042. But if you attempt to convert a text string that is not numeric, such as Hogwarts, an exception will be thrown.

By the way, the code performing the conversion uses the CInt function, rather than the Convert class methods we've used earlier to perform conversion. CInt is functionally equivalent to the Convert.ToInt32 method, although CInt is compiled inline and is nominally faster than the comparable Convert method.

You should also know that CInt (or another conversion method, such as Convert.ToInt32) is required when running code with Option Strict turned on (as I recommend). If Option Strict were off, you could rely on implicit conversion, and a conversion function or method would not be needed. However, even in this case, the attempt to implicitly convert from a nonnumeric text string to a number would cause an invalid type cast exception.

Appendix C, "Visual Basic .NET Types and Type Conversion," provides a great deal of information about VB .NET type conversion alternatives.

To cause an invalid type cast exception:

1. Double-click the Exception button to create an event handler procedure for the button's click event:

```
Private Sub btnExc_Click(ByVal _
    sender As System.Object, _
    ByVal e As System.EventArgs) _
    Handles btnExc.Click


End Sub
```

2. Within the click event handler procedure, declare an integer variable named answer:

```
Dim answer As Integer
```

3. Assign the text that the user will enter, converted to the integer type, to the answer variable:

```
answer = 42 \ CInt(txtInput.Text)
```

   (The division into 42 is included so that we can subsequently cause a division-by-zero error.)

   The code needed to cause the exception is now complete and is shown in **Listing 9.1**.

4. Run the project.

5. Enter a nonnumeric text string in the text box (**Figure 9.2**).

6. Click Exception.

   The development environment displays an unhandled exception message (**Figure 9.3**). As you can see in Figure 9.3, the line of code that causes the problem is highlighted in the Code Editor.

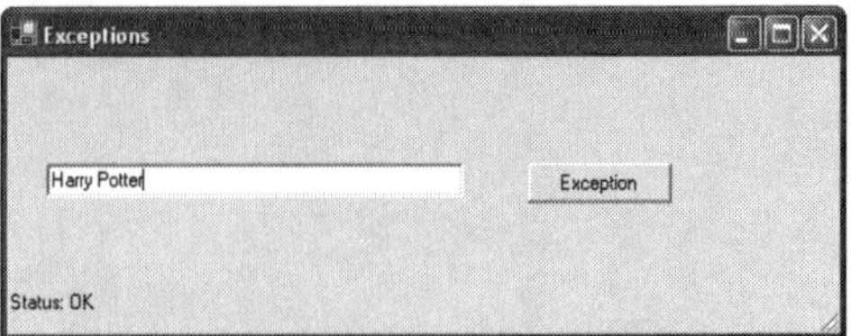

Figure 9.2 If the user enters text that is not numeric, an exception will occur.

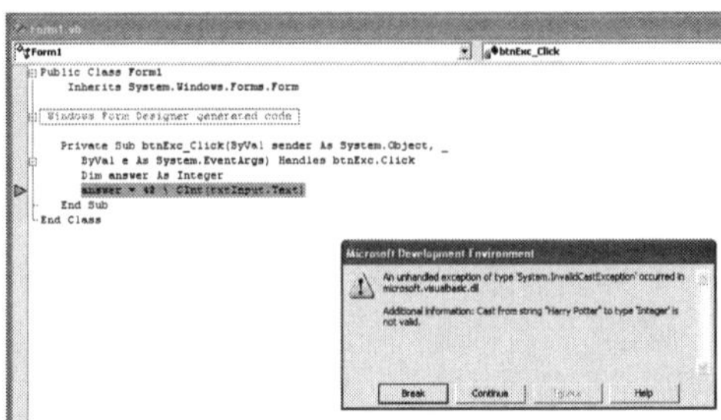

Figure 9.3 When an exception occurs in the development environment, the program code that caused the exception is flagged.

Listing 9.1 Code that causes an exception (depending on user input).

```
Private Sub btnExc_Click(ByVal sender As System.Object, ByVal e As System.EventArgs) _
    Handles btnExc.Click
    Dim answer As Integer
    answer = 42 \ CInt(txtInput.Text)
End Sub
```

USING TRY STATEMENTS

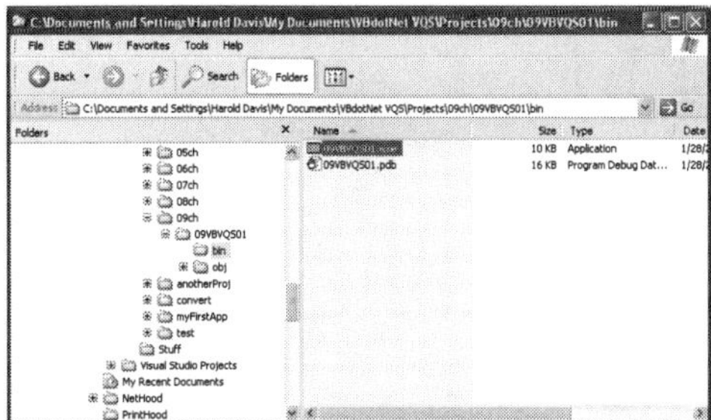

Figure 9.4 The compiled executable file for a program is placed in the bin directory for the project.

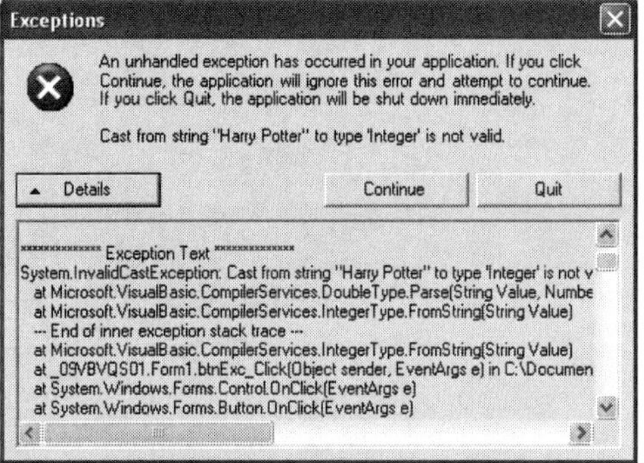

Figure 9.5 If the exception is not handled, the error message produced when the exception occurs is not very user friendly.

This gives us a pretty good idea of what an unhandled exception looks like in the Code Editor when run from the Visual Studio development environment, but what will it look like to the end user? The end user runs a stand-alone executable file and will not see the internal diagnostic messages displayed by the development environment. Let's see what the stand-alone unhandled exception looks like outside of the Visual Studio development environment.

To view an unhandled exception as seen by the end user:

1. Open Windows Explorer.
2. Locate the compiled program created in the previous task.

   As you can see in **Figure 9.4**, Visual Studio places this program file in the bin directory it creates for each project.
3. Double-click the file to launch it.
4. In the text box, enter a nonnumeric text string.
5. Click Exception.

   An exception occurs, and a general Exceptions message box appears.
6. Click Details to see more information about the exception.

   The top pane in **Figure 9.5** is the general Exceptions message box; the Details pane is at the bottom.

There's nothing really wrong with the information shown in the Exceptions message box, but it is not the kind of thing you probably want an end user to see. (To most end users, it will probably look like complete gobbledy-gook.) Using structured exception handling, assuming that you take care to handle exceptions that come from left field as well as the ones you can think of, you can make sure that the end users of your program never see anything like this.

As a first step, let's properly handle the invalid cast exception so that the user sees only a message that explains the problem (and how to correct it).

To handle an invalid cast exception:

1. With the Code Editor open, locate the click event procedure used to generate the unhandled exception.
2. Within the event handling framework, but before any other code, add a Try statement.
3. At the end of the event handling framework, just before the End Sub statement, add an End Try statement.
4. Before the End Try statement, but after the other code, start a Catch clause.
5. As you declare a variable, excep, in the Catch clause, auto-completion will supply a list of possible types (**Figure 9.6**). Select the InvalidCastException type from the list.

   The Catch clause now looks like this:

   ```
   Catch excep As InvalidCastException
   ```

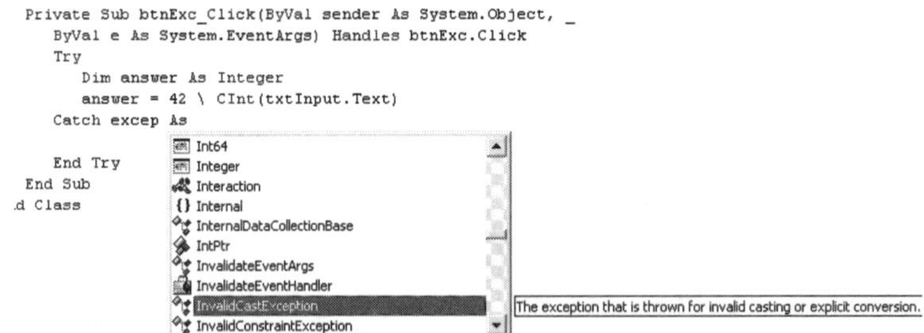
Private Sub btnExc_Click(ByVal sender As System.Object, _
ByVal e As System.EventArgs) Handles btnExc.Click
Try
Dim answer As Integer
answer = 42 \ CInt(txtInput.Text)
Catch excep As
End Try
End Sub
.d Class
Int64
Integer
Interaction
Internal
InternalDataCollectionBase
IntPtr
InvalidateEventArgs
InvalidateEventHandler
InvalidCastException
InvalidConstraintException
The exception that is thrown for invalid casting or explicit conversion.

Figure 9.6 You can select the kind of exception to catch from the drop-down list provided by auto-completion in the Code Editor.

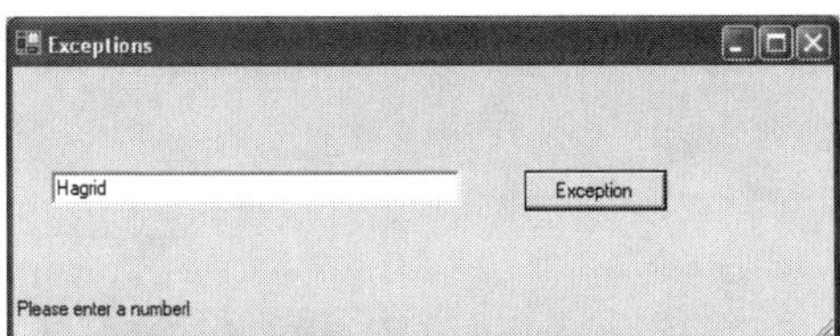

Figure 9.7 If you catch an exception, you can display a descriptive message to users and suggest how to fix the problem.

6. After the Catch clause, add code that displays for the end user an intelligible directive in the status bar:

```
StatusBar1.Text = _
    "Please enter a number!"
```

   Here's the complete code for the Try block as it now stands:

```
Try
    Dim answer As Integer
    answer = 42 \ CInt(txtInput.Text)
Catch excep As InvalidCastException
    StatusBar1.Text = _
        "Please enter a number!"
End Try
```

7. Run the project.
8. In the text box, enter a text string, such as `Hagrid`, that will cause the exception.
9. Click OK.

   A message telling the user to enter a number appears on the status bar (**Figure 9.7**), and there is no incomprehensible error message to be seen!

One of the most useful features of a Try statement is that you can add a Finally block. This code goes in the block following the Finally clause, and it is always executed, whether or not an exception has occurred in the application. Therefore, the Finally block is the ideal place to put cleanup code. This kind of code takes care of operations that you want to occur under all circumstances, such as closing open databases.

To see how these blocks work, we'll add a Finally block that displays a message box. Bear in mind that in production code, you should use Finally blocks for the serious business of closing open resources, maintaining security, and so on.

To test the functionality of the blocks by adding a Finally block:

1. In the click event procedure used to generate exceptions, before the End Try statement, but after the other code, add the keyword Finally to start the Finally block.
2. Within the Finally block, add a MessageBox statement.

   Here's how the entire Try...End Try statement now looks:

```
Try
   Dim answer As Integer
   answer = 42 \ CInt(txtInput.Text)
Catch excep As InvalidCastException
   StatusBar1.Text = _
      "Please enter a number!"
Finally
   MessageBox.Show _
 ("I am processed no matter what!", _
   "Finally!",MessageBoxButtons.OK, _
   MessageBoxIcon.Information)
End Try
```

3. Run the project.
4. Enter a number in the text box (so that an exception will not occur).
5. Click Exception.

   The message box appears.
6. Click OK.
7. Enter a text string in the text box (to cause an exception).
8. Click Exception.

   The message box still appears (**Figure 9.8**).

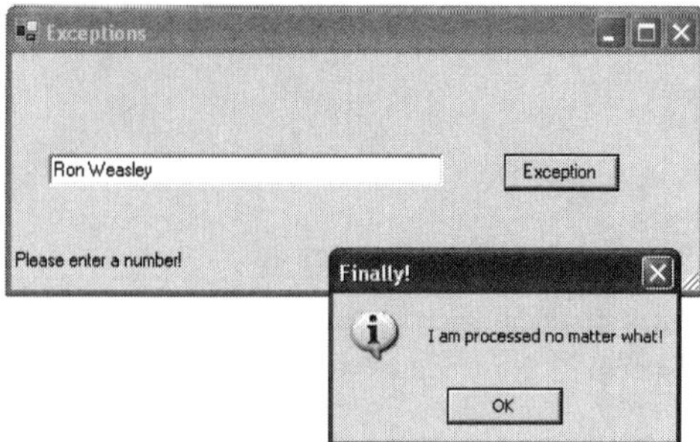

Figure 9.8 Code placed in the Finally block gets executed no matter what.

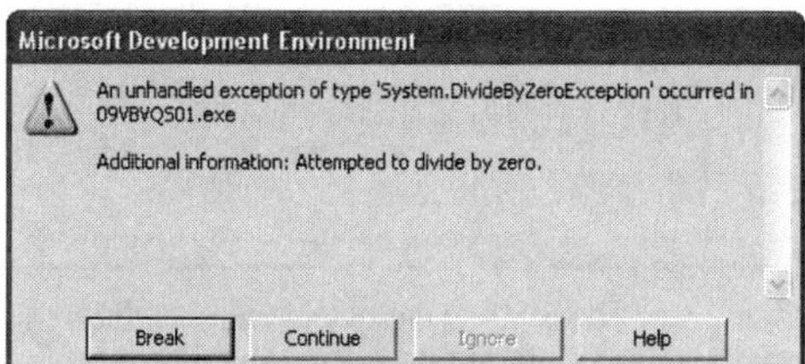

Figure 9.9 If the divide-by-zero exception is not handled, the Microsoft Development Environment displays this message.

As mentioned earlier, the code in the click event procedure is designed to cause an exception when the user enters 0 (because division by zero is forced). Part of the power of the Try...End Try statement is that it can handle unexpected exceptions as well as those you specifically think possible.

To see how this works, suppose that you never considered the possibility that the user might cause an exception by entering 0. If the user enters 0 in the text box and clicks Exception, the Visual Studio development environment will display a message like the one shown in **Figure 9.9**.

But suppose you never saw this divide-by-zero exception coming. Here's how to "expect the unexpected" and handle all exceptions.

To handle all exceptions by adding a general Catch clause:

1. Within the Try...End Try statement, after all other Catch clauses, but before the Finally clause (if there is one), add a new Catch clause (called the *general* Catch clause):

   ```
   Catch excep As Exception
   ```

   This Catch clause is intended to handle all uncaught exceptions, so it is declared generally as of type Exception. (If there is no Finally clause, the general Catch clause goes just before the End Try statement.)

2. Add code to the general Catch clause using the ToString method of the excep Exception object to display in the status bar the message generated by any exception thrown:

   ```
   Catch excep As Exception
      StatusBar1.Text = excep.ToString()
   ```

continues on next page

I've displayed the message generated by the Exception object because it's a good idea to provide as much information as possible when you don't know the nature of the exception that may trigger the Catch clause.

Here's the Try...End Try statement as it now stands:

```
Try
   Dim answer As Integer
   answer = 42 \ CInt(txtInput.Text)
Catch excep As InvalidCastException
   StatusBar1.Text = _
      "Please enter a number!"
Catch excep As Exception
   StatusBar1.Text = excep.ToString()
Finally
   MessageBox.Show _
 ("I am processed no matter what!", _
   "Finally!",MessageBoxButtons.OK, _
   MessageBoxIcon.Information)
End Try
```

3. Run the project.
4. Enter 0 in the text box (to cause the same divide-by-zero exception as before).
5. Click Exception.

   Information about the exception now appears in the status bar (**Figure 9.10**) rather than in the development environment's error message as you saw in Figure 9.9.

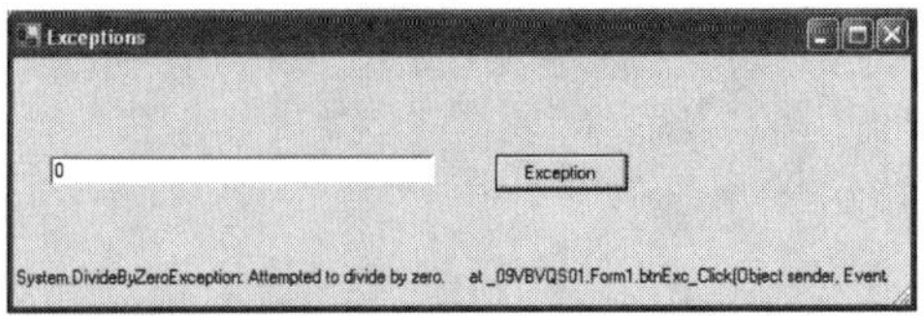

Figure 9.10 The ToString method of the exception object contains information about the exception (displayed here in the status bar).

✔ Tip

- In a real-life production application, you might want to write general Catch clause exception information to a log (or a file) for future diagnostic use, rather than displaying it to the end user.

Listing 9.2 shows the click event procedure used to cause and handle exceptions as developed so far in this section.

You likely can think of a number of exceptions that may occur. So far, our code includes one specific exception (a cast type error) and a general Catch clause (along with the Finally block). You can easily add specific Catch clauses, each taking a customized action, for each exception you can think of (leaving the general Catch clause for all of those exceptions that didn't occur to you).

To see how this works, let's add a Catch clause to handle a specific exception that has occurred to us, namely a divide-by-zero exception. (Of course, you can have as many specific Catch clauses as you need.)

Listing 9.2 Handling an invalid cast exception in a Try...Catch...Finally statement.

```
Private Sub btnExc_Click(ByVal sender As System.Object, ByVal e As System.EventArgs) _
   Handles btnExc.Click
   Try
      Dim answer As Integer
      answer = 42 \ CInt(txtInput.Text)
   Catch excep As InvalidCastException
      StatusBar1.Text = "Please enter a number!"
   Catch excep As Exception
      StatusBar1.Text = excep.ToString()
   Finally
      MessageBox.Show("I am processed no matter what!", "Finally!", MessageBoxButtons.OK, _
      MessageBoxIcon.Information)
   End Try
End Sub
```

To add another specific exception:

1. After the code in the Try block, but before the general Catch clause, add a Catch statement that handles an exception of type DivideByZeroException:

   ```
   Catch excep As DivideByZeroException
   ```

2. Within the Catch clause, take appropriate action when the exception is encountered (in this example, I simply display a message in the status bar):

   ```
   Catch excep As DivideByZeroException
      StatusBar1.Text = _
        "Dividing by zero makes me ill!"
   ```

   Listing 9.3 shows the complete code for the click event that generates and handles the exception, including both specific Catch clauses and a general Catch clause.

3. Run the project.
4. Enter `0` in the text box.
5. Click Exception.

   The Catch clause handles the divide-by-zero exception and displays the message in the status bar (**Figure 9.11**).

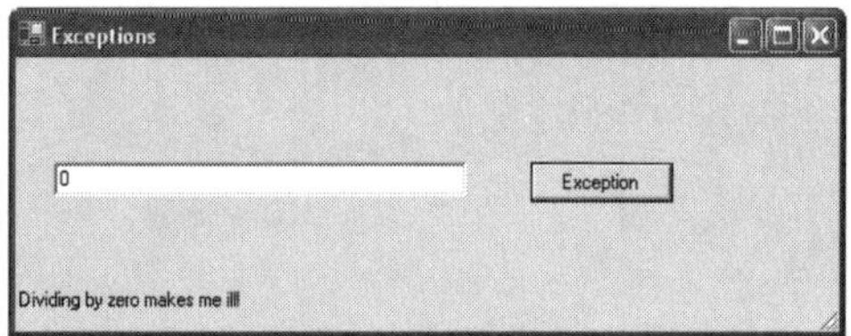

Figure 9.11 If you handle an exception in a Catch clause, you can display an intelligible message.

Listing 9.3 Handling several different kinds of exceptions.

```
Private Sub btnExc_Click(ByVal sender As System.Object, ByVal e As System.EventArgs) _
   Handles btnExc.Click
   Try
      Dim answer As Integer
      answer = 42 \ CInt(txtInput.Text)
   Catch excep As InvalidCastException
      StatusBar1.Text = "Please enter a number!"
   Catch excep As DivideByZeroException
      StatusBar1.Text = "Dividing by zero makes me ill!"
   Catch excep As Exception
      StatusBar1.Text = excep.ToString()
   Finally
      MessageBox.Show("I am processed no matter what!", "Finally!", MessageBoxButtons.OK, _
         MessageBoxIcon.Information)
   End Try
End Sub
```

Throwing Exceptions

Programmers can also throw their own custom exceptions and often do this when they know in advance that an exception is likely to occur in a particular situation.

For example, the programmer may have figured out that in some complicated piece of code, a divide-by-zero exception will occur if the user enters the number 512. Rather than just letting the program throw a divide-by-zero exception (handled or unhandled) in this situation, the programmer may decide to add code that throws a custom exception when the user enters 512. Catching and handling this specific custom exception allows the programmer to add an appropriate message to be displayed to the end user ("Don't enter 512!").

Note from this example that throwing a custom exception is usually used *in conjunction with* a generic exception handler. Throwing the custom exception allows you to provide more information to the user because you can't really give this kind of specific guidance when handling a general divide-by-zero exception. However, the generic exception handler is still present because you need to be sure that the general exception is handled, not just those specific divide-by-zero exceptions caused by the entry of 512.

Custom exceptions are also an excellent mechanism for providing advance warning to a program that a required resource, such as a network drive or a database server, is not available.

To see how to throw and handle a custom exception, we'll throw and then handle a custom exception when the user enters the text string `Ghost`.

To throw a custom exception:

1. In the click event procedure used to demonstrate exceptions, add an If statement to the Try block that checks to see if the user entered the string Ghost:

```
If txtInput.Text = "Ghost" Then _
End If
```

2. Within the If statement, use the Throw keyword to cause an exception, creating the exception using the New constructor for an ApplicationException object (which is passed the string Ghost to identify it):

```
If txtInput.Text = "Ghost" Then _
   Throw New _
      ApplicationException("Ghost")
End If
```

Note that the custom exception that is thrown is of type ApplicationException, rather than type Exception. The ApplicationException class is derived from the Exception class, so the two are closely related. We based the custom exception that is thrown on the ApplicationException type rather than the Exception type so that the general Catch clause, explained earlier in "To add a general Catch clause," can still work properly (as the exception handler of last resort).

You should also be aware that if you need to add specialized facilities to an exception object (for example, to properly communicate with a specific application or database server), you can add these facilities by deriving your own exception class from Exception, or from the ApplicationException class, adding the required members to meet your needs.

Listing 9.4 Throwing, handling, and catching exceptions.

```
Private Sub btnExc_Click(ByVal sender As System.Object, ByVal e As System.EventArgs) _
   Handles btnExc.Click
   Try
      If txtInput.Text = "Ghost" Then
         Throw New ApplicationException("Ghost")
      End If
      Dim answer As Integer
      answer = 42 \ CInt(txtInput.Text)
   Catch excep As InvalidCastException
      StatusBar1.Text = "Please enter a number!"
   Catch excep As DivideByZeroException
      StatusBar1.Text = "Dividing by zero makes me ill!"
   Catch excep As ApplicationException
      If excep.Message = "Ghost" Then
         StatusBar1.Text = "There are ghosts in the machine! It is possessed."
      End If
   Catch excep As Exception
      StatusBar1.Text = excep.ToString()
   Finally
      MessageBox.Show("I am processed no matter what!", "Finally!", MessageBoxButtons.OK, _
         MessageBoxIcon.Information)
   End Try
End Sub
```

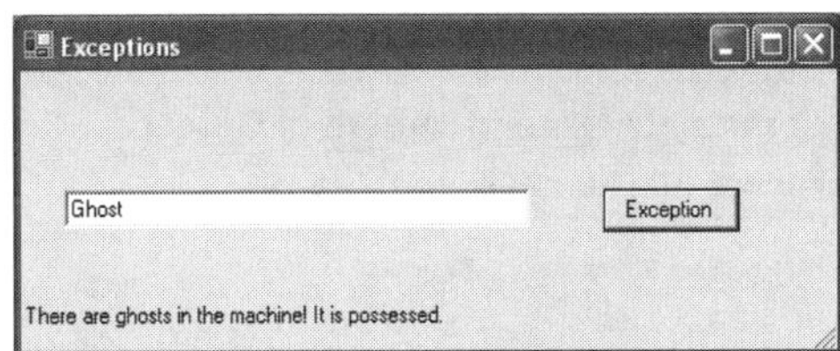

Figure 9.12 You can easily throw and catch your own exceptions.

Handling the custom exception that we've just thrown is easy.

To handle a custom exception:

1. In the click event procedure used to demonstrate exceptions, add a Catch clause to handle exceptions of type ApplicationException:

   ```
   Catch excep As ApplicationException
   ```

2. Within the Catch block, make sure that the exception being handled is the custom exception we want by checking its Message property to make sure that it contains the string value Ghost:

   ```
   Catch excep As ApplicationException
      If excep.Message = "Ghost" Then

      End If
   ```

3. Within the If statement, add code to display a message in the status bar to demonstrate that the exception has been handled; the message will appear if the value of the Message property of the custom exception is Ghost:

   ```
   Catch excep As ApplicationException
      If excep.Message = "Ghost" Then _
         StatusBar1.Text = _
   "There are ghosts in the machine!" & _
         " It is possessed."
      End If
   ```

4. Run the project.
5. Enter `Ghost` in the text box.
6. Click Exception.

   The status bar displays the message that shows that the custom exception has been handled (**Figure 9.12**).

Listing 9.4 shows the complete code for the click event procedure designed to demonstrate exceptions, with throwing and catching the custom exception added.

Working with Exception Objects

Exception objects are instances of the Exception class, or—more commonly—classes that derive from the Exception class. This means that exception objects inherit the properties and methods that are members of the Exception class.

You've already seen how to use two of these members of the Exception class: its Message property and its ToString method. **Table 9.1** shows these and a few other exception object members.

The Exception class has two major subclasses within the .NET Framework: the ApplicationException class and the SystemException class.

Exceptions thrown by your application are supposed to be derived from the ApplicationException class (see the example in "Throwing Exceptions" earlier in this chapter).

In contrast, exceptions generated by the .NET Framework, its runtime library (called the *common language runtime*, or CLR), and other pieces of the platform that your programs run on are supposed to be derived from the SystemException class. You've already seen a couple of these exceptions, including the InvalidCastException class and the DivideByZeroException class.

Probably the best place to learn about all of the exception classes derived from the SystemException class, and their taxonomy, is the Object Browser. (You'll learn how to get the most out of using the Object Browser in Chapter 14, "The Object Browser.") Also, you can use the Exceptions dialog, described in the next section, to look at the exception classes that come ready-made with VB .NET.

Table 9.1

Commonly Used Members of Objects Based on the Exception Class

Property or Method	Purpose
HelpLink property	Gets or sets a link to the help file associated with the exception.
Message property	Gets or sets a message that describes the current exception.
Source property	Gets or sets the application or object that caused the exception.
StackTrace property	Returns a string that contains a trace (or analysis) of the stack immediately before the exception was thrown.
TargetSite property	Gets the method that threw the current exception.
ToString method	Returns a string that contains the name of the exception and a great deal of other information, such as the error message and the stack trace.

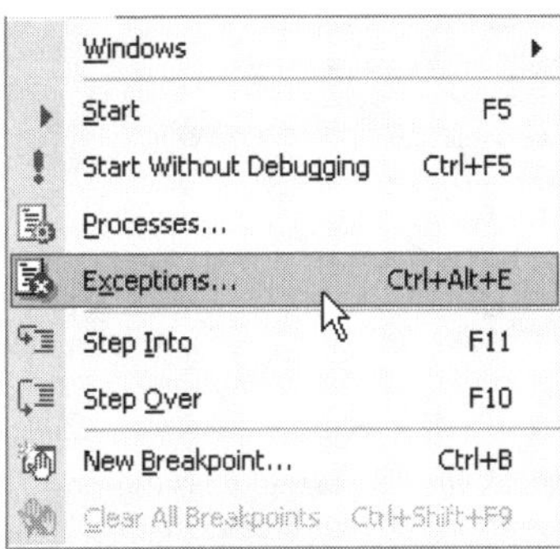

Figure 9.13 From the Debug menu, select Exceptions to open the Exceptions dialog.

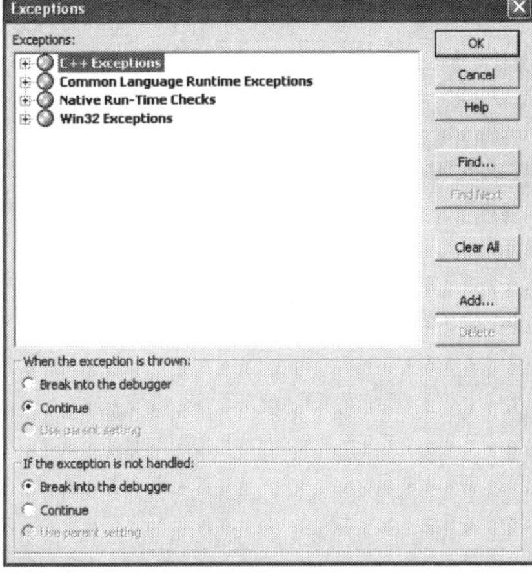

Figure 9.14 The Exceptions dialog displays a number of top-level nodes.

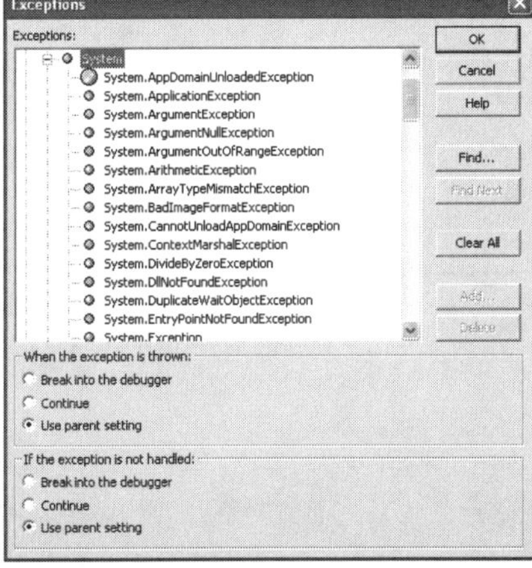

Figure 9.15 Exceptions derived from the System-Exception class appear under the System node.

Using the Exceptions Dialog

You can use the Exceptions dialog to change the behavior in the development environment when an exception is thrown and when a thrown exception is not handled.

To view a list of exceptions:

1. From the Visual Studio Debug menu, choose Exceptions (**Figure 9.13**).

   The Exceptions dialog opens (**Figure 9.14**).

2. Click the plus sign to the left of Common Language Runtime Exceptions to expand the node.

3. Click the plus sign to the left of the System node to expand the node.

   You will see a list of system exception classes (**Figure 9.15**).

The default behavior of the development environment when an exception occurs is to continue processing. Instead, you may want to break into the Code Editor so that you can see what is happening in the code when the exception is thrown.

To break when an exception is thrown:

1. In the Exceptions dialog, select the exception class.
2. For the When the Exception Is Thrown setting, select the Break into the Debugger radio button.

   The icon next to the exception class changes to indicate that it now breaks when thrown, as you can see in **Figure 9.16**.
3. Click OK.

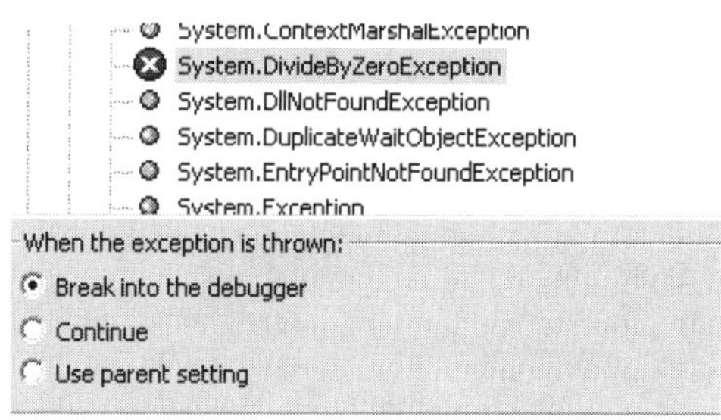

Figure 9.16 To break when an exception is thrown, select the exception and choose Break into the Debugger.

You may notice in the Exceptions dialog that the When Exception Is Thrown settings also include a Use Parent Setting option (which is the default in most cases). If you select this radio button, then to modify the behavior of all System exceptions, you can simply change the option for their parent node, which is the Common Language Runtime Exceptions node.

You can also easily change the behavior of a program in the development environment when an exception that is not handled is thrown. Normally, by default, the exception will cause the program to halt and indicate the code that threw the exception. However, you may just want to continue and ignore the exception—for example, if you were concerned with debugging other parts of a program.

To continue when an exception is not handled:

1. In the Exceptions dialog, select the exception class.
2. For the If the Exception Is Not Handled setting, select the Continue radio button (**Figure 9.17**).
3. Click OK.

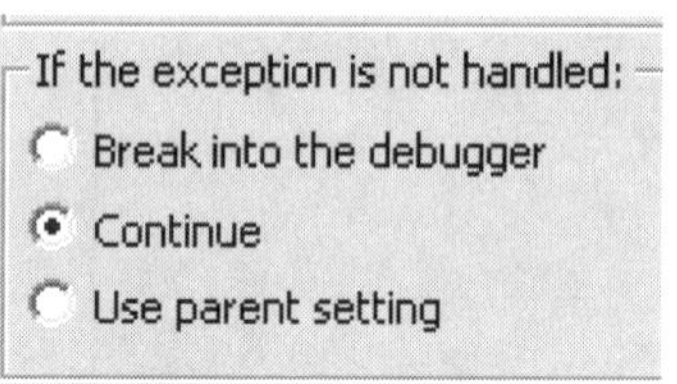

Figure 9.17 To continue when an exception is not handled, select the exception and choose Continue.

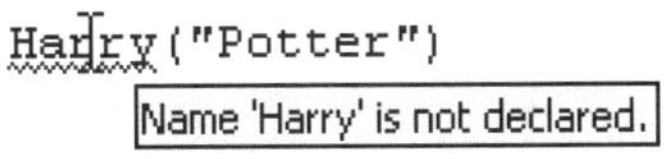

```
Harry("Potter")
        Name 'Harry' is not declared.
```

Figure 9.18 Syntax errors are underlined and described in the Code Editor as they occur.

Understanding Different Kinds of Bugs

So far in this chapter, we've discussed exceptions, examined some variations of them, and illustrated how to bullet-proof applications using structured exception handling. Exception handling is an important topic; every production program should use structured exception handling, implemented using Try...Catch...Finally statements.

The final sections of this chapter discuss a related topic: the debugging tools that are available to programmers as part of the Visual Studio .NET environment.

But before we go there, you need to understand the different kinds of bugs, also called errors or problems, that can occur in programs.

Generally speaking, three kinds of errors can occur in a program: syntax errors, runtime errors, and logical errors.

Syntax errors

Syntax errors, which are the most easily dealt with, are caused by improperly constructed code. Put a little more formally, a syntax error occurs when a statement in a program fails to meet the requirements of the language definition (and therefore cannot be compiled).

Obviously, there are many ways to create syntax errors. The good news is that the Visual Studio development environment intercepts syntax errors for you. Almost as soon as you type the offending statement in the Code Editor, it is underlined and an explanatory message displayed (**Figure 9.18**).

Why Are They Called Bugs?

It's well-known computer folklore that the term *bug* comes from a literal insect that was creating havoc with the innards of an old-time computer. Admiral Grace Hopper, an early programmer and one of the creators of the language COBOL, first used the term *bug* in the 1950s to describe a moth that was causing a vacuum tube monster to malfunction. These days, a bug refers to any error that causes computer software or hardware to malfunction (it is synonymous with error).

In actual historical fact, *bug* was used long before to the invention of the computer to mean a glitch or problem in an industrial or scientific process. (Thomas Edison is on record as having used the term this way.) However, Admiral Hopper is probably the first to use the term in connection with a computer (it's also likely that the moth was figurative rather than literal).

Also, if you attempt to compile the program (by running the project), the development environment will let you know that there is a syntax problem, or build error (**Figure 9.19**). The Task List will then display a list of all syntax (build) errors (**Figure 9.20**). These errors must be fixed before the project can be compiled.

Figure 9.19 If you attempt to compile a program containing syntax errors, you will be notified that it contains build errors.

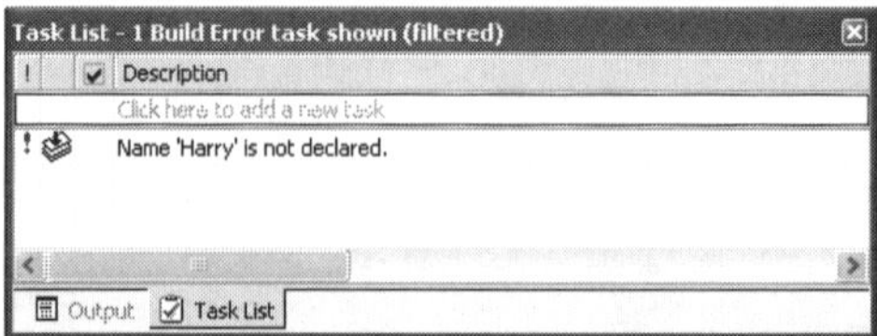

Figure 9.20 The Task List displays any build, or syntax, errors in a program.

In other words, since you can't even get a program to run if it contains syntax errors, and since the development environment accurately pinpoints the location of these errors in code, finding these problems is a trivial matter. They are also pretty easy to resolve using product documentation and aids such as this book.

Runtime errors

Runtime errors occur when a program that was successfully compiled attempts to perform an impossible operation. The simple, but classic, example, shown earlier in this chapter, is the error that occurs when user input causes a successfully compiled program to attempt to divide by zero.

Divide-by-zero errors do occur, but other kinds of unexpected runtime errors are more problematic. Typical examples include the errors that occur when you attempt to write to a full disk, read a file that doesn't exist, use a network resource that isn't available, or log onto a database with incorrect credentials.

There is nothing syntactically illicit about any of these things; they just cannot be done. They also cannot all be easily anticipated.

The embarrassing thing about runtime errors is that they usually don't appear on your desktop when you are testing a program (but see the sidebar "How to Test a Program" for some help with this). Runtime errors generally start to make themselves known only after your programs are installed and in use by important clients.

Runtime errors are the error category that structured exception handling is meant to deal with. By handling all exceptions, including those that are not anticipated, structured exception handling lets you insulate end users from the worst consequences of runtime problems (and also helps you pinpoint the issues involved).

Logical errors

Logical errors occur when a program runs properly, but produces the wrong results. This kind of error can be the hardest of all errors to debug, because, unlike runtime errors, a logical error will often not produce a dramatic or obvious symptom like a program crash. (In contrast, there is no doubt that a program will crash if you try to perform an unhandled division by zero.)

In fact, logical errors can cause inconsistent results that are sometimes correct and sometimes wrong. This situation can be particularly frustrating to debug. The subtler the problem, the harder it may be to fix (or to be sure that an error even exists).

Thinking carefully about how your program works is one of the best ways to resolve logical errors. However, VB .NET also provides a great many tools to help you debug logical errors, some of which are explained in the remainder of this chapter.

How to Test a Program

The following guidelines will help you effectively test your programs:

- Rigor and discipline in the testing process are good things.
- Be diligent in working to break your application. In real life, everything that can go wrong will. Be relentless in attempting to reproduce this truism in your testing process.
- Track your testing process carefully, possibly using software designed for the testing process. Pay particular attention to the test values of variables.
- Consider bounding values (those at the upper and lower ends of the possible ranges that can be assigned to variables).
- One-off errors are a great source of problems, particularly in looping. You should suspect a one-off error in the loop counter whenever a logical error occurs and a loop is present.
- Test for runtime errors under as great a variety of operating conditions as possible.

Using Debug Object Methods

You can use the shared methods of the Debug object to display messages in the Watch window, including variable values, while a program is running. (Since the methods are shared, you don't have to create instances of the Debug object to use the methods.)

Table 9.2 lists the commonly used methods of the Debug object.

Since the values of the counter in a loop often are a cause of logical errors, you might want to display the values assigned to loop counter variables.

To display loop counter values in the Output window:

1. Open a new Windows Application project.
2. Open the Windows form in its designer.
3. Use the Toolbox to add a Button control to the form.
4. Change the name of the Button control to `btnLoop` and its Text value to `Loop`.
5. Double-click the button to create a click event handler procedure in the Code Editor.
6. Within the click event handler, create a number of nested loops using For statements:

```
Dim x, y, z As Integer
For x = 1 To 4200
   For y = 1500 To -1000 Step -1
     For z = -15000 To 15000 Step 100
     Next
   Next
Next
```

Table 9.2

Debug Object Methods

Method	Purpose
Assert	Used to check whether an assertion (a logical condition) evaluates to False when a program is running.
Write	Writes to the Watch and Output windows.
WriteLine	Writes a line to the Watch and Output windows.
WriteIf	Writes to the Watch and Output windows if a condition is True.
WriteLineIf	Writes a line to the Watch and Output windows if a condition is True.

7. Within the innermost loop, add a series of Debug.WriteLine method calls that display the value of each loop counter variable:

```
Debug.WriteLine _
   ("The value of x is " & _
   x.ToString())
Debug.WriteLine _
   ("The value of y is " & _
   y.ToString())
Debug.WriteLine _
   ("The value of z is " & _
   z.ToString())
```

Note that the Output window displays string values, so the numeric loop counter variables have been converted to the string type using the ToString method. Also, I've included explanations with each variable value displayed (otherwise the contents of the Output window can be confusing to read). **Listing 9.5** shows the complete click event procedure code with the loops and the Debug.WriteLine statements.

continues on next page

Listing 9.5 Three nested loops, with Debug.WriteLine statements that display the value of each loop counter.

```
Private Sub btnLoop_Click(ByVal sender As System.Object, ByVal e As System.EventArgs) _
   Handles btnLoop.Click
   Dim x, y, z As Integer
   For x = 1 To 4200
      For y = 1500 To -1000 Step -1
         For z = -15000 To 15000 Step 100
            Debug.WriteLine("The value of x is " & x.ToString())
            Debug.WriteLine("The value of y is " & y.ToString())
            Debug.WriteLine("The value of z is " & z.ToString())
         Next
      Next
   Next
End Sub
```

8. Run the project.
9. Click Loop.
10. From the Visual Studio View menu, choose Other Windows.
11. Choose Output.

    The Output window opens, displaying the value of the loop counter variables as the program runs (**Figure 9.21**).

✔ Tip

- Depending on the resources of your system, code of this sort with extensive nested looping can take a while to complete.

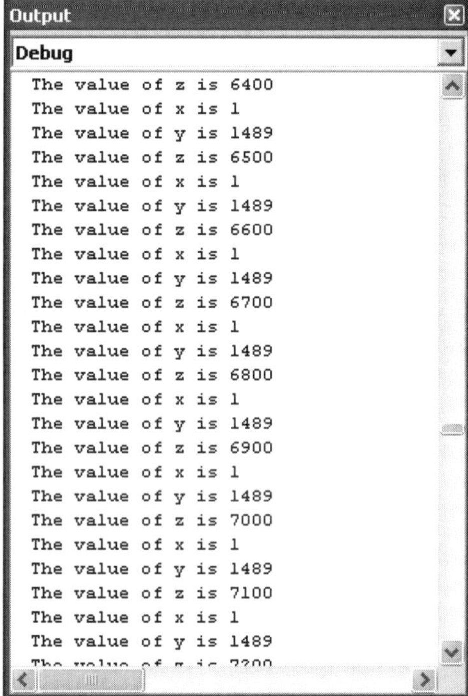

Figure 9.21 The Output window displays values written by the methods of the Debug object.

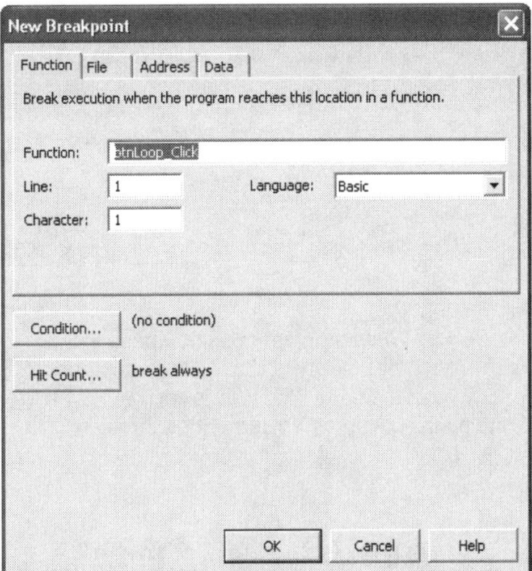

Figure 9.22 You can use the New Breakpoint dialog to set various characteristics of a breakpoint.

```
Public Class Form1
    Inherits System.Windows.Forms.Form

 Windows Form Designer generated code

    Private Sub btnLoop_Click(ByVal sender As System.Object, _
       ByVal e As System.EventArgs) Handles btnLoop.Click
       Dim x, y, z As Integer
       For x = 1 To 4200
          For y = 1500 To -1000 Step -1
             For z = -15000 To 15000 Step 100
                Debug.WriteLine("The value of x is " & _
                   x.ToString())
                Debug.WriteLine("The value of y is " & _
                   y.ToString())
                Debug.WriteLine("The value of z is " & _
                   z.ToString())
             Next
          Next
       Next
    End Sub
End Class
```

Figure 9.23 Breakpoints are indicated in the Code Editor with a round icon in the left margin.

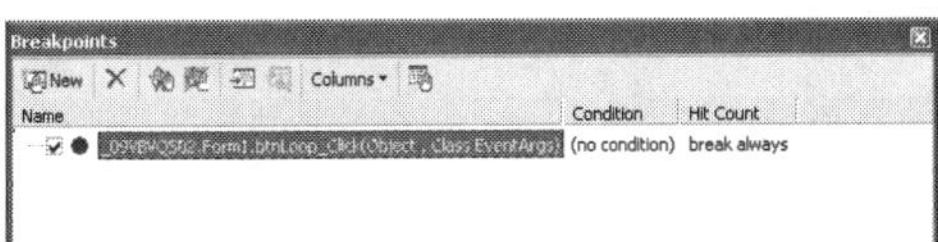

Figure 9.24 The Breakpoints window allows you to view and modify all operational breakpoints.

Stepping and Watching

Using the methods of the Debug object to display values in the Output window works well, but it can be quite a cumbersome way to determine the value of a variable at a particular point in the execution of a program. To overcome this limitation, you can use *stepping*, which allows you to move statement by statement through a program, and *watching*, which displays the variable values of a program running in debug mode in the Visual Studio development environment. This section explains the basics of stepping and watching.

Generally, before you can begin to step, you need to set a *breakpoint*, so you can halt program execution at a specific statement.

To set a breakpoint:

1. Open the Code Editor.
2. Place the cursor in the statement you want to use as a breakpoint.
3. From the Visual Studio Debug menu, choose New Breakpoint.

   The New Breakpoint dialog opens (**Figure 9.22**).
4. Click OK.

   In the Code Editor, a round icon will appear in the left margin next to the statement that is the breakpoint (**Figure 9.23**).

✔ Tip

- You can view and modify all existing breakpoints by choosing Windows > Breakpoints from the Debug menu to open the Breakpoints dialog (**Figure 9.24**).

Now you can advance the program to the breakpoint and start stepping through the program.

To step through the program:

1. Run the project.
2. Click the Loop button.

   The breakpoint engages, and program execution comes to a halt. The statement that triggered the breakpoint is highlighted in the Code Editor (**Figure 9.25**).
3. To step through each statement in the program, from the Debug menu choose Step Into (or press the F11 key). One statement will be processed, and then execution will halt. The processed statement is highlighted in the Code Editor.
4. To process the next statement, again choose Step Into from the Debug menu (or press the F11 key).

   Once again, the statement is highlighted in the Code Editor.
5. Continue stepping through the program until you've found the information you need.

```
Private Sub btnLoop_Click(ByVal sender As System.Object, _
    ByVal e As System.EventArgs) Handles btnLoop.Click
    Dim x, y, z As Integer
    For x = 1 To 4200
        For y = 1500 To -1000 Step -1
            For z = -15000 To 15000 Step 100
                Debug.WriteLine("The value of x is " & _
                    x.ToString())
                Debug.WriteLine("The value of y is " & _
                    y.ToString())
                Debug.WriteLine("The value of z is " & _
                    z.ToString())
            Next
        Next
    Next
End Sub
```

Figure 9.25 When program execution halts at a breakpoint, the statement that halted execution is displayed in the Code Editor (as is each subsequent statement as the program is stepped through).

More Debugging Tools

This chapter has only begun to touch on the debugging tools that are available within Visual Studio .NET. Here are some other debugging tools that you may want to know about:

- The Autos window allows you to display and modify the values of variables in running statements.
- The Call Stack window displays the functions (or procedures) currently on the stack. In other words, if you are running a procedure called from another procedure, both will be on the stack and displayed in the Call Stack window.
- The Command window allows you to run code statements interactively against programs in breakpoint mode.
- The Modules window shows the modules used by a program running in the development environment.
- The Trace object works like the Debug object, except that (unlike the Debug object) it is compiled into final distributed code. Trace object methods are used for monitoring a program after it has been released to end users.

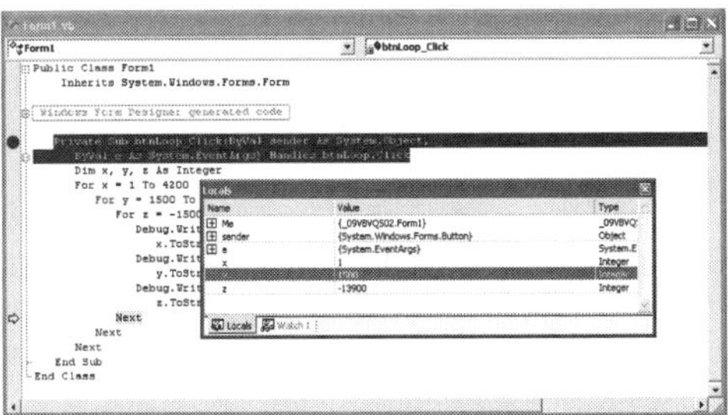

Figure 9.26 The Locals window displays the values of all local variables when a program is in breakpoint mode.

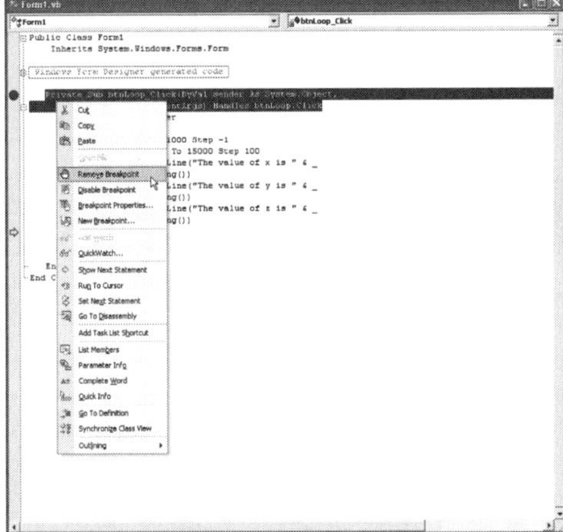

Figure 9.27 To remove a breakpoint, you use the breakpoint's context menu.

There are many ways to discover the values of variables while you are stepping through a program. (One is to read the values written to the Output window by the methods of the Debug object as explained in the previous section.) But perhaps the easiest method of discovering variable values is to read them in the Locals window.

To view variable values in the Locals window:

1. Make sure that a breakpoint has been set.
2. Run the project to advance to the breakpoint.
3. Start stepping through the project (so that your variables have some values).
4. From the Debug menu, choose Windows > Locals.

   The current values of the local variables (that is, variables within the scope of the procedure that is running) will be displayed in the Locals window (**Figure 9.26**).

When you are through debugging, you should know how to remove your breakpoints so that your program can execute normally.

To remove a breakpoint:

1. In the Code Editor, right-click the breakpoint you want to remove.
2. From the context menu that appears, select Remove Breakpoint (**Figure 9.27**).

Summary

In this chapter, you learned how to:

- Use structured exception handling to create bullet-proof programs
- Work with Try...Catch...Finally statements
- Add a general Catch clause
- Throw a custom exception
- Handle a custom exception
- Work with Exception objects
- Use the Exceptions dialog
- Define syntax, runtime, and logical errors and describe how they differ
- Work with the methods of the Debug object
- Set and remove breakpoints
- Step through a program
- Use the Locals window to view variable values as a program is stepped through

Controls That Accept User Input

Now it's time to turn our focus to creating user interfaces that allow the user to provide input.

So far you've learned how to work with forms and buttons (Chapter 5, "Windows Forms"), as well as group boxes, radio buttons, and check boxes (Chapter 7, "Message Boxes and If Statements"). This chapter continues on the topic of creating front end applications by showing you how to work with some of the tools and controls that VB .NET provides to build a professional Windows user interface.

We'll focus on a number of VB .NET interface elements: First we'll examine how to get the most out of the Visual Studio Toolbox by customizing it to suit your own preferences. Second, we'll look at how to use the Visual Studio Format menu to easily arrange controls in a pleasing fashion. Next, we'll explore how to use a single click event procedure to handle the click events of multiple controls. And finally, we'll take a close look at some of the most important Windows controls that accept user input, including the ToolBar, TabControl, TrackBar, and ListBox controls.

This is great and fun material, which I'm sure you'll be able to use to great advantage in your Windows applications, so hang on for a wonderful ride!

Customizing the Toolbox

So far in this book, we've made extensive use of the Visual Studio Toolbox. This, of course, will continue: the Toolbox offers the only easy way to add controls and components to a module in its designer. (See Chapter 5 for the definitions of *control* and *component* and for discussion of how the two objects differ.)

The Toolbox is organized by tabs. Each tab contains a set of related controls and components. For example, the Windows Form tab contains controls for creating a Windows user interface. The Data tab contains components for connecting to a database, as you'll see in Chapter 15, "XML, Data, and ADO.NET."

In keeping with Visual Studio terminology, we'll generally refer to objects that can be placed on a Toolbox tab as *items*. For the most part, these items are controls and components (but see "To store code in a Toolbox item" later in this chapter for an example of an item that can be added to a Toolbox tab that is neither a control nor a component).

In some cases, a particular Toolbox tab, and the items the tab contains, will not appear in the Toolbox unless a module that can use the Toolbox items is open in its designer. For example, the Windows Form tab of the Toolbox will not be displayed unless a Windows form is open in its designer in the Visual Studio development environment. Similarly, the Web Forms tab of the Toolbox and its items will not be displayed unless a Web form is open in its designer.

In other words, you should not expect at any given time to see all of the Toolbox tabs because the tabs displayed depend on the Visual Studio development environment context. However, if you ever need to, you can display all of the tabs in the Toolbox by selecting Show All Tabs from the Toolbox context menu.

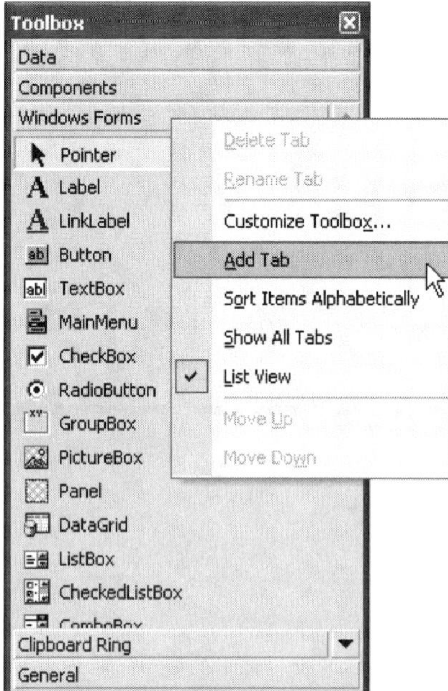

Figure 10.1 Use the Toolbox context menu to add custom tabs.

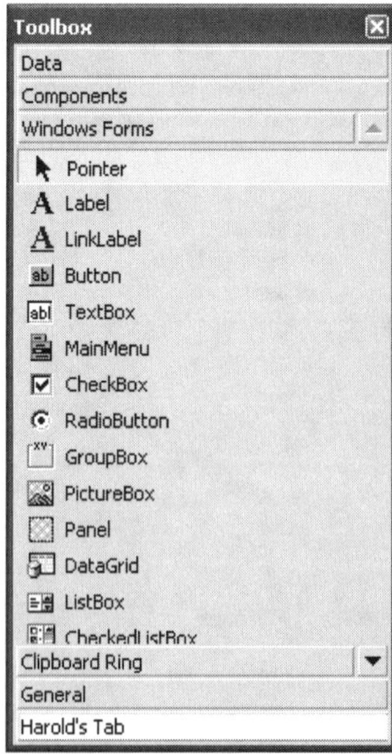

Figure 10.2 The new custom tab appears at the bottom of the Toolbox.

Figure 10.3 The new custom tab is empty, except for the Pointer tool.

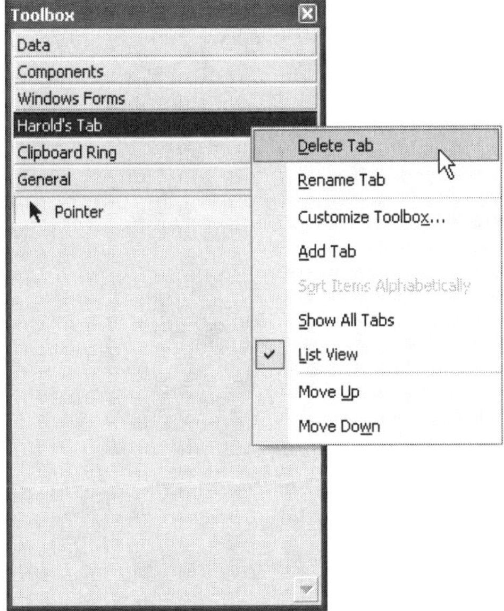

Figure 10.4 You can use the Toolbox context menu to delete tabs.

In fact, the entire Toolbox is highly configurable. You can set up the Toolbox so that it works the way you do. For example, for a particular project, you may use only a small number of controls. So why not add a Toolbox tab that contains just the controls you need?

This section shows you the basics of customizing the Toolbox.

To create a new Toolbox tab:

1. From the Visual Studio View menu, choose Toolbox to open the Toolbox.
2. Right-click within the Toolbox to display the Toolbox context menu.
3. From the Toolbox context menu, choose Add Tab (**Figure 10.1**).

   A new custom tab is added to the Toolbox.
4. Enter a name for the new tab: for example, *Harold's Tab*, as shown in **Figure 10.2**.
5. Press Enter.

   The tab will appear containing the Pointer tool and no other items (**Figure 10.3**).

To delete a custom Toolbox tab:

1. With the Toolbox open, right-click the name of the tab you want to delete.
2. Select Delete Tab from the Toolbox context menu (**Figure 10.4**).

   The tab will be deleted.

You can easily store text, such as program code, in a Toolbox item. You may want to do this for bits of program code that you use over and over again, such as a boilerplate comment. However, a code item in the Toolbox will be accessible only when the Visual Studio development environment is in a context in which code can be used, such as when the Code Editor is open.

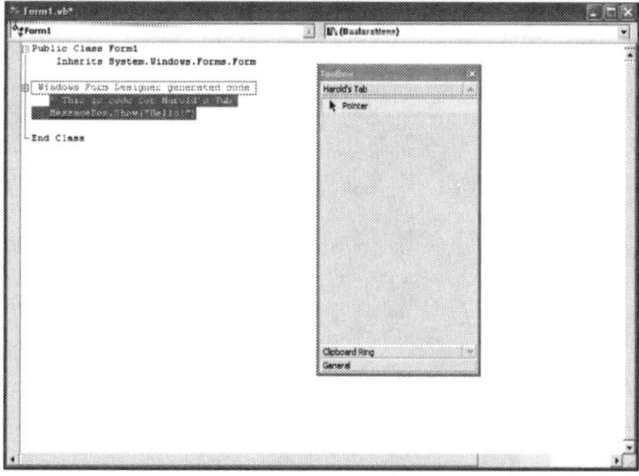

Figure 10.5 To add a code snippet to a Toolbox panel, first select the code snippet in the Code Editor.

To store code in a Toolbox item:

1. Open the Code Editor.
2. Open the Toolbox.
3. Select the Toolbox tab to which you want to add the code snippet.
4. In the Code Editor, select the code snippet (**Figure 10.5**).
5. Drag the selected code and drop it on the Toolbox tab.

   The code snippet will now appear as an item, marked as text, on the Toolbox tab (**Figure 10.6**).

Figure 10.6 Code or other text appears as an item on a Toolbox tab.

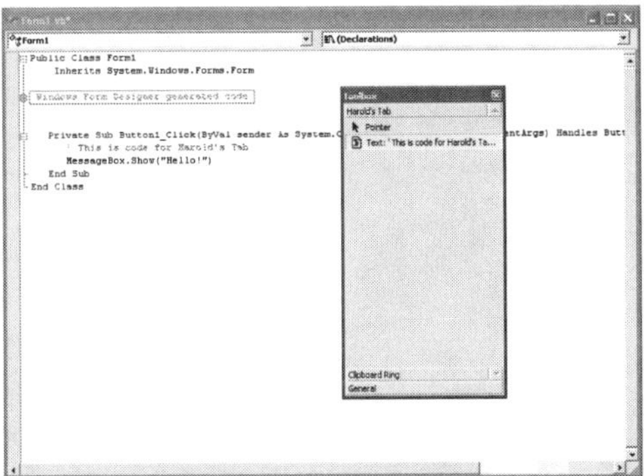

Figure 10.7 A code snippet stored as a Toolbox item can be added to a program by dragging the snippet to the location where you want to place it in the Code Editor.

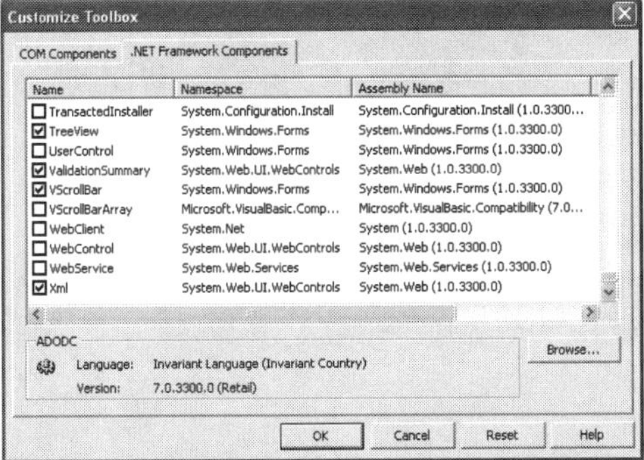

Figure 10.8 Use the Customize Toolbox dialog to add components and controls to the Toolbox.

To retrieve code from a Toolbox item:

1. Open the Code Editor.
2. Open the Toolbox.
3. Select the tab that contains the code snippet.
4. Drag the code snippet from the Toolbox and drop it on the destination location in the Code Editor (**Figure 10.7**).

To add a component or a control to a Toolbox tab:

1. Open the Toolbox.
2. Select the Toolbox tab to which you want to add a component or control.
3. Right-click the Toolbox tab and choose Customize Toolbox from the context menu.

   The Customize Toolbox dialog opens.
4. Click the .NET Framework Components tab (**Figure 10.8**).
5. Place a check mark in the box next to the component or control you want to add.
6. Click OK.

   The item is added to the active Toolbox tab.

✔ Tips

- To remove a component or control from the Toolbox, clear the check box next to the item in the Customize Toolbox dialog shown in Figure 10.8 and click OK.
- You can add an item not listed in the Customize Toolbox dialog by clicking the Browse button and locating the file that contains the item.
- The Reset button restores the Toolbox to its factory settings, but you should use this button with caution as any changes you have made to customize the Toolbox will be lost.

To delete an item from a Toolbox tab:

1. Select the item you want to remove from the Toolbox tab.
2. Right-click to open the Toolbox context menu.
3. Choose Delete from the context menu.
4. Click OK to confirm the deletion.

To move an item from one Toolbox tab to another:

- Drag the item you want to move from a Toolbox tab to the top of another Toolbox tab.

To copy an item from one Toolbox tab to another:

1. Select the item you want to copy.
2. Right-click to open the Toolbox context menu.
3. Choose Copy.
4. Select the tab to which you want to copy the item.
5. Right-click to open the context menu with the destination tab selected.
6. Choose Paste.

   You can use copying and pasting to easily create custom tabs for special purposes; for example, the tab shown in **Figure 10.9** shows the new controls that will be explained in this chapter.

Figure 10.9 You can move (or copy) items from one tab to another.

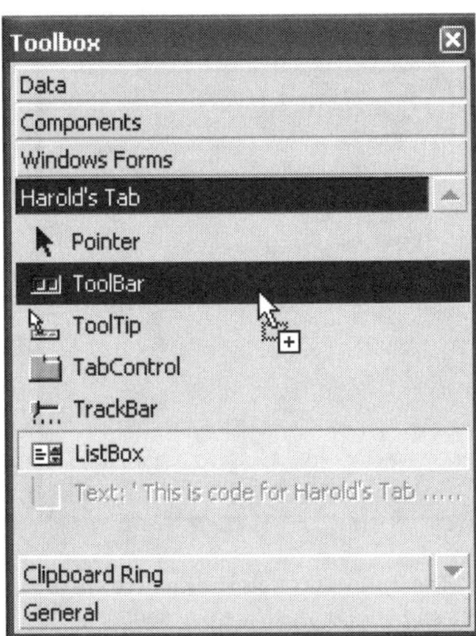

Figure 10.10 You can position items on a Toolbox tab by dragging them to the desired location.

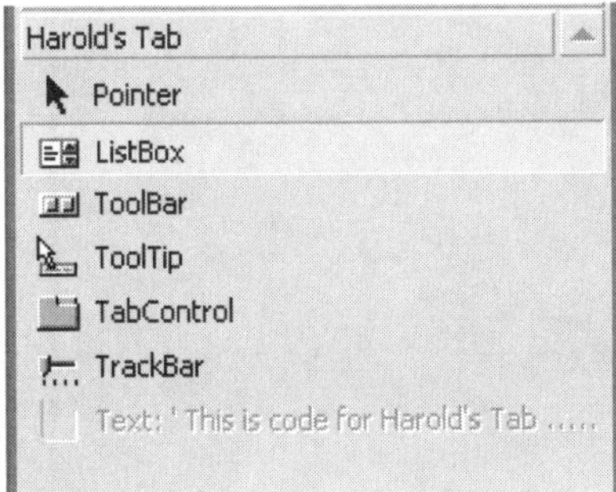

Figure 10.11 An item, such as a control, appears on a tab where it was dropped.

To reposition an item on a Toolbox tab:

1. Select the item you want to move.
2. Drag the item to the desired location. The toolbox items will become highlighted as you drag the item over them. When you drop the item, it will appear above the highlighted item. (**Figure 10.10**).
3. Drop the item.

   It will now appear in the new position (**Figure 10.11**).

Using the Format Menu

The Visual Studio .NET Format menu provides access to tools for arranging controls on a form in its designer. You use these formatting tools in much the same way that you use the tools in a page layout program to arrange the text and other items that make up a printed page.

In professional user interfaces, controls are generally all the same size and intelligently aligned. The tools that you can access through the Format menu make it easy to achieve these objectives in VB .NET.

To make multiple controls the same size:

1. With a form open in its designer, use the Toolbox to add a number of different controls to the form.
2. Drag and drop the control borders so that they are different sizes.

   Figure 10.12 shows Button controls, but you can make controls of any type the same size.
3. Select the controls that you want to make the same size, either by choosing the Pointer tool from the Toolbox and using it to marquee select the controls (**Figure 10.13**) or by holding down the Ctrl key and selecting each control in turn.

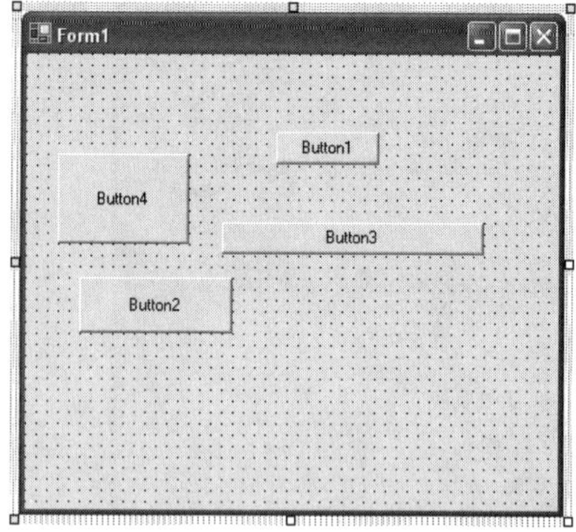

Figure 10.12 The Button controls shown here are of diverse sizes and do not present a pleasant user interface.

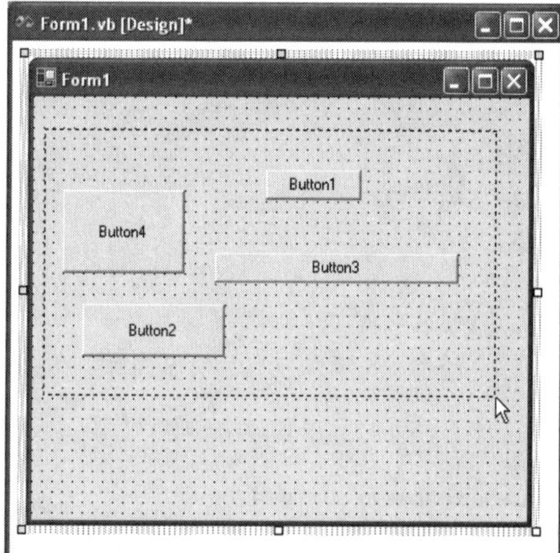

Figure 10.13 You can use the Pointer tool to select multiple controls at the same time.

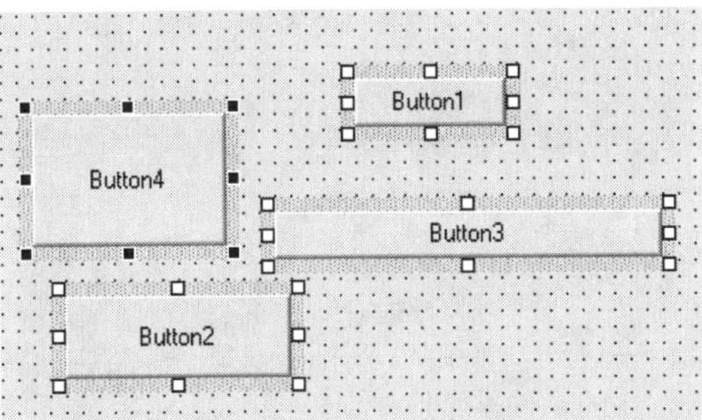

Figure 10.14 The four Button controls are selected.

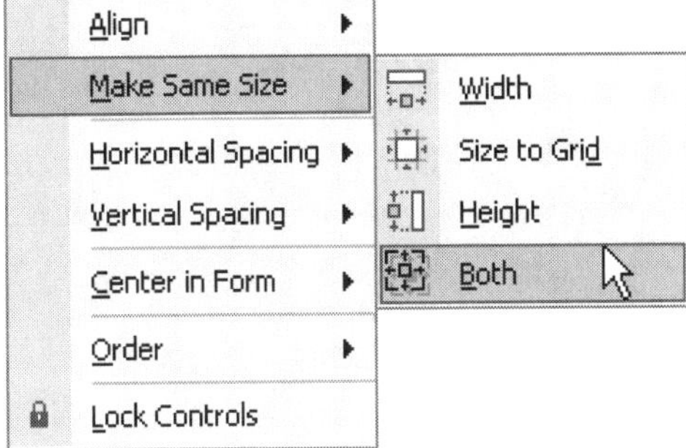

Figure 10.15 Choose Both from the Make Same Size submenu to make the height and width of the selected controls the same.

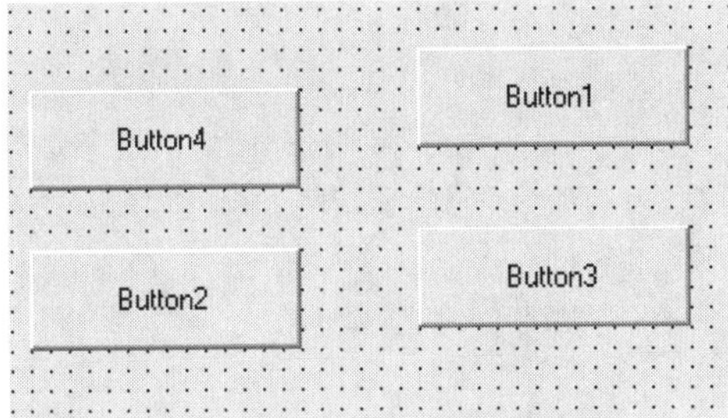

Figure 10.16 The four Button controls are now the same size (although misaligned).

4. With the controls selected (**Figure 10.14**), from the Visual Studio Format menu, choose Make Same Size (**Figure 10.15**).

5. As shown in Figure 10.15, from the Make Same Size submenu, choose Both to make the controls the same size in both dimensions (**Figure 10.16**).

   Alternatively, you can make the controls only the same height or width, or you can choose Size to Grid to snap all selected controls to the nearest points on the grid.

✔ Tip

- If you marquee select the controls you want to resize, the first selected control is used as the basis for the size of all of the controls to be resized. If, instead, you hold down the Ctrl key and select the controls in turn, the last control selected is the one used as the basis for the size of the other selected controls.

In addition to resizing, you will often want to align multiple controls.

To align controls:

1. With a form open in its designer, use the Toolbox to add a number of different controls to the form. Make sure that the controls are not aligned.

   Figure 10.17 shows a group of RadioButton controls, but you can align controls of any type.

2. Select the controls that you want to align, either by choosing the Pointer tool from the Toolbox and using it to marquee select the controls or by holding down the Ctrl key and selecting each control in turn.

3. With the controls selected that you want to align, from the Visual Studio Format menu, choose Align > Lefts (**Figure 10.18**).

   The controls become left-aligned (**Figure 10.19**).

   Alternatively, you can align the controls using the centers, rights, tops, middles, or bottoms for alignment, or you can choose To Grid to align all selected controls to the nearest points on the grid.

✔ Tip

- If you marquee select the controls you want to resize, the first selected control is used as the basis for the alignment of all of the controls to be aligned. If, instead, you hold down the Ctrl key and select the controls in turn, the last control selected is the one used as the basis for the alignment of the other selected controls.

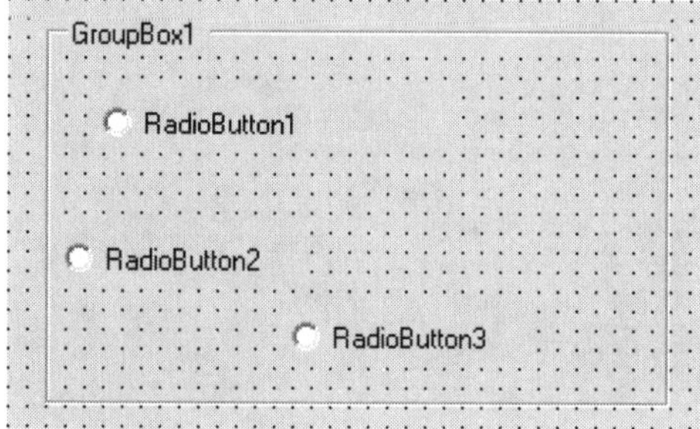

Figure 10.17 This group of RadioButton controls is misaligned.

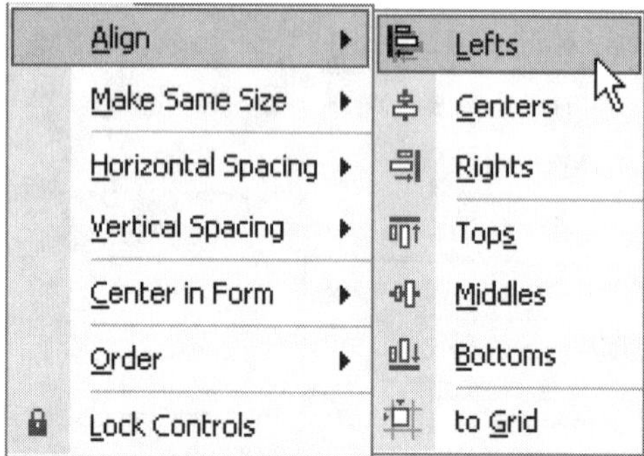

Figure 10.18 Choose Lefts from the Align submenu to left-align the radio buttons.

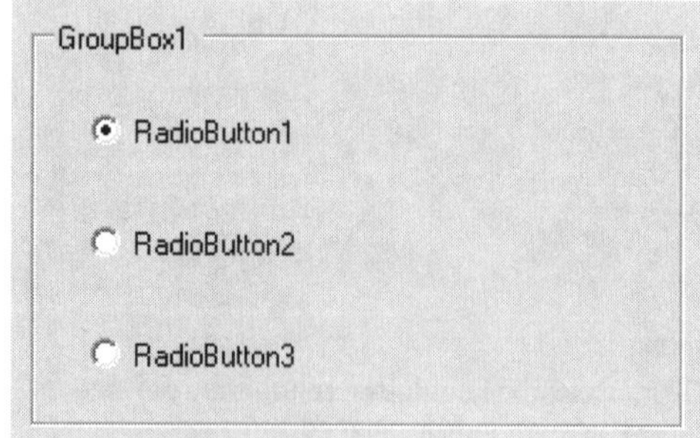

Figure 10.19 RadioButton controls in a group should usually be left-aligned.

The Format menu provides access to a number of items besides control size and alignment that you can use to design the appearance of controls on a form. The use of these tools is fairly intuitive, so we won't examine how they work in detail. You should know, though, that you can also use the Format menu to do the following:

- Adjust horizontal and vertical spacing between controls.
- Center a control or group of controls in a form.
- Bring a control to the front or send a control to the back. This ability, which is also called changing the *z-order* of a control, is particularly useful when one control is hidden behind another one.
- Lock the controls in their current positions on the form so that they can't be moved by accident as you work with the form. This setting is a toggle, so that you can unlock the controls if you discover later that you need to adjust the size or position of a control.

Working with Groups of Controls

In the previous section, in learning how to use the formatting tools provided by the Format menu, you added a number of Button and RadioButton controls to a form. In this section, you'll learn how to use a single click event procedure to process and evaluate the user's input to both kinds of controls. The benefit of using a single event handler to process multiple controls is efficiency: you have to create only one code procedure rather than one for each control.

To process the click events of a group of buttons in a single procedure:

1. Double-click one of the buttons you created in the previous section—for example, Button3—to create a click event handler in the Code Editor:

```
Private Sub Button3_Click _
    (ByVal sender As System.Object, _
    ByVal e As System.EventArgs) _
    Handles Button3.Click


End Sub
```

2. In the click event procedure in the Code Editor, add a comma at the end of the Handles clause and add each click event that you want the procedure to handle, separated by a comma (the three other buttons are shown in this example):

```
Handles Button3.Click, _
    Button1.Click, Button2.Click, _
    Button4.Click
```

3. Within the click event procedure, declare a variable, myButton, of type Button:

```
Dim myButton As Button
```

4. Cast, or convert, the sender argument of the original click event procedure to Button and assign it to myButton:

```
myButton = CType(sender, Button)
```

5. Use the value referenced by myButton (the Button control that fired the click event procedure) to display the firing Button's name in the caption bar of the form:

```
Me.Text = _
    myButton.Name & _
    " was clicked!"
```

   Here's the complete multiple click event handler:

```
Private Sub Button3_Click _
    (ByVal sender As System.Object, _
    ByVal e As System.EventArgs) _
    Handles Button3.Click, _
    Button1.Click, Button2.Click, _
    Button4.Click
    Dim myButton As Button
    myButton = CType(sender, Button)
    Me.Text = _
        myButton.Name & _
        " was clicked!"
End Sub
```

6. Run the project.
7. Click a button.

   The name of the button is displayed in the caption bar of the form (**Figure 10.20**).

8. Verify that the code works by clicking another button and making sure that the name of the newly clicked Button control appears in the caption bar.

You should observe several points about the code in this task.

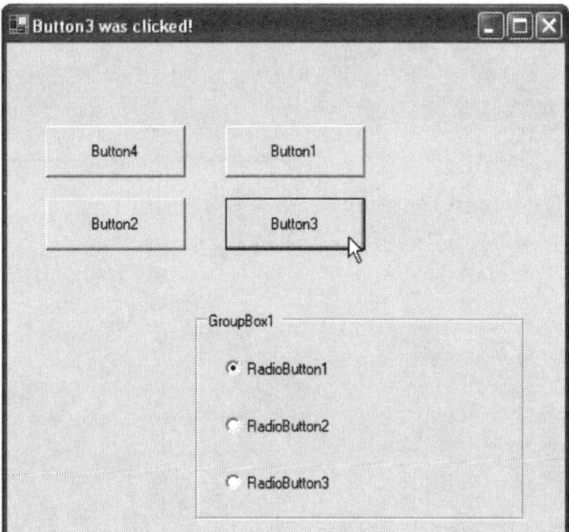

Figure 10.20 The name of the Button control that was clicked appears in the form caption bar.

First, most professional developers recommend running VB .NET projects with Option Strict turned on because this leads to fewer errors in code. (For more information, see "Setting property pages for a project" in Chapter 1.)

However, if you turned Option Strict off, you would no longer need to explicitly convert the object referenced by the sender variable to a Button type. Instead, the program would practice late binding—meaning that it would determine the type of object referenced by the sender argument at runtime. This implies that you could directly use the value sender.Name without any conversion.

In contrast, with Option Strict turned on, you're restricted to early binding, meaning that you need to know the types of objects you use at compile time (rather than runtime)—hence, the need for an explicit conversion using the CType function. For more information about Option Strict and type conversion, see Appendix C, "Visual Basic .NET Types and Type Conversion" at the back of the book.

Next, a procedure that handles multiple events is not limited to handling events fired by a particular type of object or to a particular event. Thus, the single event handler used to handle the button click events could also be used to process, for example, a Resize event fired by a Form class. You would do this by adding the form event to the original Button control click event Handles clause (Resize is a base class event for a Form class, so it is referred to using the MyBase keyword):

```
Private Sub Button3_Click _
   (ByVal sender As System.Object, _
   ByVal e As System.EventArgs) _
   Handles Button3.Click, _
   Button1.Click, Button2.Click, _
   Button4.Click, MyBase.Resize
```

However, if you run this code, you'll get a syntax error (**Figure 10.21**) because of the attempt to convert the sender variable to a Button type (sender might contain a Form type).

You can side-step this syntax error by using a conditional statement and the Is keyword to check the type referenced by the sender variable. You'll see how to use the Is keyword in the next task, which evaluates which RadioButton control in a group of RadioButton controls is selected, using the one event procedure to determine which is selected.

You may recall that only one RadioButton control in a group can be selected (see Chapter 7, "Message Boxes and If Statements"). A RadioButton control is selected if its Checked property evaluates to True.

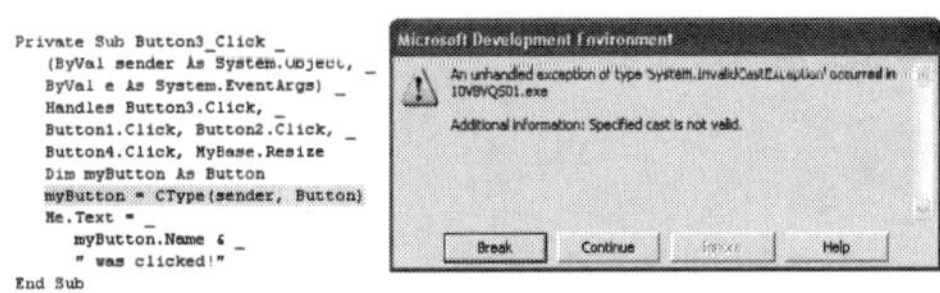

Figure 10.21 The attempt to convert a Form type to a Button type produces a syntax error.

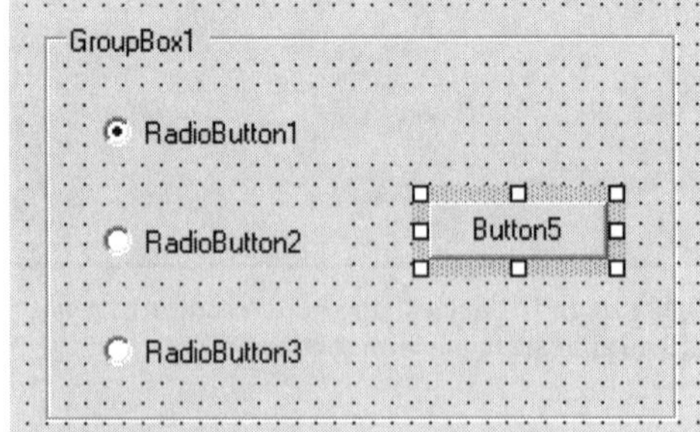

Figure 10.22 The GroupBox control contains a number of RadioButton controls and a Button control.

To determine which RadioButton control is selected:

1. Use the Toolbox to add a GroupBox control to a form.
2. Add some RadioButton controls to the GroupBox container.

   (The RadioButton controls shown in Figure 10.22 are the same ones shown earlier in this chapter in "To align controls.")
3. Use the Properties window to make sure that one of the RadioButton controls is initially selected by setting its Checked property to True.
4. Add another type of control, such as a Button control, to the group box control as shown in **Figure 10.22**.

   As you can see, this technique doesn't require that radio buttons be the only control type present in the GroupBox container control.

5. Add the new Button control's click event to the handler for multiple buttons that you developed earlier in this section:

```
Private Sub Button3_Click _
   (ByVal sender As System.Object, _
   ByVal e As System.EventArgs) _
   Handles Button3.Click, _
   Button1.Click, Button2.Click, _
   Button4.Click, Button5.Click
```

I've added the code that evaluates which RadioButton control was selected to the general button click event procedure, as you can see in **Listing 10.1**, which shows the complete code for processing all Button control click events on the form and evaluating which RadioButton control is selected. However, in your own applications, you could add this code anywhere that it will get processed.

continues on next page

Listing 10.1 Using one event handler for many buttons and determining the selected RadioButton control.

```
Private Sub Button3_Click (ByVal sender As System.Object, ByVal e As System.EventArgs) _
   Handles Button3.Click, Button1.Click, Button2.Click, Button4.Click, Button5.Click
   Dim myButton As Button
   myButton = CType(sender, Button)
   Me.Text = myButton.Name & " was clicked!"
   Dim c As Control
   For Each c In GroupBox1.Controls
      If TypeOf (c) Is RadioButton Then
         Dim rb As RadioButton = CType(c, RadioButton)
         If rb.Checked = True Then
            MessageBox.Show(rb.Name & " is selected!", "Groups of controls", _
               MessageBoxButtons.OK, MessageBoxIcon.Information)
         End If
      End If
   Next
End Sub
```

6. Wherever you choose to place the code, declare a variable of type Control, so that any type of control can be referenced in it without causing a syntax error:

   ```
   Dim c As Control
   ```

7. Use a For loop and the variable c to process each control contained by the GroupBox control:

   ```
   For Each c In GroupBox1.Controls

   Next
   ```

8. Check to see if the control referenced by the c loop variable is a RadioButton control:

   ```
   If TypeOf (c) Is RadioButton Then

   End If
   ```

9. If the control is a RadioButton control, convert it formally to the RadioButton type and save a reference to it in the variable rb:

   ```
   Dim rb As RadioButton = _
       CType(c, RadioButton)
   ```

10. Add the code to display the name of the checked radio button in a message box:

   ```
   If rb.Checked = True Then
      MessageBox.Show(rb.Name & _
         " is selected!", _
         "Groups of controls", _
         MessageBoxButtons.OK, _
         MessageBoxIcon.Information)
   End If
   ```

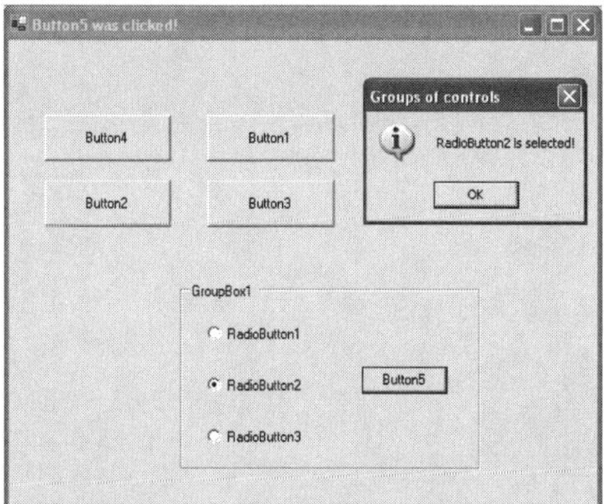

Figure 10.23 Clicking any of the buttons on the form displays a message box that shows the name of the selected RadioButton control.

Here's the complete code for determining the selected RadioButton control:

```
Dim c As Control
For Each c In GroupBox1.Controls
   If TypeOf (c) Is RadioButton Then
      Dim rb As RadioButton = _
         CType(c, RadioButton)
      If rb.Checked = True Then
        MessageBox.Show(rb.Name & _
          " is selected!", _
          "Groups of controls", _
          MessageBoxButtons.OK, _
         MessageBoxIcon.Information)
      End If
   End If
Next
```

11. Run the project.
12. Select a radio button.
13. Click any button.

    The selected RadioButton control is displayed in a message box (**Figure 10.23**).

✔ Tip

- You can use a more general loop variable, containing a reference to the Object type, if you are not sure whether all objects contained within the GroupBox are of type Control.

Working with the ToolBar Control

You can use toolbars to let users make choices by clicking buttons. Generally, users can click toolbar buttons in lieu of selecting menu items or clicking standard buttons. Toolbars can be positioned in the most convenient places in a window for users. They are often used in multiple-document interface applications. (For information about MDI applications, see Chapter 8, "Working with MDI Forms.")

In Visual Basic .NET, you can add a toolbar to a form by adding a ToolBar control to the form. The actual process is slightly more complicated than just adding the control, however, because a ToolBar control itself does not host any of the images that will be used as toolbar buttons.

The images are provided by an ImageList control. An ImageList control is designed to be a repository, or library, of images. The ImageList control is added to your form and used to store images, but it is invisible at run-time to the users of your application.

Once images have been loaded in the ImageList control, it can be associated with a ToolBar control, and the images stored in the ImageList control can then be used to create the ToolBar buttons on the screen. The process involves the following general steps (which will be discussed in detail):

- Load an ImageList control with images.
- Associate the ImageList control with a ToolBar control.
- Use the images stored in the ImageList control to populate the ToolBar control's buttons.

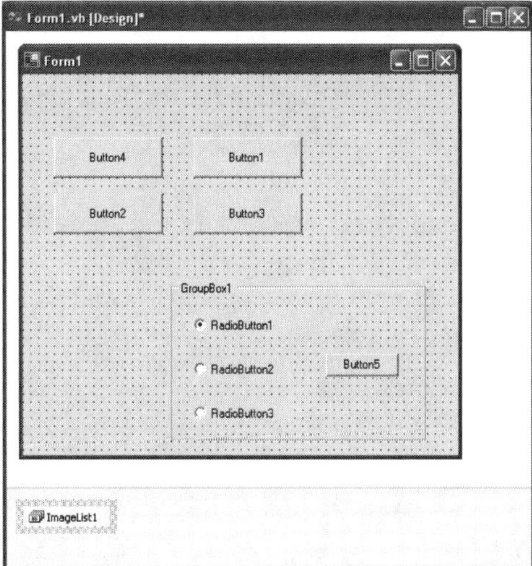

Figure 10.24 The ImageList control, which is invisible at runtime, appears at design time in the tray below a form.

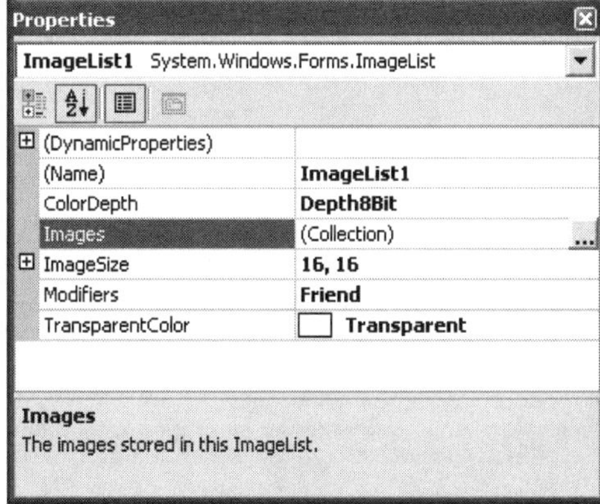

Figure 10.25 Click the button in the right column next to the Images property of an ImageList control to open the Image Collection Editor.

If this process sounds complex, don't worry: it's not. In this section, I'll guide you through each of these steps.

To load an ImageList control with images:

1. Open a form in its designer.
2. From the View menu, choose Toolbox to open the Toolbox.
3. In the Toolbox, double-click the ImageList control to add it to the form. (The ImageList control is about midway down the controls on the Windows Form tab of the Toolbox.)

   Once the ImageList control has been added to the form, this control, unlike controls that are visible at runtime, appears in the tray beneath the form (**Figure 10.24**) rather than on the form itself.
4. Select the ImageList control in the tray, right-click, and choose Properties from the context menu to open the Properties window with the ImageList control displayed.

   Alternatively, you can choose Properties Window from the View menu and select the ImageList control from the objects list at the top of the Property window.
5. In the left column of the Properties window, select Images (**Figure 10.25**).

continues on next page

6. Click the ... button in the right column.

   The Image Collection Editor opens (**Figure 10.26**).

7. Click Add.

   The Open dialog (**Figure 10.27**) allows you to browse to locate the images you want to use for your toolbar buttons.

8. Select an image and click Open to accept the first toolbar button image.

   The image is displayed in the Members pane of the Image Collection Editor (**Figure 10.28**).

9. Repeat the process of clicking Add and selecting an image file until all of the images you need appear in the Members pane (**Figure 10.29**).

10. Click OK.

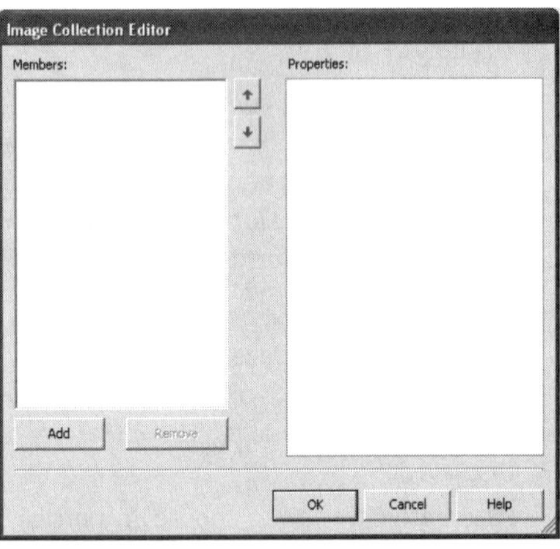

Figure 10.26 Use the Image Collection Editor to add images to the ImageList control's library.

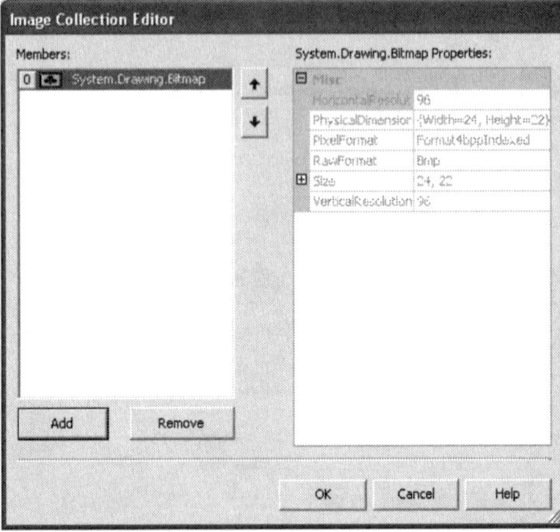

Figure 10.28 Once an image has been added, it appears in the Members pane of the Image Collection Editor.

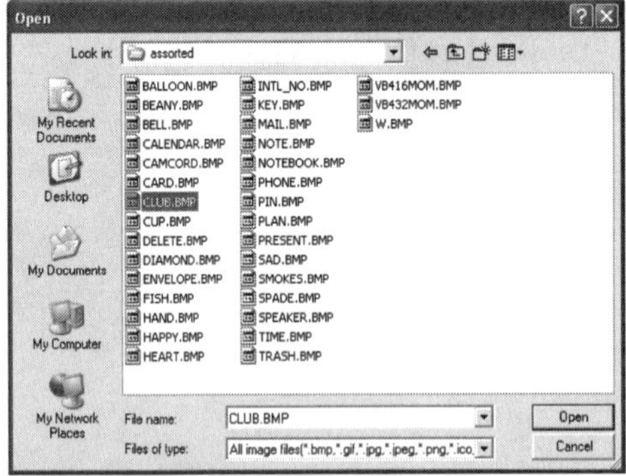

Figure 10.27 Use the Open dialog, accessed by clicking Add in the Image Collection Editor, to locate image files.

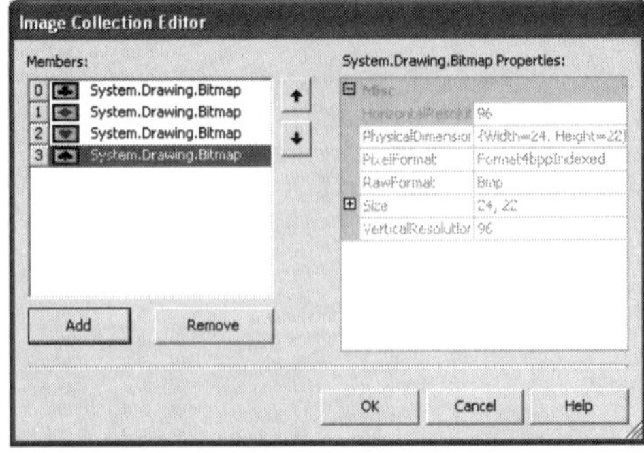

Figure 10.29 All of the images contained by an ImageList control appear in the Members pane of the Image Collection Editor.

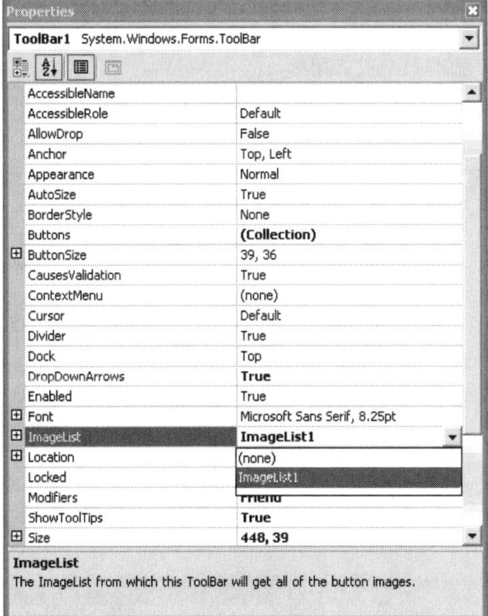

Figure 10.30 Use the ImageList property of a ToolBar control to link the ToolBar control with an ImageList control.

Visual Studio .NET ships with many graphics files that you can use for purposes such as building toolbars (or creating icons). In a default installation, these files are located in folders beneath Program Files\Microsoft Visual Studio .NET\Common7\Graphics. For instance, the image files used for the buttons shown in this section can be found in the Program Files\Microsoft Visual Studio .NET\Common7\Graphics\bitmaps\assorted folder.

To link an ImageList control with a ToolBar control:

1. With the form open in its designer, use the Toolbox to add a ToolBar control to the form.
2. In the Properties window, select the ToolBar control from the Objects list.
3. In the left column of the Properties window, select ImageList.
4. In the right column of the Properties window, choose the ImageList control from the drop-down list (**Figure 10.30**).

With the ImageList control linked to the ToolBar control, the next step is to add the buttons that use the images stored in the image list to the toolbar.

To add buttons to the ToolBar control:

1. With the ToolBar control still selected in the Properties window, select Buttons in the left column.
2. Click the ... button in the right column of the Properties window.

   The ToolBarButton Collection Editor opens.

continues on next page

3. Click Add to add the first button to the Members pane of the ToolBarButton Collection Editor.

   Note that the members of the ToolBar-Button collection use a zero-based index, so the first button that is a member of the collection has an index of 0, the second member will have an index of 1, and so on. (The index value appears to the left of button name in the Members list.)

4. With the button selected in the Members pane of the ToolBarButtton Collection Editor, select the ImageIndex property in the left column of the ToolBarButton Properties pane.

5. From the drop-down list in the right column of the ToolBarButton Properties pane, choose the image from the ImageList control that you want to use with the first button (**Figure 10.31**).

6. In the left column of the ToolBarButton Properties pane, select ToolTipText.

7. In the right column of the ToolBarButton Properties pane, enter the text that you want to appear when the user pauses the mouse over the button.

8. For all of the buttons that you want added to the toolbar, repeat the same process of clicking Add and assigning an image and a value that you used for the ToolTipText property.

   Buttons that have been added to the toolbar appear in the Members pane of the ToolBarButton Collection Editor, as you can see in **Figure 10.32**.

9. Click OK.

   The toolbar appears at the top of the form. The bitmaps chosen in the ImageList control represent the buttons, and the value of the ToolTipText property setting is displayed when the mouse pauses over a button (**Figure 10.33**).

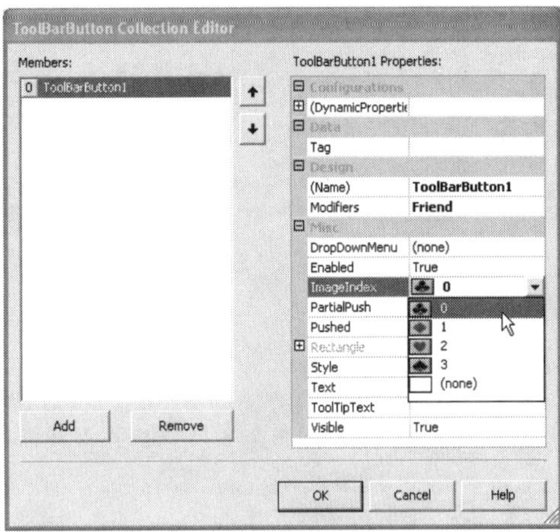

Figure 10.31 Use the ToolBarButtons Collection Editor to link tool bar buttons with specific image list items.

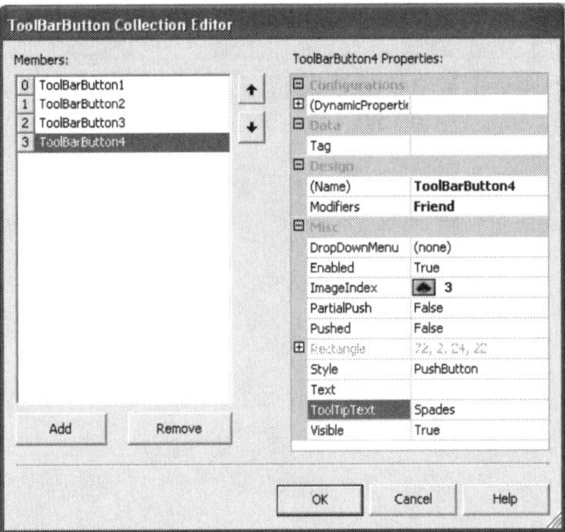

Figure 10.32 Text entered as the ToolTipText property for each button that is a member of the ToolBarButtons collection will appear on the screen when the user's mouse hovers over the button.

Figure 10.33 The ToolBar control at runtime with ToolTip text displayed.

You now need to provide a way to determine which button the user clicked on the toolbar. A ToolBar control provides a ButtonClick event. One of the arguments passed to the ButtonClick event procedure is of type ToolBarButtonClickEventArgs. A ToolBarButtonClickEventArgs argument has a property, Button, that you can use to determine which button the user clicked.

To determine which toolbar button was clicked:

1. With the form open in its designer, double-click the ToolBar control to create a click event procedure in the Code Editor.

   Here's what the framework for the procedure looks like:

```
Private Sub ToolBar1_ButtonClick _
   (ByVal sender As System.Object, _
   ByVal e As System.Windows.Forms. _
   ToolBarButtonClickEventArgs) _
   Handles ToolBar1.ButtonClick

End Sub
```

2. Within the click event procedure, create a Select Case statement that uses the IndexOf collection function to evaluate the index of the clicked button using the Button property of the ToolBarButtonClickEventArg argument passed to the procedure:

```
Select Case _
   ToolBar1.Buttons.IndexOf(e.Button)

End Select
```

continues on next page

Select Case Statements

Select Case statements are used extensively in Visual Basic code. They cause execution to branch to the first Case condition within the statement that evaluates to True.

Anything that can be written with a Select Case statement can also be written using a series of If statements (and vice versa). However, a single Select Case statement tends to be easier to read (and maintain) than a whole bunch of If statements.

The general form of the Select Case statement is:

```
Select Case Expression
   Case Value0
   ...
   Case ValueN
   Case Else
End Select
```

The expression at the beginning of the statement is evaluated, and execution branches to the code within the first Case clause that matches the value. If no match is found, then the code in the optional Case Else clause is processed.

3. Create a Case clause for each button that displays information about the button in the form's caption bar—for example:

   ```
   Case 0
       Me.Text = "You clicked Clubs!"
   ```

   Listing 10.2 shows the complete code for the toolbar click event procedure.

4. Run the project.

5. Click a button on the toolbar.

   The text relating to the button clicked will appear in the caption bar of the form (**Figure 10.34**).

Figure 10.34 You can add code to a ToolBar control click event that conditionally executes, depending on which button you clicked.

Sometimes you need to add a toolbar button to a toolbar at runtime, usually dynamically in response to a user action. For example, the user might open a document in the interface that requires an additional tool, represented by a new button on the toolbar.

Fortunately, it is fairly easy to add a button to a toolbar at runtime.

Listing 10.2 Determining which toolbar button was clicked.

```
Private Sub ToolBar1_ButtonClick(ByVal sender As System.Object, _
   ByVal e As System.Windows.Forms.ToolBarButtonClickEventArgs) Handles ToolBar1.ButtonClick
   Select Case ToolBar1.Buttons.IndexOf(e.Button)
      Case 0
         Me.Text = "You clicked Clubs!"
      Case 1
         Me.Text = "You clicked Diamonds!"
      Case 2
         Me.Text = "You clicked Hearts!"
      Case 3
         Me.Text = "You clicked Spades!"
   End Select
End Sub
```

To add a toolbar button at runtime:

1. Add a new Button control to the form.
2. Use the Properties window to name the Button control **btnAdd** and give its Text property a value of **Add**.
3. Double-click the Add button to create a click event procedure in the Code Editor:
```
Private Sub btnAdd_Click(ByVal _
    sender As System.Object, _
    ByVal e As System.EventArgs) _
    Handles btnAdd.Click

End Sub
```
4. In the Code Editor, within the button's click event procedure, declare a variable, myImg, of type System.Drawing.Image and use the Image class's shared FromFile method to load myImg from the image file FISH.BMP:
```
Dim fn As String = "FISH.BMP"
Dim myImg As Drawing.Image = _
    Image.FromFile(fn)
```
For this procedure to work, the file FISH.BMP needs to be located in the executable, or bin, directory of the project (I copied the file to this location from the Microsoft common graphics library mentioned earlier in this section). Otherwise, you can supply a full file path as well as the file name in the FromFile method argument.
5. Add the image reference by myImg to the ImageList control:
```
ImageList1.Images.Add(myImg)
```
6. Create a new toolbar button instance:
```
Dim myButton As New _
    ToolBarButton()
```
7. Use the Add method to add the new toolbar button to the ToolBar control's Buttons collection:
```
ToolBar1.Buttons.Add(myButton)
```
8. Assign a string value to the ToolTipText property, and an index value to the new toolbar button:
```
myButton.ToolTipText = _
    "This is a fish, but it is" & _
    " hard to see."
myButton.ImageIndex = 4
```
Listing 10.3 shows the complete code for the Add button's click event handler.

continues on next page

Listing 10.3 Adding a toolbar button at runtime.

```
Private Sub btnAdd_Click(ByVal sender As System.Object, ByVal e As System.EventArgs) _
    Handles btnAdd.Click
    Dim fn As String = "FISH.BMP"
    Dim myImg As Drawing.Image = Image.FromFile(fn)
    ImageList1.Images.Add(myImg)
    Dim myButton As New ToolBarButton()
    ToolBar1.Buttons.Add(myButton)
    myButton.ToolTipText = "This is a fish, but it is hard to see."
    myButton.ImageIndex = 4
End Sub
```

9. Run the project.
10. Click the Add button.

    You'll see that a new button has been added to the toolbar with the ToolTip text provided and in the position indicated by the index value (**Figure 10.35**).

Figure 10.35 You can easily add (and delete) tool bar buttons at runtime in response to an action taken by a user.

You may also need to remove a toolbar button at runtime: for example, if a tool accessed by the button is not supposed to be available to a user.

You can easily use the RemoveAt method of the Buttons collection associated with the toolbar to remove a specific button using the index number of the button.

To remove a toolbar button at runtime:

- In code, use the RemoveAt method with the index of the button supplied as an argument. For example, to remove the fifth button (which has an index value of 4) from a toolbar, you use the following code:

```
ToolBar1.Buttons.RemoveAt(4)
```

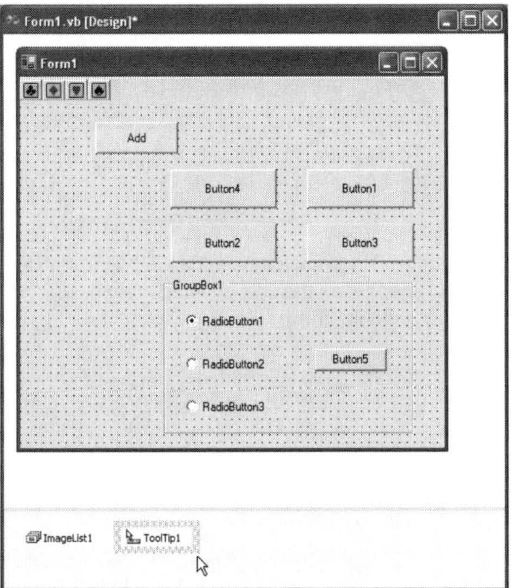

Figure 10.36 The ToolTip control appears in the tray of the form to which it is added.

Figure 10.37 The ToolTip on ... property appears in the Properties window only after a ToolTip control has been added to a form.

Telling a Tale with the ToolTip Control

As you saw in the previous section, buttons on a toolbar come with ToolTip text string that appears when the user hovers the mouse over a button. You can easily add a similar facility for any control by using the ToolTip control.

To add ToolTip text to a control:

1. With a form open in its designer, use the Toolbox to add a ToolTip control to the form by double-clicking the ToolTip control.

   The ToolTip control appears in the tray at the bottom of the form (**Figure 10.36**).

2. In the Properties window, use the objects list to select the control to which you want to add ToolTip text (in this case, the Add button control, which is named btnAdd).

3. In the left column of the Properties window, locate the property named ToolTip on ToolTip1 (**Figure 10.37**).

   Note that this property will not appear in the Properties window for a control until an instance of the ToolTip control has been added to the form that contains the control. Also, ToolTip1 is the default name for the first instance of a ToolTip control added to a form (and there is no particularly good reason to change this). However, if the ToolTip control instance had been given another name, for example, myTT, then the property name shown in the Properties window for the Button control will correspond: for example, ToolTip on myTT.

4. In the right column of the Properties window corresponding to the ToolTip on ToolTip1 property, enter the text value that you want to use as the ToolTip text, as shown in Figure 10.37.

continues on next page

5. Run the project.

6. Hover the mouse over the Add button.

   The designated ToolTip text appears (**Figure 10.38**).

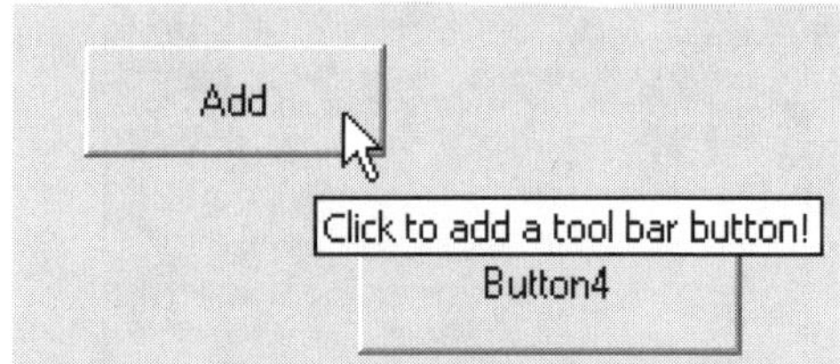

Figure 10.38 The ToolTip text added in the Properties window appears on the screen when the mouse hovers over the control.

✔ Tips

- You can use one ToolTip control to provide different ToolTip text for as many different controls as you like.
- You can use the Delay settings of the ToolTip control to determine how long the ToolTip text takes to appear under various conditions. For example, the default value of InitialDelay is 500, which means that it takes 500 milliseconds (or half a second) for the ToolTip text to appear the first time a user hovers the mouse over a control that generates text.

Sometimes you may want to add or change ToolTip text dynamically at runtime (for instance, if the function of a user interface control changes midstream). This is easy to do using the SetToolTip method of the ToolTip control.

To add ToolTip text to a control at runtime:

1. Add a ToolTip control to the form.

2. In code, execute a call to the ToolTip control's SetToolTip method. Use the name of the control whose ToolTip text is to be added as the first argument, and use the text to be added as the second argument—for example:

```
ToolTip1.SetToolTip(btnAdd, _
   "I've changed the tool tip text!")
```

   When this code is run, the new ToolTip text is added, or it replaces any existing ToolTip text (**Figure 10.39**).

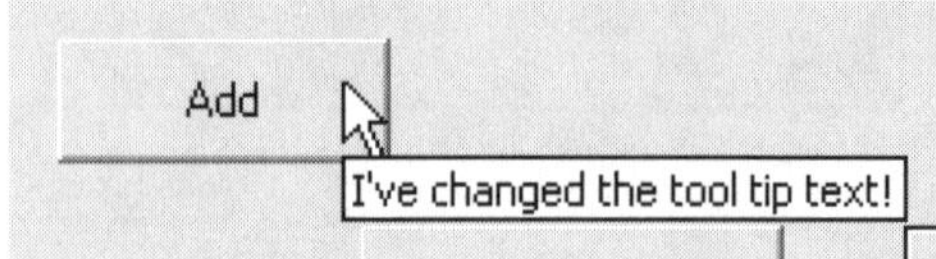

Figure 10.39 The ToolTip text added in code appears on the screen.

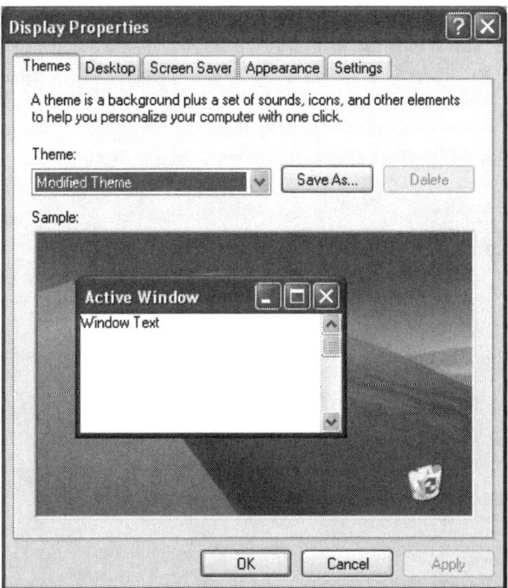

Figure 10.40 The Windows XP Display Properties dialog is an example of a tabbed dialog.

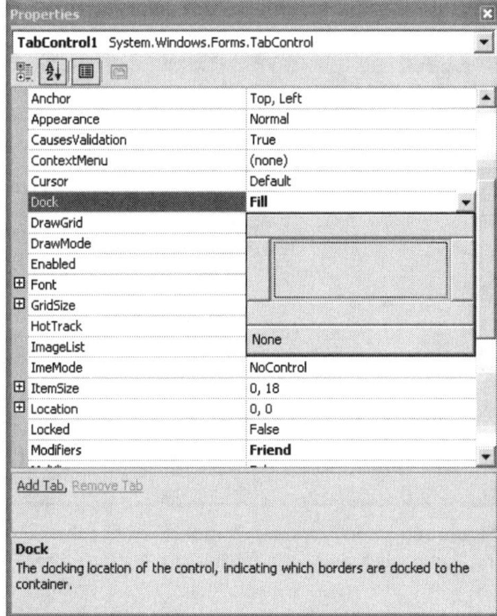

Figure 10.41 Setting the Dock property of the TabControl control to Fill makes the tab control expand to fill the client space of the form it is seated upon.

Using the TabControl

In a tabbed dialog, the user clicks to open different pages (each page is called a tab).

You can use tabbed dialogs not only to save space but also to intelligently group related controls, with each related group of controls on its own tab page.

Tabbed dialogs are used in a great many Windows applications and are very useful. For example, you may have used the Windows XP Display Properties dialog, shown in **Figure 10.40**, which consists of five tab pages (represented by the tabs you can see running horizontally across the top of the dialog).

In Visual Basic .NET, you use the TabControl control to create tabbed dialogs. This control contains a collection of TabPage objects. Each TabPage object corresponds to a tab page in the tabbed dialog created by TabControl. In addition, each TabPage object contains a collection of the controls that are positioned on the corresponding tab page.

To add a TabControl to a form:

1. With a form open in its designer, double-click TabControl to add this control to the form.
2. Using the Properties window, set the Dock property of the tab control to Fill (**Figure 10.41**).

✔ Tip

- Typically, TabControls are set to take up the full client area of a form, which is accomplished by setting the control's Dock property to Fill as you just did. However, there is no law preventing you from using a tab control in only a portion of a form.

To add TabPage objects to a tab control:

1. With a tab control added to a form, open the Properties window.
2. In the left column of the Properties window, select TabPages (**Figure 10.42**).
3. Click the ... button in the right column. The TabPage Collection Editor opens.
4. Click Add to add the first tab page to the Members pane of the TabPage Collection Editor (**Figure 10.43**).

   Note that the members of the TabPages collection use a zero-based index, so the first tab page that is a member of the collection has an index of 0, the second member would have an index of 1, and so on. (The index value appears to the left of the tab page name in the Members pane in Figure 10.43.)

Figure 10.42 The TabPages property of a tab control contains a collection of TabPage objects.

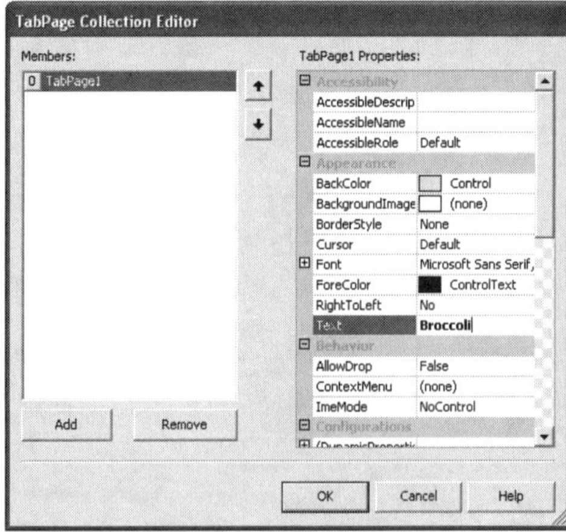

Figure 10.43 You can set the properties of each TabPage object using the TabPage Collection Editor.

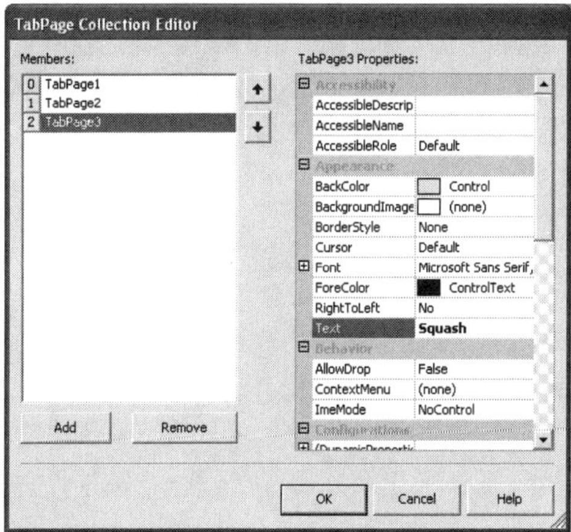

Figure 10.44 The members of the tab control's TabPages collection appear in the Members pane of the TabPage Collection Editor.

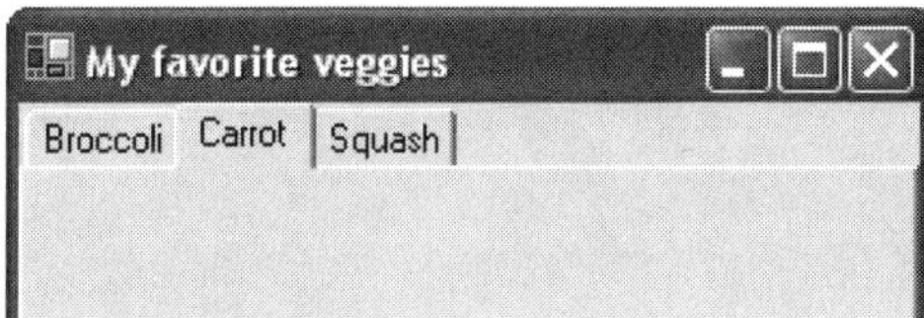

Figure 10.45 Users can click between the tabs of a tab control with no further work required.

5. In the left column of the Properties pane for the tab page, select Text.
6. In the right column of the Properties pane, enter the text that you want to appear on the tab presented by the tab page.
7. For each tab page that you want to add to the TabPages collection, repeat the process of clicking Add and assigning a value for the Text property.

   Tab pages that have been added to the collection appear in the Members pane of the TabPage Collection Editor, as you can see in **Figure 10.44**.
8. Click OK.
9. The tab control is fully functional at this point without any further wiring. To observe this, run the project and check whether you can move back and forth between tab pages by clicking the tabs (**Figure 10.45**).

To add controls to a tab page:

1. Open a control in its designer.
2. Add a tab control to the form.
3. Add some TabPage objects to the tab control's TabPage collection, as explained earlier in "To add TabPage objects to a tab control."
4. In the designer, click the tab representing the TabPage object to which you want to add controls (to make the tab page active).
5. Drag controls from the Toolbox and drop them on the active tab page (**Figure 10.46**).

✔ Tip

- You cannot double-click a control in the Toolbox to add it to a TabControl tab page (this is the way you might normally add controls to a form). Instead, you must drag the control to the tab page on which you want it seated.

As the needs of your user interface change, you may want to move controls from one tab page to another at runtime. This is simple to do in code once you realize that you can refer to an individual TabPage object using the index for that tab page in the TabControl TabPages collection. The controls on a particular TabPage object are also the members of a collection: the Controls collection for that tab page.

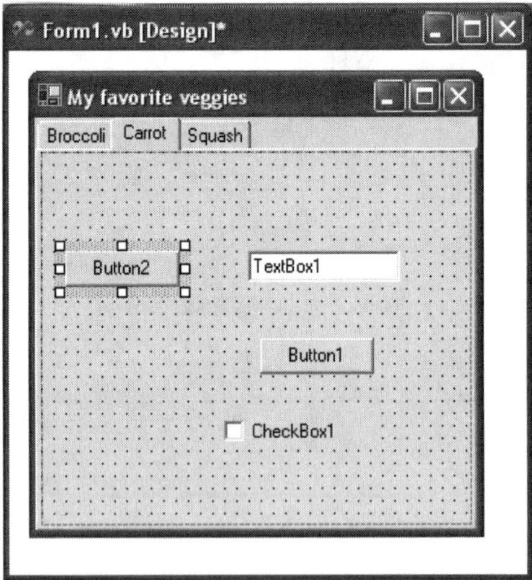

Figure 10.46 Controls can be added to any of a tab control's TabPage objects (here, the controls are shown positioned on the Carrot tab).

Here is an example using a click event procedure to move the controls on the second TabPage object (Carrot) in Figure 10.46 to the first TabPage object (Broccoli).

To move controls from one tab page to another at runtime:

1. Add a Button control to the first tab of the tab control.
2. Use the Properties window to change the name of the Button control to `btnMove` and the value of its Text property to `Move` (**Figure 10.47**).
3. Double-click the Move button to create a click event procedure in the Code Editor:

```
Private Sub btnMove_Click(ByVal _
   sender As System.Object, _
   ByVal e As System.EventArgs) _
   Handles btnMove.Click

End Sub
```

continues on next page

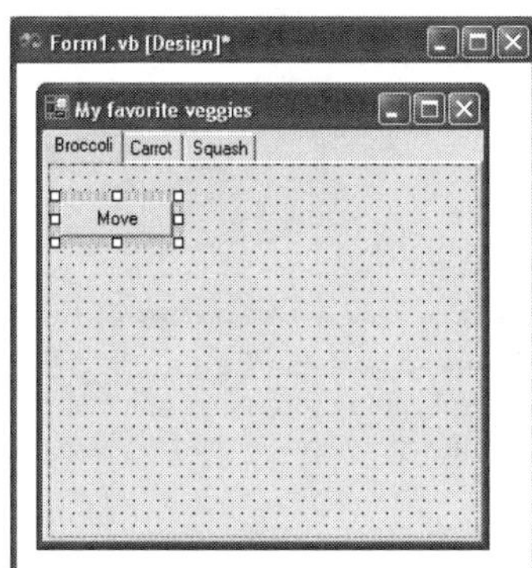

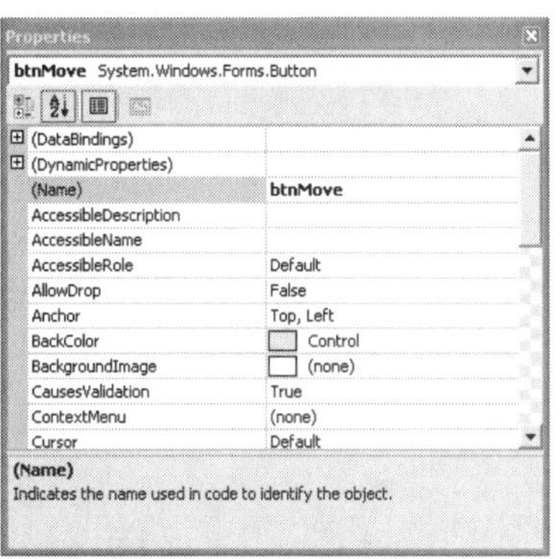

Figure 10.47 A Move Button control is added to the first tab (Broccoli).

4. Within the click event procedure, use the zero-index TabPages object to refer to the first tab page, and employ the AddRange method of the TabPage controls collection to add an array of controls:

```
TabControl1.TabPages(0).Controls. _
   AddRange(New Control() _
   {Me.Button2, Me.CheckBox1, _
   Me.TextBox1, Me.Button1})
```

   Listing 10.4 shows the complete code for moving the controls.

5. Run the project.

   The Broccoli tab page shows only the Move button (**Figure 10.48**).

6. Click Move.

   The other controls have been moved and now appear on the Broccoli tab page (**Figure 10.49**).

Figure 10.48 When the project is run, the Broccoli tab is displayed with just the Move button.

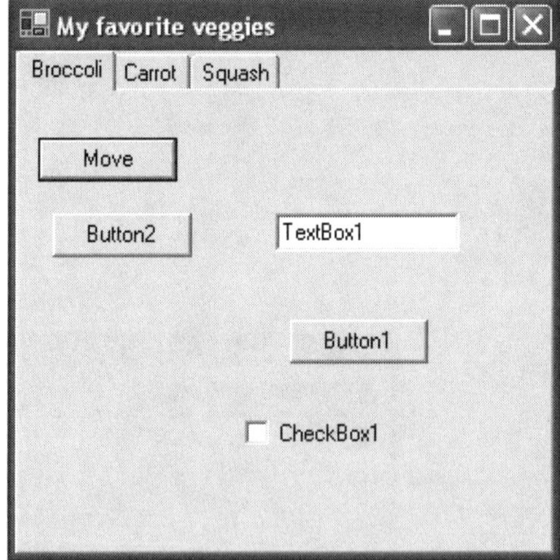

Figure 10.49 When the user clicks the Move button, the specified controls are moved from the Carrot tab to the Broccoli tab.

✔ Tip

- You can add controls to a collection in a number of ways besides using the AddRange method. For example, you can use the Add method to add one control at a time.

Listing 10.4 Moving controls from one tab page to another at runtime.

```
Private Sub btnMove_Click(ByVal sender As System.Object, ByVal e As System.EventArgs) _
   Handles btnMove.Click
   TabControl1.TabPages(0).Controls.AddRange(New Control() _
      {Me.Button2, Me.CheckBox1, Me.TextBox1, Me.Button1})
End Sub
```

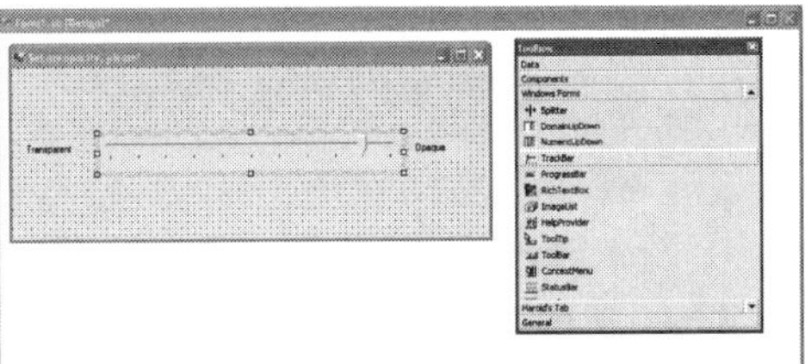

Figure 10.50 You can use a TrackBar control to accept input from the user.

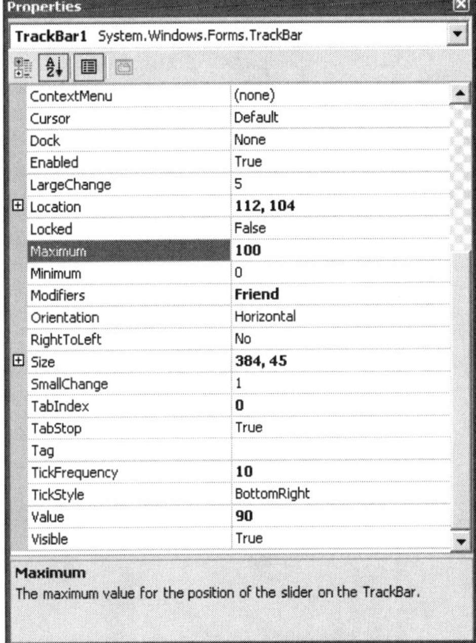

Figure 10.51 The Minimum and Maximum properties of the TrackBar control determine the range of values that the control can accept.

Using the TrackBar Control

The TrackBar control is an excellent tool for managing user input in a situation in which the user can enter choices within a strictly limited range. The TrackBar control provides a visual metaphor for this situation and is analogous to widgets that users encounter in everyday life: thermostats, volume controls, and so on. In addition, there is absolutely no way a user can enter a value outside the range allowed by the TrackBar control.

For example, in Chapter 5, you learned how to set a form's Opacity property at runtime in code when the user entered a number between `0` and `1` in a text box. In the example in Chapter 5, I noted that it is unwise to allow a user to directly enter an Opacity value because of potential problems if the user enters an out-of-range value and suggested that a TrackBar control would solve the problem by ensuring that the user could enter only valid values.

Here's how to use a TrackBar control to let the user set a value for a form's Opacity property.

To use a TrackBar control to set a form's Opacity property:

1. With a form open in its designer, use the Toolbox to add a TrackBar control to the form (**Figure 10.50**).
2. With the TrackBar control selected in the Properties window, set the Maximum property to `100`, the TickFrequency property to `10`, and the Value property to `90` (**Figure 10.51**). Leave the other property values unchanged (in particular, the value of the Minimum property should remain at its default value, 0).

continues on next page

We will be dividing the value derived from the user's manipulation by 100, which explains the need to set the Maximum property to 100 (100 divided by 100 is 1). The TickFrequency property controls the number of tick marks that appear next to the TrackBar control, and the track bar's Value property sets the initial value for the track bar.

3. Double-click the TrackBar control to create a Scroll event procedure for the control in the Code Editor:

```
Private Sub TrackBar1_Scroll _
   (ByVal sender As System.Object, _
   ByVal e As System.EventArgs) _
   Handles TrackBar1.Scroll


End Sub
```

This event is fired every time the user moves the track bar's slider.

4. Within the Scroll event, divide the current TrackBar control value by 100 and assign the results to the form Opacity property:

```
Me.Opacity = TrackBar1.Value / 100
```

Listing 10.5 shows the complete code for the TrackBar control's Scroll event.

5. Run the project.

6. Use the TrackBar control's slider to change the opacity of the running form (**Figure 10.52**). Move the slider to verify that the form's opacity changes as it should.

✔ Tip

- The code that changes the value of the form's Opacity property could alternatively be placed in the TrackBar control's ValueChanged event, rather than the Scroll event.

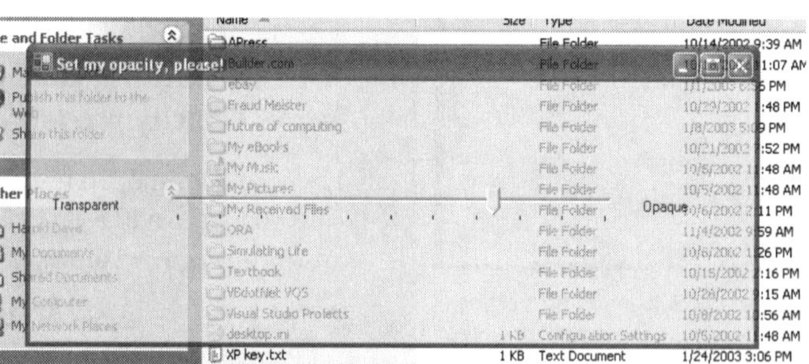

Figure 10.52 If you use the TrackBar control to set form opacity to about 75 percent, you can see the form, but it is transparent.

Listing 10.5 Using a TrackBar control to set form opacity.

```
Private Sub TrackBar1_Scroll(ByVal sender As System.Object, ByVal e As System.EventArgs) _
   Handles TrackBar1.Scroll
   Me.Opacity = TrackBar1.Value / 100
End Sub
```

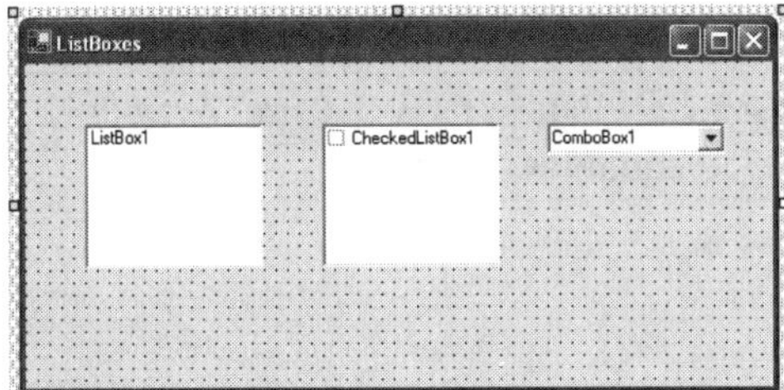

Figure 10.53 In design mode, from left to right, a ListBox control, a CheckedListBox control, and a ComboBox control.

Managing Lists with the ListBox Control

List boxes are the best thing since sliced bread! ListBox controls slice and dice and, best of all, give users lists that (depending on the needs of your application) they can modify.

Seriously, since computer programs almost always involve lists of things—numbers or text—it is rare to see a user interface that does not provide some kind of list box control.

The .NET ListBox control, depicted in the Toolbox as [icon], presents a series of items in a box. Depending on the size of the control on the form and the number of items in the list, the control may include scroll bars to access items not visible on the screen. Users can choose one or more items from a ListBox control by selecting them.

In your Toolbox, you will find two controls closely related to the ListBox control: the CheckedListBox control [icon] and the ComboBox control [icon]. All three controls are derived from the .NET ListControl class and are closely related.

A ComboBox control is like a ListBox control with an added text box that allows users to directly enter items. (The text box for adding text to the ComboBox control appears at the top of the control, and, although it appears the same, it behaves differently than the top boxes in the ListBox and CheckedListBox controls, which cannot be used to enter text.) A CheckedListBox control is like a ListBox control except that a check box appears to the left of each item. **Figure 10.53** shows a design-time example of each of these controls.

Since these controls all operate in much the same way, we won't go over the same ground multiple times. This section focuses on the most basic and common of these controls, the ListBox control because, for the most part, you can apply the techniques used with the ListBox control to the other two controls as well. (However, you will learn how to retrieve checked items from a CheckedListBox control and how to make the text entered by the user become items in a ComboBox.)

The user selects items in a ListBox control by clicking them. When an item has been selected, it is highlighted.

The SelectMode property of a ListBox control determines how the user can make selections in a list box. **Table 10.1** shows the four possible values for the SelectionMode property.

If you want to prepopulate a ListBox control, you can easily do so by accessing the String Collection Editor from the Properties window, as you'll see in a moment. However, the great power of ListBox controls generally comes from some form of dynamic response at runtime, so prepopulating a list box will get you only so far. You should also know that it is very common to bind controls such as list boxes to the data returned from a database (see Chapter 15 for details.)

Table 10.1

Possible Values for a ListBox Control's SelectionMode Property

Value	Meaning
None	No user selection is possible.
One	This is the default value for the SelectionMode property; the user can make one, and only one, selection.
MultiSimple	The user can select multiple items by clicking.
MultiExtended	The user can select multiple items by clicking or by using Ctrl, Shift, or an arrow key.

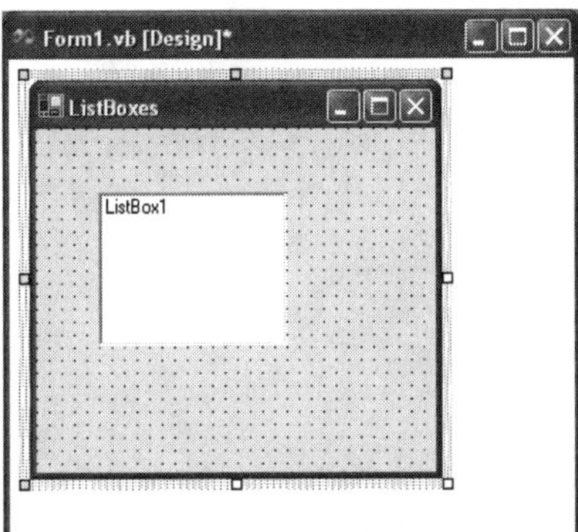

Figure 10.54 The ListBox control is positioned on the form in design mode.

Figure 10.55 By selecting the Items property in the Properties window, you can open the String Collection Editor.

To add items to a ListBox control using the String Collection Editor:

1. With a form open in its designer, use the Toolbox to add a ListBox control to the form.

   Figure 10.54 shows the ListBox control seated on the form.

2. Open the Properties window.

3. In the left column of the Properties window, select Items (**Figure 10.55**).

continues on next page

4. In the right column of the Properties window, click the ... button.

   The String Collection Editor opens (**Figure 10.56**).

5. Enter the text for the items that will be displayed in the ListBox control, one item per line (**Figure 10.57**).

6. Click OK.

   The items now appear in the ListBox control (shown in runtime mode in **Figure 10.58**).

The Sorted property of a ListBox control determines whether the items in a ListBox control's Items collection are displayed alphabetically (by default, they are not, as you can see in Figure 10.58).

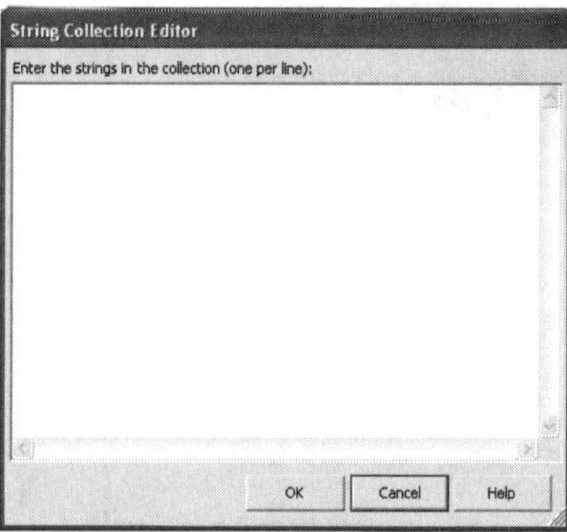

Figure 10.56 You can use the String Collection Editor to add text strings, one per line.

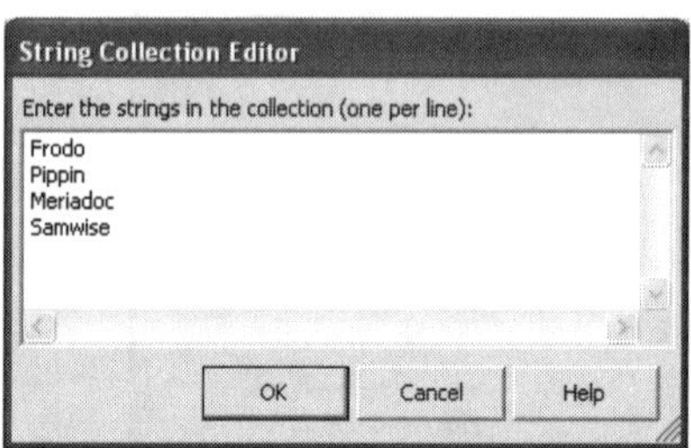

Figure 10.57 When you have entered all of the string items you want, click OK.

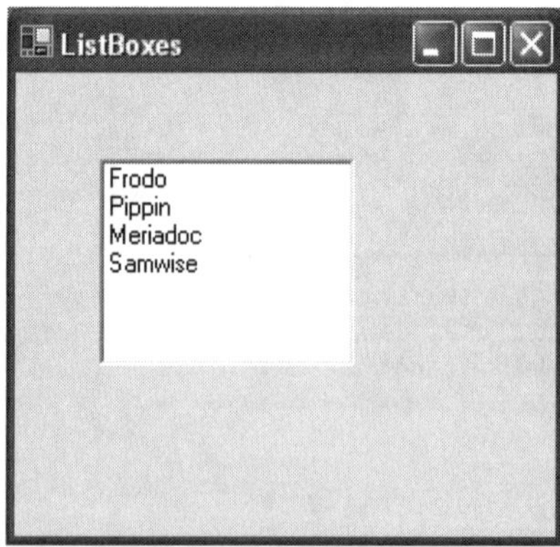

Figure 10.58 The items entered in the String Collection Editor show in the ListBox control at runtime.

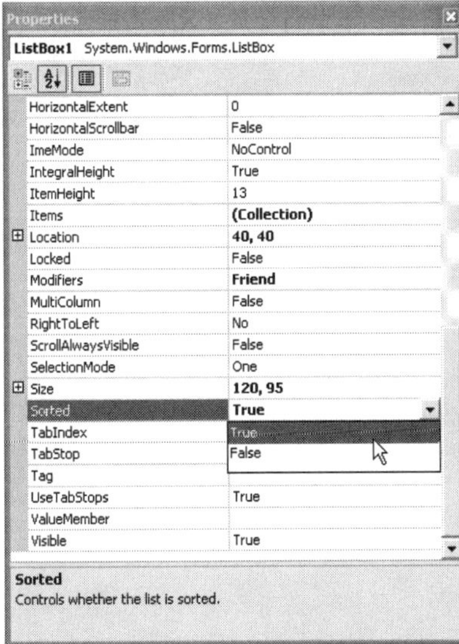

Figure 10.59 The ListBox control's Sorted property determines whether items appear in alphabetical order.

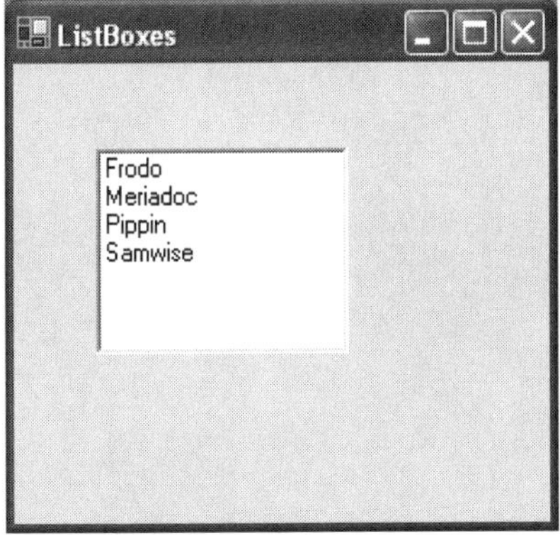

Figure 10.60 If the ListBox control's Sorted property is set to True, then the items in the ListBox Items collection are listed alphabetically.

To alphabetize a list box using the Properties window:

- With the ListBox control seated on a form in its designer, use the Properties window to set the ListBox control's Sorted property to True (**Figure 10.59**).

  The items in the ListBox control's Items collection now appear in alphabetical order (**Figure 10.60**).

You can easily alphabetize an unsorted ListBox control at runtime by setting the control's Sorted property in code.

To alphabetize a list box using code:

Set the Sorted property of the ListBox control to True—for example:

```
ListBox1.Sorted = True
```

You can let users add items to a list box by entering text in a TextBox control; then when the user clicks a button, the text is added as an item to the ListBox control's Items collection.

To add an item to a ListBox control using code:

1. With a ListBox control seated on a form in its designer, use the Toolbox to add a Button control and a TextBox control to the form.
2. Use the Properties window to set the Button control's Name property to `btnDemo` and its Text property to `Demo`.
3. Use the Properties window to set the TextBox control's Name property to `txtItem` and its Text property to the empty string.

continues on next page

4. Double-click the Button control to create a click event handler for it in the Code Editor:

```
Private Sub btnDemo_Click(ByVal _
   sender As System.Object, ByVal e _
   As System.EventArgs) _
   Handles btnDemo.Click

End Sub
```

5. Within the event handler, use the Add method of the ListBox control's Items collection to add the text value of the text box to the Items collection when the user clicks the button:

```
ListBox1.Items.Add(txtItem.Text)
```

Here's the complete code for the click event:

```
Private Sub btnDemo_Click(ByVal _
   sender As System.Object, ByVal e _
   As System.EventArgs) _
   Handles btnDemo.Click
   ListBox1.Items.Add(txtItem.Text)
End Sub
```

6. Run the project.

7. Enter some text in the text box.

8. Click Demo and verify that the text you entered has been added to the list box (**Figure 10.61**).

Note that if the ListBox control is not sorted, this code adds the new item at the bottom of the list box. You can also add items at a specific location, using the Insert method of the ListBox control's Items collection along with an index value for the location in the collection where you want the item to appear.

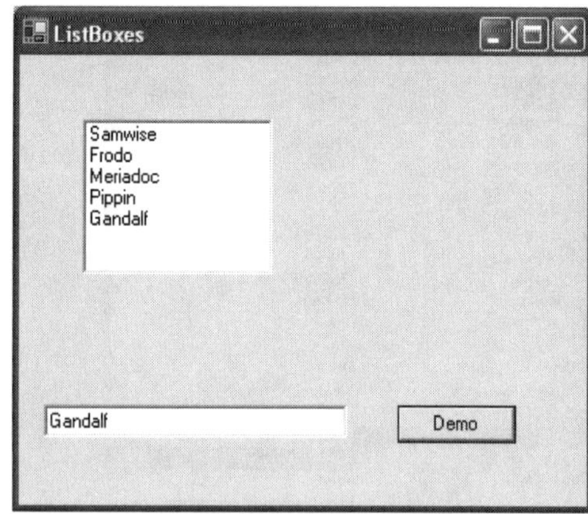

Figure 10.61 You can easily add a text item to the Items collection of the ListBox control at runtime.

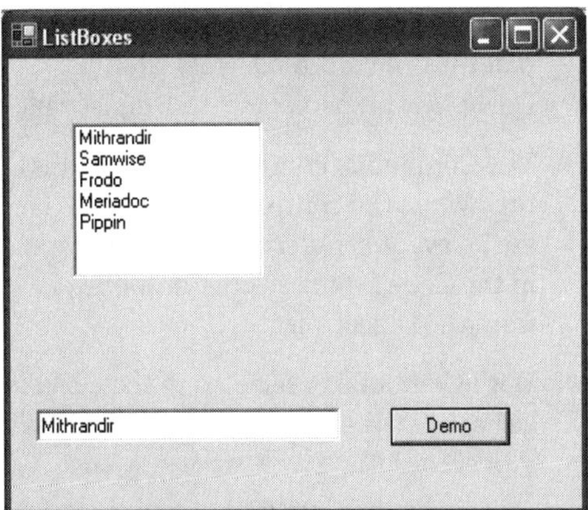

Figure 10.62 Use the ListBox control's Items collection Insert method and an index value of 0 to position the new item at the beginning of the list.

To add an item to a list box at a specific location:

1. Replace the line of code shown in Step 5 of the click event procedure in "To add an item to a ListBox control using code" with the following line of code:

   ```
   ListBox1.Items.Insert _
      (0, txtItem.Text)
   ```

2. Run the project.
3. Enter some text.

   The text item is added as the first item in the list box (**Figure 10.62**) because the Insert method's first argument was 0, indicating the beginning of the Items collection list.

To place the text item at some location other than the beginning of the list, you would use the index value of the location as the first argument passed to the Insert method.

Note that the ListBox control's Item collection list is zero based (like all collections in .NET), so the index values for items run from 0 to the count of items in the list minus 1. If you need to, you can determine the number of items in a ListBox control's Items collection by getting the value of the Item's collection Count property—for example:

```
ListBox1.Items.Count
```

This procedure is often useful for iterating through all of the items in a ListBox control's Items collection.

By the way, if the ListBox control is sorted, it really doesn't matter where you insert a new item. It will be added in alphabetic order.

As mentioned earlier in this section, the ComboBox control is a very close relative of the ListBox control. The only substantive difference is that the ComboBox provides facilities similar to those of a TextBox control, allowing the user to enter text that can be programmatically retrieved. By the way, for this facility to be operational, the DropDownStyle property of the ComboBox control must be set to Simple or DropDown (the default). If the DropDownStyle property is set to DropDownList, then the user will not be able to enter text.

As they say, nothing in life is free—or at least, very little. The ComboBox control's text entry facility does not come prewired. This means that you must add code to make it work.

As part of enabling the text entry facility of the ComboBox control, you should consider what ComboBox events to add code to in light of your user interface. In the following example, the text that the user enters in the ComboBox control is added to the control's items list when the user presses the Enter key or when the ComboBox control loses focus (because the user has pressed the Tab key or used the mouse to click somewhere outside the ComboBox control). Therefore, you will want to place code in the ComboBox control's Leave event (fired when the control loses focus) and the control's KeyDown event (fired when a key is pressed).

To allow users to add items to a combo box:

1. With a form open in its designer, use the Toolbox to add a ComboBox control to the form. Don't change the default name of this ComboBox control, which is ComboBox1.
2. Use the Properties window to make sure that the ComboBox control's DropDownStyle property is set to DropDown.
3. The ComboBox control's Leave event is fired when the control loses focus. To create an event handler for the Leave event, in the Code Editor, select ComboBox1 from the Objects list.
4. With ComboBox1 selected in the Objects list, select the Leave event from the Procedures list.

   An event procedure framework for the Leave event is generated in the Code Editor:

   ```
   Private Sub ComboBox1_Leave _
      (ByVal sender As Object, _
      ByVal e As System.EventArgs) _
      Handles ComboBox1.Leave

   End Sub
   ```
5. Within the click event procedure, make sure that the Text property of the combo box is not empty (meaning that the user has entered some text in the top part of the combo box):

   ```
   If ComboBox1.Text <> _
      String.Empty Then

   End If
   ```
6. If the user has entered some text in the top part of the combo box, add the text to the Items collection of the ComboBox control:

   ```
   ComboBox1.Items.Add(ComboBox1.Text)
   ```
7. Clear the Text property of the combo box so the user can enter another item without having to delete the existing contents:

   ```
   ComboBox1.Text = String.Empty
   ```

8. The ComboBox control's KeyDown event is fired when the user presses a key. To create an event handler for the KeyDown event, in the Code Editor, select ComboBox1 from the Objects list.

9. With ComboBox1 selected in the Objects list, select the KeyDown event from the Procedures list.

   An event procedure framework for the KeyDown event is generated in the Code Editor:

```
Private Sub ComboBox1_KeyDown _
   (ByVal sender As Object, ByVal e _
   As System.Windows.Forms. _
   KeyEventArgs) _
   Handles ComboBox1.KeyDown


End Sub
```

10. In the KeyDown event procedure, use the KeyEventArgs value passed to the procedure to see if the key pressed was the Enter key:

```
If e.KeyCode = Keys.Enter Then


End If
```

11. If the Enter key was pressed, add the same code as in the Leave event to add the current Text value as an item to the ComboBox Items collection:

```
ComboBox1.Items.Add(ComboBox1.Text)
ComboBox1.Text = String.Empty
```

   Listing 10.6 shows the complete code for both event procedures.

12. Run the project.

continues on next page

Listing 10.6 Wiring a combo box so that text entered is added to the list of items.

```
Private Sub ComboBox1_Leave(ByVal sender As Object, ByVal e As System.EventArgs) _
   Handles ComboBox1.Leave
   If ComboBox1.Text <> String.Empty Then
      ComboBox1.Items.Add(ComboBox1.Text)
      ComboBox1.Text = String.Empty
   End If
End Sub

Private Sub ComboBox1_KeyDown(ByVal sender As Object, _
   ByVal e As System.Windows.Forms.KeyEventArgs) Handles ComboBox1.KeyDown
   If e.KeyCode = Keys.Enter Then
      If ComboBox1.Text <> String.Empty Then
         ComboBox1.Items.Add(ComboBox1.Text)
         ComboBox1.Text = String.Empty
      End If
   End If
End Sub
```

13. Enter some text in the top portion of the combo box (**Figure 10.63**).
14. Press the Enter key or the Tab key.
15. Enter some more text as in Step 13.
16. Press the Enter key or the Tab key to add the new text to the Items collection.
17. Repeat Steps 15 and 16 a number of times.
18. Click the down arrow on the right-side of the combo box to make sure that the text items you entered have been added to the combo box's items list (**Figure 10.64**).

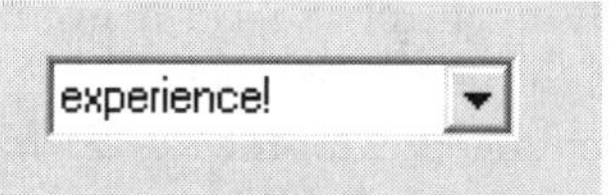

Figure 10.63 The user can enter text in the upper part of the ComboBox control.

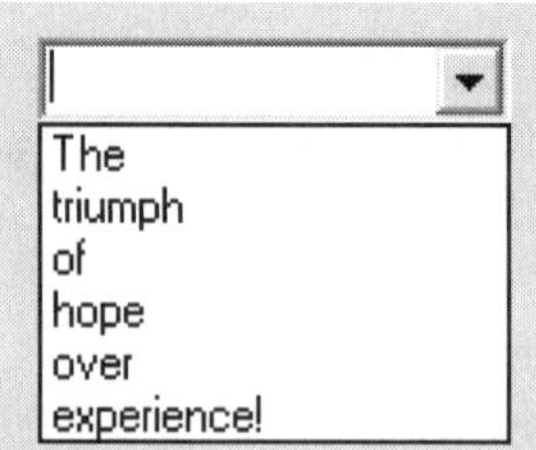

Figure 10.64 Text entered by the user is added to the ComboBox control's Items collection.

Whether you are working with a ComboBox control or a plain-vanilla ListBox control, the techniques for removing items are the same. Here, you'll work with a ListBox control, but the same methods would work for a ComboBox or CheckedListBox control.

To delete a list box item using the index value:

- Use the RemoveAt method of the ListBox control's Items collection with the index value of the item you want to remove. For example, to remove the second item (remember that the Items collection index is zero based) enter the following:

```
ListBox1.Items.RemoveAt(1)
```

To delete a list box item using the text value:

- Use the Remove method of the ListBox control's Items collection with the text value of the item you want to remove—for example:

```
ListBox1.Items.Remove("Frodo")
```

removes the first item in the Items collection list with a text value of "Frodo."

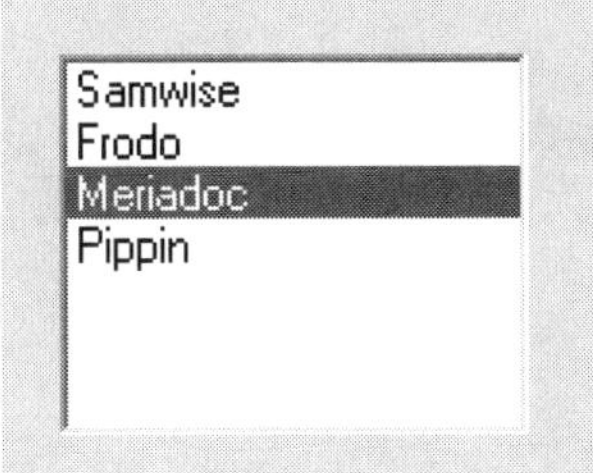

Figure 10.65 In single-selection mode, one item can be selected in a ListBox control.

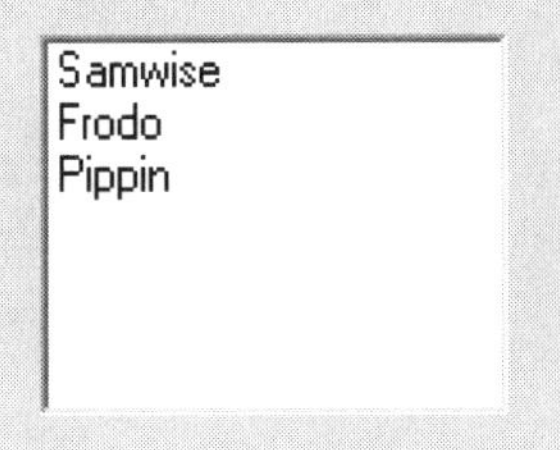

Figure 10.66 The selected item has been removed.

The selected item in a single-select ListBox control is returned using the list box's SelectedItem property, so you can use this property to remove a selected item.

To delete the selected list box item:

1. In a Button control's click event, check to see that the selection mode of the ListBox control is single selection:

```
If ListBox1.SelectionMode = _
   SelectionMode.One Then

End If
```

2. If the list box is set to single selection, use the Remove method of the ListBox control's Items collection with the ListBox control's SelectedItem property to remove the selected item:

```
ListBox1.Items.Remove _
   (ListBox1.SelectedItem)
```

   Here's the complete conditional code to delete the selected item:

```
If ListBox1.SelectionMode = _
   SelectionMode.One Then
   ListBox1.Items.Remove _
      (ListBox1.SelectedItem)
End If
```

3. Run the project.
4. Select an item in the ListBox control (**Figure 10.65**).
5. Execute the click event code and verify that the selected item has been removed (**Figure 10.66**).

If you need to retrieve the selected item (as opposed to deleting it), you easily do so. The next task shows how to retrieve a selected item from a ListBox control and display it as the value of the Text property in a TextBox control.

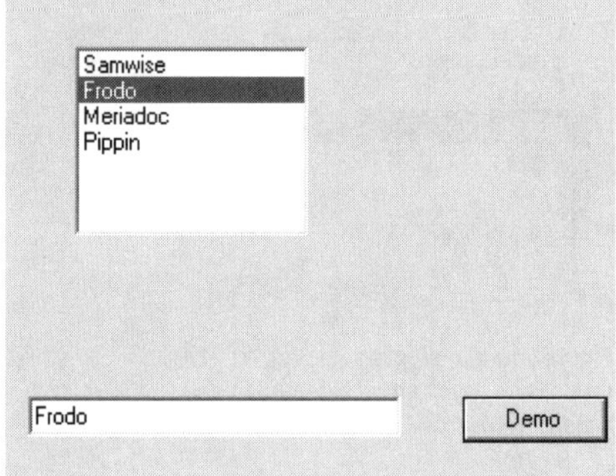

Figure 10.67 You can use a text box to display the value of the selected item in a list box.

To retrieve the selected item (single selection):

1. In a Button control's click event, check to see that the selection mode of the ListBox control is single selection:

   ```
   If ListBox1.SelectionMode = _
      SelectionMode.One Then


   End If
   ```

2. If the list box is set to single selection, use the ToString method to assign the text value of the selected item in the list box to the Text property of the text box:

   ```
   txtItem.Text = _
     ListBox1.SelectedItem.ToString()
   ```

   Here's the complete conditional code to retrieve the selected item:

   ```
   If ListBox1.SelectionMode = _
      SelectionMode.One Then
      txtItem.Text = _
        ListBox1.SelectedItem.ToString()
   End If
   ```

3. Run the project.
4. Select an item in the ListBox control (**Figure 10.67**).
5. Execute the click event code and verify that the selected item has been added to the TextBox control as shown in Figure 10.67.

If a ListBox control's selection mode has been set so that multiple items can be selected at once (achieved by setting the control's SelectionMode property to either MultiSimple or MultiExtended), then retrieving all selected items is a straightforward process.

The following task shows how to retrieve all selected items from a ListBox control and add them to the Items collection list of a CheckedListBox control.

To retrieve multiple selected items:

1. With a ListBox control seated on a form in its designer, use the Properties window to check that the SelectionMode property of the list box is set to MultiSimple or MultiExtended.
2. Use the Toolbox to add a CheckedListBox control to the form, accepting the default name of CheckedListBox1 for the control.
3. Use the Toolbox to add a Button control to the form.
4. Use the Properties window to change the Name of the Button to `btnMulti` and its Text property value to `Multi`.
5. Double-click the Multi button to create a click event procedure framework in the Code Editor:

```
Private Sub btnMulti_Click _
   (ByVal sender As System.Object, _
   ByVal e As System.EventArgs) _
   Handles btnMulti.Click

End Sub
```

6. Within the click event procedure, declare an integer variable, i, to serve as an iteration counter:

```
Dim i As Integer
```

continues on next page

7. Check to see that multiselection mode is enabled:

```
If ListBox1.SelectionMode = _
   SelectionMode.MultiSimple Or _
   ListBox1.SelectionMode = _
   SelectionMode.MultiExtended Then

End If
```

8. If multiselection is enabled, iterate through the SelectedItems collection of the ListBox control, adding each item in the SelectedItems collection to the Items collection of the CheckedListBox control:

```
For i = 0 To _
   ListBox1.SelectedItems.Count - 1
   CheckedListBox1.Items.Add _
      (ListBox1.SelectedItems(i))
Next
```

Listing 10.7 shows the complete code for the click event procedure.

9. Run the project.
10. Select some items in the list box.
11. Click the Multi button.

The selected items now appear as items in the CheckedListBox control (**Figure 10.68**).

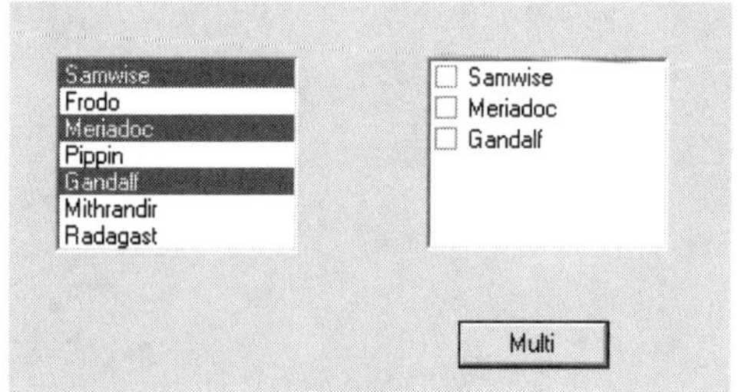

Figure 10.68 The selected items in a multiselection list box have been added to the CheckedListBox control.

Listing 10.7 Adding selected items in a multiselection ListBox control to a CheckedListBox control.

```
Private Sub btnMulti_Click(ByVal sender As System.Object, ByVal e As System.EventArgs) _
   Handles btnMulti.Click
   Dim i As Integer
   If ListBox1.SelectionMode = SelectionMode.MultiSimple Or ListBox1.SelectionMode = _
      SelectionMode.MultiExtended Then
      For i = 0 To ListBox1.SelectedItems.Count - 1
         CheckedListBox1.Items.Add(ListBox1.SelectedItems(i))
      Next
   End If
End Sub
```

Now that we have a CheckedListBox control, let's retrieve the items checked by the user. This is done using the CheckedListBox control's GetItemChecked method.

Here, you'll see how to pull the checked items from a CheckedListBox control and add them to the collection list of a combo box (you can use the ComboBox control added to the form earlier in this section).

To retrieve checked items from a CheckedListBox control:

1. With a CheckedListBox control positioned on a form in its designer, make sure that a ComboBox control instance is available for receiving checked items (add a ComboBox control to the form if necessary).
2. Use the Toolbox to add a Button control to the form.
3. Use the Properties window to change the name of the button to `btnChecked` and the Text property value to `Checked`.
4. Double-click the Multi button to create a click event procedure framework in the Code Editor:
   ```
   Private Sub btnChecked_Click _
      (ByVal sender As System.Object, _
      ByVal e As System.EventArgs) _
      Handles btnChecked.Click

   End Sub
   ```
5. Within the click event procedure, declare an integer variable, i, to serve as an iteration counter:
   ```
   Dim i As Integer
   ```

continues on next page

6. Iterate through the Items collection of the CheckedListBox control:

   ```
   For i = 0 To _
      CheckedListBox1.Items.Count - 1

   Next
   ```

7. For each item in the CheckedListBox Items collection, determine if it is checked by using the GetItemChecked method:

   ```
   If CheckedListBox1. _
      GetItemChecked(i) = True Then

   End If
   ```

8. If an item is checked, add it to the Items collection of the ComboBox control:

   ```
   ComboBox1.Items.Add _
      (CheckedListBox1.Items(i). ToString())
   ```

   Listing 10.8 shows the complete code for the click event procedure.

9. Run the project.

10. Populate the CheckListBox control (in the example shown in **Figure 10.69** by retrieving multiple selected items from the ListBox control).

11. Check some of the boxes next to items in the CheckedListBox control.

12. Click the Checked button.

13. Verify, as shown in Figure 10.69, that the checked items from the CheckedListBox Items collection have been added to the Items collection of the ComboBox control.

Listing 10.8 Getting checked items from a CheckedListBox control and adding them to the items list of a combo box.

```
Private Sub btnChecked_Click(ByVal sender As System.Object, ByVal e As System.EventArgs) _
   Handles btnChecked.Click
   Dim i As Integer
   For i = 0 To CheckedListBox1.Items.Count - 1
      If CheckedListBox1.GetItemChecked(i) = True Then
         ComboBox1.Items.Add(CheckedListBox1.Items(i).ToString())
      End If
   Next
End Sub
```

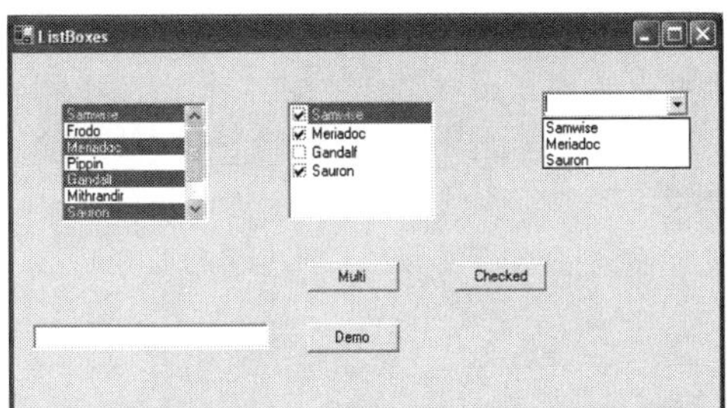

Figure 10.69 The checked items in the CheckedListBox control have been added to the combo box items list.

Summary

In this chapter, you learned how to:

- Customize the Toolbox
- Create Toolbox tabs
- Move controls from one Toolbox tab to another
- Use one click event procedure to handle events fired by multiple controls
- Iterate through a group of RadioButton controls to find the checked control
- Create toolbars using the ToolBar control
- Use the ImageList control for a library of images
- Determine which toolbar button has been clicked
- Work with the ToolTip control to provide users with information
- Use the TabControl control to create tabbed dialogs
- Use a TrackBar control to create rheostat-like user interfaces
- Work with list boxes and with the Item collections of the ListBox, ComboBox, and CheckedListBox controls

11 The Timer Component

Pity the poor Timer component! At first glance, it looks like a lightweight: It's invisible at runtime, and its members include only a few methods, one event, and two significant properties. Yet this slender reed supports the scaffolding necessary for a great many applications—applications that wouldn't be possible without it—including games, simulations, and any program that has to track the passing of time (including those that model real-world systems like the weather or the stock market).

The idea behind the Timer component is really quite simple: It's used to fire an event at specified, regular intervals. There is nothing more or less to it. You place the code you want executed in the event that is fired, called the Elapsed event.

This chapter focuses on three key areas of the Timer component. You'll learn about its members and how to count the number of times a timer has fired, how to use a Timer component to display the current time on a status bar, and how to use a Timer component to animate a sprite, or small graphic image (the kind of animation that is the basis for most arcade games).

This is a fun chapter, so let's get started!

Understanding the Timer

Code placed in the Elapsed event of an enabled Timer component is fired when the time period specified in the Timer component's Interval property passes. The firing of code continues to occur at the specified time interval so long as the Timer component is enabled.

The time period you specify in the Interval property is expressed in milliseconds (thousandths of a second). The shorter the time interval, the more often the code in the Elapsed event is executed. In applications where code executed in the Elapsed event moves objects onscreen (as in the program shown later in this chapter), the objects will appear to move faster when the code is executed at shorter time intervals. Conversely, the longer the time interval you specify, the fewer times the code is executed in a given period; thus the objects will appear to move more slowly on the screen.

If different objects or processes within a program need to move at different speeds, each object (or process) is moved with its own Timer component. Complex programs can thus employ multiple Timer components, each one propelling a different process or object that may only occasionally interact with the other processes or objects.

Static Variables

You can declare a variable using the Static keyword, rather than with Dim (or one of the scope access modifiers explained in Chapter 3, "Working with Classes.")

When you use the Static keyword in a variable declaration instead of the Dim keyword within a procedure, you are saying that the variable is supposed to retain its value as long as the project is running. Without the Static keyword, a variable declared in a procedure loses its value when the procedure finishes processing, even though the project is still running.

The task "To count the number of times a timer has fired" uses a static variable, which is declared within the Elapsed event, to track the number of times the timer fires. On each successive execution of the Elapsed event code, the static variable retains its value from the previous execution of the event.

A comparable effect could have been achieved by declaring the counter variable in the normal fashion, using the Dim keyword at the class level rather than within the Elapsed event procedure.

Table 11.1

Timer Component Members

Member	Description
Elapsed	Code placed in the Elapsed event is processed when the time Interval specified in the Interval property elapses.
Enabled	When the Enabled property is set to True, the Timer component is on and fires Elapsed events at the specified interval. When the Enabled property is set to False, the Timer component is off and does not fire Elapsed events.
Interval	The time interval, in milliseconds, between firings of an enabled Timer component's Elapsed event.
Start	Starts the Timer component; equivalent to setting the Enabled property to True.
Stop	Stops the Timer component; equivalent to setting the Enabled property to False.

In addition to the Interval property, which determines the Timer component's firing interval, and the Elapsed event, in which code is placed for processing when the event is fired, each Timer component has members that turn the timer off and on:

- The Enabled property turns a Timer component on or off, depending on whether it's set to True or False, respectively.
- The Start method, when it's invoked, starts the Timer component (it's the equivalent of setting the Enabled property to True).
- The Stop method, when it's invoked, stops the Timer component (it has the same impact as setting the Enabled property to False).

With only five members, the Timer component is not at all complicated. **Table 11.1** summarizes these members to help you see at a glance how they function.

To get a feel for the way the Timer component operates, we'll create a simple Timer component application that counts and displays in a form caption bar the number of times an Elapsed event has fired.

To count the number of times a timer has fired:

1. In a Windows Application project, open a form in its designer.
2. From the View menu, choose Toolbox to open the Toolbox.
3. Click the Components tab.
4. On the Components tab of the Toolbox, double-click Timer to add the Timer component (**Figure 11.1**) to the form.

   It will appear in the tray beneath the form (**Figure 11.2**), which is reserved for components and controls that have no visual interface at runtime.
5. From the View menu, choose Properties Window to open the Properties window.
6. In the Properties window, use the Objects list to select the Timer component.
7. Use the Properties window to set the Timer component's Enabled property to False. Leave the Timer component's Interval property at the default, 100, which is 100 milliseconds, or one-tenth of a second (**Figure 11.3**).
8. Back in the form designer, double-click the Timer component in the tray to create an event handler procedure for the Timer component's Elapsed event:

```
Private Sub Timer1_Elapsed _
   (ByVal sender As System.Object, _
   ByVal e As _
   System.Timers.ElapsedEventArgs) _
   Handles Timer1.Elapsed

End Sub
```

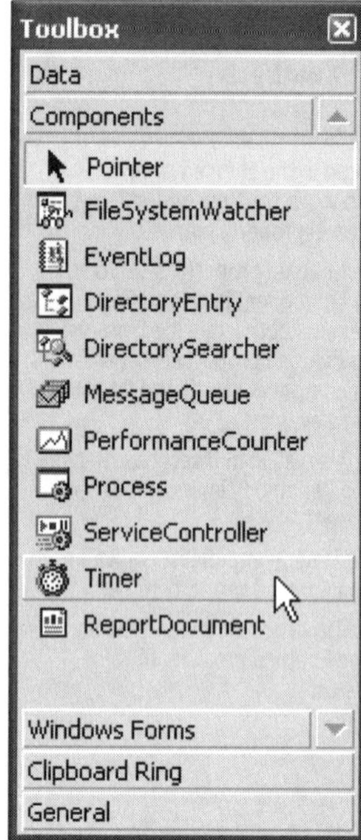

Figure 11.1 The Timer component is located on the Components tab of the Toolbox.

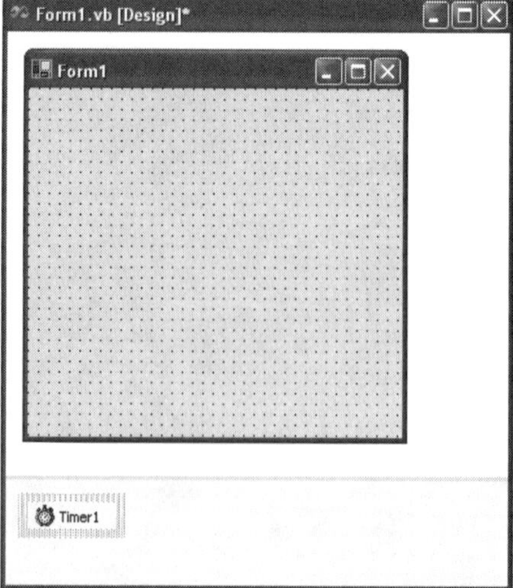

Figure 11.2 When you add a Timer component to a form in its designer, the component appears in the tray below the form.

UNDERSTANDING THE TIMER

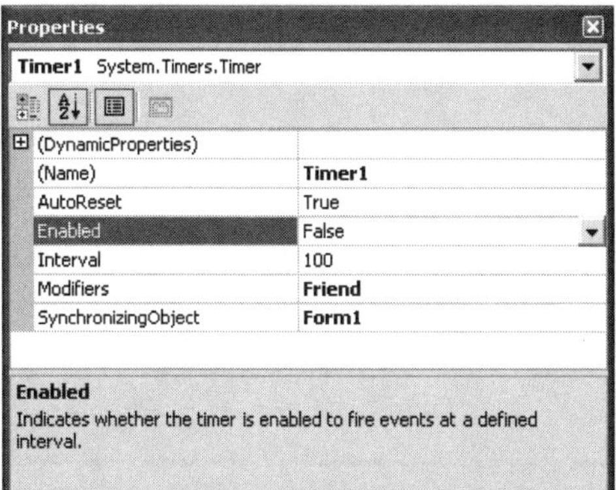

Figure 11.3 The Property window shows the values of the Timer component's Enabled and Interval properties.

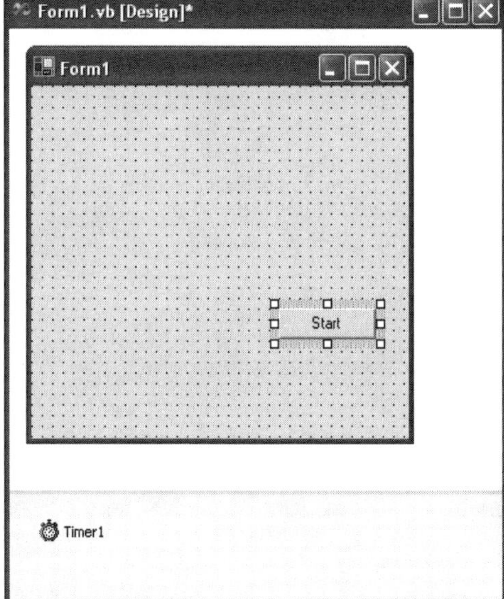

Figure 11.4 The Button control that will be used to start and stop the timer is positioned on the form.

9. In the Code Editor, within the Elapsed event, declare a static variable, `i`, that will be used to count the number of times that the Elapsed event fires:

```
Static i As Long
```

10. Display the current value of the variable i in the form's caption bar:

```
Me.Text = _
    "The Timer has been fired " & _
    i.ToString() & " times!"
```

11. Increment the counter:

```
i = i + 1
```

12. From the View menu, choose Designer to return to the form designer.

13. Use the Toolbox to add a Button control to the form.

    This Button control will be used to start and stop the Timer component.

14. Use the Properties window to change the name of the Timer component to `btnTimer` and its Text value to `Start` (**Figure 11.4**).

15. Double-click the Start button to create a click event handler procedure for it:

```
Private Sub btnTimer_Click_
    (ByVal sender As System.Object, _
    ByVal e As System.EventArgs) _
    Handles btnTimer.Click


End Sub
```

16. If the Timer component's Text value is Start, then start the timer and set the Text value to `Stop`:

```
If btnTimer.Text = "Start" Then
    Timer1.Start()
    btnTimer.Text = "Stop"
Else
...
```

continues on next page

Understanding the Timer

17. If the Timer component's Text value is not Start, then stop the timer and set the Text value to `Start`:

```
...
Else
   Timer1.Stop()
   btnTimer.Text = "Start"
End If
```

Listing 11.1 shows the complete code for the Timer component's Elapsed event and the Button click event that starts and stops the timer.

18. Run the project.

19. Click Start.

The display in the form's caption bar will start counting up as the Timer component fires its Elapsed event (**Figure 11.5**).

20. Click Stop and Start a few times, to make sure that the counter stops when the timer is disabled and starts again when it is reenabled.

✔ Tip

- I've used a single button that toggles between Start and Stop rather than two separate buttons.

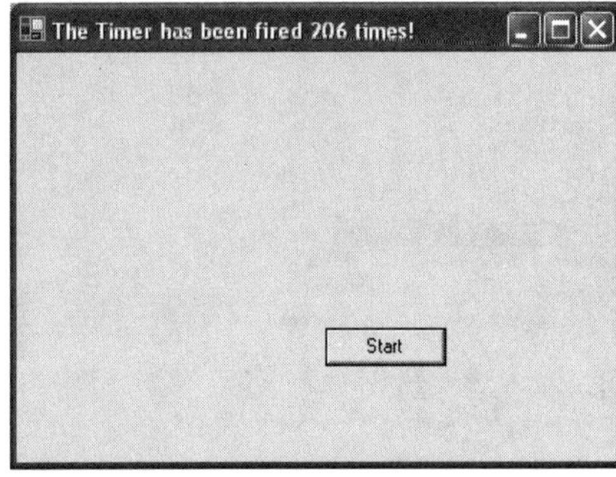

Figure 11.5 The form caption reports the number of times that the Timer component has been fired, which is the number of times that the code in the Timer component's Elapsed event has been executed.

Listing 11.1 Counting the number of times that a timer has been fired.

```
Private Sub Timer1_Elapsed(ByVal sender As System.Object, _
   ByVal e As System.Timers.ElapsedEventArgs) Handles Timer1.Elapsed
   Static i As Long
   Me.Text = "The Timer has been fired " & i.ToString() & " times!"
   i = i + 1
End Sub

Private Sub btnTimer_Click(ByVal sender As System.Object, ByVal e As System.EventArgs) _
   Handles btnTimer.Click
   If btnTimer.Text = "Start" Then
      Timer1.Start()
      btnTimer.Text = "Stop"
   Else
      Timer1.Stop()
      btnTimer.Text = "Start"
   End If
End Sub
```

Displaying the Current Time

Displaying the current time on an application's status bar (or any other control) is very common and very easy to accomplish. But to keep the time up to date, you need to employ a mechanism that refreshes the time and keeps it current: the Timer component. (For information on how to add status bars to an application using the StatusBar control, see Chapter 8, "Working with MDI Forms.")

This section explains how to use a Timer component to display the current date and time on a status bar. The first task, "To add a timer and panels to a status bar," shows you how to add three panels to a status bar. (You may recall that the application presented in Chapter 8 showed you how to add a status bar without panels.) Panels added to the Panels collection of a StatusBar control can be visually effective because they allow selective grouping of information. The leftmost panel will display the date, and the rightmost panel will display the current time. You could use the middle panel to display application-specific information.

Keeping the Time Clock in Synch

The task in this section uses the Now property of the System.DateTime structure to get the current time and date information from the system clock of the computer that is running the program. (By the way, the Microsoft.VisualBasic.DateAndTime class provides the same functionality as the DateTime structure.)

The classic computer term for this situation is GIGO—or garbage in, garbage out. If the computer's clock is inaccurate, then the time displayed using the Now property will also be wrong.

Advanced users might be interested in adding code that uses a Web service to keep the computer's time clock in synch with the time given by a central authority. You can find several Web services that return the time accurately using the Find a Service tab on the XML Web Services page of the Visual Studio Start Page (as explained in "To find a Web service" in Chapter 2). Alternatively, when you open the Add Web Reference dialog by choosing Web Reference from the Project menu, you can search the Microsoft UDDI directory for Web services such as one that returns the correct time.

To add a timer and panels to a status bar:

1. In a Windows Application project, open a form in its designer.
2. From the View menu, choose Toolbox to open the Toolbox.
3. Click the Components tab.
4. On the Components tab of the Toolbox, double-click Timer to add the Timer component to the form.

   It will appear in the tray beneath the form.
5. On the Windows Forms tab of the Toolbox, double-click the StatusBar control to add it to the form.

   Figure 11.6 shows the Form designer with the timer in the tray and the StatusBar control on the form.
6. From the View menu, choose Properties Window to open the Properties window.
7. Select the StatusBar control in the Objects list at the top of the Properties window.
8. Select Panels in the left column of the Properties window (**Figure 11.7**).

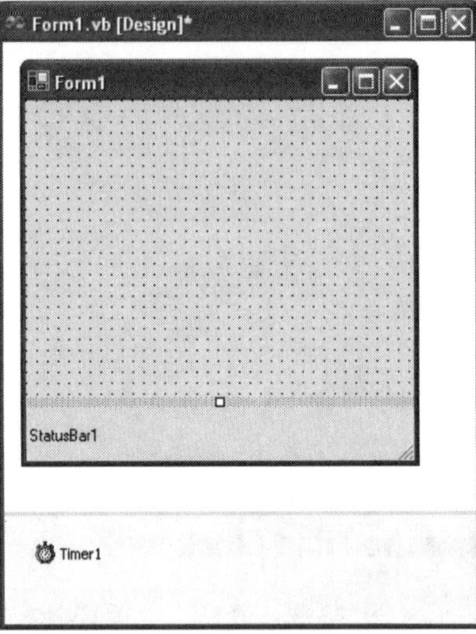

Figure 11.6 A StatusBar control and a Timer component have been added to the form.

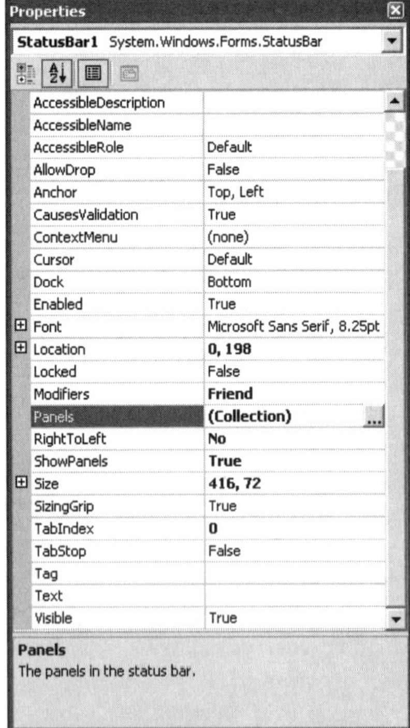

Figure 11.7 In the Properties window, click the button next to the Panels property to add status bar panels.

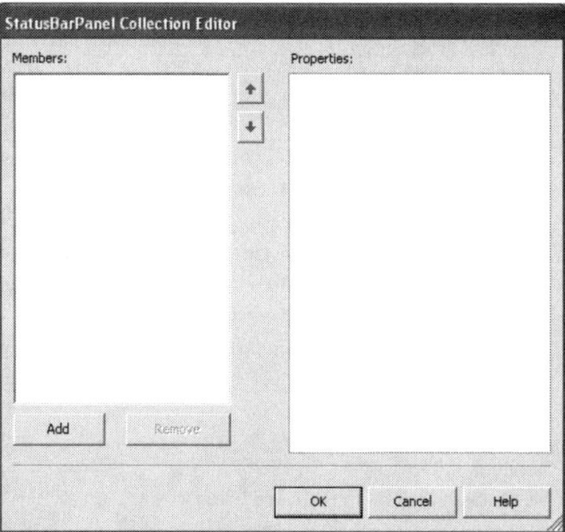

Figure 11.8 You use the StatusBarPanel Collection Editor to add panels to the Panels collection of the StatusBar control.

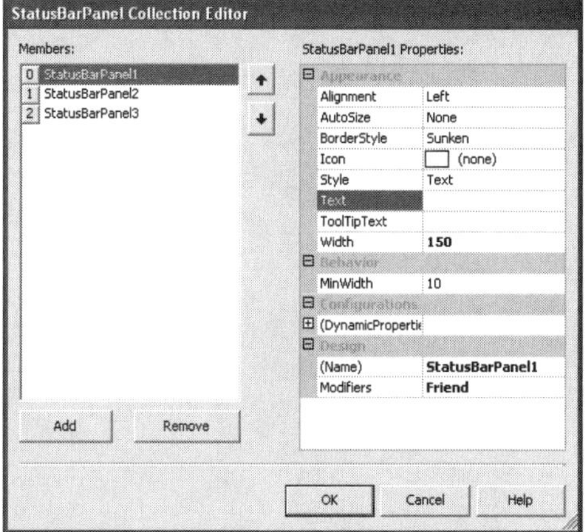

Figure 11.9 Each panel in the collection can be customized.

9. In the right column, click the ... button. The StatusBarPanel Collection Editor opens (**Figure 11.8**).
10. Click Add to add the first panel to the Panels collection.
11. Make sure that the Text property value for the first panel is set to the empty string (**Figure 11.9**).
12. Repeat Steps 10 and 11 for the second panel.
13. Click Add to add a third panel. This time, in addition to setting the Text property value to the empty string, set the Alignment property of the panel to Right, so that the time will appear aligned with the right edge of the status bar.
14. Click OK.

To display the current date and time on status bar panels:

1. Using the Properties window, make sure that the Timer component's Interval property is set to one-tenth of a second (100 milliseconds) and that its Enabled property is set to True (**Figure 11.10**).
2. Double-click the Timer component in the tray to create an event handler procedure for the Timer component's Elapsed event:

```
Private Sub Timer1_Elapsed _
    (ByVal sender As System.Object, _
    ByVal e As _
    System.Timers.ElapsedEventArgs) _
    Handles Timer1.Elapsed

End Sub
```

3. In the Code Editor, within the Elapsed event, use the zero-based index value of the third panel in the StatusBar control's Panels collection to reference the third panel: that is, StatusBar1.Panels(2). Assign the current time, in long time string format, to the Text property of the panel.

```
StatusBar1.Panels(2).Text = _
    DateTime.Now.ToLongTimeString
```

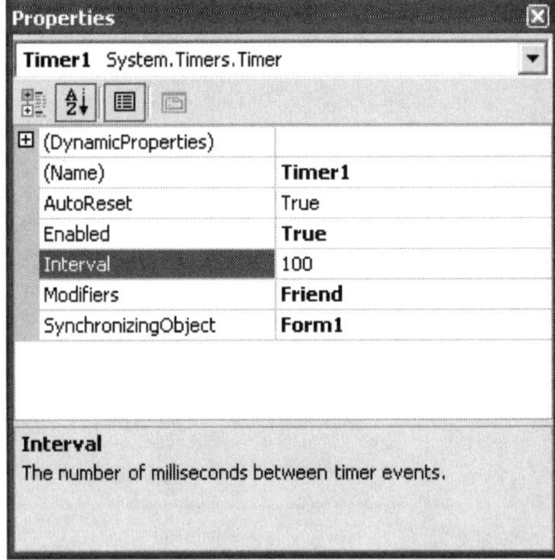

Figure 11.10 In the Properties window, you can view the initial default properties for the Timer component.

Figure 11.11 The date and the updated, current time appear on the status bar.

4. Assign the current date, in long date string format, to the Text value of the first panel:

   ```
   StatusBar1.Panels(0).Text = _
      DateTime.Now.ToLongDateString
   ```

   There's no need to update the date every 100 milliseconds, so I've put the code that displays the date on the status bar panel in the Form class New constructor, meaning that it is executed when the form opens in the application. (So if you keep the form open overnight, the date will become, well, dated.)

   Listing 11.2 shows the code that displays the date in position in the Form New constructor as well as the Timer component's Elapsed event (used to update the current time).

5. Run the project.

   The date and updated time appear on the status bar (**Figure 11.11**).

Listing 11.2 Displaying and updating the current time (and date) on a status bar.

```
#Region " Windows Form Designer generated code "


    Public Sub New()
        MyBase.New()


        'This call is required by the Windows Form Designer.
        InitializeComponent()
      StatusBar1.Panels(0).Text = DateTime.Now.ToLongDateString
        'Add any initialization after the InitializeComponent() call
   End Sub
...
Private Sub Timer1_Elapsed(ByVal sender As System.Object, _
   ByVal e As System.Timers.ElapsedEventArgs) Handles Timer1.Elapsed
   StatusBar1.Panels(2).Text = DateTime.Now.ToLongTimeString
End Sub
```

Animating a Sprite

A *sprite* is a small graphics file used as the basis for an animation. As the sprite moves around the screen, it appears to be animated. Sprites are the foundation for numerous animated effects, including the visual effects in many arcade-style games.

In the example in this section, we'll load a graphics file into a Label control. The Label control will become the sprite, and moving it around the screen using a Timer component will achieve the animation effect. The code in the Timer component's Elapsed event will move the Location property of the Label control to achieve the effect of motion.

Label controls are often used in this way because they are simple and consume the least resources, or have the least overhead, of any control that can display an image.

One general and solid approach to programming involves first creating a single example that functions the way you want it to, and then generalizing it to make multiple instances of that element work the way you want them to. We'll follow that strategy in this section by first animating a single sprite—in this case, a Label control displaying an image—and then generalizing from this example to animate multiple Label controls.

Single vs. Multiple Timers

In the interest of simplicity, this example uses a single Timer component to animate five sprites, but bear in mind that in your own real-world applications, whether you are moving a sprite on the screen or showing the progress of a simulation through time, you will likely need to use a separate Timer component for each task. This way, each sprite can move at its own pace.

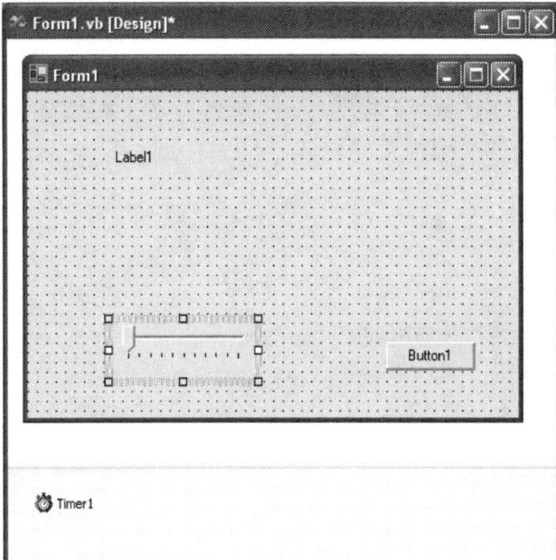

Figure 11.12 The Timer component, a TrackBar control, a Button control, and the Label control that will serve as the basis for the animated sprite have been added to the form.

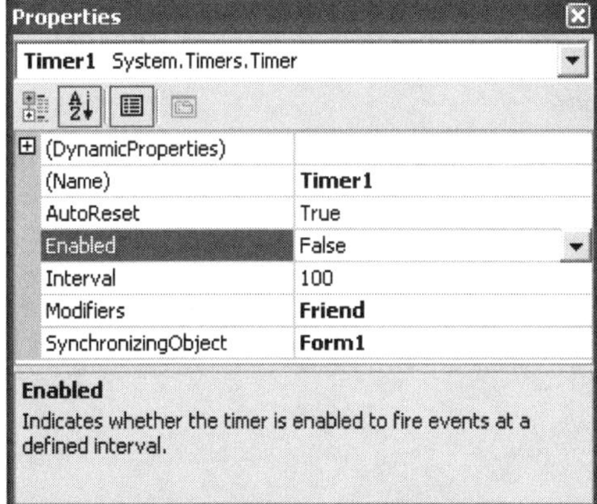

Figure 11.13 In the Properties window, the Timer component's Enabled property is set to False.

Animating a single Label control

In the first exercise we use the SNOW.ICO file for the graphic that will be displayed. Later exercises in this section use the SUN.ICO, CLOUD.ICO, LITENING.ICO, and RAIN.ICO files. You can find these files in the \Program Files\Microsoft Visual Studio .NET\Common7\Graphics\icons\Elements folder (assuming that you have a default installation). I copied them into the executable, or bin, directory of the application we'll be creating so that they can be referred to without path information. (You can, of course, place the files anywhere you like, provided that you give full path information when you load them into the Label control.)

It's cool to let the user determine the speed of the animation. You may remember from Chapter 10, "Controls That Accept User Input," that the TrackBar control allows the user to specify a setting within a range. In the animation examples in this section, you'll provide a TrackBar control to let the user set the speed of sprite movement by directly setting the Interval property of the Timer component.

To animate a single Label control:

1. Open a Windows form in its designer.
2. Use the Toolbox to add a Label control, a TrackBar control, a Timer component, and a Button control to the form (**Figure 11.12**).
3. Use the Properties window to set the Text value for the Label control to the empty string and the Name property to `Sprite1`.
4. Use the Properties window to set the Enabled property of the Timer component to False (**Figure 11.13**).

continues on next page

5. Use the Properties window to set the Text property of the button to `Start` and the Name property to `btnAnimate`.

   This button will be used to start and stop the animation.

6. Use the Properties window to set the TrackBar control's Maximum property to `1000`, its Minimum property to `10`, and its TickFrequency to `100` (**Figure 11.14**).

   As I explained at the beginning of the chapter, the higher the value of the Interval property of a Timer component, the more slowly a sprite moved by that timer will go. Normally, programs use track bars that progress from the slowest setting on the left to the fastest setting on the right. Ideally, we want our track bar to progress from 1000 on the left (which is the slowest setting) to 10 on the right (which is the fastest setting). Since this is an inverse relationship (the larger the number, the slower the motion), the track bar currently moves from fastest to slowest.

   This means that, later, we'll need to perform a calculation to reverse the track bar value before we apply it to the Interval property of the Timer component.

7. Double-click the Button control to create a click event handler for it:

```
Private Sub btnAnimate_Click _
   (ByVal sender As System.Object, _
   ByVal e As System.EventArgs) _
   Handles btnAnimate.Click

End Sub
```

Figure 11.14 The TrackBar control will be used to increase or decrease the frequency at which the timer fires.

8. Within the click event handler, add code similar to that shown earlier in this chapter in the task "To count the number of times the Timer has fired" to start and stop the Timer component:

```
If btnAnimate.Text = "Start" Then
   Timer1.Start()
   btnAnimate.Text = "Stop"
Else
   Timer1.Stop()
   btnAnimate.Text = "Start"
End If
```

9. Still in the Code Editor, declare variables that will represent the horizontal and vertical movements of the sprite at the Form class level:

```
Dim xInc As Integer
Dim yInc As Integer
```

10. In the Form New constructor, add code to initialize the increment variables:

```
xInc = 5
yInc = 10
```

11. Still in the New constructor, load the image into the file:

```
Dim fn As String = "SNOW.ICO"
Sprite1.Image = Image.FromFile(fn)
```

12. Select the Timer component from the Objects list at the upper left of the Code Editor.

13. With the Timer component selected, select the Elapsed event from the Procedures list at the upper right of the Code Editor.

    An event procedure for the Timer component's Elapsed event will be created:

```
Private Sub Timer1_Elapsed _
   (ByVal sender As Object, _
   ByVal e As _
   System.Timers.ElapsedEventArgs) _
   Handles Timer1.Elapsed

End Sub
```

14. Add code to move the Location property of the sprite (the Label control) 5 pixels along the X axis and 10 pixels along the Y axis, using the increment variables previously declared:

```
If Sprite1.Location.X <= 0 Then
   xInc = 5
End If
If Sprite1.Location.Y <= 0 Then
   yInc = 10
End If
Sprite1.Location = New _
   Point(Sprite1.Location.X + xInc, _
   Sprite1.Location.Y + yInc)
```

15. Add code to reverse the direction for the sprite (the Label control) when it reaches the top or right side of the form:

```
If Sprite1.Location.X > _
   Me.Size.Width - 30 Then
   xInc = -5
End If
If Sprite1.Location.Y > _
   Me.Size.Height - 50 Then
   yInc = -10
End If
```

16. In the Objects list, select the TrackBar control.

continues on next page

17. In the Procedures list, select the ValueChanged event to create an event procedure:

```
Private Sub TrackBar1_ValueChanged _
   (ByVal sender As System.Object, _
   ByVal e As System.EventArgs) _
   Handles TrackBar1.ValueChanged


End Sub
```

18. In the TrackBar control's ValueChanged event, add code that uses the Math object's absolute value method to reverse the range of TrackBar values and assign the reversed value to the Timer component's Interval property:

```
Timer1.Interval = _
   Math.Abs(TrackBar1.Value - 1010)
```

Listing 11.3 shows the complete code for animating the sprite.

19. Run the project.

20. Click Start.

    The snowflake is smoothly animated (**Figure 11.15**).

21. Play with the TrackBar control to verify that the animation speed changes to reflect your track bar setting.

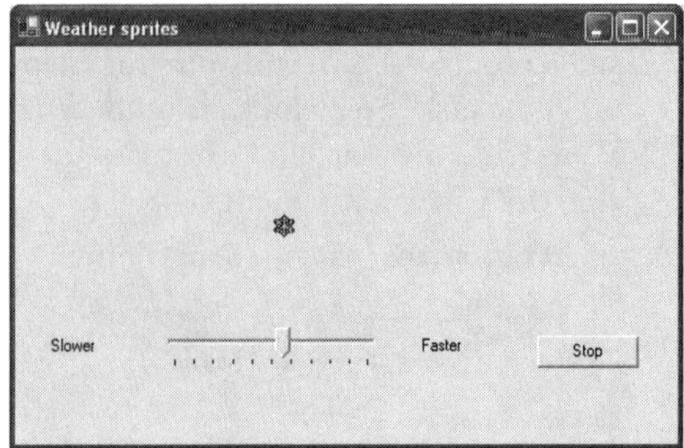

Figure 11.15 A single sprite is animated to move around the form.

To animate multiple sprites—or Label controls—we can generalize the code used for creating a single sprite. To make things reasonably interesting, we want each Label control sprite to move each time the Timer component is fired by that sprite's own increment.

We can easily declare a structure that can be used to track a Label control sprite with its corresponding increment variables, and we can use an array, so that animating multiple Label control sprites is not appreciably harder than animating a single one.

Listing 11.3 Using a Timer component to animate a single sprite.

```
Public Sub New()
   MyBase.New()
   'This call is required by the Windows Form Designer.
   InitializeComponent()
   xInc = 5
   yInc = 10
   Dim fn As String = "SNOW.ICO"
   Sprite1.Image = Image.FromFile(fn)
   'Add any initialization after the InitializeComponent() call
End Sub
...
Dim xInc As Integer
Dim yInc As Integer

Private Sub btnAnimate_Click(ByVal sender As System.Object, ByVal e As System.EventArgs) _
   Handles btnAnimate.Click
   If btnAnimate.Text = "Start" Then
      Timer1.Start()
      btnAnimate.Text = "Stop"
   Else
      Timer1.Stop()
      btnAnimate.Text = "Start"
   End If
End Sub

Private Sub Timer1_Elapsed(ByVal sender As Object, ByVal e As System.Timers.ElapsedEventArgs) _
   Handles Timer1.Elapsed
   If Sprite1.Location.X > Me.Size.Width - 30 Then
      xInc = -5
   End If
   If Sprite1.Location.Y > Me.Size.Height - 50 Then
      yInc = -10
   End If
   If Sprite1.Location.X <= 0 Then
      xInc = 5
   End If
   If Sprite1.Location.Y <= 0 Then
      yInc = 10
   End If
   Sprite1.Location = New Point(Sprite1.Location.X + xInc, Sprite1.Location.Y + yInc)
End Sub

Private Sub TrackBar1_ValueChanged (ByVal sender As System.Object, ByVal e As System.EventArgs) _
   Handles TrackBar1.ValueChanged
   Timer1.Interval = Math.Abs(TrackBar1.Value - 1010)
End Sub
```

To animate multiple Label controls:

1. Start with the project and code developed in the previous task, "To animate a single Label control."
2. Use the Toolbox to add four more Label controls to the form.
3. Use the Properties window to set the Text property value for each Label control to the empty string.
4. Name the new Label controls `Label2`, `Label3`, `Label4`, and `Label5`.
5. In the Code Editor declare a structure, `Sprite`, that contains a Label control and two integer variables representing the increment of movement as applied to a particular Label control sprite:
   ```
   Structure Sprite
      Dim lbl As Label
      Dim xInc As Integer
      Dim yInc As Integer
   End Structure
   ```
6. Declare a zero-based array consisting of four Sprite structure objects:
   ```
   Dim spriteArray(4) As Sprite
   ```
7. In the Form New constructor, load each element of the sprite array with an image and increment values. For example, here are the first and fifth elements:
   ```
   spriteArray(0).xInc = 5
   spriteArray(0).yInc = 10
   Dim fn As String = "SNOW.ICO"
   Sprite1.Image = Image.FromFile(fn)
   spriteArray(0).lbl = Sprite1
   ...
   spriteArray(4).xInc = 5
   spriteArray(4).yInc = 10
   fn = "RAIN.ICO"
   Sprite5.Image = Image.FromFile(fn)
   spriteArray(4).lbl = Sprite5
   ```

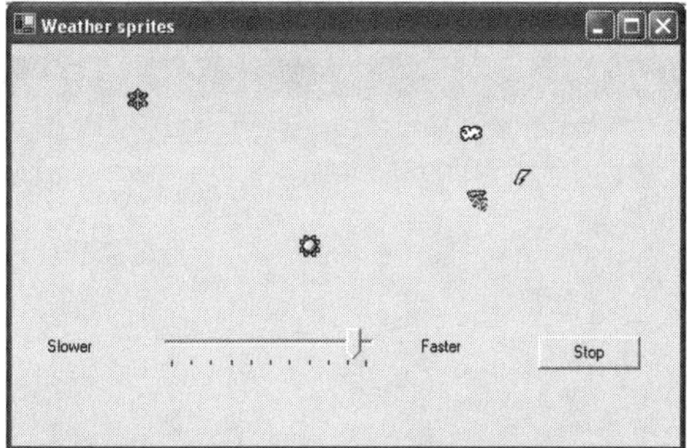

Figure 11.16 One timer can animate many sprites!

8. In the Timer component's Elapsed event, use a For loop to move each sprite array element, referring to the elements by their index values:

```
For i = 0 To 4
 If spriteArray(i).lbl.Location.X > _
     Me.Size.Width - 30 Then
     spriteArray(i).xInc = -5
 End If
 If spriteArray(i).lbl.Location.Y > _
     Me.Size.Height - 50 Then
     spriteArray(i).yInc = -10
 End If
 If spriteArray(i).lbl.Location.X _
     <= 0 Then
     spriteArray(i).xInc = 5
  End If
  If spriteArray(i).lbl.Location.Y _
     <= 0 Then
     spriteArray(i).yInc = 10
  End If
  spriteArray(i).lbl.Location = _
    New Point(spriteArray(i). _
    lbl.Location.X + _
    spriteArray(i).xInc, _
    spriteArray(i).lbl.Location.Y + _
    spriteArray(i).yInc)
Next i
```

   Listing 11.4 on the next page shows the complete code for animating multiple Label control sprites.

9. Run the project.

10. Click Start.

    The Label control sprites move around the screen (**Figure 11.16**).

Listing 11.4 One timer can animate a whole array of sprites!

```
Public Sub New()
   MyBase.New()
   'This call is required by the Windows Form Designer.
   spriteArray(0).xInc = 5
   spriteArray(0).yInc = 10
   Dim fn As String = "SNOW.ICO"
   Sprite1.Image = Image.FromFile(fn)
   spriteArray(0).lbl = Sprite1

   spriteArray(1).xInc = 8
   spriteArray(1).yInc = 12
   fn = "SUN.ICO"
   Sprite2.Image = Image.FromFile(fn)
   spriteArray(1).lbl = Sprite2

   spriteArray(2).xInc = 10
   spriteArray(2).yInc = 5
   fn = "CLOUD.ICO"
   Sprite3.Image = Image.FromFile(fn)
   spriteArray(2).lbl = Sprite3

   spriteArray(3).xInc = 8
   spriteArray(3).yInc = 12
   fn = "LITENING.ICO"
   Sprite4.Image = Image.FromFile(fn)
   spriteArray(3).lbl = Sprite4

   spriteArray(4).xInc = 5
   spriteArray(4).yInc = 10
   fn = "RAIN.ICO"
   Sprite5.Image = Image.FromFile(fn)
   spriteArray(4).lbl = Sprite5
   'Add any initialization after the InitializeComponent() call
End Sub
...
Structure Sprite
   Dim lbl As Label
   Dim xInc As Integer
   Dim yInc As Integer
End Structure
Dim spriteArray(4) As Sprite
```

continues on next page

Listing 11.4 *(continued)*

```
Private Sub btnAnimate_Click(ByVal sender As System.Object, ByVal e As System.EventArgs) _
   Handles btnAnimate.Click
   If btnAnimate.Text = "Start" Then
      Timer1.Start()
      btnAnimate.Text = "Stop"
   Else
      Timer1.Stop()
      btnAnimate.Text = "Start"
   End If
End Sub

Private Sub Timer1_Elapsed(ByVal sender As Object, ByVal e As System.Timers.ElapsedEventArgs) _
   Handles Timer1.Elapsed
   Dim i As Integer
   For i = 0 To 4
      If spriteArray(i).lbl.Location.X > Me.Size.Width - 30 Then
         spriteArray(i).xInc = -5
      End If
      If spriteArray(i).lbl.Location.Y > Me.Size.Height - 50 Then
         spriteArray(i).yInc = -10
      End If
      If spriteArray(i).lbl.Location.X <= 0 Then
         spriteArray(i).xInc = 5
      End If
      If spriteArray(i).lbl.Location.Y <= 0 Then
         spriteArray(i).yInc = 10
      End If
      spriteArray(i).lbl.Location = _
         New Point(spriteArray(i).lbl.Location.X + spriteArray(i).xInc, _
         spriteArray(i).lbl.Location.Y + spriteArray(i).yInc)
   Next i
End Sub

Private Sub TrackBar1_ValueChanged(ByVal sender As System.Object, ByVal e As System.EventArgs) _
   Handles TrackBar1.ValueChanged
   Timer1.Interval = Math.Abs(TrackBar1.Value - 1010)
End Sub
```

Summary

In this chapter, you learned how to:

- Use the members of the Timer component
- Place code in the Elapsed event of the Timer component
- Turn a Timer component off and on
- Count the number of times that a Timer component has fired
- Display the current time on a status bar panel
- Use a Timer component to animate a Label control so that it behaves like a sprite
- Use a TrackBar control to let the user set the value of a Timer component's Interval property
- Generalize the sprite animation program to extend it to an array of Label control sprites

12

Menus

The veritable menu—nearly every application has one. In fact, as a general principle of user interface design, any program feature that is accessible through a user interface control, such as code activated by a button control's click event, should also be accessible to users via a menu item. Fortunately, as you'll see in this chapter, it's very easy to handle a menu item click event in the same procedure that handles a button click event.

This chapter shows you how to visually add menus, submenus, and context menus to an application and respond to menu events programmatically. It also shows you how to add menus in code without using the visual menu designer that VB .NET provides. (You'll need to know how to do this, for example, to dynamically change menus and menu items at runtime.) Finally, you'll explore menus in a real-world context: Using an MDI text editing application as an example, you'll see how to implement an Edit menu and an MDI Window menu, which arranges MDI child forms on the screen.

Adding Menus

Each top-level menu consists of a list of menu items. Each of these menu items can have its own list of menu items, referred to as a *submenu*. The items in a submenu may have their own submenus as well (in which case the submenu is sometimes referred to as a menu).

While there is no theoretical limit to the number of nested submenus you can have, from a user interface standpoint, you should not have more than two levels of submenus below the main menu.

When a menu item has a submenu, an arrow appears next to it. For example, the Other Windows menu item on the Visual Studio View menu sports this arrow (**Figure 12.1**). When you hover the mouse over the Other Windows menu item, its submenu appears.

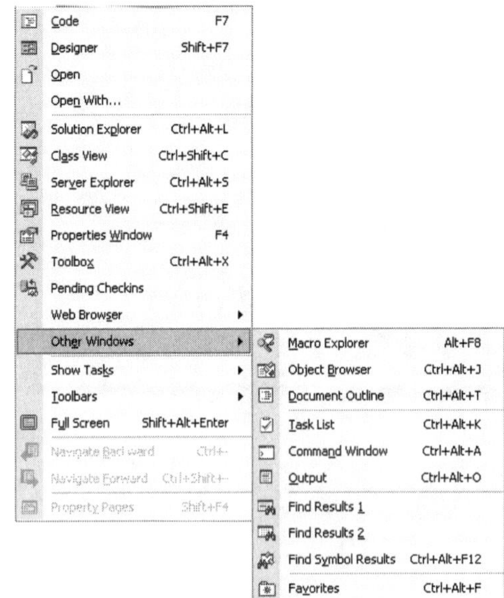

Figure 12.1 The arrow to the right of the Other Windows menu item indicates that a submenu is present.

In VB .NET, when you add a MainMenu control to a form, a visual interface opens that allows you to add menus to the form. Once you've added at least one top-level menu to the form, you can use the visual interface to add menu items as well (and menu items to the menu's submenu items, to create submenus).

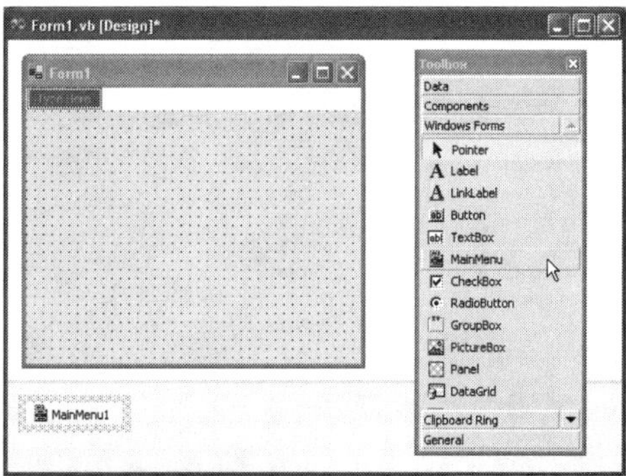

Figure 12.2 When a MainMenu control is added to a form, it appears in the form's tray.

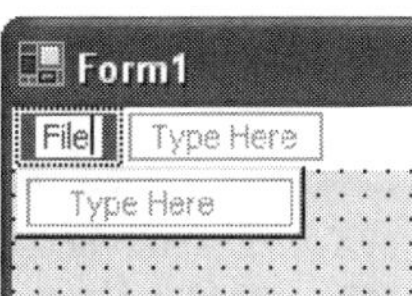

Figure 12.3 With the Text value for the first menu entered, you can enter another menu or a menu item.

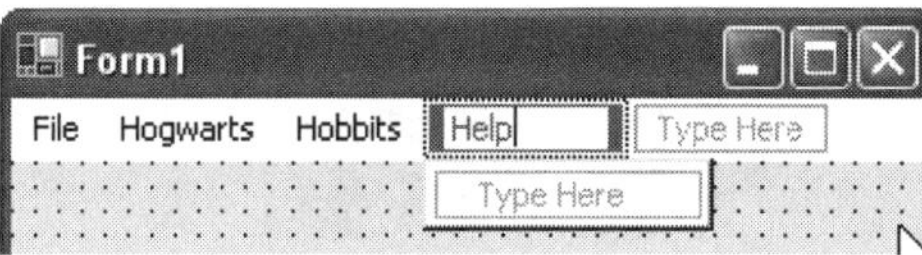

Figure 12.4 The menus appear along the top of the form, just below the caption bar.

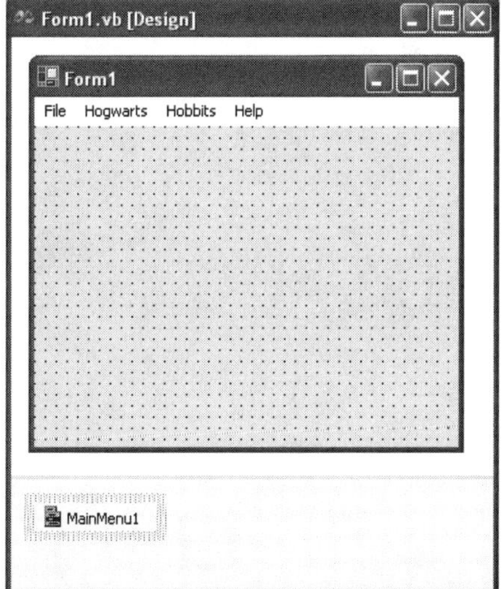

Figure 12.5 You can see the menus that were added in the Form designer.

Internally, the top-level menus comprise the MenuItems collection of the MainMenu control. Menu items form another MenuItems collection, each attached to the menu they are a part of. Under the covers, top-level menus are MenuItem objects just like any ordinary-Joe menu or submenu item that is much farther down the menu hierarchy.

To add menus to a form:

1. With a form open in its designer, choose Toolbox from the View menu to open the Toolbox.
2. Double-click the MainMenu control, located on the Windows Forms tab of the Toolbox, to add it to the form.

   The control will appear in the tray below the form (**Figure 12.2**).
3. With the Type Here box selected on the form, as shown in Figure 12.2, type the text value, also called the menu's caption, for the first menu.

   If the Type Here box is not displayed, select the MainMenu control to activate it.

   After you have entered the text for the first menu, new Type Here boxes appear so that you can enter either a submenu item or another top-level menu (**Figure 12.3**).
4. Add several top-level menus by typing each in the Type Here box to the right of the caption of the previous menu (**Figure 12.4**).

   The top-level menus now appear on the form in its designer (**Figure 12.5**).

   You might think that you have successfully added a number of top-level menus to the form, but, in fact, if you run the project at this point, you will not see the menus. Another step is necessary.

continues on next page

5. From the Visual Studio View menu, choose Properties Window.
6. In the Properties window that appears, make sure the form is selected in the Objects list.
7. In the left column of the Properties window, choose Menu (**Figure 12.6**).
8. Use the drop-down list in the right column of the Properties window, as shown in Figure 12.6, to assign the MainMenu control that you added to the form in Step 2 of this task as the value of the form's Menu property.
9. Run the project to make sure that the top-level menus now appear on the form at runtime (**Figure 12.7**).

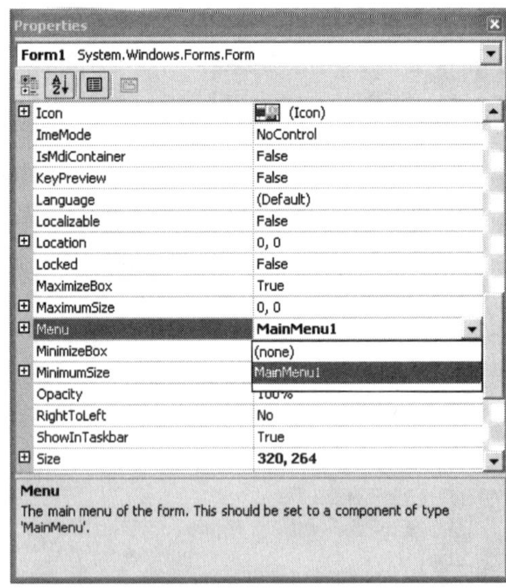

Figure 12.6 For a form to display a menu at runtime, its Menu property must be assigned the MainMenu control that stores the menu hierarchy.

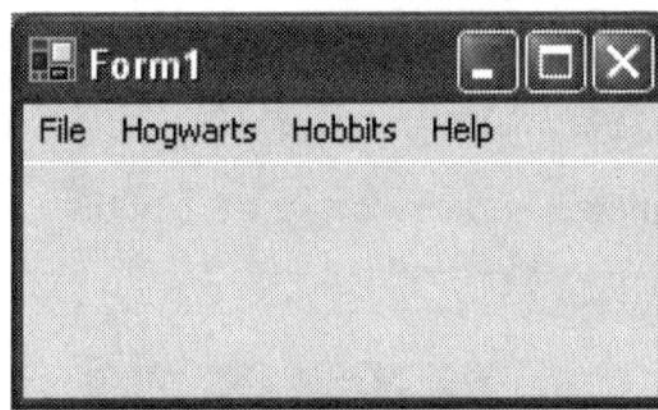

Figure 12.7 With the form's Menu property assigned, the top-level menus are displayed at runtime.

Figure 12.8 Select a menu to add a submenu item to it.

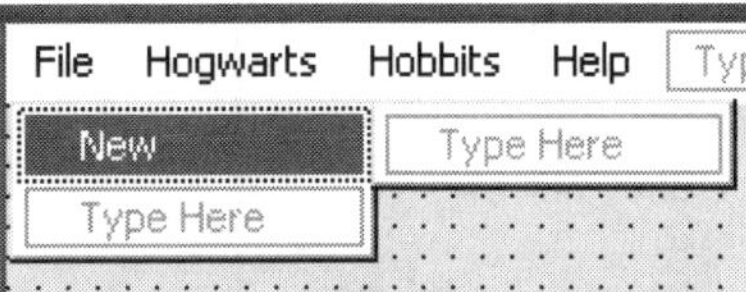

Figure 12.9 After you add one menu item by entering a text value in the Text Here box, the Text Here box for the next menu item appears.

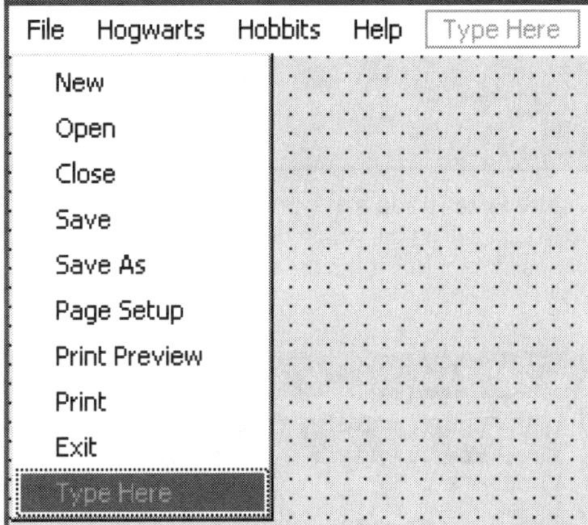

Figure 12.10 You can add as many menu items as you like to a menu.

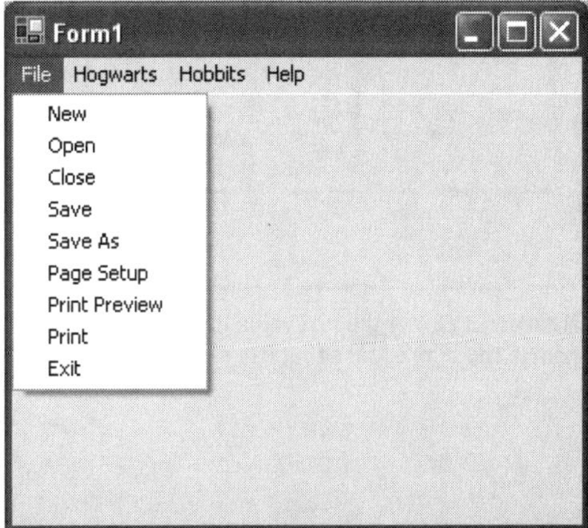

Figure 12.11 The File menu items are displayed at runtime.

To add menu items:

1. Make sure that a MainMenu control has been added to a form, that the text value for at least one top-level menu has been entered, and that the Menu property of the form has been assigned the MainMenu control as its value, as explained in "To add menus to a form" and as shown in Figure 12.7.
2. Choose the menu to which you want to add a menu item; for example, choose the File menu shown in Figure 12.7.

   A Type Here box appears (**Figure 12.8**).
3. In the Type Here box, enter a text value; for example, enter `New` (**Figure 12.9**).
4. Repeat the process until all desired File menu items have been added (**Figure 12.10**).
5. Run the project to verify that the File menu with its menu items appears at runtime (**Figure 12.11**).

To insert a menu item:

1. On the menu in which you want to insert a menu item, choose the menu item *below* the location where you want to insert a new menu item. For example, choose Page Setup to insert a menu item above that item (**Figure 12.12**).
2. Right-click and choose Insert New from the context menu, as shown in Figure 12.12.

   A new, blank text entry field for the inserted menu item will be added above the menu item you chose in Step 1.
3. Type the text value for the new menu item; for example, type `Widgets`.

   Figure 12.13 shows a new Widgets menu item inserted before Page Setup on the File menu.

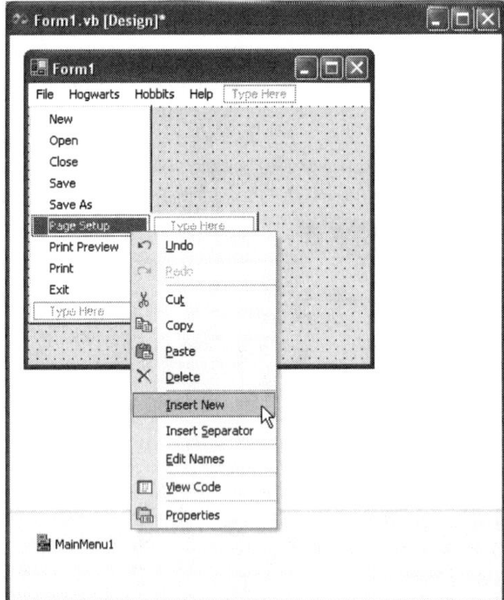

Figure 12.12 To add a new menu item, select the menu item that will be below the new item, right-click, and choose Insert New from the context menu.

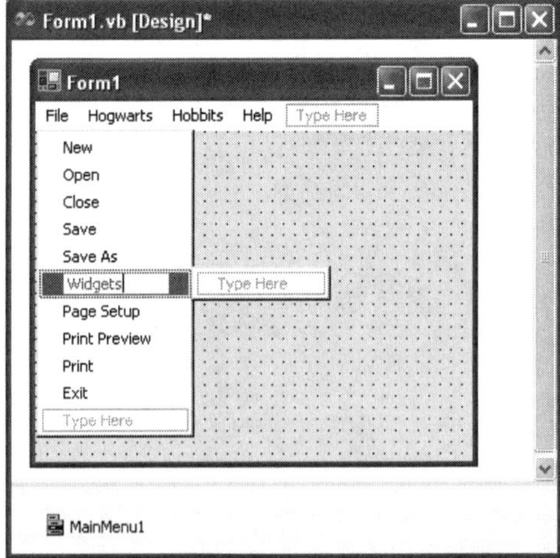

Figure 12.13 Enter the text value for the new menu item in the blank space that has been inserted.

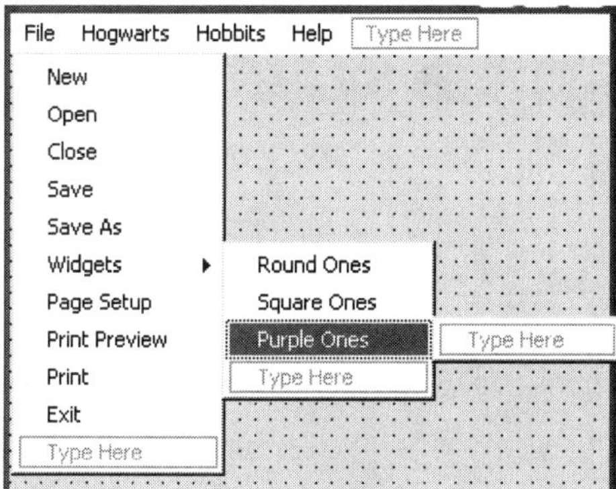

Figure 12.14 With a menu item selected, you can enter text values for submenu items in the Text Here boxes provided.

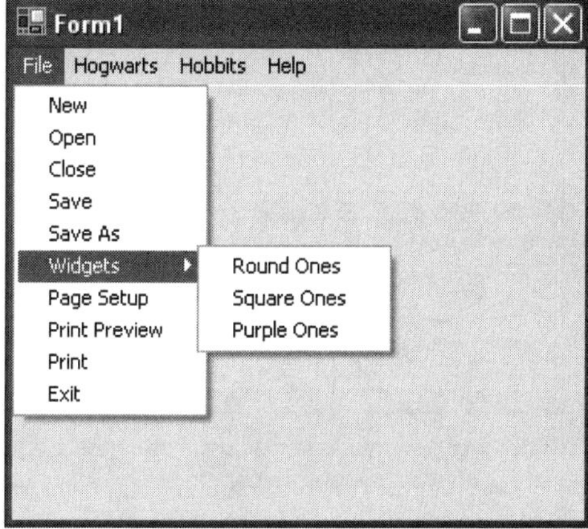

Figure 12.15 The new submenu is displayed at runtime.

To add a submenu:

1. Select the menu item to which you want to add a submenu; for example, select the Widgets menu item.

   A Text Here box appears to the right of the menu item, as shown in Figure 12.13.

2. Enter the text value for the first submenu item in the Text Here box.

   New Text Here boxes appear to the right and below the first submenu item.

3. Repeat the process by adding items below the initial submenu item until the submenu is complete (**Figure 12.14**).

4. Run the project to view the menu item and submenu at runtime (**Figure 12.15**).

To delete a menu item:

1. Right-click the menu item you want to delete and choose Delete from the context menu (**Figure 12.16**).

   If the menu item that you want to delete has submenu items, these will be deleted along with the menu item. Before making the deletion, VB .NET will ask you for confirmation (**Figure 12.17**).

2. Click Yes to continue with the deletion.

   The menu item and any submenu items will be deleted.

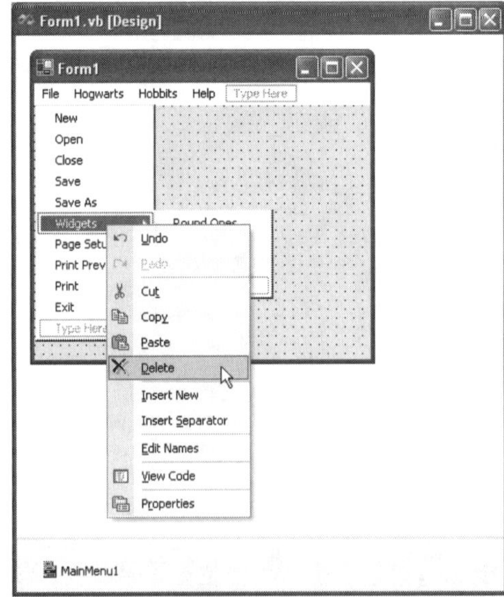

Figure 12.16 To delete a menu item, select the item and choose Delete from the context menu.

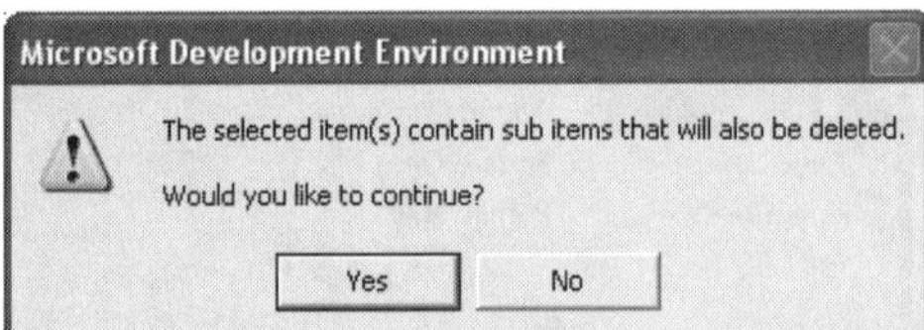

Figure 12.17 If the menu item you are attempting to delete contains submenu items, you will be asked to confirm the deletion.

Naming Menus

The text values you've been entering in the Text Here boxes are not, in fact, the names of menus or menu items. Rather, these text values—such as File or Edit—are the menu or menu item *captions* that appear on the form. A menu item's *name,* on the other hand, is a programmatic label for the Menu object that users never see. If you let VB .NET assign the name of the menu or menu item for you, it will be something completely opaque like MenuItem1. (Here's the formula: The name of each menu or menu item is the word *MenuItem* followed by an integer that represents the order in which the menu or item was added to the form.)

A much better approach is to name menu items recognizably—at least those that you intend to use programmatically—so that you know what they are. One good convention is to use the prefix *mnu* for menus, followed by the menu's caption—for example, mnuFile and mnuEdit. For menu items, append the item's caption to the menu name—for example, name the New menu item of the File menu mnuFileNew; name the Open menu item of the File menu mnuFileOpen.

Because the Objects list in the Code Editor is alphabetical, this practice also groups together all of the menu items on a particular menu.

VB .NET gives you several ways to provide a programmatic name for a menu item.

To name a menu item using the Properties window:

1. Select the menu or menu item you want to name and right-click to open its context menu.
2. From the context menu, choose Properties (**Figure 12.18**).
3. In the left column of the Properties window, select the Name property (**Figure 12.19**).
4. In the right column of the Properties window, enter the text value for the new name; for example, enter `mnuFileNew` as in Figure 12.19.

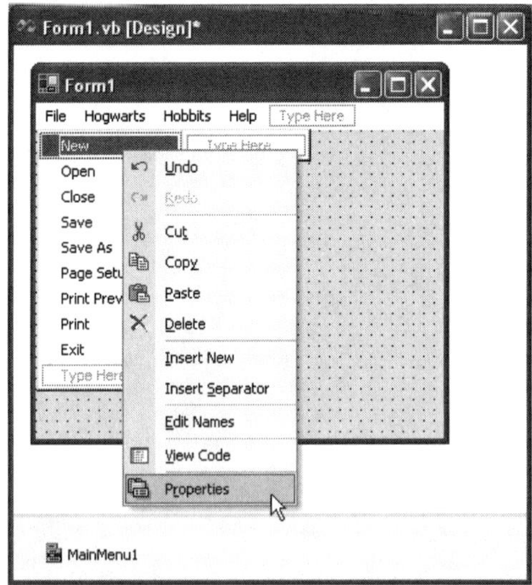

Figure 12.18 Choose Properties from a menu item's context menu to open the Properties window for the item.

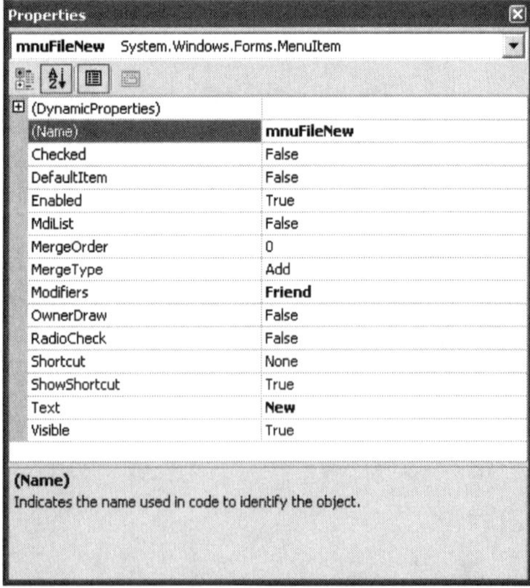

Figure 12.19 You can use the Properties window, with a MenuItem object selected, to change the name of the menu item.

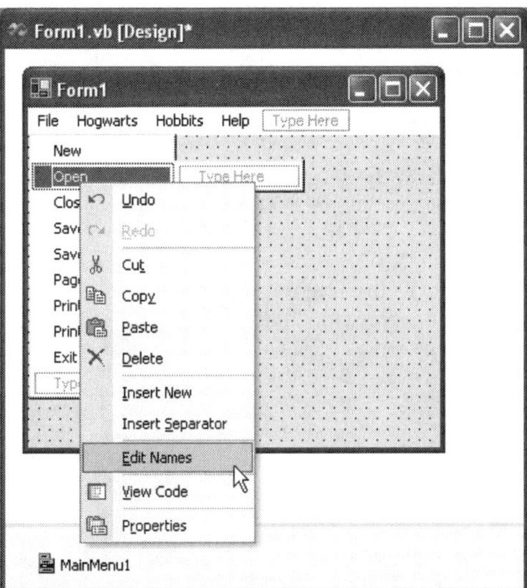

Figure 12.20 Choosing Edit Names from the context menu for a menu item toggles Edit Names mode on (and off).

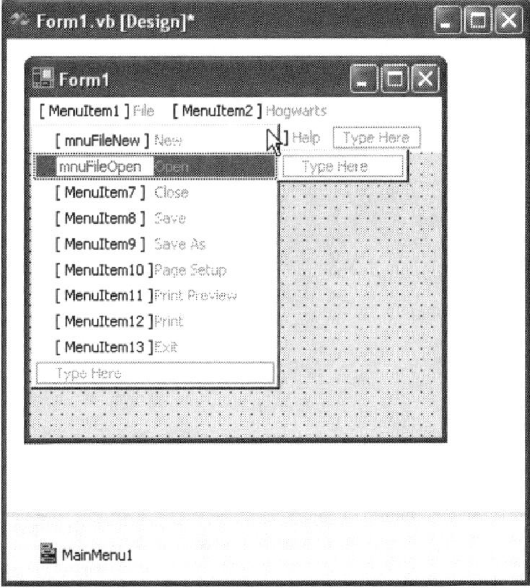

Figure 12.21 In Edit Names mode, you can directly enter a name for each menu item.

To name a menu item using Edit Names mode:

1. Select the menu or menu item you want to name and right click to open its context menu.
2. From the context menu, choose Edit Names (**Figure 12.20**).

   Edit Names mode toggles on, allowing you to enter programmatic names for all menu items (**Figure 12.21**).
3. Enter the desired name for your menu item (or items); for example, as shown in Figure 12.21, enter `mnuFileOpen`.
4. When you are through entering programmatic names, select a menu item, right-click, and choose Edit Names from its context menu to close Edit Names mode.

Polishing Menus

Access keys allow users to navigate a menu hierarchy by pressing the specified key in conjunction with the Alt key. For example, if the access key for the File menu is F and the access key for the New item in the File menu is N, pressing Alt+F followed by Alt+N has the same effect as selecting the New menu item from the File menu.

A standard principle of interface usability is that every menu item should be accessible via a combination of access keys.

It's important that access keys be unique at each menu level. (If you don't follow this guideline, the results are unpredictable.) The upper-level menu access keys must not be duplicated, for example, and all access keys for menu items within each menu must be unique. The Save menu item in the File menu and the Select All menu item in the Edit menu, however, can both use S as the access key. Although access keys are often the first letter of the caption, to avoid duplication, you can use a subsequent letter—for example, you might use X for Exit, making Alt+X the access key for the Exit menu item.

To set a menu item access key:

- When entering the text value for a menu item, place an ampersand (&) before the letter that you want to use as the access key.

  For example, to access the File menu using Alt+F, you would enter the caption as `&File`. To access the New menu item using Alt+N, you would enter the caption as &New (**Figure 12.22**). (Of course, you can edit an existing menu caption to add the ampersand (&) character.)

  Note that in Figure 12.22, the underscore already appears under the F in the text value for the File menu, indicating that this letter has been specified as the access key.

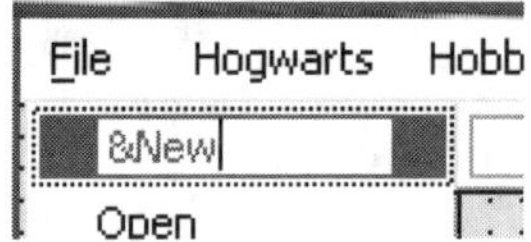

Figure 12.22 By placing an ampersand (&) before a letter that is part of the text value of a menu item, you assign that letter as the access key (in combination with Alt) for the menu item.

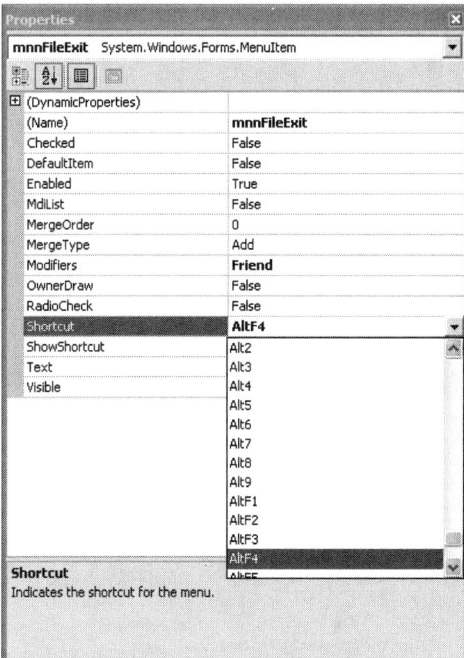

Figure 12.23 The Alt+F4 key combination is assigned as the shortcut key for the menu item.

Shortcut keys differ from access keys in that they immediately invoke the functionality of a menu item, whereas to reach a menu item using access keys, you must navigate the menu hierarchy.

Shortcut keys—actually, keyboard combinations, such as Ctrl+P, which is generally used to start printing from a Windows application—must be unique across an entire application.

To assign a shortcut key:

1. On the Form designer, select the menu item for which you want to assign a shortcut.
2. Right-click and from the context menu, choose Properties.

   The Properties window opens with the menu item selected.
3. In the left column of the Properties window, select Shortcut, and in the right column, choose a shortcut key from the drop-down menu. (**Figure 12.23**).

   In this case, the key combination Alt+F4 is being assigned to the Exit menu item on the File menu.

Separators are blank menu items that appear on the screen as lines. They are used to visually organize groups of menu items.

To add a separator:

1. On the Form designer, select the menu item that the separator is to appear above.

   In **Figure 12.24**, the separator will appear between the Save menu item and the Close menu item.
2. Right-click the menu item and choose Separator from the context menu.
3. Repeat Steps 1 and 2 for each separator that you want to add.
4. Run the project to see how the separators look at runtime (**Figure 12.25**).

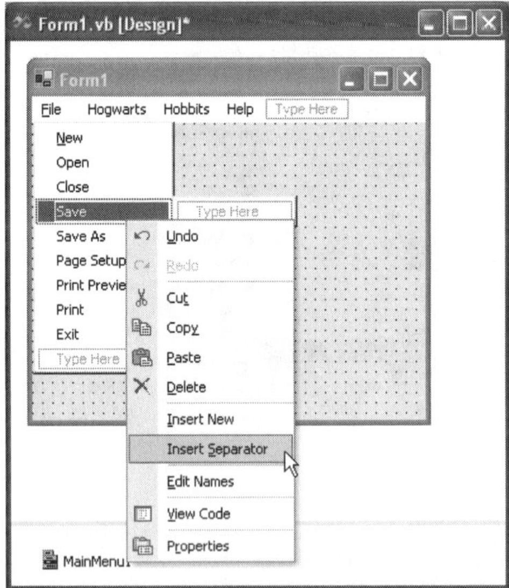

Figure 12.24 To insert a separator, select the item that is to be just below the separator, right-click, and choose Separator from the context menu.

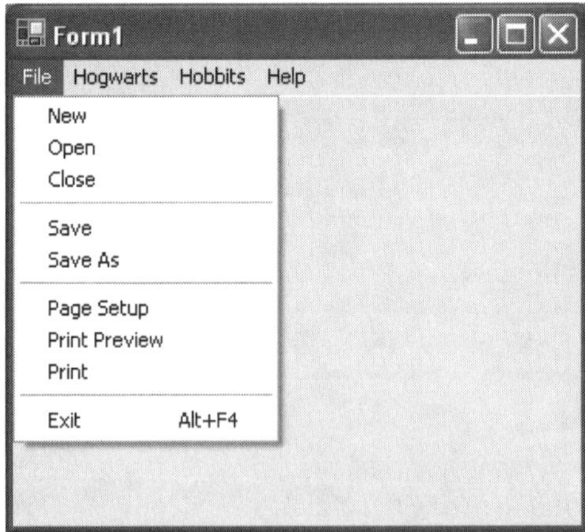

Figure 12.25 The File menu is shown with separators in place.

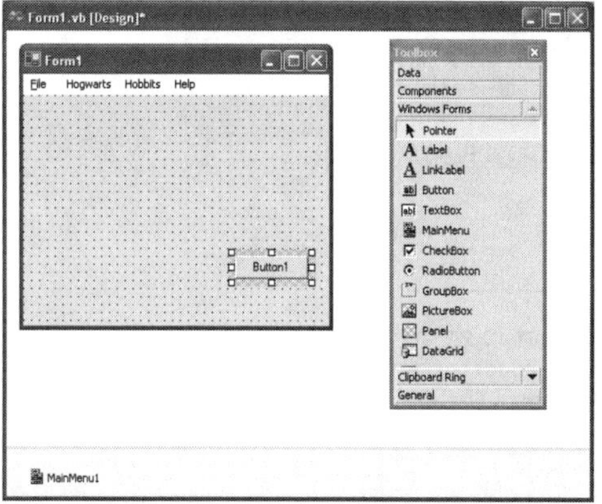

Figure 12.26 A context menu appears when the user right-clicks a form or a control (such as the button shown).

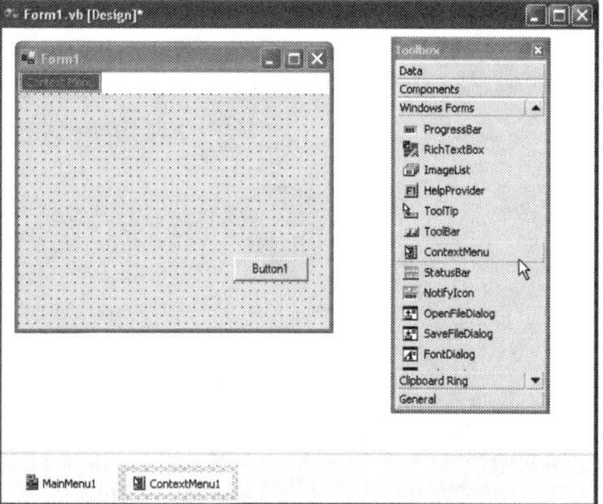

Figure 12.27 When you add the ContextMenu control to the form, it appears in the form's tray.

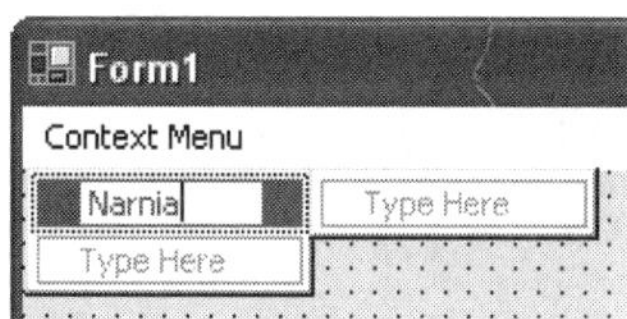

Figure 12.28 Select the ContextMenu control to add text values for context menu items.

Context menus, sometimes called pop-up menus, are menus that appear when the user right-clicks a form or control. Although context menus are added using the ContextMenu control, rather than with the MainMenu control that is used for adding an application's standard menu system, you add, delete, and insert text values for context menu items exactly as you do for regular menu items.

To add a context menu and context menu items:

1. With a form open in its designer, use the Toolbox to add a Button control to the form (**Figure 12.26**).

   This button will be linked to the context menu, so that the context menu items will appear when the user right-clicks the button.

2. Double-click the ContextMenu control, which is located on the Windows Forms tab of the Toolbox, to add it to the form.

   The control will appear in the tray beneath the form (**Figure 12.27**).

3. If it is not already selected, select the ContextMenu control.

4. In the text box under the Context Menu heading, enter the text value for the first context menu item (**Figure 12.28**).

continues on next page

5. Enter as many text values for context menu items and submenu items as you like (**Figure 12.29**).

6. When you've finished entering context menu items, choose Properties Window from the Visual Studio View menu to open the Properties window.

7. Using the Objects list at the top of the Properties window, select the button control that will be linked to the context menu (**Figure 12.30**).

8. In the left column of the Properties window, choose the ContextMenu property, and in the right column, select the ContextMenu control from the drop-down menu (Figure 12.30).

9. Run the project. Right-click the control. The context menu items that you entered will appear (**Figure 12.31**).

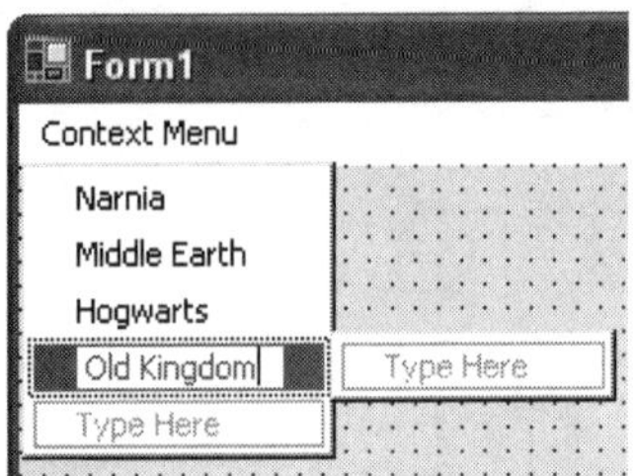

Figure 12.29 You can enter the text values for context menu items and submenu items.

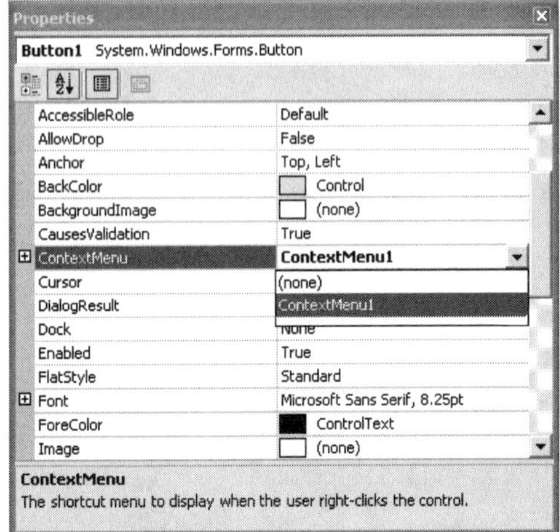

Figure 12.30 For the context menu to be displayed, you must set the control's ContextMenu property to the ContextMenu control that stores the context menu hierarchy.

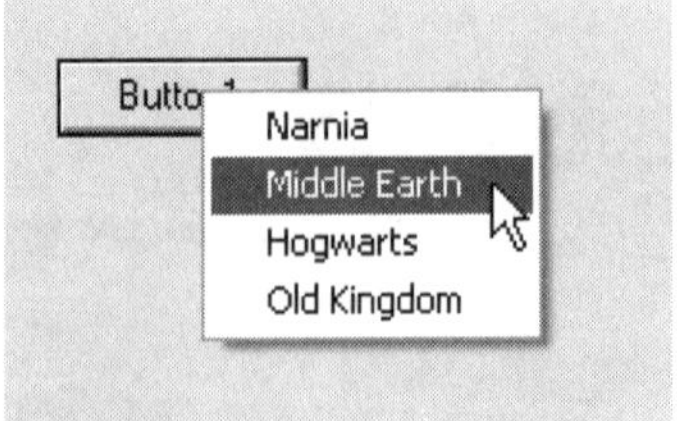

Figure 12.31 The context menu items are displayed at runtime when the user right-clicks the Button control.

POLISHING MENUS

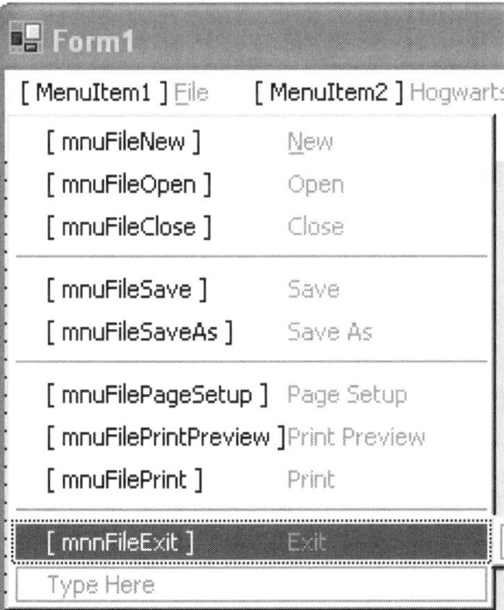

Figure 12.32 In Edit Names mode, the programmatic names of menu items, as well as their text values, are shown.

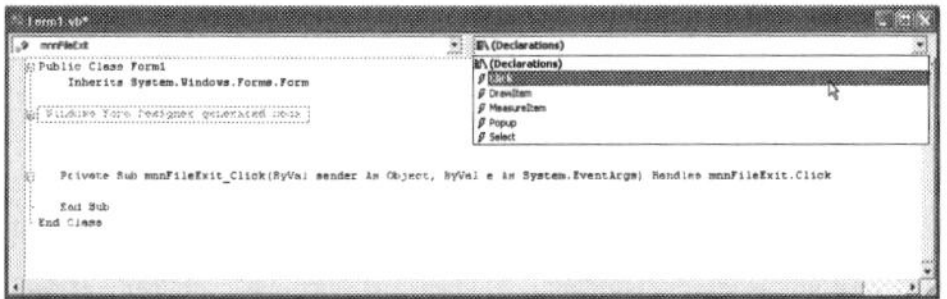

Figure 12.33 To create a click event handler for the menu item in the Code Editor, select the menu item from the Objects list and the Click event from the Procedures list.

Responding to Menu Events

Creating the items that comprise a menu is, of course, only part of the story. You also need an easy way to programmatically respond when the user chooses a menu item. In fact, when the user chooses a menu item, a menu item click event is fired. Responding to this event in code is as easy as responding to the click event generated by a control such as a button.

To add a menu item click event procedure:

1. Note the programmatic name of the menu item to which you want to add a click event.

   For example, the name of the Exit menu shown in **Figure 12.32** in Edit Names mode is mnuFileExit.

2. To create a menu item click event handler, *do one of the following:*

   On the Form designer, double-click the menu item.

   or

   From the View menu, choose Code to open the Code Editor. From the Objects list, select the menu item's programmatic name; and from the Procedures list, choose the Click event (**Figure 12.33**).

   A click event procedure for the menu item will be created in the Code Editor (as you can see in Figure 12.33).

   Here's the code for the framework:

```
Private Sub mnnFileExit_Click _
   (ByVal sender As Object, _
   ByVal e As System.EventArgs) _
   Handles mnnFileExit.Click

End Sub
```

continues on next page

RESPONDING TO MENU EVENTS

3. Add code within the menu item click event to display a message box and, since this is the Exit menu item, to close the form:

```
MessageBox.Show _
   ("Exit menu clicked!", _
   "Menus", MessageBoxButtons.OK, _
   MessageBoxIcon.Exclamation)
Me.Close()
```

   Listing 12.1 shows the complete code for the menu item click event handler.

4. Run the project.
5. Choose the Exit menu item from the File menu.
   The message box will appear (**Figure 12.34**).
6. Click OK.
   The form will close.

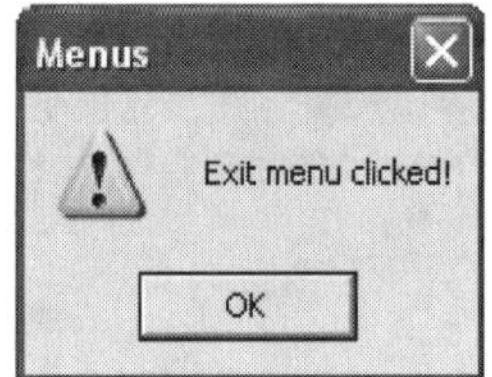

Figure 12.34 The message box appears when the menu item's click event is fired.

To keep your program code well organized, you may want to use a single event procedure to manage multiple items rather than employing a large number of separate procedures. You can easily do this by adding each menu item that is handled by a central procedure to the Handles clause of the procedure.

Listing 12.1 The Exit menu item's click event.

```
Private Sub mnnFileExit_Click(ByVal sender As Object, ByVal e As System.EventArgs) _
   Handles mnnFileExit.Click
   MessageBox.Show("Exit menu clicked!", "Menus", MessageBoxButtons.OK, _
   MessageBoxIcon.Exclamation)
   Me.Close()
End Sub
```

Table 12.1

Hobbits Menu Items	
Programmatic Name	**Text Value**
mnuHobbitsFrodo	Frodo
mnuHobbitsMerry	Merry
mnuHobbitsPippin	Pippin
mnuHobbitsSam	Sam

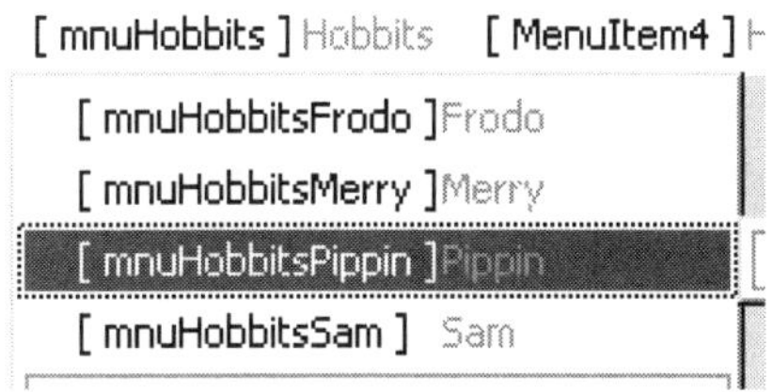

Figure 12.35 The Hobbits menu is shown in Edit Names mode.

```
:k(ByVal sender As System.Object, _
 Handles mnuHobbitsFrodo.Click,
```

MenuItem8
MenuItem9
mnnFileExit
mnuFileNew
mnuFileOpen
mnuHobbitsFrodo
mnuHobbitsMerry
mnuHobbitsPippin
mnuHobbitsSam
MyBase

Figure 12.36 The Code Editor supplies a drop-down list of objects that can be added to an event's Handles clause.

To see how this works, let's use as a test case a Hobbits menu, with programmatic names and text values for the menu items as shown in Edit Names mode in **Figure 12.35** and in **Table 12.1**.

To add a central menu item processing procedure:

1. Create a menu item click event procedure in the Code Editor for one of the menu items as explained in Step 2 of the previous task.

   Assuming that you used the Frodo menu item to create the click event procedure, the procedure should look like this in the Code Editor:

   ```
   Private Sub mnuHobbitsFrodo_Click _
      (ByVal sender As System.Object, _
      ByVal e As System.EventArgs) _
      Handles mnuHobbitsFrodo.Click


   End Sub
   ```

2. In the Code Editor, for each menu item you want to handle in the event procedure, add a comma at the end of the Handles clause (following mnuHobbitsFrodo.Click).

   The Code Editor will display a drop-down list of objects with events that can be handled (**Figure 12.36**).

3. Choose a menu item whose click event you want to handle: for example, mnuHobbitsMerry.

4. After the menu item's programmatic name, add a dot operator (`.`).

5. From the drop-down list supplied by the Code Editor, choose the Click event (or just type it).

continues on next page

6. Repeat the process for each menu item with a click event that you want the procedure to handle.

   When you are finished and all the Hobbits menu item click events have been added, the procedure declaration should look like this:

```
Private Sub mnuHobbitsFrodo_Click _
   (ByVal sender As System.Object, _
   ByVal e As System.EventArgs) _
   Handles mnuHobbitsFrodo.Click, _
   mnuHobbitsMerry.Click, _
   mnuHobbitsPippin.Click, _
   mnuHobbitsSam.Click


End Sub
```

7. Convert the sender variable in the event procedure to the MenuItem type (so that its Text property can be inspected):

```
Dim mi As MenuItem = _
   CType(sender, MenuItem)
```

8. Use a Select Case statement to branch according to the value of the Text property:

   Select Case mi.Text

```
End Select
```

9. For each menu item selection, display a message box whenever the item is clicked. For example, for the Sam menu item, use the following code to set up a message box:

```
...
Case "Sam"
   MessageBox.Show _
   ("Sam menu clicked!", "Menus", _
   MessageBoxButtons.OK, _
   MessageBoxIcon.Exclamation)
...
```

   Listing 12.2 shows the complete central procedure code for the Hobbits menu.

Listing 12.2 A central menu item event processing procedure.

```
Private Sub mnuHobbitsFrodo_Click(ByVal sender As System.Object, ByVal e As System.EventArgs) _
   Handles mnuHobbitsFrodo.Click, _
   mnuHobbitsMerry.Click, mnuHobbitsPippin.Click, mnuHobbitsSam.Click
   Dim mi As MenuItem = CType(sender, MenuItem)
   Select Case mi.Text
      Case "Frodo"
         MessageBox.Show("Frodo menu clicked!", "Menus", MessageBoxButtons.OK, _
            MessageBoxIcon.Exclamation)
      Case "Merry"
         MessageBox.Show("Merry menu clicked!", "Menus", MessageBoxButtons.OK, _
            MessageBoxIcon.Exclamation)
      Case "Pippin"
         MessageBox.Show("Pippin menu clicked!", "Menus", MessageBoxButtons.OK, _
            MessageBoxIcon.Exclamation)
      Case "Sam"
         MessageBox.Show("Sam menu clicked!", "Menus", MessageBoxButtons.OK, _
            MessageBoxIcon.Exclamation)
   End Select
End Sub
```

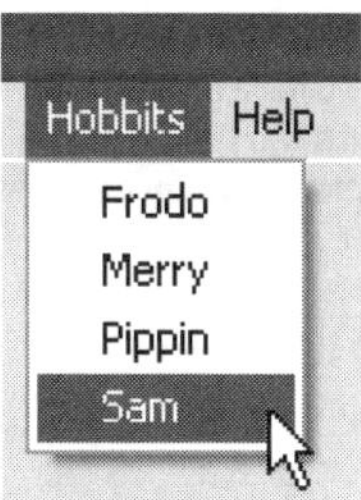

Figure 12.37 The Hobbits menu at runtime.

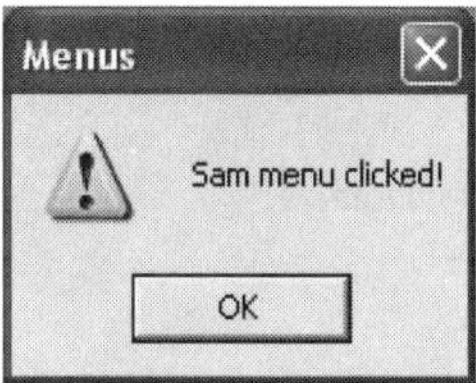

Figure 12.38 When you select a Hobbits menu item, the appropriate message box is displayed.

10. Run the project.
11. Choose the Hobbits menu and click a menu item such as Sam (**Figure 12.37**).
12. Verify that the appropriate message box is displayed (**Figure 12.38**).

The central procedure we just created is a little unrealistic because usually the point of having different menu items is that you want different code processed depending on the user's selection of a menu item. If all you wanted to do was display a message box showing the menu item that fired the event, you wouldn't need the Select Case statement. Instead, you would display the menu item that invoked the procedure:

```
Dim mi As MenuItem = _
   CType(sender, MenuItem)
MessageBox.Show(mi.Text)
```

In fact, you can consider the message boxes in the task "To add a central menu item processing procedure" merely stand-ins for the code that would perform specific functions depending on the menu item selected by the user.

However, there's one case where you definitely want a click event to process the same code no matter what object originated the event. As mentioned at the beginning of this chapter, anything that can be accessed through controls placed on a form should also be accessible from a menu item. So if, for example, a menu item click event has the same functionality as a Button control's click event, the same procedure presumably should implement this functionality. There's likely no reason to branch within this combined procedure depending on the object that invoked it (unlike in the Select...Case statement in the task "To add a central menu item processing procedure").

To handle a menu click event in another event procedure:

1. Add a Button control named Button1 to a form, if the control is not already present (**Figure 12.39**).
2. Add a menu item to the form with a text value of `Button` and the name `mnuButton` (**Figure 12.40**).
3. Double-click the Button control to add a click event procedure for the control in the Code Editor:

```
Private Sub Button1_Click _
   (ByVal sender As System.Object, _
   ByVal e As System.EventArgs) _
   Handles Button1.Click


End Sub
```

4. Add a comma after the Handles clause and add mnuButton's click event:

```
Private Sub Button1_Click _
   (ByVal sender As System.Object, _
   ByVal e As System.EventArgs) _
   Handles Button1.Click, _
   mnuButton.Click


End Sub
```

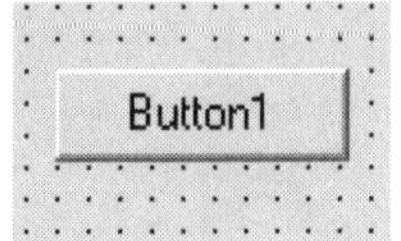

Figure 12.39 The Button control's click event procedure will handle both the event fired when the user clicks the button and the event fired when the user chooses the menu item.

Figure 12.40 The Button menu item is shown in Edit Names mode.

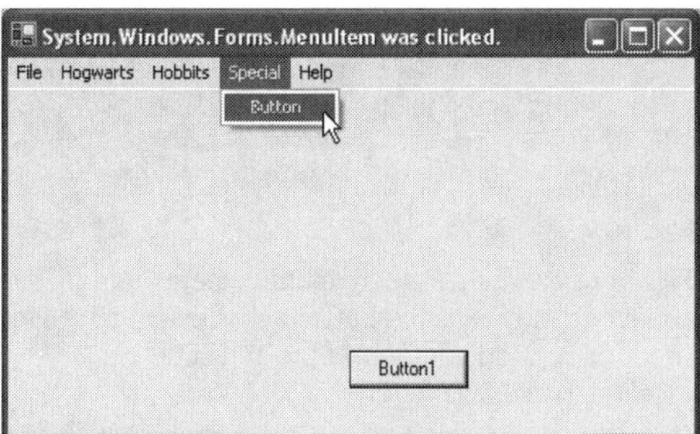

Figure 12.41 The form caption reports the type of object that fired the event.

5. In case there's a programmatic need to know, display the kind of object that fired the event procedure in the caption bar of the form (using the sender object's GetType method):

   ```
   Me.Text = sender.GetType.ToString & _
      " was clicked."
   ```

   Listing 12.3 shows the complete code for the click event.

6. Run the project.

7. Select the Button menu item and also click the actual button (Button1). Make sure that the correct object type appears in the form caption bar (**Figure 12.41**).

✔ Tip

- A Button control's click event can be handled by a MenuItem control's click event handler just as easily as the other way around.

You can hedge your bets by calling one event procedure from another. For example, a menu item click event could call a Button control's click event.

The advantage of this scheme over the one described in the task "To handle a menu click event in another click event procedure" is that this scheme is a little more flexible. You still get the functionality of the button's click event procedure, but before execution transfers to the button's click event, you have an opportunity to implement menu-item-specific code to the menu item's click event, should you so desire.

Listing 12.3 Displaying the type of object that fired the event.

```
Private Sub Button1_Click(ByVal sender As System.Object, ByVal e As System.EventArgs) _
   Handles Button1.Click, mnuButton.Click
   Me.Text = sender.GetType.ToString & " was clicked."
End Sub
```

To use a menu click event procedure to call another event procedure:

1. Add a menu item to the form; for example, add a menu item named `mnuCall` with the text value `Call`.
2. Double-click the Call menu item to create an event procedure for it in the Code Editor:

```
Private Sub mnuCall_Click _
    (ByVal sender As System.Object, _
    ByVal e As System.EventArgs) _
    Handles mnuCall.Click

End Sub
```

3. Within the Call menu item's click event procedure, invoke the Button1 click event procedure, using the sender object and the EventArgs values that were passed to the menu item's click event as the arguments in the call to the menu click event:

```
Button1_Click(sender, e)
```

   Listing 12.4 shows the complete menu item click event code.

4. Run the project to make sure that clicking the Call menu item invokes the Button1 click event.

   You'll know because the Button1 click event displays a message in the form caption bar indicating the type of object that invoked the event (**Figure 12.42**).

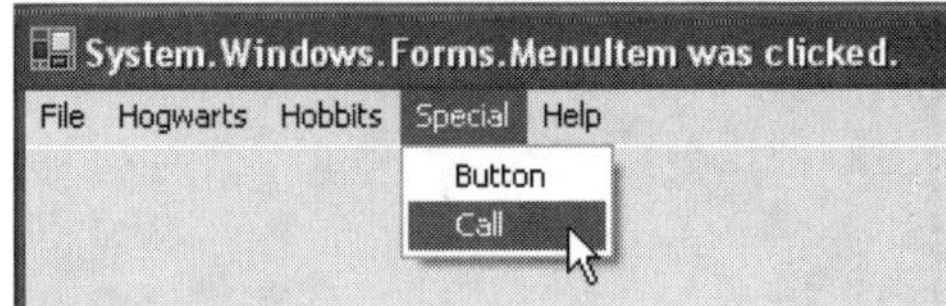

Figure 12.42 You can verify that the menu item click event correctly calls the Button1 click event, because the form caption bar reports the object type that invoked the event.

Listing 12.4 Calling a button click event from a menu item click event.

```
Private Sub mnuCall_Click(ByVal sender As System.Object, _
   ByVal e As System.EventArgs) Handles mnuCall.Click
   Button1_Click(sender, e)
End Sub
```

Using Code to Manipulate Menus

So far in this chapter, you've been working with the visual interface provided by VB .NET to add menus, context menus, and menu items to a project, and you've explored a number of techniques for responding in code to the event fired when the user selects a menu item (the menu item's click event). To provide a project with a truly professional menu, however, you need to know a little bit more.

In this section, you'll learn how you can use code to perform the following operations:

- Check and uncheck menu items
- Enable and disable menu items
- Toggle an application between two menu hierarchies

In fact, you can use code to replace the entire functionality of the visual menu designer. Whether you choose to do so is up to you. To help make this an informed decision on your part and to start you down the road to creating menus and menu items programmatically, this section also shows you how to add a menu item in code dynamically at runtime—a function you may need to implement in a real-world application.

We'll first explore how to check and uncheck a menu item. A check mark on a menu item indicates that the item is selected.

You can easily add an initial check mark to a menu item using the Properties window. However, if you want to display a check mark next to an item *after* the user selects it or uncheck an item that is checked, you'll need to use code.

To check and uncheck a menu item:

1. Add a menu item to a menu with the text value `To check or not to check` (after all, that *is* the question!) (**Figure 12.43**).
2. Use the Properties window to name the menu item `mnuCheck` and set the initial Checked property for the mnuCheck menu item to True (**Figure 12.44**).
3. Double-click the menu item to create a click event for it:

```
Private Sub mnuCheck_Click _
   (ByVal sender As System.Object, _
   ByVal e As System.EventArgs) _
   Handles mnuCheck.Click


End Sub
```

4. Add a conditional statement that toggles the menu item's Checked property:

```
If mnuCheck.Checked = True Then
   mnuCheck.Checked = False
Else
   mnuCheck.Checked = True
End If
```

Listing 12.5 shows the complete click event that toggles the menu item's Checked property.

Figure 12.43 The "To check or not to check" menu item is unchecked.

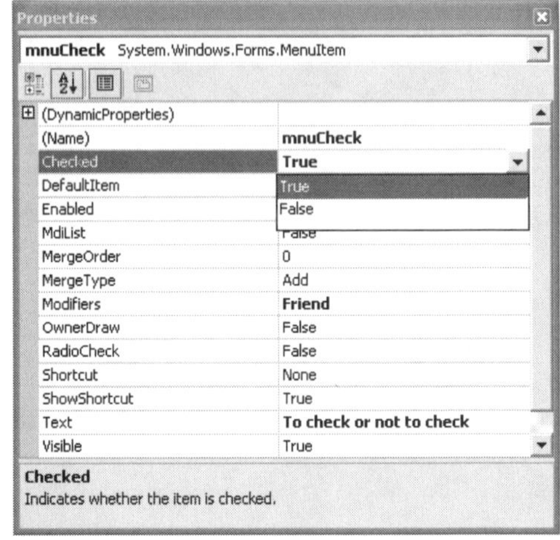

Figure 12.44 Using the Properties menu, you can set a menu item to initially appear with a check mark.

Listing 12.5 Toggling a menu check mark.

```
Private Sub mnuCheck_Click(ByVal sender As System.Object, ByVal e As System.EventArgs) _
   Handles mnuCheck.Click
   If mnuCheck.Checked = True Then
      mnuCheck.Checked = False
   Else
      mnuCheck.Checked = True
   End If
End Sub
```

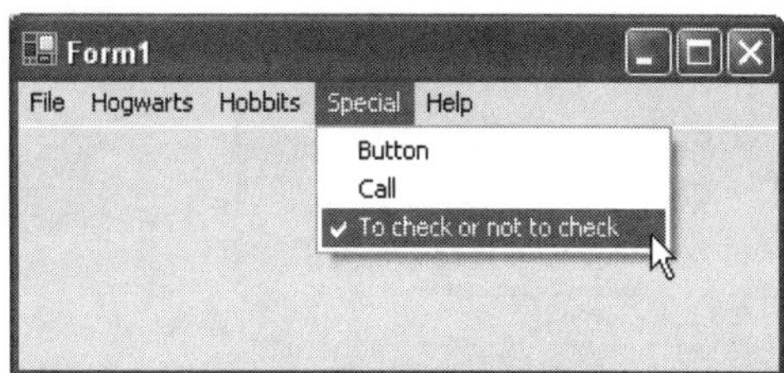

Figure 12.45 At runtime, the menu toggles between a checked and an unchecked state (checked is shown).

5. Run the project.
6. Verify that clicking the To Check or Not to Check menu item toggles the check mark on and off (**Figure 12.45** shows the item checked).

When you disable a menu item, it can no longer fire events. In addition, disabled menu items appear dimmed.

Disabling a menu item is a way of signaling the user that the action that the menu item initiates cannot be performed. At the same time, when you disable a menu item (rather than not showing it at all), you let the user to know that the action is available under some circumstances.

You can easily disable a menu item initially using the Properties window. However, a menu item that is always disabled is pretty useless (because code placed in a disabled menu item's click event will never be processed). If there is nothing programmatic that would enable the menu item, then you should probably remove it completely, rather than showing it disabled.

Therefore, if a menu item starts with its Enabled property set to False, you will likely want to be able to change this property at runtime (perhaps in response to changing program conditions).

To enable and disable a menu item:

1. Add a menu item with the text value `Am I able?` (**Figure 12.46**).
2. Use the Properties window to set the Name property for the menu item to `mnuEnable` and its Enabled property to False (**Figure 12.47**).
3. Use the Toolbox to add a Button control to the form.
4. Use the Properties window to set the button's Name property to `btnEnable` and its Text property to `Enable` (**Figure 12.48**).
5. Double-click the Button control to create a click event handler for it.
6. Within the event procedure, add code that toggles both the Button control's text and the Enabled property of the menu:

```
If btnEnable.Text = "Enable" Then
    mnuEnable.Enabled = True
    btnEnable.Text = "Disable"
Else
    mnuEnable.Enabled = False
    btnEnable.Text = "Enable"
End If
```

7. Double-click the Am I Able? menu item to create a click event procedure in the Code Editor.

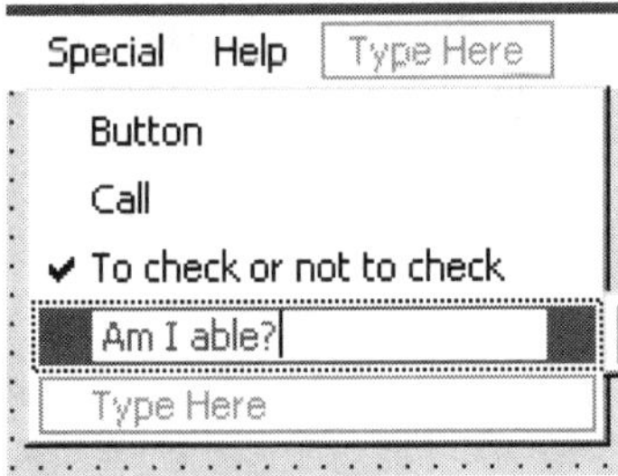

Figure 12.46 The Am I Able? menu item will be used to demonstrate the toggling of the menu item's Enabled property.

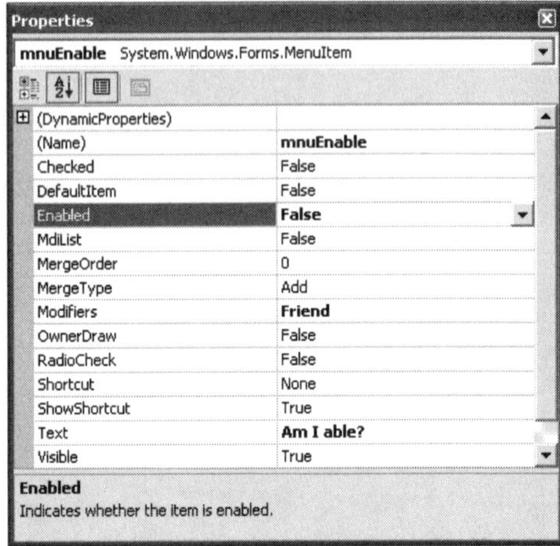

Figure 12.47 Using the Properties window, you can set a menu item's Enabled property to False.

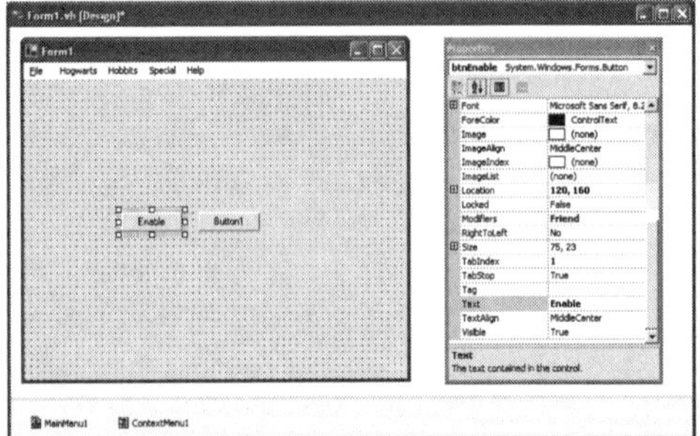

Figure 12.48 The Enable Button control will be used to toggle the Enabled property of the menu item.

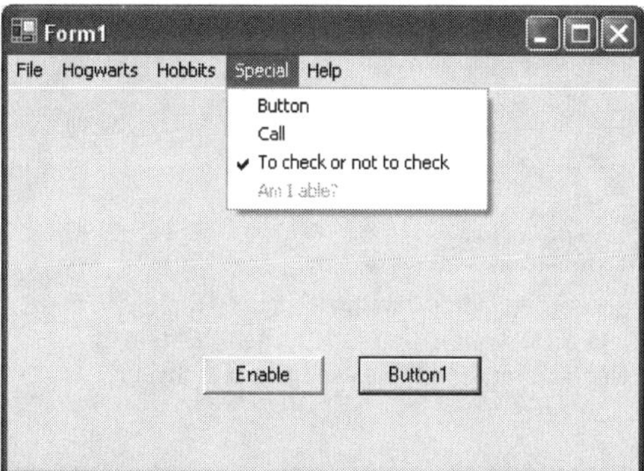

Figure 12.49 When the menu item's Enabled property is set to False, it appears dimmed at runtime.

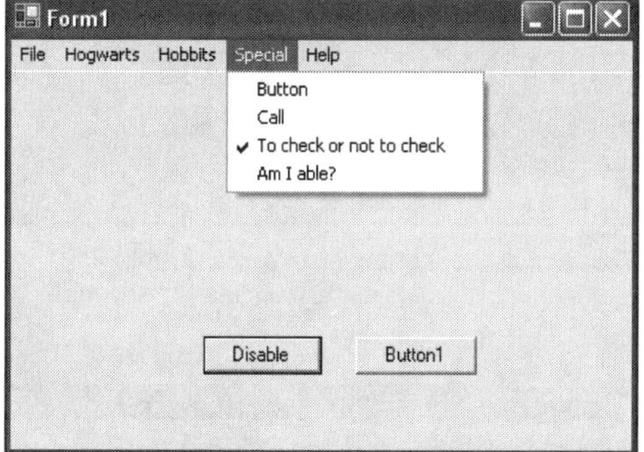

Figure 12.50 Clicking the Enable button toggles the Enabled property of the menu item.

8. Within the menu item's click event procedure, add code that displays a message box (which will be used to demonstrate that code placed in a menu item's click event is fired only if the menu item is enabled):

   ```
   MessageBox.Show("I am enabled!", _
      "Menus", MessageBoxButtons.OK, _
      MessageBoxIcon.Exclamation)
   ```

   Listing 12.6 shows the complete code for the two event procedures.

9. Run the project.

   The menu item will be disabled (**Figure 12.49**).

10. Select the menu item to verify that the code placed in its click event is not processed and that no message box appears.

11. Click the Enabled button.

    The menu item is now enabled (**Figure 12.50**).

continues on next page

Listing 12.6 Enabling and disabling a menu item.

```
Private Sub btnEnable_Click(ByVal sender As System.Object, ByVal e As System.EventArgs) _
   Handles btnEnable.Click
   If btnEnable.Text = "Enable" Then
      mnuEnable.Enabled = True
      btnEnable.Text = "Disable"
   Else
      mnuEnable.Enabled = False
      btnEnable.Text = "Enable"
   End If
End Sub

Private Sub mnuEnable_Click(ByVal sender As System.Object, ByVal e As System.EventArgs)
   Handles mnuEnable.Click
   MessageBox.Show("I am enabled!", "Menus", MessageBoxButtons.OK, _
   MessageBoxIcon.Exclamation)
End Sub
```

12. Select the menu item to verify that the code in its click event will now run and that a message box now appears (**Figure 12.51**).

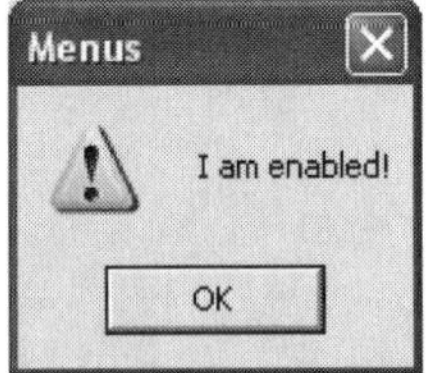

Figure 12.51 When a menu item is enabled, the code in its click event is processed when the item is selected and then the message box is displayed.

Probably one of the best dynamic menu effects, and certainly one of the easiest to implement, switches the entire menu hierarchy at runtime. This is accomplished by adding multiple MainMenu controls to a form and creating menu items for each. At runtime, the Menu property of the form is assigned from one MenuMenu control to another.

To switch between menus dynamically:

1. With a MainMenu control and menu items in place on a form, use the Toolbox to add a second MainMenu to the control (**Figure 12.52**).

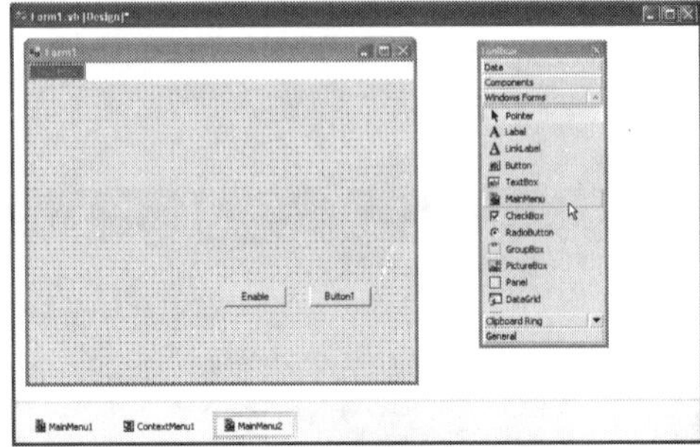

Figure 12.52 The second MainMenu control, MainMenu2, appears in the tray below the form.

2. Select the second MainMenu control.
3. Use the visual editing tools provided by the second MainMenu control to provide text values for its menus and menu items (**Figure 12.53**).

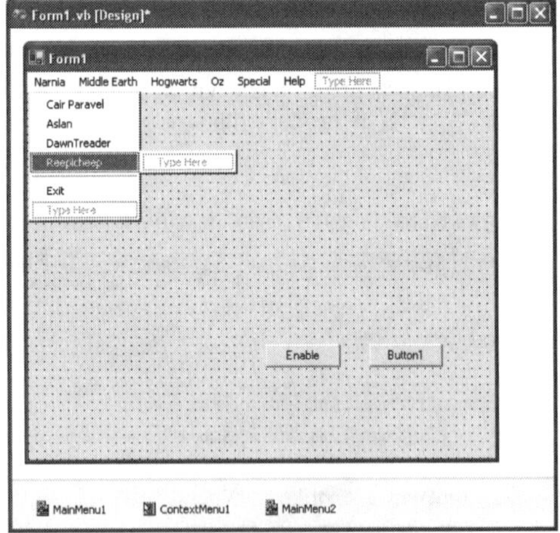

Figure 12.53 With MainMenu selected, you can start entering text values for menu items.

4. Add a Button control to the form.
5. Use the Properties window to name the button `btnToggle` and give its Text property a value of `Toggle` (**Figure 12.54**).
6. Double-click the Toggle button to create a click event procedure for it.
7. Within the click event procedure, use the Is operator to check whether the first MainMenu control is the value of the form Menu property and, if it is, assign the second MainMenu control as the value of the form's Menu property:

```
If Me.Menu Is MainMenu1 Then
   Me.Menu = MainMenu2
End If
```

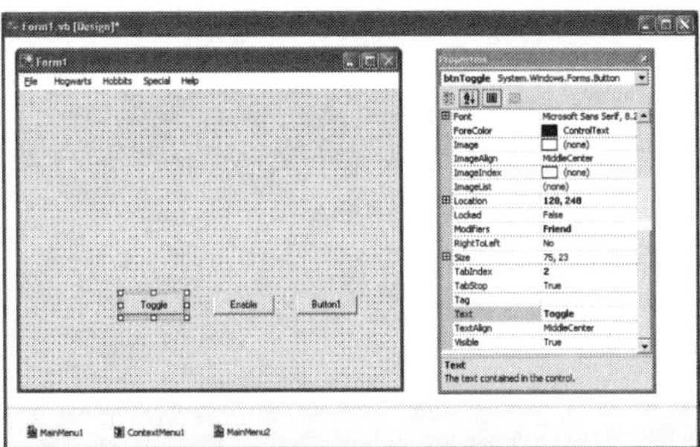

Figure 12.54 The Toggle button will be used to switch between menus stored in MainMenu1 and MainMenu2.

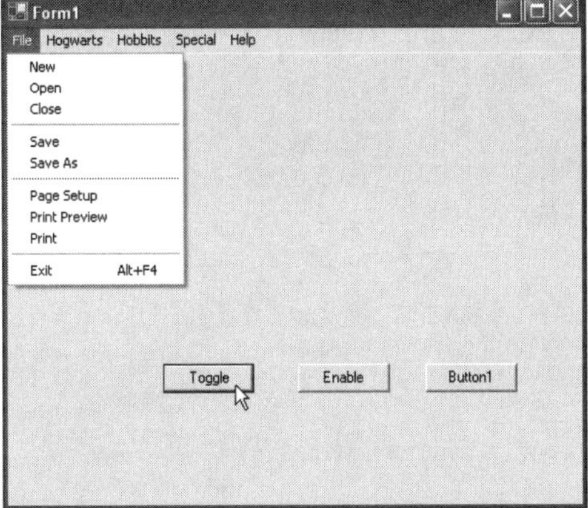

Figure 12.55 When the form opens, the menu stored in MainMenu1 is displayed.

8. If the first MainMenu control is not the value of the form Menu property (meaning that the second MainMenu control is), assign the first MainMenu control as the value of the form's Menu property:

```
If Me.Menu Is MainMenu1 Then
   Me.Menu = MainMenu2
Else
   Me.Menu = MainMenu1
End If
```

   Listing 12.7 shows the complete click event procedure.

9. Run the project.

   The menu hierarchy stored in the first MainMenu control is displayed (**Figure 12.55**).

continues on next page

Listing 12.7 Toggling menu hierarchies stored in MainMenu controls.

```
Private Sub btnToggle_Click(ByVal sender As System.Object, ByVal e As System.EventArgs) _
   Handles btnToggle.Click
   If Me.Menu Is MainMenu1 Then
      Me.Menu = MainMenu2
   Else
      Me.Menu = MainMenu1
   End If
End Sub
```

10. Click Toggle.

    Now the menu hierarchy stored in the second MainMenu control is displayed (**Figure 12.56**).

11. Click Toggle again to demonstrate that the user can return to the original menu.

✔ Tip

- The Is comparison operator, rather than the equals comparison operator (=), is used to check whether two objects—in this case, the value of the form's Menu property and the MainMenu1 object—are the same. If you were comparing two variables containing numeric values, you would use the equals comparison operator (=) since Is can be used only with objects.

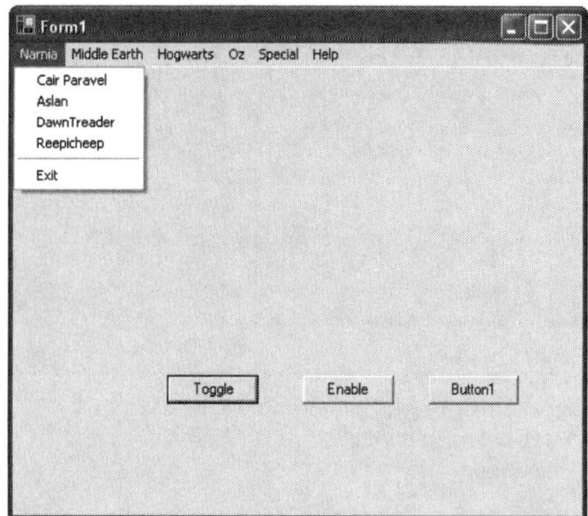

Figure 12.56 After the Toggle button is clicked, the menu stored in MainMenu2 is displayed.

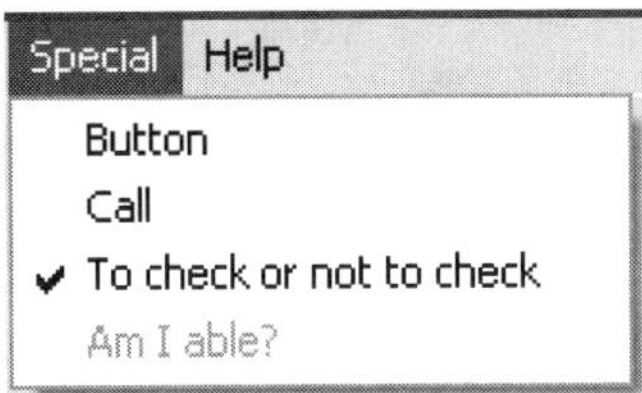

Figure 12.57 The Special menu.

Using Code to Add Menus

Visual Basic .NET being Visual Basic .NET, there is nothing that you can do using the visual interface of a MainMenu control that you can't do in code. (One good way to discover what you need to do to create and manipulate menus in code is to look at the code added to your form when you add a MainMenu control, menus, and menu items to a form.)

This section won't guide you through the entire process of adding menus and menu items in code. However, it will give you a sense of what's involved in the context of a task that you may need to perform even if you add your menus visually. The task is to add a menu item dynamically, which you often need to do so that your programs are able to respond to changing conditions. As you'll see, the only tricky part is responding to the menu item's click event when the item has been created programmatically.

Specifically, you'll add a Hello menu item to the Special menu shown in **Figure 12.57** when the user clicks an Add button. The Hello menu item will be declared using the AddressOf operator to point to the click event that contains the code that is processed when the Hello item is selected at runtime.

To add a menu item in code:

1. With the form containing the Special menu open in its designer, use the Toolbox to add a Button control to the form.
2. Use the Properties window to change the name of the button to `btnAdd` and its text value to `Add` (**Figure 12.58**).
3. Double-click the Add button to add a click event procedure to it:
```
Private Sub btnAdd_Click _
   (ByVal sender As System.Object, _
   ByVal e As System.EventArgs) _
   Handles btnAdd.Click


End Sub
```
4. In the Code Editor, within the event handler, declare a new MenuItem object that has a text value of `Hello` and that uses the AddressOf operator to point to a procedure named helloClick that will handle its click event:
```
Dim newItem As New MenuItem _
   ("Hello", New _
   System.EventHandler _
   (AddressOf Me.helloClick))
```
5. Determine the index number value of the Special menu by counting top-level menus, starting at 0, from left to right, as shown in Figure 12.58.
   (The index number value of the Special menu is 3.)
6. Use the index value of the Special menu to reference it, and use the Add method of the Special menu's MenuItems collection to add the new item to the Special menu:
```
MainMenu1.MenuItems(3). _
   MenuItems.Add (newItem)
```

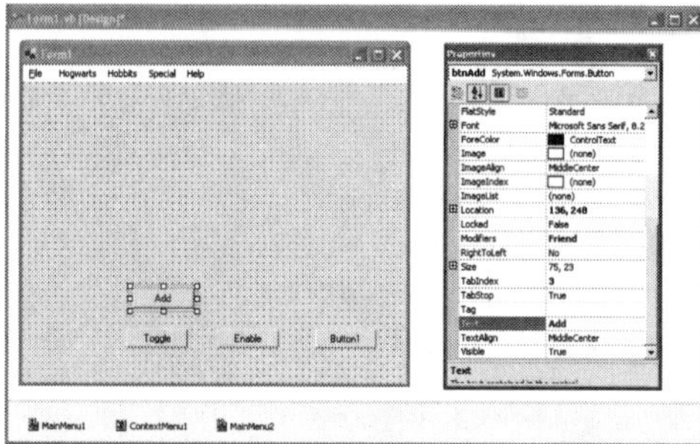

Figure 12.58 The Add button will be used to add a menu item to the Special menu.

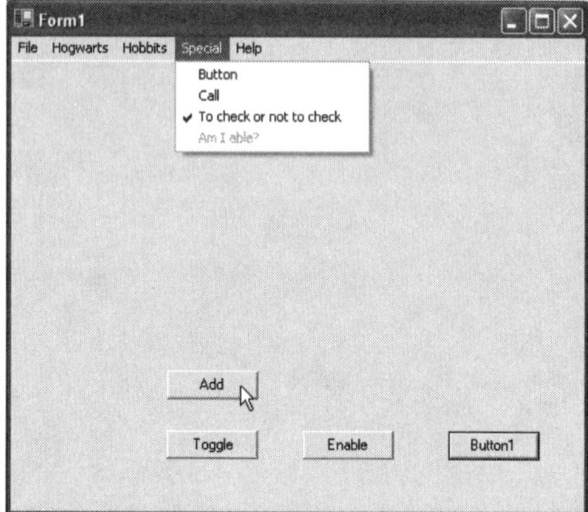

Figure 12.59 At runtime, the Special menu appears normally.

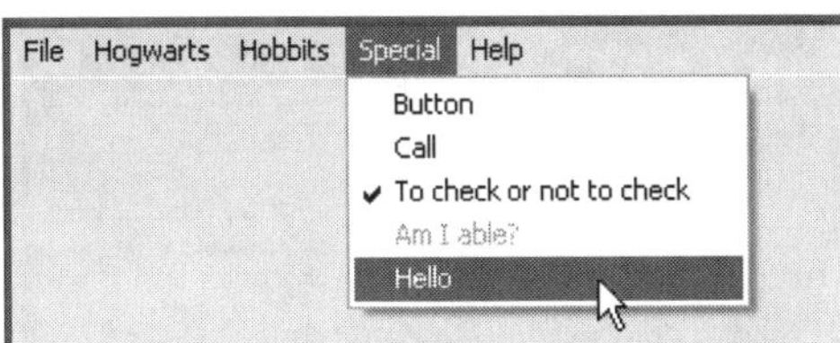

Figure 12.60 When the user clicks the Add button, the new menu item, Hello, is added to the Special menu.

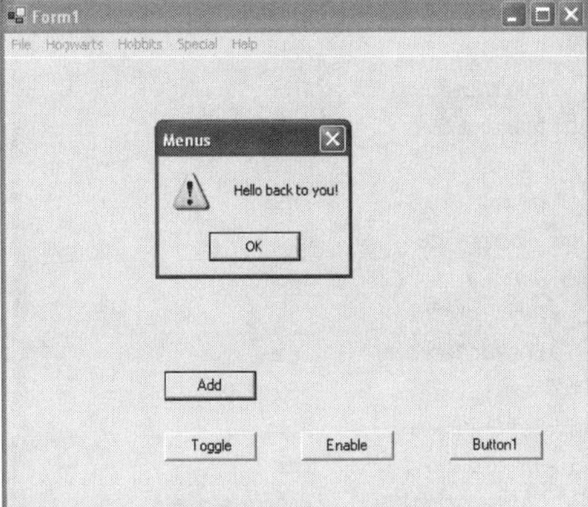

Figure 12.61 Choosing Hello on the Special menu causes the code in the Hello menu item's click event to be processed, displaying a message box.

7. At the Form class level, create a declaration for the helloClick procedure that will handle the click event generated when the Hello menu item is selected:

```
Private Sub helloClick(ByVal _
   sender As Object, ByVal e As _
   System.EventArgs)


End Sub
```

8. Within the helloClick procedure, add code to display a message box:

```
MessageBox.Show _
   ("Hello back to you!", "Menus", _
   MessageBoxButtons.OK, _
   MessageBoxIcon.Exclamation)
```

   Listing 12.8 shows the complete code for adding the Hello menu item and responding to its click event.

9. Run the project.

   The Special menu appears normally, without the Hello menu item (**Figure 12.59**).

10. Click the Add button.

    The Hello item is added to the bottom of the Special menu (**Figure 12.60**).

11. Choose Hello from the Special menu.

    This causes the Hello menu item's click event to be fired, processing the code that displays the message box shown in **Figure 12.61**.

Listing 12.8 Creating a menu item, adding it to a menu, and creating a click event handler for the menu item.

```
Private Sub btnAdd_Click(ByVal sender As System.Object, ByVal e As System.EventArgs) _
   Handles btnAdd.Click
   Dim newItem As New MenuItem("Hello", New System.EventHandler(AddressOf Me.helloClick))
   MainMenu1.MenuItems(3).MenuItems.Add(newItem)
End Sub

Private Sub helloClick(ByVal sender As Object, ByVal e As System.EventArgs)
   MessageBox.Show("Hello back to you!", "Menus", MessageBoxButtons.OK, _
   MessageBoxIcon.Exclamation)
End Sub
```

Implementing MDI Menus

In Chapter 8, "Working with MDI Forms," you learned how to create MDI—or multiple document interface—applications. Let's turn our attention now to creating an MDI Window menu, which allows easy management of MDI child forms.

Before we can work with MDI Window menus, however, we've got to get a few preliminaries out of the way. Obviously, we need to create an MDI application to work with. Chapter 8 discussed in detail how to create an MDI program that tracks child forms. The first task in this section walks you through this procedure again (if you have any questions about the details of the code, you should refer to Chapter 8). Next, we'll look at how to implement New, Close, and Exit menu items, and how to add a RichTextBox control to an MDI child form, which gives you a great deal of editing and text formatting capability right out of the box. Then we'll examine how to add and implement an Edit menu for the MDI child form before finally adding and implementing an MDI Window menu.

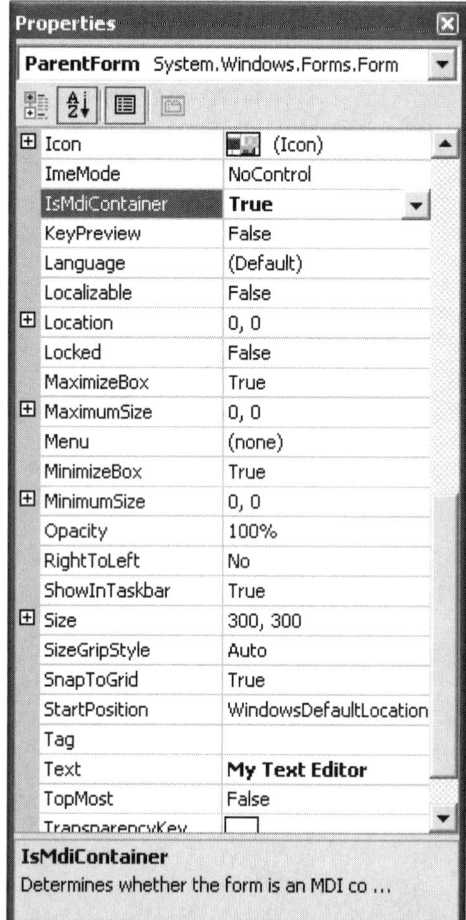

Figure 12.62 The IsMdiContainer property of the parent form is set to True.

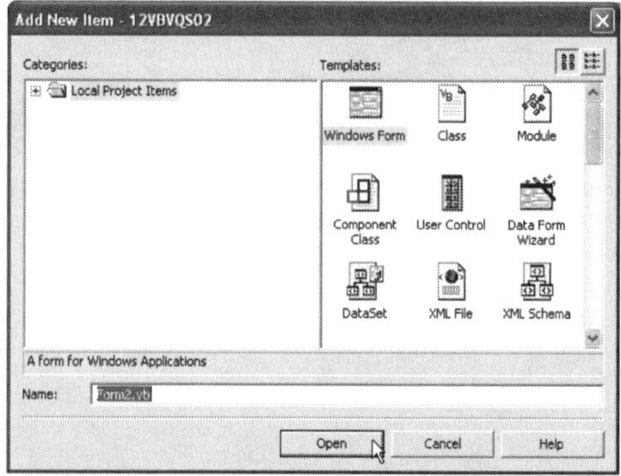

Figure 12.63 A new Windows form is added to the application.

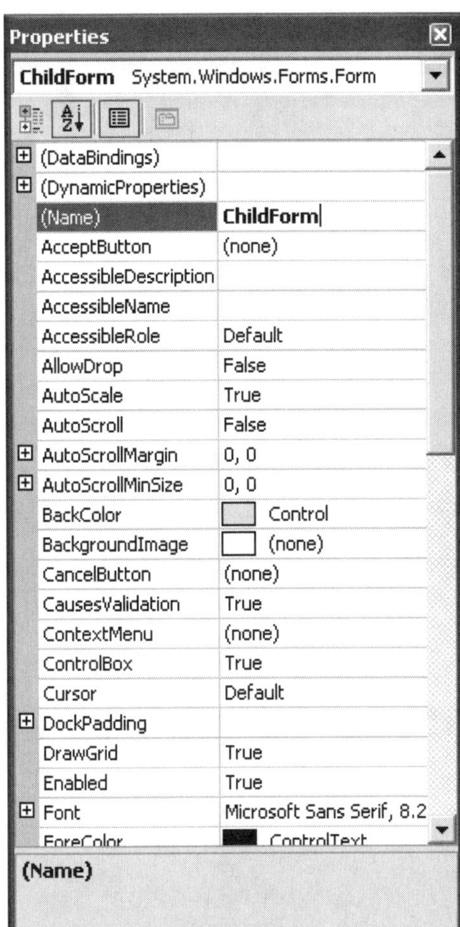

Figure 12.64 Use the Properties window to set the name of the new form to `ChildForm`.

To create an MDI application:

1. Open a new Windows Application project.
2. With the application's form open in its designer, use the Properties window to set the name of the form to `ParentForm`, its text value to `My Text Editor`, and its IsMdiContainer property to True (**Figure 12.62**).
3. From the Visual Studio Project menu, choose Add Windows Form.

   The Add New Item dialog opens (**Figure 12.63**).
4. Make sure that Windows Form is selected in the Templates pane and click Open.
5. Open the new form in its designer and use the Properties window to set its name to `ChildForm` (**Figure 12.64**).
6. In the child form, use the Code Editor to add code to implement the form's Closing event and to support the MDI application, as shown in **Listing 12.9** on the next page (and explained in Chapter 8).
7. In the parent form, use the Code Editor to add code to implement the NumForms property, as shown in **Listing 12.10** on the next page (and explained in Chapter 8).

Listing 12.9 The MDI child code.

```
Public theDad As ParentForm
Private Sub ChildForm_Closing(ByVal sender As Object, _
   ByVal e As System.ComponentModel.CancelEventArgs) Handles MyBase.Closing
   theDad.NumForms = theDad.NumForms - 1
   Me.Renumber()
End Sub

Private Sub Renumber()
   Dim frmArray(theDad.MdiChildren().GetUpperBound(0)) As Form
   frmArray = theDad.MdiChildren()
   Dim i As Integer
   Dim j As Integer = 0
   For i = 0 To theDad.MdiChildren().Length - 1
      If (frmArray(i) Is Me) Then
         j = i
         Exit For
      End If
   Next i
   For i = j + 1 To theDad.MdiChildren().Length - 1
      frmArray(i).Text = "Document " & CStr(i)
   Next i
End Sub
```

Listing 12.10 In the MDI parent, tracking the children, opening a new child, closing the active child, and exiting the application.

```
Private m_numForms As Integer = 0
Public Property NumForms() As Integer
   Get
      NumForms = m_numForms
   End Get
   Set(ByVal Value As Integer)
      m_numForms = Value
   End Set
End Property

Private Sub mnuFileNew_Click(ByVal sender As System.Object, ByVal e As System.EventArgs) _
   Handles mnuFileNew.Click
   Dim theKid As New ChildForm()
   Me.NumForms += 1
   theKid.MdiParent = Me
   theKid.theDad = Me
   theKid.Text = "Document " & CStr(Me.NumForms)
   theKid.Show()
End Sub

Private Sub mnuFileExit_Click(ByVal sender As System.Object, ByVal e As System.EventArgs) _
   Handles mnuFileExit.Click
   Application.Exit()
End Sub

Private Sub mnuFileClose_Click(ByVal sender As System.Object, ByVal e As System.EventArgs) _
   Handles mnuFileClose.Click
   Me.ActiveMdiChild.Close()
End Sub
```

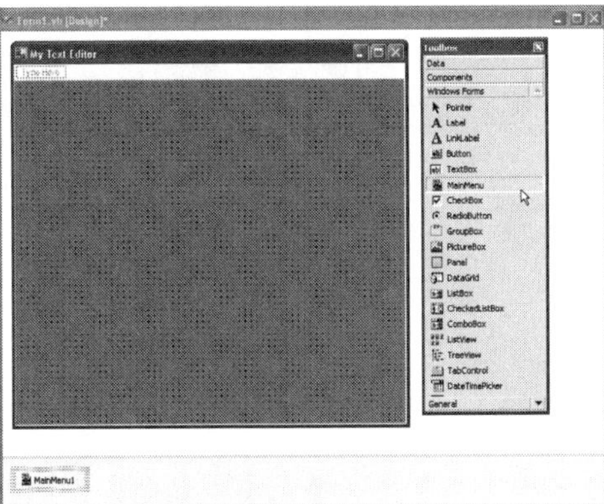

Figure 12.65 Use the Toolbox to add a MainMenu control to the parent form.

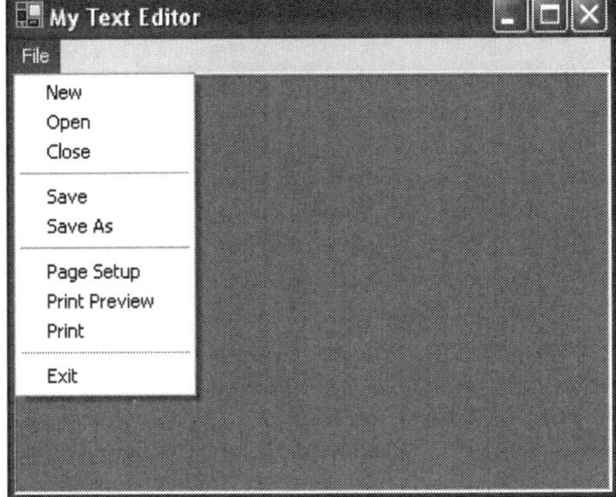

Figure 12.66 The File menu includes a New menu item.

To implement the New menu item:

1. With the parent form open in its designer, use the Toolbox to add a MainMenu control to the form (**Figure 12.65**).
2. Add menu items with the text values shown in **Figure 12.66**.

   The New, Close, and Exit menu items will be implemented in this section, and the other items on this menu will be implemented in Chapter 13, "The Common Dialog Controls."
3. Use the Properties window or Edit Names mode to provide a programmatic name of `mnuFileNew` for the New menu item.
4. Double-click the New menu item in the Form designer to create a click event handler for it:

   ```
   Private Sub mnuFileNew_Click _
      (ByVal sender As System.Object, _
      ByVal e As System.EventArgs) _
      Handles mnuFileNew.Click


   End Sub
   ```
5. Within the click event, add the code (explained in Chapter 8) for opening a new MDI child document:

   ```
   Dim theKid As New ChildForm()
   Me.NumForms += 1
   theKid.MdiParent = Me
   theKid.theDad = Me
   theKid.Text = "Document " & _
      CStr(Me.NumForms)
   theKid.Show()
   ```

   Listing 12.10 shows the complete code for the New click event.

To implement the Close menu item:

1. Use the Properties window or Edit Names mode to provide a programmatic name of `mnuFileClose` for the Close menu item.
2. Double-click the Close menu item in the Form designer to create a click event handler for it:
   ```
   Private Sub mnuFileClose_Click _
      (ByVal sender As System.Object, _
      ByVal e As System.EventArgs) _
      Handles mnuFileClose.Click

   End Sub
   ```
3. Within the click event, close the active MDI child:
   ```
   Me.ActiveMdiChild.Close()
   ```
   Listing 12.10 shows the complete code for the Close click event.

To implement the Exit menu item:

1. Use the Properties window or Edit Names mode to provide a programmatic name of `mnuFileExit` for the Exit menu item.
2. Double-click the Exit menu item in the Form designer to create a click event handler for it:
   ```
   Private Sub mnuFileExit_Click _
      (ByVal sender As System.Object, _
      ByVal e As System.EventArgs) _
      Handles mnuFileExit.Click

   End Sub
   ```
3. Within the click event, use the application's Exit method to shut down the running application:
   ```
   Application.Exit()
   ```
   Listing 12.10 shows the complete code for the Exit click event.

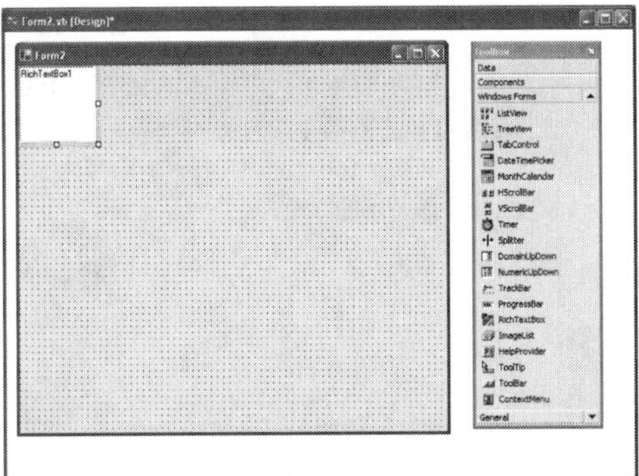

Figure 12.67 Use the Toolbox to add a RichTextControl to the child form.

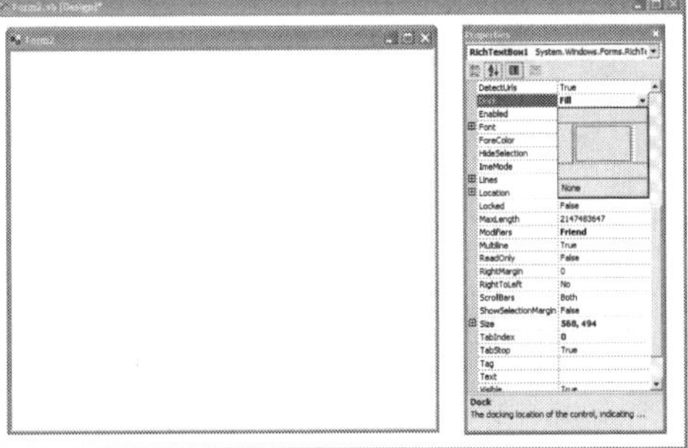

Figure 12.68 Use the Properties window to set the Dock property of the RichTextBox control to Fill.

To add a RichTextBox control to the child form:

1. With the child form open in its designer, use the Toolbox to add a RichTextBox control to the form as shown in **Figure 12.67** (the RichTextBox control is listed toward the middle of the controls on the Windows Forms tab of the Toolbox).

2. Use the Properties window to set the Text property of the RichTextBox control to the empty string.

3. With the RichTextBox still selected in the Properties window, set its Dock property to Fill (**Figure 12.68**).

   The RichTextBox control will now expand and contract to occupy the entire client area of the child form.

It's time to test what you've done so far. But first, before running the project, use the Property Pages for the project to make sure that the parent form is set as the Startup object for the project (**Figure 12.69**).

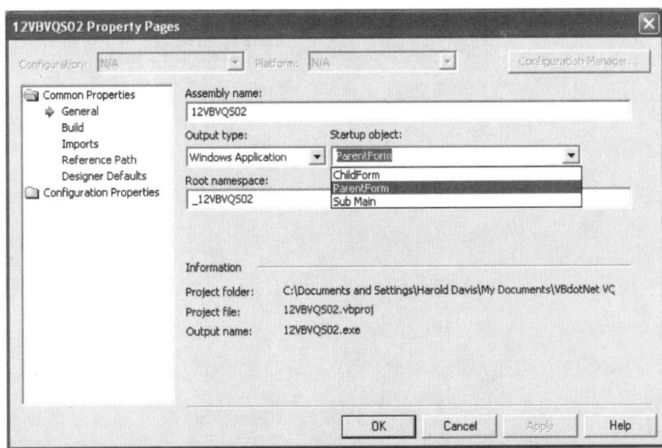

Figure 12.69 Make sure that the parent form is set as the Startup object in the project Property pages.

When you run the project, you'll see that you can create (and close) multiple child forms, each of which have basic text editing capabilities (**Figure 12.70**).

The next step is to implement an Edit menu with the menu items shown in **Figure 12.71**. These menu items and their programmatic names and standard shortcut keys are listed in **Table 12.2**.

To add an Edit menu:

1. Use the MainMenu control to add an Edit menu.
2. Add the menu items shown in Figure 12.71 and Table 12.2 to the Edit menu.
3. Use Edit Names mode or the Properties window to assign the programmatic names to the menu items as shown in Table 12.2.
4. Use the Properties window to assign the shortcut keys to the menu items as shown in Table 12.2.

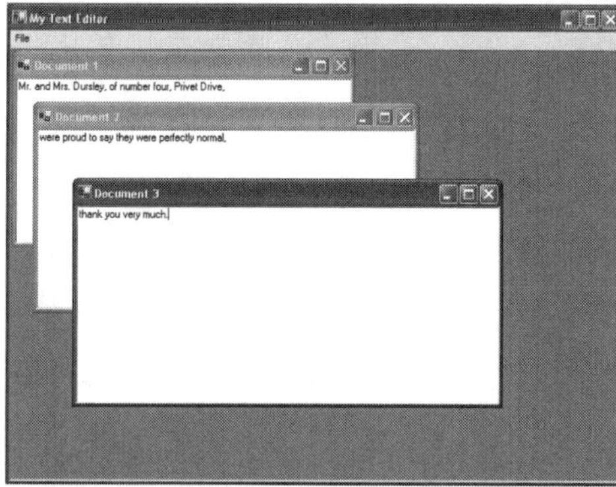

Figure 12.70 Clicking the New menu item opens a new text document.

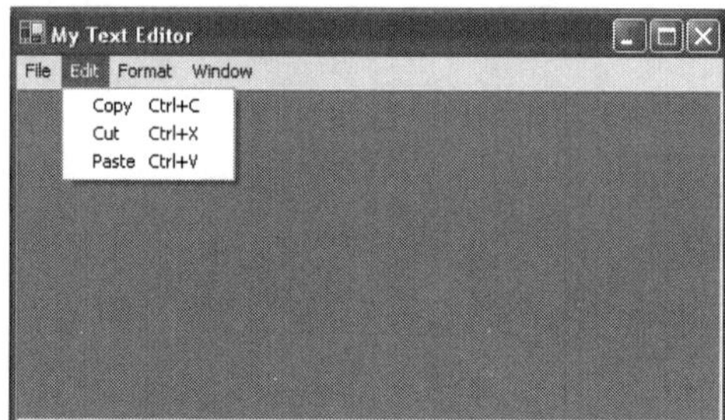

Figure 12.71 The Edit menu (with standard shortcut keys).

Table 12.2

Edit Menu Items

MENU ITEM/ TEXT VALUE	PROGRAMMATIC NAME	SHORTCUT KEYS
Copy	mnuEditCopy	Ctrl+C
Cut	mnuEditCut	Ctrl+X
Paste	mnuEditPaste	Ctrl+V

To implement the Edit menu:

1. Double-click one of the menu items—for example, Copy—to create a click event handler for the menu item:

```
Private Sub mnuEditCopy_Click _
   (ByVal sender As System.Object, _
   ByVal e As System.EventArgs) _
   Handles mnuEditCopy.Click, _

End Sub
```

2. In the Code Editor, add the click events for the two other menu items to the handler:

```
Private Sub mnuEditCopy_Click _
   (ByVal sender As System.Object, _
   ByVal e As System.EventArgs) _
   Handles mnuEditCopy.Click, _
   mnuEditCut.Click, _
   mnuEditPaste.Click

End Sub
```

3. Convert the type of the sender argument to determine the menu item that caused the click event and store a reference to it in the variable mi:

```
Dim mi As MenuItem = _
   CType(sender, MenuItem)
```

4. Convert the active MDI child to type ChildForm:

```
Dim cf As ChildForm
cf = CType(Me.ActiveMdiChild, _
   ChildForm)
```

continues on next page

5. Use the Cut, Copy, or Paste method of the RichTextBox control (depending on the sender):

```
Select Case mi.Text
   Case "&Copy"
      cf.RichTextBox1.Copy()
   Case "Cu&t"
      cf.RichTextBox1.Cut()
   Case "&Paste"
      cf.RichTextBox1.Paste()
End Select
```

   Listing 12.11 shows the complete code for the Edit menu implementation.

6. Run the project.

7. Verify that the Edit menu items cut, copy, and paste selected text on the active child form (**Figure 12.72**).

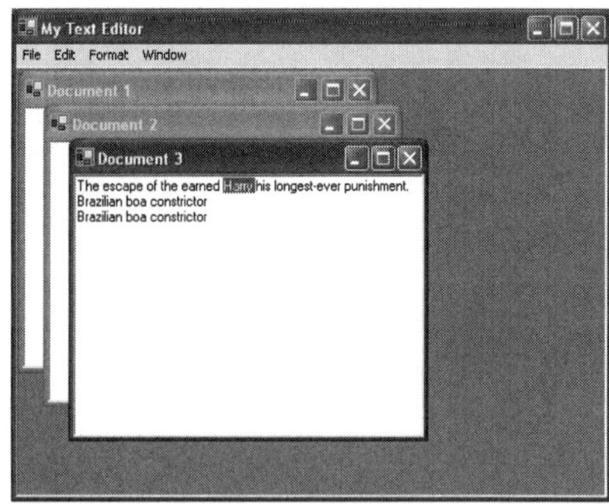

Figure 12.72 Cut, copy, and paste are now working.

✔ Tip

- The Select Case statement branches on the text value for the menu item, but note that the text value includes the ampersand (&) used to create an access key for each item: for example, Cu&t.

Listing 12.11 Implementing the Edit menu.

```
Private Sub mnuEditCopy_Click(ByVal sender As System.Object, ByVal e As System.EventArgs) _
   Handles mnuEditCopy.Click, _
   mnuEditCut.Click, mnuEditPaste.Click
   Dim mi As MenuItem = CType(sender, MenuItem)
   Dim cf As ChildForm
   cf = CType(Me.ActiveMdiChild, ChildForm)
   Select Case mi.Text
      Case "&Copy"
         cf.RichTextBox1.Copy()
      Case "Cu&t"
         cf.RichTextBox1.Cut()
      Case "&Paste"
         cf.RichTextBox1.Paste()
   End Select
End Sub
```

Table 12.3

Window Menu Items		
MENU ITEM/ TEXT VALUE	PROGRAMMATIC NAME	SHORTCUT KEYS
Cascade	mnuWindowCascade	Displays child windows in cascading fashion.
Tile Horizontal	mnuWindowTileH	Arranges child windows horizontally.
Tile Vertical	mnuWindowTileV	Arranges child windows vertically.
Arrange Icons	mnuWindowArrange	Lines up child forms that have been iconized.

The next step is to implement a Window menu with the menu items shown in **Table 12.3**. The table also lists programmatic names and purpose of the menu items.

In addition, when you set the MdiList property of a top-level menu to True, the menu displays a list of all open child forms beneath the menu items that belong to the menu. This list of child forms can be used to navigate between children. The active child form will be checked in the list.

To add an MDI Window menu:

1. Use the MainMenu control to add a Window menu to the form in its designer.
2. With the top-level Window menu item selected in the Properties window, choose MdiList in the left column, and then set the MdiList property to True (**Figure 12.73**).
3. Add the menu items to the Window menu as shown in Table 12.3 and **Figure 12.74**.
4. Use Edit Names mode or the Properties window to assign the programmatic names to the menu items as shown in Table 12.3.

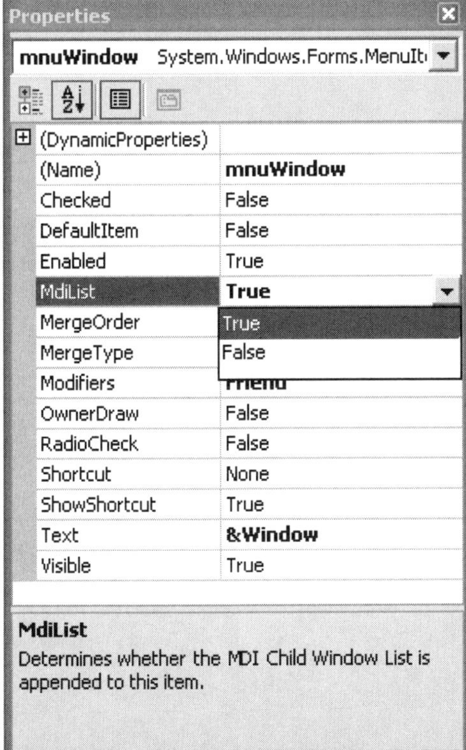

Figure 12.73 Use the Properties window to set the MdiList property for the MDI Window menu to True.

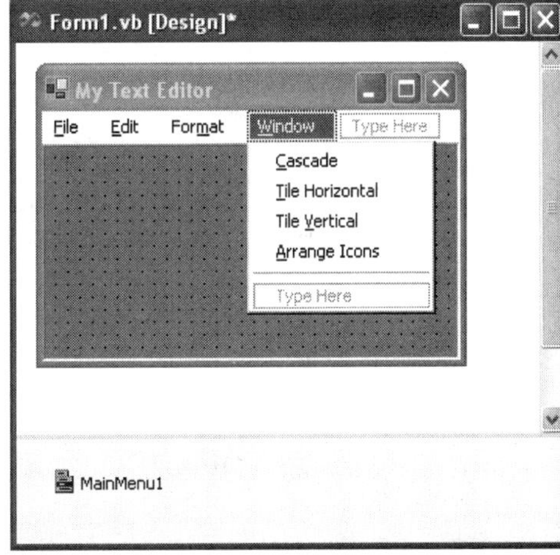

Figure 12.74 The MDI Window menu on the Form designer.

IMPLEMENTING MDI MENUS

To implement the MDI Window menu:

1. Double-click one of the menu items—for example, Cascade—to create a click event handler for the menu item:

```
Private Sub mnuWindowCascade_Click _
   (ByVal sender As System.Object, _
   ByVal e As System.EventArgs) _
   Handles mnuWindowCascade.Click, _
   mnuWindowTileH.Click

End Sub
```

2. In the Code Editor, add the click events for the other menu items to the handler:

```
Private Sub mnuWindowCascade_Click _
   (ByVal sender As System.Object, _
   ByVal e As System.EventArgs) _
   Handles mnuWindowCascade.Click, _
   mnuWindowTileH.Click, _
   mnuWindowTileV.Click, _
   mnuWindowArrange.Click

End Sub
```


Listing 12.12 Implementing the MDI Window menu.

```
Private Sub mnuWindowCascade_Click(ByVal sender As System.Object, ByVal e As System.EventArgs) _
   Handles mnuWindowCascade.Click, _
   mnuWindowTileH.Click, mnuWindowTileV.Click, mnuWindowArrange.Click
   Dim mi As MenuItem = CType(sender, MenuItem)
   Select Case mi.Text
      Case "&Cascade"
         Me.LayoutMdi(MdiLayout.Cascade)
      Case "&Tile Horizontal"
         Me.LayoutMdi(MdiLayout.TileHorizontal)
      Case "Tile &Vertical"
         Me.LayoutMdi(MdiLayout.TileVertical)
      Case "&Arrange Icons"
         Me.LayoutMdi(MdiLayout.ArrangeIcons)
   End Select
End Sub
```

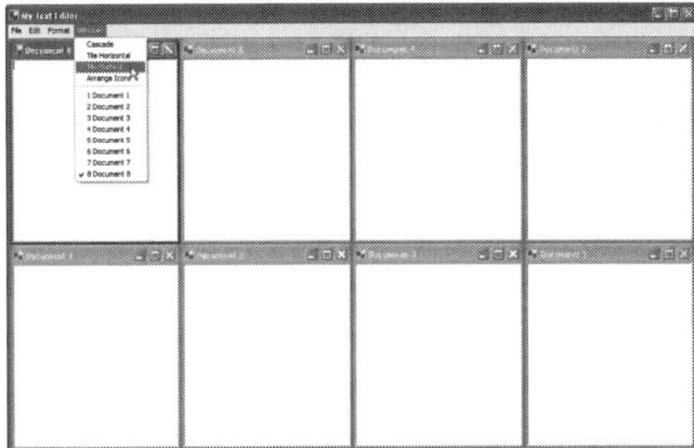

Figure 12.75 Using the MDI Window menu, you can arrange the child forms (a check appears next to the active child document in the MDI list at the bottom of the menu).

3. Convert the type of the sender argument to determine the menu item that caused the click event and store a reference to it in the variable mi:

```
Dim mi As MenuItem = _
   CType(sender, MenuItem)
```

4. Use the MdiLayout method with a constant value to arrange the child forms:

```
Select Case mi.Text
   Case "&Cascade"
      Me.LayoutMdi _
         (MdiLayout.Cascade)
   Case "&Tile Horizontal"
      Me.LayoutMdi _
         (MdiLayout.TileHorizontal)
   Case "Tile &Vertical"
      Me.LayoutMdi _
         (MdiLayout.TileVertical)
   Case "&Arrange Icons"
      Me.LayoutMdi _
         (MdiLayout.ArrangeIcons)
End Select
```

Listing 12.12 shows the complete code for the Window menu implementation.

5. Run the project.

6. Verify that the Window menu items arrange the child forms and display a list of open children below the menu items (**Figure 12.75**).

✔ Tip

- The Select Case statement branches on the text value for the menu item, but note that the text value includes the ampersand (&) used to create an access key for each item: for example, &Cascade.

Summary

In this chapter, you learned how to:

- Add a menu to a form
- Add submenus to a menu
- Add menu items
- Insert and delete menu items
- Provide programmatic names for menu items
- Set access keys for a menu item
- Assign shortcut keys for a menu item
- Add separators to a menu
- Add a context menu and context menu items to controls and forms
- Add menu item click event procedures
- Create a central menu item click event processor
- Handle a menu item click event as part of another event procedure
- Check and uncheck menu items in code at runtime
- Enable and disable menu items in code at runtime
- Create a menu item, including a click event procedure, at runtime in code
- Implement an Edit menu
- Implement an MDI Window menu

13 The Common Dialog Controls

The common dialog controls provided by the .NET Framework are a magnificent way to lend professional polish to your applications and give users the familiar, standardized interface they've come to expect.

These controls make it extremely easy to include dialogs, referred to as the *common dialogs*, that are already "baked into" the Windows operating system. Each common dialog control can be configured using control properties, which are set via the Properties window or in code. We'll be setting them in code for the most part in this chapter —this is a better practice, since it makes more clear to someone glancing at the code listing what is going on (because you don't also need to know Properties window settings).

Keep in mind that the common dialog controls do not actually do anything other than *display* professional-quality dialogs. The dialog displayed by a common dialog control generally lets the user select something (such as a file name for opening or saving). It's up to you, the programmer, to add the wiring necessary to make the user's selection actually do something (such as saving or opening the specified file).

The common dialog controls explained in this chapter will be explained in the context of a sample application. Along the way, you'll learn how to implement some of the functionality suggested by the common dialogs to print, open, and save files.

Dialog control functionality

This chapter shows you how to use the dialogs provided by the following common dialog controls:

- **FontDialog** control, which provides a dialog that allows the user to select a font
- **ColorDialog** control, which provides a dialog that allows the user to choose a color
- **SaveFileDialog** and **OpenFileDialog** controls, which provide dialogs that allow the user to select a file for saving or opening
- **PrintDialog, PrintPreviewDialog,** and **PageSetupDialog** controls, which—along with the PrintPreviewControl and PrintDocument controls—provide dialogs that allow the user to configure page setup, preview documents, and print documents

Table 13.1

File Menu	
Menu item/text value	**Programmatic name**
New	mnuFileNew
Open	mnuFileOpen
Close	mnuFileClose
Save	mnuFileSave
Save As	mnuFileSaveAs
Page Setup	mnuFilePageSetup
Print Preview	mnuFilePrintPreview
Print	mnuFilePrint
Exit	mnuFileExit

Table 13.2

Format Menu	
Menu item/text value	**Programmatic name**
Font	mnuFormatFont
Color	mnuFormatColor

The Sample Application

In the last chapter you learned how to construct a multiple document interface (MDI) text editing application that implemented Edit and MDI Window menus. In this chapter, however, we don't need to involve the complexity of the MDI application to learn how to work with the common dialog controls, so we'll be using a single document interface (SDI) text editor. (If you prefer to work through the tasks using the MDI application from Chapter 12 you can; it's equivalent to the SDI text editor used here.)

As you'll see, the text editor application uses a RichTextBox control for most formatting and editing functions. The File and Format menus, shown in **Tables 13.1** and **13.2**, will be used to display the common dialogs and to implement the functionality suggested by the menu items.

Of the menu items on the File menu, New and Close are not implemented—they make more sense in the context of an MDI application. (See "Implementing MDI Menus" in Chapter 12 for more information on the New, Close, and Exit menu items.)

Another menu—the Edit menu, which contains the Copy, Cut, and Paste menu items—is a very useful feature of any text editor, including the one we're creating here. You saw how to implement this functionality in Chapter 12, so we won't delve into that again here.

Let's get started building the simple application that will show you how to use the common dialog controls.

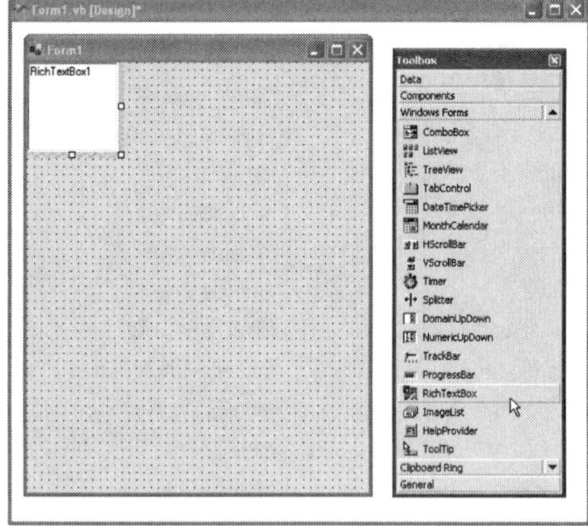

Figure 13.1 Double-click the RichTextBox control in the Toolbox to add it to a form.

To add a RichTextBox control:

1. Open a new Windows Application project.
2. With the Windows form open in its designer, use the Toolbox to add a RichTextBox control to the form as shown in **Figure 13.1**.
3. Use the Properties window to set the Text property of the RichTextBox control to the empty string.
4. With the RichTextBox control still selected in the Properties window, set its Dock property to Fill (**Figure 13.2**).

   The RichTextBox control now expands and contracts to occupy the entire client area of the child form.

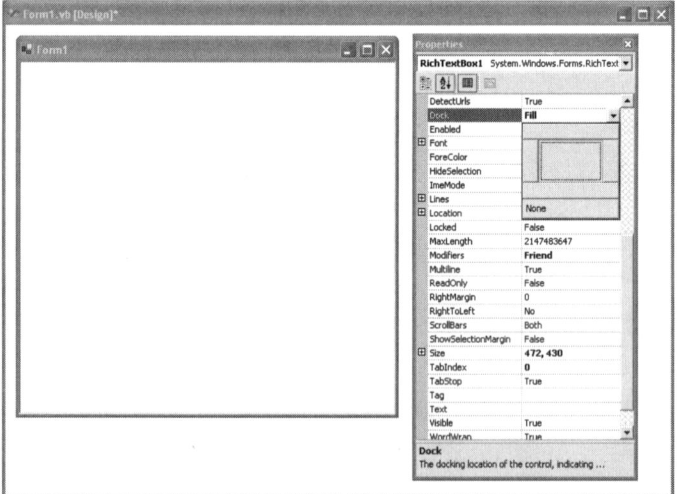

Figure 13.2 When you set the Dock property of the RichTextBox control to Fill, the RichTextBox control will expand to fill the client area of the form.

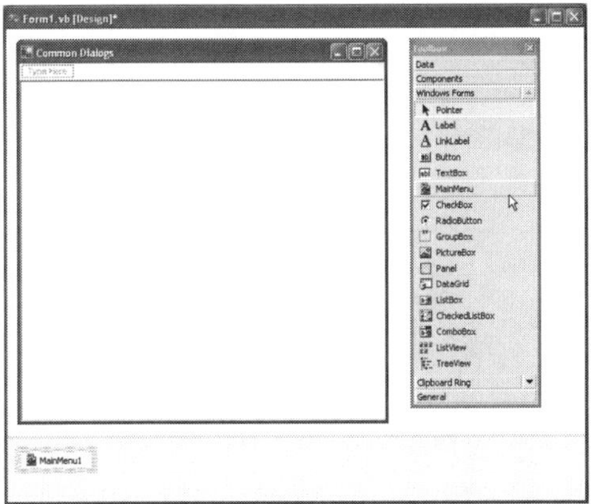

Figure 13.3 Double-click the MainMenu control to add it to the form (it appears in the tray beneath the form).

Figure 13.4 The File menu shows the text values of the menu items on it.

Next we'll be using the MainMenu control to add menus and menu items, as explained in detail in "Adding Menus" in Chapter 12.

To add File and Format menus:

1. With the Windows form open in its designer, use the Toolbox to add a MainMenu control to the form (**Figure 13.3**).
2. Add menu items with the text values shown in Table 13.1 for the File menu and Table 13.2 for the Format menu.

   The menu items on the File menu are also shown in **Figure 13.4**.
3. Use the Properties window or Edit Names mode, as explained in Chapter 12, to provide programmatic names for each of the menu items on the File and Format menus as shown in Tables 13.1 and 13.2.

You'll now create centralized procedures to handle menu click events; for detailed instructions, see "To add a central menu item processing procedure" in Chapter 12.

To add a central menu item processing procedure (Format menu):

1. With the form open in its designer, select the Font menu item to create a click event handler for it:

   ```
   Private Sub mnuFormatFont_Click _
      (ByVal sender As System.Object, _
      ByVal e As System.EventArgs) _
      Handles mnuFormatFont.Click

   End Sub
   ```

2. In the Code Editor, add the Color menu item to the Font menu handler, so that the one procedure handles both items' click events:

   ```
   Private Sub mnuFormatFont_Click _
      (ByVal sender As System.Object, _
      ByVal e As System.EventArgs) _
      Handles mnuFormatFont.Click, _
      mnuFormatColor.Click

   End Sub
   ```

3. Convert the sender variable in the event procedure to the MenuItem type (so that its Text property can be evaluated):

   ```
   Dim mi As MenuItem = _
      CType(sender, MenuItem)
   ```

4. Use a Select Case statement to branch according to the value of the Text property:

   ```
   Select Case mi.Text

   End Select
   ```

5. Add a Case clause for the Font and Color menu items (remember to include the ampersand used to indicate an access key in the text value):

   ```
   Select Case mi.Text
      Case "&Font"
      Case "&Color"
   End Select
   ```

To add a central menu item processing procedure (File menu):

1. With the form open in its designer, select the Open menu item to create a click event handler for it:

```
Private Sub mnuFileOpen_Click _
   (ByVal sender As System.Object, _
   ByVal e As System.EventArgs) _
   Handles mnuFileOpen.Click _

End Sub
```

2. In the Code Editor, add the Save, Save As, Page Setup, Print Preview, and Print menu items to the Open menu handler, so that the one procedure handles all items' click events:

```
Private Sub mnuFileOpen_Click _
   (ByVal sender As System.Object, _
   ByVal e As System.EventArgs) _
   Handles mnuFileOpen.Click, _
   mnuFileSave.Click, _
   mnuFileSaveAs.Click, _
   mnuFilePageSetup.Click, _
   mnuFilePrintPreview.Click, _
   mnuFilePrint

End Sub
```

3. Convert the sender variable in the event procedure to the MenuItem type (so that its Text property can be evaluated):

```
Dim mi As MenuItem = _
   CType(sender, MenuItem)
```

4. Use a Select Case statement to branch according to the value of the Text property:

```
Select Case mi.Text

End Select
```

5. Add Case clauses for the Open, Save, Save As, Page Setup, Print Preview, and Print menu items (remember to include the ampersand [&] used to indicate an access key in the text value):

```
   Select Case mi.Text
      Case "&Open"

      Case "&Save"

      Case "Save &As"

      Case "Page Set&up"

      Case "Print Pre&view"

      Case "Print"
   End Select
```

The Font Dialog

We'll start with the Font common dialog control: FontDialog.

To add a FontDialog control:

- With a form open in its designer, double-click the FontDialog control in the Toolbox to add it to the tray beneath the form (**Figure 13.5**).

To display the Font common dialog:

- With a FontDialog control added to a form, in the Code Editor, call the ShowDialog method of the FontDialog control—for example:

  `FontDialog1.ShowDialog()`

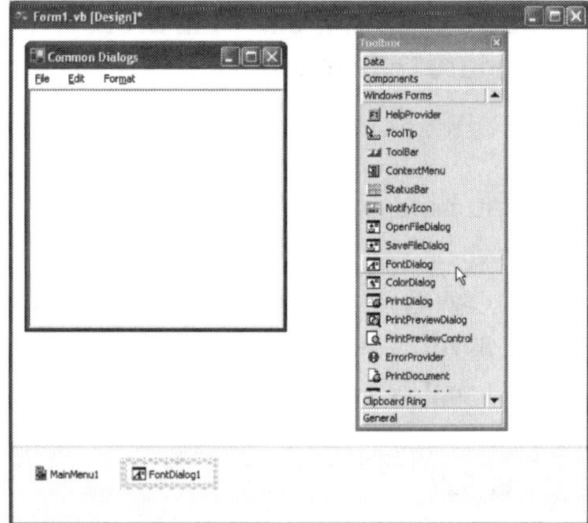

Figure 13.5 When you add a FontDialog control to a form, it appears in the form's tray.

Listing 13.1 The central processing procedure for the Format menu.

```
Private Sub mnuFormatFont_Click(ByVal sender As System.Object, ByVal e As System.EventArgs) _
   Handles mnuFormatFont.Click, mnuFormatColor.Click
   Dim mi As MenuItem = CType(sender, MenuItem)
   Select Case mi.Text
      Case "&Font"
         FontDialog1.ShowDialog()
         Dim theFont As System.Drawing.Font = FontDialog1.Font
         RichTextBox1.SelectionFont = theFont
      Case "&Color"
         ColorDialog1.AllowFullOpen = True
         ColorDialog1.AnyColor = True
         ColorDialog1.ShowDialog()
         Dim theColor As System.Drawing.Color = ColorDialog1.Color
         RichTextBox1.SelectionColor = theColor
         Me.ForeColor = theColor
   End Select
End Sub
```

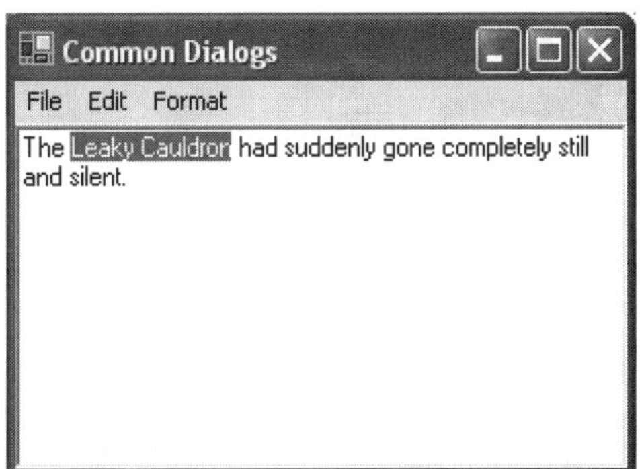

Figure 13.6 Select text to change its characteristics.

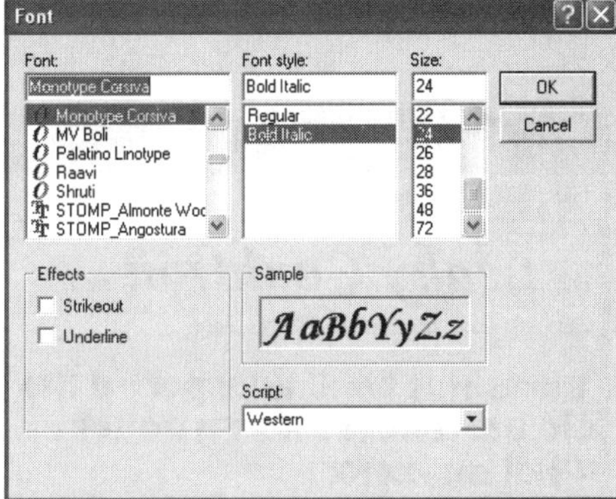

Figure 13.7 The Font dialog lets you choose a font and set its style and size.

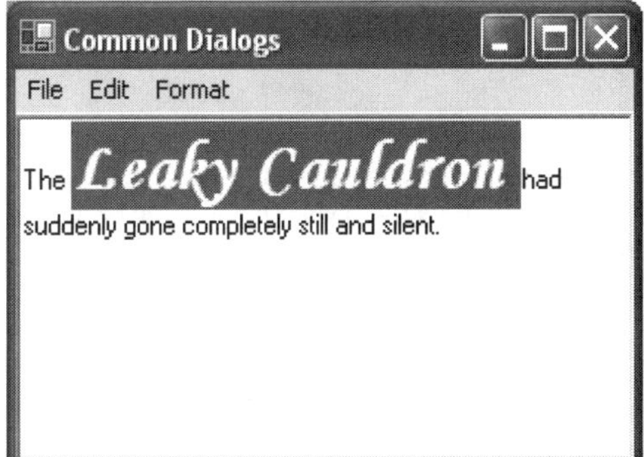

Figure 13.8 The selected text is set in the font, font style, and size selected in the Font dialog.

To set the font for selected text in a RichTextBox control:

1. Open the Code Editor
2. Within the "&Font" Case clause of the Format menu's central processing procedure, show the Font common dialog:
   ```
   FontDialog1.ShowDialog()
   ```
3. Declare a variable, theFont, of type System.Drawing.Font, and assign the Font property of the font common dialog to the variable:
   ```
   Dim theFont As _
      System.Drawing.Font = _
      FontDialog1.Font
   ```
4. Assign the value referenced in the variable named theFont to the SelectionFont property of the RichTextBox:
   ```
   RichTextBox1.SelectionFont = theFont
   ```
   The complete code for setting the selected font is shown as part of the central processing procedure for the Format menu in **Listing 13.1**.
5. Run the project.
6. Enter some text.
7. Select some text, such as the phrase "Leaky Cauldron" (**Figure 13.6**).
8. Choose Font from the Format menu.
   The Font dialog opens (**Figure 13.7**).
9. In the Font dialog, choose a font, font style, and size.
10. Click OK.
    The selected text is now changed to the font you specified (**Figure 13.8**).

To set the font starting at the insertion point:

1. Before entering text in the RichTextBox, choose Font from the Format menu.

   The Font dialog opens (**Figure 13.9**).

2. Select a font, font style, and size.
3. Click OK.
4. Start typing text in the RichTextBox control.

   The text following the original insertion point will be in the selected font (**Figure 13.10**).

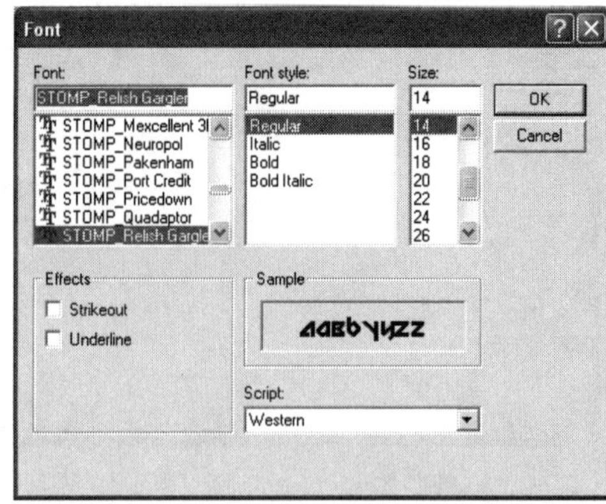

Figure 13.9 You can use the Font dialog to set font characteristics for text entered after the insertion point.

Figure 13.10 The text entered after the insertion point is formatted using the choices made in the Font dialog.

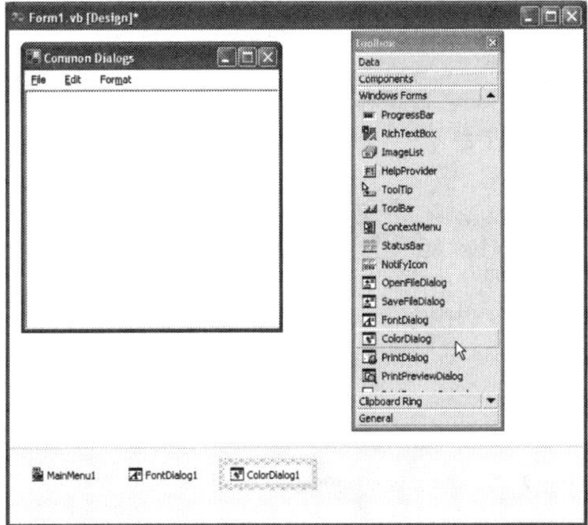

Figure 13.11 When the ColorDialog control is added to a form, it appears in the tray beneath the form.

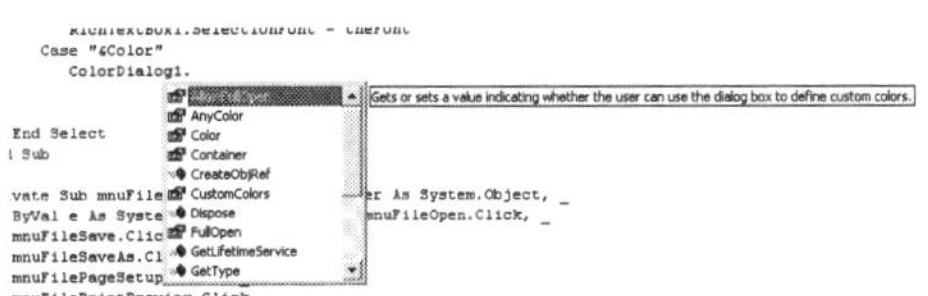

Figure 13.12 It is often good practice to set common dialog properties in code in the Code Editor rather than using the Properties window (the auto-completion feature of the Code Editor is shown here supplying ColorDialog properties that can be set).

The Color Dialog

The Color common dialog control, ColorDialog, works in pretty much the same way as the FontDialog control, except that you will probably want to change a few of the properties that control the way the Color common dialog is displayed.

To add a ColorDialog control:

- With a form open in its designer, double-click the ColorDialog control in the Toolbox to add it to the tray beneath the form (**Figure 13.11**).

To display the Color common dialog:

- With a ColorDialog control added to a form, in the Code Editor, call the ShowDialog method of the ColorDialog control—for example:

  ```
  ColorDialog1.ShowDialog()
  ```

To set the color for selected text in a RichTextBox control:

1. Open the Code Editor.
2. Within the "&Color" Case clause of the Format menu's central processing procedure, set the AllowFullOpen property of the ColorDialog control to True (**Figure 13.12**):

   ```
   ColorDialog1.AllowFullOpen = True
   ```

   This will allow the user to access the portion of the Color dialog that permits the definition of custom colors.
3. Set the AnyColor property of the ColorDialog to True:

   ```
   ColorDialog1.AnyColor = True
   ```
4. Use the ShowDialog method to display the Color dialog:

   ```
   ColorDialog1.ShowDialog()
   ```

continues on next page

5. Declare a variable, theColor, of type System.Drawing.Color, and assign the Color property of the Color common dialog to the variable:

```
Dim theColor As _
   System.Drawing.Color = _
   ColorDialog1.Color
```

6. Assign the value referenced in theColor variable to the SelectionColor property of the RichTextBox control:

```
RichTextBox1.SelectionColor = _
   theColor
```

   The complete code for setting the selected color is shown as part of the central processing procedure for the Format menu in Listing 13.1.

7. Run the project.
8. Enter some text.
9. Select some text, such as the name "Harry Potter" (**Figure 13.13**).
10. Choose Color from the Format menu.
    The Color dialog opens (**Figure 13.14**).
11. Click Define Custom Colors to expand the Color dialog to permit the selection of a custom color (**Figure 13.15**).
12. Select a basic or custom color.
13. Click OK.
    The selected text will now be changed to the chosen color.

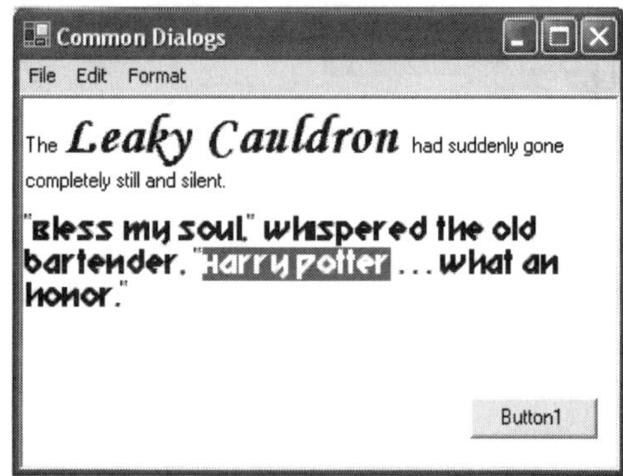

Figure 13.13 Select some text to display its color.

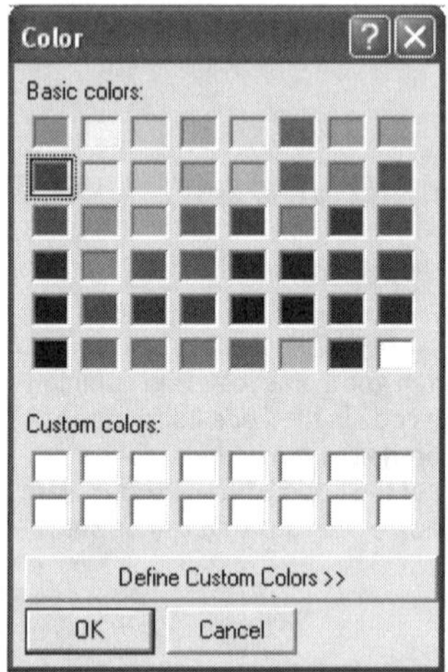

Figure 13.14 The Color dialog allows the user to select a color.

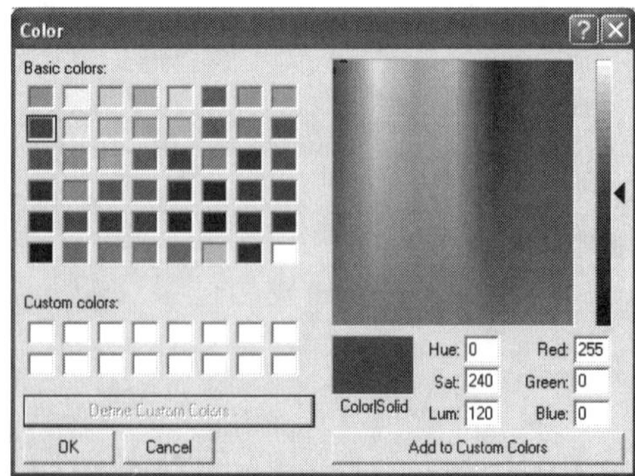

Figure 13.15 If the ColorDialog control's AllowFullOpen property is set to True, the user can define custom colors using the dialog.

Figure 13.16 A Button control has been added to the form (the color selected by the user in the Color dialog will be used to set the Button control's ForeColor property).

If the user sets the ForeColor property of a form, the color of the text of all controls seated on the form change to the color selected (unless the ForeColor property of the seated control has been set individually). You can use the Color dialog to allow the user to set color values for control text (and background, if you choose, using the BackColor property rather than the ForeColor property).

To use a Color common dialog to set the form ForeColor property:

1. Add a control such as a button to the form that contains the RichTextBox control (**Figure 13.16**).
2. In the Code Editor, assign the ColorDialog control's Color property value to the form's ForeColor property:
   ```
   Me.ForeColor = theColor
   ```
3. Run the project.
4. Choose Color from the Format menu to open the Color dialog.
5. In the Color dialog, select a color, such as red.
6. Click OK.
   The text color of the Button control changes to the selected color.

The File Dialogs

The Save and Open common dialogs, displayed using the SaveFileDialog and OpenFileDialog controls, provide a standard user interface for selecting a file to save or open.

To add a SaveFileDialog control:

- With a form open in its designer, double-click the SaveFileDialog control in the Toolbox to add it to the tray beneath the form (**Figure 13.17**).

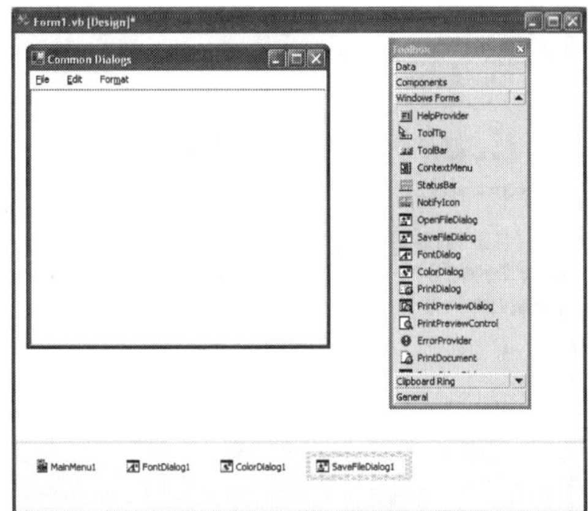

Figure 13.17 When the SaveFileDialog control is added to a form, it appears in the tray beneath the form.

To display the Save common dialog:

- With a SaveFileDialog control added to a form, in the Code Editor, call the ShowDialog method of the SaveFileDialog control—for example:

```
SaveFileDialog1.ShowDialog()
```

To save the contents of the RichTextBox control:

1. In the form with the RichTextBox and SaveFileDialog controls and the File menu, choose Code from the View menu to open the Code Editor.
2. In the File menu's central processing procedure, within the "Save &As" Case clause, set the initial directory displayed in the Save As dialog to the application's executable directory (the bin directory in the case of a VB .NET application running in the development environment):

```
SaveFileDialog1.InitialDirectory _
   = Application.ExecutablePath
```

3. Set the initial file name displayed by the dialog (in this example, "LeakyCauldron"):

```
SaveFileDialog1.FileName = _
   "LeakyCauldron"
```

4. Set the Filter property of the SaveFile-Dialog control to specify the choices presented to the user in the Save as Type drop-down list in the Save As dialog:

```
SaveFileDialog1.Filter = _
   "Rich Text Files" & _
"(*.rtf)|*.rtf|All files (*.*) | *.*"
```

The first choice on this list is the Rich Text File (.rtf) format.

5. Display the Save As dialog and save the dialog results in a variable named answer:

```
Dim answer As DialogResult = _
   SaveFileDialog1.ShowDialog()
```

6. Check to see if the user clicked Save, indicated by a dialog result value of DialogResult.OK:

```
If answer = DialogResult.OK Then


End If
```

7. If Save was clicked, then save the contents of the RichTextBox control, using the RichTextBox control's SaveFile method with the FileName property of the SaveFileDialog control as its argument:

```
If answer = DialogResult.OK Then
   RichTextBox1.SaveFile _
      (SaveFileDialog1.FileName)
End If
```

The complete code for letting the user select a file name and location using the Save As dialog and for saving the contents of the RichTextBox control is shown as part of the central processing procedure for the File menu in **Listing 13.2**.

8. Run the project.

continues on next page

The Filter Property

The Filter property is a text string with items separated by the pipe character (|). An item consists of a description, followed by a pipe, followed by the file suffix using DOS wildcard file naming notation. Another pipe is used to start the next item.

Be careful not to include extra spaces between the end of one item and the beginning of the next item. Extra spaces may cause the filter not to work properly.

Consider the Filter property used with the SaveFileDialog control in the text:

```
Rich Text Files (*.rtf)|*.rtf|All
files (*.*) | *.*
```

In this list, the following is one item:

```
Rich Text Files (*.rtf)|*.rtf
```

It consists of a description followed by the specification: `*.rtf`.

The second item is

```
All files (*.*) | *.*
```

In this item, `All Files (*.*)` is the description, and `*.*` is the wildcard specification, meaning files of all types.

Listing 13.2 The central processing procedure for the File menu (and related code).

```
...
Public Sub New()
    MyBase.New()
    InitializeComponent()
    Me.Saved = False
End Sub
...
Dim Saved As Boolean
Private Sub mnuFileOpen_Click(ByVal sender As System.Object, ByVal e As System.EventArgs) _
   Handles mnuFileOpen.Click, mnuFileSave.Click, mnuFileSaveAs.Click, mnuFilePageSetup.Click, _
   mnuFilePrintPreview.Click, mnuFilePrint.Click
   Dim mi As MenuItem = CType(sender, MenuItem)
   Select Case mi.Text
      Case "&Open"
         OpenFileDialog1.InitialDirectory = Application.ExecutablePath
         OpenFileDialog1.DefaultExt = "rtf"
         OpenFileDialog1.FileName = "LeakyCauldron"
         OpenFileDialog1.Filter = "Rich Text Files" & "(*.rtf)|*.rtf|All files (*.*) | *.*"
          Dim answer As DialogResult = OpenFileDialog1.ShowDialog()
          If answer = DialogResult.OK Then
             RichTextBox1.LoadFile(OpenFileDialog1.FileName)
          End If
      Case "&Save"
         If Me.Saved = False Then
            GoTo SaveAs
         Else
            RichTextBox1.SaveFile(Me.Text)
         End If
      Case "Save &As"
SaveAs:
         SaveFileDialog1.InitialDirectory = Application.ExecutablePath
         SaveFileDialog1.FileName = "LeakyCauldron"
         SaveFileDialog1.Filter = "Rich Text Files" & "(*.rtf)|*.rtf|All files (*.*) | *.*"
         Dim answer As DialogResult = SaveFileDialog1.ShowDialog()
         If answer = DialogResult.OK Then
            RichTextBox1.SaveFile(SaveFileDialog1.FileName)
            Me.Text = SaveFileDialog1.FileName
            Me.Saved = True
         End If
      Case "Page Set&up"
         PageSetupDialog1.ShowDialog()
      Case "Print Pre&view"
         PrintPreviewDialog1.ShowDialog()
      Case "&Print"
         ' PrintDocument1.Print()
         Dim answer As DialogResult = PrintDialog1.ShowDialog()
         If answer = DialogResult.OK Then
            PrintDocument1.Print()
         End If
   End Select
End Sub

Private Sub PrintDocument1_PrintPage(ByVal sender As System.Object, _
   ByVal e As System.Drawing.Printing.PrintPageEventArgs) Handles PrintDocument1.PrintPage
   e.Graphics.DrawString(RichTextBox1.Text, New Font("Arial", 14, FontStyle.Regular), _
      Brushes.Black, 100, 100)
End Sub
```

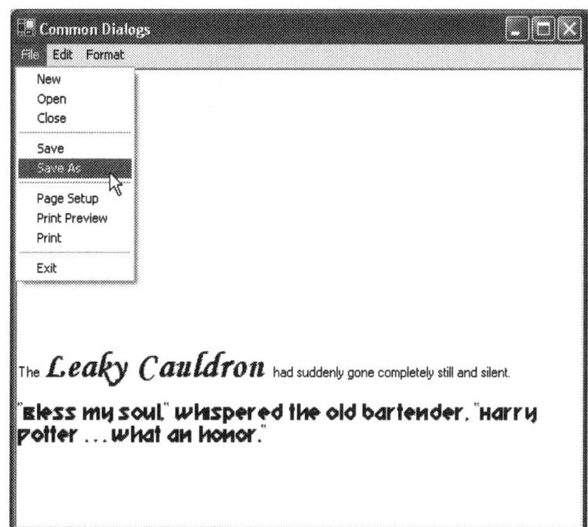

Figure 13.18 Select Save As from the File menu to open the Save As dialog.

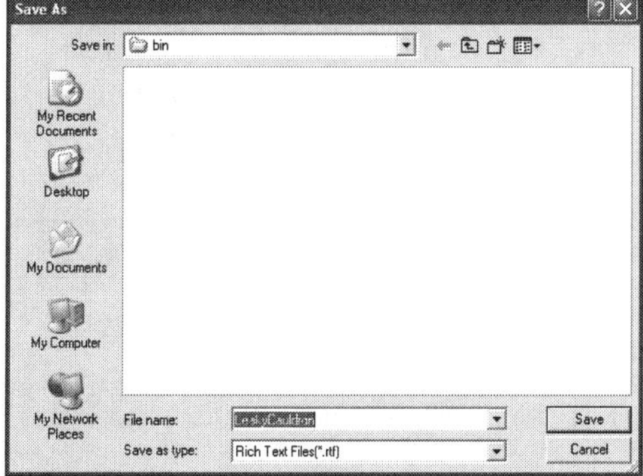

Figure 13.19 The default location, file name, and extension are preset in the Save As dialog.

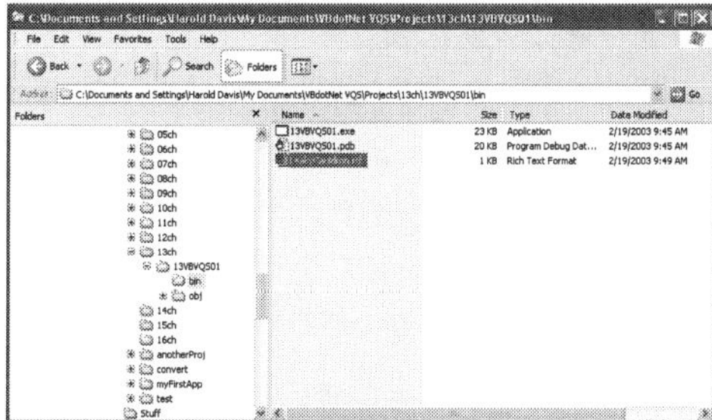

Figure 13.20 You can use Windows Explorer to verify that the file has been saved.

9. Enter and format some text and then choose Save As from the File menu (**Figure 13.18**).

   The Save As dialog opens.

10. Verify that the Save As dialog works in the familiar way; then choose a file location, file name, and file type (such as the suggested defaults) and click Save (**Figure 13.19**).

11. Use Windows Explorer to verify that a file was saved in the specified location (**Figure 13.20**).

12. Open the file in Microsoft Word to verify that it has been saved with the formatting intact (**Figure 13.21**).

When a user attempts to simply save a file, the results depend on whether the file has been saved before. If the file has already been saved, then a file name and location will be selected by default, and changes will be saved to this same file unless the user specifies otherwise by choosing another file name and location. If the file has not been previously saved, then the Save As dialog will be displayed to allow the user to choose a file name and location.

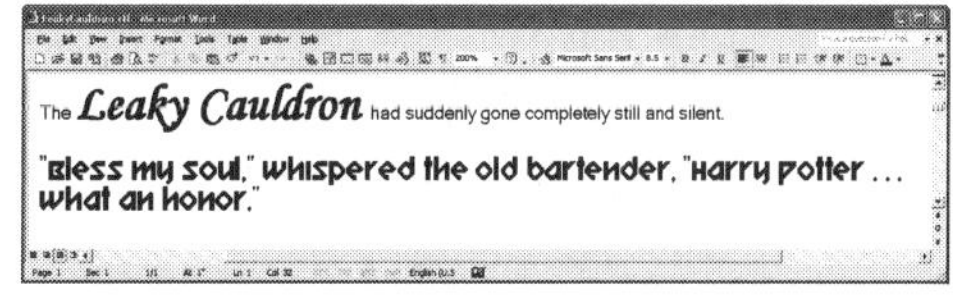

Figure 13.21 If you open the saved file in Microsoft Word, you can verify that the formatting is intact.

To implement a Save menu item:

1. In the Code Editor, at the Form class level, declare a Boolean variable, Saved, that will track whether the file has been saved:

   ```
   Dim Saved As Boolean
   ```

2. In the New constructor for the form, initialize Saved to False, meaning that from the viewpoint of this application, when it opens, it assumes that the contents of the RichTextBox control has not been saved:

   ```
   ...
   Public Sub New()
       MyBase.New()
       InitializeComponent()
       Me.Saved = False
   End Sub
   ...
   ```

3. In the "Save &As" Case clause of the File menu's central processing procedure, before any code in the clause, add a label so that execution can branch to this clause:

   ```
           ...
           Case "Save &As"
   SaveAs:
           ...
   ```

4. At the end of the this clause—after the user selects a file name and location and the contents of the RichTextBox control are saved—set the value of the Saved variable to True within the `answer = DialogResult.OK` conditional statement. Then store the path and file name selected in the Text property of the form:

   ```
   If answer = DialogResult.OK Then
      RichTextBox1.SaveFile _
         (SaveFileDialog1.FileName)
      Me.Text = SaveFileDialog1.FileName
      Me.Saved = True
   End If
   ```

5. Within the "&Save" Case clause of the File menu's central processing procedure, check to see whether the contents have previously been saved:

   ```
   If Me.Saved = False Then

   Else

   End If
   ```

6. *Do one of the following:*
   - ▲ If the contents have been saved, save the current contents of the RichTextBox control using the path and file name that are the values of the form's Text property:

     ```
     RichTextBox1.SaveFile(Me.Text)
     ```

   - ▲ If the contents have not previously been saved, use a GoTo statement to branch to the "&Save As" Case clause to display the Save As dialog. Then save the file in exactly the same fashion as if the user had selected Save As rather than Save:

     ```
     GoTo SaveAs
     ```

   The use of GoTo statements in code is generally a bad idea because it produces "spaghetti code" that is hard to maintain. In this case, however, it doesn't seem to create unduly complex code, and it avoids duplication of the statements that display the Save As dialog.

   The complete code for implementing a Save menu item is shown as part of the central processing procedure for the File menu in Listing 13.2.

7. Run the project.
8. Enter and format some text.
9. Choose Save from the File menu.

   Because this is the first time since the application opened that you are saving its contents, the Save As dialog will open.

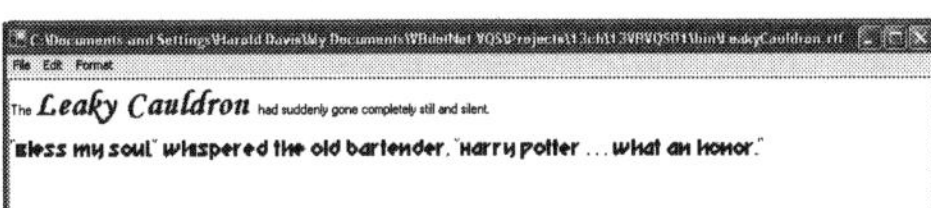

Figure 13.22 If the file has been saved, its path and name appear in the form's caption bar.

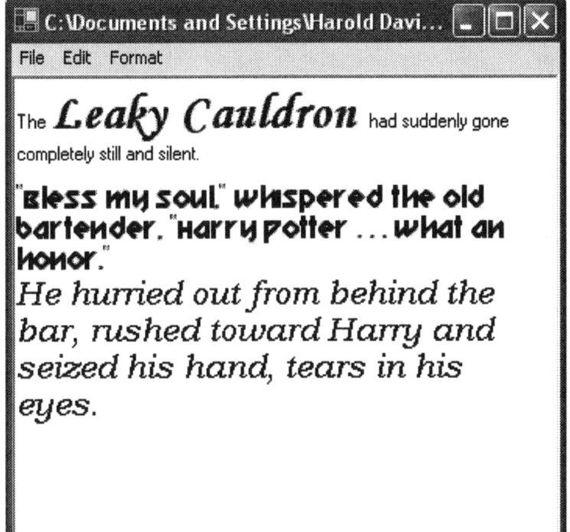

Figure 13.23 Add some more text to the saved file and choose Save from the File menu.

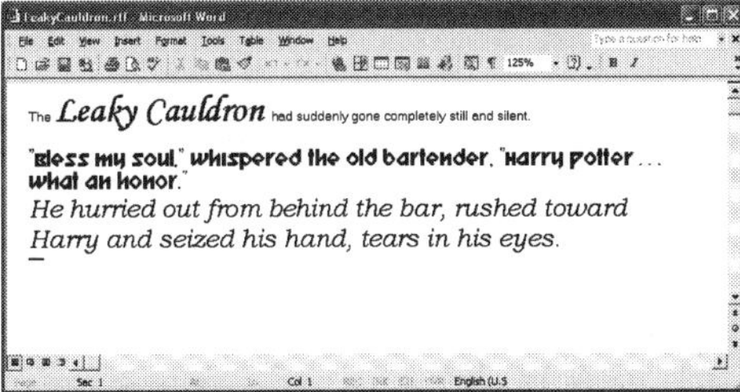

Figure 13.24 When the user chooses Save and the file has been saved previously, changes are saved without the appearance of a File dialog.

10. Select a file name and location.

11. Click Save.

12. If you accept the default file name and location, you will be prompted to overwrite the existing file (since a file with that name was created and saved in the previous task, "To save the contents of a RichTextBox control." Click OK.

The path and file name used to save the RichTextBox contents now appear in the form's caption bar (**Figure 13.22**).

13. Enter and format some more text (**Figure 13.23**).

14. Choose Save from the File menu.

This time, since the file has already been saved, the Save As dialog will not open.

15. Use Microsoft Word to verify that the additions to the file were, in fact, saved (**Figure 13.24**).

✔ Tips

- In some cases, you may want to implement the file saving process so that the flag that indicates whether a file has been saved, along with the path and file name information, are available when the application is closed and then opened. One way to make these items persist is to use the Windows Registry to save the information, in key=value pairs. For more information, look up the topic "Registry Class" in the online help.
- A more robust approach to storing information about a path and file name is to create a custom property to hold the path and file information selected in the Save As dialog (rather than using the Form class's Text property).

In much the same way that the SaveFileDialog allows the user to select a file name and location for saving, the OpenFileDialog control allows the user to choose a file to open.

To add an OpenFileDialog control:

- With a form open in its designer, double-click the OpenFileDialog control in the Toolbox to add it to the tray beneath the form (**Figure 13.25**).

To display the Open common dialog:

- With an OpenFileDialog control added to a form, in the Code Editor, call the ShowDialog method of the OpenFileDialog control—for example:

```
OpenFileDialog1.ShowDialog()
```

To retrieve the contents of a file into the RichTextBox control:

1. In the form with the RichTextBox and OpenFileDialog controls and the File menu, choose Code from the View menu to open the Code Editor.
2. In the File menu's central processing procedure, within the "&Open" Case clause, set the initial directory displayed in the Open file dialog to the application's executable directory (the bin directory in the case of a VB. NET application running in the development environment):

```
OpenFileDialog1.InitialDirectory _
    = Application.ExecutablePath
```

3. Set the initial file extension and file name displayed by the dialog (in this example, to "LeakyCauldron.rtf"):

```
OpenFileDialog1.DefaultExt = "rtf"
OpenFileDialog1.FileName = _
    "LeakyCauldron"
```

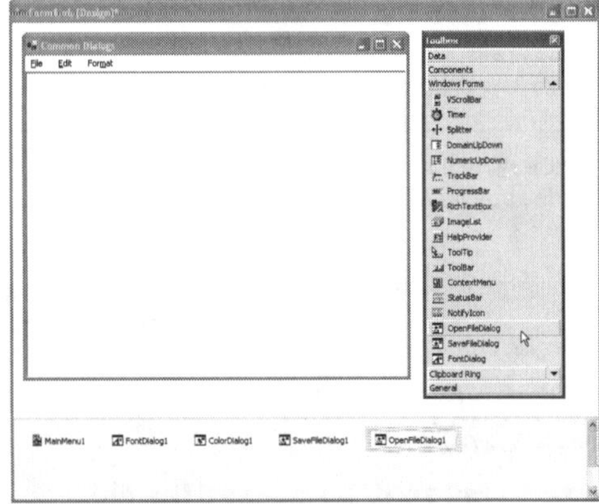

Figure 13.25 When the OpenFileDialog control is added to a form, it appears in the tray beneath the form.

4. Set the Filter property of the OpenFile-Dialog control to specify the choices presented to the user in the Files of Type drop-down list in the Open dialog:

```
OpemFileDialog1.Filter = _
   "Rich Text Files" & _
"(*.rtf)|*.rtf|All files (*.*) | *.*"
```

For more information about the Filter property, see "The Filter Property" sidebar earlier in this chapter.

5. Display the Open dialog and save the dialog results in a variable named answer:

```
Dim answer As DialogResult = _
   OpenFileDialog1.ShowDialog()
```

6. Check to see if the user clicked Open, indicated by a dialog result value of DialogResult.OK:

```
If answer = DialogResult.OK Then

End If
```

7. If Open was clicked, load the contents of the file into the RichTextBox control, using the RichTextBox control's LoadFile method with the FileName property of the OpenFileDialog as its argument:

```
If answer = DialogResult.OK Then
   RichTextBox1.LoadFile _
      (OpenFileDialog1.FileName)
End If
```

The complete code for letting the user select a file using the Open dialog and for loading the contents of the file into the RichTextBox control is shown as part of the central processing procedure for the File menu in Listing 13.2.

8. Run the project.

continues on next page

9. With the contents of the RichTextBox control empty, choose Open from the File menu (**Figure 13.26**).

   The Open dialog appears (**Figure 13.27**).

10. In the Open dialog, choose a file with the Rich Text File (.rtf) format.

11. Click Open.

    The RichTextBox control displays the contents of the file (**Figure 13.28**).

✔ Tip

- Of course, using the LoadFile method of the RichTextBox control works only if the file selected is actually formatted with the Rich Text File format.

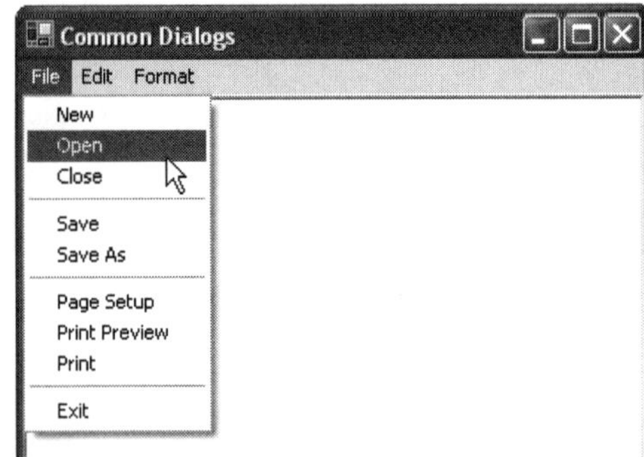

Figure 13.26 Choose Open from the File menu.

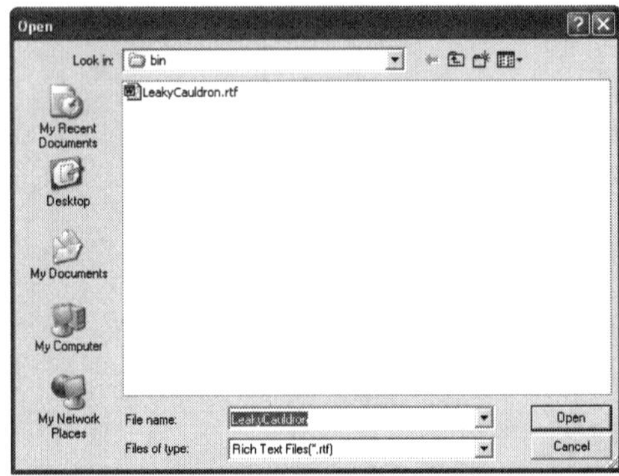

Figure 13.27 The Open dialog displays files that can be opened.

Figure 13.28 The contents of the selected file are displayed in the RichTextBox control.

Using a FileStream Object

The examples in the previous section, "The File Dialogs," use the methods of the RichTextBox control to save and open content (which must be in Rich Text File format). This approach is easy and works fine with the RichTextBox control, but it somewhat begs the more general question of how to save content to a file.

The general topic of saving content to a file in .NET is a big one because the process involves many different types of content and many different .NET classes that can be used to manipulate files. This section provides an overview of how to save text information to a file and open a file for display without using the RichTextBox methods. This alternative approach is important because much of the time you will not be working with RichTextBox controls—and won't have available the easy-to-use methods that by the RichTextBox control provides for saving and opening files.

However, if you need more extensive information about working with the .NET Framework file classes, refer to the File and FileStream classes in the online help or read through Chapter 10, "Working with Streams and Files," in another one of my books, *Visual C# .NET Programming.*

We'll be exploring this alternative approach to saving content to a file using content that has been entered (and displayed) by the RichTextBox control; however, it will work the same way with any text string—for example, the value of the Text property of a TextBox control or a text string created as part of a code procedure.

Although the approach discussed here involves reading text files directly, "directness" is a matter of degree. You are still shielded from the nitty-gritty that would be involved in directly reading the bits that make up a file.

About System.IO namespace classes

The examples in this section use three classes that are members of the System.IO namespace (for more about .NET namespaces, see Chapter 14, "The Object Browser"): FileStream, StreamReader, and StreamWriter.

The **FileStream** class is derived from the abstract Stream base class, which uses the concept of a stream. A *stream* represents a digital flow of information coming from a source such a network, the Web, memory, or a file. An object created using the FileStream class represents a stream and supports reading from and writing to files.

The **StreamReader** and **StreamWriter** classes provide members that make it easy to read from and write to a text-based FileStream object (the comparable classes BinaryReader and BinaryWriter are used to read to and write from a binary-encoded FileStream object).

It is convenient to import the System.IO namespace into a project that will use FileStream and related classes. We can then refer to the classes simply (for example, FileStream). If the System.IO namespace were not imported, we would need to use a fully qualified name for the class (for example, System.IO.FileStream).

To import the System.IO namespace:

1. In the project containing the RichTextBox, open the form module in the Code Editor.
2. As the very first line of code in the module, even before the Form class declaration, add an Imports statement:
   ```
   Imports System.IO
   ```

To save a text file using a FileStream object:

1. In the Code Editor, in the "Save &As" Case clause of the File menu's central processing procedure, comment out the line of code that uses the SaveFile method of the RichTextBox control so that this statement will no longer be processed.
2. In place of the commented-out statement, declare a string variable, theFile, and store the path and file name selected in the SaveFileDialog control within it:
   ```
   Dim theFile As String = _
      SaveFileDialog1.FileName
   ```
3. Declare a variable, fs, as a FileStream object and use theFile to instantiate it in Open or Create mode:
   ```
   Dim fs As FileStream = New _
      FileStream(theFile, _
      FileMode.OpenOrCreate)
   ```
4. Declare a variable, sw, as a StreamWriter object and use the fs FileStream object to instantiate it:
   ```
   Dim sw As StreamWriter = New _
      StreamWriter(fs)
   ```
5. Use the Write method of the sw StreamWriter object to write the value of the RichTextBox control's Rtf property to the file:
   ```
   sw.Write(RichTextBox1.Rtf)
   ```
   The RichTextBox control's Rtf property is a straight text value, but it does include RTF formatting codes (the designers of the RTF format made sure that the formatting codes were all just plain text). You should understand that you could equally well save any text value to the StreamWriter object (for example, the Text property of the RichTextBox control, or the Text property of a TextBox control, or the text string "I love you!").

Figure 13.29 The file is saved using the Save As dialog, even though the methods of the RichTextBox control are not invoked.

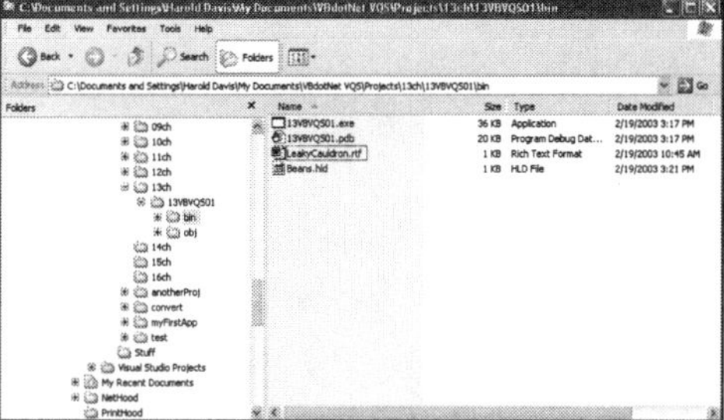

Figure 13.30 Using Windows Explorer, you can verify that the file was saved.

6. Close the StreamWriter and FileStream objects (it's important that you do this to make sure that the file actually gets written to disk and to conserve resources):

```
sw.Close()
fs.Close()
```

Here's the complete code needed to save the text values using FileStream and StreamWriter objects:

```
Dim theFile As String = _
    SaveFileDialog1.FileName
Dim fs As FileStream = New _
    FileStream(theFile, _
    FileMode.OpenOrCreate)
Dim sw As StreamWriter = New _
    StreamWriter(fs)
sw.Write(RichTextBox1.Rtf)
sw.Close()
fs.Close()
```

7. Run the project.
8. Enter and format some text.
9. Choose Save from the File menu.

   The Save As dialog opens.
10. Save the file with a non-RTF file extension—for example, as `Beans.hld`, after the author's initials (**Figure 13.29**).
11. Use Windows Explorer to verify that a file has actually been created and saved (**Figure 13.30**).

To open a text file using a FileStream object:

1. In the Code Editor, in the "&Open" Case clause of the File menu's central processing procedure, comment out the line of code that uses the LoadFile method of the RichTextBox control so that this statement will no longer be processed.
2. In place of the commented-out statement, declare a string variable, theFile, and store the path and file name selected in the OpenFileDialog within it:
   ```
   Dim theFile As String = _
      OpenFileDialog1.FileName
   ```
3. Declare a variable, fs, as a FileStream object and use theFile to instantiate it in Open mode:
   ```
   Dim fs As FileStream = New _
      FileStream(theFile, FileMode.Open)
   ```
4. Declare a variable, sr, as a StreamReader object and use the fs FileStream object to instantiate it:
   ```
   Dim sr As StreamReader = New _
      StreamReader(fs)
   ```
5. Use the ReadToEnd method of the sr StreamReader object to read the text value stored in the file and assign the text value to the Rtf property of the RichTextBox control:
   ```
   RichTextBox1.Rtf = sr.ReadToEnd
   ```
   You should understand that you could equally well read any text value from a file using the StreamReader object (for example, the Text property of the RichTextBox control, or the Text property of a TextBox control, or the text string "I love you!").

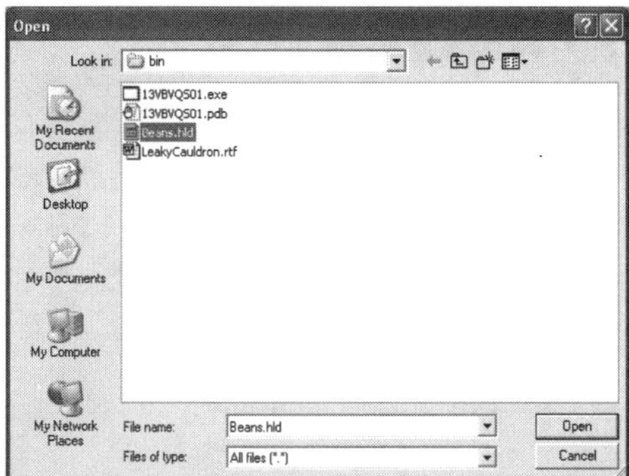

Figure 13.31 Select the Beans.hld file using the Open dialog.

Figure 13.32 The contents of the file are properly displayed in the RichTextBox control (even though the methods of the RichTextBox were not used).

6. Close the StreamReader and FileStream objects (it's important that you do this to conserve resources):

```
sr.Close()
fs.Close()
```

Here's the complete code needed to open the text value contained in a text file using FileStream and StreamReader objects:

```
Dim theFile As String = _
   OpenFileDialog1.FileName
Dim fs As FileStream = New _
   FileStream(theFile,
FileMode.Open)
Dim sr As StreamReader = New _
   StreamReader(fs)
RichTextBox1.Rtf = sr.ReadToEnd
sr.Close()
fs.Close()
```

7. Run the project.
8. Choose Open from the File menu.

   The Open dialog opens.
9. Select the Beans.hld file that you previously saved (**Figure 13.31**).
10. Click Open.

    The correctly formatted text appears in the RichTextBox control (**Figure 13.32**).

Printing

Depending on the needs of your application, printing in VB .NET can be either very easy or very hard. The difficulties arise because you are programmatically responsible for rendering the content that will be printed using the methods of the .NET Graphics object passed as an argument to the PrintPage event of a PrintDocument object.

Printing straight text in a single font is quite easy. In addition, you can create almost any two-dimensional shape using the methods of the Graphics object. However, if you need to print a multipage, formatted document that uses a variety of fonts, rendering it for printing will take a substantial bit of programming.

As you'll see in this section, the good news is that VB .NET provides a number of controls designed to provide a user interface for the printing process. These controls are easy to use, and they give your applications a polished, professional look. The only challenge is keeping the names of the controls straight in your mind, because they are so similar (and have related functionality).

To print from a document:

1. With the form containing the RichTextBox control and the File menu open in its designer, choose Toolbox from the View menu to open the Toolbox.
2. Double-click the PrintDocument control in the Toolbox to add an instance of it to the tray beneath the form (**Figure 13.33**).

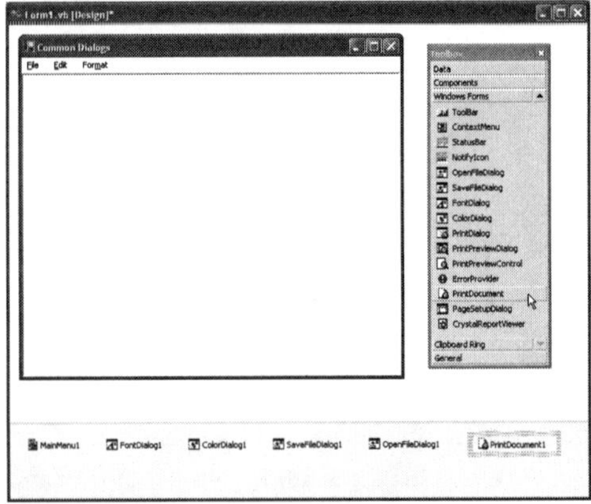

Figure 13.33 When the PrintDocument control is added to a form, it appears in the tray beneath the form.

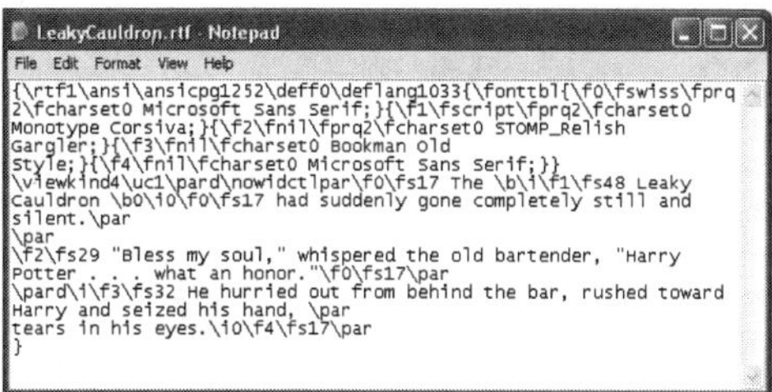

Figure 13.34 The raw RTF codes (shown here as part of the RTF document in Notepad) would have to be parsed to print an RTF document as it is displayed.

✔ Tips

- The actual RTF codes for the LeakyCauldron document are shown in Notepad in **Figure 13.34**. To print a document that looks like the display in the RichTextBox control, you would need to save the document to a file and use a FileStream object to read the file line by line. Each line would be parsed for RTF formatting codes, and the codes would be used to generate Graphics object method calls to approximate the look on the screen.
- Using the e.Graphics object, you can do a lot more than print text. For example, you could use the e.Graphics.DrawEllipse method to print a circle.

3. Double-click the PrintDocument control in the form's tray to create a PrintPage event handler procedure for the PrintDocument control in the Code Editor:

```
Private Sub _
   PrintDocument1_PrintPage _
   (ByVal sender As System.Object, _
   ByVal e As System.Drawing. _
   Printing.PrintPageEventArgs) _
   Handles PrintDocument1.PrintPage

End Sub
```

4. Within the PrintPage event handler, use the methods of the e.Graphics object to print the value of the Text property of the RichTextBox control, using 14-point Arial:

```
e.Graphics.DrawString _
   (RichTextBox1.Text, _
   New Font("Arial", 14, _
   FontStyle.Regular), _
   Brushes.Black, 100, 100)
```

5. In the "&Print" Case clause of the File menu's central processing procedure, invoke the Print method of the PrintDocument control:

```
...
Case "&Print"
   PrintDocument1.Print()
...
```

   Listing 13.2 shows the complete code for the PrintPage event and the "&Print" Case clause.

6. Run the project.
7. Open a document, such as the LeakyCauldron.rtf file shown earlier in this chapter.
8. Select File > Print and verify that the text prints on your default printer.

PRINTING

To display a Page Setup dialog:

1. With the form containing the RichTextBox control and the File menu open in its designer, choose Toolbox from the View menu to open the Toolbox.
2. Double-click the PageSetupDialog control in the Toolbox to add an instance of it to the tray beneath the form (**Figure 13.35**).
3. Right-click the PageSetupDialog control in the form tray and select Properties from its context menu to open the Properties window with the control selected (**Figure 13.36**).
4. In the Properties window, set the Document property of the PageSetupDialog control to the PrintDocument control configured earlier in the task "To print from a document." (Alternatively, you can use the statement `PageSetupDialog1.Document = PrintDocument1` to set the same property in code.)
5. In the Code Editor, in the "Page Set&up" Case clause of the File menu's central processing procedure, call the ShowDialog method of the PageSetupDialog control:

```
...
Case "Page Set&up"
    PageSetupDialog1.ShowDialog()
...
```

6. Run the project.
7. Open a document, such as the LeakyCauldron.rtf file shown earlier in this chapter.

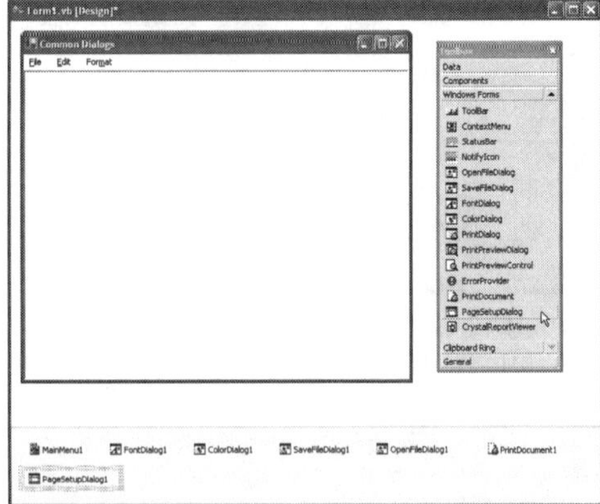

Figure 13.35 When the PageSetupDialog control is added to a form, it appears in the tray beneath the form.

Figure 13.36 The Document property of the PageSetupDialog control needs to be set to a PrintDocument object, either using the Properties window (shown here) or in code.

PRINTING

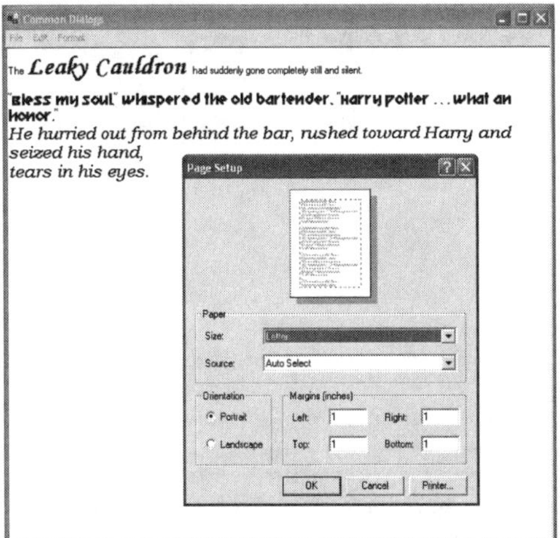

Figure 13.37 Changing the settings in the Page Setup dialog changes the way the associated PrintDocument is printed.

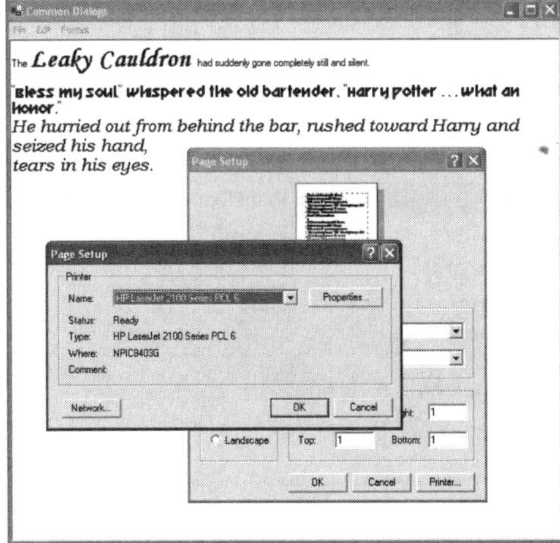

Figure 13.38 If you click Printer in the Page Setup dialog, you can select a printer.

8. Choose Page Setup from the File menu.

   The Page Setup dialog opens (**Figure 13.37**).

9. Click Printer to verify that you can choose a printer other than the default (**Figure 13.38**).

10. In the main Page Setup dialog, change a setting, such as the paper orientation, and click OK.

11. Choose Print from the File menu and verify that the changes you made in the Page Setup dialog are reflected in the printed document.

✔ Tip

- The easiest way to verify that the changes you make in the Page Setup dialog are taking effect is to change the paper orientation and then preview the page. Previewing the page is explained later in this chapter in the task "To preview a page."

Most production Windows applications, such as Microsoft Word, display a Print dialog prior to actually printing. In VB .NET, you can use the PrintDialog control to display a standard dialog of this sort, the Print dialog. Depending on how you set the PrintDialog control properties, the Print dialog allows the user to select a printer, specify the pages and number of copies to print, and more.

To display a Print dialog:

1. With the form containing the RichTextBox control and the File menu open in its designer, choose Toolbox from the View menu to open the Toolbox.
2. Double-click the PrintDialog control in the Toolbox to add an instance of it to the tray beneath the form (**Figure 13.39**).
3. Right-click the PrintDialog control in the tray and select Properties from its context menu to open the Properties window with the control selected (**Figure 13.40**).
4. In the Properties window, set the Document property of the PrintDialog control to the PrintDocument control configured earlier in the task "To print from a document." (Alternatively, you can use the statement `PrintDialog1.Document = PrintDocument1` to set the same property in code.) While the Properties window is open, you can also use it configure the features that you want it to display to the user (for example, enabling the Print to File check box).
5. In the Code Editor, in the "&Print" Case clause, delete or comment out the original `PrintDocument1.Print()` statement so that it is no longer effective.

Figure 13.39 When the PrintDialog control is added to a form, it appears in the tray beneath the form.

Figure 13.40 The Document property of the PrintDialog control needs to be set to a PrintDocument object, either using the Properties window (shown here) or in code.

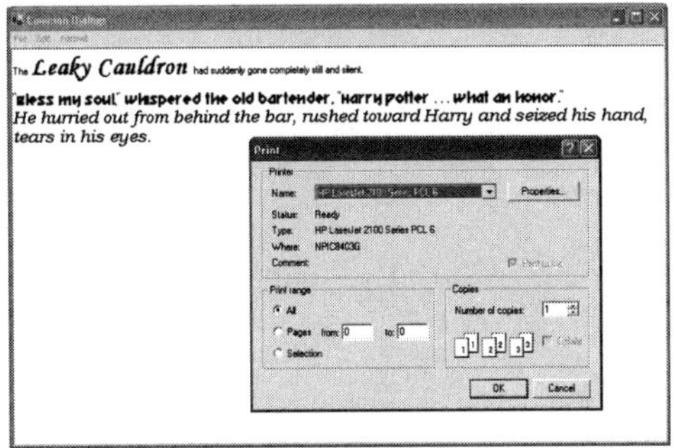

Figure 13.41 You can easily add code that displays the Print dialog before printing a PrintDocument object (imitating the behavior of application's such as Microsoft Word).

6. Declare a variable, answer, of type DialogResult and assign it the value of the PrintDialog control's ShowDialog method:

   ```
   ...
   Case "&Print"
      Dim answer As DialogResult = _
         PrintDialog1.ShowDialog()
   ...
   ```

7. If the value of the variable answer is DialogResult.OK, then call the Print method of the PrintDocument control:

   ```
   ...
   Case "&Print"
      Dim answer As DialogResult = _
         PrintDialog1.ShowDialog()
      If answer = DialogResult.OK Then _
         PrintDocument1.Print()
      End If
   ...
   ```

   Listing 13.2 shows the complete code for the modified "&Print" Case clause.

8. Run the project.

9. Open a document, such as the LeakyCauldron.rtf file shown earlier in this chapter.

10. Choose Print from the File menu.

    The Print dialog opens (**Figure 13.41**).

11. Verify that the Print dialog is functional by, for example, choosing an alternative printer.

12. Click OK to print the document.

You can use the Print Preview dialog to display a preview of a printed page. Note that a standard Print Preview dialog generated using a PrintPreviewDialog control creates a rendering using the Graphics object methods specified in the PrintPage event of the linked PrintDocument control. This rendering may differ radically from a document displayed on the screen. In particular, if the PrintPage event doesn't contain any Graphics method calls that create two-dimensional objects (or text), then the PrintPreviewDialog will display a blank document, even if the application that invoked the Print preview dialog shows a document with content on the screen.

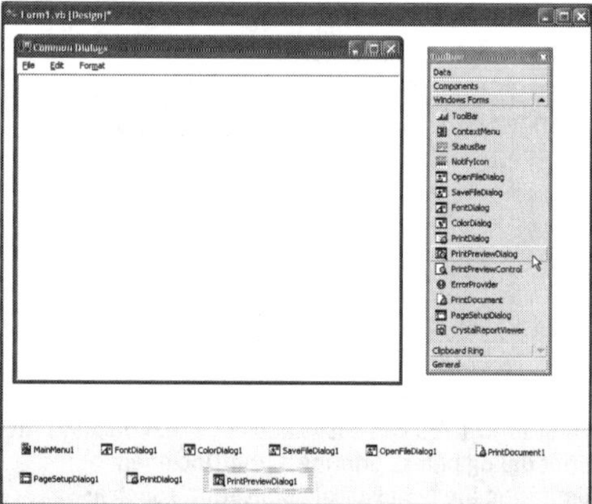

Figure 13.42 When the PrintPreviewDialog control is added to a form, it appears in the tray beneath the form.

To preview a page:

1. With the form containing the RichTextBox control and the File menu open in its designer, choose Toolbox from the View menu to open the Toolbox.
2. Double-click the PrintPreviewDialog control in the Toolbox to add an instance of it to the tray beneath the form (**Figure 13.42**).
3. Right-click the PrintPreviewDialog control in the tray and select Properties from its context menu to open the Properties window with the control selected (**Figure 13.43**).
4. In the Properties window, set the Document property of the PrintPreviewDialog control to the PrintDocument control configured earlier in the task "To print from a document." (Alternatively, you can use the statement `PrintPreviewDialog1.Document = PrintDocument1` to set the same property in code.)

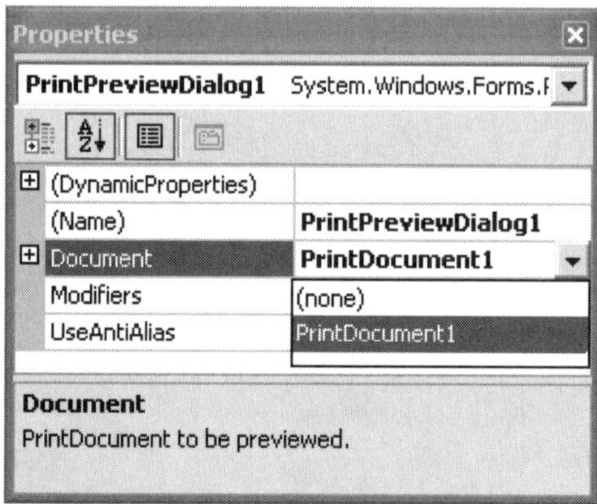

Figure 13.43 The Document property of the PrintPreviewDialog control needs to be set to a PrintDocument object, either using the Properties window (shown here) or in code.

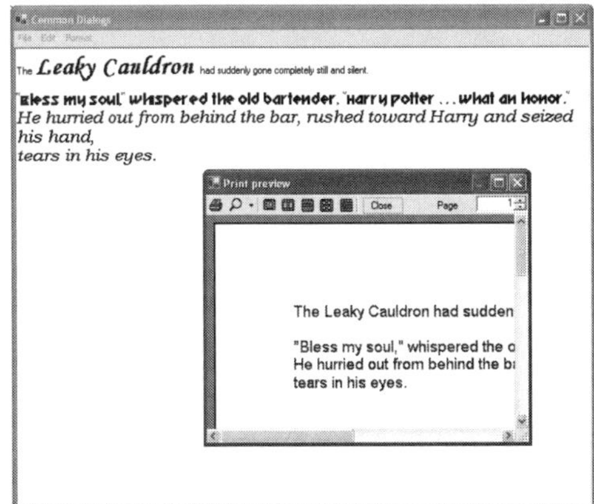

Figure 13.44 The PrintPreviewDialog control provides a rendering of the PrintDocument object (which is not in RTF format).

5. In the Code Editor, in the "Print Pre&view" Case clause, call the ShowDialog method of the PrintPreviewDialog control:

```
...
Case "Print Pre&view"
   PrintPreviewDialog1.ShowDialog()
...
```

   Listing 13.2 shows the complete code for the File menu's central processing procedure, including the "Print Pre&view" Case clause.

6. Run the project.
7. Open a document, such as the LeakyCauldron.rtf file shown earlier in this chapter.
8. Choose Print Preview from the File menu.

   The Print preview dialog opens, displaying a rendering of the document that will be printed (**Figure 13.44**).

9. You can now use controls in the Print preview dialog to, for example, enlarge the document preview and to print the document.

Summary

In this chapter, you learned how to:

- Work with central menu processing procedures
- Use the Font common dialog
- Use the Color common dialog
- Save text files using the Save common dialog and the members of a RichTextBox control
- Open text files using the Open common dialog and the members of the RichTextBox control
- Save and open text files directly using the FileStream, StreamReader, and StreamWriter classes
- Manage printing using the PrintPage event of a PrintDocument control
- Display a Page Setup dialog
- Display a Print dialog
- Use the PrintPreviewDialog control to preview a page as it will print

The Object Browser

The Object Browser is my favorite tool for discovering information about .NET classes and their members. Using the Object Browser, you can easily find the actual declaration for any structure, class, or member (such as a method, event, property, or constant). You can also determine the relationship of members and classes to each other and how they are organized in namespaces. Usually, you can also find descriptive definitions of each member or class that give you a pretty good idea of the purpose of the member or class and how to use it.

I find that I can obtain accurate information about these important matters more easily and quickly by using the Object Browser than by consulting the .NET online documentation. It's like going to the primary source for information. Of course, if the procedures for a .NET task really are obscure, you will need all the help you can get, starting with the primary source—the Object Browser—and also referring to secondary sources such as the help documentation (and this book!).

This chapter explains in detail how to use the Object Browser to examine .NET classes, members, and relationships. Delving further into the topic of .NET relationships, you'll also learn how to work with assemblies (the basic unit of .NET projects) and namespaces (the basic organizational unit of .NET classes in the .NET Framework and in your projects).

Opening the Object Browser

The Object Browser is an integral part of the Visual Studio .NET user interface (just like the Properties window or Solution Explorer).

To open the Object Browser:

- From the Visual Studio View menu, select Other Windows > Object Browser (**Figure 14.1**).

  or

- Press Ctrl + Alt + J on the keyboard.

  The Object Browser opens (**Figure 14.2**).

  You can also open the Object Browser to a particular definition from the Code Editor.

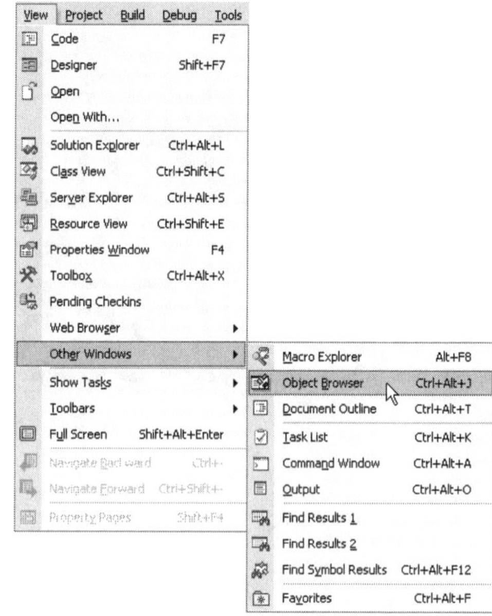

Figure 14.1 To open the Object Browser, select Object Browser from the Other Windows menu.

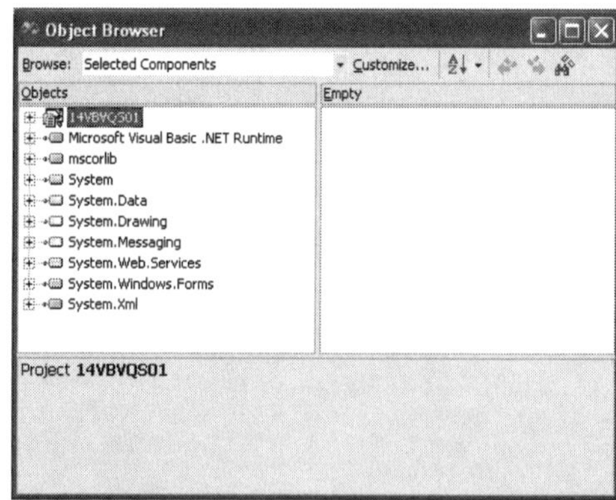

Figure 14.2 The Object Browser window (showing assemblies).

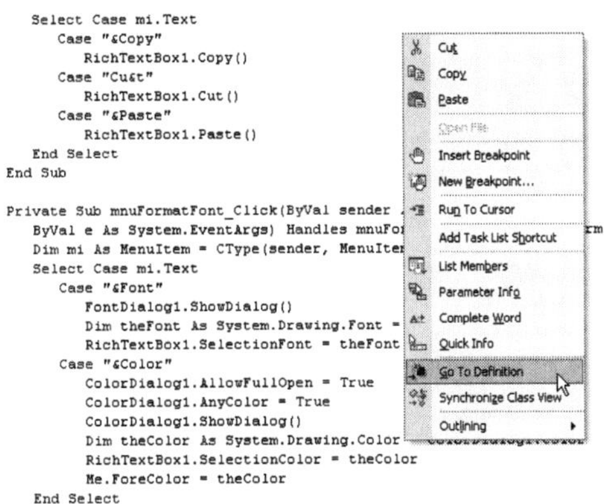

Figure 14.3 Selecting Go To Definition from the Code Editor's context menu opens the Object Browser with the definition of the class (or other object) referenced in the Code Editor.

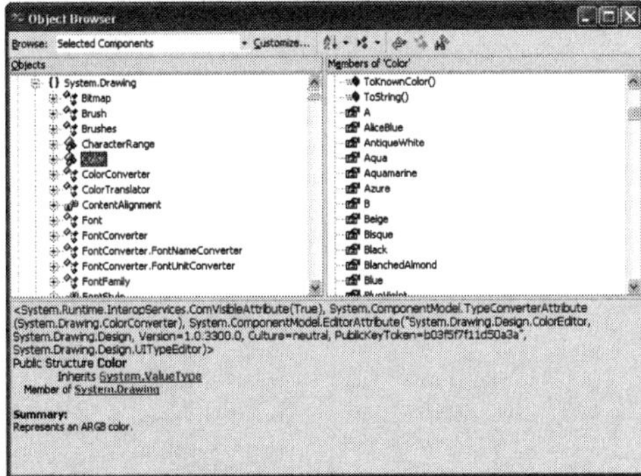

Figure 14.4 The definition of a class or structure appears in the Object Browser.

To open the Object Browser directly to a definition:

1. In the Code Editor, place the cursor over or immediately to the right or left of a .NET framework structure, class, or member and then right-click to open the context menu.

2. Choose the Go To Definition menu item from the context menu (**Figure 14.3**).

   The Object Browser opens with the item that was picked in the Code Editor selected (**Figure 14.4** shows the definition for the System.Drawing.Color structure).

Note that Go To Definition will open the Object Browser only if a .NET Framework object is selected. If, instead, you pick an object declared in your own code as a .NET type, choosing Go To Definition will take you in the Code Editor to the object declaration for that type in your code. For example, if you create the declaration `Dim theColor As System.Drawing.Color` at the Form class level and later select the Color variable and choose Go To Definition, the Object Browser will not open; instead, the declaration line will be selected in the Code Editor. Only by selecting an intrinsic .NET type—System.Drawing.Color, for instance—will choosing Go To Definition open the Object Browser.

When the Object Browser opens, you have a choice of two *scopes*, or two universes of objects that can be displayed. The default is Selected Components, which allows you to customize the components that determine the universe of objects displayed, as explained in "To Add Selected Components" later in this section.

The other Object Browser scope setting is Active Project, which includes all objects in the active project and its references. The Active Project setting cannot be customized (although you can add project references, as explained later in this chapter in "To add a reference to an assembly").

To set the Object Browser scope:

- In the Object Browser, choose Selected Components (the default) or Active Project from the Browse drop-down list (**Figure 14.5**), located at the upper left of the Object Browser window.

To add selected components:

1. Open the Object Browser.
2. Make sure Selected Components is chosen in the Browse drop-down list.
3. Click Customize, located to the right of the Browse drop-down list (and shown in Figure 14.5).

   The Selected Components dialog opens with the current project and its references selected (**Figure 14.6**).
4. Click Add to open the Component Selector dialog.

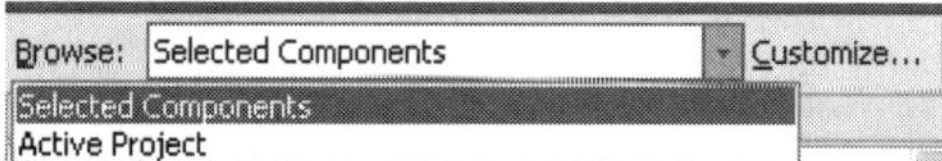

Figure 14.5 The Browse drop-down list controls the scope of the Object Browser.

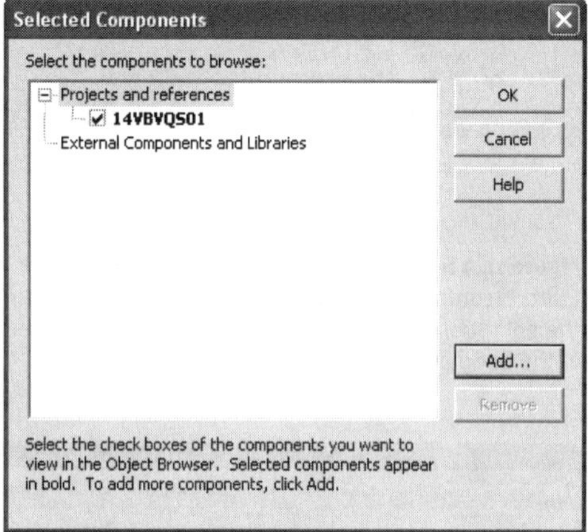

Figure 14.6 You can use the Selected Components dialog to determine which components and libraries to browse.

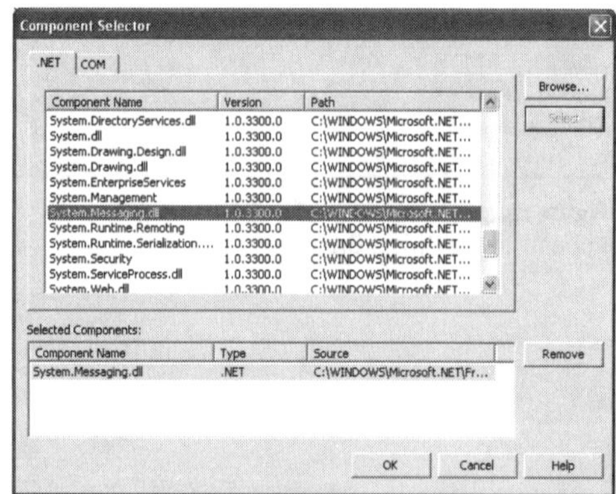

Figure 14.7 The Component Selector dialog lets you add components.

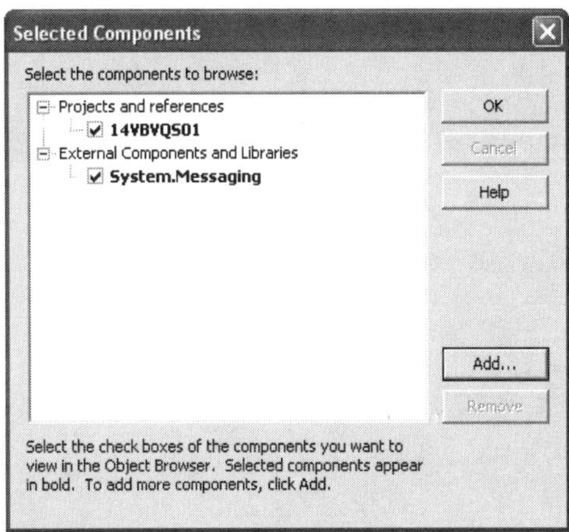

Figure 14.8 Added components appear in the Selected Components dialog.

5. In the upper pane of the Component Selector dialog, choose a component to add, such as System.Messaging.dll. Then click Select.

   The selected component is added to the Selected Components pane (**Figure 14.7**).

6. Click OK.

   The Component Selector dialog closes, and the selected component is added to the Selected Components dialog (**Figure 14.8**).

7. Click OK to add the selected component to the scope of the Object Browser.

8. Open the Object Browser and verify that the objects belonging to the selected component can now be browsed.

   Figure 14.9 shows classes and other objects belonging to the System.Messaging namespace displayed in the Object Browser.

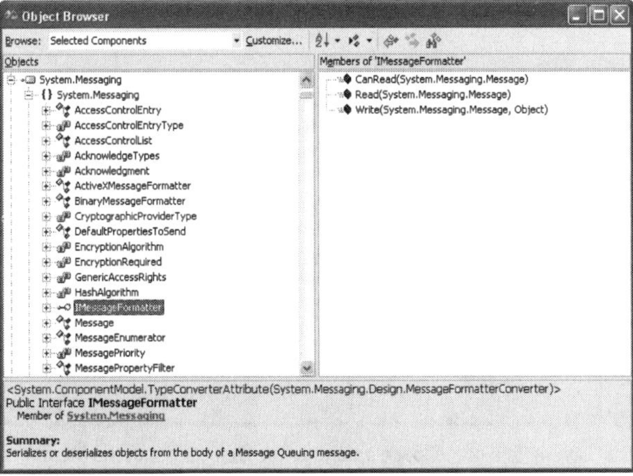

Figure 14.9 The objects that are part of the added component appear in the Object Browser.

The Object Browser Interface

The Object Browser is really easy to use once you get the hang of it. But since the way the Object Browser user interface works is not always obvious, you should spend a little time getting to know it.

The Object Browser user interface consists of a toolbar and three windows (or panes): the Objects pane, the Members pane, and the Description pane (**Figure 14.10**).

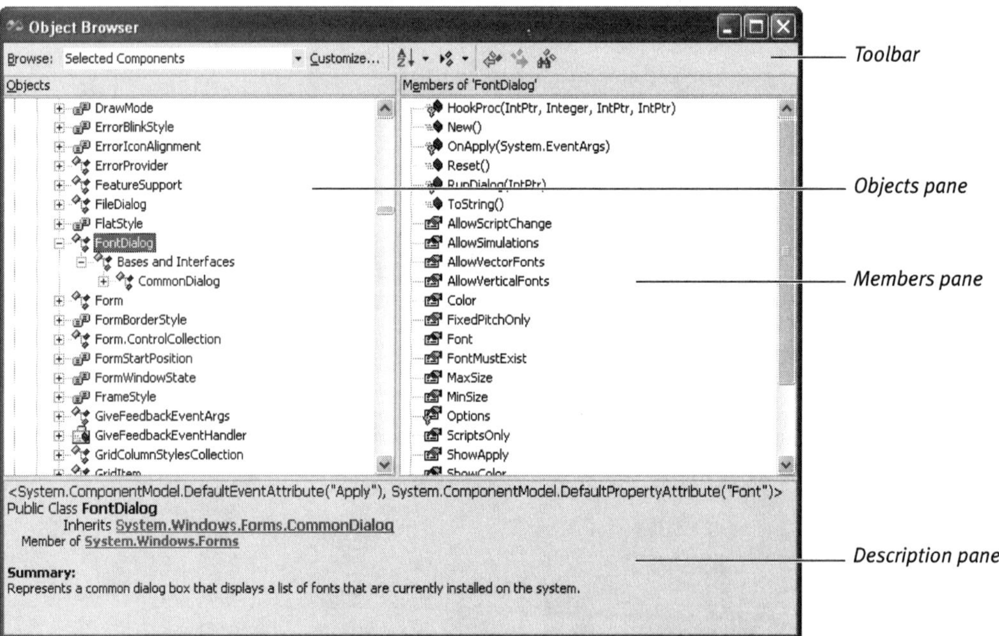

Figure 14.10 The objects that belong to a namespace appear in the Objects pane; the Members pane displays the members of these objects, and the Description pane provides information about selected objects and members.

Figure 14.11 The Objects pane.

The Objects Pane

The Objects pane provides a hierarchical view of the objects (primarily classes, but also interfaces and structures) that are within the current scope of the Object Browser.

Figure 14.11 shows the Objects pane with the FontDialog class selected and expanded to show objects within it. The FontDialog class, which is the implementation of the FontDialog control explained in Chapter 13, "The Common Dialog Controls," is a member of the System.Windows.Forms namespace.

Clicking the + or – icon in the Objects pane expands or contracts the hierarchical view of objects. For example, since the FontDialog class is a member of the System.Windows.Forms namespace, to view the FontDialog class, you would first select System.Windows.Forms, then expand it to view its members, and then scroll down the Objects pane to locate FontDialog.

Selecting and fully expanding objects such as classes in the Objects pane is the primary mechanism for discovery using the Object Browser. By selecting and expanding an object, you can learn a great deal about it, such as the classes it derives from and its members—which are shown in the Members pane.

The Members Pane

The Members pane shows the members of an object selected in the Objects pane. Members are properties, methods, events, fields, and constants (such as enumeration values). **Figure 14.12** shows the Members pane with some of the members of the FontDialog object.

If you look at the Members pane, you'll notice an icon to the left of each member. These icons provide information about the type and scope of the member. However, the meaning of each icon is not immediately obvious (at least, it wasn't to me). To help you, **Table 14.1** shows and describes the member type icons.

Some members have additional icons to the left of the member type icon. These indicate a scope access restriction. If you don't see one of these two access modifiers in the Members pane, then you can assume that the member has a public access scope. **Table 14.2** shows the member access scope icons.

For more information on the different kinds of members, and access restrictions, see Chapter 3, "Working with Classes."

Table 14.1

Member Type Icons

Icon	Represents Member Type
	Property or procedure
	Method
	Event
	Constant or enumeration value
	Field or variable

Table 14.2

Member Access Scope Icons

Icon	Scope of Member Marked with Icon
	Private (access restricted to within a class)
	Protected (accessible only from its own or a derived class)

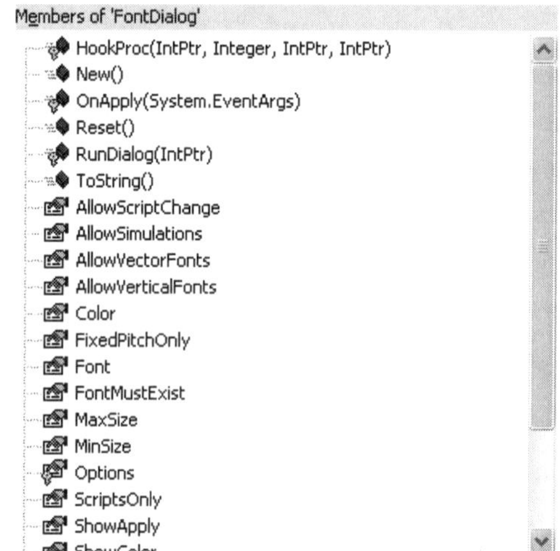

Figure 14.12 The Members pane.

The Description Pane

The Description pane provides information about an item that is selected in the Objects pane or Members pane. **Figure 14.13** shows the information in the Description pane when the FontDialog class is selected in the Objects pane.

The information shown in the Description pane varies depending on the object selected. It usually includes the following:

- A description of the object (for example, the summary of the FontDialog class shown in Figure 14.13)
- The name of the object and its parent
- The declaration for the object (which shows you the syntax for the object)

In addition, you'll usually find links to related objects and members. Clicking these links takes you to the destination object or member in the Object Browser. For example, the Description pane for the FontDialog class shown in Figure 14.13 provides a link to the class from which FontDialog derives (System.Windows.Forms.CommonDialog) and the namespaces of which FontDialog is a member (System.Windows.Forms).

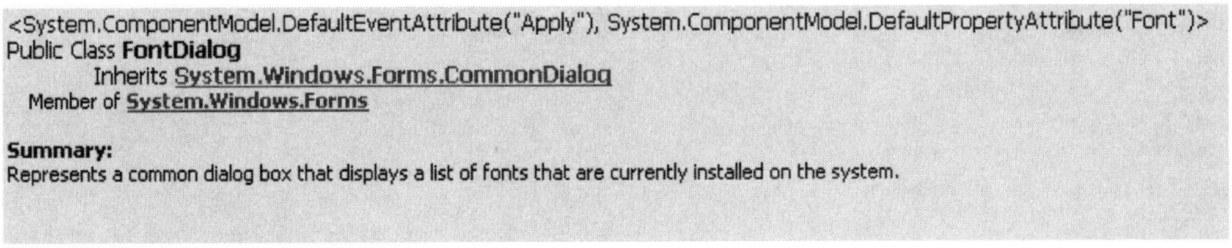

```
<System.ComponentModel.DefaultEventAttribute("Apply"), System.ComponentModel.DefaultPropertyAttribute("Font")>
Public Class FontDialog
        Inherits System.Windows.Forms.CommonDialog
  Member of System.Windows.Forms

Summary:
Represents a common dialog box that displays a list of fonts that are currently installed on the system.
```

Figure 14.13 The Description pane.

The Toolbar

You use the Object Browser toolbar (**Figure 14.14**) to set and customize the Object Browser scope (as explained earlier in this chapter in "To add selected components"). You can also use the toolbar to perform the following functions:

- Sort the items in the Objects and Members panes (the Sort Objects and Sort Members drop-down lists allow you to sort objects alphabetically, by type, and more)
- Navigate to previously selected items (using the Back and Forward buttons)
- Find identifiers (using the Find Symbol button)

Probably the most useful button on the Object Browser toolbar is Find Symbol. The Find Symbol button opens the Find Symbol dialog, which you can use to locate objects by their identifiers (called *symbols* here). The Find Symbol dialog is equivalent to the Find dialog in a word processing program. It often provides the quickest way to find an object you are looking for in the Object Browser.

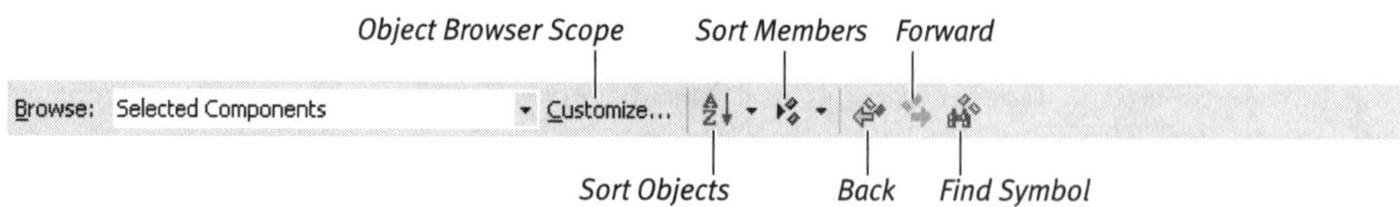

Figure 14.14 The Object Browser toolbar.

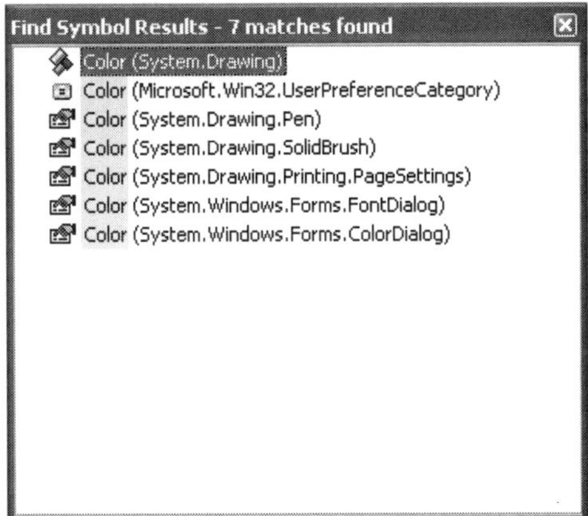

Figure 14.16 Multiple results of an Object Browser search appear in the Find Symbol Results display.

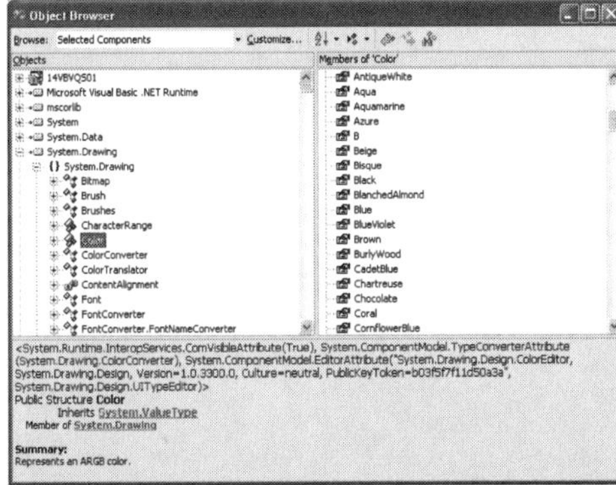

Figure 14.17 Selecting a result of a search opens the Object Browser with that object or member selected..

To find a symbol:

1. With the Object Browser open, click the Find Symbol button on the Object Browser toolbar.

   The Find Symbol dialog opens (**Figure 14.15**). Note that if an object was selected in the Object Browser, this object appears selected in the Find What field of the Find Symbol dialog, as shown in Figure 14.15.

2. In the Find What text field, enter the identifier of the object you want to locate.

3. Click Find.

   If there is exactly one match with the identifier you entered, the Object Browser will open with the corresponding object selected. If there are multiple matches with the identifier, they will be listed in the Find Symbol Results dialog (**Figure 14.16**).

4. Double-click the identifier listed in the Find Symbol Result dialog that you want to match.

   The Object Browser opens with the object that corresponds to the identifier selected in the Objects pane (**Figure 14.17**).

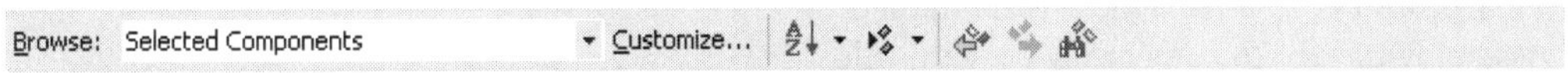

Figure 14.15 Use the Find Symbol dialog to search the Object Browser.

Assemblies

Assemblies are the basic unit for .NET application deployment, version control, security, and much more. They are, in other words, units of code that correspond to deployable programs such as stand-alone executable program files (usually with an .exe file extension) and other kinds of programs such as libraries and components (usually sporting a .dll file extension). Each compiled .NET program has at least one assembly. Every time you build an executable (EXE) file or a library or component (DLL) file in .NET, you are creating an assembly.

When you open a new VB.NET project, it is the basis for an assembly. Each assembly provides a *manifest*, or table of contents, that provides information about the assembly, including the following:

- The assembly name and version number
- A file table showing the files that makes up the assembly
- A reference list that catalogs the external assemblies that the project references

By default, the assembly name for a project is the same as the project name. However, you can change the assembly name to something different if you prefer by using the General tab of a project's Property pages.

The assembly manifest information for a VB .NET project is saved in a file project named AssemblyInfo.vb. You can easily view this file from within Visual Studio.

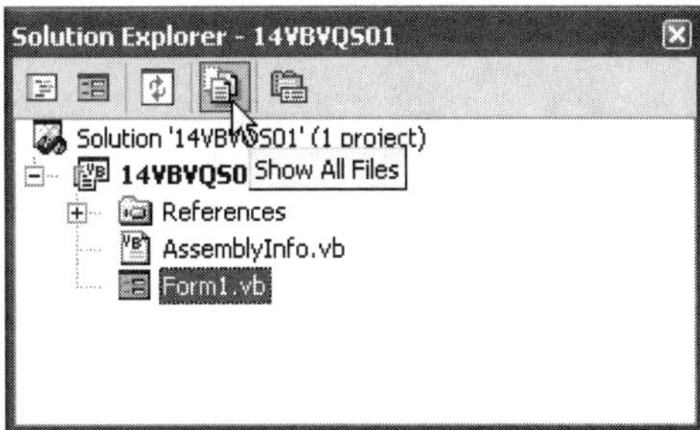

Figure 14.18 To view reference and assembly files in Solution Explorer, you may need to click the Show All Files button.

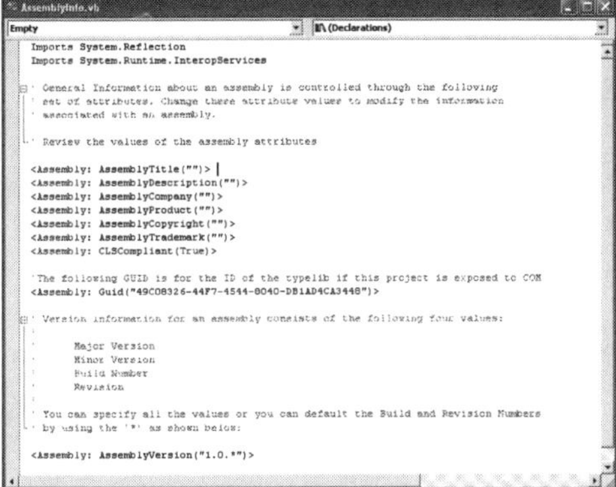

Figure 14.19 You can modify assembly information in the AssemblyInfo.vb file.

To view an assembly manifest:

1. With a VB .NET project open in Visual Studio, choose Solution Explorer from the View menu to open Solution Explorer.
2. If you do not see a file named AssemblyInfo.vb in Solution Explorer, click the Show All Files button on the Solution Explorer toolbar (**Figure 14.18**). Note that Figure 14.18 shows a form module selected, which is what you can expect in Solution Explorer if you also have a form open in its designer in the active Visual Studio project.

   The AssemblyInfo.vb file appears in Solution Explorer.
3. Double-click AssemblyInfo.vb in Solution Explorer to open the AssemblyInfo.vb manifest file for inspection and editing in the Visual Studio Code Editor (**Figure 14.19**).

You'll often want to use a class or a class member in an assembly that is not the current assembly—an approach called using an *external* assembly. The external assembly may be part of the .NET Framework, or it may be a code project that you (or someone else) have written. Note that you can use classes and their members that are part of an external assembly when that assembly is a library or component file (with a .dll file extension), but not when the classes and members are part of an executable file.

To use the classes and class members that belong to an external assembly, you first need to add a reference to the external assembly to the current project.

To add a reference to an assembly:

1. To open the Add Reference dialog, *do one of the following:*

   ▲ From the Visual Studio Project menu, choose Add Reference.

   or

   ▲ With Solution Explorer open, select the References folder.

   or

   ▲ Right-click and choose Add Reference from the context menu.

2. Select a .NET Framework component, a COM component, or a .NET project to add a reference to, using the appropriate tab for the type of object referenced.

3. Click Select.

   The object to be referenced is added to the Selected Components pane (**Figure 14.20**).

4. Click OK.

   A reference to the external project is added to the current project. You can view the new external reference in the References folder in Solution Explorer.

✔ Tip

■ If you don't see the assembly you want to reference, click the Browse button to open the Select Component dialog and locate the file that contains the assembly.

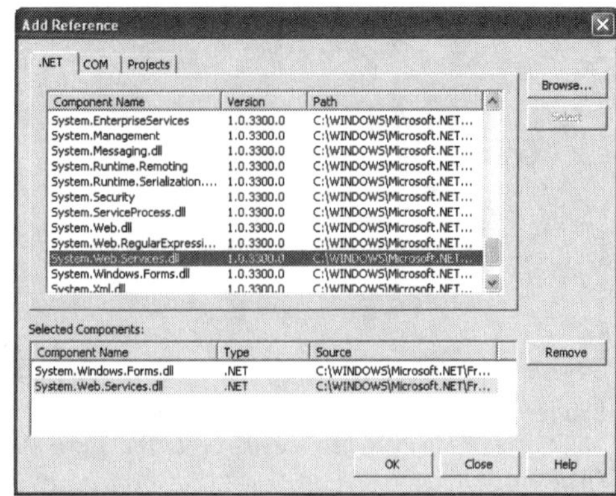

Figure 14.20 Use the Add Reference dialog to add a reference to an external project.

Namespaces

Namespaces are used to organize classes and other top-level objects such as interfaces and structures within assemblies. A single assembly can contain many namespaces, each of which can contain other namespaces. This is called *nesting* namespaces.

You use the dot operator (.) between a *root* namespace (or top-level namespace) and the namespaces it contains, as well as between namespaces to indicate that one is nested within another—for example:

```
RootNamespace.NameSpace1.NestedNamespace
```

The default name for the root namespace within an assembly is the project name preceded by an underscore (_). For example, if a project is named 14VBVQS02, then the default root namespace name is _14VBCQS02. If you need to, you can change the root namespace for a project to something different using the General tab of a project's Property pages.

Classes and other top-level objects are organized into namespaces for the following reasons:

- To make referencing items easier
- To help organize the large number of classes and other top-level objects present in the .NET Framework (and maybe in your own projects and class libraries)
- To simplify class references
- To avoid ambiguity

Namespaces themselves can contain other namespaces, but no other .NET language element can contain a namespace. In other words, namespaces can contain almost anything. The most common top-level objects you'll find in namespaces are:

- Other namespaces
- Classes
- Interfaces
- Structures

(Of course, these top-level objects themselves can contain a variety of members, including properties, methods, events, fields, enumerations, and so on.)

It's cumbersome to use a fully qualified class-and-namespace name to refer to a class (or other object). You'll likely get tired of writing `RootNamespace.NameSpace1.NestedNamespace.theClass` in your code. To avoid having to refer to a class within a nested namespace in a fully qualified fashion, you can *import* the namespace. Once you have imported a namespace, you can use the classes and other top-level objects contained in the namespace without qualifying the reference to the class with the namespace.

To import a namespace:

1. Open a new project—for example, a Class Library project, as shown in **Figure 14.21**.
2. As explained in "To add a reference to an assembly" earlier in this chapter, use the Add Reference dialog to add a reference to the System.Windows.Forms namespace to the project (**Figure 14.22**).

   The reference just added will now be displayed in the References folder for the project in Solution Explorer (**Figure 14.23**).

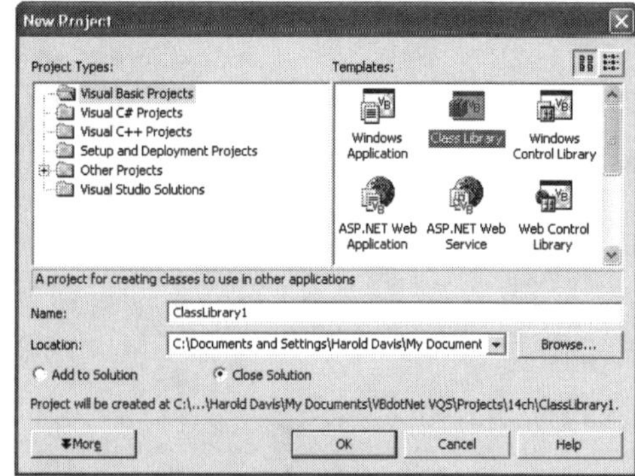

Figure 14.21 Select Class Library in the New Project dialog to create a library file.

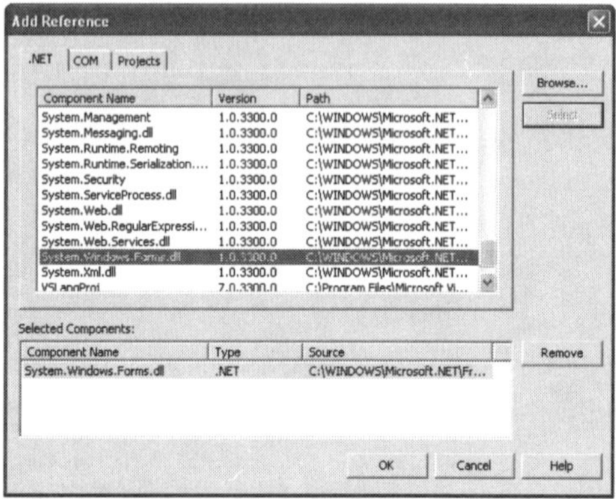

Figure 14.22 You can use the Add Reference dialog to add a reference to the System.Windows.Forms namespace.

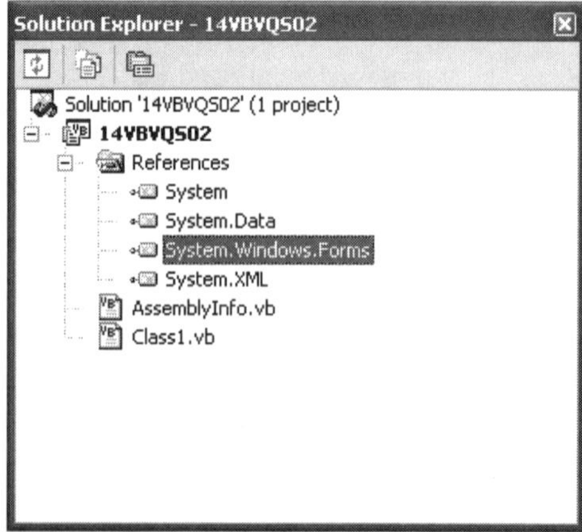

Figure 14.23 The added reference is displayed in Solution Explorer.

NAMESPACES

3. Open the class module contained in the Class Library project in the Code Editor.

4. Before any other code in the module, use the Imports keyword to import a namespace—for example:

   ```
   Imports System.Windows.Forms
   ```

   You can now refer to the members of System.Windows.Forms without qualification by namespace. For example, to invoke the Show method of the MessageBox class, you can enter the following:

   ```
   MessageBox.Show ...
   ```

An alternative to importing a namespace is to use an *alias*, which essentially means creating a variable that references the namespace and then using this variable as shorthand to refer to the namespace.

To create an alias for a namespace:

- In a module in the Code Editor, before any code other than Imports statements, use the Imports keyword with the assignment operator (=) to assign a namespace reference to an identifier.

  For example, the following statement creates an alias for the namespace System.Windows.Forms using the identifier swf:

  ```
  Imports swf = System.Windows.Forms
  ```

  A class member contained in the System.Windows.Forms namespace can now be invoked using the swf alias—for example:

  ```
  swf.MessageBox.Show _
     ("You say Hello", _
     "I say Goodbye", _
     swf.MessageBoxButtons.OK)
  ```

Now that you've seen how to reference assemblies and use the namespaces contained in those assemblies, it's time to create your own namespaces.

To create a nested namespace:

1. Within the class module of the Class Library project created in "To import a namespace," delete all code except the statement that creates an alias for the System.Windows.Forms namespace.
2. Use the Namespace and End Namespace keywords to create the namespace YouSay:

```
Namespace YouSay


End Namespace
```

3. Within the YouSay Namesapce, use the Namespace and End Namespace keywords to create the namespace Hello:

```
Namespace YouSay
   Namespace Hello


   End Namespace
End Namespace
```

4. Within the Hello Namesapce, use the Namespace and End Namespace keywords to create the namespace ISay:

```
Namespace YouSay
   Namespace Hello
      Namespace ISay


      End Namespace
   End Namespace
End Namespace
```

5. Within the ISay Namesapce, use the Namespace and End Namespace keywords to create the namespace GoodBye:

```
Namespace YouSay
   Namespace Hello
      Namespace ISay
         Namespace GoodBye


         End Namespace
      End Namespace
   End Namespace
End Namespace
```

6. Within the GoodBye Namesapce, create a public class named Greeting containing a ForYou method :

```
Namespace YouSay
   Namespace Hello
      Namespace ISay
         Namespace GoodBye
            Public Class Greeting
               Sub ForYou()


               End Sub
            End Class
         End Namespace
      End Namespace
   End Namespace
End Namespace
```

7. Implement the ForYou method using the Show method of the MessageBox class:

```
Sub ForYou()
   swf.MessageBox.Show _
      ("You say Hello", _
      "I say Goodbye", _
      swf.MessageBoxButtons.OK)
End Sub
```

NAMESPACES

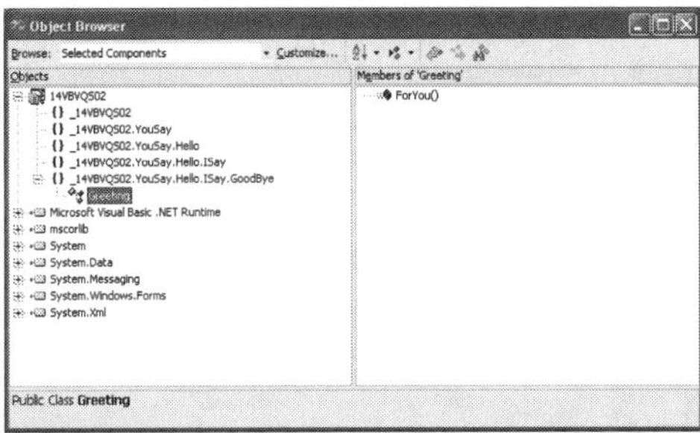

Figure 14.24 The Object Browser shows nested namespaces and the single class.

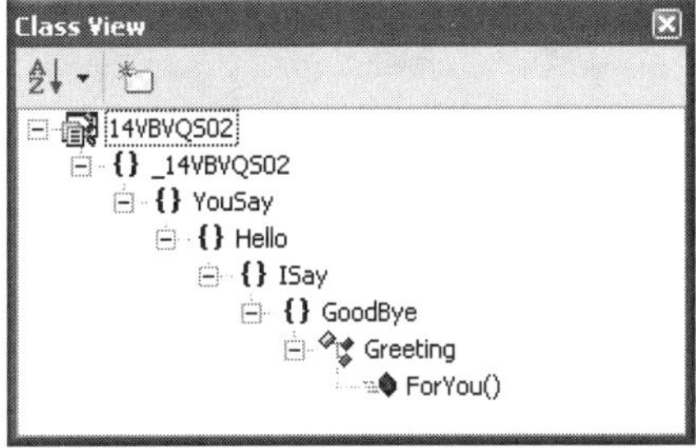

Figure 14.25 Class View provides another way of displaying the same information presented by the Object Browser.

Listing 14.1 shows the complete code for the class and member within nested namespaces.

8. Open the Object Browser (as explained earlier in this chapter) to look at the nested namespaces and the class and member (**Figure 14.24**).

   Note that _14VBVQS02, shown as the root namespace in Figure 14.24, is the default name for the root namespace, since the project is named 14VBVQS02.

9. From the Visual Studio View menu, choose Class View to see the namespace information presented visually in a different way (**Figure 14.25**).

   Unlike the Object Browser, the Class View tool can be used to inspect the namespaces and classes only in the current project.

Listing 14.1 Embedding a class deep within namespaces and calling a class method from an external project.

```
Imports swf = System.Windows.Forms
Namespace YouSay
   Namespace Hello
      Namespace ISay
         Namespace GoodBye
            Public Class Greeting
               Sub ForYou()
                  swf.MessageBox.Show("You say Hello", "I say Goodbye", swf.MessageBoxButtons.OK)
               End Sub
            End Class
         End Namespace
      End Namespace
   End Namespace
End Namespace

Private Sub btnHello_Click(ByVal sender As System.Object, ByVal e As System.EventArgs) _
   Handles btnHello.Click
   Dim x As New _14VBVQS02.YouSay.Hello.ISay.GoodBye.Greeting()
   x.ForYou()
End Sub
```

As a final step toward understanding nested namespaces, let's invoke the ForYou method of the Greeting class from an external project.

To invoke a member of a nested namespace externally:

1. With the solution containing the Class Library project that includes the namespaces and the Greeting class open, choose Build from the Visual Studio Build menu to compile the class library into a component (DLL) file.
2. Close the solution that contains the Greeting class.
3. Open a different .NET project, such as a Windows Application project.
4. As described in "To add a reference to an assembly" earlier in this chapter, open the Add Reference dialog.
5. Click the Browse button.
6. Use the Select Component dialog to locate and select the compiled library file that contains the namespaces and the Greeting class (**Figure 14.26**).
7. Click Open.

   The library file is added to the Selected Components pane of the Add Reference dialog (**Figure 14.27**).
8. Click OK.
9. Use the Toolbox to add a Button control to the Windows form contained in the Windows application.
10. Use the Properties window to change the value of the Text property of the Button control to `Hello` and the name of the Button to `btnHello` (**Figure 14.28**).

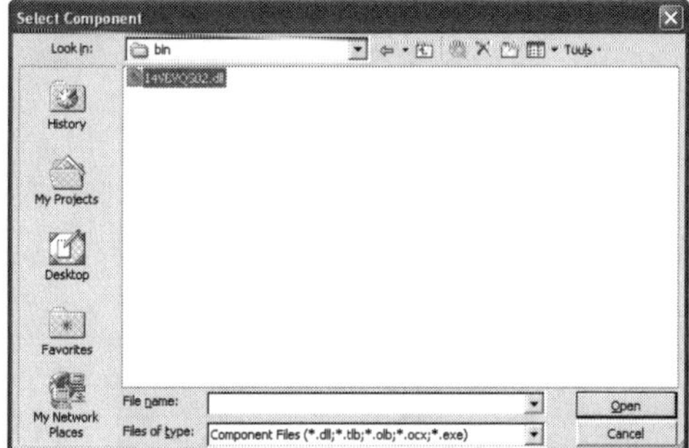

Figure 14.26 The library file containing the nested classes can be selected as a component.

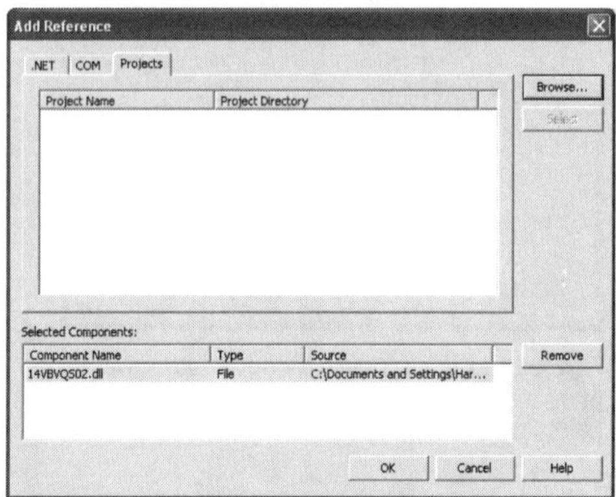

Figure 14.27 The library file has been added to the Selected Components pane of the Add Reference dialog.

Figure 14.28 A button is added (its click event will be used to reference the external library file).

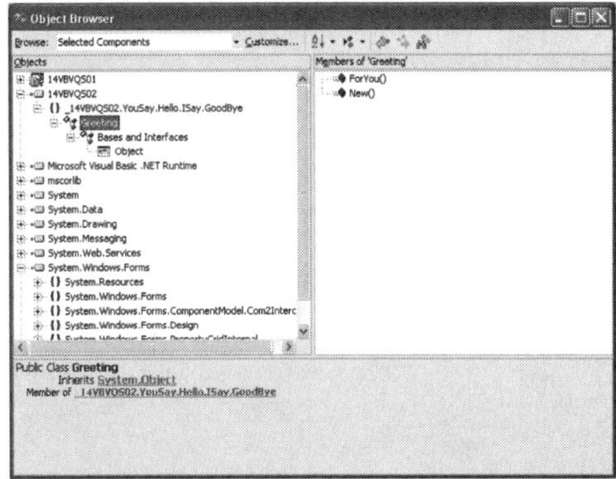

Figure 14.29 The Object browser shows the external component's nested namespaces, class, and member.

```
Private Sub btnHello_Click(ByVal sender As System.Object, _
    ByVal e As System.EventArgs) Handles btnHello.Click
    Dim x As New _14VBVQS02.YouSay.Hello.ISay.GoodBye.
    x.ForYou()                                    Greeting
End Sub
```

Figure 14.30 The auto-completion feature of the Code Editor supplies the class within the nested namespaces.

Figure 14.31 An object created from the external class correctly displays a message box.

11. Double-click the Hello button to create an event procedure for it in the Code Editor:

    ```
    Private Sub btnHello_Click _
        (ByVal sender As System.Object, _
        ByVal e As System.EventArgs) _
        Handles btnHello.Click

    End Sub
    ```

12. Open the Object Browser to inspect the namespaces and classes available to your code in the external library project (**Figure 14.29**).

13. Within the Hello event handler, declare a variable, x, as a new instance of the Greeting class; note that auto-completion in the Code Editor will correctly supply the class name after you provide the nested namespace identifiers (**Figure 14.30**).

    ```
    Dim x As New _
    _14VBVQS02.YouSay.Hello.ISay. _
    GoodBye.Greeting()
    ```

14. Invoke the ForYou method of the Greeting class instance:

    ```
    x.ForYou()
    ```

    Listing 14.1 shows the complete code for the Hello event handler, using a method of a class in nested namespaces in an external assembly.

15. Run the project.

16. Click Hello.

    The message box specified by the ForYou method appears (**Figure 14.31**).

Important .NET Namespaces

The Object Browser is a marvelous tool for learning about the .NET Framework namespaces and the objects and object members that comprise these namespaces. Now that you know how to use the Object Browser, why not spend some time using it to learn about .NET?

If you decide to follow this suggestion, you can start by inspecting the classes, interfaces, and structures that belong to the namespaces shown in **Table 14.3**, which are likely to be those that are most important to VB .NET programmers.

Table 14.3

Important .NET Namespaces

Namespace	Description
Microsoft.VisualBasic	This namespace contains the Visual Basic runtime and the classes that support compilation and code generation using the VB language. Classes used for backward compatibility with VB6 are also provided in this namespace.
System	Contains fundamental classes that define types, arrays, strings, events, event handlers, exceptions, interfaces, data-type conversion, mathematics, application environment management, and much more.
System.Collections	Includes a set of classes that you can use to manage collections of objects, such as lists, queues, arrays, hash tables, and dictionaries.
System.Data	Consists mainly of the classes that comprise the ADO.NET architecture, used for managing access to data sources as explained in Chapter 15, "XML, Data, and ADO.NET."
System.Diagnostics	Provides classes for debugging, tracing, and interacting with system processes, event logs, and performance counters.
System.Drawing	Contains classes that provide access to graphics functionality.
System.IO	Contains types and classes for reading and writing to data streams and files and for general input/output (I/O) functionality.
System.Reflection	Contains classes and interfaces that provide type inspection and the ability to dynamically bind objects.
System.Text	Contains classes for encoding characters, converting blocks of characters to and from blocks of bytes, and more.
System.Text.RegularExpressions	Contains classes that provide access to the .NET Framework regular expression engine.
System.Timer	Provides the Timer component (see Chapter 11, "The Timer Component," for more information).
System.Web	Contains classes used to facilitate browser-server communication and other Web-related functionality.
System.Web.Services	Contains classes used to build and consume Web services.
System.Web.UI	Provides classes and interfaces used in the creation of the user interface of Web pages and controls.
System.Windows.Forms	Contains classes for creating a Windows-based user interface.
System.XML	Provides classes that support XML processing.

Summary

In this chapter, you learned how to:

- Open the Object Browser
- Use Go To Definition in the Code Editor
- Set the Object Browser's scope
- Describe the items shown in the Members and Objects panes of the Object Browser
- Use the Object Browser toolbar
- View an assembly manifest
- Add a reference to an external assembly
- Import and alias namespaces
- Create a nested namespace
- Invoke a class in a nested namespace located in an external assembly
- List some of the most important .NET Framework namespaces.

XML, DATA, AND ADO.NET

15

XML—short for *eXtensible Markup Language*—is very important "under the hood" to Visual Studio, VB .NET, and the .NET Framework as a technology that facilitates interoperability, configuration, and much more. Think of the crucial role that XML plays in the creation of ASP.NET Web Services, for example (see Chapter 2, "Creating a Web Service," and Chapter 6, "Consuming the Web Service").

Fortunately, the .NET Framework provides myriad classes that make it easy to work with data stored in XML. In this chapter, you'll learn how to perform basic operations that involve XML using VB .NET and the .NET Framework classes.

You'll also learn all about *datasets*. Sometimes called a *data store*, a dataset is a cache of data consisting of relational data tables, usually generated by querying a database. In VB .NET, you can easily convert XML data back and forth to a dataset. DataSet components, used to represent datasets in the .NET Framework, are one of the most important of the .NET Data components, which together make up the .NET data connectivity layer called *ADO.NET*. This layer is used to facilitate interoperability between your programs and a database.

continues on next page

The second half of this chapter shows you the essentials of working with the ADO.NET data connectivity layer. (The more general topic of programming databases is way beyond the scope of this chapter.) Specifically, you'll learn how to use Data components to generate a dataset and *bind* the data contained in the dataset to controls used on a form. A bound control can display data from the source it is bound to, iterate through the data provided by the source, and (if programmed to do so and appropriate permissions are in place) update the data source.

Because working with XML and data in VB .NET can involve a great many classes, controls, and components, this subject may seem complicated. Actually, the mechanics of accomplishing most tasks involving XML and data are pretty easy—and not only that, but they are essential to a great many applications.

Working with XML

XML is a markup language, similar in nature to HTML, meaning that both languages consist of tags that describe content. In contrast to HTML, in which tags have a fixed descriptive meaning and a tag set such as `<h1></h1>` always denotes a level-one header, the tags used in XML are user (or custom) defined.

An XML tag set, such as `<address></address>`, identifies the contents of the tag as an address. You can invent your own XML tags and use them to mark data as you like, provided that the XML is *well-formed*, meaning that it conforms to the rules governing XML tags and documents. (You can find the full technical specifications for XML, which has recently turned five years old as a language, at www.w3c.org/XML/.)

Theoretically, one of the great benefits of XML data documents is that they are readable by both humans and computers.

Essentially, XML tags can be used to describe any structured data, meaning data that is hierarchic and consistently labeled.

But structuring data doesn't help to solve problems unless there is agreement about the structure. For example, a group of suppliers and vendors might agree that the following XML tag set can be used to define a product:

```
<Product ProdID="" ProdType="">
   <Name></Name>
   <Description></Description>
   <Inventor></Inventor>
</Product>
```

Once the agreed-upon definition is in place, the suppliers and vendors (and their computers) can all recognize a product when they see it and understand the information about the product provided by the standardized XML.

Therefore, specialized communities have grown up that have agreed-upon XML structures that are specific to their knowledge domains. For example, dentists and dental-supply businesses might, as a community, define the XML tags they use to communicate. Or a shipping company might specify the XML tags to be used in a manifest.

Abstractly, this kind of structure is called a *taxonomy*. Domain-specific taxonomies are concretely implemented as XML *schemas*. An XML schema, itself written in a form of XML, is used to standardize the structure of XML communication. As long as the XML in a document provides the data for elements (and only the elements) specified in an XML schema, then all participants in a community, be they man or machine, will know what the document is talking about. An XML data document that meets this threshold is said to be *validated* against the schema.

In the five years or so that XML has been around, a number of different schema schemes (!) have been devised. This chapter discusses only XSD schemas, which seem to have become the industry standard. (XSD is a vendor-neutral standard administered by the World Wide Web Consortium; you can find specification details online at www.w3c.org. In .NET, XSD replaces older schema standards such as Document Type Definition, or DTD, and Microsoft's proprietary XDR schema standard.)

Creating XML schemas

Schemas are the heart of XML data and bear the same relationship to the data contained in an XML data file that the tabular structure in a database does to the data stored in a database. (This comparison is literally true, as you'll see later in this chapter.)

Before we explore some of the many ways to create an XML schema in .NET, let's take a quick look at the most important .NET namespaces that contain classes related to XML development, shown in **Table 15.1.**

Table 15.1

XML Namespaces

Namespace	Purpose
System.Xml	Provides primary support for a variety of XML functions.
System.Xml.Schema	Contains the XML classes that provide support for XML Schema Definition (XSD) schemas.
System.Xml.Serialization	Contains the classes used to serialize and deserialize XML and XML schemas to and from the Simple Object Access Protocol (SOAP). SOAP is an open-standard mechanism for wrapping XML and other content so that it can be transmitted over HTTP and is used as a mechanism for invoking methods on a remote server using XML documents.
System.Xml.XPath	Provides an XPath parser and evaluation engine. XML Path Language (XPath) enables you to easily write queries that retrieve particular subsets of XML data.
System.Xml.Xsl	Provides the tools needed to work with eXtensible Stylesheet Language Transformations (XSLT). Essentially, XSLT lets you create templates that can be used to manipulate XML documents into other formats and/or tweak the XML. One use of XSLT is to transform XML into HTML so that it can be rendered in a browser.

Table 15.2

Toolbox Components and Add Submenu Items

Element	Purpose
element	Creates an element, which associates a name with a type. The element can be global, added to other elements, added to groups, or used to construct complexType elements.
attribute	Creates an attribute, which associates a name with a type and is associated with an element or complexType element. Attributes can be global, added to elements, or added to groups.
attributeGroup	Creates an attribute group, or group of attributes, that can be global, added to elements, or used in the construct of complexType elements.
complexType	Creates a complexType element to which you can add elements, attributes, attributeGroup elements, any elements, and anyAttribute elements.
simpleType	Creates a simple type to which you can add facets.
group	Creates groups that can be global and added to other groups, elements, or complexType elements.
any	Creates an any element (meaning any element or sequence of elements from a specified namespace) that can be added to elements, complexType elements, or groups.
anyAttribute	Creates an any attribute element (meaning any attribute element or sequence of attribute elements from a specified namespace) that can be added to elements, attribute groups, or complex types.
facet	Sets limits on the type of content a simpleType element can contain.
key	Launches the Edit Key dialog box, which is used to create keys when added to an element. Keys are the primary fields that tie relations together, and they work the same way in XML as they do in databases (see the sidebar "Understanding Relational Databases" later in this chapter).
Relation	Launches the Edit Relation dialog box, which is used to define relationships between elements.

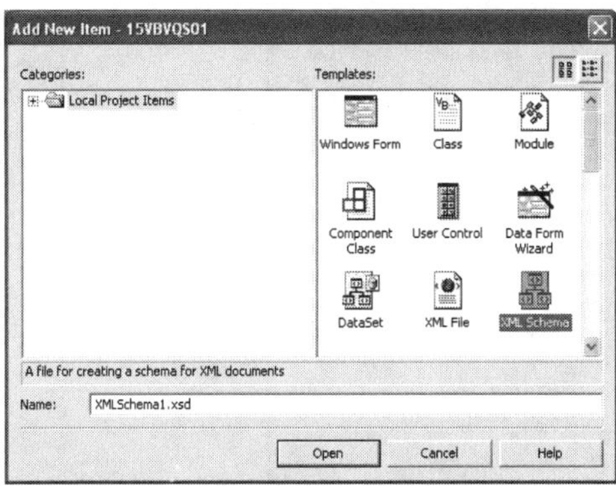

Figure 15.1 To open an XML Schema designer, choose XML Schema from the Add New Item dialog.

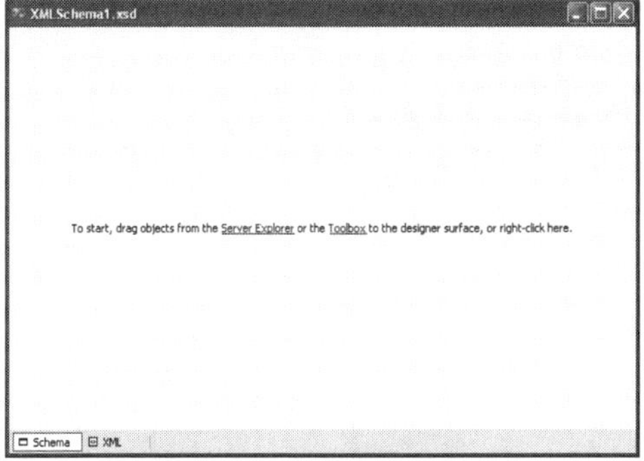

Figure 15.2 The XML Schema designer lets you create an XML schema visually using drag and drop.

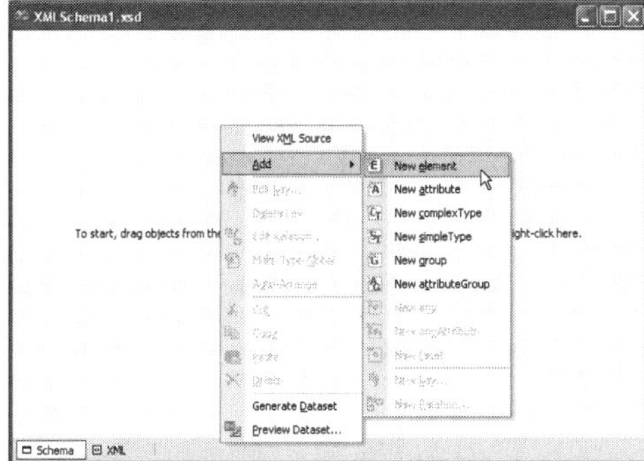

Figure 15.3 The items on the Add context menu are used to add XML schema elements to the XML schema.

You may not know what all the objects in these namespaces do, but you'll know more about them after reading this chapter, and this table will help you if you ever need to find an XML-related class or member using the Object Browser, as described in Chapter 14, "The Object Browser."

To create an XML schema using the XML Schema designer:

1. With a project open in the Visual Studio development environment, choose Add New Item from the Project menu.

   The Add New Item dialog opens (**Figure 15.1**).

2. In the Templates pane of the Add New Item dialog, select XML Schema.

3. Provide a name for the schema (or accept the default name).

4. Click Open.

   The schema opens in the XML Schema designer (**Figure 15.2**).

5. Make sure the Schema tab of the XML Schema designer is selected.

6. Right-click to open the context menu, choose Add, and then select the schema items you want from the Add submenu (**Figure 15.3**).

   Table 15.2 lists the schema items available from the Add submenu.

7. Repeat the process until your schema is complete.

   The schema will appear on the Schema tab in tabular form.

To create an XML schema using Toolbox controls:

1. Follow Steps 1-5 of the previous task.
2. Choose Toolbox from the Visual Studio View menu.

   If the XML Schema designer is active, an XML Schema tab will be available in the Toolbox (**Figure 15.4**).
3. Drag and drop XML schema elements, represented by components on the XML Schema tab of the Toolbox and listed in Table 15.2, to the Schema tab of the XML Schema designer.
4. Repeat the process until your schema is complete.

   The schema will appear on the Schema tab in tabular form.

To create an XML schema manually:

1. Follow Steps 1-4 of "To create an XML schema using the XML Schema designer."
2. Click XML to open the XML tab of the XML Schema designer.
3. Manually enter the XML code that makes up an XSD schema.

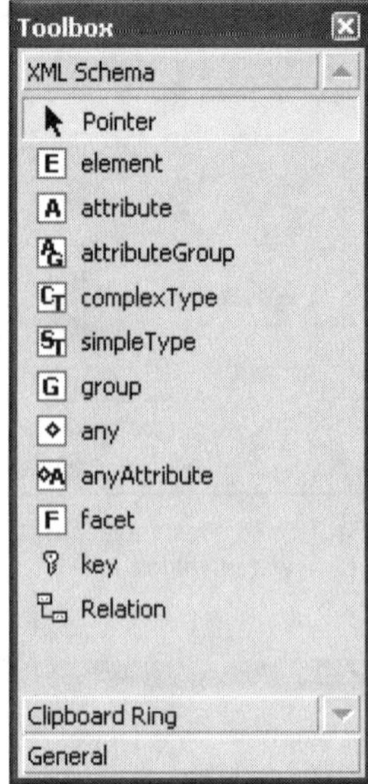

Figure 15.4 When an XML Schema designer is the active window in Visual Studio, schema elements appear as components in the Toolbox.

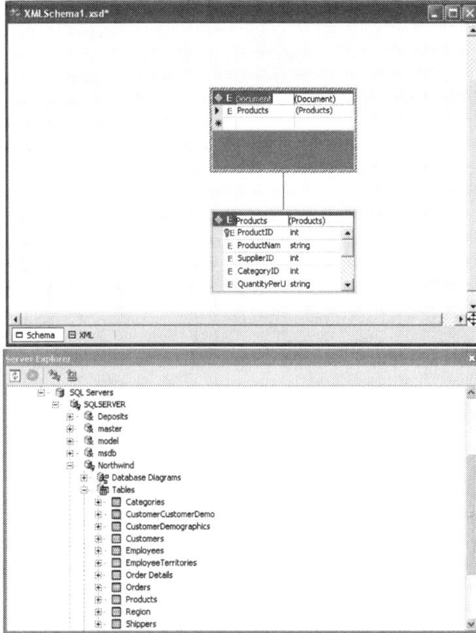

Figure 15.5 You can create an XML schema by dragging a database table from Server Explorer to the XML Schema designer.

To create an XML schema using Server Explorer:

1. Follow Steps 1-5 of "To create an XML schema using the XML Schema designer."
2. Choose Server Explorer from the Visual Studio View menu to open Server Explorer.
3. In Server Explorer, connect to a database.

   Connecting to a database in Server Explorer is explained in detail in "Working with Databases," later in this chapter.
4. Drill down in Server Explorer to locate tables within the database (**Figure 15.5**).
5. Drag and drop the table (or tables) that represent the information structure that you want the XML schema to enforce to the Schema tab of the XML Schema designer.

   As you can see in Figure 15.5, the database tables continue to be represented as tables on the Schema tab.

In addition to the ways just described to create an XML schema using the XML Schema designer, you can create an XML schema based on XML entered in the XML File designer (you'll see how this works later in this chapter in the task "To create an XML schema from an XML file.") An XML schema created in this way can then be opened in the XML Schema designer by double-clicking the newly created XML schema file in Solution Explorer.

Finally, you can also create an XML schema programmatically using the Items collection of the XmlSchema class (part of the System.Xml.Schema namespace). We won't go into the details of this process here, although it works in much the same way as creating XML data in code, explained in "To write an XML data file in code" later in this chapter.

Viewing and validating XML schemas

With an XML schema created using the XML Schema designer, using any of the alternatives in the task "To create an XML schema," you can easily view the XML code that comprises the schema.

To view the XML code that comprises the XML schema:

- With the schema loaded in the XML Schema designer, click the XML tab to view the XML code.

  The XML schema in **Figure 15.6** is the code representation of the structure provided by dragging database tables onto the Schema tab of the XML Schema designer (shown in Figure 15.5).

Validating a schema means checking to see that the schema is well formed. Another way of putting this is to say that a validated schema complies with the rules set forth in the W3C specifications for the XSD schema language. (Recall that XSD is itself a form of XML.) Bear in mind that validating a schema says nothing about any XML data that may (or may not) be valid according to the schema.

```
XMLSchema1.xsd*
<?xml version="1.0" encoding="utf-8" ?>
<xs:schema id="XMLSchema1" targetNamespace="http://tempuri.org/XMLSchema1.xsd" elementFormDefault="qualified" xmlns="ht
  <xs:element name="Document">
    <xs:complexType>
      <xs:choice maxOccurs="unbounded">
        <xs:element name="Products">
          <xs:complexType>
            <xs:sequence>
              <xs:element name="ProductID" msdata:ReadOnly="true" msdata:AutoIncrement="true" type="xs:int" />
              <xs:element name="ProductName" type="xs:string" />
              <xs:element name="SupplierID" type="xs:int" minOccurs="0" />
              <xs:element name="CategoryID" type="xs:int" minOccurs="0" />
              <xs:element name="QuantityPerUnit" type="xs:string" minOccurs="0" />
              <xs:element name="UnitPrice" type="xs:decimal" minOccurs="0" />
              <xs:element name="UnitsInStock" type="xs:short" minOccurs="0" />
              <xs:element name="UnitsOnOrder" type="xs:short" minOccurs="0" />
              <xs:element name="ReorderLevel" type="xs:short" minOccurs="0" />
              <xs:element name="Discontinued" type="xs:boolean" />
            </xs:sequence>
          </xs:complexType>
        </xs:element>
      </xs:choice>
    </xs:complexType>
    <xs:unique name="DocumentKey1" msdata:PrimaryKey="true">
      <xs:selector xpath=".//mstns:Products" />
      <xs:field xpath="mstns:ProductID" />
    </xs:unique>
  </xs:element>
</xs:schema>
Schema  XML
```

Figure 15.6 The XML code that constitutes the XML schema is shown on the XML tab of the XML Schema designer.

Validating a schema is something like saying about program code that it contains no syntax errors. This is a good thing, but it doesn't tell you that the schema will enforce the taxonomy that it is supposed to enforce.

To validate an XML schema:

1. With a schema loaded in the XML Schema designer, click the XML tab so that the XML code comprising the schema is visible.
2. From the Visual Studio Schema menu, choose Validate.

   By the way, in case you've never seen a Visual Studio Schema menu before and are wondering, the Schema menu appears along the Visual Studio top menu bar only when an XML Schema designer is active in the development environment.
3. If validation problems occur, the Task List opens with a list of the issues (**Figure 15.7**). Click an item in the Task List to go to the offending XSD statement on the XML tab of the XML Schema designer.

   If the Task List does not open and no message appears, your schema is in fine shape and has no validation problems.

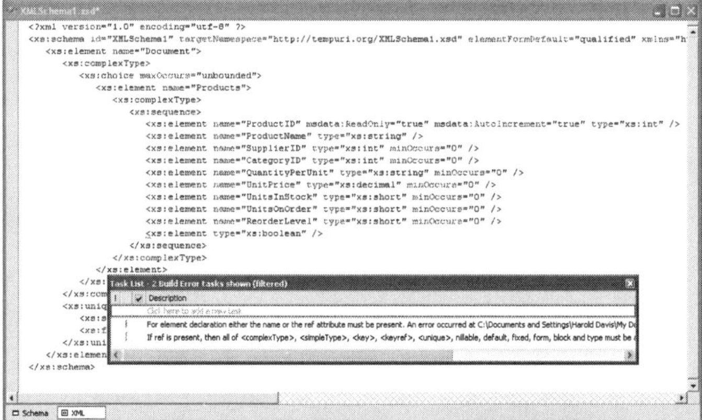

Figure 15.7 By validating an XML schema, you can determine if it is well-formed, and if not, what the problems are.

Working with XML files

In Visual Studio, you can use an XML file to create XML tags and to add data to the tags.

To open an XML file:

1. Choose Add New Item from the Visual Studio Project menu.
   The Add New Item dialog opens.
2. In the Templates pane of the Add New Item dialog, select XML File (**Figure 15.8**).
3. Provide a name for the XML file (or accept the default name).
4. Click Open.
   The XML file opens in its designer with the XML tab selected (**Figure 15.9**).

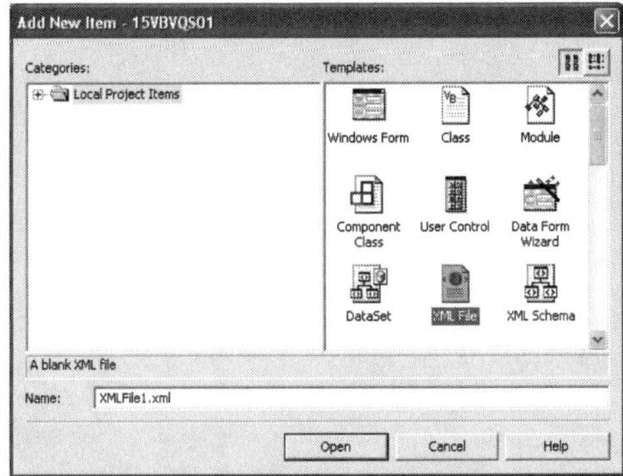

Figure 15.8 To open an XML File designer, choose XML File from the Add New Item dialog.

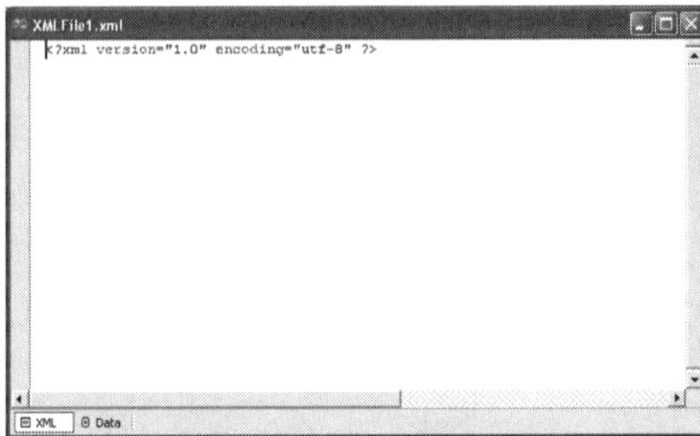

Figure 15.9 When you open the XML tab on the XML File designer, it will be empty other than the XML declaration.

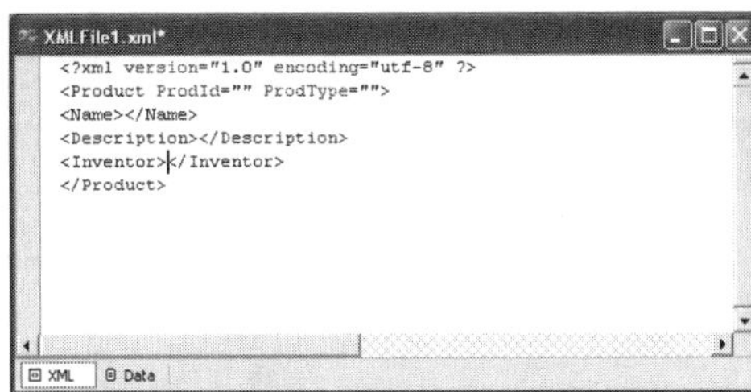

Figure 15.10 You can use the XML tab of the XML File designer to add an XML element using XML code.

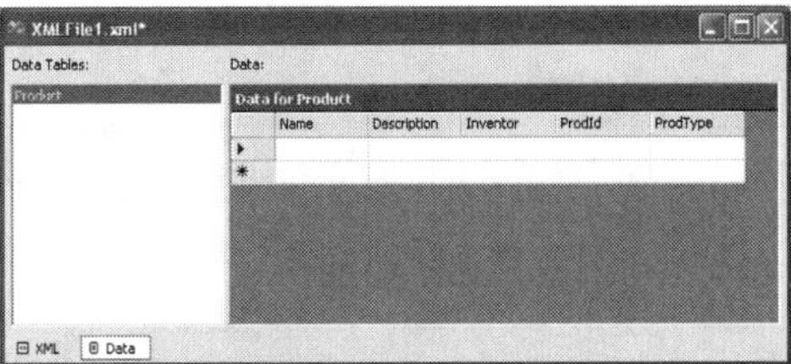

Figure 15.11 With the structure of an XML element in place, you can add XML data in tabular form using the Data tab of the XML File designer.

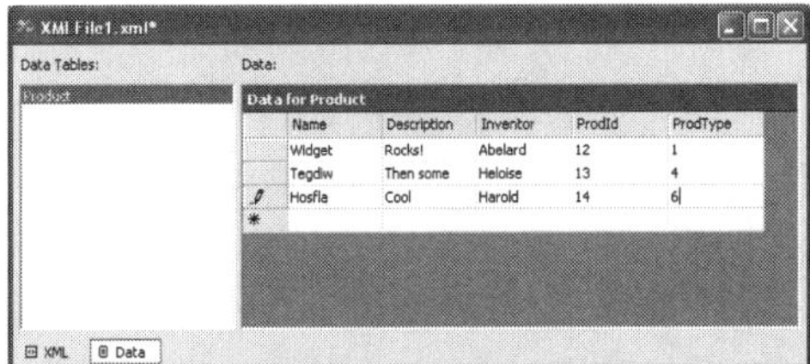

Figure 15.12 You can enter as many rows as you like using the Data tab of the XML File designer.

Figure 15.13 Data entered in the tables on the Data tab of the XML File designer is automatically rendered as XML code on the XML tab of the XML File designer.

The XML file created in the preceding task contains neither XML nor data. (As you can see in Figure 15.9, it does provide an XML comment at the top of the designer.) Thus, the next step is to add some XML, and the related data, to the XML File designer.

To add data to an XML file:

1. With an XML file open in its designer, make sure the XML tab is active as shown in Figure 15.9.
2. Type some XML tags, such as those shown in **Figure 15.10**.
3. Click Data, located at the bottom of the dialog, to open the Data tab of the XML File designer.

   The Data tab displays the XML tag structure entered on the XML tab in tabular form (**Figure 15.11**).
4. Enter as many rows of information as you like in the table or tables on the Data tab of the XML File designer (**Figure 15.12**).
5. When you are through entering data, click XML to reopen the XML tab of the XML File designer.

   The data you entered in the tables will be present as well-formed XML surrounded by the appropriate tags (**Figure 15.13**).

Once you have an XML file with data and XML, you can use it to create an XML schema. The point of creating a schema is to create a template that can be used to enforce standards in other XML documents.

To create an XML schema from an XML file:

- With an XML file containing XML and data active in its designer, choose Create Schema from the Visual Studio XML menu or from the XML File designer's context menu.

  The newly created XML schema appears in Solution Explorer (**Figure 15.14**) and can be opened in its designer. **Figure 15.15** shows the Schema tab of the generated XML schema, and **Figure 15.16** shows the XML tab.

✔ Tip

- You won't see the XML menu on the top Visual Studio menu bar unless an XML file is active in its designer.

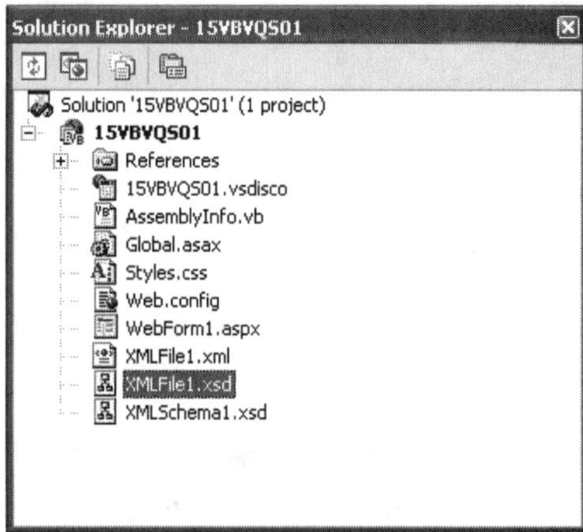

Figure 15.14 The XML schema file generated by Visual Studio appears in Solution Explorer.

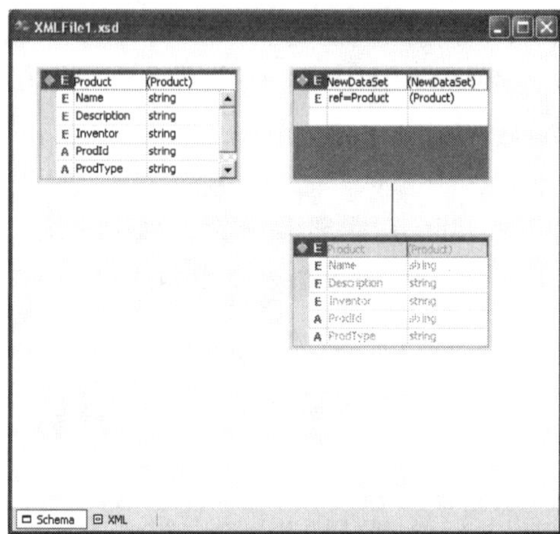

Figure 15.15 The XML schema that was generated appears in tabular form on the Schema tab of the XML Schema designer.

Figure 15.16 The generated schema appears as XML on the XML tab of the XML Schema designer.

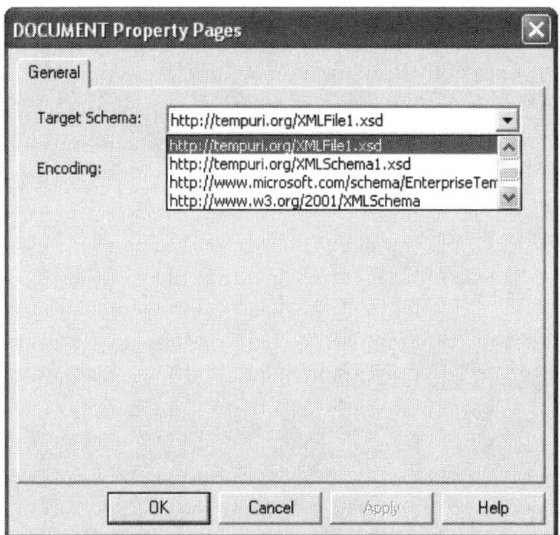

Figure 15.17 You can use the Property Pages dialog for the XML data file to change the target schema that the data file is run against.

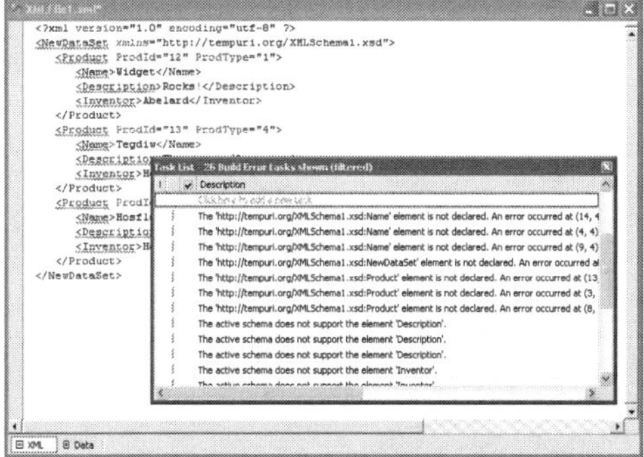

Figure 15.18 If the data in an XML data file does not match the schema specified, the validation errors for the data file are displayed in the Task List.

✔ Tip

- You won't see the XML menu on the top Visual Studio menu bar unless an XML file is active in its designer.

The *target* schema for an XML document is the schema that the XML in the document should adhere to. You can easily change the target XML schema for an XML file.

To assign an XML schema to an XML file:

1. With the XML file active in its designer, right-click to open its context menu.
2. Choose Properties from the context menu.

   The Property Pages dialog for the XML file opens (**Figure 15.17**).
3. In the Property Pages dialog for the XML file, choose a target schema from the Target Schema drop-down list as shown in Figure 15.17.
4. Click OK.

Validating an XML file against a target XML schema indicates that the XML and data in the XML file do, in fact, adhere to the schema specifications in the XML schema. This kind of validation should be viewed as more meaningful than validation of an XML schema, which merely checks whether the schema is well formed.

To validate an XML file against an XML schema:

1. Open an XML file in its designer.
2. Make sure that the XML schema is assigned as the target schema for the XML file, as explained in the preceding task, "To assign an XML schema to an XML file."
3. Choose Validate XML Data from the Visual Studio XML menu.

   If there are no validation errors, you'll see no messages. If validation problems do occur, they will be displayed in the Task List (**Figure 15.18**).
4. Click an item in the Task List to go to any validation problem in the XML file.

Writing and reading XML using VB .NET code

As you might suppose, all of the operations we've discussed so far in this chapter—creating XML schemas and files, validating, and so on—can be accomplished in code using the classes that are part of the XML namespaces listed in Table 15.1. We won't examine how to do all of these things programmatically because that would take too much space. Instead, we'll discuss how to write, and then read, an XML data file programmatically. (Writing comes before reading because it is useful to have written something to read!)

Writing and reading an XML data file programmatically is an important task that you may need to undertake in the real world. In addition, once you've learned how to read and write XML using VB .NET code, you'll probably have a pretty good sense of how to go about other XML-related tasks programmatically.

To create the user interface for writing and reading XML:

1. Open a new Windows application form.
2. Use the Toolbox to add a TextBox control to accept the name of an XML element.
3. Use the Properties window to set the name of the TextBox control to `txtElement` and its Text property to the empty string.
4. Use the Toolbox to add a TextBox control to accept the value of the XML element.
5. Use the Properties window to set the name of the TextBox control to `txtValue` and its Text property to the empty string.

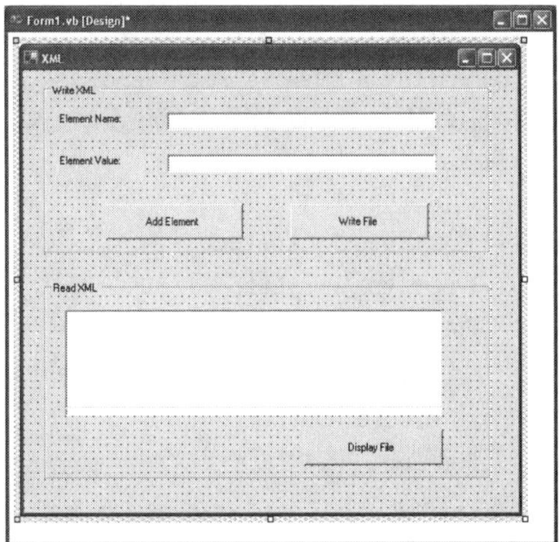

Figure 15.19 The Windows form user interface allows the user to enter XML elements names and values.

6. Use the Toolbox to add a TextBox control to display the XML that the application will read.
7. Use the Properties window to set the name of the TextBox control to `txtDislay`, its Multiline property to True, and its Text property to the empty string.
8. Use the Toolbox to add Label controls to identify the purpose of the TextBox controls.
9. Use the Properties window to set the values of the Text properties of the Label controls.
10. Use the Toolbox to add a Button control.
11. Use the Properties window to name the Button control `btnAdd` and set the value of its Text property to `Add Element`.
12. Use the Toolbox to add a Button control.
13. Use the Properties window to name the Button control `btnWrite` and set the value of its Text property to `Write File`.
14. Use the Toolbox to add a Button control.
15. Use the Properties window to name the Button control `btnDisplay` and set the value of its Text property to `Display File`.

    The completed user interface should look similar to the one shown in the Form designer in **Figure 15.19**.

Next, I'll show you one good way to write XML data to a file. This process involves a number of steps:

- Creating an XML collecton class
- Adding XML elements to an XML collection object based on the collection class
- Finally, saving the XML elements in the XML collection to a file on disk.

To create an XML collection class:

1. With the Windows form created in the previous task, choose Code from the Visual Studio View menu to open the Code Editor with the Form class code.
2. In the Code Editor, at the top of the Form class module, add an Imports statement to import the System.Collections and the System.Xml namespaces:

```
Imports System.Collections, _
   System.Xml
```

3. At the bottom of the Form class module, below the End Class statement, create a class designed to store an XML element-value pair:

```
Public Class XmlElement
   Public theElement As String
   Public theValue As String
End Class
```

4. Below the XmlElement class, create a collection class, derived from the ArrayList class, designed to be used as a collection of XmlElement objects:

```
Public Class XmlCollect
   Inherits ArrayList
   Public Overloads Sub Add _
      (ByVal anElement As XmlElement)
      MyBase.Add(anElement)
   End Sub
End Class
```

Listing 15.1 shows the complete code for the XmlElement class and the related collection class. For more about collection classes, see "Collection Classes" in Chapter 8, "Creating MDI Applications."

Listing 15.1 The XML element and collection classes.

```
Public Class XmlElement
   Public theElement As String
   Public theValue As String
End Class

Public Class XmlCollect
   Inherits ArrayList
   Public Overloads Sub Add(ByVal anElement As XmlElement)
      MyBase.Add(anElement)
   End Sub
End Class
```

To add text-value XML pairs to the collection class:

1. At the Form class level, declare an instance of the XML collection class:
   ```
   Dim myXml As XmlCollect
   ```
2. In the New constructor for the Form class, instantiate an object, myXml, based on the XmlCollect class:
   ```
   Public Sub New()
      MyBase.New()
      InitializeComponent()
      myXml = New XmlCollect()
   End Sub
   ```
3. In the form designer, double-click the Add Element button to create a click event handler for it:
   ```
   Private Sub btnAdd_Click  _
      (ByVal sender As System.Object, _
      ByVal e As System.EventArgs) _
      Handles btnAdd.Click

   End Sub
   ```
4. Within the click event handler, add code that adds a name-value XML pair to the XML collection class:
   ```
   Dim myElement As New XmlElement()
   myElement.theElement = _
      txtElement.Text
   myElement.theValue = txtValue.Text
   myXml.Add(myElement)
   ```
5. Clear the TextBox controls so the user can more easily enter the next text-value pair:
   ```
   txtElement.Text = String.Empty
   txtValue.Text = String.Empty
   ```
   Listing 15.2 on the next page shows the complete code for adding text-value XML pairs to the XmlCollect class.

Listing 15.2 Adding XML elements and writing and reading XML documents.

```
Imports System.Collections, System.Xml
Public Class Form1
   Inherits System.Windows.Forms.Form
...
Public Sub New()
   MyBase.New()
   InitializeComponent()
   myXml = New XmlCollect()
End Sub
...
Dim myXml As XmlCollect
Dim fn As String = Application.StartupPath & "\myXml.xml"

Private Sub btnAdd_Click(ByVal sender As System.Object, ByVal e As System.EventArgs) _
   Handles btnAdd.Click
   Dim myElement As New XmlElement()
   myElement.theElement = txtElement.Text
   myElement.theValue = txtValue.Text
   myXml.Add(myElement)
   txtElement.Text = String.Empty
   txtValue.Text = String.Empty
End Sub

Private Sub btnWrite_Click(ByVal sender As System.Object, ByVal e As System.EventArgs) _
   Handles btnWrite.Click
   Dim myXmlTextWriter As New XmlTextWriter(fn, Nothing)
   myXmlTextWriter.Formatting = Formatting.Indented
   myXmlTextWriter.Indentation = 4
   myXmlTextWriter.IndentChar = Chr(10)
   myXmlTextWriter.WriteStartDocument()
   myXmlTextWriter.WriteComment("This is a programmatically generated XML document. Enjoy!")
   myXmlTextWriter.WriteStartElement("MyXml")
   Dim myElement As XmlElement
   For Each myElement In myXml
      myXmlTextWriter.WriteElementString (myElement.theElement, myElement.theValue)
   Next
   myXmlTextWriter.WriteEndElement()
   myXmlTextWriter.Close()
End Sub

Private Sub btnDisplay_Click(ByVal sender As System.Object, ByVal e As System.EventArgs) _
   Handles btnDisplay.Click
   Dim myXmlTextReader As New XmlTextReader(fn)
   myXmlTextReader.ReadStartElement("MyXml")
   Do While myXmlTextReader.Read()
      If myXmlTextReader.Name = "MyXml" Then Exit Do
      txtDisplay.Text += ControlChars.CrLf & myXmlTextReader.ReadOuterXml
   Loop
   myXmlTextReader.Close()
End Sub
```

To save the XML elements in the XML collection to a file:

1. At the Form class level, create a string variable, fn, and assign the application's executable path and a hard-coded file name to it:

   ```
   Dim fn As String = _
      Application.StartupPath & _
      "\myXml.xml"
   ```

   In a real-world application, you'd probably allow the user to choose a file name and location, as explained in Chapter 13, "The Common Dialog Controls," rather than hard coding this information.

2. In the Form designer, double-click the Write File button to create a click event handler for it:

   ```
   Private Sub btnWrite_Click  _
      (ByVal sender As System.Object, _
      ByVal e As System.EventArgs) _
      Handles btnWrite.Click

   End Sub
   ```

3. Within the click event handler, create a XmlTextWriter object based on the hard-coded file name:

   ```
   Dim myXmlTextWriter As New _
      XmlTextWriter(fn, Nothing)
   ```

   The XmlTextWriter class works in much the same way as the StreamWriter class explained in Chapter 13, except that the XmlTextWriter class is optimized for use with XML.

continues on next page

4. Set a variety of formatting properties of XmlTextWriter and hard-code the root XML element so that it is named MyXml:

```
myXmlTextWriter.Formatting = _
   Formatting.Indented
myXmlTextWriter.Indentation = 4
myXmlTextWriter.IndentChar = Chr(10)
myXmlTextWriter.WriteStartDocument()
myXmlTextWriter.WriteComment _
   ("This is a programmatically " & _
   "generated XML document. Enjoy!")
myXmlTextWriter.WriteStartElement _
   ("MyXml")
```

   Fortunately, the auto-completion feature in the Code Editor is available to help fill in these properties and to let you know their possible values (**Figure 15.20**).

5. Cycle through the elements in the XmlCollect collection and write each name-value pair to the file:

```
Dim myElement As XmlElement
For Each myElement In myXml
 myXmlTextWriter.WriteElementString _
   (myElement.theElement, _
   myElement.theValue)
Next
```

6. Close the XML element and XmlTextWriter:

```
myXmlTextWriter.WriteEndElement()
myXmlTextWriter.Close()
```

   Listing 15.2 shows the complete code for writing the XML file.

7. Run the project.

8. Enter a name-value pair (**Figure 15.21**) and click.

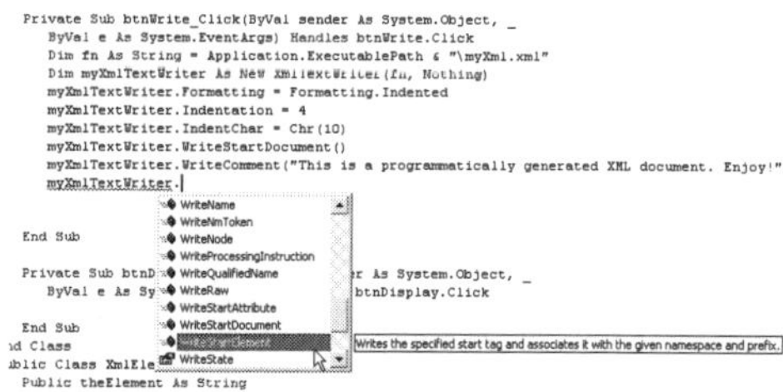

Figure 15.20 As usual, the Code Editor's auto-completion feature helps you navigate through the complex ocean of XML-related classes and members.

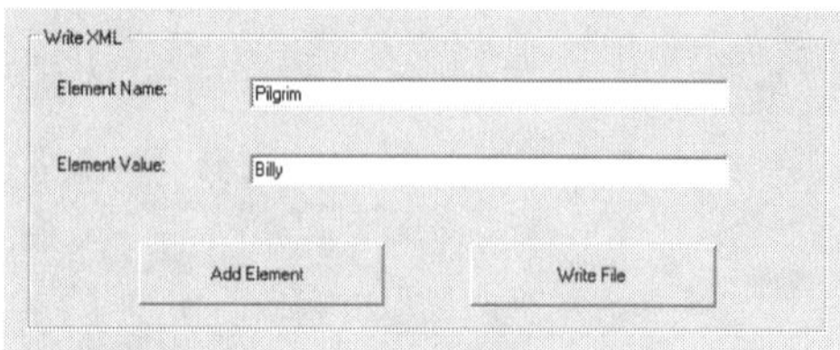

Figure 15.21 The user can add XML element name and value pairs.

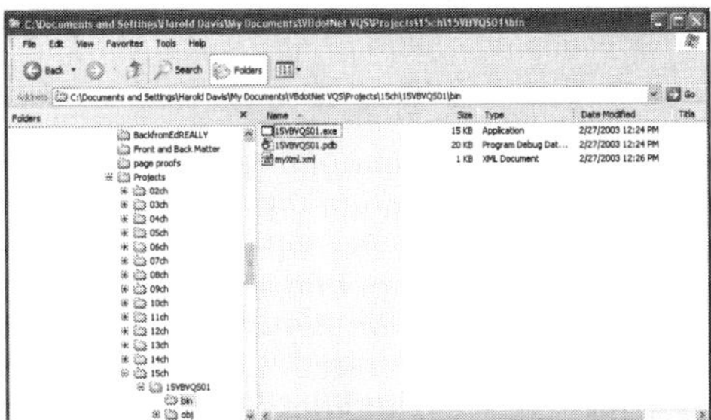

Figure 15.22 The XML file that was created appears in Windows Explorer.

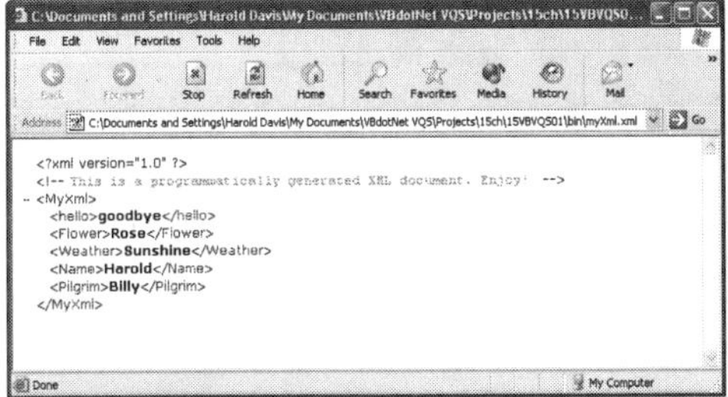

Figure 15.23 The XML file can be opened in Internet Explorer.

9. Click Add Element.
10. Repeat the process to add a number of elements.
11. Click Write File.
12. Use Windows Explorer to verify that the file was written (**Figure 15.22**).
13. Double-click the file to open it in your system's default XML editor (likely Internet Explorer, as shown in **Figure 15.23**) and verify that the XML elements have been correctly added.

Of course, you need to be able to read XML elements as well as write them. Here's how.

To read an XML data file in code:

1. With the form used for the user interface for writing and reading XML open in its designer, double-click the Display button to create a click event handler for it in the Code Editor:

```
Private Sub btnDisplay_Click _
   (ByVal sender As System.Object, _
   ByVal e As System.EventArgs) _
   Handles btnDisplay.Click


End Sub
```

2. Within the click event, create an XmlTextReader object using the hard-coded file:

```
Dim myXmlTextReader As New _
   XmlTextReader(fn)
```

The XmlTextReader object works much like the StreamReader object, explained in Chapter 13.

continues on next page

3. Provide XmlTextReader with the name of the root XML element:

```
myXmlTextReader.ReadStartElement _
   ("MyXml")
```

4. Loop through the file, adding each element to the value of the Text property of the Display TextBox control:

```
Do While myXmlTextReader.Read()
   If myXmlTextReader.Name = _
      "MyXml" Then Exit Do
   txtDisplay.Text += _
      ControlChars.CrLf & _
      myXmlTextReader.ReadOuterXml
Loop
```

5. Close XmlTextReader:

```
myXmlTextReader.Close()
```

   Listing 15.2 shows the complete code for reading the XML file

6. Run the project.

7. Click Display File and verify that the XML elements that were written to the file are correctly displayed (**Figure 15.24**).

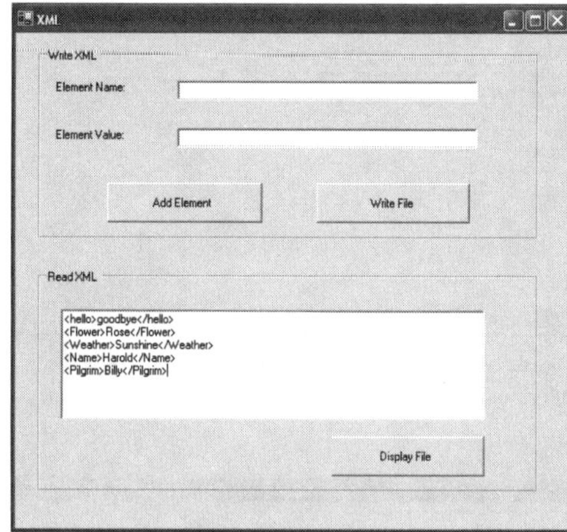

Figure 15.24 The text box displays the XML name and value pairs entered by the user.

Working with Databases

Ultimately, all programs of any sophistication require access to stored data. This access can be accomplished in ways ranging from reading and saving information in files to interacting with sophisticated database programs.

Without the ability to work with stored values, your program has no memory from one time it is run to the next. Programs that handle tasks such as managing inventory or handling accounting chores must be able to save their work—and pick up where they left off.

Sure, you could use files and the file system as a mechanism for your data storage and retrieval needs. But as your applications get more complicated, this becomes an increasingly complex proposition, particularly when you need sophisticated ways to guarantee the security, integrity, and performance of the data management solution. There's a general rule that says if existing commercial software can do something, you are better off buying it than building your own. Since database management software exists, and is, indeed, very good at its job, you can bet dollars to donuts that if you write professional software, it will end up interacting with a database.

In this section, you'll learn the essentials of working with the tools provided by Visual Studio and VB .NET for manipulating the data connectivity layer of the .NET Framework. As mentioned in the introduction to this chapter, this data connectivity layer is called ADO.NET.

There is some confusion about exactly what ADO stands for. Each new version of Microsoft's development platform has shipped with a new model for its data connectivity layer, each with a new acronym, and ADO is the latest in this progression. If thinking that the letters *A, D,* and *O* stand for ActiveX data objects helps you remember what ADO is, then go ahead and do so—although Microsoft has denied that the letters stand for anything specific, and "ActiveX" is no longer in Microsoft's marketing lexicon.

Programming, and even just working with, databases is a big topic, or rather, topics. Indeed, some of these topics—for instance, ADO.NET, programming databases, administering databases, and SQL—easily merit entire separate books. So understand that the tasks and explanations in this section will only get you started on the road to incorporating database interactions into your applications.

As discussed in detail later in this section, ADO.NET ships with two *managed providers*. These managed providers are the heart of ADO.NET, and one of the two is specifically intended to work with Microsoft's enterprise database product, SQL Server. (The other managed provider that ships is generally intended for the rest of the databases out there.) Essentially, this means that SQL Server is the native database for .NET programming. Therefore, the examples in this chapter are based on working with a SQL Server database. But don't worry if you don't have SQL Server installed; you work with the ADO.NET connectivity layer in much the same way no matter what database you use (although class and component names change). And if you don't have access to a database server at all, I'll show you how to open an Access database file so that you can use to learn how to program a database connectivity layer. (Access database files are present on almost any Windows system that has an installed copy of Microsoft Office.)

Understanding Relational Databases

The most important thing to know about databases is that they are organized in tables. Each table contains rows and columns, called *fields*, of information. A row across a table is called a *record*.

Each table usually contains a primary key, which is used to uniquely identify records. In other words, within a table, the value of a primary key cannot be duplicated across records. For example, a primary key might be a social security number, an e-mail address, or some other unique identifier. An example of a poorly chosen primary key would be a customer's last name, as duplication is possible (two people can have the same last name).

In addition to primary keys, *foreign keys*, which do not need to be unique, are used to establish relationships between the data in tables. For example, suppose you have a Customers table in which cust_ID is the primary key. You could also have an Orders table in which the same cust_ID showed up several times as a foreign key because one customer made multiple orders. (This is called a *one-to-many* relationship.)

Data organized in this fashion in independent tables is called *relational*. The software used to contain it is, logically, a *relational database*. Structured Query Language (SQL) is the common language used to manipulate and retrieve information stored in relational databases.

Good database architecture funnels data access through special programs internal to the database, written in an internal, database-specific language intended for this purpose, called *stored procedures*. While stored procedures are far beyond the scope of this chapter, as is SQL, you should know that, from the viewpoint of a VB .NET program, what you want to do to a database is either execute SQL statements against it or run a stored procedure in the database (in large part, the stored procedure itself executes SQL).

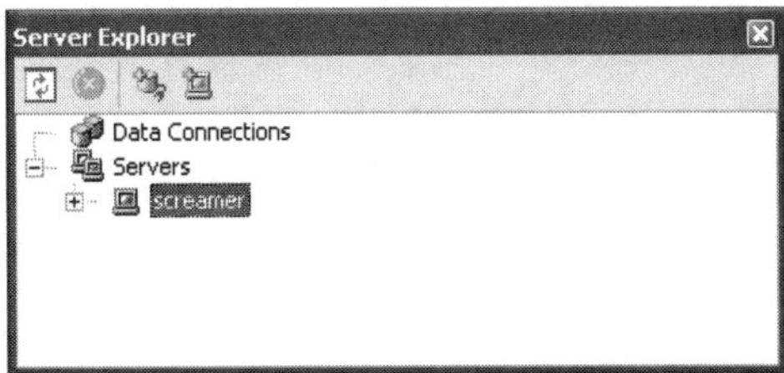

Figure 15.25 Server Explorer shows the servers that are currently connected to the system that is hosting the Visual Studio development environment.

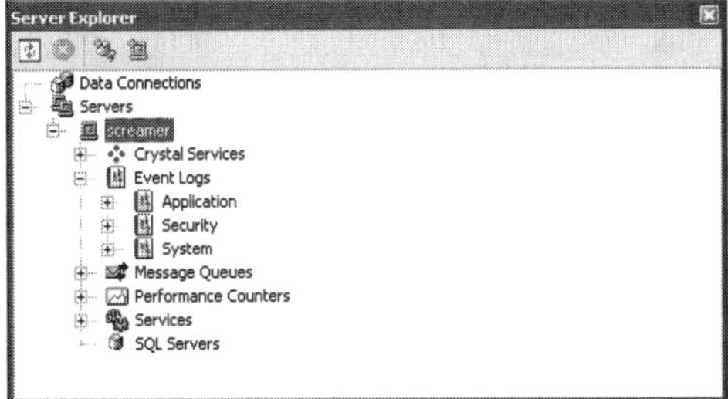

Figure 15.26 Expanding the nodes in Server Explorer provides access to a variety of server functionality.

Server Explorer is a visual interface used in Visual Studio to make it easier to connect to servers, such as database servers, conduct discovery (meaning, find out about the structure and content of information provided) in relation to the database servers, and perform simple tasks with database servers. For example, you saw earlier in this chapter how Server Explorer can be used drag a database table or tables to an XML Schema designer, thereby creating an XML schema.

To open Server Explorer:

1. In Visual Studio, choose Server Explorer from the View menu.

   Server Explorer opens, showing available server computers (depending on its configuration, including the system hosting Visual Studio .NET), as shown in **Figure 15.25**.

2. Click the plus icon to the left of a server name to expand the node and discover the server software that is actually available on the server, such as event logs, message queues, servers, and—yes—database servers (**Figure 15.26**).

Connecting to a database server requires administrative permission—in other words a logon ID and password. Logon IDs in Microsoft SQL Server can be the same as those used to log on to Windows (using Windows integrated security). Alternatively, SQL Server can manage its own set of logon names and passwords. In either case, a given logon is administratively assigned to a group within SQL Server, with different groups having different privilege and access levels. You need to be sure that your user name has the privileges and accesses you need for your program to work. What this boils down to, if you are not administering SQL Server yourself, is that it behooves you to get to know and befriend your SQL Server administrator.

The tasks in this section are based on the sample Northwind database that ships with SQL Server.

To connect to a SQL Server database:

1. With Server Explorer open in Visual Studio, right-click to open the Server Explorer context menu.
2. Choose Add Connection from the context menu.

   The Data Link Properties dialog opens (**Figure 15.27**).
3. In the Data Link Properties dialog, enter a server name, or choose a server from the drop-down list (**Figure 15.28**).

   The server name drop-down list should display all available servers on your network, but if you don't see the server you are looking for and don't know its name, try clicking the Refresh button to refresh the list of servers in the drop-down list.
4. With a server selected in the Data Link Properties dialog, select Use Windows NT Integrated Security if you want the user name and password you are logged on with to be used to access SQL Server, or select Use a Specific User Name and Password and provide a user name and password in the appropriate boxes.
5. If you selected Use a Specific User Name and Password and don't want to have to provide a password each time a SQL Server logon is attempted, check the Allow Saving Password box under Step 2 in the Data Link Properties dialog.

   The downside to checking this box is that your password will be saved as part of the database connection string and will be readable in plain text by anyone with access to the source code of your project.

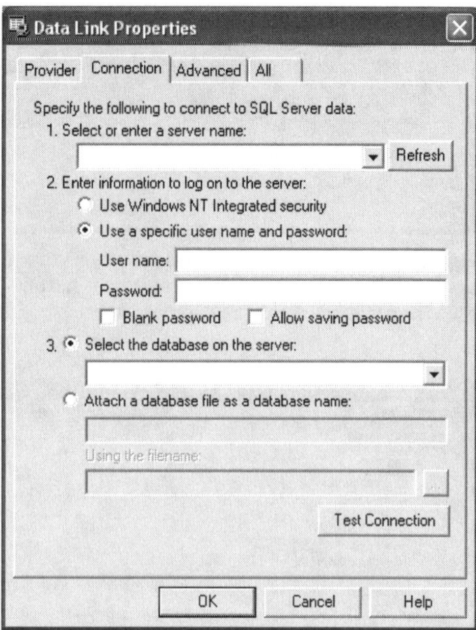

Figure 15.27 Attempting to connect to a new database server causes the DataLink Properties dialog to open.

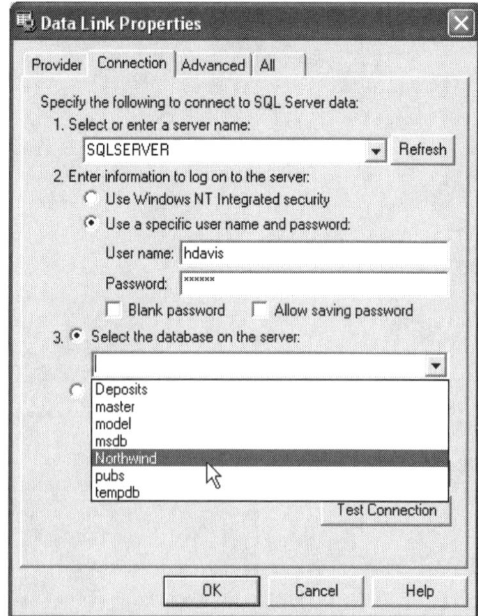

Figure 15.28 The DataLink Properties dialog lets you supply a database server, logon information, and a database.

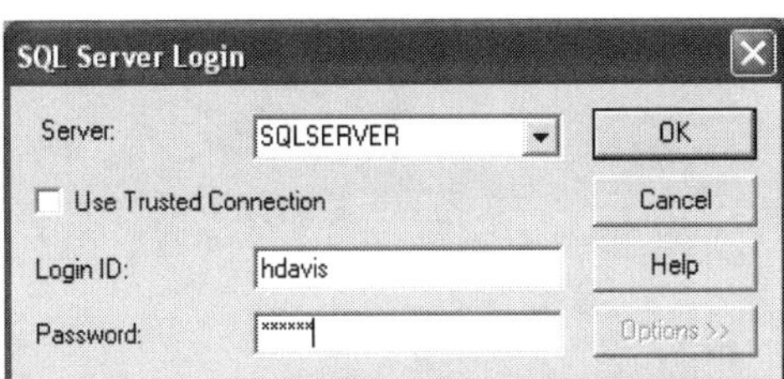

Figure 15.29 If you don't allow password saving, you'll have to log on each time you connect to the database server.

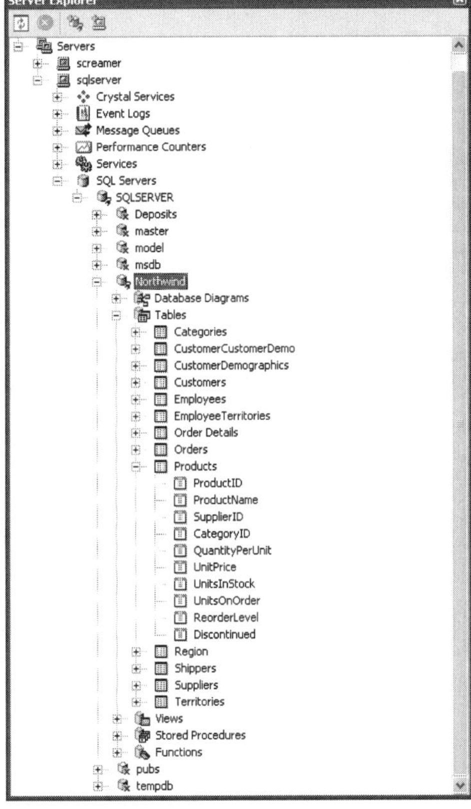

Figure 15.30 Once you are connected, the tables in the remote database are displayed in Server Explorer.

6. Under Step 3 of the Data Link Properties dialog, select a database on the server from the drop-down list.
7. If you like, click Test Connection to make sure that the database connection is working properly.

   If the connection is working, a message box will display information to that effect.
8. If you tested the connection. click OK to close the test connection message.
9. If you are satisfied with your settings, and if the connection passed its test, click OK.
10. If you chose not to allow password saving, you will be prompted to reenter your password. Enter your password again (**Figure 15.29**) and click OK.

    The server is now displayed in Server Explorer in addition to the servers that were already displayed.
11. Drill down through the nodes of the new server to find the Northwind database.
12. Expand the Northwind database node to find the Table node for the database.

    You'll see all of the tables that the Northwind database contains (**Figure 15.30**).

As mentioned earlier, not everyone can access a running version of SQL Server—but almost everyone running Windows has a version of the Northwind Access database file, since it ships with Microsoft Office. The samples in this section are based on the sample Northwind database and SQL Server, but to use the Northwind Access database instead (if you don't have SQL Server), all you have to do is connect to the sample Access database, as described in the next task, "To connect to an Access database file," rather than to SQL server.

If you have Microsoft Office XP installed, you will find a copy of the Northwind database at C:\Program Files\Microsoft Office\Office10\1033\FPNWind.mdb. If you have an older copy of Office installed, most likely you will find the Northwind database at C:\Program Files\Microsoft Office\Office\Samples\Northwind.mdb. Note that you do not need to have the Microsoft Access program installed on your system to be able to interact with the Access database file.

To connect to an Access database file:

1. With Server Explorer open in Visual Studio, right-click to open the Server Explorer context menu.
2. Choose Add Connection from the context menu.

   The Data Link Properties dialog opens (see Figure 15.27).
3. Click Provider to open the Provider tab of the Data Link Properties dialog (**Figure 15.31**).
4. In the Select the Data You Want to Connect To list, select Microsoft Jet 4.0 OLE DB Provider, which is used with Microsoft Access databases.
5. Click Next.

   The Connection tab of the Data Link Properties dialog opens, configured to connect to Access data (**Figure 15.32**).

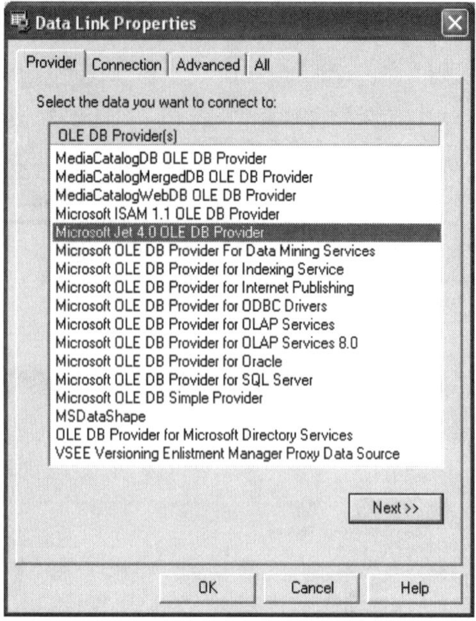

Figure 15.31 Select Microsoft Jet as the OLE DB provider to connect to an Access database.

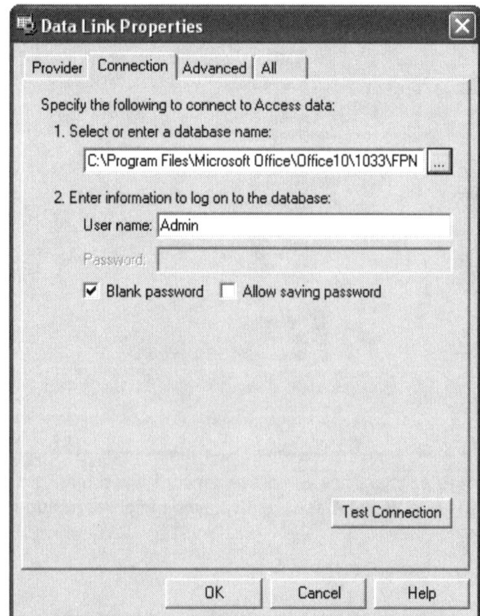

Figure 15.32 You can choose the Access file (it will have the .mdb file extension) from the Select Access Database dialog.

Working with Databases

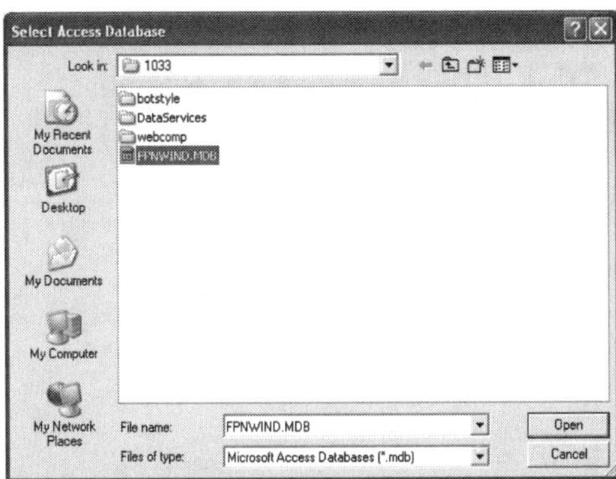

Figure 15.33 Clicking the Text Connection button lets you verify that you are properly connected to a database.

Figure 15.34 Server Explorer displays the tables in the Access database.

6. Click the button ... to the right of the Select or Enter a Database Name text box to open the Select Access Database dialog (**Figure 15.33**).
7. In the Select Access Database dialog, choose an Access database file (usually, a file with an .mdb file extension), such as the sample Northwind database (see the introduction to this task for its usual locations).
8. Click Open.
9. Click Test Connection to make sure the connection with the Access database is working.

   If everything is working, a message box appears saying so.
10. Click OK to close the test connection message box.
11. Click OK to add the Access database to Server Explorer (**Figure 15.34**).

    As you can see, as you drill down through the sample Northwind Access database, it has tables named (and structured) in exactly the same way as the sample Northwind database that ships with SQL Server.

If all your application needs to do is read some rows of a database table, using a DataReader component may be the simplest way to go. Visual Studio (and VB .NET) ships with two versions of the DataReader: the SqlDataReader class, which is intended for use with Microsoft SQL Server, and the OleDbDataReader class, which is intended for use with a general Open Database Connectivity (ODBC) source, such as an Access database or database server from a vendor besides Microsoft. In the next task, you will see how to use a DataReader component to display the data in the CompanyName column of the Suppliers column of the sample

Northwind database in SQL Server. If you are using the Access Northwind database, you will need to replace the classes and members that belong to the System.Data.SqlClient namespace with classes and members belonging to the System.Data.OleDb namespace. (For more information on the components intended to work with specific data sources, see "Managed providers" later in this chapter.)

To display data with a DataReader component:

1. In a Windows Application project, open a Windows form in its designer.
2. Use the Toolbox to add a ListBox control to the form.
3. Use the Toolbox to add a Button control to the form.
4. Use the Properties window to change the name of the ListBox control to `lstData`.
5. Use the Properties window to change the name of the TextBox control to `btnReadData` and its Text value to `Read Data`.

   Your user interface should now look like the one shown in the designer in **Figure 15.35**.
6. Double-click the Read Data button to create a click event handler for it in the Code Editor:

```
Private Sub btnReadData_Click _
   (ByVal sender As System.Object, _
   ByVal e As System.EventArgs) _
   Handles btnReadData.Click

End Sub
```

7. In the Code Editor, at the top of the form code, before the Form class declaration, import the System.Data.SqlClient namespace:

```
Imports System.Data.SqlClient
```

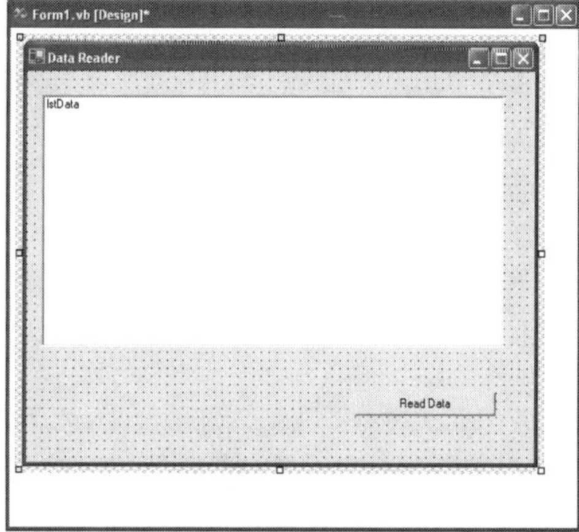

Figure 15.35 Use a ListBox control to display data obtained using a DataReader component.

WORKING WITH DATABASES

8. In the btnReadData click event handler, create a SQL query that will return the CompanyName column of the Suppliers table and store the SQL in a string variable named myQuery:

```
Dim myQuery As String = _
  "SELECT CompanyName FROM Suppliers"
```

9. Create a connection string, using an object of the SqlConnection class, and store the connection string in the variable myConnect:

```
Dim myConnect As New SqlConnection _
("data source=SQLSERVER;initial" & _
" catalog=Northwind;" & _
"password=hdavis; user id=hdavis")
```

Of course, the connection string will be different for you. For more information about creating (or determining) a connection string, see "To create a connection" later in this chapter.

10. Create a new SqlCommand object named myCommand, based on the SQL string and the connection string:

```
Dim myCommand As SqlCommand = _
   New SqlCommand(myQuery, myConnect)
```

11. Open the connection:

```
myConnect.Open()
```

12. Declare a new SqlDataReader named myReader using the ExecuteReader method of the myCommand object to return the query results specified by the myQuery SQL object:

```
Dim myReader As SqlDataReader = _
   myCommand.ExecuteReader
```

13. Use myReader to loop through the returned results, adding them one by one to the Items collection of the lstData control:

```
Do While myReader.Read()
  lstData.Items.Add _
    (myReader.GetString(0))
Loop
```

continues on next page

Listing 15.3 Displaying data using a DataReader object.

```
Imports System.Data.SqlClient
...
Private Sub btnReadData_Click(ByVal sender As System.Object, ByVal e As System.EventArgs) _
   Handles btnReadData.Click
   Dim myQuery As String = "SELECT CompanyName FROM Suppliers"
   Dim myConnect As New SqlConnection("data source=SQLSERVER;initial" & _
      " catalog=Northwind;password=hdavis;user id=hdavis")
   Dim myCommand As SqlCommand = New SqlCommand(myQuery, myConnect)
   myConnect.Open()
   Dim myReader As SqlDataReader = myCommand.ExecuteReader
   Do While myReader.Read()
      lstData.Items.Add(myReader.GetString(0))
   Loop
   myReader.Close()
   myConnect.Close()
End Sub
```

14. Close the SqlDataReader and SqlConnection objects:

```
myReader.Close()
myConnect.Close()
```

Listing 15.3 on the previous page shows the complete code for reading the CompanyName column of the Suppliers table of the SQL Server Northwind database and displaying the data read in a ListBox control.

15. Make sure your system is connected to the instance of SQL Server specified in the connection string.
16. Run the project.
17. Click Read Data.

Each item in the CompanyName column is displayed in the ListBox control (**Figure 15.36**).

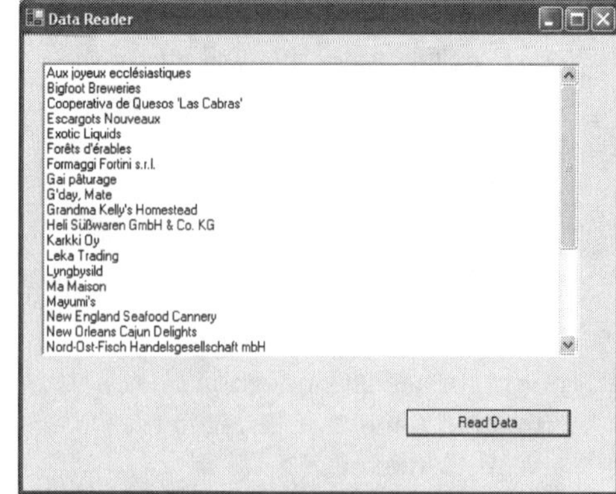

Figure 15.36 The data from the Customers table is displayed using the DataReader component.

✔ Tip

- Much can go wrong when your program requires database connectivity. The database may be down, there may be network communication problems, your logon and password may not be authorized (or may have insufficient permissions), the database administrator may have deleted the sample Northwind database—and much more. For this reason, any program dependent on database connectivity should employ structured exception handling, as explained in Chapter 9, "Exceptions and Debugging." You will also find an example of how to do this in the task "To bind a ListBox control to a dataset" later in this chapter.

Managed providers

VB .NET ships with two sets of components for each data source: Microsoft SQL Server and every other data source (via the OLE DB set of components). Each of these sets of components is called a *managed provider*. Managed providers are the heart of the ADO.NET data connectivity layer.

While these two sets of managed providers are functionally identical, they are aimed at differing data sources. The data connectivity components (or managed providers) for both data sources appear on the Toolbox. These components can be added in the usual fashion to a form. They then appear in the tray beneath the form.

Table 15.3 lists the managed providers available from the Toolbox.

The only thing simple about a connection string is determining whether it works. Obtaining a working connection string is more an act of what hackers term "social engineering" than it is an act of programming. (In the best situation, you administer SQL Server in your own domain, in which case, providing yourself with logons, passwords, and appropriate permissions should not present a substantive problem.)

Table 15.3

ADO.NET Data Components (Managed Providers) Available from the Toolbox

Component	Purpose
OleDbDataAdapter and SqlDataAdapter	Contain and control Command objects such as a SelectCommand object, which retrieve data from a database.
OleDbConnection and SqlConnection	Provide a connection to a database server (or source such as a flat Access table).
OleDbCommand and SqlCommand	Execute SQL statements (or stored procedures). The ExecuteReader method of the Command object is used to create a DataReader object (as explained in "To display data with a DataReader component" earlier in this chapter).
DataSet	Stores an in-memory cache of data (sometimes called a *data store*) made up of one or more tables. This object is the heart of ADO.NET. It is filled using one or more managed provider data adapters.
DataView	Contains filtered and sorted data based on a DataSet component. Controls can be bound to a DataView component.

Nonetheless, there is some art involved in specifying a connection string, even if you have the logon and password (either because you administer the database or because the system administrator or database administrator provided you with the information).

If, in Server Explorer, you've connected to a data source for SQL Server or an Access database file, as explained earlier in this chapter, then you can open the Properties window for the data source by right-clicking it and choosing Properties from the context menu. The connection string used is the value of the ConnectString property (**Figure 15.37**). You can read this property value and use it as the connection string in program code. Bear in mind, however, that a connection string obtained in this way is probably longer and contains *more* information than you actually need. This is an inconvenience, not a tragedy, and you can experiment with shortening a connection string obtained in this way to remove extraneous information.

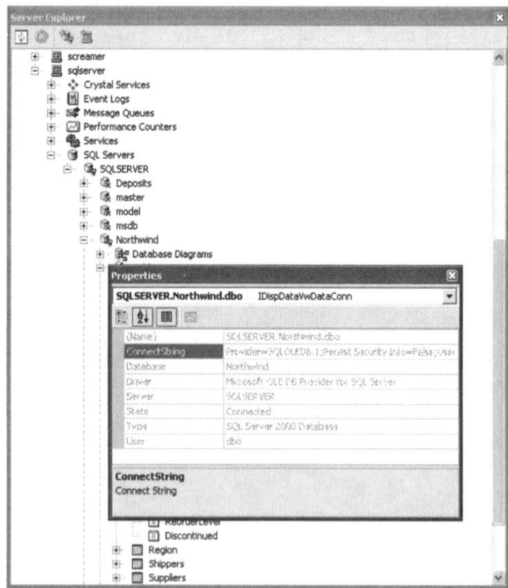

Figure 15.37 You can use the ConnectString property of a database (shown here in the Properties window) to determine an effective connection string for the database.

More ADO.NET Managed Data Providers

You may be interested to know that there are more managed providers available than those in the two component sets that ship with Visual Studio and VB .NET.

An ODBC managed provider is available from Microsoft. The OLE DB managed provider addresses an update to the ODBC standard. To connect to some older data sources, you'll need the ODBC managed drivers. To download them, go to http://msdn.micrososft.com and search for ODBC .NET Data Provider.

You can find information about the IBM .NET managed data provider for IBM's DB2 database and download it from http://www7b.software.ibm.com/dmdd/downloads/dotnetbeta/index.html. (Note that as this book goes to press, the .NET DB2 managed provider is still in the beta version.)

A .NET managed data provider is available for Oracle databases. You can find more information about it at http://otn.oracle.com/sample_code/tech/windows/odpnet/content.html and download it from http://otn.oracle.com/software/content.html.

Sybase has a managed provider for its Adaptive Server product. For information, go to http://www.sybase.com/detail?id=1023454. Download information is available at the following link: http://www.sybase.com/detail?id=1022085.

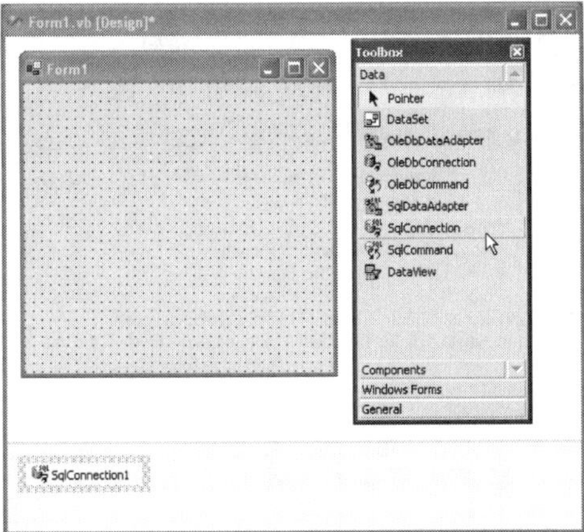

Figure 15.38 When you add a SqlConnection component to a form, it appears in the tray beneath the form.

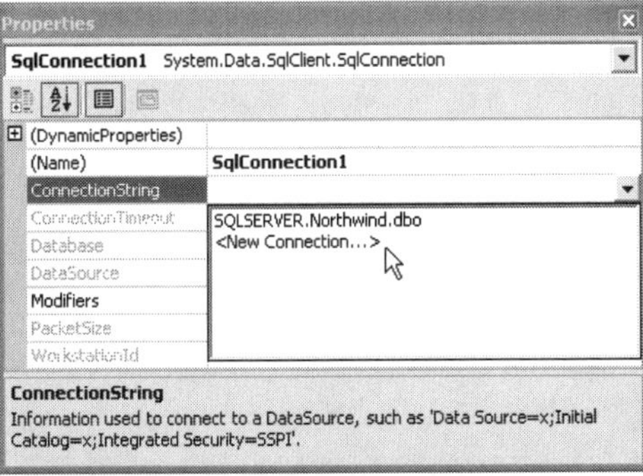

Figure 15.39 With the SqlConnection component selected in the Properties window, you can choose the ConnectString property to select an existing connection or create a new connection.

A little more formally, you can use a Connection component (either SqlConnection or OleDbConnection) to create (or obtain) a connection (and a connection string). This process uses the Data Link Properties dialog to obtain the connection, so in many ways it is similar to connecting to a data source via Server Explorer as explained earlier in this chapter.

To create a connection:

1. With a form open in its designer, choose Toolbox from the View menu to open the Toolbox.
2. Click the Data tab of the Toolbox so that the managed provider data components are displayed (**Figure 15.38**).
3. Double-click the SqlConnection component to add it to the tray beneath the form as shown in Figure 15.38. (If you are using the OLE DB managed provider, substitute the OleDbConnection component.)
4. Right-click the SqlConnection component in the tray to open its context menu.
5. Choose Properties to open the Properties window with the SqlConnection component selected (**Figure 15.39**).
6. In the left column of the Properties window, select ConnectionString.

continues on next page

7. Choose <New Connection...> from the drop-down list in the right column as shown in Figure 15.39.

   The Provider tab of the Data Link Properties dialog opens (**Figure 15.40**).

8. Choose an OLE DB Provider.

   Microsoft OLE DB Provider for SQL Server, shown in Figure 15.40, is the correct source for SQL Server.

9. Click Next.

   The Connection tab of the Data Link Properties dialog opens (**Figure 15.41**).

10. Select a server, provide login information, and select a database on the server as shown in Figure 15.41 (and as explained earlier in "To connect to a SQL Server database").

11. Click OK.

12. Right-click the SqlConnection component in the tray to open its context menu.

13. Read (or copy and paste to your code) the text value of the connection string stored in the SqlConnection component to set it as the value of the ConnectionString property (**Figure 15.42**).

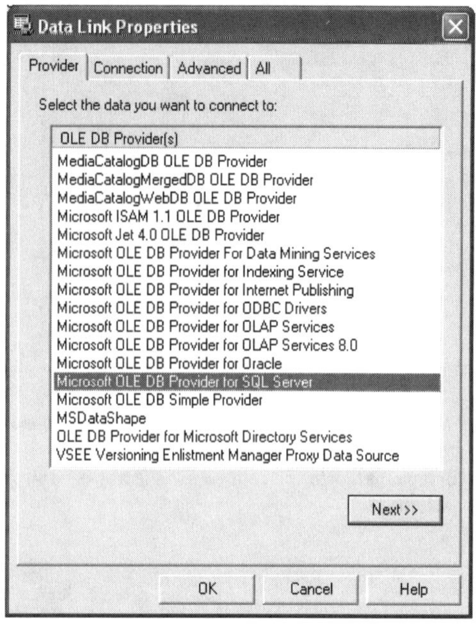

Figure 15.40 The first step in creating a connection string is to pick a provider.

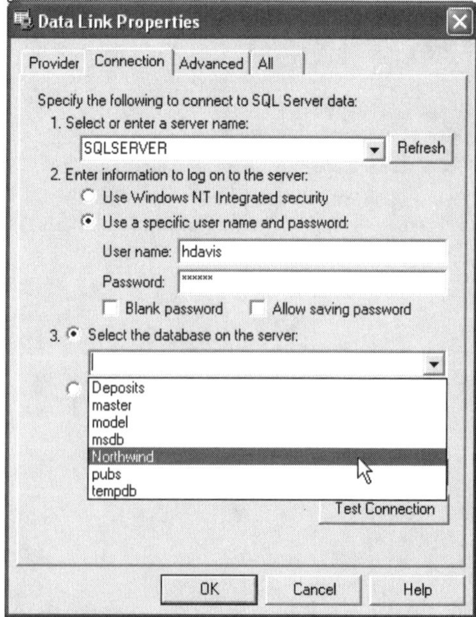

Figure 15.41 With the provider selected, you will be asked to give the other required information; you can also, if desired, test the connection.

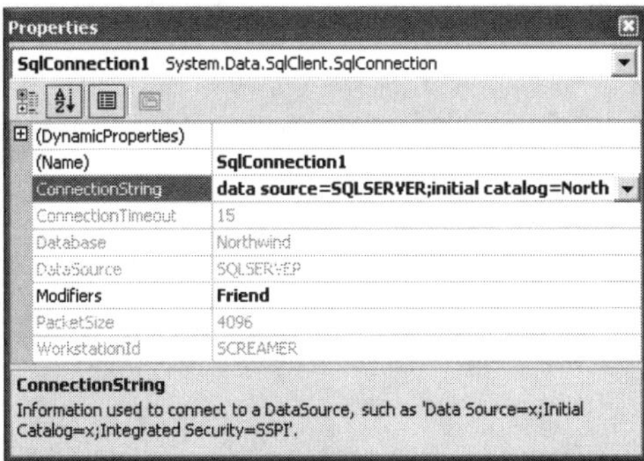

Figure 15.42 The connection string is displayed as the value of the SqlConnect component's ConnectString property.

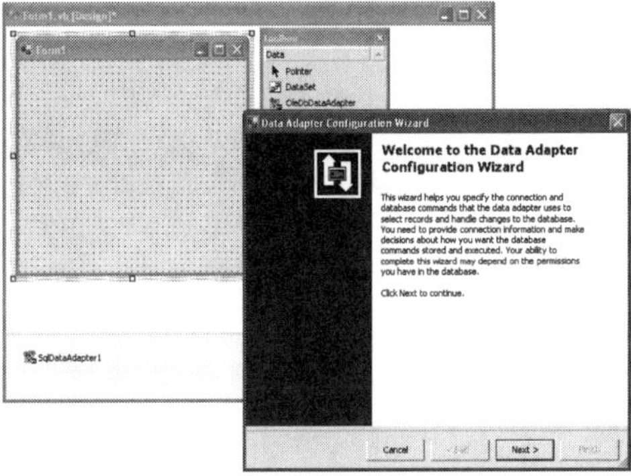

Figure 15.43 When you add a SqlAdapter component to a form, the Data Adapter Configuration Wizard opens.

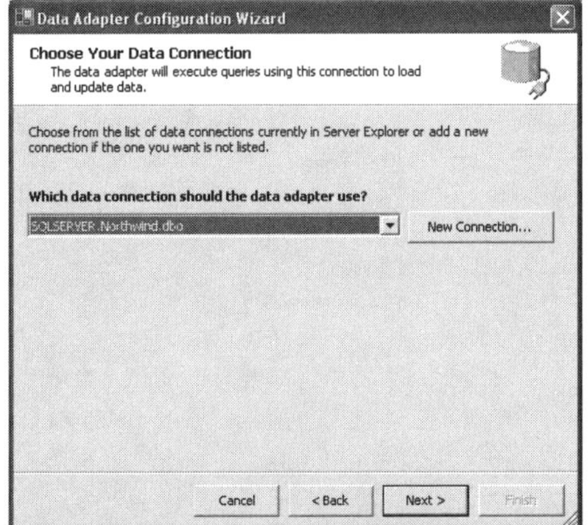

Figure 15.44 You can specify an existing connection or create a new connection.

Using datasets

As noted earlier, a dataset is one or more tables of data, represented in .NET by a DataSet component. Datasets are the most powerful use of the ADO.NET connectivity layer. As you'll see a little later, you can easily create a DataSet component programmatically.

The process for adding a DataSet component using the Visual Studio visual development interface starts with the addition of a SqlDataAdapter component. (In this and the subsequent tasks, you should substitute the OleDbDataAdapter for the SqlDataAdapter if appropriate for your data source.) Then the next step is to create a SQL query for the dataset.

To create a dataset:

1. With a form open in its designer, choose Toolbox from the View menu to open the Toolbox.
2. Click the Data tab of the Toolbox so that the managed provider data components are displayed (refer to Figure 15.38).
3. Double-click the SqlDataAdapter component to add it to the tray beneath the form. (If you are using the OLE DB managed provider, substitute the OleDbDataAdapter component.)

   When the SqlDataAdapter component is added to the form, the Data Adapter Configuration Wizard automatically opens (**Figure 15.43**).
4. Click Next.

   The Choose Your Data Connection pane of the wizard (**Figure 15.44**) opens.

continues on next page

5. In the Choose Your Data Connection pane, *do one of the following:*
   - ▲ Choose a data connection from the existing data connections in the drop-down list.

   or

   - ▲ Create a new data connection by clicking the New Connection button. The Data Link Properties dialog opens, and the process is exactly as described in the previous task, "To create a connection."

   In either case, a SqlConnection component is created and added to the tray beneath the form.
6. Click Next.

   The Choose a Query Type pane of the wizard (**Figure 15.45**) opens.
7. In the Choose a Query Type pane of the wizard, select Use SQL Statements, Create New Stored Procedures, or Use Existing Stored Procedures as the means of database access.

   As noted in the sidebar "Understanding Relational Databases," SQL statements are easier to use in an ad hoc fashion, but stored procedures (which are programs within the database) are architecturally more robust.
8. Click Next.

   Assuming that you chose to use SQL queries or create stored procedures, the Generate the SQL Statements pane of the wizard opens (**Figure 15.46**). (If you chose to use existing stored procedures, you will be asked to select the existing stored procedures to use.)
9. Enter a SQL query as shown in Figure 15.46 and proceed to Step 18. If you want to use the Query Builder to create your SQL query, proceed to the next step.

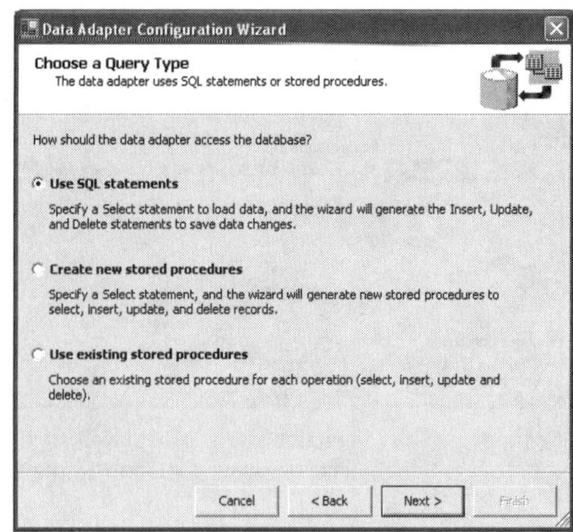

Figure 15.45 You can generate queries using SQL statements or stored procedures.

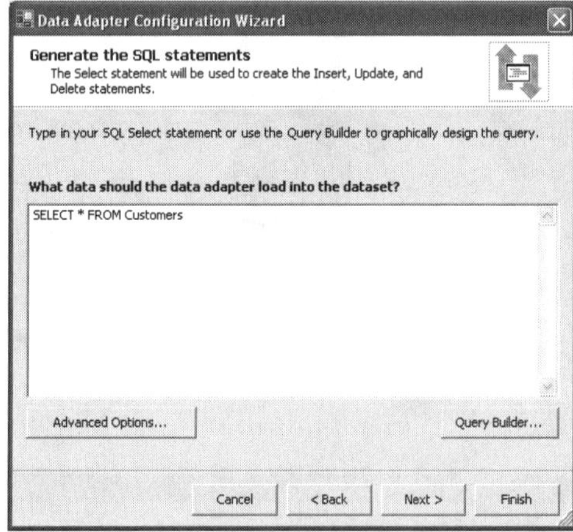

Figure 15.46 You can enter SQL statements directly.

Working with Databases

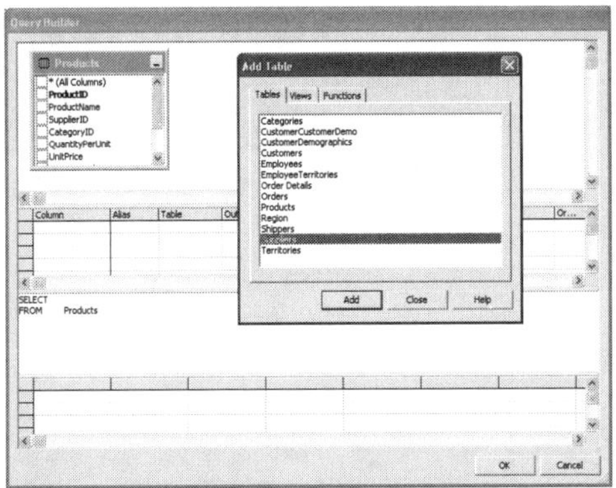

Figure 15.47 The Query Builder provides visual tools for constructing queries.

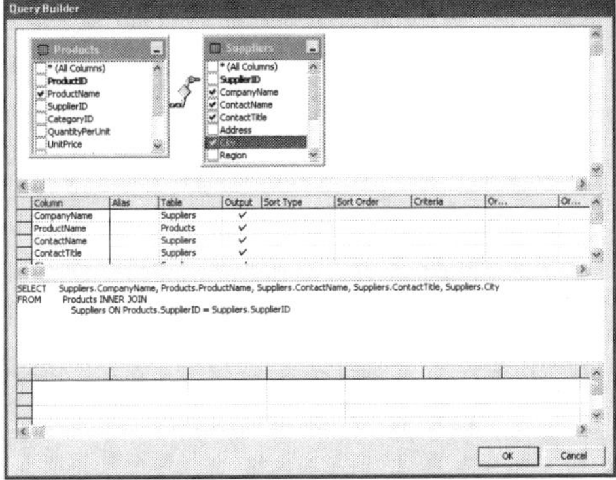

Figure 15.48 After you specify the tables and columns, the Query Builder constructs the corresponding SQL statement.

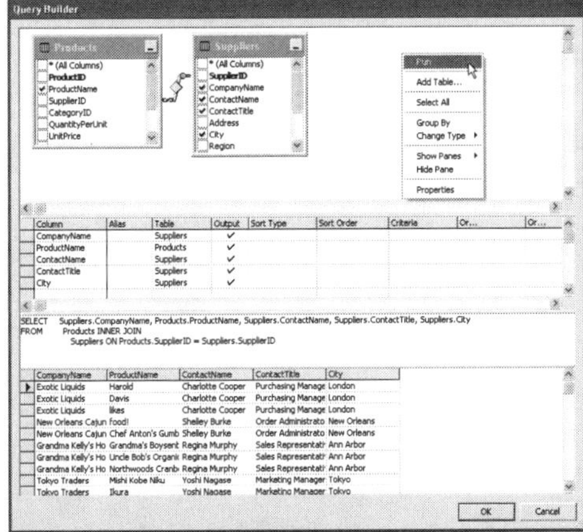

Figure 15.49 You can run the SQL statement created by the Query Builder to see the data it generates.

10. Click Query Builder to open the Query Builder dialog .
11. Right-click in the top pane of the Query Builder dialog to open the Add Table dialog (**Figure 15.47**).
12. Select a table to be part of the query: for example, the Suppliers table.
13. Click Add.
14. In the Suppliers table that appears in the top pane of the Query Builder, check the boxes next to the columns you want to include.
15. Repeat the process for all of the tables and rows you want to include in your query.

    The columns and tables you select will be displayed in tabular form on the middle pane of the Query Builder, and the SQL that the Query Builder will generate will be shown in the next pane down (**Figure 15.48**).
16. To preview the dataset that will result from the query, right-click the Query Builder dialog and choose Run from the context menu.

    The dataset will be displayed in the table at the bottom of the Query Builder (**Figure 15.49**).

continues on next page

17. When you are done, click OK.

The Generate the SQL Statements pane of the Data Adapter Configuration wizard reopens, showing the generated SQL (or stored procedure) (**Figure 15.50**).

18. Click Next.

The View Wizard Results pane details the activities of the Data Adapter Configuration wizard (**Figure 15.51**).

19. Click Finish.

If you check the tray below the form in its designer, you'll see that a SqlConnection component, representing the connection you choose or created, has been added to the tray.

✔ Tip

- To start the Data Adapter Configuration wizard for a SqlDataAdapter component that is already seated in the tray of a form, right-click the SqlDataAdapter and choose Configure Data Adapter from the context menu or choose Configure Data Adapter from the Visual Studio Data menu.

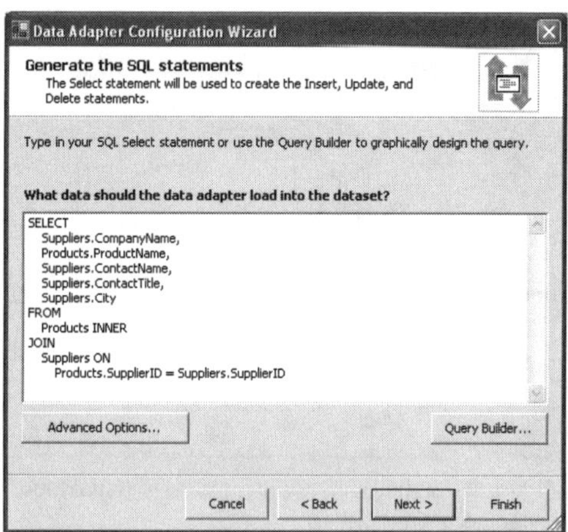

Figure 15.50 The Data Adapter Configuration Wizard uses the SQL supplied by the Query Builder.

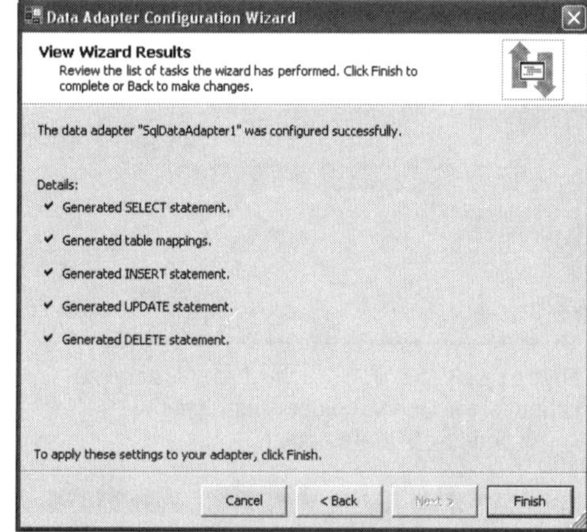

Figure 15.51 The final wizard panel shows the results obtained.

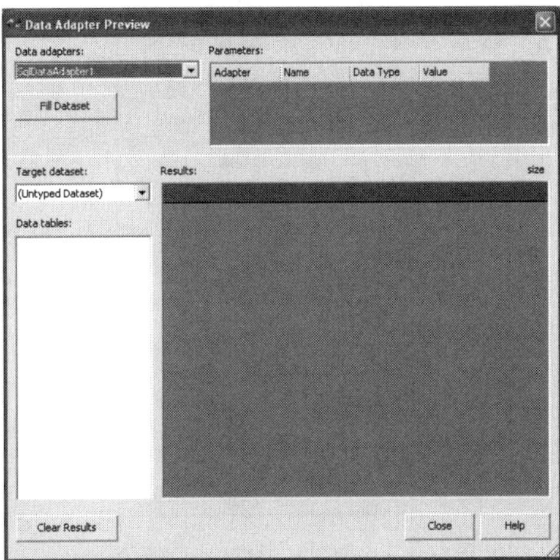

Figure 15.52 When the Data Adapter Preview window opens, it doesn't display any data.

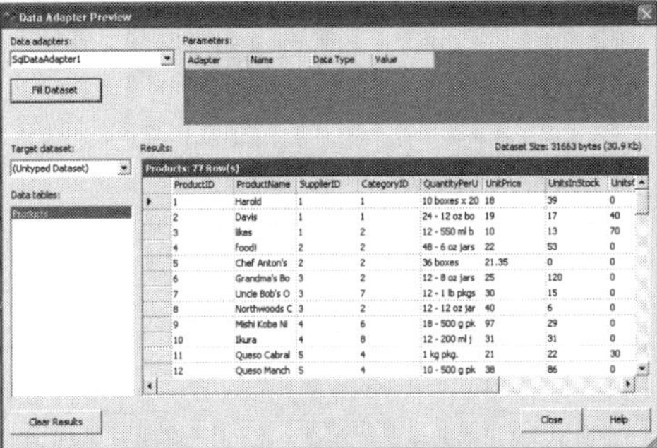

Figure 15.53 Once the Data Adapter Preview window has been filled, the dataset that the SqlAdapter component will generate is displayed.

You can preview the dataset to make sure that it includes the data you need.

To preview a dataset:

1. With SqlConnection and SqlDataAdapter components seated on a form, either choose Preview Data from the Visual Studio Data menu or right-click the SqlDataAdapter component and select Preview Data from its context menu.

   The Data Adapter Preview dialog opens (**Figure 15.52**).

2. Make sure that the SqlDataAdapter component is selected in the Data Adapters drop-down list.

3. Click Fill Dataset.

   A preview of the dataset appears in the Results pane (**Figure 15.53**).

4. After examining the data, click Close to close the Data Adapter Preview dialog.

✔ Tip

- Data does not appear as a top-level Visual Studio menu unless data components have been added to a form.

As you might (or might not) expect, previewing a dataset does not a generated dataset make. Before you can use the dataset created with the Data Adapter Configuration Wizard (and previewed in the task "To preview a dataset"), you must generate the dataset, which adds a DataSet component to the tray of the form.

This is an easy task to accomplish, but also an easy one to forget. If you forget to generate the dataset, it won't contain any data—and you'll probably be wondering why.

To generate a dataset:

1. With SqlConnection and SqlDataAdapter components seated on a form, either choose Generate Data from the Visual Studio Data menu or right-click the SqlDataAdapter component and select Generate Data from its context menu.

   The Generate Dataset dialog opens (**Figure 15.54**).

2. Either accept the default name provided for the new DataSet component or enter a name of your choice.

3. Make sure that Add This Dataset to the Designer is checked.

4. Click OK.

   The DataSet component now appears in the tray beneath the Form in its designer (**Figure 15.55**).

✔ Tip

- This chapter started by showing you how a database table can be used to generate an XML schema. It should not be surprising, then, that internally, a DataSet component, which consists of database tables, is represented by an XML schema. You can see this by selecting the newly generated DataSet component in the tray and choosing View Schema from its context menu. The designer for the DataSet component presents data in tabular form, and on its XML tab, it presents the XML schema that controls generation of the dataset (**Figure 15.56**).

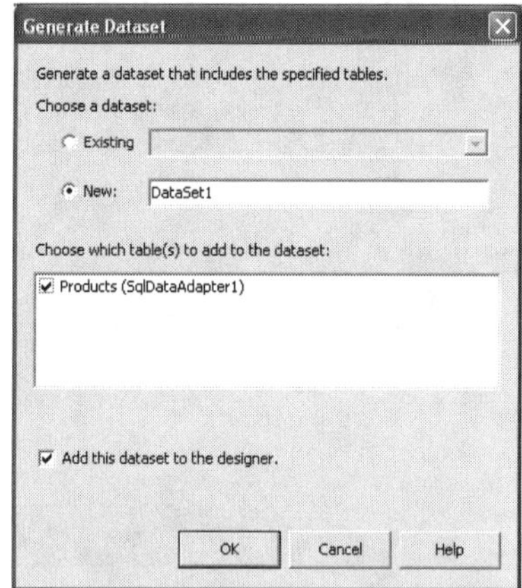

Figure 15.54 When the DataSet component is generated, you have the option of adding it to a form designer.

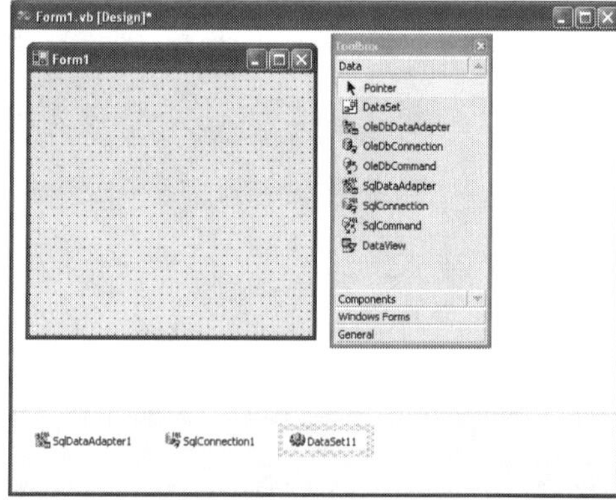

Figure 15.55 The generated DataSet component appears in the tray beneath the form.

Figure 15.56 You can view the underlying tabular structure of the dataset in the form of its equivalent XML schema.

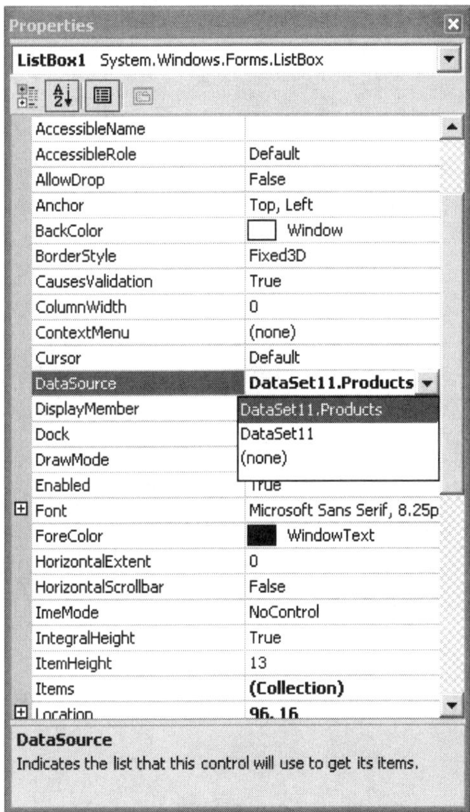

Figure 15.57 To bind a control to a data source, set the DataSource property of the control.

As most developers know, an easy and powerful procedure is to bind a control to a dataset. The content of the control then will be determined by the data in the dataset. As the data in the dataset (or database table) changes, the data displayed in the control can change dynamically; if the dataset is configured to allow insertions, it can also be updated by user entries in the bound control. In other words, the control and the dataset are synchronized so that when one is changed, so is the other—and this is accomplished with very little work on the part of the programmer.

You can use the Properties window to bind a control, such as a ListBox, to a DataSet component.

To bind a ListBox control to a dataset:

1. Use the Toolbox to add a ListBox control to the form that hosts the DataSet component created in the preceding task, "To generate a DataSet."
2. Use the Toolbox to add a Button control to the form.
3. Use the Properties window to change the name of the Button control to `btnFill` and the value of its Text property to `Fill`.
4. In the Properties window, select the ListBox control in the Objects drop-down list.
5. In the left column of the Properties window, choose DataSource.
6. In the drop-down list in the right column, choose the table that belongs to the DataSet component that you want to use to fill the ListBox control.

   Figure 15.57 shows the Products table selected. Note that the Products table is shown in Figure 15.57 modifying that DataSet component DataSet11 (which is the default name assigned to the component).

continues on next page

7. In the left column of the Properties window, choose DisplayMember, and in the right column, choose the column you want to bind to the ListBox control (**Figure 15.58**).

8. On the form in its designer, double-click the Fill button to create a click event handler for it:

```
Private Sub btnFill_Click _
    (ByVal sender As System.Object, _
    ByVal e As System.EventArgs) _
    Handles btnFill.Click


End Sub
```

9. Within the click event, use the Fill method of the SqlDataAdapter component to fill the DataSet component:

```
SqlDataAdapter1.Fill _
    (DataSet11, "Products")
```

This code is shown as part of **Listing 15.4**.

10. Run the project.

11. Click the Fill button.

Provided there are no connection problems with the data source, the data in the ProductNames column will appear in the ListBox control (**Figure 15.59**).

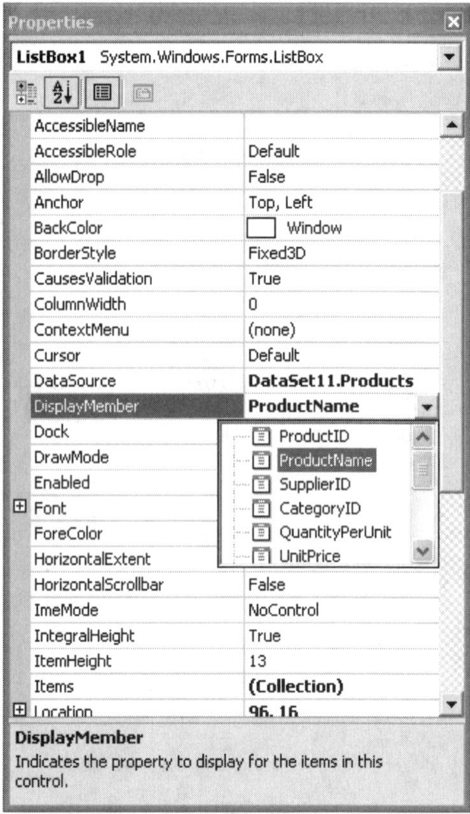

Figure 15.58 To bind a control to a column, set the DataMember property of the control.

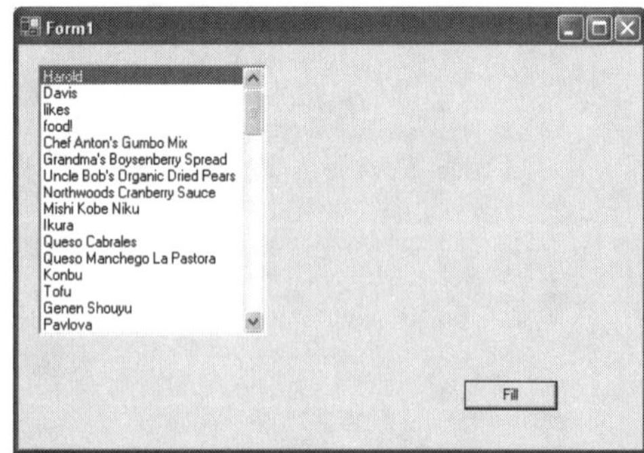

Figure 15.59 The data in the ProductName column is displayed in the bound ListBox control.

✔ Tips

- You can place the SqlDataAdapter Fill method in the Form New constructor so that no user action is required to fill the list box. Then the ProductName column data will be loaded when the form opens.
- Any program that requires database connectivity, including one as short as this, should include structured exception handling, as explained in Chapter 9. If you don't include structured exception handling, what happens—to take a very simple example—when the database is down? There are many possible problems that can arise when a program requires access to data, and your code should function well when the simple and foreseeable happens (the database is down), and also when other, more complex, error conditions arise.
- You'll see how to embed database connectivity code within structured exception handling in the next task.

Listing 15.4 Binding ListBox controls to a dataset.

```
Imports System.Data.SqlClient
...
Private Sub btnFill_Click(ByVal sender As System.Object, ByVal e As System.EventArgs) _
   Handles btnFill.Click
   Try
      ' Bind the first ListBox
      SqlDataAdapter1.Fill(DataSet11, "Products")
      ' Generate a second dataset in code and bind to second ListBox:
      Dim myQuery As String = "SELECT * FROM CUSTOMERS"
      Dim myConnect As New SqlConnection("data source=SQLSERVER;initial" & _
         " catalog=Northwind;password=hdavis;user id=hdavis")
      Dim myDataSet As New DataSet()
      Dim myAdapter As New SqlDataAdapter(myQuery, myConnect)
      myAdapter.Fill(myDataSet, "Customers")
      ListBox2.DataSource = myDataSet.Tables("Customers")
      ListBox2.DisplayMember = "CompanyName"
   Catch excep As System.Data.SqlClient.SqlException
      MessageBox.Show("There was a SQL error. Please check your connection. " & _
         "Here is the exception text: " & excep.Message)
   End Try
End Sub
```

Working with datasets in code

Visual interfaces are very nice—I love them more than beans and rice—but in some respects, it's just as easy to generate SqlDataAdapter and DataSet components and bind them to a control in code as it is to accomplish the same thing visually. The procedure you use is to some degree a matter of taste (and depends in part on how helpful you find the Query Builder).

In the next task, you'll see how to generate and fill DataSet and SqlDataAdapter components in code and bind them to a ListBox. This time, we'll bind the CompanyName column of the Northwind Customers table (rather than the ProductName column of the Products table as in the previous task).

To generate a DataSet object and bind it to a ListBox control in code:

1. Using the same form as in the preceding task, "To bind a ListBox control to a dataset," use the Toolbox to add a new ListBox control to the form.
2. Accept the default name for the new ListBox, ListBox2.

   The ListBox2 control is bound to the DataSet object in code.
3. Choose Code from the Visual Studio View menu to open the Code Editor.

   All of the code for this task will go within the click event for the Fill button, which was generated in the preceding task.
4. Within the Fill button click event handler created in the preceding task, create a Try...Catch...End Try statement:

   ```
   Try

   Catch

   End Try
   ```

   The Catch clause within the Try statement is intended to handle the very common exception generated when, for one reason or another, database connectivity fails. For a detailed explanation of Try statements, see Chapter 9.
5. Add code to the Catch clause to catch a SqlException, a member of the System.Data.SqlClient namespace:

   ```
   Catch excep As _
   System.Data.SqlClient.SqlException
   ```
6. Within the Catch clause, handle the SqlException by displaying a message box suggesting that the user check the database connection and displaying the text of the original exception that triggered the Catch clause, in case it contains useful information:

   ```
   Catch excep As _
   System.Data.SqlClient.SqlException
   MessageBox.Show _
   ("There was a SQL error. Please" & _
   " check your connection. " & _
   "Here is the exception text: " & _
   excep.Message)
   End Try
   ```
7. At the top of the Try block, create the SQL query and store it in a string variable named myQuery:

   ```
   Dim myQuery As String = _
      "SELECT * FROM CUSTOMERS"
   ```
8. Create the connection string and store it in the string variable myConnect:

   ```
   Dim myConnect As New _
      SqlConnection("data " & _
      source=SQLSERVER;initial" & _
      " catalog=Northwind;password" & _
      "=hdavis;user id=hdavis")
   ```

WORKING WITH DATABASES

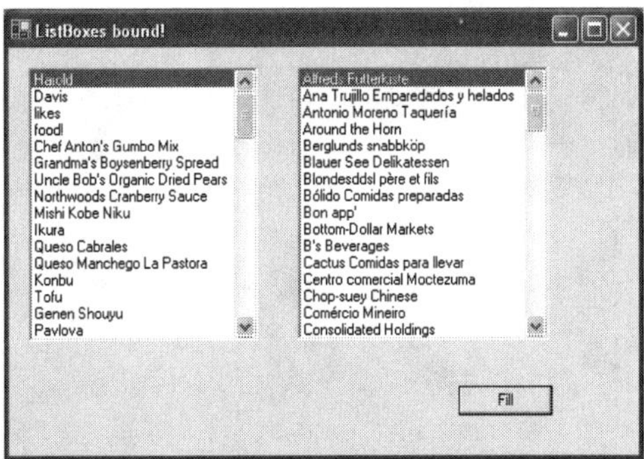

Figure 15.60 You can generate a DataSet and bind a control (such as the ListBox shown on the right) using code.

9. Instantiate a new DataSet object in the variable myDataSet:

   ```
   Dim myDataSet As New DataSet()
   ```

10. Instantiate a new SqlDataAdapter object using the myQuery and myConnect strings in the variable myAdapter:

    ```
    Dim myAdapter As New _
       SqlDataAdapter(myQuery,
    myConnect)
    ```

11. Fill the DataSet object using the Fill method of the SqlDataAdapter object and the Customers table:

    ```
    myAdapter.Fill(myDataSet, _
       "Customers")
    ```

12. Set the DataSource property of ListBox2 to the Customers table of the DataSet object.

    ```
    ListBox2.DataSource = _
       myDataSet.Tables("Customers")
    ```

13. Set the DisplayMember property of ListBox2 to CompanyName

    ```
    ListBox2.DisplayMember = _
       "CompanyName"
    ```

    Listing 15.4 shows the complete code for binding the ListBox control to the DataSet object in code.

14. Run the project.

15. Click Fill.

    The ListBox control bound in code will be filled with the CompanyName column of the Customers table, as shown on the right of **Figure 15.60**.

Almost any kind of control with a user interface can be bound to a data source such as a dataset. (One common approach not shown in this chapter is to allow the user to update the data source using a bound control, if this is appropriate in the context of the given application.)

It's particularly common to bind a DataGrid control to a dataset, because the DataGrid control can display an entire table, meaning rows as well as columns, all at once.

To bind a DataGrid control:

1. With the form containing the two bound ListBox controls open in its designer, choose Toolbox from the View menu to open the Toolbox.
2. Double-click the DataGrid control on the Windows Forms tab of the Toolbox to add an instance of the control to the form (**Figure 15.61**).
3. Choose Properties Window from the View menu to open the Properties window.
4. Select the DataGrid control in the Objects list at the top of the Property window.
5. In the Properties window, set the DataSource property to the DataSet object already created on the form.
6. In the Properties window, set the DataMember property to the Products table (**Figure 15.62**).

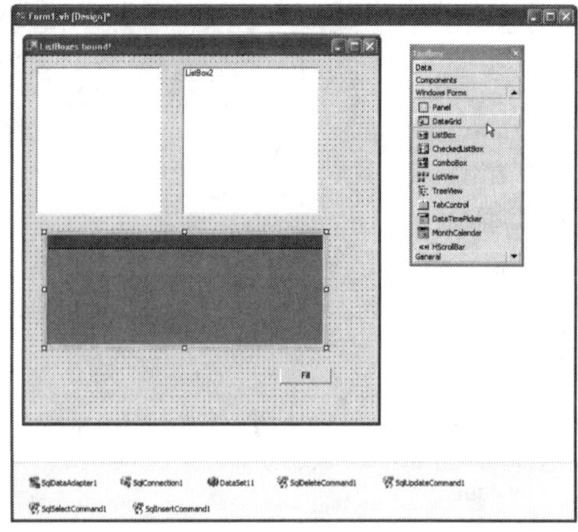

Figure 15.61 Double-click the DataGrid control in the Toolbox to add an instance of the control to a form.

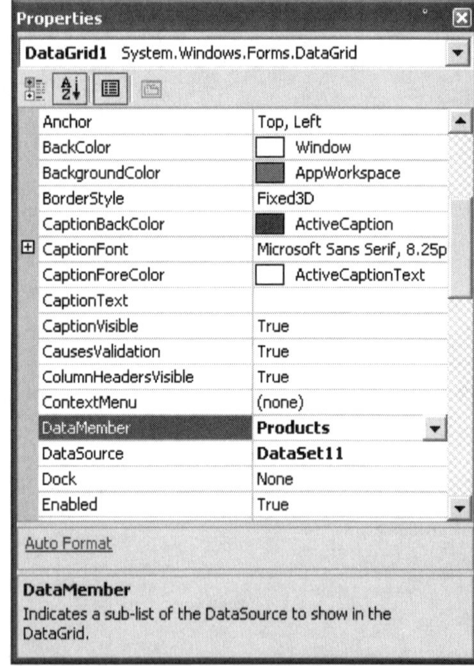

Figure 15.62 You can bind the DataGrid control to a dataset by setting the DataGrid control's DataSource and DataMember properties.

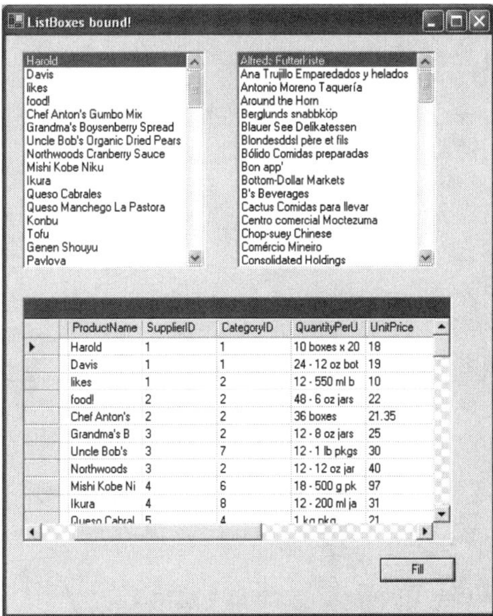

Figure 15.63 With the DataGrid control bound, the rows and columns in the specified table in the dataset source appear as the rows and columns of the grid.

7. Run the project.
8. Click Fill.

   The DataGrid control will be populated with the Products table, as shown at the bottom of **Figure 15.63**.

✔ Tip

- The example in this task relies on the fact that a DataAdapter component, a DataSet object, and related components have already been created on the form (otherwise, you would have to add them as explained in the previous two tasks). In addition, the code in the Fill click event uses the Fill method of the SqlAdapter component to load the DataSet object:

  ```
  SqlDataAdapter1.Fill _
     (DataSet11, "Products")
  ```

  If this line of code weren't already present, you would need to arrange for its execution before the data would be displayed in the DataGrid control.

You may be interested to know that Visual Basic .NET ships with a Data Form Wizard, which will construct a bound form for you. This wizard generates several varieties of fairly sophisticated forms, each featuring a number of bound controls. You can use these forms as is in your projects, or you can use the controls (and code) as a jump-start for creating data-bound controls and then add your own modifications.

To use the Data Form wizard:

1. With a Windows application open in Visual Studio, choose Add New Item from the Project menu.

   The Add New Item dialog opens (**Figure 15.64**).

2. In the Templates pane of the Add New Item dialog, choose Data Form Wizard as shown in Figure 15.64.
3. Accept the default name given for the form that will be generated or provide your own name for the data-bound form.
4. Click Open.

   The Data Form wizard opens (**Figure 15.65**).

5. Click Next to open the Choose the Dataset You Want to Use pane (**Figure 15.66**).
6. Choose to create a new dataset (in which case, you will complete a process like that described earlier in this chapter in the task "To create a dataset"), or, as shown in Figure 15.66, select a dataset that exists in the current project.
7. Click Next to open the Choose Methods to Load and Update Data pane.
8. In the Choose Methods to Load and Update Data pane, choose stored procedures or SQL statements.

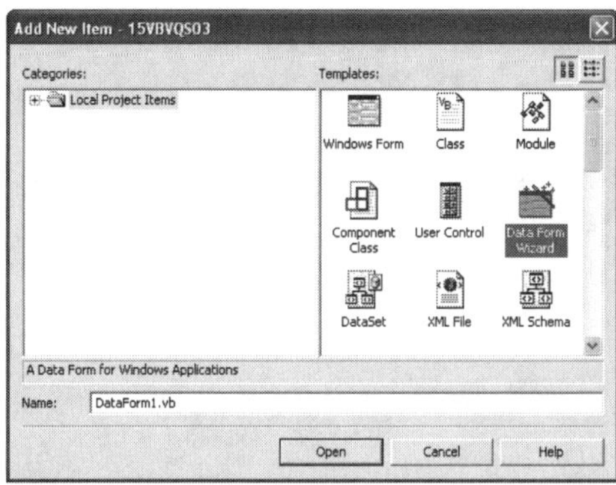

Figure 15.64 Select Data Form Wizard in the Add New Item dialog to start the wizard.

Figure 15.65 The opening screen of the Data Form wizard.

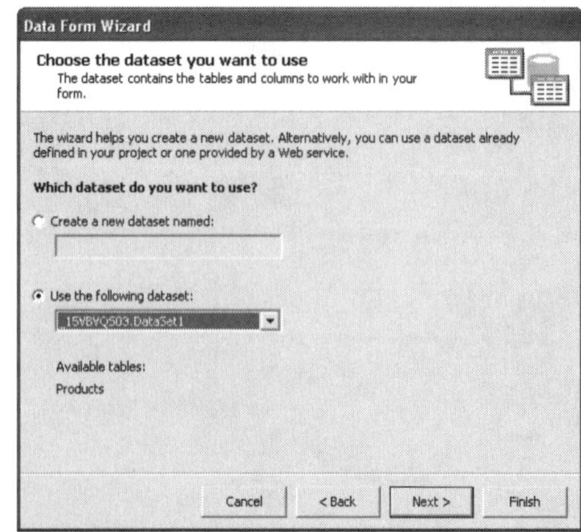

Figure 15.66 You can use an existing dataset or generate a new dataset.

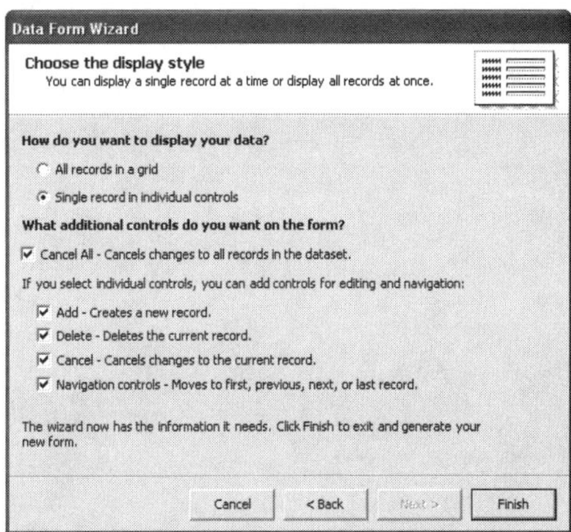

Figure 15.67 You can specify a grid interface or one involving multiple individual controls (shown here).

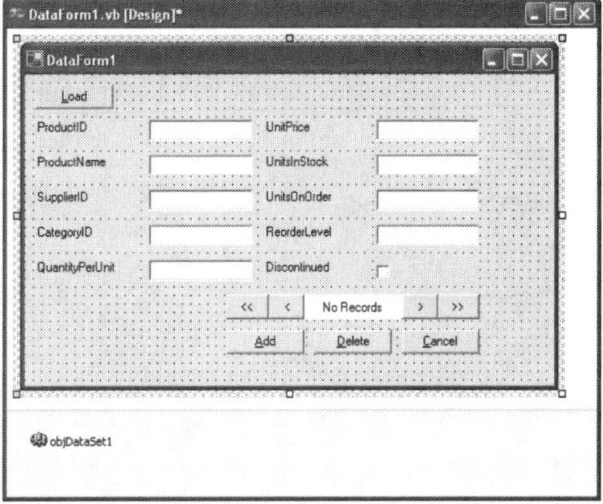

Figure 15.68 When the wizard finishes, a fairly complex data-bound form is generated in its designer.

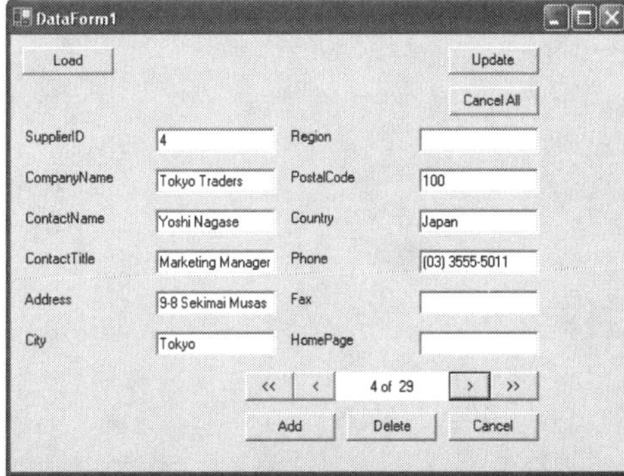

Figure 15.69 You can use the controls on the form to cycle through the bound database table.

9. Click Next to open the Choose the Display Style pane (**Figure 15.67**).
10. Choose to display records (rows) in a grid or, as shown in Figure 15.67, to display one record at a time, using individual controls.
11. Click Finish.

    The new form, containing data-bound controls and appropriate code, opens in its designer (**Figure 15.68**).
12. Add mechanism for displaying the form containing the data-bound controls.

    For example, if the project includes another form, you could do one of the following:

    Add a Button control to the other form.

    Use the Properties window to name the Button control `btnDataForm` and assign a Text property value of `Show Data` to the Button control.

    Double-click the Button control to create a click event handler in the Code Editor.

    Add code to the click event handler to display an instance of the form containing the data-bound controls:

```
Private Sub btnDataForm_Click _
   (ByVal sender As System.Object, _
   ByVal e As System.EventArgs) _
   Handles btnDataForm.Click
   Dim x As New DataForm1()
   x.Show()
End Sub
```

13. Run the project.
14. Click the Show Data button.

    The form generated by the Data Form Wizard opens, containing the data-bound controls.
15. Click Load.

    You can now use the controls on the form to scroll through the records in the dataset (**Figure 15.69**).

Summary

In this chapter, you learned how to:

- Create an XML schema
- Validate an XML schema
- Add data to an XML file
- Create a schema from an XML file
- Assign a schema to an XML file
- Validate an XML file against a schema
- Read and write XML elements in code
- Connect to a SQL Server database
- Connect to an Access database file
- Display data with a DataReader component
- Create a database connection
- Create a dataset
- Preview a dataset
- Generate a dataset
- Bind a ListBox control to a dataset
- Bind a ListBox control to a dataset programmatically
- Bind a DataGrid control to a dataset
- Use the Data Form Wizard to generate forms containing data-bound controls

ASP.NET Web Applications

16

ASP.NET is the part of the .NET Framework that developers use to create Web applications. From the viewpoint of a programmer, ASP.NET represents a great improvement over its predecessor technology, ASP (short for Active Server Pages). In contrast to the older ASP technology, in which uncompiled Web scripts were processed in a linear top-to-bottom fashion and code was mingled with HTML tags and content, ASP.NET accomplishes a number of important goals:

- You can now create ASP.NET Web applications from within the Visual Studio development environment, taking advantage of the world-class development and debugging facilities that Visual Studio.NET provides.
- Within Visual Studio, you can separate program code from HTML tags and content.
- You can write ASP.NET Web applications using the full strength of the VB.NET language in an event-driven and object-oriented fashion.
- You can build and compile ASP.NET projects just like any other .NET program.

There is only one thing that can be said against the wonderful ASP.NET technology: It is fully integrated with the Microsoft Internet Information Services (IIS) Web server, meaning that an ASP.NET Web application cannot be deployed with any other Web server (such as Apache).

ASP.NET Web application development is a vast topic. (There are quite a few thick books devoted solely to ASP.NET, although I can't really recommend any of them.) In the context of a big, fat topic like ASP.NET, the goal of this chapter is simply to introduce you to some of the key concepts and techniques used in ASP.NET development and to present some tasks that give you a feel for the process of creating ASP.NET Web applications.

Understanding ASP.NET

Before we take a look at how ASP.NET works, let's back up and explore the general scenario for server-side Web applications.

A Web browser, such as Internet Explorer, can display, or *render*, only static HTML and client-side scripts, such as client-side JavaScript code. Server-side programs produce dynamic HTML, often using database access for this purpose and employing fairly complex programming models. However, the output of a server-side Web program can only be the static HTML (and client-side scripting) that a browser is capable of rendering.

In this model, an HTTP form that is part of a Web page displayed in the browser submits an HTTP form Get or Post request back to the Web server. Usually, this happens when the user clicks a button that activates the HTTP Get or HTTP Post request. The Web server—or specialized software attached to the Web server, sometimes called an *application server*—then processes the form; executes program code against it; perhaps accesses a database server to obtain, update, or query data; and returns custom-generated HTML. (In some cases, HTML, or XML, is even stored in the database.) This whole setup is generally known as a *dynamic* Web application.

From the perspective of a developer, the typical source code file for a dynamic Web application has generally consisted of HTML with embedded custom tags and program commands. There are many examples of this kind of development scenario, including Web applications built using ColdFusion, Java Server Pages (JSP), and earlier versions of Active Server Pages (ASP). In these Web development environments, the following takes place:

- Source code files are processed on the server side.
- Custom tags and script commands are expanded and straight HTML is dynamically generated to replace them.
- Straight HTML (along with occasional client-side script) is returned for rendering by the browser.

ASP.NET applications work in this way to some extent: the real action occurs on the server side, and as you'll see later in this chapter, the browser just renders plain old HTML. But working with ASP.NET in Visual Studio allows the programmer to create code in a more sophisticated way than the single source file containing HTML, custom tags, and script implies.

It's true (but not covered in this chapter) that you can still operate in the good old-fashioned way and create a single source code file containing HTML, ASP.NET tags, and VB .NET code, although I don't advise you to do so if you want to do anything at all complicated.

Invoking an ASP.NET application

You invoke an ASP.NET application by opening an ASP.NET Web Form module (which has the .aspx file extension) over HTTP. The first time it is invoked, the .aspx file (sometimes called an .aspx *page*) is used to compile a related program into a library file.

Internally, the .aspx page interacts programmatically with the Web server (IIS) by using an HTTP form Post command to request an .aspx page (which, once an application is running, is quite likely to be a *post back* request, or a page that issues a request for itself). So far, the process is no different than in the older model.

The great difference is in the way ASP.NET programs are created using Visual Studio and the .NET Framework:

- A custom, compiled program is created for each .aspx file that outputs HTML to the client. When the .aspx file is invoked, the HTML form commands and ASP.NET control tags in the source code are processed by the custom, compiled program.
- Within the compiled program, flow control is organized around objects and events; it is not limited to top-down processing as in the older model.
- Visual Studio provides complete separation of HTML and program code. The Web Form designer, as you'll see in this chapter, provides three interfaces: one for designing controls visually, much like the Windows Form designer; one for editing the HTML that is part of the Web form; and one—the full-featured Visual Studio Code Editor—for creating the *code-behind* module (program code that runs with the Web form).

ASP.NET and Browser Wars? Not!

A common misconception is that Internet Explorer is the only Web browser that works with ASP.NET. Since the browser is rendering straight HTML, however, this just is not so. ASP.NET applications will work with any reasonably current Web browser.

Building an ASP.NET Web application

ASP.NET Web applications are built around Web Form modules in the same way that .NET Windows applications are built around Windows Forms modules. A Web form represents a page in a Web browser in the same ways that a Windows form represents a window in a Windows application. Both kinds of modules have properties, methods, and events that can be used to modify the appearance and behavior of the page in the Web browser (or the window on the desktop). Just as a Windows Application project has out of the box one Windows form module, an ASP.NET Web Application project has by default one Web Form module, which becomes a Web page in the Web browser when the compiled project is run. (As with Windows Application projects, you can add as many Web Form modules to a project as you like.) Although Windows form and Web Form modules cannot inhabit the same project, you can add many other kinds of modules, such as class modules, to each of these kinds of projects.

It's worth bearing in mind the so-called *statelessness* of a Web program. What this means is that once a Web server serves HTML to a Web browser (which is also called a Web *client*), the client and the server are disconnected until the client uses an HTTP Get or HTTP Post request to send an HTTP form back to the server. For the programmer, this gives Web application development a very different feel than Windows application development.

Using (or not using) cookies

Since a Web server may have multiple clients (browsers) connected to it at any given time, server programs need a way of determining the state of each individual client. The general solution is to use a *cookie*, a small file that contains an identification string, stored on each client system to identify the client to the server. However, if cookies are not available—say, the user has disallowed them in the browser—alternative techniques like the use of hidden form fields or of a *mangled URL* (a URL modified to include a session identifier) can enable a server-side Web program to know exactly what client session it is interacting with.

The good news from the viewpoint of an ASP.NET programmer is that, for the most part, ASP.NET automatically keeps track of the state for you. In other words, the underlying mechanism for maintaining the state is transparent to the programmer. Cookies and mangled URL mechanisms are all completely under the hood. Basically, you can assume that the values of control properties will persist across the client-server state gap. For example, if the user enters text in a TextBox server control, when the page containing the HTTP form that contains the server control posts back to the server, the ASP.NET program on the server side will know the new TextBox control property value.

You do have to keep execution order in mind when creating an ASP.NET Web application. Does the code get executed when a Web page first loads? Or is it intended for execution when a click event has been fired (and, therefore, the HTTP form is posted back)? Do you need to set up special precautions so that code is not executed when a form is refreshed by the user in a Web browser? As you'll see, these special considerations are what make ASP.NET programming different from other kinds of programming in the .NET Framework.

Okay—with these basics in mind, let's get started!

Requirements for Running ASP.NET

To create ASP.NET applications in the Visual Studio .NET development environment, you will need Internet Information Services (IIS) version 5 or later installed on your development system, in addition to Visual Studio. You'll also need to have installed an extension to IIS known as the FrontPage Server Extensions. These requirements should not pose a problem, since the operating systems that Visual Studio .NET runs on (primarily Windows XP Professional and Windows 2000) ship with both IIS and the FrontPage Server Extensions, and Visual Studio should properly configure this software for you when it installs. However, if you did not install the FrontPage Server Extensions when you first installed IIS, you may need to uninstall Visual Studio, install the FrontPage Server Extensions, and reinstall Visual Studio.

ASP.NET Web applications are designed to run locally using a Web browser with the URL http://localhost/ followed by the name of your project and an .aspx file. (As you'll see in this chapter, the .aspx file corresponds to a Web Form module.) The URL http://localhost/ is a *virtual* URL, meaning that it corresponds to a location in your file system, normally C:\Inetpub\wwwroot (if C:\ is the designation of the drive on which Windows is installed). This file location then becomes the root for storing the ASP.NET project source files. It is where you need to go to find the per-project directory created by Visual Studio .NET, and it is also where ASP.NET projects and source files need to be located to run on your system. (You can change the mapping of the http://localhost/ virtual URL to the physical /Inetpub/wwwroot physical directory to another physical directory using the Home Directory tab of the Default Website Properties dialog, accessed from the IIS administrative utility.)

You should also know that if you deploy an ASP.NET Web application on a remote server, the external server needs to have IIS, the FrontPage Server Extensions, and the .NET Framework libraries installed.

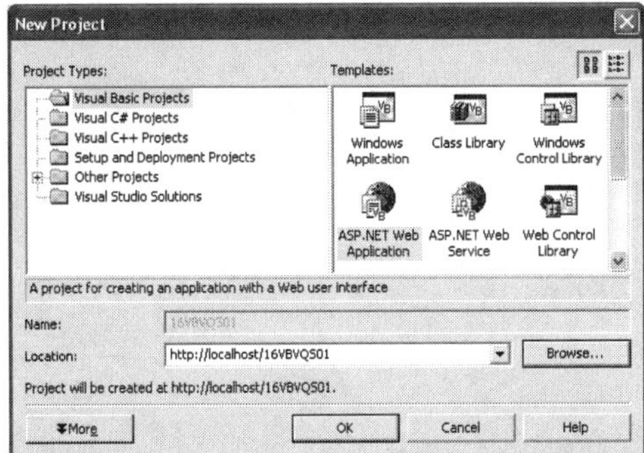

Figure 16.1 Choose ASP.NET Application to open a new ASP.NET Web project.

Creating Web Forms Applications

You create an ASP.NET Web application project, sometimes called a *Web Forms application*, in pretty much the same fashion as you create any other project type in Visual Studio and VB .NET, such as a Windows Application project.

To open a new ASP.NET Web Application project:

1. Open the New Project dialog (**Figure 16.1**) in one of the ways explained in Chapter 1, "Introducing Visual Studio .NET."
2. In the Templates pane of the New Project dialog, choose ASP.NET Web Application as the project type.

   When you select ASP.NET Web application as the project type, the Name text box is disabled, as shown in Figure 16.1.
3. Name the project in the Location text box.

   The Location text box will show the server name, usually http://localhost. The part of the Location entry following the server name (16VBVQS01 in Figure 16.1) becomes the project name.

continues on next page

4. Click OK.

   A new ASP.NET application project will be created, with its source files placed in a folder with the project name (the project created in Figure 16.1 will have source files created in a directory named 16VBVQS01). The directory will be created in the virtual root folder for the localhost IIS Web server, normally \Inetpub\wwwroot (so the source files for the project shown in Figure 16.1 will be saved in the \Inetpub\wwwroot\16VBVQS01 directory).

   When the newly created project opens in Visual Studio, the first thing you will see is the Web Form module associated with the project open in its designer (**Figure 16.2**).

5. From the Visual Studio View menu, choose Solution Explorer.

   Solution Explorer (**Figure 16.3**) shows you the source code and other files associated with the project in Visual Studio.

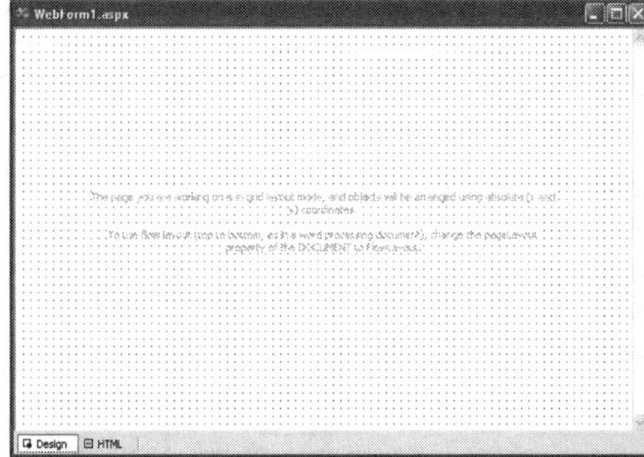

Figure 16.2 The Design tab of the Web Form designer is used for placement of controls.

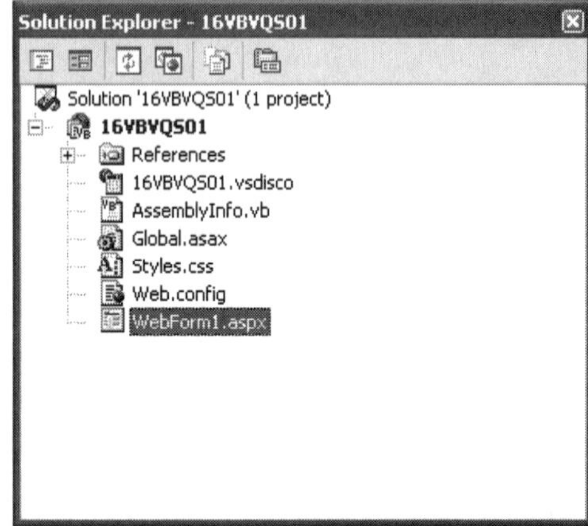

Figure 16.3 A new ASP.NET Web project in Solution Explorer (the Web Form module is shown with an .aspx file extension).

To open an ASP.NET Web application in a browser:

- With the project open in Visual Studio, choose Run from the Debug menu or press F5 on the keyboard.

  The project will be compiled, and the HTML generated by the Web Form module will appear in Internet Explorer, which is operating within the Visual Studio development environment.

  or

- Choose Run from the Debug menu or Build Solution or Build Project from the Build menu, or press F5 on the keyboard. Open a Web browser, such as Internet Explorer and specify the URL for the project followed by the .aspx file name.

  For example, for the project and Web Form module shown in Figures 16.1, 16.2, and 16.3, the URL would be http://localhost/16VBVQS01/WebForm1.aspx.

✔ Tip

- If you rename WebForm1.aspx as Default.aspx, this file can be opened using the URL http://localhost/16VBVQS01/ without mentioning the page name explicitly. This feature is configured and controlled using the Documents tab of the Default Website Properties dialog, accessed from the IIS administrative utility.

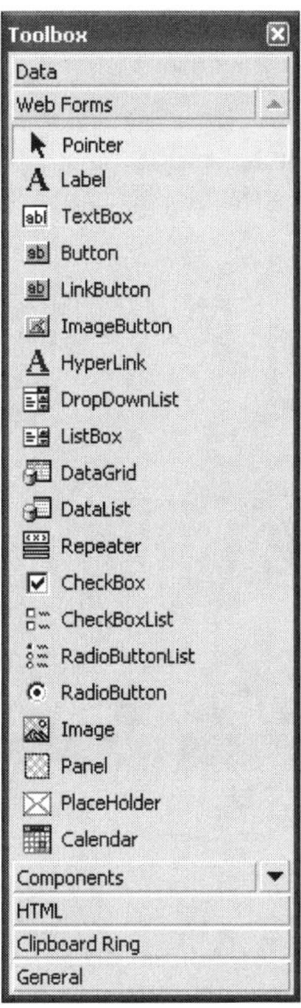

Figure 16.4 When a Web form is active in its designer, the Toolbox tabs show controls and components that can be used to create a Web application.

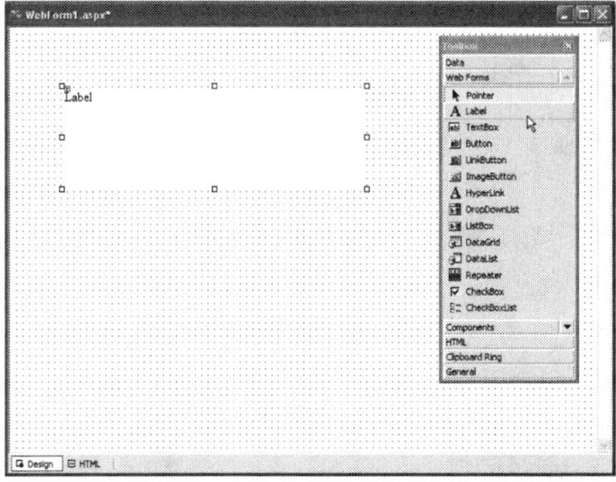

Figure 16.5 Double-click a Label control in the Toolbox, or drag and drop it, to add the Label control to a Web form.

To create a "Hello, VQS!" Web application:

1. With a new ASP.NET Application project open in Visual Studio and a Web Form module open in its designer, choose Toolbox from the Visual Studio View menu.

   The Toolbox opens, showing a number of tabs containing controls specifically intended to work with ASP.NET Web applications (**Figure 16.4**).

2. On the Web Forms tab of the Toolbox, double-click the Label control to add it to the Web form, or drag and drop the Label control to position it on the Web form (**Figure 16.5**).

3. From the Visual Studio View menu, choose Properties Window to open the Properties window.

continues on next page

4. Make sure that the Label control is selected in the Object list at the top of the Properties Window. Then, in the left column of the Properties window, select the Text property (**Figure 16.6**).

5. In the right column of the Properties window, supply the following value for the Text property: `Hello, VQS!`

6. In the left column of the Properties window, select the Font object.

7. Click the plus (+) icon to the left of the Font object to expand it so that its members are accessible in the Properties window (**Figure 16.7**).

8. Set the Font Name property, the Font Size property, the Font Bold property, and the Font Italic property to your taste.

Properties

Label1 System.Web.UI.WebControls.Label

(DataBindings)	
(ID)	**Label1**
AccessKey	
BackColor	
BorderColor	
BorderStyle	NotSet
BorderWidth	
CssClass	
Enabled	True
EnableViewState	True
⊞ Font	
ForeColor	
Height	**119px**
TabIndex	0
Text	**Hello, VQS!**
ToolTip	
Visible	True
Width	**375px**

Text
The text to be shown for the label.

Figure 16.6 Use the Properties window to set the Text property of the Label control.

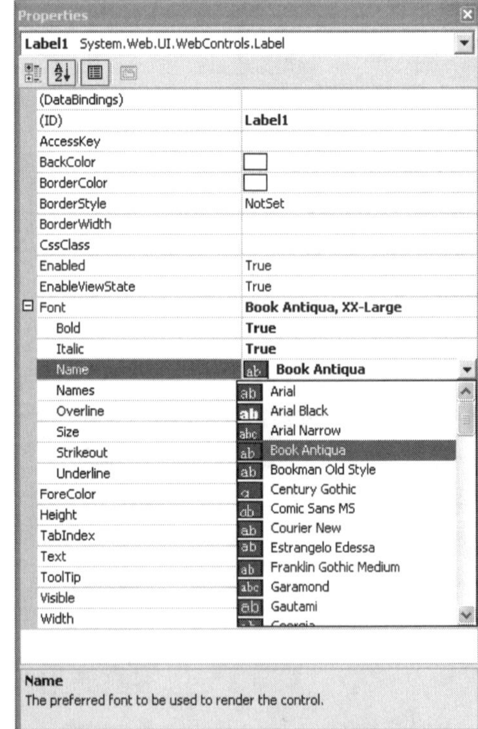

Figure 16.7 You can use the members of the Label control's Font objects to choose a font, font size, and font style.

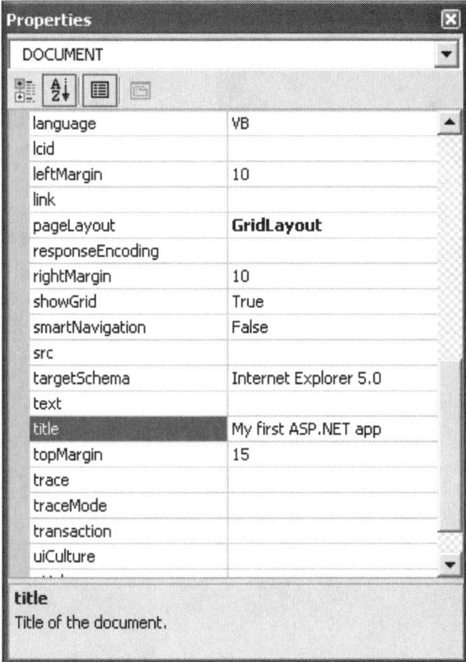

Figure 16.8 The Document title property, shown here in the Properties window, appears in the title bar of the HTML generated by the Web form.

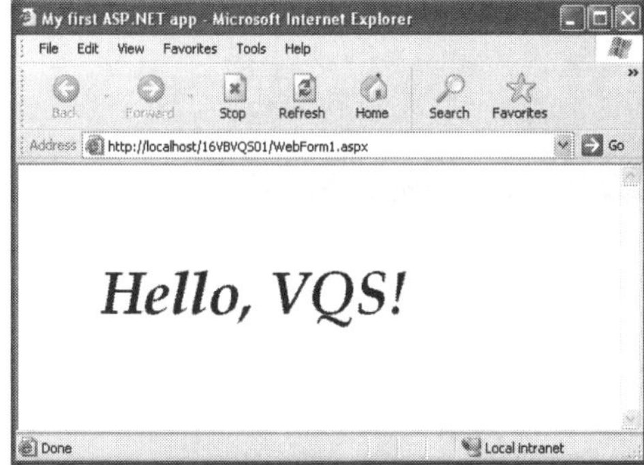

Figure 16.9 The Text value of the Label control is displayed in a Web browser when the application is run.

9. In the Objects list, at the top of the Properties window, select the Document object (**Figure 16.8**).

10. In the left column of the properties window, choose the title property.

11. In the right column of the Properties window, set the value of the title property to *My first ASP.NET app* as shown in Figure 16.8.

    The value of the Document title property will be displayed in the Web browser as the title of the Web page.

12. Run the project.

    The Web Form module modified with the Label control will appear in the browser (**Figure 16.9**). Note that the text value entered as the value of the Document title property in Step 11 appears in the title bar of Internet Explorer in Figure 16.9.

To view the HTML displayed in the browser:

1. Open a running ASP.NET Web application in Internet Explorer, either by running a project in Visual Studio as explained earlier in the task "To create a 'Hello, VQS' Web application" or by opening a compiled ASP.NET Web application via URL directly in the browser as explained in the task "To open an ASP.NET Web application in a browser."
2. With the ASP.NET Web Application Web Form module running in Internet Explorer, choose Source from the Internet Explorer View menu.

   The HTML that was served back to the client (Internet Explorer) opens in Notepad (**Figure 16.10**).

If you look at the HTML shown in Figure 16.10 you'll see that it is unvarnished client-side HTML. There's nothing programmatic here, other than an HTTP form, which, sure enough, when submitted, sends an HTTP Post request to webForm1.aspx.

WebForm1[1] - Notepad

File Edit Format View Help

```
<!DOCTYPE HTML PUBLIC "-//W3C//DTD HTML 4.0 Transitional//EN">
<HTML>
	<HEAD>
		<title>My first ASP.NET app</title>
		<meta name="GENERATOR" content="Microsoft Visual Studio.NET 7.0">
		<meta name="CODE_LANGUAGE" content="Visual Basic 7.0">
		<meta name="vs_defaultClientScript" content="JavaScript">
		<meta name="vs_targetSchema"
content="http://schemas.microsoft.com/intellisense/ie5">
	</HEAD>
	<body MS_POSITIONING="GridLayout">
		<form name="Form1" method="post" action="WebForm1.aspx" id="Form1">
<input type="hidden" name="__VIEWSTATE" value="dDwtMTU3ODAzNTQ4MDs7PuWrGg03K2tJzFh21VglTToJmDav"
/>

			<span id="Label1" style="font-family:Book
Antiqua;font-size:XX-Large;font-weight:bold;font-style:italic;height:119px;width:375px;Z-INDEX:
101; LEFT: 69px; POSITION: absolute; TOP: 75px">Hello, VQS!</span>
		</form>
	</body>
</HTML>
```

Figure 16.10 The HTML source code rendered by the browser is displayed in Notepad.

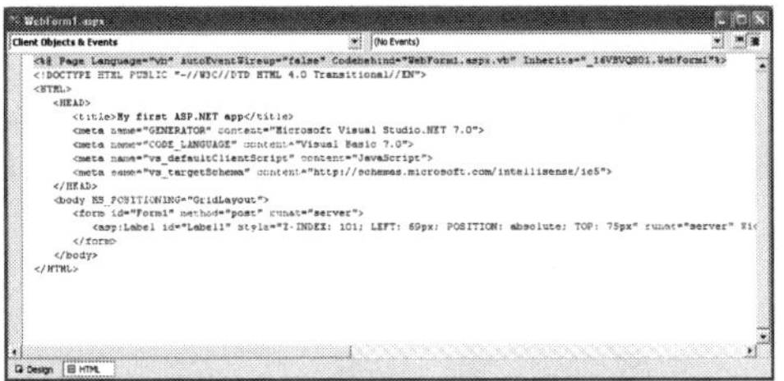

Figure 16.11 Click the HTML tab of the Web Form designer to work with the HTML rather than visually adding controls.

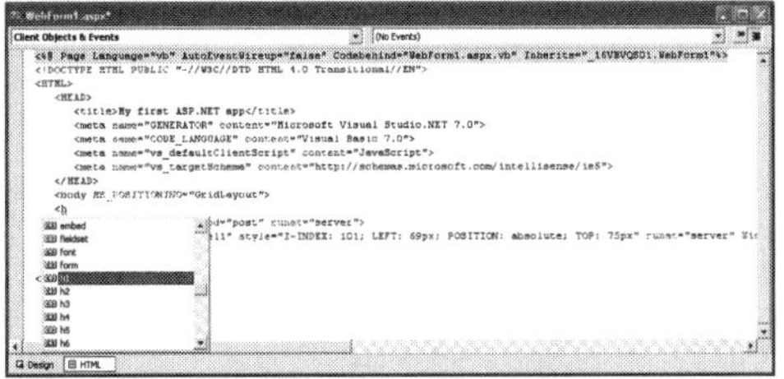

Figure 16.12 You can use auto-completion to add HTML elements to the HTML tab of the Web Form designer.

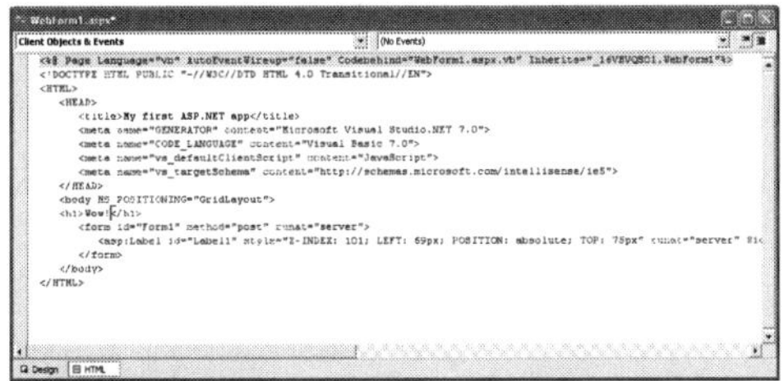

Figure 16.13 Straight HTML (an H1 tag) has been added to the HTML tab of the Web Form designer.

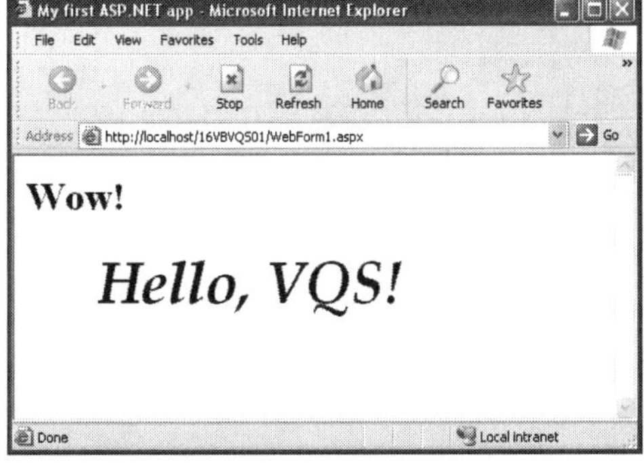

Figure 16.14 The HTML added to the HTML tab of the Web Form designer appears along side the Label control text value when the project is run.

As you'll see in a moment, the server-side HTML, which can be edited using the HTML tab of the Web form in its designer, looks a bit different.

To work with HTML in the Web Form designer:

1. With an ASP .NET Web application project open in Visual Studio and a Web Form module open in its designer, click the HTML tab at the lower left of the designer.

   The HTML tab of the Web Form designer opens (**Figure 16.11**).

2. Enter your HTML tags and content directly on the HTML tab of the Web Form designer.

   In fact, Visual Studio's auto-completion feature will even help you supply the correct syntax for HTML tags via a drop-down list. For example, as shown in **Figure 16.12**, you might enter a new H1 header using straight HTML: <h1>Wow!</h1>. **Figure 16.13** shows the results.

3. Run the project to make sure that the added HTML is displayed when the Web form is displayed on the client side (**Figure 16.14**).

If you compare the HTML shown on the client side in the browser (Figure 16.10) with the Web form HTML in the server-side development environment (Figure 16.11), the most prominent difference you'll see is the Page directive, shown at the top of Figure 16.11 and 16.12. This Page directive tells the compiler what language to use (VB), and the location of the *code-behind*, or the module that contains the actual VB source code for the ASP.NET Web application (in this example, the name of the file that contains the module is WebForm1.aspx.vb). If you look closely, you'll also notice some significant differences in HTTP form construction and the way server-side controls are referenced compared to controls in the client-side HTML.

Writing client-side code

Whose says you can't have it all? Often, it makes sense to add client-side scripts to ASP.NET Web applications that execute on the server side. Client-side code, usually written in JavaScript, can perform a great deal of the work of creating user interfaces in the browser and validating user input. As a matter of Web application architecture, the more you can offload to the client side, the less load there is on your Web server, and the less time the user has to spend waiting for the Web server to respond to a request.

Fortunately, ASP.NET and Visual Studio provide an excellent mechanism for adding client-side scripts to your ASP.NET programs.

In the next task, you'll see how to add a very simple client-side piece of JavaScript functionality: the browser will display an alert box—the JavaScript name for a message box—when the user clicks the page in the browser.

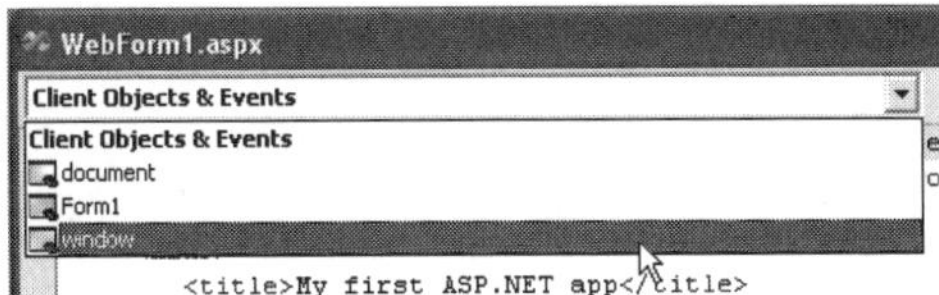

Figure 16.15 Use the Objects list on the HTML tab of the Web Form designer to choose a client object.

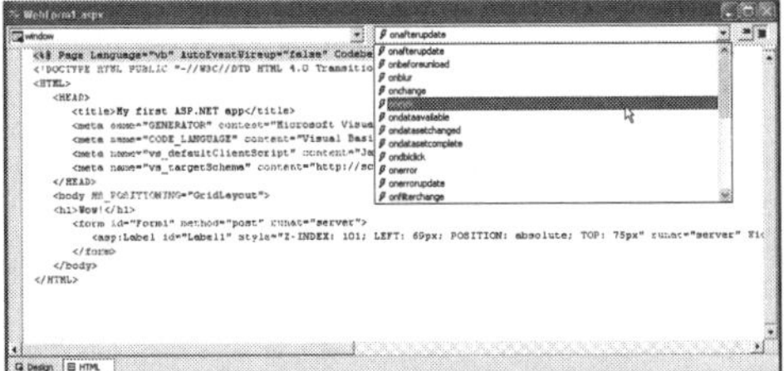

Figure 16.16 With a client object selected in the Objects list, you can choose an event in the Procedures list to create a client-side event framework.

Figure 16.17 Auto-completion on the HTML tab of the Web Form designer will supply client-side JavaScript syntax.

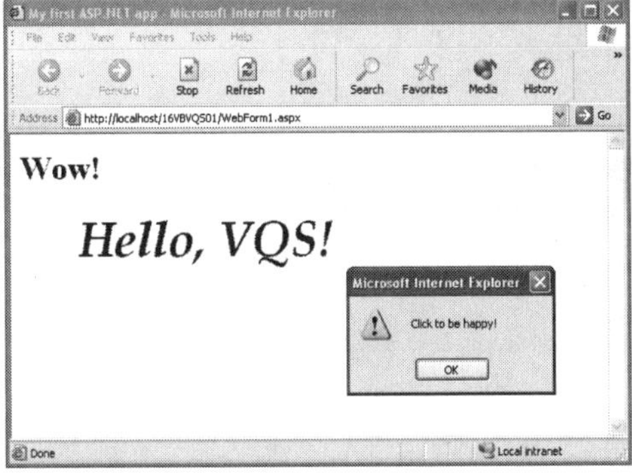

Figure 16.18 In the browser, the client-side script displays a JavaScript alert box when the user clicks the browser window.

To add a client-side script:

1. With a Web form open in its designer in Visual Studio, select the HTML tab.
2. On the HTML tab of the Web Form designer, select the window object from the Client Objects and Events drop-down list at the upper left of the designer (**Figure 16.15**).
3. Select the onClick event from the Procedures list at the upper right of the designer (**Figure 16.16**).

   Visual Studio will create an addition to the HTML <body> tag that adds a function call when the JavaScript onclick event is fired:

   ```
   <body language="javascript"
   onclick="return window_onclick()">
   ```

   Visual Studio will also create a framework for the JavaScript function:

   ```
   function window_onclick() {


   }
   ```

4. Within the HTML tab of the designer, add the JavaScript commands you want executed within the function (auto-completion will help you with JavaScript syntax, as shown in **Figure 16.17**).

   For example, here's the complete function code to display the JavaScript alert box:

   ```
   function window_onclick() {
      alert ("Click to be happy!");
   }
   ```

5. Run the project.
6. Click the page in the Web browser.

   The alert box appears (**Figure 16.18**).

   By the way, if you check the browser source code, as explained earlier in the task "To view the HTML displayed in the browser," you'll see the JavaScript event code and function exactly as entered in the Web Form designer (processing of the JavaScript code is handled by the Web browser).

Accessing the Web form code-behind

So far, we have nibbled around the periphery of the ASP.NET Web application. Now it is time to cut to the chase. From a programmer's viewpoint, the most interesting and powerful feature of the Visual Studio development environment for creating ASP.NET Web applications is the Web form's code-behind module, opened in the Code Editor.

To view the Web form code-behind:

1. With a Web form open in its designer in Visual Studio, choose Code from the Visual Studio View menu, or View Code from the designer's context menu.

   The code-behind opens in the Code Editor (**Figure 16.19**). The code is exactly what you will see when you open the Code Editor if you accepted the default name for your Web Form module (WebForm1). However, just like a Windows form, a Web form contains code in a hidden region.

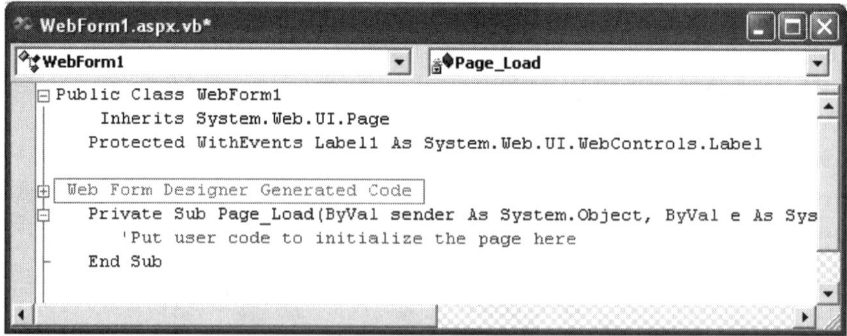

Figure 16.19 When you open the Code Editor, you'll see the out-of-the-box code-behind module.

2. To view the full Web Form module code (including that within the hidden region), click the plus sign (+) shown in gray to the left of the text "Web Form Designer Generated Code."

   Listing 16.1 shows the out-of-the box default code-behind for a Web form, including the code in the hidden region.

✔ Tip

- It is interesting to compare the default code for a Web form with the default code for a Windows form, shown in Listing 5.1, in Chapter 5, "Windows Forms."

Listing 16.1 Default WebForm class code.

```
Public Class WebForm1
    Inherits System.Web.UI.Page

#Region " Web Form Designer Generated Code "

'This call is required by the Web Form Designer.
 <System.Diagnostics.DebuggerStepThrough()> Private Sub InitializeComponent()
End Sub

Private Sub Page_Init(ByVal sender As System.Object, ByVal e As System.EventArgs) _
   Handles MyBase.Init
   'CODEGEN: This method call is required by the Web Form Designer
   'Do not modify it using the code editor.
   InitializeComponent()
End Sub

#End Region

Private Sub Page_Load(ByVal sender As System.Object, ByVal e As System.EventArgs) _
   Handles MyBase.Load
   'Put user code to initialize the page here
End Sub

End Class
```

Working with Controls

Creating an ASP.NET Web Application project, just like creating a VB .NET Windows Application project and a Windows Form module, generally involves visually adding controls to a Web Form module in its designer. You set the control properties using the Properties window, and you set the size and location of the control visually. Then you wire the controls in the Code Editor.

Before we explore some examples of this process, let's sit back for a moment and talk about the different kinds of controls available to an ASP.NET Web Form module.

If you look at the Toolbox when the Design tab is open in Web Form designer, you will not see the Toolbox tab for the familiar Windows Forms controls. Instead, you'll see Toolbox tabs for Web Forms controls and HTML controls. The Toolbox with these tabs is shown in Figure 16.4 and **Figure 16.20**. (In addition, the Data tab makes available the ADO.NET components and controls explained in Chapter 15, "XML, Data, and ADO.NET." These objects are very important in ASP.NET development, since most Web applications involve accessing databases.

Starting with the controls available on the Toolbox tabs just mentioned, let's categorize the server-side controls that you are likely to work with as an ASP.NET developer:

- Web Forms controls are the intrinsic .NET Framework ASP.NET server-side controls. These are the controls you are mostly likely to work with when creating an ASP.NET application. HTML controls found on the HTML tab of the Toolbox are the server-side HTML equivalent of the HTML <INPUT> elements that make up an HTML form. The HTML elements have been rejiggered to work as server-side controls by adding a runat=server attribute to the HTML elements.

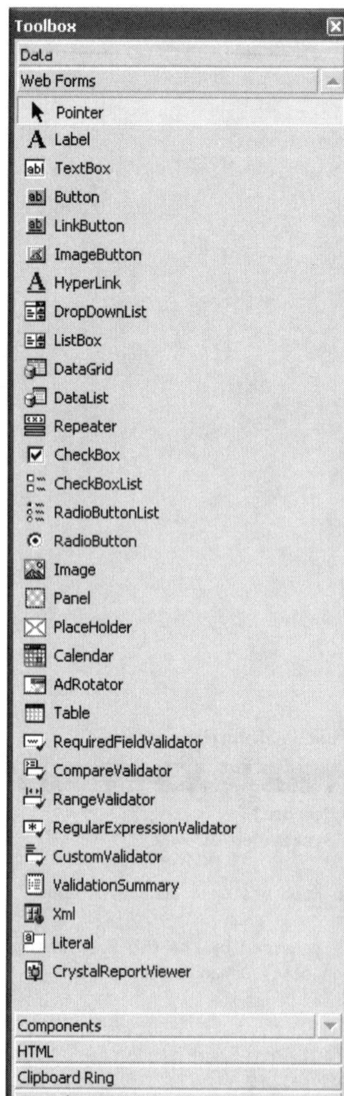

Figure 16.20 The Web Forms tab of Web Forms controls shown in its entirety.

- Web User controls are custom-created, reusable portions of an .aspx page, including the related code-behind module. Web user controls are pretty easy to create and can be thought of as analogous to server-side includes. For more information, look up the topic "Walkthrough: Creating a Web User control" in the online help. Web User Controls should not be confused with custom controls, which can be created from scratch or by derivation from an existing control for both Windows and Web applications.

All of the Web Forms controls are shown on the Web Forms tab of the Toolbox in Figure 16.20 and described in **Table 16.1**.

Table 16.1

Web Forms (ASP.NET) Controls

Control	Description
Label	Displays text
TextBox	Displays user-editable text
Button	Displays a button that the user can click
LinkButton	Displays a hyperlink; behaves like a button
ImageButton	Displays a button with an image rather than text
Hyperlink	Creates a hyperlink for navigation
DropDownList	Displays a list in a drop-down box
ListBox	Displays a scrollable list of items
DataGrid	Displays a table of information
DataList	Displays a list of items using templates
Repeater	Displays a rendered list of items
CheckBox	Displays a check box, which can be checked on or off
CheckBoxList	Displays a group of check box items
RadioButton	Displays an option button
RadioButtonList	Displays a group of option buttons
Image	Displays an image
Panel	Creates a container for other controls on a Web form
Calendar	Displays an interactive calendar
AdRotator	Displays a sequence of images, either in random or predetermined order
Table	Displays a table
RequiredFieldValidator	Makes sure that the user does not leave a field blank
CompareValidator	Compares the user's entry in a field with a value such as a variable or constant
RangeValidator	Makes sure that the user's entry is between a specified range of values
RegularExpressionValidator	Validates the user's entry against a regular expression
CustomValidator	Makes sure that the user's entry complies with validation logic you have coded
ValidationSummary	Displays a summary of all validation errors
Xml	Reads XML and displays it on a Web form page, optionally applying an XSLT transformation before rendering the XML
Literal	Used to place text on a Web form page, which can be programmatically manipulated on the server side. (For static text that is not programmatically changed, you can use HTML rather than this control)
CrystalReportViewer	Allows you to create, manipulate, and view reports

Let's start by doing something simple with Web Forms controls. The next few tasks show you how to add a TextBox control and a Button control to the Web form that already contains the Label control used to display the text "Hello, VQS." When the user enters text in the TextBox control and clicks the Button control, the Label control will display that text instead of "Hello, VQS!"

To add controls and create a click event handler for a Button control:

1. With the Design tab of the Web Form designer used in the "Hello, VQS" application open in Visual Studio, choose Toolbox from the View menu to open the Toolbox.
2. On the Web Forms tab of the Toolbox, double-click the Label control, or drag and drop it onto the Web form, to add a Label control instance to the form (**Figure 16.21**).
3. On the Web Forms tab of the Toolbox, double-click the Button control, or drag and drop it onto the Web form, to add a Button control instance to the form (**Figure 16.22**).
4. From the Visual Studio View menu, choose Properties Window to open the Properties window.
5. In the Object list at the top of the Properties window, choose the Button control.
6. In the left column of the Properties window, select (ID).
7. In the right column of the Properties window, provide a value of *btnChange* for the ID for the Button control.
8. In the left column of the Properties window, select Text.

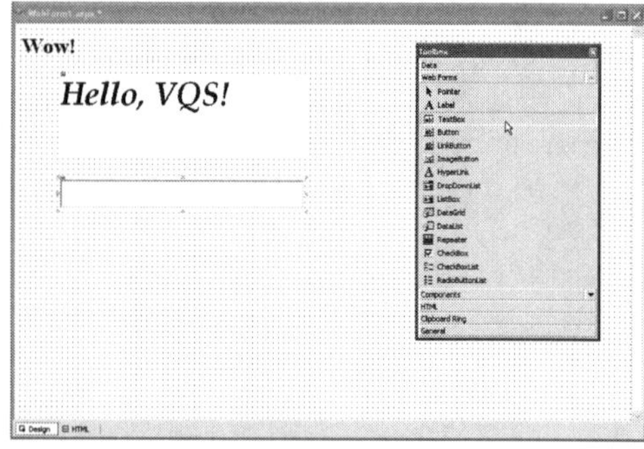

Figure 16.21 Select TextBox on the Web Forms tab of the Toolbox and double-click (or drag and drop) to add a TextBox control to the Web form.

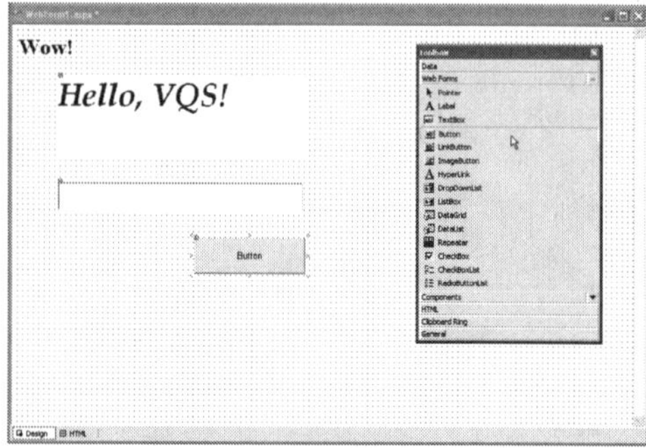

Figure 16.22 Select Button on the Web Forms tab of the Toolbox and double-click (or drag and drop) to add a Button control to the Web form.

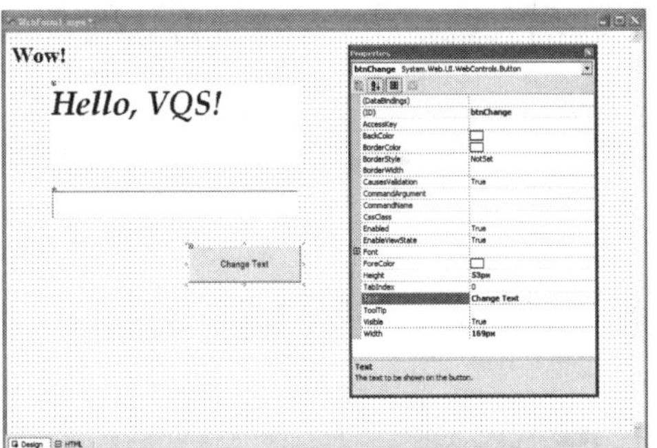

Figure 16.23 You can use the Properties window to change the name and Text property values of controls such as the Button control shown here.

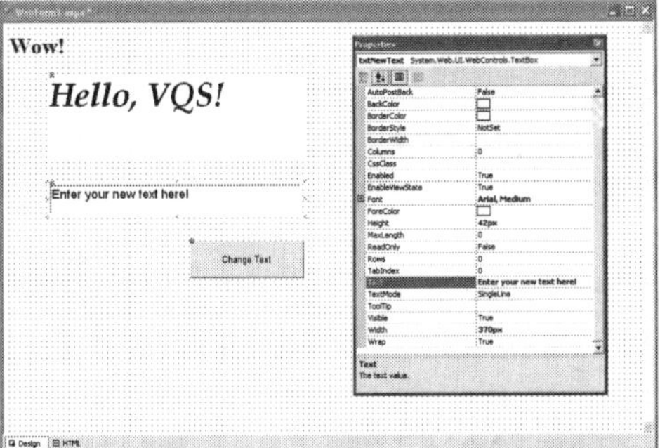

Figure 16.24 You can use the Properties window to change the value of the Text property of the TextBox control.

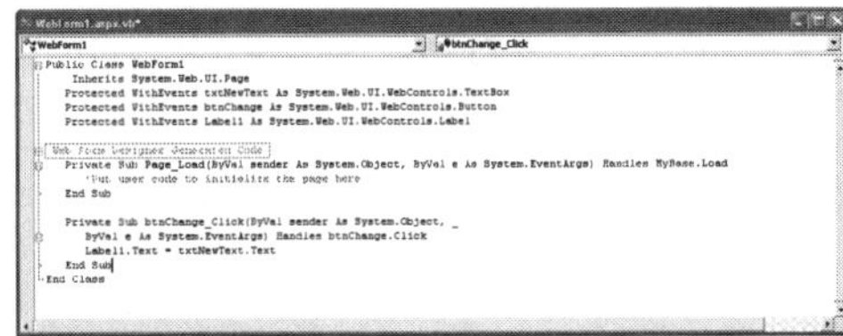

Figure 16.25 When you double-click the Button control, a click event procedure is created for it in the Code Editor.

9. In the right column of the Properties window, set the value of the Text property to *Change Text.*

   Figure 16.23 shows the Properties window with the ID and Text properties entered.

10. In the Object list at the top of the Properties window, choose the TextBox control.

11. In the left column of the Properties window, select (ID).

12. In the right column of the Properties window, provide a value of *txtNewText* for the ID for the TextBox control.

13. In the left column of the Properties window, select Text.

14. In the right column of the Properties window, set the value of the Text property to *Enter your new text here!* as shown in **Figure 16.24**.

15. Double-click the Change Text button to create a click event handler for the Button control.

    The code-behind will open in the Code Editor, positioned at the click event (**Figure 16.25**).

To change the Text value of a Label control based on user input:

1. Within the click event handler, add code that changes the value of the Label control's Text property to the value of the TextBox control's Text property:

   ```
   Label1.Text = txtNewText.Text
   ```

   Here's the complete click event procedure:

   ```
   Private Sub btnChange_Click _
      (ByVal sender As System.Object, _
      ByVal e As System.EventArgs) _
      Handles btnChange.Click
      Label1.Text = txtNewText.Text
   End Sub
   ```

2. Run the project.

   The Web form opens in the browser.

3. Enter some text in the TextBox (**Figure 16.26**).

4. Click Change Text.

   The text you entered now appears in the Label control (**Figure 16.27**).

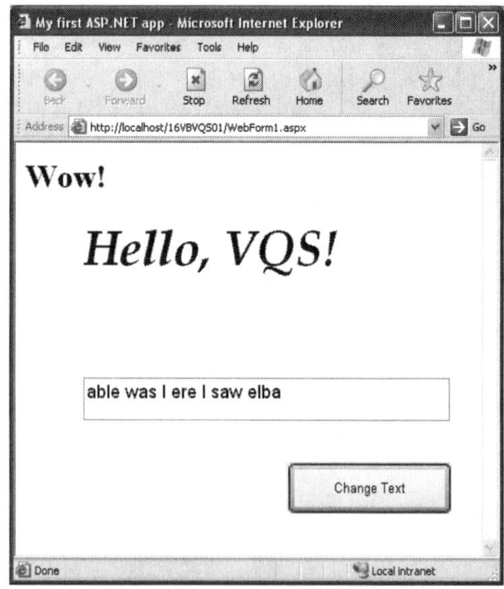

Figure 16.26 When the project is run, the Web form is displayed in the browser.

Figure 16.27 Text entered in the TextBox control is displayed in the Label control when the user clicks the Button control.

Multiform applications are very common in Windows. They are a little less common in ASP.NET applications, which tend instead to post back multiple times to one Web form, which appears in different guises depending on which controls are visible. (You'll see an example of this later in this chapter in the tasks "To save session information" and "To save application information.")

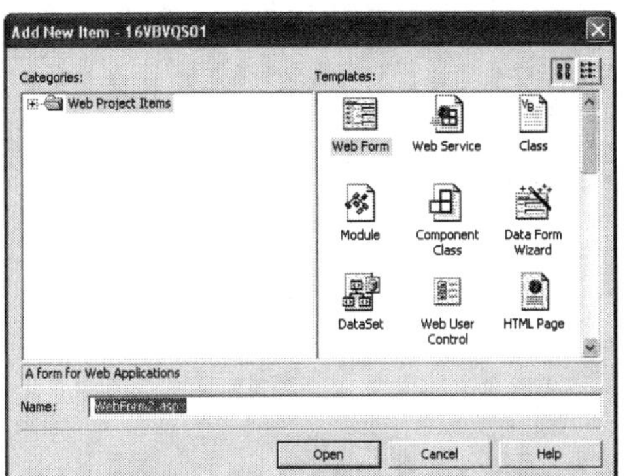

Figure 16.28 Use the Add New Item dialog to add a second Web form to a project.

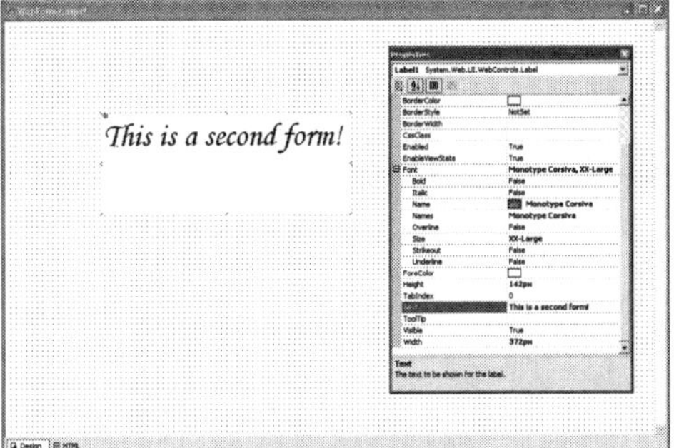

Figure 16.29 Use a Label control to identify the second form.

Nevertheless, you will sometimes want to open one Web form from another. This next task shows you how to do so. We'll start with the "Hello, VQS!" project and add a new form that opens from a click event in the original "Hello, VQS" Web form.

To open a new instance of a Web form from a click event:

1. With the "Hello, VQS!" project still open in Visual Studio, choose Add Web Form from the Project menu to open the Add New Item dialog (**Figure 16.28**).
2. In the Add New Item dialog, make sure Web Form is selected in the Templates pane.
3. In the Name text box, enter a name with a .aspx file suffix for the Web form, or accept the suggested default name.
4. Click Open.

   The new Web form opens in its designer (**Figure 16.29**).
5. Use the Toolbox to add a Label control to the new Web form.
6. Use the Properties window to set the value of the Label control's Text property to *This is a second form!* as shown in Figure 16.29.
7. Choose DOCUMENT in the Objects drop-down list at the top of the Properties window.

continues on next page

8. In the left column of the Properties window, select title (**Figure 16.30**).

9. In the right column of the Properties window, set the value of the title property to *The second form.*

10. Open the first "Hello, VQS!" Web form (named WebForm1.aspx if you haven't changed the default name) in its designer *by doing one of the following:*

    Select the form from the Visual Studio Window menu if it is available on the Window menu.

    or

    From the Visual Studio View menu, choose Solution Explorer and double-click WebForm1.aspx to open it in its designer.

11. With the "Hello, VQS" Web form open in its designer, use the Toolbox to add a Button control to the Web form.

12. Use the Properties window to change the name of the Button control to *btn2Form* and the value of its Text property to *Second Form* (**Figure 16.31**).

13. Double-click the Second Form button to create a click-event handler for it in the code-behind module in the Code Editor:

```
Private Sub btn2form_Click _
   (ByVal sender As System.Object, _
   ByVal e As System.EventArgs) _
   Handles btn2form.Click


End Sub
```

Figure 16.30 Use the DOCUMENT title property in the Properties window to set the HTML title value for the HTML that will be returned to the browser.

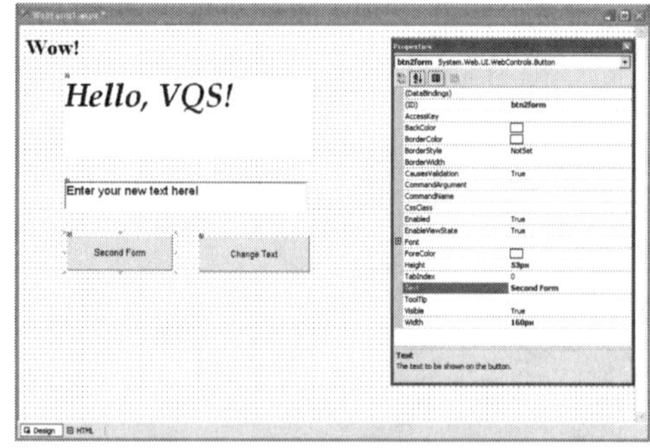

Figure 16.31 A Button control is added to the first form, to be used to open the second form.

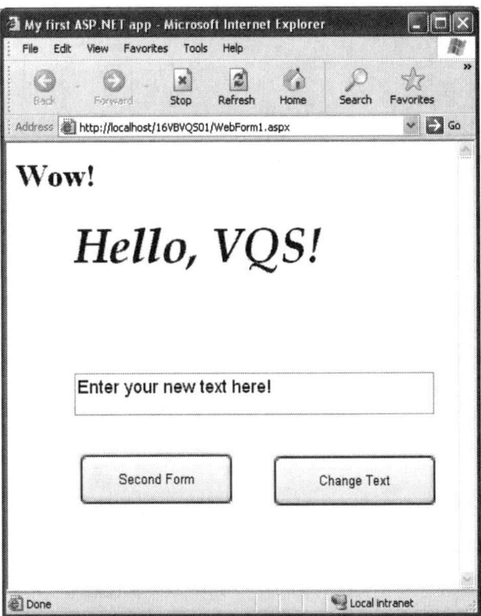

Figure 16.32 The Second Form Button control has been added to the application.

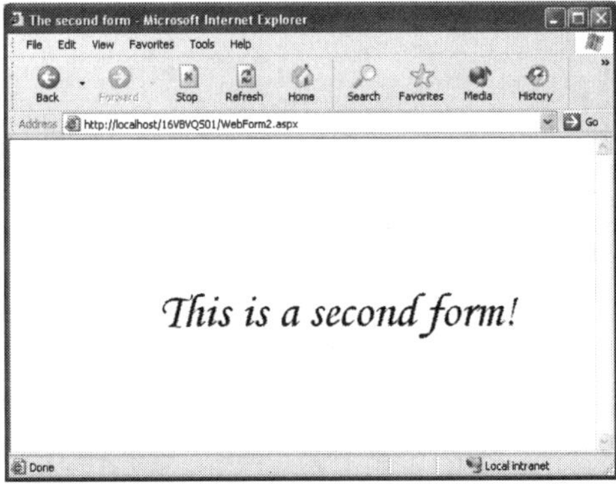

Figure 16.33 When the user clicks the Second Form button, the second Web form is displayed in the browser.

14. Within the click event handler, use the Redirect method of the Response object to open the second Web form:

```
Response.Redirect("WebForm2.aspx")
```

Here's the complete click event handler:

```
Private Sub btn2form_Click _
   (ByVal sender As System.Object, _
   ByVal e As System.EventArgs) _
   Handles btn2form.Click
   Response.Redirect("WebForm2.aspx")
End Sub
```

15. Run the project.

The first Web form (WebForm1.aspx) opens in the browser (**Figure 16.32**).

16. Click Second Form.

The second Web form (WebForm2.aspx if you didn't change the default name) opens (**Figure 16.33**).

Displaying an interactive calendar

There are so many Web Forms controls that it would certainly take an entire Visual QuickStart book to show you how to use them all. (If you don't believe me, take another look at the controls on the Web Forms Toolbox tab, shown in Figure 16.20 and described in Table 16.1.) So we can't possibly cover the use of all these controls in the remainder of this chapter. But it seems fair to give you a taste of something a little more exotic (and powerful) than Button, Label, and TextBox controls.

In the next task, you'll see how to display a month-by-month calendar in a Web browser. When the application opens, the current date will be selected. The user can select another date and another month to display. The application will display the current date and the selected date.

In a real-world Web application, you'd probably want to do a lot more with a calendar. The point here is to show you how easy it is to put the basic functionality of a calendar in your ASP.NET Web applications. (Think how long it would take you to hand-code the HTML returned to the browser by this control, used to render the calendar!)

To create the calendar interface:

1. Open a new ASP.NET Web application.
2. With the default Web form open in its designer, choose Toolbox from the View menu.
3. Double-click the Calendar control, or drag and drop it, to place an instance of the Calendar control on the Web form (**Figure 16.34**).
4. Use the Toolbox to add Label controls to display the current and selected dates, a DropDownList control to allow the user to select a month, and a Button control (**Figure 16.35**).

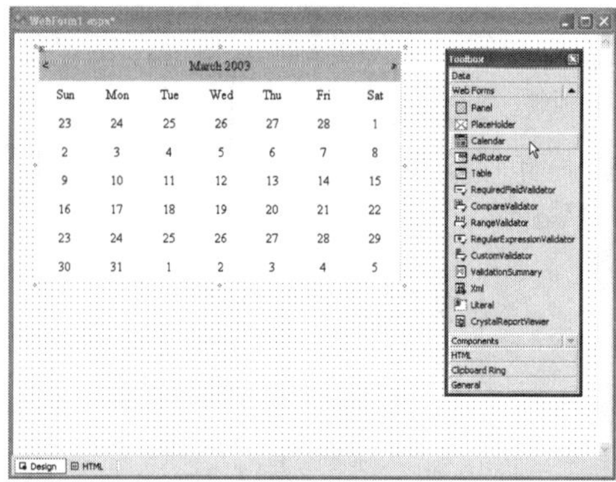

Figure 16.34 Double-click the Calendar control on the Web Forms tab of the Toolbox to add it to a Web form.

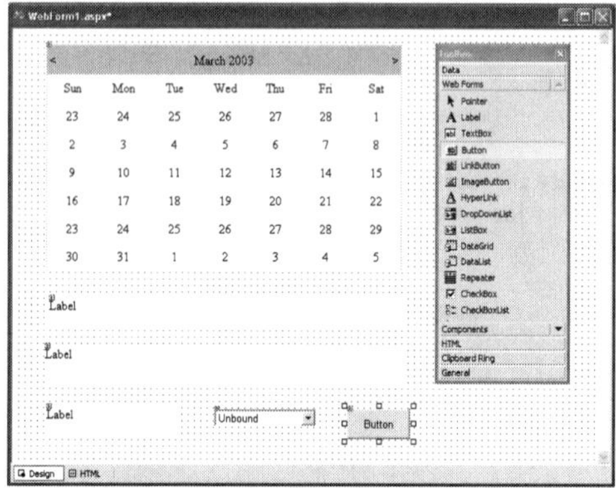

Figure 16.35 When the user interface is complete, it should look like this on the Design tab of the Web Form designer.

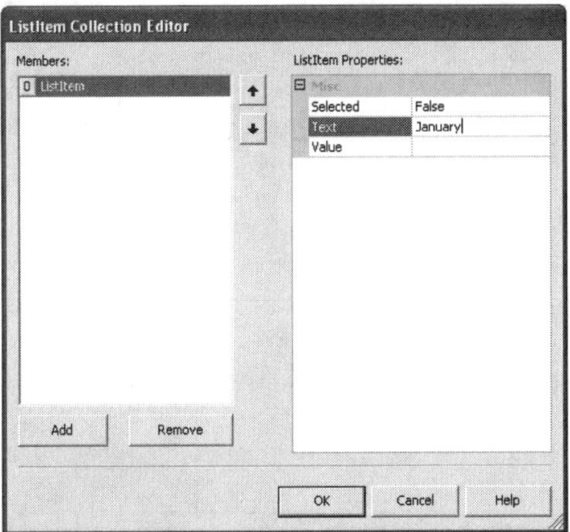

Figure 16.36 You can use the ListItem Collection Editor to add items to the Items collection of the DropDownList control.

To add items to the interface:

1. Use the Properties window to set the name of the first label to *lblToday*, the name of the second label to *lblDateSelected*, the name of the drop-down list to *lstMonths*, and the name of the button to *btnSetMonth*.
2. Use the Properties window to set the value of the Text property of the third label to *Choose a month:* and the value of the Text property of the Button control to *Choose*.
3. In the Objects list at the top of the Properties window, select the lstMonths DropDownList control.
4. In the left column of the Properties window, select the Items property.
5. In the right column of the Properties window, click the ... button.
   The ListItem Collection Editor will open (**Figure 16.36**).
6. In the ListItem Collection Editor, enter *January* as the value of the Text property for the first item in the Items collection (as you can see in Figure 16.36, the index for the first item is 0, rather than 1).

continues on next page

7. Click Add.

8. Repeat the process until all 12 months have been added as items to the Items collection (**Figure 16.37**).

   Looking at Figure 16.37, you can see that the index values for the 12 months range from 0 to 11, not 1 to 12. As you likely know, it is a matter of personal preference whether you add initial items in this fashion using the ListItem Collection Editor or in program code. (For more information about list boxes and the Items collections of ListBox controls, see Chapter 10, "Controls That Accept User Input.")

9. Click OK.

   Your user interface should now look like **Figure 16.38**. The contents of the HTML tab of the Web form designer (the .aspx file) is shown in **Listing 16.2**.

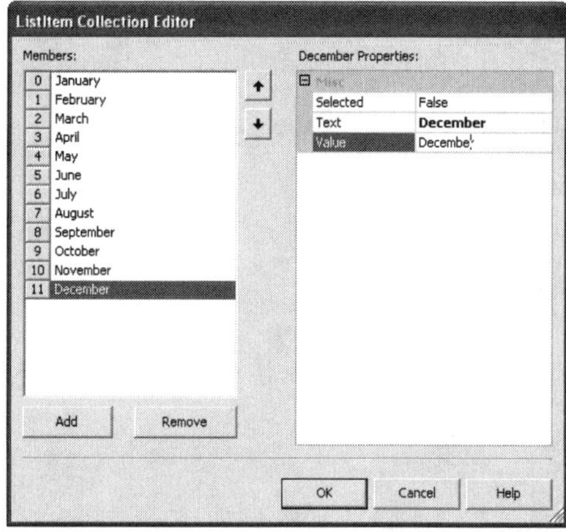

Figure 16.37 All 12 months have been added to the Items collection of the drop-down list (note that the items are indexed starting with 0).

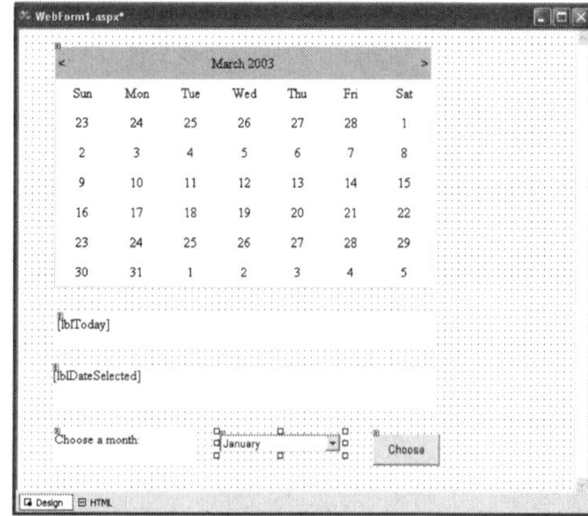

Figure 16.38 The first month, January, now appears in the DropDownList control on the Web Form designer.

Listing 16.2 The Calendar ASPX file (edited for clarity).

```
<%@ Page Language="vb" AutoEventWireup="false" Codebehind="WebForm1.aspx.vb"
Inherits="_16VBVQS02.WebForm1"%>
<!DOCTYPE HTML PUBLIC "-//W3C//DTD HTML 4.0 Transitional//EN">
<HTML>
   <HEAD>
   <title>WebForm1</title>
   <meta name="GENERATOR" content="Microsoft Visual Studio.NET 7.0">
   <meta name="CODE_LANGUAGE" content="Visual Basic 7.0">
   <meta name="vs_defaultClientScript" content="JavaScript">
<meta name="vs_targetSchema" content="http://schemas.microsoft.com/intellisense/ie5">
   </HEAD>
   <body MS_POSITIONING="GridLayout">
      <form id="Form1" method="post" runat="server">
         <asp:Calendar id="Calendar1" style="Z-INDEX: 101; LEFT: 43px; POSITION: absolute; TOP:
20px" runat="server" Height="283px" Width="453px"></asp:Calendar>
         <asp:Label id="lblToday" style="Z-INDEX: 102; LEFT: 47px; POSITION: absolute; TOP: 336px"
runat="server" Height="35px" Width="450px"></asp:Label>
         <asp:Label id="lblDateSelected" style="Z-INDEX: 103; LEFT: 42px; POSITION: absolute; TOP:
396px" runat="server" Height="47px" Width="454px"></asp:Label>
         <asp:Label id="Label3" style="Z-INDEX: 104; LEFT: 44px; POSITION: absolute; TOP: 471px"
runat="server" Height="35px" Width="167px">Choose a month:</asp:Label>
         <asp:DropDownList id="lstMonths" style="Z-INDEX: 105; LEFT: 242px; POSITION: absolute;
TOP: 474px" runat="server" Height="32px" Width="147px">
         <asp:ListItem Value="January">January</asp:ListItem>
         <asp:ListItem Value="February">February</asp:ListItem>
         <asp:ListItem Value="March">March</asp:ListItem>
         <asp:ListItem Value="April">April</asp:ListItem>
         <asp:ListItem Value="May">May</asp:ListItem>
         <asp:ListItem Value="June">June</asp:ListItem>
         <asp:ListItem Value="July">July</asp:ListItem>
         <asp:ListItem Value="August">August</asp:ListItem>
         <asp:ListItem Value="September">September</asp:ListItem>
         <asp:ListItem Value="October">October</asp:ListItem>
         <asp:ListItem Value="November">November</asp:ListItem>
         <asp:ListItem Value="December">December</asp:ListItem>
         </asp:DropDownList>
         <asp:Button id="btnSetMonth" style="Z-INDEX: 106; LEFT: 427px; POSITION: absolute; TOP:
473px" runat="server" Height="38px" Width="80px" Text="Choose"></asp:Button>
      </form>
   </body>
</HTML>
```

To create and test the code-behind:

1. Double-click the Choose button to create a click event handler for it and to open the Code Editor with the code-behind module loaded.

2. You first need to set up the Calendar control when it initially loads. The code that does this goes within the Page_Load event, which is automatically created for you (see Listing 16.1). Within the Page_Load event, two possibilities need to be considered: is the page being loaded for the first time, or is this a post-back event? Start with an If statement that checks to determine this:

```
Private Sub Page_Load(ByVal sender _
   As System.Object, ByVal e As _
   System.EventArgs) Handles _
   MyBase.Load
   If Not IsPostBack Then

   End If
End Sub
```

3. If the event is not a post-back, meaning that the page is loading for the first time, set the date selected in the Calendar control to the current date, use the VisibleDate property of the Calendar control to set the month shown by the calendar to the current month, set the lstMonths DropDownList control to select the month shown in the calendar, and display the date selected:

```
If Not IsPostBack Then
   Calendar1.SelectedDate = _
      Calendar1.TodaysDate
   Calendar1.VisibleDate = _
      Calendar1.TodaysDate
   lstMonths.SelectedIndex = _
      Calendar1.VisibleDate.Month - 1
   lblDateSelected.Text = _
      "Date selected is " & _
      Calendar1.SelectedDate. _
      ToLongDateString & "."
  End If
```

4. Regardless whether the event is a post-back, display today's date:

```
lblToday.Text = "Today is " & _
     Calendar1.TodaysDate. _
     ToLongDateString & "."
```

Here's the complete Page_Load event procedure:

```
Private Sub Page_Load(ByVal sender _
   As System.Object, ByVal e As _
   System.EventArgs) Handles _
   MyBase.Load
   If Not IsPostBack Then
     Calendar1.SelectedDate = _
       Calendar1.TodaysDate
     Calendar1.VisibleDate = _
       Calendar1.TodaysDate
     lstMonths.SelectedIndex = _
       Calendar1.VisibleDate.Month - 1
     lblDateSelected.Text = _
        "Date selected is " & _
        Calendar1.SelectedDate. _
        ToLongDateString & "."
   End If
   lblToday.Text = "Today is " & _
     Calendar1.TodaysDate. _
     ToLongDateString & "."
 End Sub
```

5. In the Objects list at the upper left of the Code Editor, choose the Calendar control.

6. With the Calendar control selected in the Objects list, choose the SelectionChanged event to create an event handler that is fired when the user selects a new date:

```
Private Sub _
Calendar1_SelectionChanged _
(ByVal sender As Object, _
ByVal e As System.EventArgs) _
Handles Calendar1.SelectionChanged

End Sub
```

7. Within the SelectionChanged event handler, display the date selected:

```
lblDateSelected.Text = _
   "Date selected is " & _
   Calendar1.SelectedDate. _
   ToLongDateString & "."
```

Here's the complete SelectionChanged event handler:

```
Private Sub _
Calendar1_SelectionChanged _
(ByVal sender As Object, _
 ByVal e As System.EventArgs) _
Handles Calendar1.SelectionChanged
  lblDateSelected.Text = _
     "Date selected is " & _
     Calendar1.SelectedDate. _
     ToLongDateString & "."
End Sub
```

8. Turn to the event handler you created earlier for the Choose button:

```
Private Sub btnSetMonth_Click _
   (ByVal sender As System.Object, _
   ByVal e As System.EventArgs) _
   Handles btnSetMonth.Click

End Sub
```

continues on next page

Within the event handler, check to see if the user selected a month in the DropDownList control that is not the same as the month selected in the Calendar control. If the months differ, create a new DateTime object using the month selected in the drop-down list to set the selected month in the calendar. To set the calendar month, you need to add 1 to the index value of the selected month in the Items collection of the drop-down list to match the number of the month as the Calendar control understands it (in the Calendar control, the numbers range from 1 to 12, rather than 0 to 11 as in the DropDownList Items collection):

```
If Not _
(CInt(Calendar1.VisibleDate.Month) _
 = lstMonths.SelectedIndex + 1) Then
   Calendar1.VisibleDate = New _
DateTime(Calendar1.TodaysDate.Year, _
lstMonths.SelectedIndex + 1, 1)
lblDateSelected.Text = _
   "Date selected is "
End If
```

Listing 16.3 shows the complete code for the code-behind module (without the hidden code region).

9. Run the project.
10. Choose a month and a date.

    The calendar allows you to make selections and displays both the current date and the date you selected (**Figure 16.39**).

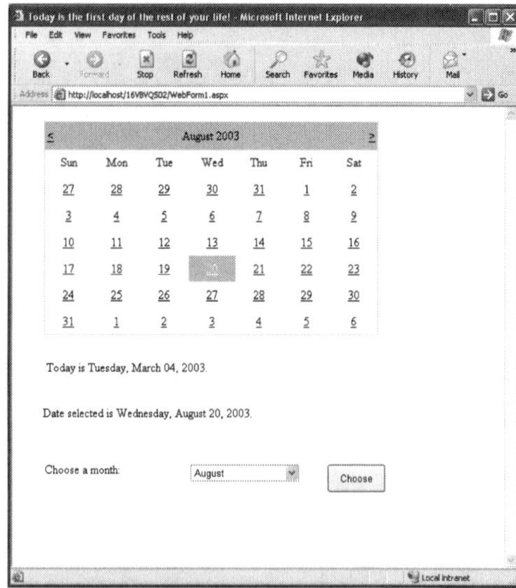

Figure 16.39 The Web calendar application lets the user choose a month for display and displays the current day as well as a day selected by the user.

Listing 16.3 The Calendar code-behind module (hidden-code region omitted).

```
Public Class WebForm1
   Inherits System.Web.UI.Page
   Protected WithEvents Calendar1 As System.Web.UI.WebControls.Calendar
   Protected WithEvents lblToday As System.Web.UI.WebControls.Label
   Protected WithEvents lblDateSelected As System.Web.UI.WebControls.Label
   Protected WithEvents Label3 As System.Web.UI.WebControls.Label
   Protected WithEvents lstMonths As System.Web.UI.WebControls.DropDownList
   Protected WithEvents btnSetMonth As System.Web.UI.WebControls.Button
   ...
   Private Sub Page_Load(ByVal sender As System.Object, ByVal e As System.EventArgs) _
      Handles MyBase.Load
      'Put user code to initialize the page here
      If Not IsPostBack Then
         Calendar1.SelectedDate = Calendar1.TodaysDate
         Calendar1.VisibleDate = Calendar1.TodaysDate
         lstMonths.SelectedIndex = Calendar1.VisibleDate.Month - 1
         lblDateSelected.Text = "Date selected is Calendar1.SelectedDate.ToLongDateString."
      End If
      lblToday.Text = "Today is Calendar1.TodaysDate.ToLongDateString."
    End Sub

   Private Sub btnSetMonth_Click(ByVal sender As System.Object, ByVal e As System.EventArgs) _
      Handles btnSetMonth.Click
      If Not (CInt(Calendar1.VisibleDate.Month) = lstMonths.SelectedIndex + 1) Then
         Calendar1.VisibleDate = New DateTime (Calendar1.TodaysDate.Year, lstMonths.SelectedIndex + 1, 1)
         lblDateSelected.Text = "Date selected is "
      End If
   End Sub
   Private Sub Calendar1_SelectionChanged(ByVal sender As Object, _
      ByVal e As System.EventArgs) Handles Calendar1.SelectionChanged
      lblDateSelected.Text = "Date selected is Calendar1.SelectedDate.ToLongDateString."
   End Sub
End Class
```

Saving session and application information

Now, in the final section of this chapter, you'll learn how to save session and application information. If you ran the calendar application in the previous task, you saw that information stored as the property values of controls is saved (or *persisted*) across form post-backs. From a coding viewpoint, this means that you may not have to worry much about persisting this kind of information. But what if you have information that you want to save with a session, such as a user's login information, that you can't or don't want to save as control property values?

In the tasks that follow, you'll first see how to save the user name associated with a given session (by *session*, I mean the period in which the browser is connected to the ASP.NET server). Note that this task is not meant to provide a road map for secure user logins, which involve issues related to authentication, credentials, and the saving of user information to databases. In fact, the login here does not even require a password or check that the user name is unique! This task is meant only to show you how to save and retrieve session information.

The last task shows you how to save and retrieve application information. In the sample application, you'll see how to keep track of the number of logged users (each of whom has his or her own session).

ASP.NET automatically keeps track of state information for you via the Session and Application objects. These objects are implemented as a Dictionary-style collection class, which was briefly described as one of the classes implementing the ICollection interface back in Chapter 8, "Creating MDI Applications." A Dictionary collection class consists of key/value pairs. The value is saved or obtained using the key. (The appellation *dictionary* may have come about because the key is used to look up the value.)

It is important to understand that the keys used in these tasks, Session("username") and Application("loggedInUsers"), are not built into the Session and Application objects. I just invented them and named them so that I could use them for the purpose of the two tasks.

The key/value pairs stored in a Session object remain available as long as the session continues (in other words, while an instance of a browser is connected to an application). In contrast, the key/value pairs stored in an Application object are available as long as the application is running on the server, regardless of whether any particular clients are connected to the application (having a session with it), or indeed, whether any clients are connected at all.

Note that you should not use either the Session or Application object to store copious quantities of data. That's not the purpose of these objects, and doing so would slow down an application considerably. If you have a lot of data, use a database, as explained in Chapter 15.

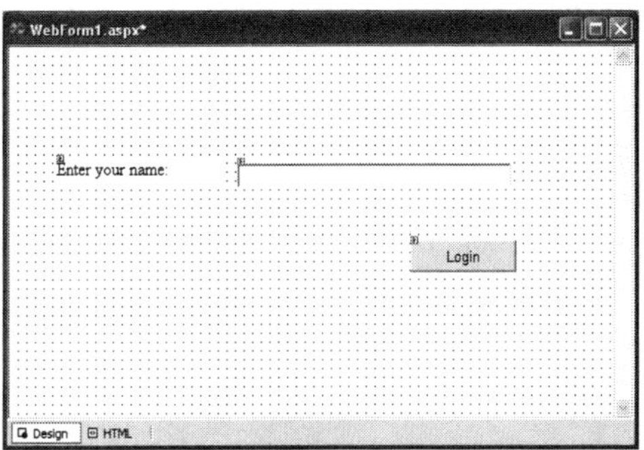

Figure 16.40 The user interface allowing a login in the Web Form designer.

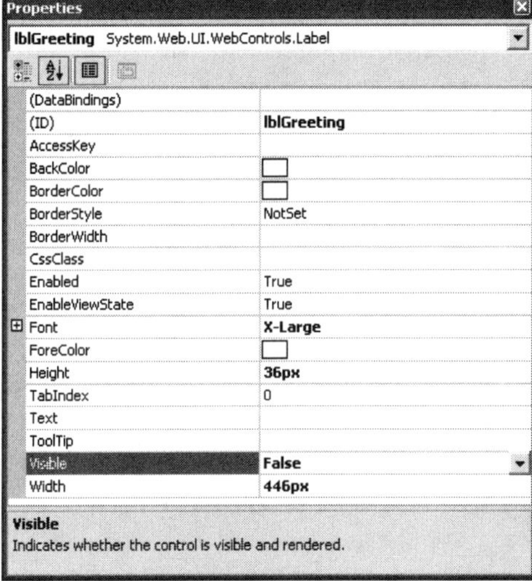

Figure 16.41 The initial Visible property value of the Label control used to acknowledge a successful login is set to False in the Properties window.

To save session information:

1. Open a new ASP.NET Web Application project.
2. Add a TextBox control and a Button control to the Web form in its designer created by the new project (**Figure 16.40**).

   The user will use the text box to enter a name and the button to log in.
3. Use the Properties window to change the name of the Button control to *btnLogin* and the value of its Text property to *Login*.
4. Use the Properties window to set the TextBox control's name to *txtName* and the value of its Text property to the empty string.
5. Add another Label control to the Web form.

   This Label control will not be visible until the user logs in, after which it will display the user name.
6. In the Properties window, set the name of the Label control to *lblGreeting*, the value of its Text property to the empty string, and the value of its Visible property to False (**Figure 16.41**).
7. Double-click the Login button to create an event handler for it in the code-behind in the Code Editor:

```
Private Sub btnLogin_Click _
   (ByVal sender As System.Object, _
   ByVal e As System.EventArgs) _
   Handles btnLogin.Click

End Sub
```

continues on next page

8. Within the click event, check to determine whether the user has logged in, using the Text property value of the Login button as the determinant (if the value is *Login*, then the user is not logged in and wants to; if the value is *Logout*, then the user is logged in but wants to log out):

```
If btnLogin.Text = "Login" Then

Else 'User is logging out

End If
```

9. If the user is logging in, check to see if a user name is entered in the text box:

```
If txtName.Text <> "" Then

End If
```

10. Assuming that a user name was entered (and this is the only validation performed here!), use the key "username" to store the value in the Session object:

```
Session("userName") = _
   txtName.Text
```

11. Change the Visible property of the logon controls to False:

```
Label1.Visible = False
txtName.Visible = False
```

12. Create a greeting for the logged-in user, save it as the value of the *lblGreeting* label's Text property, and change the Visible property of the label to True:

```
lblGreeting.Text = _
   "Hello, " & _
   Session("userName").ToString() _
   & "!"
lblGreeting.Visible = True
```

13. In the log out portion of the conditional statement, change the Text value of *btnLogin*:

```
btnLogin.Text = "Login"
```

14. Change the Visible property of the logon controls to True:

```
Label1.Visible = True
txtName.Text = ""
txtName.Visible = True
```

15. Change the Visible property of the *lblGreeting* label to False:

```
lblGreeting.Visible = False
```

16. Set the value corresponding to the Session key to Nothing (which tells the Session object to erase the entry stored for this user):

```
Session("userName") = Nothing
```

Here's the complete code for the conditional statement:

```
If btnLogin.Text = "Login" Then
   If txtName.Text <> "" Then
      btnLogin.Text = "Logout"
      Session("userName") = _
         txtName.Text
      Label1.Visible = False
      txtName.Visible = False
      lblGreeting.Text = _
         "Hello, " & _
     Session("userName").ToString() _
         & "!"
     lblGreeting.Visible = True
   End If
Else 'User is logging out
   btnLogin.Text = "Login"
   Label1.Visible = True
   txtName.Text = ""
   txtName.Visible = True
   lblGreeting.Visible = False
   Session("userName") = Nothing
End If
```

The complete code-behind module is shown as part of **Listing 16.4** (this listing also shows working with an Application object value).

Listing 16.4 The state and session management class (hidden-code region omitted).

```
Public Class WebForm1
   Inherits System.Web.UI.Page
   Protected WithEvents txtName As System.Web.UI.WebControls.TextBox
   Protected WithEvents Label1 As System.Web.UI.WebControls.Label
   Protected WithEvents lblGreeting As System.Web.UI.WebControls.Label
   Protected WithEvents lblTotUsers As System.Web.UI.WebControls.Label
   Protected WithEvents btnLogin As System.Web.UI.WebControls.Button
...
   Private Sub Page_Load(ByVal sender As System.Object, ByVal e As System.EventArgs) _
      Handles MyBase.Load
      'Put user code to initialize the page here
   End Sub

   Private Sub btnLogin_Click(ByVal sender As System.Object, ByVal e As System.EventArgs) _
      Handles btnLogin.Click
      If btnLogin.Text = "Login" Then
         If txtName.Text <> "" Then
            If Application("loggedInUsers") Is Nothing Then
               Application("loggedInUsers") = 1
            ElseIf Session("userName") Is Nothing Then
               Application("loggedInUsers") = _
                  CType(Application("loggedInUsers"), Integer) + 1
            End If
            lblTotUsers.Text = "There is/are " & _
               Application("loggedInUsers").ToString() & _
               " user(s) logged in on the system currently."
            btnLogin.Text = "Logout"
            Session("userName") = txtName.Text
            Label1.Visible = False
            txtName.Visible = False
            lblGreeting.Text = "Hello, " & Session("userName").ToString() & "!"
            lblGreeting.Visible = True
         End If
      Else  ' User is logging out
         btnLogin.Text = "Login"
         Label1.Visible = True
         txtName.Text = ""
         txtName.Visible = True
         lblGreeting.Visible = False
         If Application("loggedInUsers") Is Nothing Then
            lblTotUsers.Text = "There are no users logged in on the system currently."
         End If
         If Not Session("userName") Is Nothing Then
            If CType(Application("loggedInUsers"), Integer) <= 1 Then
               Application("loggedInUsers") = Nothing
               lblTotUsers.Text = "There are no users logged in on the system currently."
            Else
               Application("loggedInUsers") = _
                  CInt(Application("loggedInUsers")) - 1
               lblTotUsers.Text = "There is/are " & _
                  Application("loggedInUsers").ToString() & _
                  " user(s) logged in on the system currently."
            End If
         ElseIf Not Application("loggedInUsers") Is Nothing Then
            lblTotUsers.Text = "There is/are " & _
                Application("loggedInUsers").ToString() & _
                " user(s) logged in on the system currently."
         End If
         Session("userName") = Nothing
      End If
   End Sub
End Class
```

To test session information:

1. Run the project.

   The login form opens in the browser (**Figure 16.42**).

2. Enter a user name in the TextBox control (**Figure 16.43**).

3. Click Login.

   The text on the Button control changes to *Logout*, and a personalized greeting is displayed (**Figure 16.44**).

4. Refresh the browser (in Internet Explorer, select Refresh from the View menu) to check that the user name persists after the browser has been refreshed.

   Since any ASP.NET application is powered by HTTP form Post commands, you'll see the message box shown in **Figure 16.45** when you refresh your browser.

5. Click Retry and verify that your login information has been retained.

6. Click Logout and verify that the application returns to its pre-login state (shown in Figure 16.42.

The Application object will be used, with the same application that used the Session object to implement a login, to keep track of the total number of logged-in users. Like the Session object, the Application object is based on a Dictionary base class. Information is saved to and retrieved from the Application object using key/value pairs. In contrast to the Session object, the Application object "stays alive" as long as the application is running on the server, regardless of whether there are any current sessions.

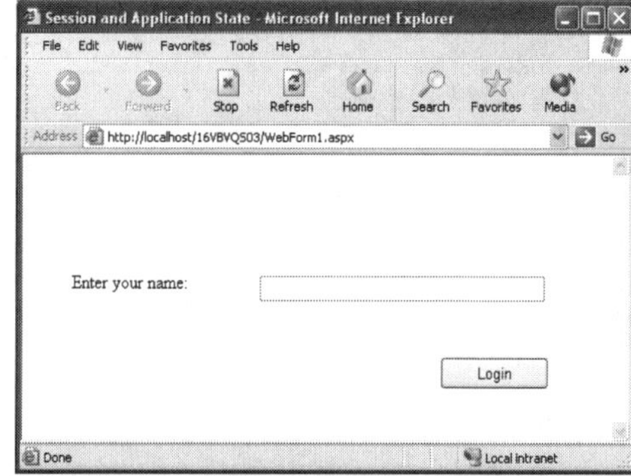

Figure 16.42 The session login project running in a Web browser.

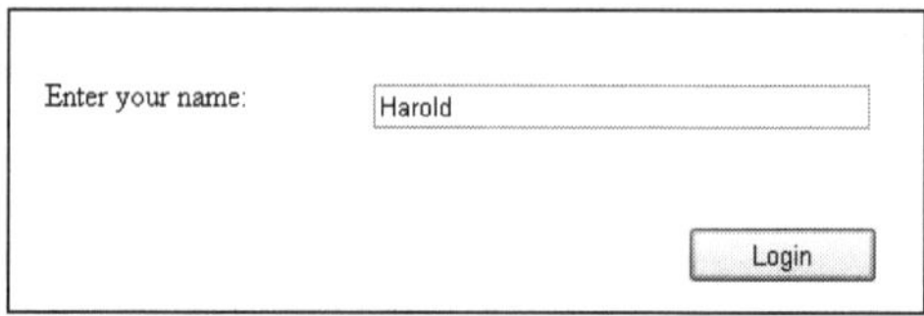

Figure 16.43 The user enters a name in the TextBox control and clicks Login.

Figure 16.44 With a user logged in, a greeting is displayed along with a Logout button.

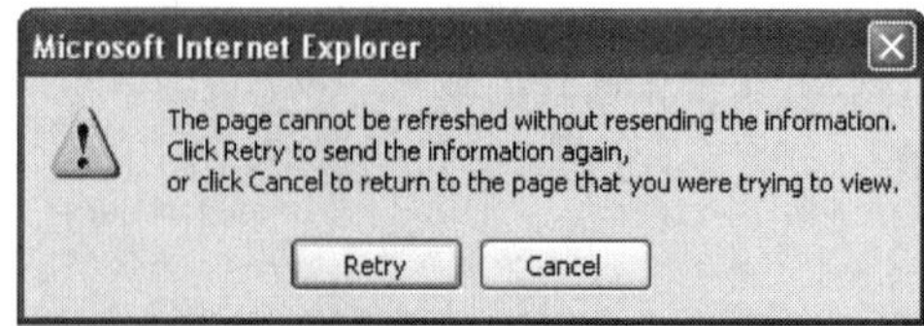

Figure 16.45 Since all ASP.NET Web applications are activated via an HTTP form Post command, when you refresh the application in the Web browser, you see this dialog box.

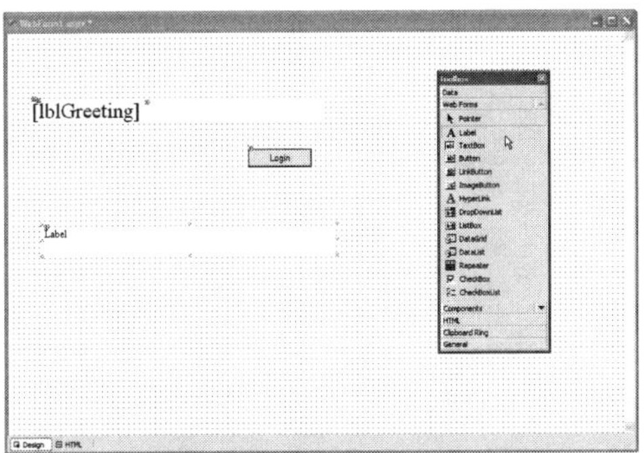

Figure 16.46 A new Label form is added to the Web form in its designer to track the number of users logged in to the application.

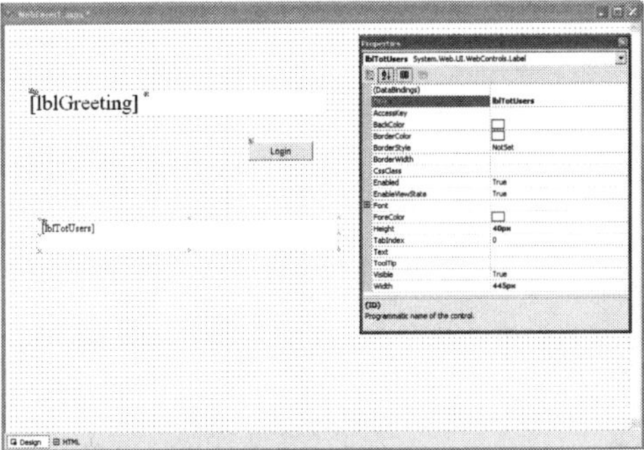

Figure 16.47 You can use the Properties window to change the name of the Label control.

To save application information:

1. Starting with the application created in the task "To save session information," open the Web form in its designer.
2. Use the Toolbox to add a Label control to the Web form.

   This Label control will be used to display total logged-in user count information (**Figure 16.46**)
3. Use the Properties window to change the name of the Label control to *lblTotUsers* and its Text value to the empty string (**Figure 16.47**).
4. From the Visual Studio View menu, choose Code to open the Code Editor with the Web form code-behind loaded.
5. In the If conditional statement explained in the task "To save Session information," add code when the user is logging in to set the value of the Application object's loggedInUsers key to 1 if this is the first user; otherwise, add 1 to the value of the loggedInUsers key:

```
If Application("loggedInUsers") _
   Is Nothing Then
      Application("loggedInUsers") _
      = 1
ElseIf Session("userName") Is _
   Nothing Then
   Application("loggedInUsers") _
   = CType(Application _
   ("loggedInUsers"), Integer) + 1
End If
```

6. Display the total user count in the *lblTotUsers* label:

```
lblTotUsers.Text = "There is/are " _
   & Application _
   ("loggedInUsers").ToString() & _
" user(s) logged in on the system."
```

continues on next page

Working with Controls

7. In the clause of the conditional statement used when a user logs out that subtracts 1 from the loggedInUsers value and displays the user count, enter the following:

```
If Application("loggedInUsers") _
   Is Nothing Then
   lblTotUsers.Text = _
      "There are no users logged in on the system."
End If
If Not Session("userName") Is _
      Nothing Then
   If CType(Application _
      ("loggedInUsers"), Integer) _
      <= 1 Then
      Application("loggedInUsers") _
         = Nothing
      lblTotUsers.Text = "There are no users logged in on the system."
   Else
      Application("loggedInUsers") = _
         CInt(Application _
         ("loggedInUsers")) - 1
      lblTotUsers.Text = _
     "There is/are" & Application("loggedInUsers").ToString() & _
     " user(s) logged in on the system currently."
   End If
ElseIf Not
   Application("loggedInUsers") _
   Is Nothing Then
   lblTotUsers.Text = _
   "There is/are" & Application("loggedInUsers").ToString() & _
   " user(s) logged in on the system currently."
End If
```

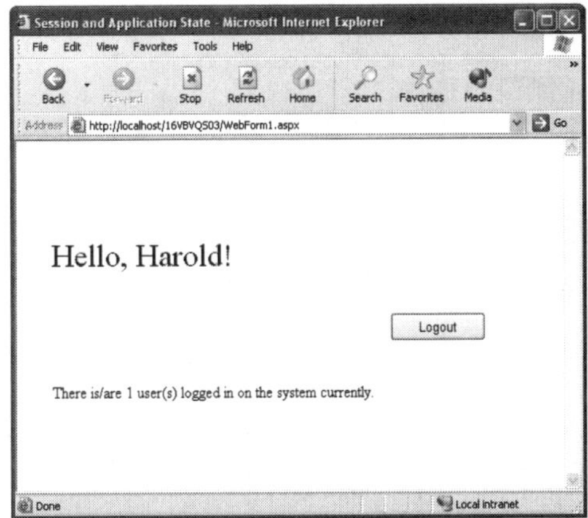

Figure 16.48 When the project is first run and a user logs in for the first time, the Label control tracking the application usage shows one user.

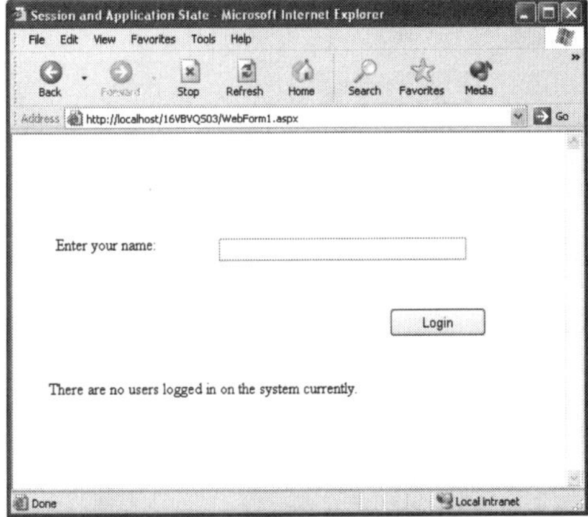

Figure 16.49 If the user logs out, the Label control displays a message saying that there are no logged-in users.

Listing 16.4 shows the complete code for managing the Application session object.

8. Run the project.
9. Enter a user name.
10. Click the Login button.

    The application now reports that a single user is logged in (**Figure 16.48**).
11. Log in again.
12. Open a browser on your system such as Internet Explorer.
13. In the browser, open the URL for the application. (You can read this in the instance running under Visual Studio; in Figure 16.48, it is http://localhost/16VBVQS03/WebForm1.aspx. Enter the URL in the new browser instance exactly as it appears in the instance running under Visual Studio.)

    A new client version of the application opens (**Figure 16.49**).

continues on next page

14. Log in to the application.

15. Repeat the process with a number of other browser instances and verify that the correct number of total users logged in to the application is displayed (**Figure 16.50**).

✔ Tip

- The type conversion in the code shown in Listing 16.4 is required because VB .NET is running with Option Strict turned on, as explained in Chapter 1. I do recommend requiring strict typing by turning on Option Strict to reduce the possibility of errors. However, working with Option Strict turned off is an easy way out that, in this case, would lead to code that appears simpler—because many of the type conversion functions can be omitted, and you can slide by with implicit type conversion. For more information about type conversion, see Appendix C, "Visual Basic .NET Types and Type Conversion."

Figure 16.50 If you open multiple copies of the application using different browser windows, the Application object correctly tracks the total number of users logged in.

Summary

In this chapter, you learned how to:

- Describe ASP.NET Web applications and application architecture
- Describe the requirements for creating and running an ASP.NET Web application
- Create an ASP.NET Web application in Visual Studio
- View HTML generated by an ASP.NET Web application in a browser
- Create client-side scripts in a Visual Studio ASP.NET Web application
- View and understand code-behind modules in the Code Editor
- Describe the different kinds of ASP.NET controls
- Describe the controls available on the Web Forms tab of the Toolbox
- Work with Label, TextBox, and Button controls
- Create an ASP.NET Web application with interactive calendaring
- Work with the ASP.NET Session and Application objects.

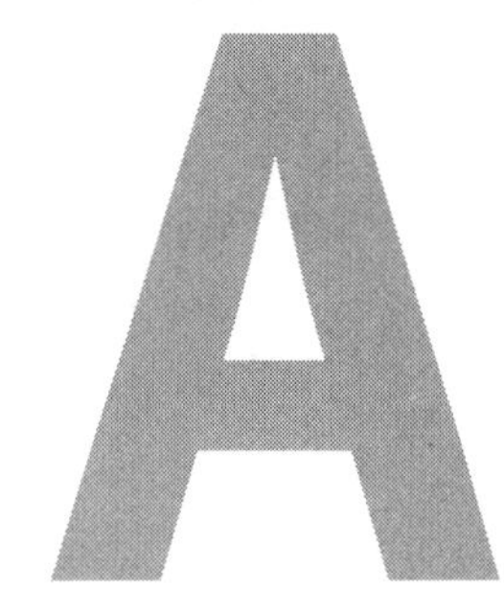

GETTING HELP

This appendix explains where (and how) to look for more information about specific Visual Studio features, the VB .NET language, and the .NET Framework classes. The first place to look for answers if you are stuck is this book. Next, check out the excellent tools that are part of the development environment (such as auto-completion in the Code Editor and the Object Browser, explained in Chapter 14, "The Object Browser"). If these tools don't, well, help, the next place to turn is the online Help system, which is also sometimes called the Microsoft Help Document Explorer.

Using the Online Help System

In the previous edition of this book, I called the VB6 online Help system "the good, the big, and the ugly." With VB .NET, the online Help situation has gotten better, bigger, and uglier. Online Help is truly comprehensive, overwhelming, and disorganized. The last point is mitigated somewhat, as you'll see in this appendix, by the power of online searching.

The biggest problem is finding what you need quickly—because the information is probably in there, somewhere. This problem is compounded by the fact that online Help provides information not only for Visual Basic .NET, but also for all the other .NET languages (C#, Visual C++, and so on). In addition, development of a huge variety of types of applications and platforms is covered. It doesn't do you much good to obtain information about creating Web applications when you need to know about programming for Windows (or vice versa).

For those who do not find navigating VB .NET's online Help system trivial (and I confess that I am in this category), this appendix will provide information that demystifies the process. For those who have no problem using the online Help, by all means skip this portion of the book!

This appendix explains the mechanics of Dynamic Help and how the Contents, Index, Search, and filtering features of the .NET online Help system work.

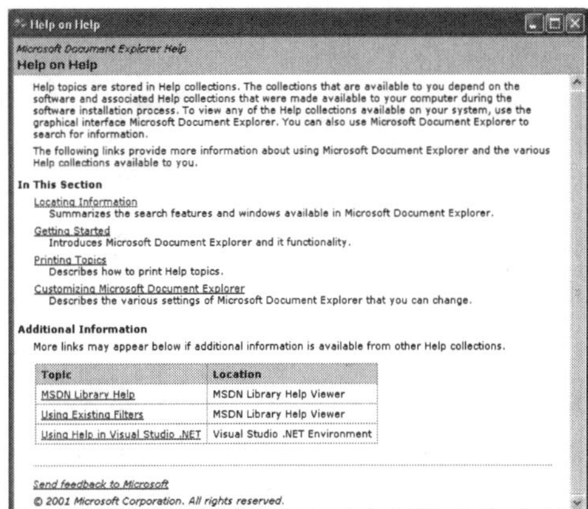

Figure A.1 The Microsoft Document Explorer Help screen (Help on Help) provides links that give information about using the features of the online Help system.

But first, you may need help on Help! The features that this appendix describes are not always obvious in my opinion. You may need some help with them. Not to worry—Help on Help is available to come to the rescue!

To open Help on Help:

- From the Visual Studio Help menu, choose Help on Help.

  The Microsoft Document Explorer Help screen (Help on Help) opens (**Figure A.1**).

Using Dynamic Help

Dynamic Help is a form of context-sensitive Help in which a window provides links to Help topics thought relevant by the system, depending on your activities in the Visual Studio development environment.

To activate Dynamic Help:

- From the Help menu, choose Dynamic Help, or press Ctrl+F1 on the keyboard.

  Dynamic Help opens, with Help links for whatever is currently active in the development environment (**Figure A.2**).

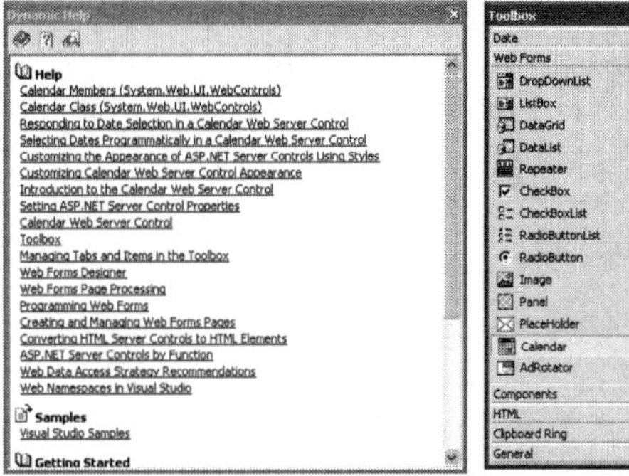

Figure A.2 Dynamic Help provides links to Help topics relevant to whatever is currently active in the development environment (here, Dynamic Help shows links relevant to the ASP.NET Calendar control that is selected in the Toolbox).

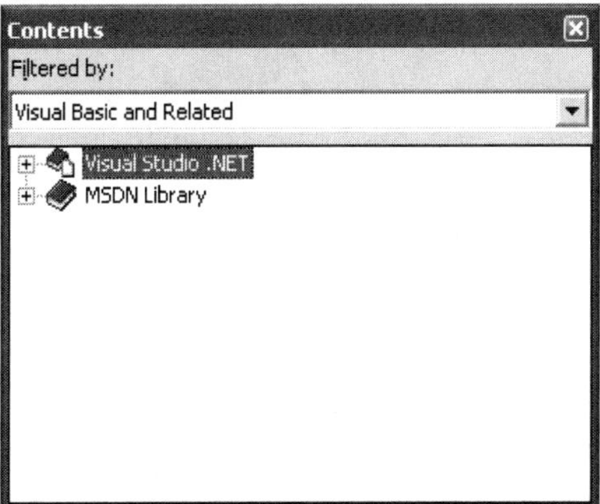

Figure A.3 When the Contents window opens, a few of the top nodes are displayed.

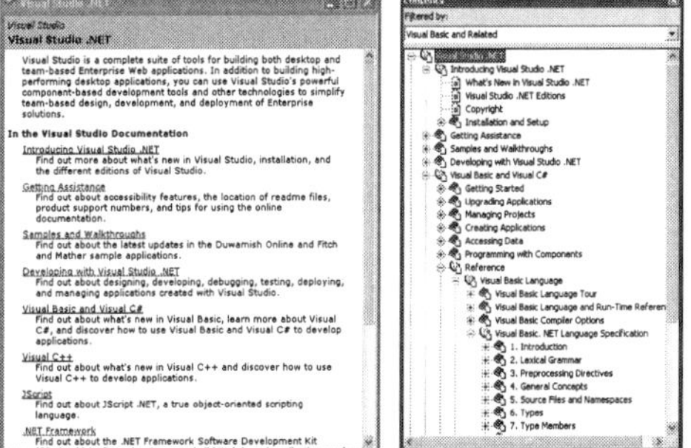

Figure A.4 Selecting the Visual Studio .NET topic page in the Contents window causes the page to open in a new window.

Using the Contents Window

You can use the Contents window to drill down through the contents of online Help to find information using nodes and links. In theory, this is analogous to using a table of contents in a hard-copy book.

To open the Contents window:

- From the Help menu, choose Contents.

  The Contents window opens with a few top nodes showing (**Figure A.3**).

To drill down through the contents:

1. Click nodes to expand them to see more nodes and topics.
2. Select a topic to display it in a separate window.

   In **Figure A.4**, the Visual Studio .NET topic page is selected in the Contents window on the right, causing the page to be displayed on the left.

No doubt, the topic displayed will contain more links, and often the best approach is to browse—and keep on browsing! (You'll never know the places you'll go, what you'll find, and what you'll learn.)

I've spent many hours usefully (or not so usefully!) employed in this fashion. If you follow in my footsteps, know that when a Help topic is displayed (as in Figure A.4), Visual Studio also opens a special toolbar, the Microsoft Document Explorer toolbar (**Figure A.5**), which provides tools that you can use to move through documents. These tools are analogous to those you use in browsing documents on the Web, with features such as Backward, Forward, and Refresh buttons.

The only toolbar button that really requires an explanation is Sync Contents. You will use this when you've been browsing and browsing through all of the exciting Help documents, and the Contents window is no longer synchronized with the topic you are browsing.

To synchronize contents:

- With the Contents window open and a Help topic open, click the Sync Contents button ⇔ on the Microsoft Document Explorer toolbar.

  The open Help topic will now be the topic selected within the hierarchy of nodes and links in the Contents window.

You should also know that the Contents window, like the Index and Search windows, can be filtered by topic, so that it will show only information related to the filter (at least in theory). You can choose a filter from the drop-down list at the top of any of these windows (Visual Basic or Visual Basic and Related are perhaps the filters you'll use most often). You can also create custom filters, as you'll see later in this appendix.

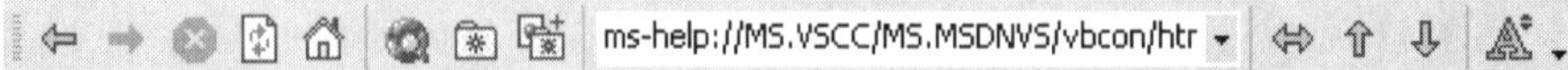

Figure A.5 The Document Explorer toolbar provides Web navigation features within the Help system.

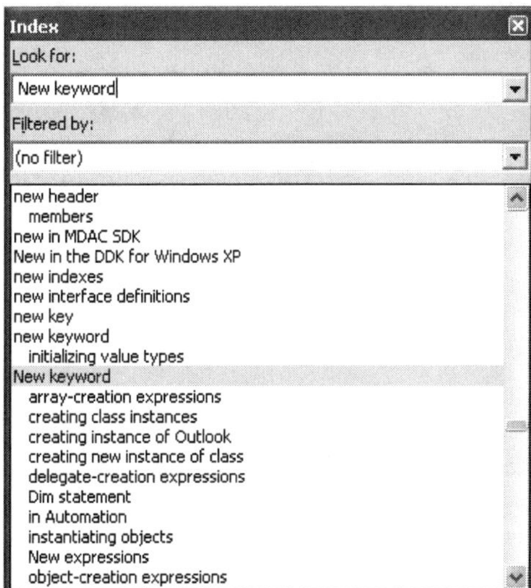

Figure A.6 A list of indexed items based on the phrase you entered in the Look For field appears in the bottom pane of the Index window.

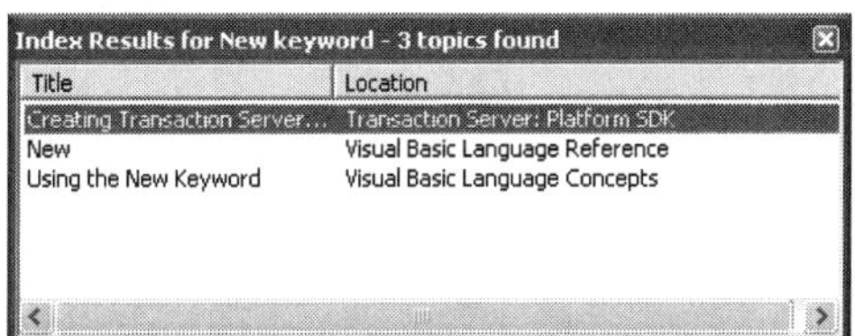

Figure A.7 If a term has multiple indexed listings, the Index Results window displays all of the listings.

Using the Index Window

The Index window allows you to search for specific information. It is analogous to the index in a hard-copy book and is, of course, most useful when the exact term you are searching for has been indexed. Only the titles of items are used to provide index terms, and I've personally found the Help Index feature of .NET quite frustrating to use.

To open the Index window:

1. From the Help menu, choose Index.

   The Index window opens.

2. In the Look For box, enter the term you are searching for (**Figure A.6**).

   A list of indexed terms, based on the phrase you entered, will appear in the bottom pane of the Index window.

3. Select a term in the bottom pane of the Index window.

   The Index Results window opens, showing all of the indexed listings for the term (**Figure A.7**).

4. Double-click a term in the Index Results window to open a topic for viewing.

   Note that if only one topic is indexed for a given term, it will open for viewing immediately when you select it in the bottom pane of the Index window (the Index Results window won't open).

✔ Tip

- Once you've searched for a term using the Index window, you can open the Index Results window directly by choosing Index Results from the Help menu.

Using the Search Window

The Search window works like the Index window, except that it returns a broader result set, since it conducts full-text searches within the text of Help documents as well as within item titles. (If you wish, you can check the box to search only within titles, thereby improving performance and degrading results.) Search is the Help window that I personally use most often to find information.

To use the Search window:

1. Choose Search from the Help menu.

   The Search window opens (**Figure A.8**).

2. In the Look For box, enter a search term.

3. Choose any of the four Search window options by clicking on the check box located to the left of each option.

4. Click Search.

   The Search Results window opens (**Figure A.9**). Unlike the Index Results window, the Search Results window will likely display a great many hits, quite possibly in the hundreds.

5. Double-click an item in the Search Results window to open the corresponding topic for viewing.

✔ Tip

- Once you've searched for a term using the Search window, you can open the Search Results window directly by choosing Search Results from the Help menu. This feature is extremely useful, because you often have to look at quite a few of the items in the Search Results window before you find the information you need.

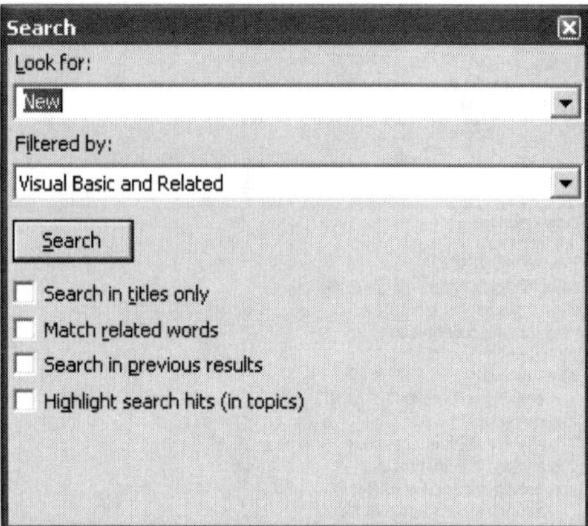

Figure A.8 The Search window can retrieve Help topics based on their content, not just the item's title.

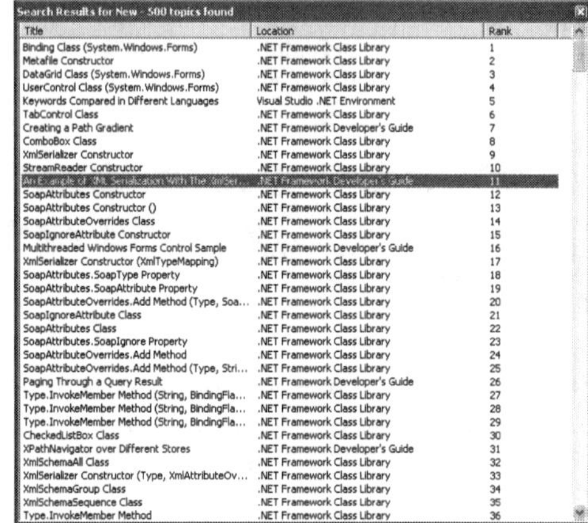

Figure A.9 The Search Results window often finds hundreds of topics that match the term searched for.

Many of the topics that result from a search are buried deep within the links-and-nodes hierarchy of the Microsoft Help Document Explorer. Sometimes the information you really need will be up one node or parallel to the topic you opened after searching, so it can be very helpful to see where a topic you found as the result of a search fits in the overall Help hierarchy. You can accomplish this as explained in the task "To synchronize contents" earlier in this appendix.

For example, let's say you used the Search window to look for the term "New," as shown in Figure A.8, with the results in the Search Results window as shown in Figure A.9. You might decide to view the topic "An Example of XML Serialization" shown selected in Figure A.9 and double-click it to open it for viewing, as in the right pane in **Figure A.10**. At this point, you might want to know where this topic fits in the Help hierarchy and the related topics that are available. To obtain this information, click the Sync Contents button on the Microsoft Document Explorer toolbar as explained in the "To synchronize contents" task earlier in this appendix. The Contents window will open, as shown on the right side of Figure A.10. The item currently open will be shown selected in the Contents window, and you can easily determine its place in the Help hierarchy and see links to closely related items.

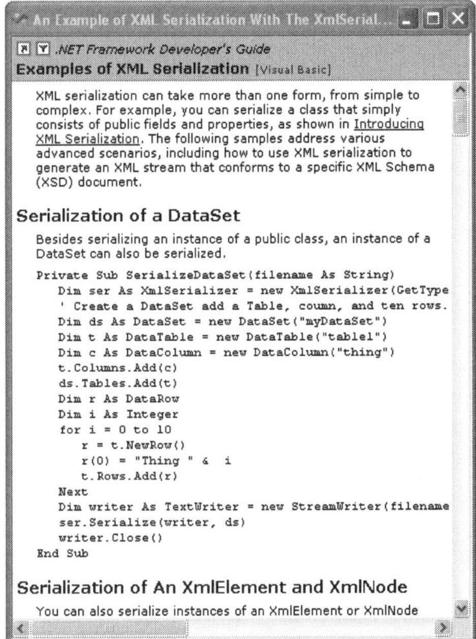

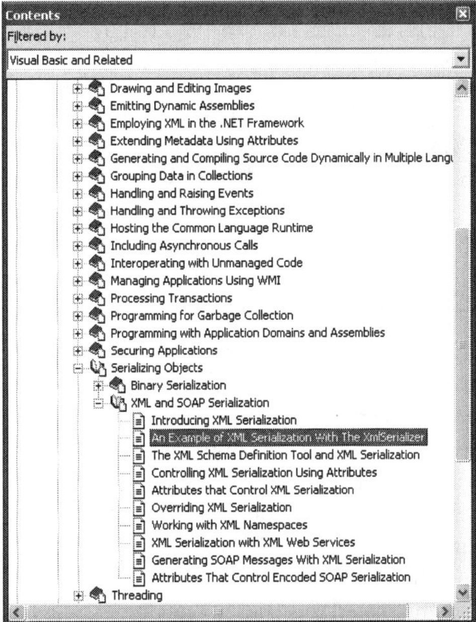

Figure A.10 The Sync Contents feature allows you to see where an item retrieved from a search fits in the overall Help hierarchy.

Filtering

You can filter Help results by choosing a filter from the Filtered By drop-down list that appears at the top of the Contents, Index, and Search windows (**Figure A.11**). (You can also set the default Help filter on the My Profile tab of your Start page.)

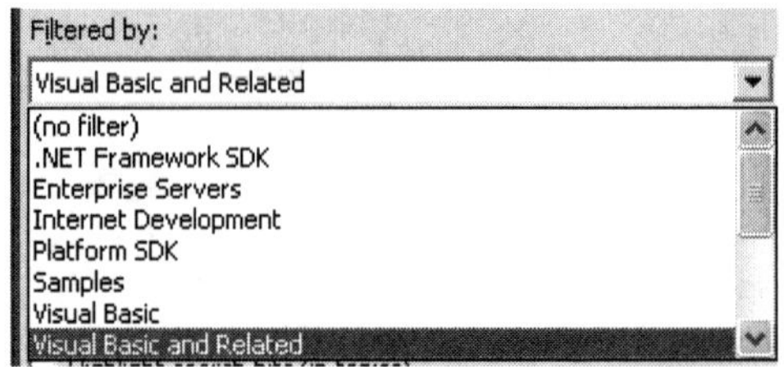

Figure A.11 You can filter Help results by selecting a filter from the Filtered By drop-down list.

Although you can turn off filtering (see the task "To turn off filtering" that follows), you probably don't want to—madness lies ahead if you do. To keep searches manageable, most of the time Visual Basic .NET programmers prefer to filter Help by one of these filters:

- Visual Basic
- Visual Basic and Related
- .NET Framework SDK

To turn off filtering:

1. Open the Contents, Index, or Search window.
2. Select (No Filter) from the Filtered By drop-down list at the top of the window.

While using Help without a filter is really not a very good way to get help (there are too many results, and the list is too unruly), sometimes it is very useful to create a custom filter. You create a custom filter using Boolean criteria, much as if you were writing the WHERE clause of a SQL query.

Custom filters are useful if you need to do a repeated search within a particular set of topics, and all the predefined topics are too broad. For example, you might want to search for topics within the .NET Framework SDK that include Visual Basic but not C#. This search requires a custom filter. Custom filters also come in handy if you need to join two topics that are not listed together in one predefined filter.

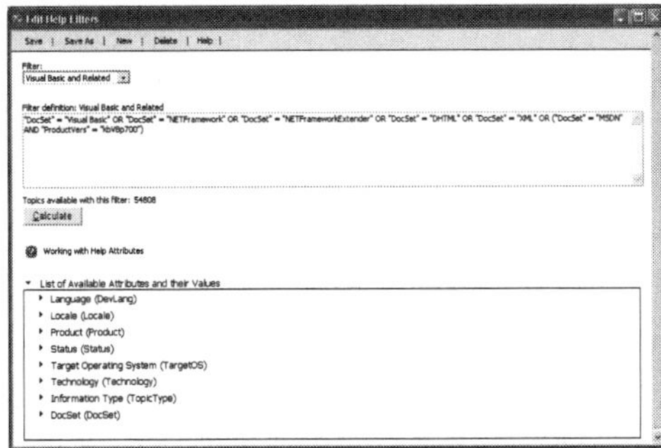

Figure A.12 Use the Edit Help Filters window to modify a Help filter or to create a new Help filter.

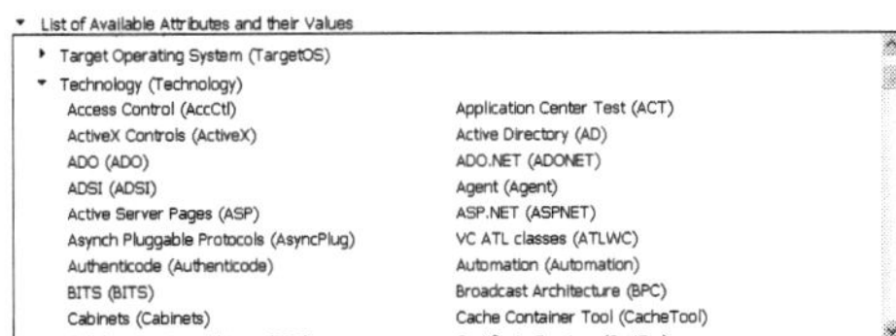

Figure A.13 The attributes in the box at the bottom of the Edit Help Filters window can be expanded to list individual topics, which you can click to add them to the search criteria.

✔ Tip

- If you select a high-level attribute in the box at the bottom of the Edit Help Filters window, it will expand to show a list of individual topics (**Figure A.13**). Selecting a value in the List of Attributes box adds it to the filter definition in a Boolean OR clause. Once you've added an attribute value to the filter definition, you can manually edit the Boolean connectors that surround it.

To create a custom Help filter:

1. From the Help menu, choose Edit Filters.

   The Edit Help Filters window opens (**Figure A.12**).

2. *Do one of the following:*
   - ▲ To modify an existing filter (such as the Visual Basic and Related filter shown in Figure A.12), choose the filter from the Filter drop-down list at the top of the Edit Help Filters window.
   - ▲ To create a new custom filter, click New.

   If you choose an existing filter, the Filter definition will appear in the Filter definition box.

3. If you choose to modify an existing filter, click Calculate to see the number of items that are searched when the filter is selected.

   As you can see in Figure A.12, you are searching through 54,808 items when the Visual Basic and Related Help filter is applied.

4. Modify (or create) search filter definitions in the Filter Definition box by hand-coding using Boolean OR and Boolean AND operators and the available attributes and values shown in the List of Available Attributes and Their Values list (at the bottom of Figure A.12).

5. *Do one of the following:*
   - ▲ To save modifications to an existing filter, click Save.
   - ▲ To save changes to a filter under a different name, click Save As.

Visual Basic.NET Keywords

This appendix lists VB .NET keywords. Keywords are the building blocks of code statements. (Statements, in turn, are combined to create programs that can be compiled into an application.)

This appendix does *not* list the meaning of each keyword—for a number of reasons. The main reason is that this appendix would become a mini-book of its own. However, an easy way for you to find the meaning of each of these keywords is to look up the topic "Visual Basic Language Keywords" in the online Help. Each keyword is listed in this topic with a link to a syntax definition and explanation.

The keywords shown in **Table B.1** are all *reserved*, meaning that they cannot be used as identifiers or for any purpose other than their defined role in the syntax of a statement. (Two of the keywords shown, Let and Variant, were used in VB6 but are not used in VB .NET. They remain reserved as keywords, however, even though they no longer have functions.)

Table B.1

Visual Basic .NET Keywords				
AddHandler	Default	Imports	Optional	Step
AddressOf	Delegate	In	Or	Stop
Alias	Dim	Inherits	OrElse	String
And	DirectCast	Integer	Overloads	Structure
AndAlso	Do	Interface	Overridable	Sub
Ansi	Double	Is	Overrides	SyncLock
As	Each	Let	ParamArray	Then
Assembly	Else	Lib	Preserve	Throw
Auto	ElseIf	Like	Private	To
Boolean	End	Long	Property	True
ByRef	Enum	Loop	Protected	Try
Byte	Erase	Me	Public	TypeOf
ByVal	Error	Mod	RaiseEvent	Unicode
Call	Event	Module	ReadOnly	Variant
Case	Exit	MustInherit	ReDim	When
Catch	#ExternalSource	MustOverride	#Region	While
CBool	False	MyBase	REM	With
CByte	Finally	MyClass	RemoveHandler	WithEvents
CChar	For	Namespace	Resume	WriteOnly
CDate	Friend	New	Return	Xor
CDec	Function	Next	Select	#Const
CDbl	Get	Not	Set	#ExternalSource
Char	GetType	NotInheritable	Shadows	#If...Then...
CType	GoTo	NotOverridable	Shared	#Else
Date	Handles	Object	Short	#ElseIf
Decimal	If	On	Single	#End
Declare	Implements	Option	Static	#Region

C

Types and Type Conversion

To be a good Visual Basic .NET programmer, you must have a clear understanding of types and type conversion techniques. This appendix explains everything you always wanted to know about types and type conversion but were afraid to ask.

There are several pieces of good news about types and type conversions. First, whatever you may have feared, this is not really very difficult material. After reading this appendix, you should have no problem correctly working with types and type conversion in your programs. As Nietzsche once said, "that which does not kill me, makes me stronger." Learning about types won't kill you, and it will make you a better programmer.

Second, you'll learn all you need to know in the pages of this appendix. Of course, you'll often need to look up the details of each VB .NET conversion function and type in online Help—including them all here would take an entire additional Visual QuickStart Guide! But reading this appendix will help you quickly grasp the sense and gist of how types and type conversion methods work.

Visual Basic .NET Types

Visual Basic .NET has a fundamental hierarchy of different kinds of elements called *types*. These types are used, in combination with keywords, in statements to accomplish the goals of a program.

With the exception of the root type, Object, all types are either value types or reference types.

Value types, such as primitive types (except strings), enumerations, and structures, hold their values, or data, within their own memory allocation. These values are stored in memory allocated to the particular value type within a program's stack, or data structure, and can be accessed from within the program as long as they are in scope.

In contrast, *reference* types, such as classes, strings, interfaces, and arrays, are implemented using global memory called the runtime heap. The important point to understand is that reference types contain instances: for example, an instance of a class. These instances are pointers to objects stored in memory on the heap and do not themselves contain the actual values of the instances. Of course, you can instantiate an object based on a reference type that you've created (such as a class); you are not limited to the types that come with .NET.

The root type, Object, is the System.Object class in the .NET Framework. As noted, it is unique because it is neither a value type nor a reference type. Ultimately, all types derive from Object, which cannot be instantiated. A variable of type Object can contain either a value type or a reference type.

Primitive types are the simple, built-in types that are predefined in VB .NET. Each primitive type is identified by a keyword, which is actually an alias to a class in the System namespace. For example, the keyword String identifies the System.String class.

Table C.1 lists the Visual Basic .NET primitive types. All primitive types shown in the table, except Object and String, are reference types.

Table C.1

Visual Basic .NET Primitive Types

Type	.NET Structure or Class	Contains
Boolean	System.Boolean	Boolean value; True or False
Byte	System.Byte	Byte; 0 through 255 (unsigned)
Char	System.Char	Single Unicode character; 0 through 65535 (unsigned)
Date	System.DateTime	Date time value; 0:00:00 on January 1, 0001 through 11:59:59 PM on December 31, 9999
Decimal	System.Decimal	Decimal number; 0 through +/–79,228,162,514,264,337,593,543, 950,335 with no decimal point; 0 through +/–7.9228162514264337593543950335 with 28 places to the right of the decimal; smallest nonzero number is +/–0.0000000000000000000000000001 (+/–1E-28)
Double	System.Double	Double-precision floating-point number; –1.79769313486231570E+308 through 4.94065645841246544E–324 through 1.79769313486231570E+308 for positive values
Integer	System.Int32	–2,147,483,648 through 2,147,483,647
Long	System.Int64	Long integer value; –9,223,372,036,854,775,808 through 9,223,372,036,854,775,807
Object	System.Object	Any type can be stored in a variable of type Object.
Short	System.Int16	–32,768 through 32,767
Single	System.Single	Single-precision floating-point number; -3.4028235E+38 through -1.401298E-45 for negative values; 1.401298E-45 through 3.4028235E+38 for positive values
String	System.String	Variable-length character string; 0 to approximately 2 billion Unicode characters

Setting Option Strict

Option Strict, a Visual Basic .NET compiler option, can be set to On or Off. When set to On, Option Strict requires explicit type conversion for any type conversion that might conceivably cause loss of data. In effect, when Option Strict is set to On, Visual Basic .NET behaves like a strongly typed language (for more about what this means, see "Understanding Strong Typing" later in this appendix).

By default, Option Strict is set to Off, which means that the VB .NET compiler will do its best to perform conversions from one type to another, even if there is a possible loss of data (another way of saying that the compiler may not always be sure what you intend).

The trade-off involved is that programming with Option Strict set to On, as I recommend, requires more rigor, a full understanding of types, and (in some cases) more work—but setting this option to On reduces the chances of an unintended bug during a type conversion operation. A side benefit is that when you run with Option Strict turned on, you will likely find type conversion errors as syntax errors during the compilation process, rather than as far trickier to find and fix logical errors, when your program works but returns wrong results. (For more about the distinction between different kinds of program bugs, see Chapter 9, "Exceptions and Debugging.")

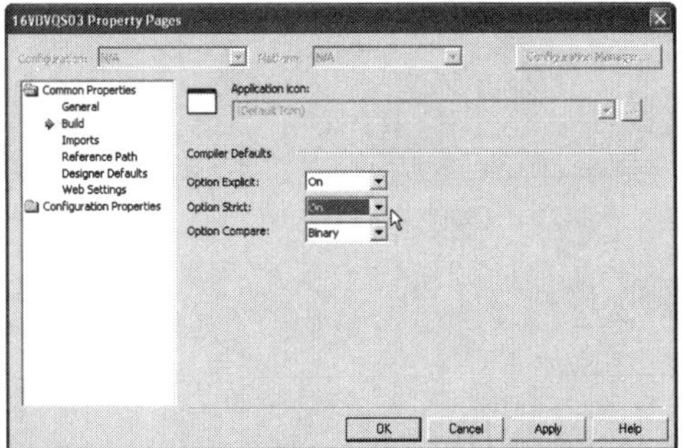

Figure C.1 You can use the Build Page of a project's Property Pages to turn on Option Strict on a per-project basis.

Here's how to engage Option Strict on a per-project basis.

To set Option Strict to On:

1. On the Build page of a project's Property Pages dialog, use the drop-down list to set Option Strict to On (**Figure C.1**).
2. Click OK when your selections are complete.

You should also know that Option Strict can be set in code on a per-source-file (or module) basis.

To turn on Option Strict in code:

1. Open the Code Editor.
2. At the top of the module in the Code Editor, before any other code, add the following statement:

```
Option Strict On
```

Understanding Strong Typing

With Option Strict on, VB .NET is a strongly typed language, which means that all variables have a type that must be declared, and that the compiler verifies the type consistency of expressions. Expressions always are of a type built in to the VB .NET language or are user-defined types.

When working in a strongly typed environment, you need to be very clear about the type of information that will be stored in a variable. Strong typing enforces good programming discipline and clarity on the part of the programmer about the contents of variables. It also prevents bugs that can occur when a weakly typed compiler "makes a mistake" about the kind of value in a type—and incorrectly converts it.

To put this another way, weak typing allows a programmer to be lazy—by not clearly thinking about the types of variables, and not specifying the appropriate conversion if there is any possible doubt. In this scenario, the compiler "guesses" what the programmer meant, most of the time correctly, but sometimes introducing errors.

The trade-off for the benefit of extra accuracy introduced by strong typing is more work for the programmer. Of course, you must explicitly declare all variables (a good practice even in weakly typed environments). In addition, you must pay close attention every time your code converts a value of one type to another—in many cases providing explicit conversion guidance to the compiler using a type conversion function, as explained later in this appendix.

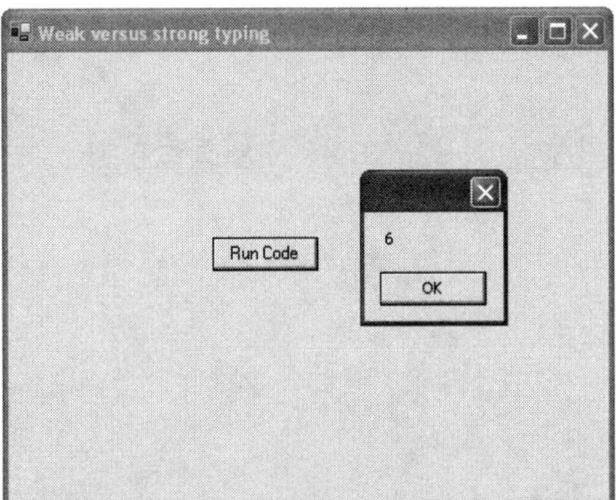

Figure C.2 The weakly typed code runs without syntax errors and rounds up 5.5 to 6.

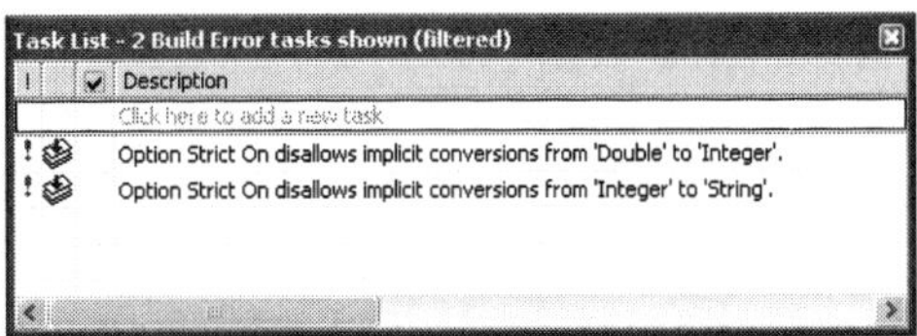

Figure C.3 Once Option Strict is turned on, type conversion syntax errors appear in the Task List window when the program is run.

To get a better understanding of the difference between weakly and strongly typed code in practice, let's look at an example. Suppose you're running in a Windows Form module with Option Strict turned off. You want to place code to a button click event that adds 3.5 and 2. The code in your form module will look something like this:

```
Option Strict Off
Public Class Form1
   Inherits System.Windows.Forms.Form
...
Private Sub Button1_Click(ByVal sender _
   As System.Object, _
   ByVal e As System.EventArgs) _
   Handles Button1.Click
      Dim theFloat As Double = 3.5
      Dim x As Integer = 2
      x = x + theFloat
      MessageBox.Show(x)
   End Sub
End Class
```

If you run the project, it will compile without incident. Clicking the button will display the results generated by the program, as shown in **Figure C.2**. In other words, 2.5 is rounded up to 3 and then added to 3, to get 6. This is not an utterly crazy result, but you might not expect it, and you might be less happy with the results of adding 2.5, 3.5, and 2 (which sum to 9, not 8). One argument in favor of strong typing is that you are more likely to know exactly what result you'll get.

Next, try replacing the Option Strict Off statement at the beginning of the module with an Option Strict On statement. When you run the revised code and attempt to compile the code, you'll be warned about a number of type conversion syntax errors (**Figure C.3**).

continues on next page

Unlike some really, really strongly typed languages (such as C#), VB .NET would compile this program in this situation despite the warnings, and it would run okay. But you'd be well advised to fix the program to avoid the possibility of logical errors. Here's the code rewritten to run in a strongly typed environment:

```
Option Strict On
Public Class Form1
   Inherits System.Windows.Forms.Form
...
Private Sub Button1_Click(ByVal sender _
   As System.Object, _
   ByVal e As System.EventArgs) _
   Handles Button1.Click
      Dim theFloat As Double = 3.5
      Dim x As Integer = 2
      x = x + CInt(theFloat)
      MessageBox.Show(x.ToString)
   End Sub
End Class
```

By the way, the conversion function used, CInt, still rounds 2.5 up to 3. But it's harder to explicitly use a conversion function such as CInt without understanding what will happen. And if you add 2.5 and 3.5 together, then convert the result to integer type, and then add this result to 3, using code like this:

```
Dim theFloat As Double = 3.5
Dim otherFloat As Single = 2.5
Dim x As Integer = 2
x = x + CInt(theFloat + otherFloat)
MessageBox.Show(x.ToString)
```

you'll get 8 (**Figure C.4**). This is the result you want to obtain. So the point is that working with strong typing gives you control over how conversions are done.

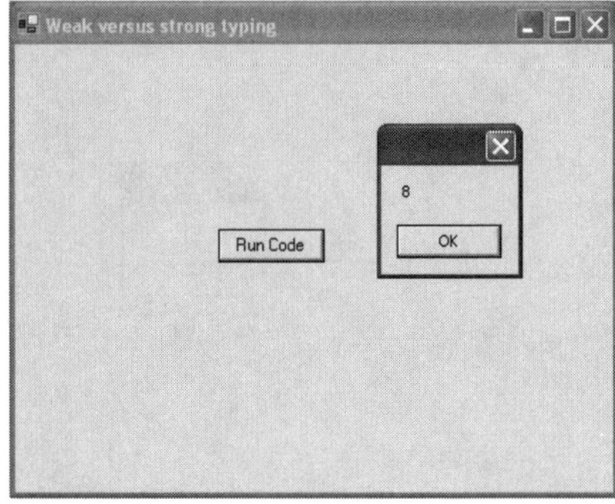

Figure C.4 Adding the floating-point numbers and then explicitly converting the result to an integer leads to the display of the correct sum.

Using Implicit Conversion

Working in a strongly typed environment doesn't mean that you can't use implicit conversion. The compiler will implicitly convert types for you (which means performing a conversion even though no conversion method or function has been specified) when there is no possibility of losing data during the conversion. This is also called a *widening conversion.*

In contrast, in a weakly typed environment, the compiler will attempt a conversion for you under almost any circumstances, even if the conversion could result in the loss of data. An implicit conversion in which some data could be lost is called a *narrowing conversion.*

Table C.2 shows the legal implicit conversions, or widening conversions, that can be used when VB .NET is running in its strongly typed mode with Option Strict engaged.

Narrowing conversions *cannot* be used in a strongly typed VB .NET project (when Option Strict has been turned on) without generating syntax errors at compile time. The following are all narrowing conversions:

- The reverse direction of the conversion shown in Table C.2 (for example, Single to Double)
- Conversions in either direction between a Boolean type and a numeric type
- Any numeric type to any enumerated type
- A conversion in either direction between a String type and any numeric type, Boolean type, Date type, or Char() array type
- Conversions from a type to a type derived from it

Note that these narrowing conversions can usually be used implicitly in VB .NET when Option Strict has been disengaged. However, by doing so, you run the risk of failure at runtime. Failure can consist of data loss, resulting in hard-to-debug logical errors. A narrowing conversion can also cause other kinds of runtime problems (a narrowing numeric conversion could result in an overflow error, for example).

Table C.2

Implicit Conversions for VB .NET Types

Type	Can Be Implicitly Converted To
Byte	Byte, Short, Integer, Long, Decimal, Single, Double
Short	Short, Integer, Long, Decimal, Single, Double
Integer	Integer, Long, Decimal, Single, Double
Long	Long, Decimal, Single, Double
Decimal	Decimal, Single, Double
Single	Single, Double
Double	Double
Any enumerated type	Its underlying integer type and any type to which that widens
Char	Char, String
Any type	Object
Any derived type	Any base type from which it is derived
Any type	Any interface it implements

Using the CType Function

The CType function, in the System.CType class, is probably the most generally useful explicit conversion function in VB .NET. CType explicitly returns an expression converted to the specified type. Here's the general syntax:

```
Ctype(Expression, Type)
```

Here's a simple example using CType that converts a Double type to an Integer type:

```
Option Explicit On
...
Dim MyDouble As Double = 41.72
Dim MyInt As Integer = _
   CType(MyDouble, Integer)
' MyInt has the value of 42.
```

CType can be used as an alternative to many of the inline conversion functions that shown in the next section (which are mostly used to explicitly convert a simple type as in the example just given).

However, CType is often also used in conjunction with user-defined types. For example, the following line of code (taken from Chapter 4, "Class Interfaces") converts the expression obj, previously declared as type Dinosaur, to the type AbstractDinosaur:

```
dino = CType(obj,AbstractDinosaur)
```

As you might suspect, both Dinosaur and AbstractDinosaur are user-defined types.

Table C.3

Type Conversion Functions

Function Name	Return Type	Range for *Expression* Argument
CBool	Boolean	Any valid String or numeric expression
CByte	Byte	0 through 255; fractions are rounded
CChar	Char	Any valid String expression; value can be 0 through 65535
CDate	Date	Any valid representation of a date and time
CDbl	Double	-1.79769313486231E+308 through –4.94065645841247E–324 for negative values; 4.94065645841247E–324 through 1.79769313486231E+308 for positive values
CDec	Decimal	+/–79,228,162,514,264,337,593,543,950,335 for zero-scaled numbers—that is, numbers with no decimal places. For numbers with 28 decimal places, the range is +/–7.9228162514264337593543950335. The smallest possible nonzero number is 0.0000000000000000000000000001
CInt	Integer	-2,147,483,648 through 2,147,483,647; fractions are rounded
CLng	Long	-9,223,372,036,854,775,808 through 9,223,372,036,854,775,807; fractions are rounded
CObj	Object	Any valid expression
CShort	Short	–32,768 through 32,767; fractions are rounded
CSng	Single	–3.402823E+38 through –1.401298E–45 for negative values; 1.401298E–45 through 3.402823E+38 for positive values
CStr	String	Returns for CStr depend on the *expression* argument—see Table C.4

Table C.4

CStr Return Values

Return Type	Expression Used
Boolean	A string containing "True" or "False"
Date	A string containing a date in the short date format of your system
Numeric	A string representing the number

Using Inline Type Conversion Functions

The type conversion functions shown in **Table C.3** are compiled inline, meaning that evaluation of the expression and code generation for conversion take place at the same time. This means that execution is faster than when a member of the Convert class is used for conversion (as explained in the next section of this appendix).

Each function explicitly converts an expression to one specific type.

Note that the argument passed to the conversion function must fall within the range shown in the third column of Table C.3, or a syntax error will result.

The return value type when an expression is passed to the CStr function depends on the expression. **Table C.4** shows the CStr function return value types and possible expression arguments

Using Other Conversion Methods

This section briefly discusses the members of the Convert class and the ToString method. As you might expect, considering the vastness of the class libraries that make up the .NET Framework, there are still other conversion methods, functions, and techniques to be found. (For example, the Asc function returns a character code corresponding to a string, and the Chr function returns the character as a string associated with a code.) However, this appendix has described the most important conversion methods.

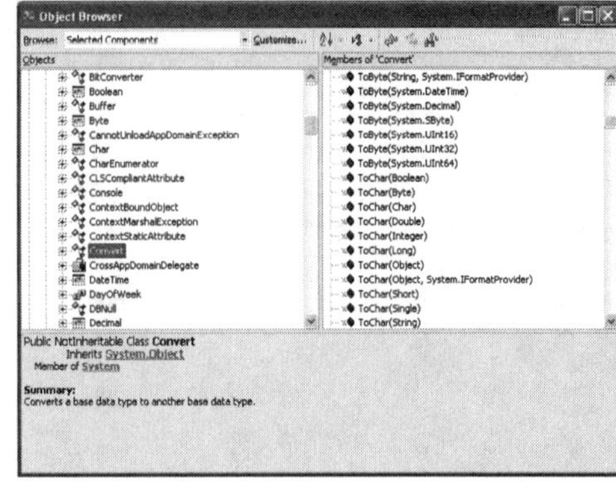

Figure C.5 You can use the Object Browser to inspect the overloaded methods that are members of the Convert class.

The Convert class

The shared public members of the Convert class, System.Convert, can be used to explicitly convert from one type to another type. For the most part, methods that are members of the Convert class correspond to the inline type conversion functions. For example, instead of the CInt function, you can use one of the overloaded versions of the Convert.ToInt32 methods. (Which overloaded method you use depends upon the type of the expression being converted.) And the overloaded versions of the Convert.ChangeType method are the equivalent of the CType conversion function explained earlier, since both can be used to convert an expression to a specified type.

You can find all of the methods of the Convert class, along with the possible overloads for the methods, by looking up the topic "Convert Members" in the online Help. You can also use the Object Browser to view them and to discover the methods and overloads available. As you can see in **Figure C.5**, there are indeed quite a few. (For more information about the Object Browser, see Chapter 14.)

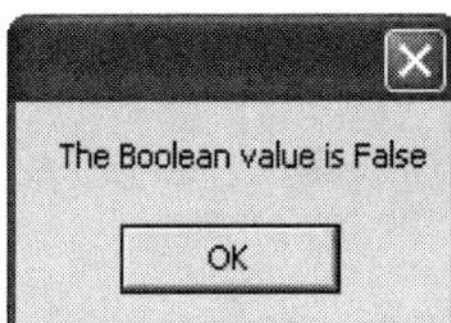
The Boolean value is False
OK

Figure C.6 Using a member of the Convert class, the string "False" is converted to the Boolean value False.

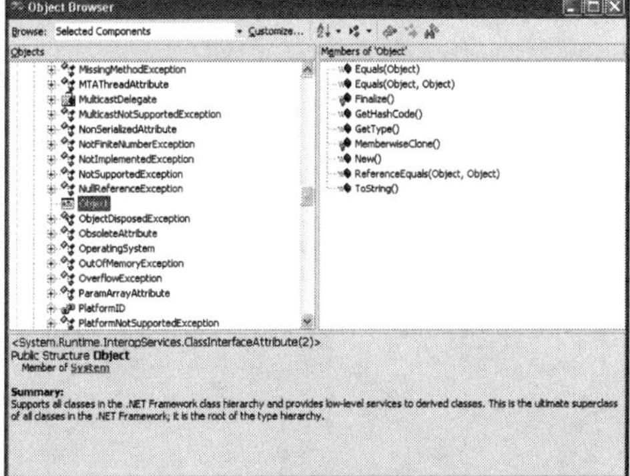

Figure C.7 The Object type is the root of the .NET type hierarchy (shown here in the Object Browser).

Here's a somewhat trivial example that uses the Convert.ToBoolean method to convert a string type with a value of "False" to a Boolean type with a value of False:

```
Option Strict On
...
If (Convert.ToBoolean("False") = False) _
   Then
      MessageBox.Show _
         ("The Boolean value is False")
Else
   MessageBox.Show _
      ("The Boolean value is True")
End If
```

A message box is displayed showing the results of the conversion; as you can see in **Figure C.6**, and as you'd expect, the string "False" converts to the Boolean value False.

You should know that the Convert methods throw an exception (and don't do any conversion) when meaningful results cannot be obtained. For example, calling any of the methods that convert the reference type System.DateTime to or from anything other than a String type always causes an exception to be thrown (and no conversion takes place).

The ToString method

The VB .NET Object type, System.Object, from which all other types derive, provides a ToString method. This means that whatever your object is, and whether or not it is user defined or intrinsic to the .NET Framework, it has a ToString method that returns a value of the String type. By the way, it's quite interesting to inspect the members of the System.Object class in the Object Browser (**Figure C.7**), since Object is the root of the .NET type hierarchy.

One thing that ToString is always good for is converting numbers to their string representation—a common task in displaying numbers, among other things. For example, you can use the ToString method to display the first four places of the expansion of π (**Figure C.8**):

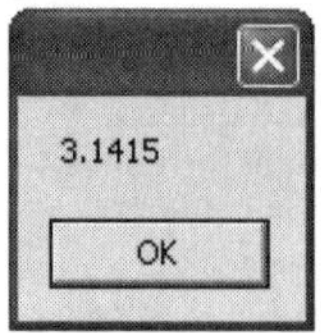

Figure C.8 You can use the ToString method to convert numbers to their string representation for display purposes.

```
Option Strict On
...
Dim theNumber As Double = 3.1415
MessageBox.Show(theNumber.ToString())
```

While the ToString method of any object will always deliver a string, it may not always be the string you want. By definition, the ToString method of an object returns a string that represents the object. The problem is that it is up to the implementer of a class to determine what is returned by objects based on the class. Usually, ToString is implemented so that it returns something reasonable, but you won't know for sure until you try.

For example, if you invoke a form's ToString method, you'll get the fully qualified form name followed by the literal ", Text:" followed by the contents of the form's Text property (its caption).

Now, most likely what you really want is the unqualified name of the form—and it is true that you could parse this out of the string returned by the ToString method—but the point stands that with complex objects, you need to be careful about exactly what ToString returns.

You should also bear in mind when creating your own classes that you are responsible for implementing the ToString method in a useful way—other programmers using your class libraries will expect to use your ToString method implementation and will be irritated if it doesn't return what they expect.

INDEX

INDEX

INDEX

INDEX

K

L

M

P

Q

R

S

U

V

W

INDEX